Issues,
Debates and
Controversies

An Introduction to Sociology

Consulting Editor: Amitai Etzioni

Issues, Debates and Controversies

An Introduction to Sociology

edited by

George Ritzer

Department of Sociology
The University of Kansas

ALLYN AND BACON, Inc.   Boston

Library of Congress Catalog Card Number: 75-186617

To
David and Jeremy

Table of Contents

Preface

In 1950 there were five books of readings advertised for sale in the *American Sociological Review*, while in 1970 the number had jumped to more than one hundred. We are clearly in the age of the anthology, and an author must have an awfully good reason to inflict still another one on his colleagues in sociology. I think I *have* such a reason. In the area of introductory sociology there are two basic types of anthologies available. The first type covers each of the major topics covered in an introductory course, with several readings designed to give the reader a broad introduction to each of the topics. These readings are generally drawn from major journals and books in the field. The problem with such anthologies is that each reading bears little relationship to those that precede or follow it. This makes the anthology very jumpy, but more important, the student is not exposed to the context in which each article arose and the excitement it generated. It is my belief that almost every piece of work in sociology arises in response to some work that preceded it. The basic format for this reader has developed from that belief. For each of the sixteen topics most frequently covered in an introductory course in sociology the student is presented with an important topic of controversy. I feel this is a more realistic way of introducing the student to sociology, since it reflects the reasons for, and contexts of, sociological work. Furthermore, it seems like a much more exciting way to present sociology. Articles which when read alone may seem "dry as dust" take on a new excitement when they are presented as critiques of earlier work and followed by the new analyses and criticisms that they have generated.

There is a second type of anthology that has recently made significant inroads in the introductory market; this might be labelled the "hip" reader. In general, this type of book strives for "relevance" and, in the process, often goes outside of sociology for its material. I simply do not believe that one must go outside the confines of sociology to find relevance and excitement. The subject matter of sociology is inherently relevant and, when looked at in the context of controversy, is also intrinsically exciting.

This anthology, then, is different from all others aimed at the introductory market. The rest convey the impression that sociology is composed of a universally agreed upon set of concepts, theories, methods, and social facts. While such an approach makes for a coherent introduction to the field, it grossly underestimates the amount of controversy in sociology.

Sociology is unified in a variety of ways, but it is also characterized by such elements as diversity, dissensus, controversy, and conflict. In many cases sociologists do not agree on the definition of concepts, do not accept the same theories, do not use the same methods, and do not agree on many social facts. Why, then, have introductory courses presented a unified conception of the field and virtually ignored our inherent controversies? I think it is fair to say that most instructors feel that students in introductory sociology want and need a coherent introduction to the field. The students are felt to have limited interest in, and commitment to, sociology. Given this limited interest and commitment, it is believed that students want a neat package that can be easily digested. The student who goes on to advanced work in sociology soon learns that the discipline is not nearly as coherent as he had been led to believe in the introductory course. For those few who go on to graduate school, the reality of sociology as a controversial discipline is clearly brought to the fore. Thus there is great discontinuity in sociological training, with the coherence of introductory sociology quickly giving way to the dissensus of advanced course work. Sociologists seem to feel that it is only the advanced students who can tolerate such a confusing view of the field.

Needless to say, I have a very different philosophy of introductory sociology and a very different view of the typical student who takes that course. I believe that the sociology we teach introductory students should be the same sociology we teach our advanced students. We tend to underestimate the beginning student. Many of them, especially the good ones, *do not* desire unity and closure; rather, they crave excitement. Most introductory books (and courses) are long on unity and closure but woefully short on excitement. Sociology is an exciting discipline made even more stimulating by the controversies that rage within it. Yet this excitement is rarely communicated to the introductory student, and consequently we lose many of our better students to the disciplines that provide more provocative introductory courses. I think students want excitement, and that they can handle a more controversial introduction to the field. Furthermore, I think it is dysfunctional to teach one way to introductory students and another way to advanced students. This is hard on the teacher and even harder on the student—who experiences "reality shock" when he moves from the basic course to more advanced courses. Sociology *is* a controversial discipline. We *know* this. Our advanced students *know* it. I think it is high time introductory students *knew* it.

There is much more behind this book, though, than simply communicating a more realistic and exciting view of the field to introductory students. Controversies are not presented for their own sake, but rather because they communicate some essential insights about sociology and the topics with which sociologists concern themselves. Thus, through the device of controversy, I hope the student will learn more about sociology. Since the student is learning his subject "in the heat of battle," it is my hope that what he learns will make a more permanent impression on him. This book represents a somewhat different approach to introductory sociology. The premises on which it is based may prove to be wrong, but I think it is well worth a try.

Plan of the Book

This anthology begins with an essay that I have written especially for it. In that essay I attempt to outline the many sources of controversy in contemporary sociology, as well as to demonstrate that sociology is not alone in being controversial—all sciences may be characterized in this way. In fact, controversy is an integral part of the scientific method, and a discipline that is lacking in debate will cease to progress. The remainder of the book is divided into sixteen sections corresponding to the topics most frequently covered in an introductory course in sociology. *It is hoped that this book will be used in conjunction with a textbook, and that the instructor will assign a chapter in this book which corresponds to the appropriate one in the textbook.* In this way the student will be exposed to the basic principles defined and illustrated in each subarea within sociology, as well as a stimulating controversy in each of these areas.

One final point. An effort has been made herein to present a wide range of types of debate. Articles have been drawn from such widely different journals as *Trans*-action and the *American Sociological Review*. Most of the authors are sociologists, but there is a smattering of people from other disciplines and even a popular writer or two. An effort has been made to be relevant and timely in terms of the controversies included, but there are some classical theoretical and empirical controversies as well. Some of the timely debates include those concerning radical sociology, snooping, race and intelligence, the urban crisis, population control, Summerhill, and the culture of poverty. On the other hand, a number of classic controversies are included such as the debate over the Davis-Moore theory of stratification, Weber's views on bureaucracies and religion, and whether America is elitist or pluralistic. Some of the controversies are very well-known; some are more obscure. The objective has been to expose the reader to the great variety of controversy in sociology. In this way he will gain a better grasp of the nature of sociology and the significance of controversy to its history and its future.

Acknowledgments

A number of my colleagues here at the University of Kansas and at Cornell University, where I spent the summer of 1971, have made contributions to this volume, and I would like to express my appreciation to them. All of my colleagues at Kansas played a role in its development, but I would particularly like to thank Ken Kammeyer, Stan Eitzen, Norm Yetman, Bob Antonio, Chuck Warriner, and Lew Mennerick for a number of very helpful suggestions. At Cornell I was greatly helped by Len Reissman, as well as by Bernie Rosen, Hal Mizruchi, and Marcello Truzzi. Barbara Johnson, Debbie Supancic, and Sharon Haskins all helped in the typing, and all deserve much more than a mere "Thank you." Finally, those marvelous faces that belong to my wife and sons David and Jeremy all deserve a big hug for continuing to shine despite the hours I spent away from home and at this typewriter.

GEORGE RITZER
Lawrence, Kansas

Issues,
Debates and
Controversies

An Introduction to Sociology

Introduction:
Sources of Controversy
in Sociology

GEORGE RITZER

"CONFLICT IS THE GADFLY OF TRUTH"

Sociologists are often controversial men who use controversial methods to study controversial topics. Recently, for example, a university tried to revoke a Ph.D. (the university later reversed itself and allowed the Ph.D. to stand) it had granted to a sociologist who had studied homosexual behavior in public restrooms by using techniques in which he disguised his intent and his identity.[1] Not all sociologists study such racy topics in such debatable ways, but in general the topics they study and the methods they use are likely to engender controversy. However, sociology is not alone in being controversial—all sciences are controversial. Controversy is an integral part of the scientific method, and we are all very much aware of many of the debates which rage within all of the sciences. In psychology there is, for example, the spectacle of the conflict between the Freudians and the neo-Freudians (Fromm, Horney, etc.) over, among other things, the causes of mental disorder. In economics there is widespread disagreement on how a society should cope with such problems as unemployment and inflation. Even in the so-called "hard sciences" we find similar disagreements. Biochemists debate the role of DNA in heredity, physicists the

---

1. That research has recently appeared in book form. See Laud Humphreys, *Tearoom Trade: Impersonal Sex in Public Places*. Chicago: Aldine Publishing Co., 1970.

nature of the atom, and geologists conflict over the composition of the moon and the planets. Thus sociologists are not alone in 'controversy, yet sociologists seem more ashamed of their controversies than those in other disciplines. Inkeles makes exactly this point: "Sociologists are often embarrassed and distressed by their pervasive disagreements, thinking that this reflects poorly on the maturity of the field."[2] The fact that controversies rage in various disciplines was confirmed in a study by Joseph Schwab, in which he examined 4,000 published American and European articles over a period of five centuries primarily in biology, psychology and the behavioral sciences.[3] Focusing on debates over methods, Schwab found them to be pervasive and remarkably constant across disciplines and over time spans.

Controversy is a critical process in the advancement of any science, since it relates to the questioning attitude required of all scientists. If scientists were to accept theories or empirical findings unquestioningly, we would still be in the dark ages scientifically. A similar process is followed in all sciences, hard or soft. A researcher (or theoretician) produces results (or ideas) which are questioned by others in the discipline. They may point up failings in the research (or the theory) and seek to replicate the earlier study or develop an alternative theory. The controversy rages as conflicting theoretical and empirical articles appear in the scientific journals. As the debate goes on many things become clarified, and ultimately some measure of consensus on at least some of the issues is reached. But even in those controversies in which consensus is achieved the debate is far from ended. In the course of the debate a number of new issues are brought to light and controversies arise around these new issues. This process is just as likely to occur in physics as it is in sociology. It follows that sociology need not be ashamed of its controversies, yet some sociologists seek to cover up the dissent in the field. The reason lies in a mistaken conception of what a science is supposed to be. Some sociologists seem to think that science is supposed to have answers, not unresolved questions. But science is not defined by its answers; rather, it is a *method* of obtaining reliable information about any natural phenomena. Thus sociology is a science to the degree that it uses the scientific method, not because it has answers about social life.

The sources of dissent in sociology are similar to the sources in any science. In the remainder of this essay I will focus on the sources of sociological controversy, but the reader should keep in mind that these points apply as well to any other science.

---

2. Alex Inkeles, *What Is Sociology?* Englewood Cliffs, N.J.: Prentice-Hall, Inc., 1964, p. 104.
3. Joseph Schwab, "What Do Scientists Do?" *Behavioral Science*, vol. 5, 1960, pp. 1–27.

THE NATURE OF THE FIELD

A number of the controversies which exist in contemporary American sociology can be traced to the highly diverse origins of the field.[4] American sociology is the resultant of a variety of intellectual and geographic inputs. Historically, sociology grew in a parallel fashion in a number of countries. The sociology which developed in England in the 1800s was heavily steeped in political economy, social administration and philosophy. German sociology had many of the same origins as well as a strong background in comparative law. In France the budding discipline of sociology was heavily influenced by philosophy and psychology. The English, German and French brands of sociology were all exported to the United States, and each found American adherents. As these different streams of thought fed into America they were met by an indigenous type of sociology which was greatly influenced by practical reform, economics and anthropology. With so many different intellectual origins, it is not surprising that sociology in the United States soon split into a variety of schools of thought. Among these schools were (and still are) the phenomenologists, the behaviorists, the functionalists and the conflict theorists. The varied history of contemporary sociology is an important source of contemporary controversy.

Stemming from these diverse origins are a number of contemporary theoretical controversies. A good example of the many theoretical controversies which could be discussed here is the seemingly endless debate between the functionalists and the conflict theorists. As the name implies, the functionalists tend to see order, consensus and integration wherever they look in society. The adherents of this theoretical school are primarily concerned with the issue of what holds society together. In contrast, the conflict theorists tend to see disorder, dissent and disintegration wherever they look in society. To the functionalists, order in society stems from the consensus of the population on basic norms and values, but to conflict theorists whatever order there is in society occurs as a result of the coercive power of the dominant group. Although this depiction is a gross oversimplification of the two theoretical positions, it does serve to underscore the basic differences between the two schools. The more general point here is that the basic differences between these theoretical schools, as well as all of the others which exist today, are major sources of controversy in modern sociology.

The sheer variability of human behavior and social organization leads the sociologist into the study of a lengthy list of topics, a list which is growing enormously each year. To get some idea of the range of topics, a list of the courses most frequently taught in sociology follows, with the percentage of colleges and universities offering them:

---

4. Robert K. Merton, "Social Conflict over Styles of Sociological Work," in Larry T. Reynolds and Janice M. Reynolds (eds.), *The Sociology of Sociology*. New York: David McKay Co., 1970, p. 175.

TABLE 1.   Rank Ordering of Sociology Course Areas by Percentage
of Institutions Offering Them (537 Schools)

Rank Order	Course Area	Percentage of Institutions Offering Courses
1.	Introductory	95.9
2.	Marriage and Family	84.9
3.	Social Problems	80.4
4.	Theory	77.1
5.	Race Relations	70.2
6.	Criminology and Penology	67.6
7.	Research Methods	65.9
8.	Anthropology-Sociology	62.8
9.	Social Welfare and Reform	60.1
10.	Social Psychology	55.3
11.	Urban Sociology	54.7
12.	Demography and/or Population Problems	46.4
13.	Community	40.0
14.	Social Institutions and Social Organization	38.9
15.	Social Stratification	37.1
16.	Anthropology	36.5
17.	Sociology of Religion	33.1
18.	Statistics	30.2
19.	Juvenile Delinquency	28.7
20.	Industrial-Labor Relations and Problems	28.5
21.	Social Change	24.6
22.	Small Groups	19.7
23.	Educational Sociology	18.2
24.	Collective Behavior	17.1
25.	Political Sociology	16.8
26.	Communications	14.9
27.	Other Specific Problems	13.6
28.	Rural Sociology	12.3
29.	Social Control	7.6
30.	Social Movements	6.7
31.	Regional Sociology	4.1
32.	Economic Sociology	2.6
33.	Miscellaneous	69.3

Source: Sue Titus Reid and Alan P. Bates, "Undergraduate Sociology Programs in Accredited Colleges and Universities," *The American Sociologist,* Vol. 6, No. 2, p. 167.

Although this list is long, it excludes literally hundreds of more esoteric topics to which sociologists have addressed themselves. This is reflected by the fact that almost 70 percent of the schools surveyed offered courses included in the miscellaneous category. Included are such areas as the sociology of medicine, the sociology of sport and even the sociology of sociology.

The diversity of topics in sociology does not, in itself, contribute to controversy in the discipline. It does, however, have an indirect effect, since it has led to a growing specialization among sociologists. We are not simply sociologists, but demographers, criminologists, statisticians, etc. It is this specialization which has helped to make sociology controversial. This may operate in two very different ways. On the one hand, sociologists are so expert in a particular area that they are able to pick out any weakness in a study done, or theory developed, in their area. The publication of their critiques in article or letter form often begins a new controversy. On the other hand, specialization makes sociologists less capable of criticizing work in areas other than their own. Nevertheless, they frequently think they see failings in work done in other areas and write critiques of them. These critiques, unlike those of experts in the area, are often off base and therefore lead to responding attacks* by the original author or one of his colleagues within that area of specialization. Thus we find specialization leading to many controversies in sociology, some of which are useful and some of which are dead ends.

A similar source of controversy stems from the diverse levels of concern of sociologists. Some sociologists are *macroscopic,* dealing with the broad sweep of society as a whole. They are concerned with such questions as how the subsystems within society unite to form the whole, how societies relate to each other and how societies change. On the opposite end of the spectrum are the sociologists who work on *microscopic* questions. Examples include Robert Bales, who is interested in charting the interaction of individuals in small groups;[5] George Homans, who focuses on the exchanges between people;[6] and the ethnomethodologists, who analyze "everyday life."[7] Those who work at the opposite ends of this spectrum often conflict. Macroscopic sociologists criticize the triviality of the work of their microscopic colleagues, and the latter respond with a critique of the lack of scientific rigor of those who seek to explain society as a whole. In

---

* It should be pointed out that sociologists also respond to critiques authored by experts in their own areas. In fact, one is hard pressed to find any attacks which are not met by counterattacks.

5. Robert Bales, *Interaction Process Analysis: A Method for the Study of Small Groups.* Reading, Mass.: Addison-Wesley, 1950.

6. George C. Homans, *Social Behavior: Its Elementary Forms.* New York: Harcourt, 1961.

7. Harold Garfinkel, *Studies in Ethnomethodology.* Englewood Cliffs, N.J.: Prentice-Hall, Inc., 1967.

the middle are sociologists who focus on such things as formal organizations, aging, the family and the like, but they have not been able to resolve the conflict between macro and micro sociology. They have simply added another dimension to the conflict. Now macroscopic, microscopic and middle-range sociologists all conflict with each other, with each claiming that theirs is the proper level of sociological analysis.

A final source of controversy is on the uses of sociology.[8] Here we come to grips with the debate between pure and applied sociology. Pure sociologists believe that sociology should be concerned with the advance of knowledge for knowledge's sake, without regard for the uses to which that knowledge is put. They seek to advance knowledge and leave its application to government, business or labor leaders. On the other hand, the applied sociologist believes that he must put his knowledge to practical use by writing for the public, translating what others write for the layman, and serving as consultant and advisor to the government, industry, labor and the like. This kind of involvement is criticized by the purists, who argue that it has a profound effect on what applied sociologists study, how they study it, what they find and how they interpret what they find. Thus Daniel Patrick Moynihan is attacked for misinterpreting the black family (he argued it was a matriarchy and pathological) in part because of his role in the government. Similarly, industrial sociologists who labored for management were castigated for developing a whole school of thought (the Human Relations school) whose major objective was the manipulation of the worker in order to make him more productive. The purists, on the other hand, are criticized for having their heads in the clouds and having no relevance to the pressing problems of the day.

In summary, there are five basic characteristics of sociology which make it controversial:

1. Sociology developed historically from widely different sources.
2. Sociology includes a wide variety of theoretical orientations.
3. Sociology encompasses a wide array of topics or substantive areas.
4. Sociology is concerned with various levels, ranging from the individual to society as a whole.
5. Sociology is split on its uses.

THE NATURE OF THE SOCIOLOGIST

There are currently about 13,000 members of the American Sociological Association. Given such a large number of sociologists, it should come as no surprise that they come from very different backgrounds in terms of social class, family, region of the country, etc. Glenn and Weiner (1969) found

---

8. Paul Lazarsfeld, William H. Sewell, and Harold Wilensky (eds.), *The Uses of Sociology*. New York: Basic Books, Inc., 1967.

45 percent of the sociologists they studied came from lower-middle class backgrounds, a third from lower class origins and almost a quarter from upper-middle or upper class families.[9] In terms of region of origin about 30 percent came from the Northeast, 30 percent from the North Central, 14 percent from the South, 15 percent from the West and 8 percent from outside the United States. About 30 percent had a rural background, and 70 percent were of urban origins. Over a third are Protestant, 13 percent are Jewish, and more than a third reported that they had no religious preference. Sociologists also came from heterogeneous backgrounds in terms of political orientation; about 40 percent of their fathers were liberal, 19 percent were middle of the road and 35 percent were conservative. A large percentage (40.6) majored in sociology as undergraduates, but many majored in such fields as the other social sciences, arts, psychology, biology and the physical sciences. This diversity of social background has made for diversity and controversy among practicing sociologists.

It is interesting to note that although sociologists spend a considerable portion of their time studying the effect of such background factors on their subjects, they have blithely ignored the effect of their own background on their work. Alvin Gouldner has recently castigated sociologists for feeling that they are immune to the factors which they are convinced affect the behavior of everyone else.[10] Clearly the sociologist, like those he studies, is affected by these factors. His class background, place of birth, religion and early political orientation are all going to have a profound impact on the kind of sociologist he becomes. The more general point is that different backgrounds lead sociologists to different positions and thereby into potential, and sometimes real, conflict.

Social background is important, but there are many other factors which help explain differences among sociologists. Of great importance is the intellectual background of each sociologist (the sociologists and sociological ideas which were influential early in his career). Obviously, the ideas that are most influential early in one's career are determined, to a large extent, by social background. The sociologist's background predisposes him to accept some ideas and reject others. Talcott Parsons, for example, was most heavily influenced by the ideas of such sociological theorists as Weber, Durkheim and Pareto. These men were far more conservative in their thinking than, for example, Karl Marx. In fact, much of their work can be viewed as an attack on Marxian theory. In his early classic on trends in sociological thought, *The Structure of Social Action*,[11]

9. Norval D. Glenn and David Weiner, "Some Trends in the Social Origins of American Sociologists," *The American Sociologist,* vol. 4, no. 4, November, 1969, pp. 291–302.
10. Alvin Gouldner, *The Coming Crisis of Western Sociology.* New York: Basic Books, Inc., 1970.
11. Talcott Parsons, *The Structure of Social Action.* New York: The Free Press, 1937.

Parsons spent hundreds of pages on these conservative theorists and dismissed Marx in only a few pages. Says Gouldner of Parsons: "Parsons, therefore, never engaged himself as directly and deeply with Marxism as had the Europeans. He never really came to a conception of its full analytic complexity and, indeed, had committed himself to a view on Marxism before he had any sensitivity to its own internal development. There is little doubt that Parsons always had a better acquaintance with Marx's critics than with Marx himself."[12] (150) In contrast, C. Wright Mills, who was most active during the years 1940 to 1960, was confronted with two wings of American sociology. On the right was the ideology of order and consensus, with Parsons as its major exponent. But Mills could not accept this position, which talked of the inevitability of class inequities and abuses of bureaucracies. Instead, Mills was drawn more to the other wing, the socialist ideology of class struggle. Although Mills had much to say against Marxism and socialism, it was clear that his own thinking was much more heavily influenced by the thinkers on the sociological left than those on the right. Again, there is a more general point here: the disciples of different sociologists often find themselves in conflict. Thus Weberians argue with Marxians, Parsonians with Millsians, etc.

Different social and intellectual backgrounds lead sociologists to different ideological positions, and differences in ideology also contribute to dissent in sociology. Parsons, because of his social and intellectual background, is on the right ideologically—while Mills, with a different background, stands to the left. Ideology colors what a sociologist says and contributes to the development of controversies. Thus Parsons, in his essay on the professions, talks of their functions for society,[13] while Mills examines business, political and military leaders and finds a conspiracy to rule society.[14] But the sociologist's ideology often leads him astray. Parsons sometimes sees functions where none exist, and Mills occasionally sees conspiracy where there is none. There are innumerable examples of ideological controversies in sociology. The right attacks the left, the left the right, and both attack those in the middle.

Another source of dissent lies in the nature of the careers of sociologists. Like those in most occupations, many sociologists are busy trying to make it to the top of their profession. At the top is a full professor at Harvard, and at the bottom is an instructor at Podunk. In order to make it to the top one must in sociology, and every other discipline, publish books and articles in learned journals. The emphasis typically is not on the quality of what one writes, but on quantity and the places (major journals, major book

---

12. Gouldner, *op. cit.,* p. 150.
13. Talcott Parsons, "The Professions and Social Structure," *Social Forces,* vol. 17, May, 1939, pp. 457–467.
14. C. Wright Mills, *The Power Elite.* New York: Oxford University Press, 1956.

publishers)[15] in which it is published. Since relatively few sociologists (like those in any other occupation) have truly original ideas, they make their mark by critiquing the work of others. It is far easier to criticize others than to do original thinking. I should hasten to add that criticism is an important way of advancing knowledge, but some of the criticism which appears in print is motivated more by careerism than by the desire to advance knowledge. The goal of the careerist is to attack the biggest name he can think of because it is this kind of attack which is more likely to be published. Thus many sociological lightweights have advanced their careers by writing critiques of such stars as Talcott Parsons.

To summarize, there are four basic facts about sociologists which make for controversy in the discipline:

1. They come from diverse social backgrounds.
2. They have very different intellectual backgrounds.
3. They are different ideologically.
4. In order to advance their careers many find it easiest to publish critiques of the works of others.

THE NATURE OF SOCIOLOGICAL METHODS

Sociologists are not only different kinds of people who look at various topics in different ways, they also have very different methodological orientations to what they do. Some sociologists see society as totally determinable, while others see much indeterminacy in the world. Many sociologists seek to emulate the hard sciences in terms of methodological rigor and techniques, while others find these techniques inappropriate to the kinds of issues with which sociologists concern themselves. Instead, they seek to gain a broad, subjective "understanding" of what goes on in the societal unit in which they are interested. Thus C. Wright Mills employed few methodologically rigorous techniques, but much understanding, in his analysis of American society in which he found it to be dominated by a power elite. Lacking "hard" data, Mills's thesis was roundly attacked, especially by those who felt that sociology should be methodologically rigorous. There are many other methodological differences in sociology, most of which revolve around the kinds of techniques used.

Some of the major sociological methods are the mail questionnaire, interview, experiment, observation and content analysis. Further, within each of these diverse methods is further differentiation. Thus one who interviews may use open-ended or closed-ended questions. In an open-

---

15. Theodore Caplow and Reece McGee, *The Academic Marketplace*. Garden City, N.Y.: Anchor Books, 1965.

ended interview the respondent is allowed to supply his own answer in his own terms. In a closed-ended interview the subject must choose his reply from a preselected list of alternatives. To add greater variability many researchers doing interviews might combine both open-ended and closed-ended questions. Similarly, in using the observation technique one may be a participant or a nonparticipant observer. The participant observer studies the group in which he is interested as a member of that group, while the nonparticipant observes from the sidelines. To make things even more complex, many researchers attempt to use several different methods in one study. For example, they might use a mail questionnaire, interview and participant observation. The source of controversy here is over the "best" method. Just as sociologists become tied to particular theories, they also come to prefer certain methods. Thus we are treated to endless debates over the preferred method for a certain problem. In addition, studies are attacked for their methodological inadequacies.

The way a sociologist does a study shapes the results that he obtains. Asking the same research question using two different techniques is likely to produce very different results. Thus the replication of a study using a different technique is likely to lead to different findings and the beginnings of a new debate. Instead of talking about this in general terms, let me illustrate the point from my own research (coauthored with Harrison Trice). The starting point for my study was research conducted by Neal Gross, Ward Mason and Alexander McEachern on the modes of resolving a role conflict situation.[16] They were concerned with what actions an individual could take when he is faced with conflicting expectations about what he should do. They hypothesized theoretically that there were four alternatives open to such an individual: conform to one expectation, conform to the other, compromise or withdraw. They conducted open-ended interviews with their respondents and categorized their responses under the four alternatives. In our follow-up study we sought to retest the work of Gross *et al.*[17] Instead of deciding a priori that there were only four alternative resolutions in a role conflict situation, it was decided to allow the alternatives to flow from the responses, rather than imposing them on the responses. Open-ended pretest interviews were conducted and the responses confirmed the viability of the four alternatives developed by Gross *et al.*, but it also became clear from the responses that there was a fifth alternative which they had overlooked—independent action, or ignoring what those involved say and doing what you think to be best. These five alternatives were then used as choices in role conflict situations used in the actual study. The findings from this study not only confirmed that inde-

---

16. Neal Gross, Ward Mason, and Alexander McEachern, *Explorations in Role Analysis: Studies of the School Suprintendency Role*. New York: John Wiley, 1958.
17. George Ritzer and Harrison M. Trice, *An Occupation in Conflict*. Ithaca, N.Y.: Cornell University, 1969.

pendent action was a viable alternative, it turned out to be the most frequently chosen one. In this case, letting the choices flow from the respondents rather than imposing them theoretically on the responses made a crucial difference in the results.

The preceding example points up another source of variation and controversy in sociology, the nature of one's respondents. Gross and his associates used school superintendents as subjects, while Ritzer and Trice used personnel managers. It may well be that school superintendents cope with role conflict differently than personnel managers. Generally, using different populations to test a theory may lead to different results, yet it is rare to find a replication of a study using the same population as in the original study. Even if one tried, individuals will have left the group in question or passed away between the time of the original study and the replication.

A related source of disagreement, alluded to above, is changes over time. If we restudy a group in 1972 that was first studied in 1962, we are likely to get very different results. Yet, because of the great time lapses between when a study is done, the results published and the replication begun, a five- to ten-year gap is not unusual. How can we replicate a study today of students which was carried out ten years ago? Students in the early sixties were characterized by their apathy, today by their activism. Similarly, black Americans in 1960 were fighting hard for integration. Today, large segments of the black community are eschewing integration for separatist goals such as black power.

Finally, there is the issue of the interpretation of results. The data sociologists collect do not speak for themselves; they must be interpreted, and it is the possibility of different interpretations of the same data which contributes to sociological controversies. Let me illustrate this with a critique of the interpretation made recently by the authors of a study of those who participated in the Detroit race riots.[18] Based on their data, the authors concluded that those who rioted were the more deprived members of the black community. They were found to have lower occupational status, lower weekly incomes and greater unemployment. But I believe that these authors misinterpreted their own data. The subjects they used for the study were not a sample of all those who rioted, but simply those who were arrested as a result of the disturbances. There is a considerable body of literature which indicates that it is the more deprived elements of the community who are *more likely to be arrested.* Thus the authors discovered some characteristics of those race rioters who were arrested, *not all race rioters.* They could have talked about race rioters in general if they had studied *both* those who were arrested as a result of the riot *and* those who

---

18. James A. Geschwender and Benjamin D. Singer, "Deprivation and the Detroit Riot," *Social Problems,* vol. 17, Spring, 1970, pp. 457–463.

escaped arrest. It may well be that those who escaped arrest were those who were better off occupationally and economically than those who were arrested. It is precisely this kind of alternative interpretation of the same data which contributes to making sociology the controversial discipline that it is.

In summary, the following are some of the major methodological reasons sociology is controversial:

1. Differences in methodological orientation of sociologists.
2. A wide variety of methods which are employed in various combinations.
3. Variations in the way questions are asked.
4. Use of different populations.
5. Changes in a population over time.
6. Alternative interpretation of the same data.

CONCLUSIONS

Some debates in sociology have been going on ever since the founding of the discipline, but most tend to be comparatively short-lived. When, in the larger society, an issue becomes "hot" we frequently find an outpouring of sociological literature on that topic. The journals are full of articles on that topic for a while, but as the issue cools the number of journal articles drops. For example, there is currently much debate over the Women's Liberation movement and, consequently, many sociological articles have appeared on the subject. But as women gain their objectives and the issue loses its popularity we can predict that sociological work on the topic will decline. As it declines there will undoubtedly be a new "hot" public issue which will attract the attention of sociologists. While some controversies are long-lived and others short-lived, there are still others which seem to ebb and flow. For example, Weber's work on the rationality of bureaucracy seems to receive a great deal of attention for a while, then interest abates only to be revived again. In contrast, Weber's work on the Protestant Ethic and the spirit of capitalism has received almost constant attention since its initial publication.

Although controversy is a valuable process in sociology, it is not always functional. When conflict degenerates to name-calling or efforts to defeat one's opponents it ceases to be of utility and, in fact, often proves harmful. Too often scientists become tied to their particular position and defend it without being interested in, or able to understand, the other side. There are many examples of such dysfunctional controversies in sociology, but happily they are overshadowed by the vast number of debates which have helped in the advancement of the discipline.

Although controversy is endemic to sociology, it is important to recognize the fact that there are some common threads which hold sociology together. It is true that sociologists conflict, but conflict is possible only when there are ties which hold the participants together.[19] Sociologists all accept the fact that social events have social (and not metaphysical) causes and that we must examine man in his social setting. Further, they are committed to generalization or making "broader sense out of the specific facts they have accumulated."[20] Finally, sociologists recognize that they must submit their ideas, results and/or theories to the critical scrutiny of their colleagues. It is this last aspect of unity which paves the way for diversity. When he presents his position a sociologist fully expects to be scrutinized, and it is this process which often leads to the controversies which make up a large portion of sociology.

19. Lewis Coser, *The Functions of Social Conflict.* Glencoe, Ill.: The Free Press, 1956.
20. R. P. Cuzzort, *Humanity and Modern Sociological Thought.* New York: Holt, Rinehart and Winston, Inc., 1969.

PART I

The Discipline of Sociology

Chapter 1	The Discipline:
	Should Sociology
	Be Radical?

One of the most important debates in sociology to both practitioners and students is whether the discipline should be radical or "value free." This controversy has a long history, but it has recently come to the fore as a result of the growing number of graduate students and militant professors who are demanding the radicalization of sociology. The first essay in this section exemplifies the point of view of many militant young sociologists. Szymanski contends that what contemporary American sociologists do is shaped by the corporate system they serve. Empirical researchers provide information which is used by the "system," while theoreticians serve to legitimize that system. Students are urged to reject these alternatives and become radical sociologists dedicated to the "pursuit of understanding of the real nature of man and society and a commitment to the self-realization of human potentialities." The most controversial aspect of Szymanski's argument is his belief that radical sociologists must identify "with the victims of the routine workings of social structures." Thus sociologists should not be value free, rather they should side with the exploited members of society. Szymanski's rationalization for this position is that it is impossible to be value free. As evidence he cites the fact that while established sociologists pay lip-service to value freedom, they are really working for the system.

Berger expresses surprise at the position taken by the young radical sociologists. He points out that historically sociology has been associated with conservatism. One of the founding fathers (Comte) saw sociology as antirevolutionary, and many of the early giants in the field (Weber, Durkheim) were engaged in refutations of Marxism. Berger sees sociology as both "subversive of established patterns of thought" *and* "conservative in its implications for the institutional order." By debunking our basic assumptions sociology can threaten the established order (as well as any "new order"). In this way it can be a liberating force, but this liberation can bring to the fore certain realities which the individual may well find terrifying. On the conservative side Berger sees society in need of order, continuity and triviality (man can only stand so much excitement). With this view, it is clear why many sociologists are skeptical of violent change. On the issue of value freedom Berger makes a differentiation between sociologists and their discipline. The discipline must be value free in terms of its methodology, but the sociologist as a practitioner must not be.

I am able to differentiate the sociologist as a sociologist from the sociologist as a citizen. In making this differentiation I think that the sociologist as a citizen must take positions on various issues, but this must not interfere with his work as a sociologist in terms of the methods he uses or the interpretations he makes. I recognize that a critic like Szymanski would say that this is impossible, a practicing sociologist cannot be value free. While I confess that I find it hard to think of even one value free sociologist, this does not mean that value freedom is not a desirable goal for those who practice sociology. Looked at in this way, the issue becomes one of degrees of value freedom. I think the basic point is that sociologists should seek to be as *value free in their work* as they possibly can be. In addition, it is incumbent on the sociologist as a citizen to use what he knows and take positions on the important issues of the day.

Toward a Radical Sociology*

ALBERT SZYMANSKI

There is today a growing undercurrent of dissatisfaction with the state of contemporary sociology. Not only students but also professors throughout the country seem to be realizing that something is amiss. Readers appear on the "New Sociology." Young professors formulate or reformulate virtually every conceivable approach to sociological methodology and theory. Older professors defensively rewrite their earlier work. Students rebel against established notions, disrespectfully rejecting the work of their teachers.

* Excerpted from *Sociological Inquiry*, 40 (Winter, 1970), pp. 3–11, by permission of the author and publisher. Reprinted in revised form from *The Human Factor*, Journal of the Graduate Sociology Student Union, Columbia University, November, 1968.

In this paper rather than cataloguing the alleged failings of American Sociology or decrying the evils of a given departmental situation, I will attempt first to analyze, from the viewpoint of the sociology of knowledge, the dominant trends in the field, and second, to outline an alternative approach that I feel sociology must take if it is to regain its relevance to the understanding of man and society.[1]

I. Corporate Sociology

Following the analysis of Paul Baran and Paul Sweezy in *Monopoly Capital* (1966), and John Kenneth Galbraith in *The New Industrial State* (1967), it is our view that American society can best be categorized as corporate capitalism. Private corporations are the dominant institution in contemporary Western society, and their functional needs for security, control, and expansion determine the broad outlines of the social structure, government policy, beliefs, and values. Unfortunately we will not be able to go into this argument here; for this the reader should refer to the above cited works. Rather, we will accept this analysis for the purposes of this paper, and examine its implications for the sociological study of contemporary sociology.

The basic methodology that we will use is functionalism, supplemented by an analysis of mechanisms. That is, we will consider an element to be explained if we can show how it contributes to the maintenance of the system of corporate capitalism, and, at the same time, can isolate the structure and processes by which this function is realized.

We will maintain that the functions of sociology for the dominant institutional structure are basically twofold. That is, sociology fulfills the system's needs for legitimation and for practical knowledge. The function of legitimation is the production of a sophisticated definition of social reality that explains and justifies the existing social order and its dominant interests—it explains how well a society functions, how all the ongoing institutions are necessary, and how good the whole system is. The function of practical knowledge is for the providing of skills, techniques, and useful facts needed by the dominant institutions in the control and manipulation of their members as well as the greater social environment.

It seems appropriate, in light of our sociology of knowledge approach to sociology, to categorize the dominant trends in contemporary sociology as corporate sociology. That is, it is descriptive to refer to it as corporate sociology because, as we will attempt to demonstrate, the basic orientations, concepts, problems, and theories of American sociology are determined, at

---

1. Our analysis and proposals are especially indebted to the important work by C. W. Mills, the *Sociological Imagination* (1959), and to the work of John Horton (1964, 1966).

least in broad outline, by the needs of the corporate system of which it is a part.

There appear to be basically two major approaches within corporate sociology, which we, following Mills, will call "Abstracted Empiricism" and "Grand Theory." Abstracted Empiricism, as Mills so adequately described, is caught in the fetishism of survey methods with its concomitant of small scale and practical theory just adequate enough to interpret data to maximize its application to manipulation, intelligence, and control—that is, the system needs of those who pay for applied social research. Grand Theory, specifically the work of Talcott Parsons, the apparent antithesis of Abstracted Empiricism, is absorbed in the association and dissociation of concepts and in the elaboration of extremely "universalistic" and "diffuse" theory with little or no reference to systematic research except by way of occasional and convenient illustration.

THE FUNCTION OF TALCOTT PARSONS,

The contemporary predominance of grand theory is essentially a product of the dominant institutional system's need for a sophisticated conservative definition of social reality to legitimate the existing social structure.

Stripped of all their neo-scholastic obscurantism, Parsons' basic ideas are both very simple and very conservative:

1) People must be socialized into the prevailing value system in order to preserve the dominant system of order.

2) Those for whom this process of social manipulation does not adequately work must be subject to "second-line defense mechanisms" such as social ostracism and police control to keep them from disrupting the prevailing system of domination.

3) The "core value system" is the fundamental determinant of the organization and change of social systems. Further, political elites act to realize the societal values of "democracy," "freedom," "justice," "equality," etc. As a specific illustration, U.S. foreign policy would be considered to be motivated by a desire to spread American values to the illiterate masses of S.E. Asia, Africa, and Latin America, and has little or nothing to do with the interests of U.S. international corporations or the military establishment.

4) Each major institution functions to enhance the stability of the system as a whole. Thus, the function of the government is attainment of the society's goals, and not the pursuit of the interests of a dominant group or class. The function of economic institutions is the adaptation of the society to the social environment, and not profit making. Within this framework depressions, superfluous production, imperialism and structural

poverty become inexplicable, if not meaningless. The function of the family is, true to the conservative tradition, "tension management and latent pattern maintenance." That is, to minimize the potential disruptive effects of frustration generated by the social structure. Lastly, the function of religion, again following in the footsteps of Edmund Burke and de Tocqueville, is social integration. That is, the enhancement of social unity and order, regardless of whether the system that is being preserved is just or oppressive.

5) All history reveals the gradual development of the values of universalism, specificity, law, equality, democracy and freedom. Societies become increasingly adapted, integrated, specialized, and rich until all these tendencies are realized, as in the contemporary United States of America.

All in all, the basic Parsonian theories are neither very original nor very insightful. They are rather just a contemporary restatement in sociological neologisms and obscure prose of a long and honorable conservative tradition.[2]

In addition, the obscurity of terminology and mode of presentation employed by Parsons is itself functional. The fact that his system is incomprehensible to the uninitiated, and difficult for the sociologist, has the effect of enhancing its prestige value as a source of profundities. Further, the high level of formalization and abstraction are particularly functional as a system-legitimizing device because of the great difficulty of getting beyond vague generalizations and down to a systematic analysis of reality in order to determine whether or not the broad abstractions describe the real world in anything like a coherent fashion.

However, in spite of its powerful ideological functions, the Parsonian system is almost totally useless as a source of practical knowledge. It finds its uses solely as a legitimizing mechanism for the dominant interest structure. Neither the government nor corporations to my knowledge employ so much as one Parsonian theorist, although they employ thousands of Keynesian Economists and Opinion Pollsters.

THE FUNCTION OF ABSTRACTED EMPIRICISM

Complementary to Parsonian Grand Theory in function is Abstracted Empiricism. By shunning systematic theory and insisting on being free of moral values, Abstracted Empiricism has little bearing on the legitimacy of the current system of domination. The uses of survey methods lie rather in provision of practical knowledge for purposes of intelligence, manipulation and control. Abstracted Empiricism is organized into applied research

---

2. For further analysis of Parsonian sociology as ideology, see the articles by Horton (1966) and Szymanski (1967).

agencies to sell data gathering and analytical skills to corporate institutions interested in the control and manipulation of their members and the greater social environment.

The dominant modes of explanation employed by abstracted empiricism—role set theory, reference group theory, cross cutting cleavages, patterns of influence, etc.—are exactly the kinds of categories that interpret survey results so as to give maximum practical knowledge to those who want to use such analysis for control and manipulation. In illustration, consider the following kinds of recurring problems and answers which occupy a central place in the tradition of survey research: How can economic productivity or kill efficiency be increased?—Reduce role conflicts or status strains, or change reference groups. How can race trouble be avoided?—Give natural leadership government summer jobs, or give more welfare handouts to the poor so they can have more of society's values. Why do people buy brand X soap or vote for politician Y?—Cross cutting cleavages, status strivings, or because of patterns of influence.

The corporate government demands practical knowledge for the implementation of its domestic policies. Sociology provides information on how to reduce racial tensions and control racial outbreaks, how to recruit and advance the most suited people in its organizational structure, how to alleviate the most glaring aspects of poverty, how to increase the health of the populations, and how to control and manipulate popular attitudes on everything from milk consumption to the War in Vietnam and identification with the system in general.

The corporate government needs practical knowledge to assist in its foreign policies. It demands practical knowledge on how to prevent revolutions, and on how to crush them once they start. It needs data on the behavior of socialist countries, the probable outcomes of nuclear war, and on how to keep up military morale and increase fire power. Sociology staffs Project Camelot and the Rand Corporation, and does studies on the American soldier.

Private Corporations are fundamentally concerned with maximizing their profits. In contemporary society this takes two principle forms, sales promotion and cost reduction. Sociology provides practical knowledge on how to sell even more of a company's product (market research) and on how to reduce conflict within corporate organizations (industrial sociology) thereby increasing production. Corporations demand to know what products they can sell under existing conditions, and even more importantly, how they can manipulate the existing attitudes in favor of their products (advertising). Further, they demand to know how to increase worker identification with the firm and how to increase management control, all, of course, without modifying the basic institutional-power structure within industry.

Politicians in and out of power demand knowledge of how to stay in or get into power. The political attitude survey has become an extremely efficient knowledge gathering technique to test the popularity of individuals and issues; and further, on how to manipulate them into supporting a given issue or candidate. The survey has thus become a powerful political weapon. The results of surveys determine which candidates will decide to run for office, and which can be made popular enough to win. High popularity ratings carry with them great power to wield against one's political opponents. A low popularity rating could bring about the collapse of a political issue, at least with many marginal groups.

In summary, we have seen great system demands on sociology to produce practical knowledge to be used in manipulation and control. The tone of this demand is universally on how to adjust and how to manipulate. The great stress is not on complex understanding, but on simple, but effective techniques. It should not be surprising that those who create the demand for, and pay for, sociology, should exert great influence in determining not only its structure, but also its content.

We can see certain parallels between our analysis of Grand Theory and Abstracted Empiricism on the one hand, and the two dominant modes of contemporary economics on the other.[3] Econometrics provides highly accurate and useful practical knowledge to meet the demands of corporate institutions for information on trends of prices, costs, demand, and investment. However, more general and comprehensive matters are left to the tautological, highly abstract, formal and non-empirical theory of the price system which serves as a general legitimizing ideology for the economic system as a whole.

In our analysis, we see abstracted empiricism fulfilling the parallel function of providing highly accurate and useful practical knowledge over a narrow range to meet the demands of the dominant interest structure. At the same time, we see Parsonian Grand Theory as fulfilling a function parallel to that of the theory of the price system. That is, it is a highly abstract, formal, almost tautological, almost non-empirical system that functions as a general legitimizing ideology of the dominant interest structure.

Further, the present hegemony of our two dominant modes of sociology is also parallel to the dominance of the two major modes of economics in that neither contemporary sociology nor contemporary economics is any longer interested in laying bare the system of power and interests that organize the society. They are rather interested in obscuring these social relations in order to preserve the existing arrangements. This is done either by denying that the analysis of the total system of power and interests is the proper study of social science (the method of abstracted empiricism) or by reducing the study of total societies to formal tautologies (the method of grand theory).

---

3. For analyses of contemporary economics as ideology see especially Joan Robinson (1962) and Gunnar Myrdal (1957).

PROCESSES AND MECHANISMS

Our analysis up to now has been functional. However, many no doubt remain unconvinced, and insist that we must do more than correlate functional imperatives to elements of sociology. Therefore, we will attempt to outline the means by which the needs of the corporate system are translated into the specific outputs of sociology.

The social structure of sociology is determined by the dominant institutional structure of the society in which sociology is a part. Sociological activities take place within well-developed bureaucracies, specifically universities and research institutions, both of which are integrally tied to the interests of corporations and government.

The role of the university in American society is to provide practical knowledge, skills, and techniques to the dominant institutions, and to socialize at a sophisticated level the brighter young people and future personnel of the society into the official definition of social reality. Universities are financed by governments, corporations, or very rich individuals. Trustees and presidents are appointed largely from the ranks of the most powerful and prestigious corporations or related elites. They are expected to and do maintain, by the very nature of their jobs, close liaison with the institutions of their origin. Students are avidly recruited into the corporate and government world upon graduation. Professors and administrators shift back and forth between government, corporations and the universities. The government and corporation foundations provide a vast variety of grants, fellowships, services, and programs to students and faculty for purposes that they deem to be in the national (their) interest. Threats of budgetary cuts and loss of contributions to fund drives with the resultant loss of prestige and faculty are a constant threat forever hanging over all universities.

All in all, it is quite obvious that the university, and within it the department of sociology, is not an autonomous value-free institution dedicated to the free pursuit of pure knowledge, but rather a central and integral institution of corporate society. It is indeed difficult to see how it could be otherwise.

Beyond the direct and central importance of the factors of demand and support there are further important consequences of the bureaucratic structure of sociology itself. The life experiences of sociologists are affected by their bureaucratic activities, especially the data and problems dealt with in handling the projects of corporations and government. For many, survey research and experimental methods become the only accepted sources of data, and attitude research and social control the only important problems. Tendencies to rational systematization, high-level generalization and abstraction, and tendencies towards orientation in terms of order, rationality, harmony, and control are all reinforced by the style of bureaucratic life. All is reinforced by selective apperception and constant reinforcement from colleagues, superiors, and clients.

Sociologists assure themselves of the truth of their systems by means of the myth of self-correcting science. That is, social science is supposed to have a built-in mechanism that automatically corrects errors. The operations that any given scientist follows to come up with a given result can be repeated by another. Since science has institutionalized the value of criticism, an objective consensus is supposed to be created.

However, this logic holds only for those immersed in the same scientific paradigm.[4] That is, agreement on the significance of data can only be achieved when there is prior consensus on modes of thinking, concepts, methods, and problems. Only a given paradigm, and not social science as a whole is thus self-correcting.

The major mechanisms that reinforce the consensus among the subscribers to a hegemonic mode of sociology are: 1) the reading of the same journals, and the attendance at the same conferences; 2) the demands of one's clients and superiors to conform; 3) the informal association with one's colleagues; and 4) the necessity to adhere to the rules of the game in order to achieve rewards from the system. These mechanisms taken together put great pressure on sociologists to conform to the dominant modes of social science.

The dominant groups within a social science, further, control the departmental structure. This gives them fundamental control over the socialization of the next generation. Not only do they teach their kind of sociology, but they can offer substantial rewards to go with it, e.g., promises of jobs, recommendations, grants, etc. Further, a process of selection applies. Quite naturally members of the dominant groups are inclined to favor admission and ultimate Ph.D. acceptance to those who are most friendly to their kind of sociology (i.e., "objective social science") while weeding out those who are most hostile (that is, if they don't drop out themselves from disillusionment with sociology).

The career of the sociologist is another process of systematic selection. The dominant groups control the key institutions within sociology. Control over grants, chairs, journals, offices, advancement possibilities, etc., is in their hands. In general, adherence to the official definitions of sociological reality are rewarded, while adherence to other types of sociology negatively sanctioned.

In summary, we have analyzed a wide assortment of means by which the system demands of the dominant institutional structure are effected against sociology. The system demands practical knowledge and legitima-

---

4. For the development of this argument see Thomas Kuhn (1962).

tion. To achieve these ends, sociology is organized into universities and research centers, and sociologists are highly rewarded with material means and prestige. At the same time, the life activities and experiences of sociologists are in correspondence with the type of sociology they do. Finally, the mechanisms of socialization, selection, and control of deviance are utilized to stabilize the dominant definitions of social reality.

II. Toward a Radical Sociology

As we have seen in the previous section, the content of contemporary sociology is determined by its uses. Moreover, the structure of graduate education is also determined by the functions of sociology for the dominant system of order. Therefore, we must come to the understanding that our personal problems and frustrations as graduate students are not accidental matters, but are rather an integral part of graduate education and stem from its social functions. That is, many of our private frustrations with our education and with sociology stem directly from the social structure of sociology which is itself in turn a product of the dominant systems' needs for legitimation and manipulation.

The purpose of graduate education in sociology is not to develop our creativity or bring out our potentialities, but rather to blunt our sensitivities and curiosity. It is geared to make us into "competent professionals," content with making our small contributions to the maintenance of the system. Instead of creative thought and stimulating research we are overwhelmed with bureaucracy, formal requirements, methodology, and professionalism. The function of graduate education is to condition us to perform our system functions.

We must reject the careers being made ready for us. Our first concern as decent people and as responsible social scientists above all else must be the pursuit of understanding of the real nature of man and society and a commitment to the self-realization of human potentialities. We must not allow ourselves to be used to subvert these two fundamental commitments in the interest of material and prestige rewards. Since we produce knowledge, we must control its uses. We must insure that our theories and research contribute only to the development of understanding and to the realization of human potentialities, and that they in no way contribute to the maintenance of an oppressive system or are used for purposes of control and manipulation. In other words, we must become radical sociologists.

It will be our concern in the remainder of this paper to outline an alternative to what we have described above as corporate sociology. The presentation of our alternative will be based on a rejection of the legitimacy of the corporate system's demands on sociology. We will advocate instead a radical sociology motivated by scientific curiosity, questioning skepticism, and a commitment to human self-realization.

Corporate sociology is permeated with the ethos of professionalism. That is to say, corporate sociologists pride themselves in being specialized, "expert," and value-free; and further regard the "authoritative" corpus of sociological theory to be more or less integrated and cumulative. As an alternative to this bureaucratized orientation we propose that the following three modes of approach be substituted as the basic orientations of a radical sociology:

1) A driving and relentless curiosity to understand man and society.

2) A deep and healthy skepticism towards all received and "established" ideas, both within and without sociology.

3) A fundamental compassion for people, and an identification with the victims of the routine workings of social structures.

UNDERSTANDING

Unlike the "professional" corporate sociologist who is content to routinely study his little corner of reality with little felt concern to comprehend the whole, and/or who willingly lets his problems be determined by corporate institutions providing only that they pay enough money, the radical sociologist is impelled to understand. His involvement with sociology is not for money, social status, or professional respect, but rather to satisfy his own need to comprehend the nature of man, society, and their interrelations. He is concerned with the central questions that have concerned sensitive men since man began to think critically. Being unsatisfied with the "common sense" and official answers to these problems he is constantly concerned with applying the scientific method to them, never allowing the fetishism of concepts, or the methodological inhibition from preventing the integral unity of theory and research necessary to achieve knowledge.

What then should be the essential problems with which a radical sociology concerns itself? On this point we will follow Mills (1959:6):

. . . those who have been imaginatively aware of the promise of their work have consistently asked three sorts of questions:
(1) What is the structure of this particular society as a whole? What are its essential components, and how are they related to one another? How does it differ from other varieties of social order? Within it, what is the meaning of any particular feature for its continuance and for its change?
(2) Where does this society stand in human history? What are the mechanics by which it is changing? What is its place within and its meaning for the development of humanity as a whole? How does any particular feature we are examining affect, and how is it affected by, the historical

period in which it moves? And this period—what are its essential features? How does it differ from other periods? What are its characteristic ways of history-making?

(3) What varieties of men and women now prevail in this society and in this period? And what varieties are coming to prevail? In what ways are they selected and formed, liberated and repressed, made sensitive and blunted? What kinds of "human nature" are revealed in the conduct and character we observe in this society in this period? And what is the meaning for "human nature" of each and every feature of the society we are examining?

It is our presumption that unbiased answers to these questions would have radical implications. That is, an objective analysis in the direction that these questions point would undermine the established theories and unexamined assumptions on which corporate capitalism is based.

In establishing answers to our three kinds of questions, we would be likely to discover:

1A. That other societies are organized in quite different ways, that is, that other types of social organization, perhaps better than ours, are possible.

1B. That the institutional structure of American Society is determined by the functional needs of corporate capitalism.

2A. That our society is rapidly changing in fundamental aspects. That is, our society is being transformed into a different kind of social organization and thus is not immutable.

2B. That this process of change is determined by developments within corporate economic organizations, rather than by the free and reasoned choice of men.

3A. That the kinds of men and women that now prevail are quite different and much less happy than the variety of people existing in other kinds of historical societies.

3B. That our human potentialities are needlessly repressed in the interests of a historically unnecessary system of domination.

All of these potential findings of a truly objective and relevant sociology have, of course, revolutionary implications. It is our contention, that only by obscuring our three kinds of questions in the manner of Grand Theory, or by denying their legitimacy in the manner of Abstracted Empiricism, is it possible to avoid these radical implications.

SKEPTICISM

The dominant "professional" notion that sociology is an integrated and cumulative science implies a strong tendency to accept what the dominant men and textbooks say as authoritative. Therefore, the role of the "professional" sociologists becomes the adding of his little almost insignificant bit of research to that ever growing corpus of "scientific" knowledge, however minutely advancing man's understanding.

This notion, of course, mitigates against reexamination of the basic assumptions, orientations, methods, concepts, and problems on which the whole hegemonic edifice is based. Students are discouraged from this pursuit on the grounds that all these "philosophical" issues have already been worked out, or perhaps, are after all, not really very important. For the professional corporate sociologist students should "build," not question.

Radical sociologists, on the other hand, should accept nothing on faith and authority. Only that which can be rigorously and clearly demonstrated to each individual student should be accepted. The first task of an aspiring sociologist should be to purge his mind of everything sacred and "established" that he has come to learn and accept throughout his life, and begin anew in the manner of a Descartes, by reexamining everything in the light of rigorous science, and a basic commitment to man.

Professional sociologists might object to this procedure, arguing that if every student were to question everything, we would never get anywhere. We would argue that we are not opposed to a cumulative understanding of society, but rather, we feel the central question is *whose* definition of basic concepts, orientations, methods, and problems we are to accept as authoritative. Since our sociology of knowledge analysis has shown that acceptance of these basic assumptions rests on institutional needs and social position, we should immediately be forewarned that behind anyone who insists on the authority of tradition may be an institutional interest.

Moreover, our proposal is not significantly different from the standard procedure of education in the physical sciences. Rather than scholastically indoctrinating students in the accepted literature, every course has a parallel laboratory section which, at least ideally, systematically repeats anew the fundamental experiments that underlie the development of the physical sciences. Any critical experiment that cannot be repeated personally by a student is discussed in detail in the textbooks. As a rule, and again ideally, the student is encouraged to accept nothing that cannot be demonstrated to him personally. It is this kind of institutionalized and systematic skepticism that we propose should be one of the basic orientations of a radical sociology.

However, it should be emphasized that we are not advocating cynicism. We are not proposing that nothing can be established with a reasonable certainty, or that nothing is ultimately sacred. We are, rather, arguing in the existentialist tradition of Camus, that each individual must first reject all that is not authentic with himself, and then establish for himself what can be accepted.

HUMAN COMMITMENT

"Professional" corporate sociology argues that it is "value-free." That is, it claims that its orientations, concepts, methods, and theories are not determined by value commitments or institutional interests. It bases its case on Max Weber's overworked sophism that there is no *logical* relation between the Is and the Ought. That is, because we comprehend something in a certain way, there is no moral imperative to compel us to evaluate it in a certain other way. Nothing in the realm of ethics has any logical relation to anything in the realm of science.[5]

Logically Weber's position is, of course, impeccable, as most philosophers have realized for quite a long time. For example, because I believe murder exists does not mean that there is a logical necessity for me to evaluate it as good or bad. The two kinds of statements, as Weber clearly perceived, are not related by the rules of formal logic.

However, this argument is a classical case of a philosophical sophism which only obscures the real issue. As in most sophisms, the trick is in the posing of the problem: the way the question is asked implies the Weberian answer. But the problem posed by Weber is not the same problem which has concerned those social scientists and moral philosophers who have claimed that a relationship exists between beliefs (scientific or otherwise) and values and interests.

The problem is not one of the formal-logical relation between the Is and the Ought. It is rather a problem of the mental patterning, or consonance, between existential and evaluational ideas. The question of a relationship between beliefs and values is thus a problem for social psychology and the sociology of knowledge, and not a problem in formal logic. Furthermore, the proof of a relation or non-relation can ultimately take place only on *empirical* grounds.

As we have shown in this and in our previous paper (Szymanski, 1967), there is a close relation between the dominant modes of sociology and the values and interests of the dominant institutional structure. Therefore, the argument that corporate sociology is value-free is seen to be both formally invalid, and empirically disproven.

---

5. See Max Weber (1949):

. . . the validity of a practical imperative as a norm and the truth value of an empirical proposition are absolutely heterogeneous in character. Any attempt to treat these logically different types of propositions as identical only reduces the particular value of each of them (p. 12).

I am most emphatically opposed to the view that a realistic "science of ethics," i.e. the analysis of the influence which the ethical evaluations of a group have on their other conditions of life and of the influences which the latter, in their turn, exert on the former, can produce an "ethics" which will be able to say anything about what should happen (p. 13).

Social scientists are faced with being unable, by the very nature of their subject-matter, to escape the integral interrelation of institutional interests and their own values with their research and theory. However, we are faced with the ironical situation in which corporate sociology, by conveniently ignoring the impact of values and interests on its theories and methods is thereby determined by them, while a radical sociology, explicitly affirming basic human values, through utilizing the sociology of knowledge, is able to approach objectivity and to become free from being determined by prior value commitments.

This apparent irony has been one of the central ideas in the tradition of the sociology of knowledge. Those who first developed the sociology of knowledge (especially Marx and Mannheim) conceived of it primarily as an attempt to get under the cloak of notions that men have about themselves and society. They understood that only by recognizing and understanding the factors that make men define social reality in certain ways can it be possible to control for these factors and thus make possible a truly objective social science. To quote Karl Mannheim (1936:10):

> The desire to treat politically important problems without being a victim to bias was responsible for the development in Germany of a new brand of social science, *Wissenssoziologie*. This new branch of research, intended to be an organ of critical self-control, has already succeeded in detecting and subjecting to control important groups of sources of error.
>
> The absence of the viewpoint of *Wissenssoziologie* from a methodological analysis seems to us to be a defect, inasmuch as this branch of sociology claims to have discovered that science itself is embedded in the stream of social and historical reality . . . the available supply of terms, the techniques of questioning, the articulation and grouping of problems, may be responsible for distortion which can only be detected by means of an intimate historical acquaintance with the correspondence between the development of science and the evolution of society.

Having, we hope, gotten rid of the objection that radical sociology, unlike corporate sociology, does not aspire to be objective, we can get down to the issue at hand. That is, to what kind of fundamental value commitments must a radical sociology explicitly adhere? Historically, radicals have usually considered the most reasonable moral commitment to be the desirability of human self-realization, or the fulfillment of man's basic nature or potentiality.

One of the radical sociologist's major tasks is thus to analyze and elaborate the details of man's human nature and potentialities, and how they can be maximally fulfilled. That is, what are men's innate material and human needs, and what are the conditions of their satisfaction, i.e., what kinds of sexual arrangements, child rearing patterns, character structures, personal relations, economic organization, political forms, etc., would maximize the satisfaction of man's needs, or the fulfillment of his potential. Moreover, the radical sociologist must contribute to the development of a strategy by which a society in which man's potential would be realized could be brought into being.

The radical sociologist must serve as a constant social critic. He must incorporate into his life work an incessant critique of the dominant institutional structure to the extent that it frustrates man's human and material needs and crushes man's potentiality. The role of the radical sociologist must be to relate people's personal troubles and day-to-day concerns to the dynamics of social structures, thus translating them into political issues. This process to Mills was an integral part of the "Sociological Imagination":

> The sociological imagination enables its possessor to understand the larger historical scene in terms of its meaning for the inner life and the external careers of a variety of individuals. It enables him to take into account how individuals in the welter of their daily experience, often become falsely conscious of their social positions. Within that welter, the framework of modern society is sought, and within that framework the psychologies of a variety of men and women are formulated. By such means the personal uneasiness of individuals is focused upon explicit troubles and the indifference of publics is transformed into involvement with public issues. (1959:5)

In summary, a radical sociology must elaborate a counter definition of social reality. It must explain how badly the present society functions, how people's private frustrations stem from the social structure, how unnecessary and oppressive the present institutional arrangements are, and how much better an alternative social order would work. It must further provide the practical knowledge, techniques, and skills to the counter institutional movement that is trying to create a decent social order.

The radical sociologist must regard himself first as a human being, and as such have a basic compassion for human suffering and a basic commitment to human self-realization. To be radical, however, implies more even than this. The radical sociologist must feel a basic identity with the victims of oppressive social structures. That is, he must feel oppressed himself, and as such feel driven to join with them in their joint liberation, and in the building of a new and more human society.

III. What Should Be Done

Having developed a systematic criticism of corporate sociology and outlined an alternative orientation, we are now faced with the problem of developing some concrete suggestions as to what radically inclined sociology students should do within the presently existing departmental structures.

We maintain that radical sociologists must have an integral conception of their role as radical sociologists, and avoid a schizophrenic dissociation of their academic and political activities. Radical sociology should not mean contributing money to radical causes, nor should it mean dropping out to organize slum dwellers, draft resisters, or guerrillas. The goal of radical sociologists should be above all the formulation and propagation of a sociology relevant to the practical problems facing man. We must conceive of our contribution to the building of a decent society in terms of 1) the development of an understanding of the organization and dynamic of our society; 2) the development of an understanding of how that society can be changed and a human social organization substituted; and 3) the dissemination of these understandings to our fellow social scientists, our students, and to men in general. That is, we must act as radical intellectuals, and not as guilty liberals or union organizers.

To these ends we propose that radically inclined graduate students organize a radical sociology group which would focus on three major sorts of activities:

(1) Organize discussion groups and/or informal caucuses within the major courses offered by our departments. The function of these groups would be to systematically and reasonably present a radical point of view in each course. In those courses in which the professor or a large number of fellow students are not receptive to a radical perspective every effort ought to be made to engage them in friendly dialogue. Our goal must never be to score debating points, but always to intelligently communicate our position, win people to our viewpoint, and, of course, to develop ourselves. We should try to structure class discussion, term papers, and if possible the direction of the course itself, into a dialogue with our position. Above all, our fellow students must be treated as potential radicals, and as such never alienated, but rather always engaged in reasonable discussion.

(2) Organize a set of seminar-workshops devoted to radical sociology. We feel that these should be of basically two kinds: those working to develop a radical understanding of contemporary social structures, and those working to propagate and make this theory relevant to the radical movements of our time. The first kind of seminar-workshops should focus on such central problems as the nature of contemporary American society, imperialism and underdevelopment, and the nature of, trends in, and differences within the socialist world. The second kind of seminar-workshop should focus on radical praxis. That is, the radical understandings that are developed must be communicated to others, and made applicable to the day-to-day struggles of the New Left and Black Power movements. Relationships with such groups as S.D.S. and The Black Panthers should be established and an interchange of concerns, orientations, and knowledge engaged in. This interchange must be considered crucially important, for without it we would be in danger of losing our relevance, and the New Left in danger of failure through lack of under-

standing of the nature of the society or how to effectively change it. Without the unity of theory and practice both a radical sociology and a radical transformation of society are impossible.

(3) A publication should be organized which would have two central functions: a) continually criticize the dominant forms of sociology, either in general or through specific book reviews; b) publish articles written from a radical perspective to demonstrate to our fellow students, faculty members, and ourselves the possibilities of an alternative sociology, while at the same time encouraging an interchange of ideas, and the development of radical approaches.

Finally, sociologists must recognize that the problems they work on should have relevance to the contemporary situation of man.

Sociology and Freedom*

PETER L. BERGER

Sociology, greatly to the surprise of most of its older practitioners, has acquired the reputation of a liberating discipline. Sociology courses are crowded with students in search of the intellectual tools with which to demolish the hypocritical world of their elders and fashion for themselves, if not for society at large, a new authenticity and a new freedom. Even more astonishing expectations are directed toward sociology by students who adhere to the radical left. For them, sociology is nothing less than the theoretical arm of revolutionary praxis, that is, a liberating discipline in the literal sense of a radical transformation of the social order. It is sociology in this latter understanding that has been associated with the remarkable proportion of students of the field who are among leading activists of the New Left, both in America and in western Europe—to the point where there now are firms in Germany and in France screening job applicants in order to bar those who have taken sociology courses. Even in this country, where sociology is established more firmly in academia, there are places where the field has taken on a slightly disreputable flavor.

All this is very recent indeed. Only a few years ago most outsiders, if they thought of a sociologist at all, thought of him as a dry character, with

* Reprinted from *The American Sociologist,* 6 (February, 1971), pp. 1–5, by permission of the author and the publisher. Paper delivered January 8, 1970, at the symposium "Freedom and the Human Sciences," Loyola University, Chicago. The full proceedings of the symposium will be published by Loyola University. Permission granted by Loyola University for separate publication of this paper is gratefully acknowledged.

an insatiable lust for statistics who at best might dig up some data of use to policy makers and at worst (in the words of one malevolent commentator) might spend ten thousand dollars to discover the local house of ill repute. It would have required a wild imagination to conceive of this unexciting type as an object of interest either for young seekers after salvation or for the FBI. It has happened all the same. Especially among younger members of the profession there are now serious aspirants to drastically different images of the sociologist. There is the image of the sociologist as one of several guru types within the youth culture, in close proximity to the evangelists of psychedelia, T-group mysticism, and other fashionable gospels. There is also the image of the sociologist as a carrier of revolutionary doctrine and, potentially at least, as a character throwing Molotov cocktails through the windows of the faculty club (in either direction, depending on circumstances). Both images have provoked dismay as well as enthusiasm. The former image is especially galling for psychologists, who suddenly find themselves challenged in what so recently was a monopoly in the treatment of the metaphysical afflictions of intellectuals. The latter image is a source of alarm not only to university administrators and law enforcement officers, but to orthodox Marxists, who describe the new radical sociologists in terms that could have been borrowed from Spiro Agnew.

The greatest dismay, naturally, comes from sociologists. Placid purveyors of Parsonian theory are suddenly confronted with demands to be "relevant" to the turbulent and constantly shifting commitments of the young. Graduates of the Bureau of Applied Social Research, collectors and producers of multiple correlations with impeccable margins of error, suddenly hear themselves denounced as academic hirelings of the military-industrial complex. This confrontation between the old and the new sociology, a yawning generation gap if there ever was one, could be fully observed at the 1969 meetings of the American Sociological Association in San Francisco. There were the various caucuses of radical leftists, black militants, and (perhaps most frightening of all) liberated or wanting-to-be liberated women sociologists, each group doing its thing in the antiseptic corridors of the San Francisco Hilton. Amid this novel furor, the majority, almost furtively, went about its usual business of interviewing job candidates, drinking publishers' liquor, and reading papers in atrocious English.

Sociology should be an instrument for the existential liberation of the individual; it should be a weapon in the revolutionary struggle to liberate society. To anyone familiar with the history of the discipline, these notions are startling, if not ironic. In the origins of sociology, there was indeed a quasi-religious conception of it—the conception of Auguste Comte and his followers. Comte, however, envisaged sociology as an *anti*revolutionary doctrine, as the new church that was to restore order and progress in the wake of the havoc caused by the French Revolution. With few exceptions, however, the Comtian view of sociology as *Heilswissen* (to use Max

Scheler's term) did not survive into the classic age of the discipline, the period roughly between 1890 and 1930. None of the classic sociologists would have been able to make much sense of the current notion of sociology as a vehicle of personal liberation.

As to understanding sociology to be a doctrine of revolutionary praxis, it is noteworthy that some of the greatest classic figures (such as Max Weber, Emile Durkheim and Vilfredo Pareto) invested a good deal of effort in what they considered to be refutations of Marxism. Most classic sociology in Europe was a counterrevolutionary and (at least implicitly) conservative doctrine. Early American sociology had a strong reformist animus, but this was more congenial to YMCA secretaries than to revolutionaries or preachers of spiritual salvation. Even this mild reformism became, at most, a submerged motif as "value-freedom" and technical proficiency became established as binding norms within the profession.

I have no satisfying explanation for the recent dramatic changes in the conception of sociology. One can point, of course, to certain intellectual sources; C. Wright Mills in this country, the so-called Frankfurt School in Germany, and Marxists-turned-sociologists, such as Henri Lefebvre, in France. This, though, does not explain why these individuals and their ideas have suddenly come to exert such a powerful influence. I strongly suspect that, as is often the case in the history of ideas, there is a strong element of chance in the new affinity between sociology and political radicalism. In any case, I don't intend to devote myself here to speculation about the reasons for this slightly bizarre marriage (not the least reason being that I doubt whether it will last long). Rather than to explore historical causes, I wish to look at the theoretical question at issue, to wit: *In what sense, if at all, can sociology be called a liberating discipline?*

I shall approach the question by way of two seemingly contradictory propositions: (1) sociology is subversive of established patterns of thought, and (2) sociology is conservative in its implications for the institutional order. I suggest that *both* propositions are correct, and that understanding this entails also grasping the relationship between sociology and freedom, at least on the level of politics. (I should add here that the epistemological problem of how an empirical science can or cannot deal with man's freedom is clearly outside the scope of this paper.)

Sociology is subversive of established patterns of thought. This, of course, is today a favorite notion of those who would marry sociology to radical politics. A few years ago most sociologists would have been shocked or honestly bewildered by the proposition. Then, it was those with a vested interest in established patterns of thought who (if the inelegant simile may be forgiven) smelled the rat before those who put it there. I recall a remark made to me in 1956 by a barber in the southern town where I had just started my first teaching job. After I told him what I was teaching, he paused (more pensively than hostilely) and remarked, "Oh, I know about sociologists. You're the guys who wrote all those footnotes in the Supreme Court decision on getting the colored into the schools." He was right, of course, in an extended sense, if not literally. I wonder how many of the sociologists who busily gathered all those data on the place of the Negro in America (some of them Southerners living quite comfortably in a segregated society) imagined that they were providing the legitimations for one of the great social transformations of our time. Put differently, I suggest that there is in sociology a subversive impulse that strives for expression regardless of the intentions of individual sociologists.

Every human society has assumptions that, most of the time, are neither challenged nor reflected upon. In other words, in every society there are patterns of thought that most people accept without question as being of the very nature of things. Alfred Schutz called the sum of these "the world-taken-for-granted," which provides the parameters and the basic programs for our everyday lives. Robert and Helen Lynd, in their classic studies of *Middletown,* pointed to the same phenomenon with their concept of "of course statements"—statements that people take for granted to such a degree that, if questioned about them, they preface their answers with "of course." These socially established patterns of thought provide the individual with what we may call his basic reality kit (paraphrasing Erving Goffman), that is, with the cognitive and normative tools to build a coherent universe to live in. It is difficult to see how social life would be possible without this. But specific institutions and specific vested interests are also legitimated by such taken-for-granted patterns of thought. Thus, a threat to the taken-for-granted quality of legitimating thought patterns can very quickly become a threat to the institutions being legitimated and to the individuals who have a stake in the institutional status quo.

Sociology, willy-nilly and by its own intrinsic logic, keeps generating such threats. Simply by doing its cognitive job, sociology puts the institutional order *and* its legitimating thought patterns under critical scrutiny. Sociology has a built-in debunking effect. It shows up the fallaciousness of socially established interpretations of reality by demonstrating that the facts do not gibe with the "official" view or, even more simply by relativizing the latter, that is, by showing that it is only one of several possible views of society. *That* is already dangerous enough and would provide sufficient grounds for sociologists to become what the Prussian authorities used to call *polizeibekannt*—of interest to the cognitive if not to the actual police— and, let me add, every society has its cognitive policemen who administer the "official" definitions of reality. But sociology, at least in certain situations, is more directly subversive. It unmasks vested interests and makes visible the manner in which the latter are served by social fictions. At least in certain situations, then, sociology can be political dynamite.

A favorite term of the New Left in Europe and Latin America is derived from the vocabulary of psychoanalysis—*Bewusstmachung* in German, *concientización* in Spanish—perhaps best translated as "bringing to consciousness." This is the process of social critique by which the mystifications of "false consciousness" are demolished and the way is prepared for the demystified consciousness necessary for revolutionary praxis. I shall return shortly to the question of revolutionary praxis. As to the first aspect of the term, the subversive effects of critical social analysis on consciousness, it must be admitted that it pertains to sociology in a very basic way. Anyone who pursues the sociological perspective to its logical consequences will find himself undergoing a transformation of his consciousness of society. At least potentially, this makes him unsafe in the eyes of the guardians of law and order. It also produces unsafety, sometimes with catastrophic effects, for his own peace of mind.

"Bringing to consciousness," in this sense, does indeed have a liberating equality. But the freedom to which it leads, quite apart from its possible political effects, can be a rather terrible thing. It is the freedom of ecstasy, in the literal sense of *ek-stasis*—stepping or standing outside the routine ways and assumptions of everyday life—and this, let us recall, also includes standing apart from routine comforts and routine security. Thus, if there is a relationship between "bringing to consciousness" and the ecstasy of liberation, there is also a relationship between that ecstasy and the possibility of desperation. Toward the end of his life Max Weber was asked by a friend to whom he had been explaining the very pessimistic conclusions of his sociological analysis, "But, if you think this way, why do you continue doing sociology?" Weber's reply is one of the most chilling statements I know in the history of western thought: "Because I want to know how much I can stand." Alfred Seidel, a student of Weber's who was also greatly influenced by Freud, came to an even more pessimistic conclusion in his little book appropriately entitled *Bewusstsein als Verhaengnis—Consciousness as Doom*. Seidel concluded that the combined critical consciousness of sociology and psychoanalysis was not only politically subversive but inimical to life itself. Whatever other motives there may have been, Seidel's suicide, as a young man in the 1920s, was an existential ratification of this view of the "bringing to consciousness" of sociology.

My purpose is not to suggest that sociologists, to be consistent, should all commit suicide. I have a somewhat more benign view of the existential possibilities of sociological consciousness. Rather, I want to point out that the relationship between sociology and freedom is not as simple, or as cheerful, as the radicals in the profession would have us believe. Yes, there is a liberating quality to the discipline of sociology. Yes, there are situations where sociological understanding can be liberating in a political and (at least in terms of my own values) morally significant sense—as in the service that sociology can render to the liberation of American blacks from racial oppression. But for individual sociologists, the discipline can bring to consciousness aspects of the world that are profoundly disturbing and a freedom that, in the extreme instance, evokes truly Kierkegaardian terrors.

Sociology is conservative in its implications for the institutional order. This second proposition, put differently, means that sociology, far from leading inevitably to revolutionary praxis, actually inhibits the latter in most cases. Put differently once more, fomenters of revolution have *as* good reason to be suspicious of sociology as policemen have. This point can be made economically by way of three imperatives which, in my opinion, sociological understanding can show to be present in every human community: the imperatives of order, of continuity, and of triviality. Each of these flies in the face of some of the fondest beliefs of the contemporary left.

After a recent lecture of mine on sociological theory, a perceptive student remarked to me, "You sure have a hangup on order, don't you?" I conceded the description, but I added that my "hangup" was not arbitrary or inadvertent. Behind it is the conviction that sociology leads to the understanding that order is *the* primary imperative of social life. There is the additional conviction (which I cannot develop here) that this fact is rooted in the fundamental constitution of man, that is, that not only sociology but philosophical anthropology must lead to a "hangup on order."

Society, in essence, is the imposition of order upon the flux of human experience. Most people will first think here of what American sociologists call "social control"—the imposition of coercive power upon deviant individuals or groups—and, of course, it is in this sense that radicals will understand, and disagree with, my "hangup on order." Coercion and external controls, however, are only incidental aspects of society's imposition of order. Beginning with language, *every* social institution, no matter how "nonrepressive" or "consensual," is an imposition of order. If this is understood, it will be clear that social life abhors disorder as nature abhors a vacuum. This has the directly political implication that, except for rare and invariably brief periods, the forces of order are always stronger than those of disorder and, further, there are fairly narrow limits to the toleration of disorder in any human society.

The left, by and large, understands that all social order is precarious. It generally fails to understand that *just because of this precariousness* societies will react with almost instinctive violence to any fundamental or long-lasting threat to their order. The idea of "permanent revolution" is an anthropologically absurd fantasy. Indeed, revolutionary movements can be successful only if they succeed, and succeed fairly rapidly, in establishing new structures of order within which people can settle down with some semblance of social *and* psychic safety. Mao Tse-tung's cultural revolution can serve as a textbook example of the grotesque failure in store for any revolutionary praxis that fails to grasp this point.

The imperative of continuity is closely related to, but not identical with, the imperative of order. I suppose that, finally, it is rooted in the simple fact that people have children. If one has children, one feels a necessity to explain the past to them and to relate the present to the past. If one loves one's children (and I take it that this is the case with most people who have them), one will want to project into the future whatever good things one has possessed in one's own life—and there are very few people, even among the most oppressed, who have possessed nothing good at all. Conversely, if one loves one's parents (the current "generation crisis" nothwithstanding, I am inclined to think that this, too, is something of an anthropological constant), one will not finally want to disparage *everything* that constituted the parents' world—especially not if one comes to have children of one's own, who not only ask what will become of them but from where they come. *Children are our hostages to history.* Consequently, to be a parent means (however dimly and on whatever level of intellectual sophistication) to have a stake in the continuity of the social order. As a result, there are limits not only to social disorder but to social discontinuity. Enthusiasts for violent change (most of whom, I have noticed, don't have children) fail to recognize this. Successful revolutionaries find out about the limits of disorder, usually to their dismay, as they must settle down to govern the society over which they have gained control. The experiences of the Soviet regime with the institutions of the family and of religion are instructive in this regard.

The imperative of triviality is also, I suspect, rooted in some basic facts of the human condition—namely, the facts that man's attention span is limited and that man can tolerate only a limited amount of excitement. Perhaps the physiological foundation of this is the need for sleep. Be this as it may, social life would be psychologically intolerable if each of its moments required from us full attention, deliberate decision, and high emotional involvement. I would thus give the status of a sociological axiom to this proposition: *Triviality is one of the fundamental requirements of social life.* It is sociologically, anthropologically, and perhaps even biologically *necessary* that a goodly portion of social life take place in a state of dim awareness or semisleep. Precisely for this reason the institutional order "programs" the individual's activity. Put simply, society protects our sanity by preempting a large number of choices—not only choices of action but choices of thought. If we understand this (the understanding has been worked out systematically, by the way, in the theory of institutions by the contemporary German sociologist Arnold Gehlen), we shall see that there are limits not only to disorder and discontinuity but to the frequency of "significant events." We shall then take more seriously "meaningless rituals," "empty forms," or "mere routines" in social life—simply through recognizing that were social life in its entirety to be charged with profound meaning, we would all go out of our minds. The "meaninglessness" of so much of social life, currently decried as the source of so-called "alienation," is in fact a necessary condition for both individual and collective sanity. The currently fashionable left ideal of full participation in the sense that everybody will participate in every decision affecting his life, would, if realized, constitute a nightmare comparable to unending sleeplessness. Fortunately, it is anthropologically unrealizable, though the endless "discussion" that goes on in radical groups gives a certain approximation of the horror that its realization would signify. It is one of the mercies of human nature that, finally, all participants and all discussants must fall asleep.

I have tried to explicate the conservative bent of sociology by pointing to some basic imperatives of social life that should make the sociologist skeptical of notions of violent change and hesitant to commit himself to revolutionary praxis. I think that similar conclusions can be arrived at, by way of sociological or historical empirical analysis, for the actual processes of revolution. If all this adds up to a conservative propensity, it should be emphasized that the conservatism in question is of a peculiar kind. It is *not* a conservatism based on the conviction that the institutions of the status quo are sacred, inexorably right, or empirically inevitable. The aforementioned subversive impulse of sociology precludes this type of conservatism. Rather, it is a conservatism based on skepticism about the status quo in society *as well as* about various programs for new social orders. It is, if you wish, the conservatism of the pessimist. The seeming contradiction between our two propositions about the subversiveness and the conservatism of sociology thus resolves itself into a paradoxical but by no means irrational stance: *the stance of a man who thinks daringly but acts carefully.* This, of course, is exactly the kind of man whom our young revolutionaries will call a fink. So be it. It is probably one of the unavoidable blindnesses of youth to fail to see that acting carefully in society may, for some, be the simple result of wanting to preserve their little applecarts, but for others, motivated quite differently, it may reflect a carefully thought through concern to avoid senseless pain and to protect the good things of ordinary life. There is some irony, though, in the fact that a generation that has made a culture hero out of Albert Camus should extol his *Rebel* at the expense of his hymns of praise to the ordinary pleasures of ordinary men on sun-drenched beaches.

Sociology, therefore, is a liberating discipline in a very specific way. There can be no doubt about its liberating effects on consciousness. At least potentially, sociology may be a prelude to liberation not only of thought but of action. At the same time, however, sociology points up the social limits of freedom—the very limits that, in turn, provide the social space for any empirically viable expression of freedom. This perspective, alas, is not simple. It requires intellectual effort and is not easily harnessed to political passions. I contend that the effort is worth it and that it will serve well precisely those political purposes that come from a concern for living men rather than for abstract doctrines of liberation.

So much for sociology as a discipline. What about the sociologist? A good case can be made that there is a crisis of freedom in the world today. What is to be the place of the sociologist in this crisis?

While the place of sociology and the place of the sociologist are not identical, they are interrelated. Perhaps the easiest way to explain the difference is in terms of so-called "value-freedom," that Weberian term that has become a sort of middle-echelon devil in the conceptual hell of the sociological left. The *discipline of sociology,* I insist as emphatically as I can, must be value-free—however difficult this may be in some situations. The moment the discipline ceases to be value-free in principle, it ceases to be a science and becomes nothing but ideology, propaganda, and a part of the instrumentarium of political manipulation. The *practitioner of the discipline,* the sociologist—a living human being—must *not* be value-free. The moment he is, he betrays his humanity and (in an operation that can simultaneously be called "false consciousness" and "bad faith") transforms himself into a ghostly embodiment of abstract science. These two statements about value-freedom are made, of course, in discrete frames of reference. The statement about the value-freedom of sociology is a methodological one; the statement about the value-freedom of the sociologist is ethical. But perhaps it is appropriate to conclude these observations with a little homily.

We may return here to the two images of the sociologists that were conjured up earlier—that of the sociologist as the antiseptically neutral technician and that of the sociologist as the fiercely committed partisan. I think that the sociological left has been very largely right, ethically speaking, in its denunciations of the former type (even if it has been unfair in individual instances). In an age in which not only freedom but the very survival of man is in jeopardy, there is something obscene about the scientist who claims that he is not responsible for the uses to which his science is put. This is not to deny in any way the right of individuals to live the theoretical life or to abstain from political engagement. This right, however, can be exercised more acceptably by Byzantinologists than by most sociologists. Sociology is too much linked to the agonizing dilemmas of our time to permit most of its practitioners to pursue their theoretical interests in detachment from the struggles of their fellow-men. It is clear, beyond that, that the sociologist in the employ of politically relevant organizations cannot disclaim political responsibility for his work—a point that has been impressed on us very forcefully by the debate that followed the revelations about Project Camelot.

Because of these considerations, I emphasize my belief in the political partisanship of sociologists and concede that at times this partisanship may be quite fierce. For example, when it comes to the Pentagon's view of Latin America, my own political reactions tend to be of considerable ferociousness. It is equally important to stress, however, that the sociologist has no doctrine of redemption to bring into the political arena. What he has to contribute is the critical intelligence that is, or should be, the foundation of his discipline. This is a political *as well as* a methodological mandate. There are plenty of passions available, and the sociologist may well participate in some of them. His distinctive contribution to politics should be his consistent, unswerving application of critical intelligence—to the status quo, yes, and to any challengers of the status quo. Indeed, when a sociologist joins a revolutionary movement (an option I have indicated I would not normally prescribe), his most important political contribution to it will be his ongoing critique *of it*. Put differently, my principal objection to most of my radicalized colleagues is not that they are engaged in the business of "bringing to consciousness" but that they are not doing enough of it.

To whom will such a conception of the sociologist's role appeal? Evidently not to those who simply want a career in any kind of establishment—and not to those who see themselves as Messianic figures. It is all too clear that both such types are strongly represented in American sociology today. I have found, however, and not least among my students, that there are others—those who are still willing to commit themselves militantly to reason. And reason has its own seductiveness.

| Chapter 2 | Sociological Methods: *Should Sociologists Snoop?* |

This section on the methods employed by sociologists in their research opens with a report of the results of an important and controversial piece of recent research by Laud Humphreys. That report (which deals with homosexuals who frequent "tearooms" [public restrooms]) is drawn from a book by Professor Humphreys which was awarded the 1969 C. Wright Mills award for the best work on a critical social issue. Humphrey's paper is presented here both because of its intrinsic interest and importance and because of the methodological controversy it spawned.

Following the article, Humphreys briefly outlined the methodology he employed in his study of the tearoom trade. At strategic points in the research Humphreys disguised his true identity and it is over this deception that the controversy rages. Should a sociologist engage in research in which he deceives his respondents in order to elicit the information he needs? A journalist, Nicholas von Hoffman, argues that he should *not*, even when the information he obtains is valuable because: "No information is valuable enough to obtain by nipping away at personal liberty." Horowitz and Rainwater reply to this critique by contending that it is the political response of a journalist who is trying to restrict the encroachment of sociologists into what, heretofore, was his territory—the interpretation of the world. In effect, it is argued that journalists like von Hoffman have a stake in keeping the world a mystery, and what he is really angry about is the demystification and not the methods employed. Horowitz and Rainwater also contend that von Hoffman makes an invidious comparison between the work of sociologists and that of the police or FBI. While the police uncover information in order to prosecute, the sociologist is not interested in the individual (and certainly not in prosecuting him), but rather the collectivity. Thus Humphreys is interested in making generalizations about those who participate in the tearoom trade, and not in unmasking individual homosexuals. Finally, Horowitz and Rainwater raise what is the key issue, the "conflict between two goods: the right to privacy and the right to know." Von Hoffman has resolved this abstractly by saying that the right to privacy is *always* more important than the right to know, but Horowitz and Rainwater argue that that issue must always be resolved case by case.

This section is concluded with a more general discussion of disguised observation by Kai Erikson, in which he contends that deliberate misrepresentation in sociological research is unethical. In a more thoughtful way, Erikson agrees with von Hoffman that disguised research can hurt the subject, yet the subject is not given the option of deciding whether the possible gains outweigh the costs to him. Secondly, Erikson notes that disguised observation can hurt the sociological discipline in the eyes of the public. Here he has anticipated von Hoffman's attack in the press and the resultant harm to sociology. Thirdly, there is the burden that such research places on the graduate students who are asked to carry it out (Humphreys did not use graduate students; in fact, he was a graduate student himself when he did his research). Finally, Erikson attacks the disguised observer because he can only approximate the behavior he is imitating; he can never reproduce it. Since he can never copy the behavior, he runs the risk of "seriously disrupting the scene he hopes to study." Based on Erikson's article we can ask three questions of Humphreys:

1. Did he hurt the subjects he studied?
2. Did he hurt sociology?
3. Did his masquerade affect the behavior in the tearoom and thereby invalidate many of his observations?

Against the answers to these questions (for which we really have no answers) we must balance the gain in knowledge from Humphreys' research.

What sociologists (including Humphreys) have been guilty of is a failure to ascertain, before they begin their research, the effects of that research on the various interested parties (especially the respondents). Further, they have been guilty of not following up on the effects of their research once it is completed. From my point of view, unethical research is that which is undertaken in spite of prior knowledge (from the researcher's preliminary study of its effects and/or prior studies) that it will be harmful to those involved. Given this position, is Humphreys guilty of unethical behavior? I think not—but he *is* guilty, along with many other sociological researchers, of plunging ahead with a research project without any information about the possibility of negative effects.

Tearoom Trade:
Impersonal Sex in Public Places*

LAUD HUMPHREYS

At shortly after five o'clock on a weekday evening, four men enter a public restroom in the city park. One wears a well-tailored business suit; another wears tennis shoes, shorts and teeshirt; the third man is still clad in the khaki uniform of his filling station; the last, a salesman, has loosened his tie and left his sports coat in the car. What has caused these men to leave the company of other homeward-bound commuters on the freeway? What common interest brings these men, with their divergent backgrounds, to this public facility?

They have come here not for the obvious reason, but in a search for "instant sex." Many men—married and unmarried, those with heterosexual identities and those whose self-image is a homosexual one—seek such impersonal sex, shunning involvement, desiring kicks without commitment. Whatever reasons—social, physiological or psychological—might be postulated for this search, the phenomenon of impersonal sex persists as a widespread but rarely studied form of human interaction.

There are several settings for this type of deviant activity—the balconies of movie theaters, automobiles, behind bushes—but few offer the advantages for these men that public restrooms provide. "Tearooms," as these facilities are called in the language of the homosexual subculture, have several characteristics that make them attractive as locales for sexual encounters without involvement.

Like most other words in the homosexual vocabulary, the origin of *tearoom* is unknown. British slang has used "tea" to denote "urine." Another British usage is as a verb, meaning "to engage with, encounter, go in against." According to its most precise meaning in the argot, the only "true" tearoom is one that gains a reputation as a place where homosexual encounters occur. Presumably, any restroom could qualify for this distinction, but comparatively few are singled out at any one time. For instance, I have researched a metropolitan area with more than 90 public toilets in its parks, only 20 of which are in regular use as locales for sexual games. Restrooms thus designated join the company of automobiles and bath-

* Copyright © January, 1970, by *Trans*-action, Inc., New Brunswick, N.J., Vol. 7, pp. 11–25.

houses as places for deviant sexual activity second only to private bedrooms in popularity. During certain seasons of the year—roughly, that period from April through October that midwestern homosexuals call "the hunting season"—tearooms may surpass any other locale of homoerotic enterprise in volume of activity.

Public restrooms are chosen by those who want homoerotic activity without commitment for a number of reasons. They are accessible, easily recognized by the initiate, and provide little public visibility. Tearooms thus offer the advantages of both public and private settings. They are available and recognizable enough to attract a large volume of potential sexual partners, providing an opportunity for rapid action with a variety of men. When added to the relative privacy of these settings, such features enhance the impersonality of the sheltered interaction.

In the first place, tearooms are readily accessible to the male population. They may be located in any sort of public gathering place: department stores, bus stations, libraries, hotels, YMCAs or courthouses. In keeping with the drive-in craze of American society, however, the more popular facilities are those readily accessible to the roadways. The restrooms of public parks and beaches—and more recently the rest stops set at programmed intervals along superhighways—are now attracting the clientele that, in a more pedestrian age, frequented great buildings of the inner cities. My research is focused on the activity that takes place in the restrooms of public parks, not only because (with some seasonal variation) they provide the most action but also because of other factors that make them suitable for sociological study.

There is a great deal of difference in the volumes of homosexual activity that these accommodations shelter. In some, one might wait for months before observing a deviant act (unless solitary masturbation is considered deviant). In others, the volume approaches orgiastic dimensions. One summer afternoon, for instance, I witnessed 20 acts of fellatio in the course of an hour while waiting out a thunderstorm in a tearoom. For one who wishes to participate in (or study) such activity, the primary consideration is finding where the action is.

Occasionally, tips about the more active places may be gained from unexpected sources. Early in my research, I was approached by a man (whom I later surmised to be a park patrolman in plain clothes) while waiting at the window of a tearoom for some patrons to arrive. After finishing his business at the urinal and exchanging some remarks about the weather (it had been raining), the man came abruptly to the point: "Look, fellow, if you're looking for sex, this isn't the place. We're clamping down on this park because of trouble with the niggers. Try the john at the northeast corner of [Reagan] Park. You'll find plenty of action there." He was right. Some of my best observations were made at the spot he recommended. In most cases, however, I could only enter, wait and watch—a method that was costly in both time and gasoline. After surveying a couple of dozen such rooms in this way, however, I became able to identify the more popular tearooms by observing certain physical evidence, the most obvious of which is the location of the facility. During the warm seasons, those restrooms that are isolated from other park facilities, such as administration buildings, shops, tennis courts, playgrounds and picnic areas, are the more popular for deviant activity. The most active tearooms studied were all isolated from recreational areas, cut off by drives or lakes from baseball diamonds and picnic tables.

I have chosen the term "purlieu" (with its ancient meaning of land severed from a royal forest by perambulation) to describe the immediate environs best suited to the tearoom trade. Drives and walks that separate a public toilet from the rest of the park are almost certain guides to deviant sex. The ideal setting for homosexual activity is a tearoom situated on an island of grass, with roads close by on every side. The getaway car is just a few steps away; children are not apt to wander over from the playground; no one can surprise the participants by walking in from the woods or from over a hill; it is not likely that straight people will stop there. According to my observations, the women's side of these building is seldom used at all.

WHAT THEY WANT, WHEN THEY WANT IT

The availability of facilities they can recognize attracts a great number of men who wish, for whatever reason, to engage in impersonal homoerotic activity. Simple observation is enough to guide these participants, the researcher and, perhaps, the police to active tearooms. It is much more difficult to make an accurate appraisal of the proportion of the male population who engage in such activity over a representative length of time. Even with good sampling procedures, a large staff of assistants would be needed to make the observations necessary for an adequate census of this mobile population. All that may be said with some degree of certainty is that the percentage of the male population who participate in tearoom sex in the United States is somewhat less than the 16 percent of the adult white male population Kinsey found to have "at least as much of the homosexual as the heterosexual in their histories."

Participants assure me that it is not uncommon in tearooms for one man to fellate as many as ten others in a day. I have personally watched a fellator take on three men in succession in a half hour of observation. One respondent, who has cooperated with the researcher in a number of taped interviews, claims to average three men each day during the busy season.

I have seen some waiting turn for this type of service. Leaving one such scene on a warm September Saturday, I remarked to a man who left close behind me: "Kind of crowded in there, isn't it?" "Hell, yes," he answered, "It's getting so you have to take a number and wait in line in these places!"

There are many who frequent the same facility repeatedly. Men will come to be known as regular, even daily, participants, stopping off at the same tearoom on the way to or from work. One physician in his late fifties was so punctual in his appearance at a particular restroom that I began to look forward to our daily chats. This robust, affable respondent said he had stopped at this tearoom every evening of the week (except Wednesday, his day off) for years "for a blow-job." Another respondent, a salesman whose schedule is flexible, may "make the scene" more than once a day—usually at his favorite men's room. At the time of our formal interview, this man claimed to have had four orgasms in the past 24 hours.

According to participants I have interviewed, those who are looking for impersonal sex in tearooms are relatively certain of finding the sort of partner they want. . . .

> You go into the tearoom. You can pick up some really nice things in there. Again, it is a matter of sex real quick; and, if you like this kind, fine—you've got it. You get one and he is done; and, before long, you've got another one.

. . . and when they want it:

> Well, I go there; and you can always find someone to suck your cock, morning, noon or night. I know lots of guys who stop by there on their way to work—and all during the day.

It is this sort of volume and variety that keeps the tearooms viable as market places of the one-night-stand variety.

Of the bar crowd in gay (homosexual) society, only a small percentage would be found in park restrooms. But this more overt, gay bar clientele constitutes a minor part of those in any American city who follow a predominantly homosexual pattern. The so-called closet queens and other types of covert deviants make up the vast majority of those who engage in homosexual acts—and these are the persons most attracted to tearoom encounters.

Tearooms are popular, not because they serve as gathering places for homosexuals but because they attract a variety of men, a *minority* of whom are active in the homosexual subculture and a large group of whom have no homosexual self-identity. For various reasons, they do not want to be seen with those who might be identified as such or to become involved with them on a "social" basis.

SHELTERING SILENCE

There is another aspect of the tearoom encounters that is crucial. I refer to the silence of the interaction.

Throughout most homosexual encounters in public restrooms, nothing is spoken. One may spend many hours in these buildings and witness dozens of sexual acts without hearing a word. Of 50 encounters on which I made extensive notes, only in 15 was any word spoken. Two were encounters in which I sought to ease the strain of legitimizing myself as lookout by saying, "You go ahead—I'll watch." Four were whispered remarks between sexual partners, such as, "Not so hard!" or "Thanks." One was an exchange of greetings between friends.

The other eight verbal exchanges were in full voice and more extensive, but they reflected an attendant circumstance that was exceptional. When a group of us were locked in a restroom and attacked by several youths, we spoke for defense and out of fear. This event ruptured the reserve among us and resulted in a series of conversations among those who shared this adventure for several days afterward. Gradually, this sudden unity subsided, and the encounters drifted back into silence.

Barring such unusual events, an occasionally whispered "thanks" at the conclusion of the act constitutes the bulk of even whispered communication. At first, I presumed that speech was avoided for fear of incrimination. The excuse that intentions have been misunderstood is much weaker when those proposals are expressed in words rather than signalled by body movements. As research progressed, however, it became evident that the privacy of silent interaction accomplishes much more than mere defense against exposure to a hostile world. Even when a careful lookout is maintaining the boundaries of an encounter against intrusion, the sexual participants tend to be silent. The mechanism of silence goes beyond satisfying the demand for privacy. Like all other characteristics of the tearoom setting, it serves to guarantee anonymity, to assure the impersonality of the sex liaison.

Tearoom sex is distinctly less personal than any other form of sexual activity, with the single exception of solitary masturbation. What I mean by "less personal" is simply that there is less emotional and physical involvement in restroom fellatio—less, even, than in the furtive action that takes place in autos and behind bushes. In those instances, at least, there is generally some verbal involvement. Often, in tearoom stalls, the only portions of the players' bodies that touch are the mouth of the insertee and the penis of the insertor; and the mouths of these partners seldom open for speech.

Only a public place, such as a park restroom, could provide the lack of personal involvement in sex that certain men desire. The setting fosters the necessary turnover in participants by its accessibility and visibility to the "right" men. In these public settings, too, there exists a sort of democracy that is endemic to impersonal sex. Men of all racial, social, educational and physical characteristics meet in these places for sexual union. With the lack of involvement, personal preferences tend to be minimized.

If a person is going to entangle his body with another's in bed—or allow his mind to become involved with another mind—he will have certain standards of appearance, cleanliness, personality or age that the prospective partner must meet. Age, looks and other external variables are germane to the sexual action. As the amount of anticipated contact of body and mind in the sex act decreases, so do the standards expected of the partner. As one respondent told me:

> I go to bed with gay people, too. But if I am going to bed with a gay person, I have certain standards that I prefer them to meet. And in the tearooms you don't have to worry about these things—because it is just a purely one-sided affair.

Participants may develop strong attachments to the settings of their adventures in impersonal sex. I have noted more than once that these men seem to acquire stronger sentimental attachments to the buildings in which they meet for sex than to the persons with whom they engage in it. One respondent tells the following story: We had been discussing the relative merits of various facilities, when I asked him: "Do you remember that old tearoom across from the park garage—the one they tore down last winter?"

> Do I ever! That was the greatest place in the park. Do you know what my roommate did last Christmas, after they tore the place down? He took a wreath, sprayed it with black paint, and laid it on top of the snow—right where that corner stall had stood. . . . He was really broken up!

The walls and fixtures of these public facilities are provided by society at large, but much remains for the participants to provide for themselves. Silence in these settings is the product of years of interaction. It is a normative response to the demand for privacy without involvement, a rule that has been developed and taught. Except for solitary masturbation, sex necessitates joint action; but impersonal sex requires that this interaction be as unrevealing as possible.

People Next Door

Tearoom activity attracts a large number of participants—enough to produce the majority of arrests for homosexual offenses in the United States. Now, employing data gained from both formal and informal interviews, we shall consider what these men are like away from the scenes of impersonal sex. "For some people," says Evelyn Hooker, an authority on male homosexuality, "the seeking of sexual contacts with other males is an activity isolated from all other aspects of their lives." Such segregation is apparent with most men who engage in the homosexual activity of public restrooms; but the degree and manner in which "deviant" is isolated from "normal" behavior in their lives will be seen to vary along social dimensions.

For the man who lives next door, the tearoom participant is just another neighbor—and probably a very good one at that. He may make a little more money than the next man and work a little harder for it. It is likely that he will drive a nicer car and maintain a neater yard than do other neighbors in the block. Maybe, like some tearoom regulars, he will work with Boy Scouts in the evenings and spend much of his weekend at the church. It may be more surprising for the outsider to discover that most of these men are married.

Indeed, 54 percent of my research subjects are married and living with their wives. From the data at hand, there is no evidence that these unions are particularly unstable; nor does it appear that any of the wives are aware of their husbands' secret sexual activity. Indeed, the husbands choose public restrooms as sexual settings partly to avoid just such exposure. I see no reason to dispute the claim of a number of tearoom respondents that their preference for a form of concerted action that is fast and impersonal is largely predicated on a desire to protect their family relationships.

Superficial analysis of the data indicates that the maintenance of exemplary marriages—at least in appearance—is very important to the subjects of this study. In answering questions such as "When it comes to making decisions in your household, who generally makes them?" the participants indicate they are more apt to defer to their mates than are those in the control sample. They also indicate that they find it more important to "get along well" with their wives. In the open-ended questions regarding marital relationships, they tend to speak of them in more glowing terms.

TOM AND MYRA

This handsome couple live in ranch-style suburbia with their two young children. Tom is in his early thirties—an aggressive, muscular and virile-looking male. He works "about 75 hours a week" at his new job as a chemist. "I am *wild* about my job," he says. "I really love it!" Both of Tom's "really close" friends he met at work.

He is a Methodist and Myra a Roman Catholic, but each goes to his or her own church. Although he claims to have broad interests in life, they boil down to "games—sports like touch football or baseball."

When I asked him to tell me something about his family, Tom replied only in terms of their "good fortune" that things are not worse:

We've been fortunate that a religious problem has not occurred. We're fortunate in having two healthy children. We're fortunate that we decided to leave my last job. Being married has made me more stable.

They have been married for eleven years, and Myra is the older of the two. When asked who makes what kinds of decisions in his family, he said: "She makes most decisions about the family. She keeps the books. But I make the *major* decisions."

Myra does the household work and takes care of the children. Perceiving his main duties as those of "keeping the yard up" and "bringing home the bacon," Tom sees as his wife's only shortcoming "her lack of discipline in organization." He remarked: "She's very attractive . . . has a fair amount of poise. The best thing is that she gets along well and is able to establish close relationships with other women."

Finally, when asked how he thinks his wife feels about him and his behavior in the family, Tom replied: "She'd like to have me around more—would like for me to have a closer relationship with her and the kids." He believes it is "very important" to have the kind of sex life he needs. Reporting that he and Myra have intercourse about twice a month, he feels that his sexual needs are "adequately met" in his relationships with his wife. I also know that, from time to time, Tom has sex in the restrooms of a public park.

As an upwardly mobile man, Tom was added to the sample at a point of transition in his career as a tearoom participant. If Tom is like others who share working class origins, he may have learned of the tearoom as an economical means of achieving orgasm during his navy years. Of late, he has returned to the restrooms for occasional sexual "relief," since his wife, objecting to the use of birth control devices, has limited his conjugal outlets.

Tom still perceives his sexual needs in the symbolic terms of the class in which he was socialized: "about twice a month" is the frequency of intercourse generally reported by working class men; and, although they are reticent in reporting it, they do not perceive this frequency as adequate to meet their sexual needs, which they estimate are about the same as those felt by others of their age. My interviews indicate that such perceptions of sexual drive and satisfaction prevail among respondents of the lower-middle to upper-lower classes, whereas they are uncommon for those of the upper-middle and upper classes. Among the latter, the reported perception is of a much higher frequency of intercourse and they estimate their needs to be greater than those of "most other men."

AGING CRISIS

Not only is Tom moving into a social position that may cause him to reinterpret his sexual drive, he is also approaching a point of major crisis in his career as a tearoom participant. At the time when I observed him in an act of fellatio, he played the insertor role. Still relatively young and handsome, Tom finds himself sought out as "trade," i.e. those men who make themselves available for acts of fellatio but who, regarding themselves as "straight," refuse to reciprocate in the sexual act. Not only is that the role he expects to play in the tearoom encounters, it is the role others expect of him.

"I'm not toned up anymore," Tom complains. He is gaining weight around the middle and losing hair. As he moves past 35, Tom will face the aging crisis of the tearooms. Less and less frequently will he find himself the one sought out in these meetings. Presuming that he has been sufficiently reinforced to continue this form of sexual operation, he will be forced to seek other men. As trade he was not expected to reciprocate, but he will soon be increasingly expected to serve as insertee for those who have first taken that role for him.

In most cases, fellatio is a service performed by an older man upon a younger. In one encounter, for example, a man appearing to be around 40 was observed as insertee with a man in his twenties as insertor. A few minutes later, the man of 40 was being sucked by one in his fifties. Analyzing the estimated ages of the principal partners in 53 observed acts of fellatio, I arrived at these conclusions: the insertee was judged to be older than the insertor in 40 cases; they were approximately the same age in three; and the insertor was the older in ten instances. The age differences ranged from an insertee estimated to be 25 years older than his partner to an insertee thought to be ten years younger than his insertor.

Strong references to this crisis of aging are found in my interviews with cooperating respondents, one of whom had this to say:

Well, I started off as the straight young thing. Everyone wanted to suck my cock. I wouldn't have been caught dead with one of the things in my mouth! . . . So, here I am at 40—with grown kids—and the biggest cock-sucker in [the city]!

Similar experiences were expressed, in more reserved language, by another man, some 15 years his senior:

I suppose I was around 35—or 36—when I started giving out blow jobs. It just got so I couldn't operate any other way in the park johns. I'd still rather have a good blow job any day, but I've gotten so I like it the way it is now.

Perhaps by now there is enough real knowledge abroad to have dispelled the idea that men who engage in homosexual acts may be typed by any consistency of performance in one or another sexual role. Undoubtedly, there are preferences: few persons are so adaptable, their conditioning so undifferentiated, that they fail to exercise choice between various sexual roles and positions. Such preferences, however, are learned, and sexual repertories tend to expand with time and experience. This study of restroom sex indicates that sexual roles within these encounters are far from stable. They are apt to change within an encounter, from one encounter to another, with age, and with the amount of exposure to influences from a sexually deviant subculture.

It is to this last factor that I should like to direct the reader's attention. The degree of contact with a network of friends who share the actor's sexual interests takes a central position in mediating not only his preferences for sex role, but his style of adaptation to—and rationalization of—the deviant activity in which he participates. There are, however, two reasons why I have not classified research subjects in terms of their participation in the homosexual subculture. It is difficult to measure accurately the degree of such involvement; and such subcultural interaction depends upon other social variables, two of which are easily measured.

Family status has a definitive effect on the deviant careers of those whose concern is with controlling information about their sexual behavior. The married man who engages in homosexual activity must be much more cautious about his involvement in the subculture than his single counterpart. As a determinant of life style and sexual activity, marital status is also a determinant of the patterns of deviant adaptation and rationalization. Only those in my sample who were divorced or separated from their wives were difficult to categorize as either married or single. Those who had been married, however, showed a tendency to remain in friendship networks with married men. Three of the four were still limited in freedom by responsibilities for their children. For these reasons, I have included all men who were once married in the "married" categories.

The second determining variable is the relative autonomy of the respondent's occupation. A man is "independently" employed when his job allows him freedom of movement and security from being fired; the most obvious example is self-employment. Occupational "dependence" leaves a man little freedom for engaging in disreputable activity. The sales manager or other executive of a business firm has greater freedom than the salesman or attorney who is employed in the lower echelons of a large industry or by the federal government. The sales representative whose territory is far removed from the home office has greater independence, in terms of information control, than the minister of a local congregation. The majority of those placed in both the married and unmarried categories with *dependent* occupations were employed by large industries or the government.

Median education levels and annual family incomes indicate that those with dependent occupations rank lower on the socioeconomic scale. Only in the case of married men, however, is this correlation between social class and occupational autonomy strongly supported by the ratings of these respondents on Warner's Index of Status Characteristics. Nearly all the married men with dependent occupations are of the upper-lower or lower-middle classes, whereas those with independent occupations are of the upper-middle or upper classes. For single men, the social class variable is neither so easily identifiable nor so clearly divided. Nearly all single men in the sample can be classified only as "vaguely middle class."

As occupational autonomy and marital status remain the most important dimensions along which participants may be ranked, we shall consider four general types of tearoom customers: 1) married men with dependent occupations, 2) married men with independent occupations, 3) unmarried men with independent occupations, and 4) unmarried men with dependent occupations. As will become evident with the discussion of each type, I have employed labels from the homosexual argot, along with pseudonyms, to designate each class of participants. This is done not only to facilitate reading but to emphasize that we are describing persons rather than merely "typical" constructs.

Type I: Trade

The first classification, which includes 19 of the participants (38 percent), may be called "trade," since most would earn that appellation from the gay subculture. All of these men are, or have been, married—one was separated from his wife at the time of interviewing and another was divorced.

Most work as truck drivers, machine operators or clerical workers. There is a member of the armed forces, a carpenter, and the minister of a pentecostal church. Most of their wives work, at least part time, to help raise their median annual family income to $8,000. One in six of these men is black. All are normally masculine in appearance and mannerism. Although 14 have completed high school, there are only three college graduates among them, and five have had less than 12 years of schooling.

George is representative of this largest group of respondents. Born of second-generation German parentage in an ethnic enclave of the midwestern city where he still resides, he was raised as a Lutheran. He feels that his father (like George a truck driver) was quite warm in his relationship with him as a child. His mother he describes as a very nervous, asthmatic woman and thinks that an older sister suffered a nervous breakdown some years ago, although she was never treated for it. Another sister and a brother have evidenced no emotional problems.

At the age of 20 he married a Roman Catholic girl and has since joined her church, although he classifies himself as "lapsed." In the 14 years of their marriage, they have had seven children, one of whom is less than a year old. George doesn't think they should have more children, but his wife objects to using any type of birth control other than the rhythm method. With his wife working part time as a waitress, they have an income of about $5,000.

"How often do you have intercourse with your wife?" I asked. "Not very much the last few years," he replied. "It's up to when she feels like giving it to me—which ain't very often. I never suggest it."

George was cooking hamburgers on an outdoor grill and enjoying a beer as I interviewed him. "Me, I like to come home," he asserted. "I love to take care of the outside of the house. . . . Like to go places with the children—my wife, she doesn't."

With their mother at work, the children were running in and out of the door, revealing a household interior in gross disarray. George stopped to call one of the smaller youngsters out of the street in front of his modest, suburban home. When he resumed his remarks about his wife, there was more feeling in his description:

> My wife doesn't have much outside interest. She doesn't like to go out or take the kids places. But she's an A-1 mother, I'll say that! I guess you'd say she's very nice to get along with—but don't cross her! She gets aggravated with me—I don't know why. . . . Well, you'd have to know my wife. We fight all the time. Anymore, it seems we just don't get along—except when we're apart. Mostly, we argue about the kids. She's afraid of having more. . . . She's afraid to have sex but doesn't believe in birth control. I'd just rather not be around her! I won't suggest having sex anyway—and she just doesn't want it anymore.

While more open than most in his acknowledgement of marital tension, George's appraisal of sexual relations in the marriage is typical of those respondents classified as Trade. In 63 percent of these marriages, the wife, husband or both are Roman Catholic. When answering questions about their sexual lives, a story much like George's emerged; at least since the birth of the last child, conjugal relations have been very rare.

These data suggest that, along with providing an excuse for diminishing intercourse with their wives, the religious teachings to which most of these families adhere may cause the husbands to search for sex in the tearooms. Whatever the causes that turn them unsatisfied from the marriage bed, however, the alternate outlet must be quick, inexpensive and impersonal. Any personal, ongoing affair—any outlet requiring money or hours away from home—would threaten a marriage that is already shaky and jeopardize the most important thing these men possess, their standing as father of their children.

Around the turn of the century, before the vice squads moved in (in their never-ending process of narrowing the behavioral options of those in the lower classes), the Georges of this study would probably have made regular visits to the two-bit bordellos. With a madam watching a clock to limit the time, these cheap whorehouses provided the same sort of fast, impersonal service as today's public restrooms. I find no indication that these men seek homosexual contact as such; rather, they want a form of orgasm-producing action that is less lonely than masturbation and less involving than a love relationship. As the forces of social control deprive them of one outlet, they provide another. The newer form, it should be noted, is more stigmatizing than the previous one—thus giving "proof" to the adage that "the sinful are drawn ever deeper into perversity."

George was quite affable when interviewed on his home territory. A year before, when I first observed him in the tearoom of a park about three miles from his home, he was a far more cautious man. Situated at the window of the restroom, I saw him leave his old station wagon and, looking up and down the street, walk to the facility at a very fast pace. Once inside, he paced nervously from door to window until satisfied that I would serve as an adequate lookout. After playing the insertor role with a man who had waited in the stall farthest from the door, he left quickly, without wiping or washing his hands, and drove away toward the nearest exit from the park. In the tearoom he was a frightened man, engaging in furtive sex. In his own back yard, talking with an observer whom he failed to recognize, he was warm, open and apparently at ease.

Weighing 200 pounds or more, George has a protruding gut and tattoos on both forearms. Although muscular and in his mid-thirties, he would not be described as a handsome person. For him, no doubt, the aging crisis is also an identity crisis. Only with reluctance—and perhaps never—will he turn to the insertee role. The threat of such a role to his masculine self-image is too great. Like others of his class with whom I have had more extensive interviews, George may have learned that sexual game as a teen-age hustler, or else when serving in the army during the Korean war. In either case, his socialization into homosexual experience took place in a masculine world where it is permissible to accept money from a "queer" in return for carefully limited sexual favors. But to use one's own mouth as a substitute for the female organ, or even to express enjoyment of the action, is taboo in the Trade code.

Moreover, for men of George's occupational and marital status, there is no network of friends engaged in tearoom activity to help them adapt to the changes aging will bring. I found no evidence of friendship networks among respondents of this type, who enter and leave the restrooms alone, avoiding conversation while within. Marginal to both the heterosexual and homosexual worlds, these men shun involvement in any form of gay subculture. Type I participants report fewer friends of any sort than do those of other classes. When asked how many close friends he has, George answered: "None. I haven't got time for that."

It is difficult to interview the Trade without becoming depressed over the hopelessness of their situation. They are almost uniformly lonely and isolated: lacking success in either marriage bed or work, unable to discuss their three best friends (because they don't have three); en route from the din of factories to the clamor of children, they slip off the freeways for a few moments of impersonal sex in a toilet stall.

Such unrewarded existence is reflected in the portrait of another marginal man. A jobless Negro, he earns only contempt and sexual rejection from his working wife in return for baby-sitting duties. The paperback books and magazines scattered about his living room supported his comment that he reads a great deal to relieve boredom. (George seldom reads even the newspaper and has no hobbies to report.) No wonder that he urged me to stay for supper when my interview schedule was finished. "I really wish you'd stay a while," he said. "I haven't talked to anyone about myself in a hell of a long time!"

Type II: Ambisexuals

A very different picture emerges in the case of Dwight. As sales manager for a small manufacturing concern, he is in a position to hire men who share his sexual and other interests. Not only does he have a business associate or two who share his predilection for tearoom sex, he has been able to stretch chance meetings in the tearoom purlieu into long-lasting friendships. Once, after I had gained his confidence through repeated interviews, I asked him to name all the participants he knew. The names of five other Type II men in my sample were found in the list of nearly two dozen names he gave me.

Dwight, then, has social advantages in the public restrooms as well as in society at large. His annual income of $16,000 helps in the achievement of these benefits, as does his marriage into a large and distinguished family and his education at a prestigious local college. From his restroom friends Dwight learns which tearooms in the city are popular and where the police are clamping down. He even knows which officers are looking for payoffs and how much they expect to be paid. It is of even greater importance that his attitudes toward—and perceptions of—the tearoom encounters are shaped and reinforced by the friendship network in which he participates.

It has thus been easier for Dwight to meet the changing demands of the aging crisis. He knows others who lost no self-respect when they began "going down" on their sexual partners, and they have helped him learn to enjoy the involvement of oral membranes in impersonal sex. As Tom, too, moves into this class of participants, he can be expected to learn how to rationalize the switch in sexual roles necessitated by the loss of youthful good looks. He will cease thinking of the insertee role as threatening to his masculinity. His socialization into the Ambisexuals will make the orgasm but one of a number of kicks.

Three-fourths of the married participants with independent occupations were observed, at one time or another, participating as insertees in fellatio, compared to only one-third of the Trade. Not only do the Type II participants tend to switch roles with greater facility, they seem inclined to search beyond the tearooms for more exotic forms of sexual experience. Dwight, along with others in his class, expresses a liking for anal intercourse (both as insertee and insertor), for group activity, and even for mild forms of sadomasochistic sex. A friend of his once invited me to an "orgy" he had planned in an apartment he maintains for sexual purposes. Another friend, a social and commercial leader of the community, told me that he enjoys having men urinate in his mouth between acts of fellatio.

Dwight is in his early forties and has two sons in high school. The school-bound offspring provide him with an excuse to leave his wife at home during frequent business trips across the country. Maintaining a list of gay contacts, Dwight is able to engage wholeheartedly in the life of the homosexual subculture in other cities—the sort of involvement he is careful to avoid at home. In the parks or over cocktails, he amuses his friends with lengthy accounts of these adventures.

Dwight recounts his first sexual relationship with another boy at the age of "nine or ten":

> My parents always sent me off to camp in the summer, and it was there that I had my sexual initiation. This sort of thing usually took the form of rolling around in a bunk together and ended in our jacking each other off. . . . I suppose I started pretty early. God, I was almost in college before I had my first woman! I always had some other guy on the string in prep

school—some real romances there! But I made up for lost time with the girls during my college years. . . . During that time, I only slipped back into my old habits a couple of times—and then it was a once-only occurrence with a roommate after we had been drinking.

Culminating an active heterosexual life at the university, Dwight married the girl he had impregnated. He reports having intercourse three or four times a week with her throughout their 18 married years but also admits to supplementing that activity on occasion: "I had the seven-year-itch and stepped out on her quite a bit then." Dwight also visits the tearooms almost daily:

> I guess you might say I'm pretty highly sexed [he chuckled a little], but I really don't think that's why I go to tearooms. That's really not sex. Sex is something I have with my wife in bed. It's not as if I were committing adultery by getting my rocks off—or going down on some guy—in a tearoom. I get a kick out of it. Some of my friends go out for handball. I'd rather cruise the park. Does that sound perverse to you?

Dwight's openness in dealing with the more sensitive areas of his biography was typical of upper-middle and upper-class respondents of both the participant and control samples. Actual refusals of interviews came almost entirely from lower-class participants; more of the cooperating respondents were of the upper socioeconomic ranks. In the same vein, working-class respondents were most cautious about answering questions pertaining to their income and their social and political views.

Other researchers have encountered a similar response differential along class lines, and I realize that my educational and social characteristics encourage rapport with Dwight more than with George. It may also be assumed that sympathy with survey research increases with education. Two-thirds of the married participants with occupational independence are college graduates.

It has been suggested, however, that another factor may be operative in this instance: although the upper-class deviants may have more to lose from exposure (in the sense that the mighty have farther to fall), they also have more means at their disposal with which to protect their moral histories. Some need only tap their spending money to pay off a member of the vice squad. In other instances, social contacts with police commissioners or newspaper publishers make it possible to squelch either record or publicity of an arrest. One respondent has made substantial contributions to a police charity fund, while another hired private detectives to track down a blackmailer. Not least in their capacity to cover for errors in judgment is the fact that their word has the backing of economic and social influence. Evidence must be strong to prosecute a man who can hire the best attorneys. Lower-class men are rightfully more suspicious, for they have fewer resources with which to defend themselves if exposed.

This does not mean that Type II participants are immune to the risks of the game but simply that they are bidding from strength. To them, the risks of arrest, exposure, blackmail or physical assault contribute to the excitement quotient. It is not unusual for them to speak of cruising as an adventure, in contrast with the Trade, who engage in a furtive search for sexual relief. On the whole, then, the action of Type II respondents is apt to be somewhat bolder and their search for "kicks" less inhibited than that of most other types of participants.

Dwight is not fleeing from an unhappy home life or sexless marriage to the encounters in the parks. He expresses great devotion to his wife and children: "They're my whole life," he exclaims. All evidence indicates that, as father, citizen, businessman and church member, Dwight's behavior patterns—as viewed by his peers—are exemplary.

Five of the 12 participants in Dwight's class are members of the Episcopal church. Dwight is one of two who were raised in that church, although he is not as active a churchman as some who became Episcopalians later in life. In spite of his infrequent attendance to worship, he feels his church is "just right" for him and needs no changing. Its tradition and ceremony are intellectually and esthetically pleasing to him. Its liberal outlook on questions of morality round out a religious orientation that he finds generally supportive.

In an interview witnessed by a friend he had brought to meet me, Dwight discussed his relationship with his parents: "Father ignored me. He just never said anything to me. I don't think he ever knew I existed." [His father was an attorney, esteemed beyond the city of Dwight's birth, who died while his only son was yet in his teens.] "I hope I'm a better father to my boys than he was to me," Dwight added.

"But his mother is a remarkable woman," the friend interjected, "really one of the most fabulous women I've met! Dwight took me back to meet her—years ago, when we were lovers of a sort. I still look forward to her visits."

"She's remarkable just to have put up with me," Dwight added:

> Just to give you an idea, one vacation I brought another boy home from school with me. She walked into the bedroom one morning and caught us bare-assed in a 69 position. She just excused herself and backed out of the room. Later, when we were alone, she just looked at me—over the edge of her glasses—and said: "I'm not going to lecture you, dear, but I do hope you don't swallow that stuff!"

Although he has never had a nervous breakdown, Dwight takes "an occasional antidepressant" because of his "moodiness." "I'm really quite

moody, and I go to the tearooms more often when my spirits are low."
While his periods of depression may result in increased tearoom activity,
his deviant behavior does not seem to produce much tension in his life:

> I don't feel guilty about my little sexual games in the park. I'm not some
> sort of sick queer. . . . You might think I live two lives; but, if I do, I
> don't feel split in two by them.

Unlike the Trade, Type II participants recognize their homosexual
activity as indicative of their own psychosexual orientations. They think of
themselves as bisexual or ambisexual and have intellectualized their deviant
tendencies in terms of the pseudopsychology of the popular press. They
speak often of the great men of history, as well as of certain movie stars and
others of contemporary fame, who are also "AC/DC." Erving Goffman has
remarked that stigmatized Americans "tend to live in a literarily-defined
world." This is nowhere truer than of the subculturally oriented participants of this study. Not only do they read a great deal about homosexuality, they discuss it within their network of friends. For the Dwights there
is subcultural support that enables them to integrate their deviance with
the remainder of their lives, while maintaining control over the information that could discredit their whole being. For these reasons they look
upon the gaming encounters in the parks as enjoyable experiences.

Type III: Gay Guys

Like the Ambisexuals, unmarried respondents with independent occupations are locked into a strong subculture, a community that provides
them with knowledge about the tearooms and reinforcement in their
particular brand of deviant activity. This open participation in the gay
community distinguishes these single men from the larger group of unmar-
rieds with dependent occupations. These men take the homosexual role of
our society, and are thus the most truly "gay" of all participant types.
Except for Tim, who was recruited as a decoy in the tearooms by the vice
squad of a police department, Type III participants learned the strategies
of the tearooms through friends already experienced in this branch of the
sexual market.

Typical of this group is Ricky, a 24-year-old university student whose
older male lover supports him. Ricky stands at the median age of his type,
who range from 19 to 50 years. Half of them are college graduates and all
but one other are at least part-time students, a characteristic that explains
their low median income of $3,000. Because Ricky's lover is a good pro-
vider, he is comfortably situated in a midtown apartment, a more pleasant
residence than most of his friends enjoy.

Ricky is a thin, good-looking young man with certain movements and manners of speech that might be termed effeminate. He is careful of his appearance, dresses well, and keeps an immaculate apartment, furnished with an expensive stereo and some tasteful antique pieces. Seated on a sofa in the midst of the things his lover has provided for their mutual comfort, Ricky is impressively self-assured. He is proud to say that he has found, at least for the time being, what all those participants in his category claim to seek: a "permanent" love relationship.

Having met his lover in a park, Ricky returns there only when his mate is on a business trip or their relationship is strained. Then Ricky becomes, as he puts it, "horny," and he goes to the park to study, cruise and engage in tearoom sex:

> The bars are o.k.—but a little too public for a "married" man like me. . . . Tearooms are just another kind of action, and they do quite well when nothing better is available.

Like other Type III respondents, he shows little preference in sexual roles. "It depends on the other guy," Ricky says, "and whether I like his looks or not. Some men I'd crawl across the street on my knees for—others I wouldn't piss on!" His aging crisis will be shared with all others in the gay world. It will take the nightmarish form of waning attractiveness and the search for a permanent lover to fill his later years, but it will have no direct relationship with the tearoom roles. Because of his socialization in the homosexual society, taking the insertee role is neither traumatic for him nor related to aging.

Ricky's life revolves around his sexual deviance in a way that is not true of George or even of Dwight. Most of his friends and social contacts are connected with the homosexual subculture. His attitudes toward and rationalization of his sexual behavior are largely gained from this wide circle of friends. The gay men claim to have more close friends than do any other type of control or participant respondents. As frequency of orgasm is reported, this class also has more sex than any other group sample, averaging 2.5 acts per week. They seem relatively satisfied with this aspect of their lives and regard their sexual drive as normal—although Ricky perceives his sexual needs as less than most.

One of his tearoom friends has recently married a woman, but Ricky has no intention of following his example. Another of his type, asked about marriage, said: "I prefer men, but I would make a good *wife* for the right *man*."

The vocabulary of heterosexual marriage is commonly used by those of Ricky's type. They speak of "marrying" the men they love and want to "settle down in a nice home." In a surprising number of cases, they take their lovers "home to meet mother." This act, like the exchange of "pinky rings," is intended to provide social strength to the lovers' union.

Three of the seven persons of this type were adopted—Ricky at the age of six months. Ricky told me that his adoptive father, who died three years before our interview, was "very warm and loving. He worked hard for a living, and we moved a lot." He is still close to his adoptive mother, who knows of his sexual deviance and treats his lover "like an older son."

Ricky hopes to be a writer, an occupation that would "allow me the freedom to be myself. I have a religion [Unitarian] which allows me freedom, and I want a career which will do the same." This, again, is typical: all three of the Unitarians in the sample are Type III men, although none was raised in that faith; and their jobs are uniformly of the sort to which their sexual activity, if exposed, would present little threat.

Although these men correspond most closely to society's homosexual stereotype, they are least representative of the tearoom population, constituting only 14 percent of the participant sample. More than any other type, the Rickys seem at ease with their behavior in the sexual market, and their scarcity in the tearooms is indicative of this. They want personal sex—more permanent relationships—and the public restrooms are not where this is to be found.

That any of them patronize the tearooms at all is the result of incidental factors: they fear that open cruising in the more common homosexual market places of the baths and bars might disrupt a current love affair, or they drop in at a tearoom while waiting for a friend at one of the "watering places" where homosexuals congregate in the parks. They find the anonymity of the tearooms suitable for their purposes, but not inviting enough to provide the primary setting for sexual activity.

Type IV: Closet Queens

Another dozen of the 50 participants interviewed may be classified as single deviants with dependent occupations, "closet queens" in homosexual slang. Again, the label may be applied to others who keep their deviance hidden, whether married or single, but the covert, unmarried men are most apt to earn this appellation. With them, we have moved full circle in our classifications, for they parallel the Trade in a number of ways:

1. They have few friends, only a minority of whom are involved in tearoom activity.

2. They tend to play the insertor role, at least until they confront the crisis of aging.

3. Half of them are Roman Catholic in religion.

4. Their median annual income is $6,000; and they work as teachers, postmen, salesmen, clerks—usually for large corporations or agencies.

5. Most of them have completed only high school, although there are a few exceptionally well-educated men in this group.

6. One in six is black.

7. Not only are they afraid of becoming involved in other forms of the sexual market, they share with the Trade a relatively furtive involvement in the tearoom encounters.

Arnold will be used as the typical case. Only 22, Arnold is well below the median age of this group; but in most other respects he is quite representative, particularly in regard to the psychological problems common to Type IV.

A routine interview with Arnold stretched to nearly three hours in the suburban apartment he shares with another single man. Currently employed as a hospital attendant, he has had trouble with job stability, usually because he finds the job unsatisfactory. He frequently is unoccupied.

Arnold:

I hang around the park a lot when I don't have anything else to do. I guess I've always known about the tearooms . . . so I just started going in there to get my rocks off. But I haven't gone since I caught my lover there in September. You get in the habit of going; but I don't think I'll start in again—unless I get too desperate.

Interviewer:

Do you make the bar scene?

Arnold:

Very seldom. My roommate and I go out together once in a while, but everybody there seems to think we're lovers. So I don't really operate in the bars. I really don't like gay people. They can be so damned bitchy! I really like women better than men—except for sex. There's a lot of the female in me, and I feel more comfortable with women than with men. I understand women and like to be with them. I'm really very close to my mother. The reason I don't live at home is because there are too many brothers and sisters living there. . . .

Interviewer:

Is she still a devout Roman Catholic?

Arnold:

Well, yes and no. She still goes to Mass some, but she and I go to seances together with a friend. I am studying astrology and talk it over with her quite a bit. I also analyze handwriting and read a lot about numerology. Mother knows I am gay and doesn't seem to mind. I don't think she really believes it though.

Arnold has a health problem: "heart attacks," which the doctor says are psychological and which take the form of "palpitations, dizziness, chest pain, shortness of breath and extreme weakness." These attacks, which began soon after his father's death from a coronary two years ago, make him feel as if he were "dying and turning cold." Tranquilizers were prescribed for him, "but I threw them out, because I don't like to become dependent on such things." He quoted a book on mental control of health that drugs are "unnecessary, if you have proper control."

He also connects these health problems with his resentment of his father, who was mentally ill:

Arnold:
  I don't understand his mental illness and have always blamed him for it. You might say that I have a father complex and, along with that, a security complex. Guess that's why I always run around with older men.
Interviewer:
  Were any of your brothers gay?
Arnold:
  Not that I know of. I used to have sex with the brother closest to my age when we were little kids. But he's married now, and I don't think he is gay at all. It's just that most of the kids I ran around with always jacked each other off or screwed each other in the ass. I just seemed to grow up with it. I can't remember a time when I didn't find men attractive. . . . I used to have terrible crushes on my gym teachers, but nothing sexual ever came of it. I just worshipped them, and wanted to be around them all the time. I had coitus with a woman when I was 16 —she was 22. After it was over, she asked me what I thought of it. I told her I would rather masturbate. Boy, was she pissed off! I've always liked older men. If they are under 30, I just couldn't be less interested. . . . Nearly all my lovers have been between 30 and 50. The trouble is that *they* always want sex—and sex isn't really what I want. I just want to be with them—to have them for friends. I guess it's part of my father complex. I just want to be loved by an older man.

Few of the Type IV participants share Arnold's preference for older men, although they report poorer childhood relationships with their fathers than do those of any other group. As is the case with Arnold's roommate, many closet queens seem to prefer teen-age boys as sexual objects. This is one of the features that distinguishes them from all other participant types. Although scarce in tearooms, teen-agers make themselves available for sexual activity in other places frequented by closet queens. A number of these men regularly cruise the streets where boys thumb rides each after-noon when school is over. One closet queen from my sample has been arrested for luring boys in their early teens to his home.

Interaction between these men and the youths they seek frequently results in the sort of scandal feared by the gay community. Newspaper reports of molestations usually contain clues of the closet queen style of adaptation on the part of such offenders. Those respondents whose lives had been threatened by teen-age toughs were generally of this type. One of the standard rules governing one-night-stand operations cautions against becoming involved with such "chicken." The frequent violation of this rule by closet queens may contribute to their general disrepute among the bar set of the homosexual subculture, where "closet queen" is a pejorative term.

One Type IV respondent, an alcoholic whose intense self-hatred seemed always about to overflow, told me one night over coffee of his loneliness and his endless search for someone to love:

> I don't find it in the tearooms—although I go there because it's handy to my work. But I suppose the [hustler's hangout] is really my meat. I just want to love every one of those kids!

Later, this man was murdered by a teen-ager he had picked up.

Arnold, too, expressed loneliness and the need for someone to talk with. "When I can really sit down and talk to someone else," he said, "I begin to feel real again. I lose that constant fear of mine—that sensation that I'm dying."

STYLES OF DEVIANT ADAPTATION

Social isolation is characteristic of Type IV participants. Generally, it is more severe even than that encountered among the Trade, most of whom enjoy at least a vestigial family life. Although painfully aware of their homosexual orientations, these men find little solace in association with others who share their deviant interests. Fearing exposure, arrest, the stigmatization that might result from a participation in the homosexual subculture, they are driven to a desperate, lone-wolf sort of activity that may prove most dangerous to themselves and the rest of society. Although it is tempting to look for psychological explanations of their apparent preference for chicken, the sociological ones are evident. They resort to the more dangerous game because of a lack of both the normative restraints and adult markets that prevail in the more overt subculture. To them, the costs (financial and otherwise) of operating among street corner youths are more acceptable than those of active participation in the gay subculture. Only the tearooms provide a less expensive alternative for the closet queens.

I have tried to make it impossible for any close associate to recognize the real people behind the disguised composites portrayed in this article. But I have worked equally hard to enable a number of tearoom players to see themselves in the portrait of George, and others to find their own stories in those of Dwight, Ricky or Arnold. If I am accurate, the real Tom will wonder whether he is trade or ambisexual; and a few others will be able to identify only partly with Arnold or Ricky.

My one certainty is that there is no single composite with whom all may identify. It should now be evident that, like other next door neighbors, the participants in tearoom sex are of no one type. They vary along a number of possible continua of social characteristics. They differ widely in terms of sexual career and activity, and even in terms of what that behavior means to them or what sort of needs it may fulfill. Acting in response to a variety of pressures toward deviance (some of which we may never ascertain), their adaptations follow a number of lines of least resistance.

In delineating styles of adaptation, I do not intend to imply that these men are faced with an array of styles from which they may pick one or even a combination. No man's freedom is that great. They have been able to choose only among the limited options offered them by society. These sets of alternatives, which determine the modes of adaptation to deviant pressures, are defined and allocated in accordance with major sociological variables: occupation, marital status, age, race, amount of education. That is one meaning of social probability.

The Sociologist as Voyeur*

LAUD HUMPHREYS

The methods employed in this study of men who engage in restroom sex are the outgrowth of three ethical assumptions: First, I do not believe the social scientist should ever ignore or avoid an area of research simply because it is difficult or socially sensitive. Second, he should approach any aspect of human behavior with those means that least distort the observed phenomena. Third, he must protect respondents from harm—regardless of what such protection may cost the researcher.

Because the majority of arrests on homosexual charges in the United States result from encounters in public restrooms, I felt this form of sexual behavior to provide a legitimate, even essential, topic for sociological investigation. In our society the social control forces, not the criminologist, determine what the latter shall study.

Following this decision, the question is one of choosing research methods which permit the investigator to achieve maximum fidelity to the world he is studying. I believe ethnographic methods are the only truly empirical ones for the social scientist. When human behavior is being examined, systematic observation is essential; so I had to become a participant-observer of furtive, felonious acts.

* Copyright © January, 1970, by *Trans*-action, Inc., New Brunswick, N.J., Vol. 7, pp. 11–25.

Fortunately, the very fear and suspicion of tearoom participants produces a mechanism that makes such observation possible: a third man (generally one who obtains voyeuristic pleasure from his duties) serves as a lookout, moving back and forth from door to windows. Such a "watch-queen," as he is labeled in the homosexual argot, coughs when a police car stops nearby or when a stranger approaches. He nods affirmatively when he recognizes a man entering as being a "regular." Having been taught the watchqueen role by a cooperating respondent, I played that part faithfully while observing hundreds of acts of fellatio. After developing a systematic observation sheet, I recorded fifty of these encounters (involving 53 sexual acts) in great detail. These records were compared with another 30 made by a cooperating respondent who was himself a sexual participant. The bulk of information presented in *Tearoom Trade* results from these observations.

Although primarily interested in the stigmatized behavior, I also wanted to know about the men who take such risks for a few moments of impersonal sex. I was able to engage a number of participants in conversation outside the restrooms; and, eventually, by revealing the purpose of my study to them, I gained a dozen respondents who contributed hundreds of hours of interview time. This sample I knew to be biased in favor of the more outgoing and better educated of the tearoom population.

To overcome this bias, I cut short a number of my observations of encounters and hurried to my automobile. There, with the help of a tape recorder, I noted a brief description of each participant, his sexual role in the encounter just observed, his license number and a brief description of his car. I varied such records from park to park and to correspond with previously observed changes in volume at various times of the day. This provided me with a time-and-place-representative sample of 134 participants. With attrition, chiefly of those who had changed address or who drove rented cars, and the addition of two persons who walked to the tearooms, I ended up with a sample of 100 men, each of whom I had actually observed engaging in fellatio.

At this stage, my third ethical concern impinged. I already knew that many of my respondents were married and that all were in a highly discreditable position and fearful of discovery. How could I approach these covert deviants for interviews? By passing as deviant, I had observed their sexual behavior without disturbing it. Now, I was faced with interviewing these men (often in the presence of their wives) without destroying them. Fortunately, I held another research job which placed me in the position of preparing the interview schedule for a social health survey of a random selection of male subjects throughout the community. With permission from the survey's directors, I could add my sample to the larger group (thus enhancing their anonymity) and interview them as part of the social health survey.

To overcome the danger of having a subject recognize me as a watch-queen, I changed my hair style, attire and automobile. At the risk of losing more transient respondents, I waited a year between the sample gathering and the interviews, during which time I took notes on their homes and neighborhoods and acquired data on them from the city and county directories.

Having randomized the sample, I completed 50 interviews with tea-room participants and added another 50 interviews from the social health survey sample. The latter control group was matched with the participants on the bases of marital status, race, job classification and area of residence. This study, then, results from a confluence of strategies: systematic, firsthand observation, in-depth interviews with available respondents, the use of archival data, and structured interviews of a representative sample and a matched control group. At each level of research, I applied those measures which provided maximum protection for research subjects and the truest measurement of persons and behavior observed.

Sociological Snoopers*

NICHOLAS VON HOFFMAN

We're so preoccupied with defending our privacy against insurance investigators, dope sleuths, counterespionage men, divorce detectives and credit checkers, that we overlook the social scientists behind the hunting blinds who're also peeping into what we thought were our most private and secret lives. But they are there, studying us, taking notes, getting to know us as indifferent as everybody else to the feeling that to be a complete human involves having an aspect of ourselves that's unknown.

If there was any doubt about there being somebody who wants to know about anything any other human being might be doing it is cancelled out in the latest issue of *Trans*-action, a popular but respected sociological monthly. The lead article, entitled "Impersonal Sex in Public Places," is a résumé of a study done about the nature and pattern of homosexual activities in men's rooms. Laud Humphrey, the author, is an Episcopal priest, a duly pee-aich-deed sociologist, holding the rank of assistant professor at Southern Illinois University. The article is taken from a forthcoming book called *Tearoom Trade: Impersonal Sex in Public Places* (Aldine Publishing Company, Chicago, March 1970).

Tearoom is the homosexual slang for men's rooms that are used for

---

* Reprinted by permission from *The Washington Post,* January 30, 1970.

purposes other than those for which they were designed. However, if a straight male were to hang around a tearoom he wouldn't see anything out of the ordinary so that if you're going to find out what's happening you must give the impression that you're one of the gang.

"I had to become a participant observer of the furtive felonious acts," Humphreys writes in explaining his methodology, "Fortunately, the very fear and suspicion of tearoom participants produces a mechanism that makes such observations possible; a third man—generally one who obtains voyeuristic pleasure from his duties—serves as a lookout, moving back and forth from door to windows. Such a 'watchqueen,' as he is labeled in the homosexual argot, coughs when a police car stops nearby or when a stranger approaches. He nods affirmatively when he recognizes a man entering as being a 'regular.' Having been taught the watchqueen role by a cooperating respondent, I played that part faithfully while observing hundreds of acts of fellatio."

Most of the people Humphreys observed and took notes on had no idea what he was doing or that they, in disguised form, would be showing up in print at some time in the future. Of all the men he studied only a dozen were ever told what his real purpose was, yet as a sociologist he had to learn about the backgrounds and vital facts of the other tearoom visitors he'd seen. To do this Humphreys noted their license numbers and by tracing their cars learned their identities. He then allowed time to pass, disguised himself and visited these men under the color of doing a different, more innocuous, door-to-door survey.

He describes what he did this way: "By passing as a deviant, I had observed their sexual behavior without disturbing it. Now I was faced with interviewing these men—often in the presence of their wives—without destroying them . . . To overcome the danger of having a subject recognize me as a watchqueen, I changed my hair style, attire and automobile. At the risk of losing the more transient respondents, I waited a year between the sample gathering [in the tearoom] and the interviews, during which time I took notes on their homes and neighborhoods and acquired data on them from the city and county directories."

Humphreys said that he did everything possible to make sure the names of the men whose secrets he knew would never get out: "I kept only one copy of the master list of names and that was in a safe deposit box. I did all the transcribing of taped interviews myself and changed all identifying marks and signs. In one instance, I allowed myself to be arrested rather than let the police know what I was doing and the kind of information I had."

Even so, it remains true that he collected information that could be used for blackmail, extortion, and the worst kind of mischief without the knowledge of the people involved. *Trans*-action defends the ethics of Humphreys' methodology on the basis of purity of motive and the argument that he was doing it for a good cause, that is getting needed, reliable information about a difficult and painful social problem.

Everybody who goes snooping around and spying on people can be said to have good motives. The people whom Sen. Sam Ervin is fighting, the ones who want to give the police the right to smash down your door without announcing who they are if they think you have pot in your house, believe they are well-motivated. They think they are preventing young people from destroying themselves. J. Edgar Hoover unquestionably believes he's protecting the country against subversion when he orders your telephone tapped. Those who may want to overthrow the government are just as well motivated by their lights. Since everybody can be said to be equally well motivated, it's impossible to form a judgment on what people do by assessing their intentions.

To this Laud Humphreys replies that his methods were less objectionable than getting his data by working through the police: "You do walk a really perilous tightrope in regard to ethical matters in studies like this, but, unless someone will walk it, the only source of information will be the police department, and that's dangerous for a society. The methods I used were the least intrusive possible. Oh, I could have hidden in the ceiling as the police do, but then I would have been an accomplice in what they were doing."

Humphreys believes that the police in many cities extort bribes from homosexuals they catch in tearooms. He also thinks that "what's more common is putting an investigation report on file. Often when they catch somebody, they don't arrest him but they get his name, address and employer. There's no defense against this and no way of knowing when the information will be used in the future. I agree there may be a dangerous precedent in studying deviant behavior this way but in some places vice squads use closed circuit TV to look into tearooms and in many cities they use decoys. To my mind *these* are the people who're the dangerous observers."

Some people may answer that by saying a study on such a topic constitutes deviant sociological behavior, a giving-in to the discipline's sometimes peculiar taste for nosing around oddballs. But in the study of man anything men do should be permissible to observe and try to understand. Furthermore, Humphreys has evidence and arguments to show that, far from being a rare and nutty aberration, tearoom activity is quite common.

He cites a UCLA law review study showing that in a four-year period in Los Angeles 274 of a total of 493 men arrested for homosexual activities were picked up in tearooms. He has another study in Mansfield, Ohio, that rural fleshpot, saying that police operating with a camera behind a one-way mirror caught 65 men in the course of only two weeks. FBI national crime figures don't have a special category for tearoom arrests, but Humphreys has enough indicative evidence to allow him to say it's a big problem. Even if it weren't, so many parents are worried about their sons being approached by homosexuals that we believe it's a big problem.

Humphreys' study suggests that tearoom habitués stay clear of teenagers. "I never saw an instance of a teen-ager being approached. The men in the tearoom are scared to death of teen-agers. When a teen-ager comes in the action breaks off and everybody gets out. You have to give a definite sign before you'll be approached [in his book he goes into detail] so they never approach anyone who hasn't done so. Anyway, there's no problem of recruiting teen-agers because teen-agers are too busy trying to join."

Incontestably such information is useful to parents, teen-agers themselves, to policemen, legislators and many others, but it was done by invading some people's privacy. This newspaper could probably learn a lot of things that the public has a right and need to know if its reporters were to use disguises and the gimmickry of modern, transistorized, domestic espionage, but there is a policy against it. No information is valuable enough to obtain by nipping away at personal liberty, and that is true no matter who's doing the gnawing, John Mitchell and the conservatives over at the Justice Department or Laud Humphreys and the liberals over at the Sociology Department.

Journalistic Moralizers*

IRVING LOUIS HOROWITZ AND LEE RAINWATER

Columnist Nicholas von Hoffman's quarrel with Laud Humphreys' "Impersonal Sex in Public Places" starkly raises an issue that has grown almost imperceptibly over the last few years, and now threatens to create in the next decade a tame sociology to replace the fairly robust one that developed during the sixties. For most of their history, the disciplines of sociology and social psychology were considered a kind of joke, an oddball activity pursued by academic types who cultivated an arcane jargon that either concealed ivory tower views about human reality, or simply said things that everyone knew already.

Somehow, during the 1960s, that image began to shift quite dramatically. People suddenly began to look to sociologists and social psychologists for explanations of what was going on, of why the society was plagued with so many problems. Sociological jargon, perspectives and findings began to enter people's conversation and thinking in a way that no one

* Copyright © January, 1970, by *Trans*-action, Inc., New Brunswick, N.J.

would have imagined a few years before. All during the sixties enrollment in sociology classes in colleges and universities increased at an accelerating rate. What sociologists had to say about international relations, or race problems, or deviant behavior, or health care or the crisis of the city became standard parts of the ways Americans explained themselves to themselves.

But as the sociological enterprise grew, there also grew up a reaction against it, especially among those who are also in the business of interpreting the society to itself. For, as sociologists know (even if they sometimes forget it), any statement, even of "fact," about a society is also a political assertion in that, whatever the motivation of the speaker, his views can have an impact on the political processes of the society. But there are other kinds of occupations that have traditionally had the right to make these kinds of statements. Foremost among them have been journalists, clergymen, politicians and intellectuals generally. When his perspectives and findings began to gain wider currency, the sociologist became willy-nilly a competitor in the effort to establish an interpretation of what we are all about. And so, these past few years, sociologists have been getting their lumps from those various groups.

With increasing stridency, traditional politicians have railed against university social scientists who exercise undue influence on the way public issues are defined. Right and left militants have sought to dry up their ability to influence public definitions through derision and systematic efforts to deny them access to sources of data. Beginning in the fifties, right wing groups launched successive campaigns against behavioral scientists, as both practitioners and teachers, culminating most recently in the John Birch Society campaign against sex education. All this has had a quiet influence on the research work of social scientists. Slowly but perceptibly over the last couple of years, and with no sign of abatement, sociologists and social psychologists are being told by a varied chorus that they talk too much, or if not too much, at least that too many of the things they say had better be left unsaid, or the saying of them ought to be left to the traditional spokesmen. What has proved particularly galling about the sociologist, as these other spokesmen view him, is his claim to the mantle of science. For all the tentativeness and roughness of sociological science, it makes at least that claim, and so represents a very powerful threat to the more traditional interpreters of reality.

Perhaps the closest competitors of all are journalists. The intertwinings of journalistic and sociological enterprise are complex indeed and have been from the early days of empirical American sociology. After all, Robert Park was a working journalist, and saw sociology simply as a better journalism because it got at the "big picture." Predictably, then, journalists often feel a deep ambivalence about empirical sociology. On the one hand, it represents a resource that can be quite useful in doing journalistic work.

On the other hand, for the ambitious practitioner of personal journalism, there is always the threat to his authority, his potential punditry, by a group of fellow interpreters of the world who lay claim to science as the basis of what they say.

It is perhaps for this reason that von Hoffman so readily applies to sociologists a standard of investigative conduct that few journalists could measure up to, and why he is so unwilling to accept the relevance of the socially constructive purpose to which sociological activities are directed.

Sociologists have tended to assume that well-intentioned people fully accept the desirability of demystification of human life and culture. In the age of Aquarius, however, perhaps such a view will be recognized as naive.

"They are there, studying us, taking notes, getting to know us, as indifferent as everybody else to the feeling that to be a complete human involves having an aspect of ourselves that's unknown." Von Hoffman seems to mean this to be a statement about the right to privacy in a legal sense, but it really represents a denial of the ability of people to understand themselves and each other in an existential sense. This denial masks a fear, not that intimate details of our lives will be revealed to *others,* but rather that we may get to know *ourselves* better and have to confront what up to now we did not know about ourselves. Just as psychoanalysis was a scientific revolution as threatening to traditional conceptions as those of Galileo and Kepler had been, it may well be that the sociologist's budding ability to say something about the how's and why's of men's relationships to each other is deeply threatening not only to the established institutions in society, but also in a more personal way to all members of society.

Von Hoffman says he is talking about the invasion of privacy, but his celebration of the "aspect of ourselves that's unknown" shows a deeper worry about making rational and open what he conceives to be properly closed and dark in human reality. Von Hoffman concentrates his outrage on the methods Humphreys used to learn what he did, but we believe that at bottom he is not much different from other critics of behavioral science who make exactly the same points that von Hoffman makes with respect to research, even when it involves people who freely give their opinions, attitudes and autobiographical data to interviewers. This, too, is regarded as a threat because eventually it will remove some of the mystery from human life.

But von Hoffman recognizes that his most appealing charge has to do with privacy, and so he makes much of the fact that Humphreys collected information that could be used for "blackmail, extortion, and the worst kind of mischief without the knowledge of the people involved."

Here his double standard is most glaringly apparent. Journalists routinely, day in, day out, collect information that could be used for "blackmail, extortion, and the worst kind of mischief without the knowledge of the people involved." But von Hoffman knows that the purpose of their work is none of those things, and so long as their information is collected from public sources, I assume he wouldn't attack them. Yet he nowhere compares the things sociologists do with the things his fellow journalists do. Instead, he couples Humphreys' "snooping around," "spying on people" with similarly "well-motivated" invaders of privacy as J. Edgar Hoover and John Mitchell.

To say the least, the comparison is invidious; the two kinds of enterprises are fundamentally different. No police group seeks to acquire information about people with any other goal than that of, in some way, prosecuting them. Policemen collect data, openly or under cover, in order to put someone in jail. Whatever it is, the sociological enterprise is not that. Sociologists are not interested in directly affecting the lives of the particular people they study. They are interested in those individuals only as representatives of some larger aggregate—in Humphreys' case, all participants in the tearoom action. Therefore, in almost all sociological research, the necessity to preserve the anonymity of the respondent is not an onerous one, because no purpose at all would be served by identifying the respondents.

In this respect, journalists are in fact much closer to policemen than sociologists are. Journalists often feel that their function is to point the finger at particular malefactors. Indeed their effort to acquire information about individuals is somewhat like that of the police, in the sense that both seek to affect importantly the lives of the particular individuals who are the object of their attention. Perhaps this kind of misconception of what the sociologist is about, and the total absence of any comment on the role of the journalist, leads von Hoffman to persistently misinterpret Humphreys' research as "invading some people's privacy." Yet everything Humphreys knew about the deviant behavior of the people he studied was acquired in a public context (indeed, on public land).

We believe in the work Humphreys has done, in its principled humaneness, in its courage to learn the truth and in the constructive contribution that it makes toward our understanding of all the issues, including the moral, raised by deviant behavior in our society. *Trans-action* has always been supportive of and open to the sort of enterprise he has so ably performed; we only wish there were more of it. Furthermore, a vigorous defense of Laud Humphreys' research (and that of others before and after him) is eminently possible and glaringly needed.

Sociologists uphold the right to know in a context of the surest protection for the integrity of the subject matter and the private rights of the people studied. Other groups in society may turn on different pivots: the right of law, the protection of individuals against invasion of privacy and so forth. But whoever is "right" in the abstract, there is a shared obligation for all parties to a controversy to step forth with fullness and fairness to present their cases before the interested public—and to permit that public to enter discussions which affect them so directly. Without this, a right higher than public disclosure or private self will be denied—the right to full public discourse.

Von Hoffman's points are: that in studying the sexual behavior of men in restrooms, Humphreys violated their rights to intimacy and privacy; that the homosexuals were and remain unaware of the true purpose of Humphreys' presence as a lookout; and that in the follow-up questionnaire the researcher further disguised himself and the true nature of his inquiry. For von Hoffman the point of principle is this: that although Humphreys' intent may have been above reproach and that in point of fact his purposes are antithetical to those of the police and other public officials, he nonetheless in his own way chipped away at the essential rights of individuals in conducting his investigations. Therefore, the ends, the goals, however noble and favorable to the plight of sexual deviants, do not justify the use of any means that further undermine personal liberties. Let us respond to these propositions as directly as possible.

COPS AND KNOWLEDGE

First, the question of the invasion of privacy has several dimensions. We have already noted the public rather than the private nature of park restrooms. It further has to be appreciated that all participants in sexual activities in restrooms run the constant risk that they have among them people who have ulterior purposes. The vocabulary of motives is surely not limited or circumscribed by one man doing research but is as rich and as varied as the number of participants themselves. The fact that in this instance there was a scientific rather than a sexual or criminal "ulterior motive" does not necessarily make it more hideous or more subject to criticism, but perhaps less so.

Second, the question of disguising "the true nature" and purpose of this piece of research has to be put into some perspective. To begin with, let us assume that the research was worth doing in the first place. We know almost nothing about impersonal sex in public places, and the fact that we know so little has in no small way contributed to the fact that the cops feel that *they* know all that needs to be known about the matter. Who, then, is going to gather this countervailing knowledge? Von Hoffman implies that the research enterprise would be ethically pure if Humphreys were himself a full participant, like John Rechy. But to be able to conduct investigations of the type Humphreys performed requires a sociological imagination rare enough among his professional peers, much less homosexuals in public places. Moreover, to assume that the investigator must share all of his knowledge with those being investigated also assumes a common universe of discourse very rarely found in any kind of research, much less the kind involving sexual deviance. Furthermore, the conduct of Humphreys' follow-up inquiries had to be performed with tact and with skill precisely because he discovered that so many of the people in his survey were married men and family men. Indeed, one of the great merits of Humphreys' research is that it reveals clearly etched class, ethnic, political and occupational characteristics of sexual participants never before properly understood. Had he not conducted the follow-up interviews, we would once again be thrown back on simpleminded, psychological explanations that are truly more voyeuristic than analytic, or on the policeman's kind of knowledge. It is the sociological dimensions of sexuality in public places that make this a truly scientific breakthrough.

To take on the ethic of full disclosure at the point of follow-up interviews was impossible given the purposes of the research. If Humphreys had told his respondents that he knew they were tearoom participants, most of them would have cooperated. But in gaining their cooperation in this way he would have had to reveal that he knew of their behavior. This he could not responsibly do, because he could not control the potentially destructive impact of that knowledge. Folding the participants into a larger sample for a different survey allowed for the collection of the data without posing such a threat. And the purpose of the research was not, after all, destruction, as von Hoffman concedes. Therefore, the posture of Humphreys toward those interviewed must be viewed as humane and considerate.

But what von Hoffman is arguing is that this research ought not to have been done, that Humphreys should have laid aside his obligation to society as a sociologist and taken more seriously his obligation to society as a citizen. Von Hoffman maintains that the researcher's intentions—the pursuit of truth, the creation of countervailing knowledge, the demystification of shadowy areas of human experience—are immaterial. "Everybody who goes snooping around and spying on people can be said to have good motives," von Hoffman writes, going on to compare Humphreys' work with policemen armed with a "no-knock" statute.

This is offensive, but it is also stupid. We have called von Hoffman a moralizer, and his moralizing consists precisely in his imputing a moral equivalence to police action, under probably unconstitutional law, and the work of a scholar. Of course the road to hell is paved with good intentions, but good intentions sometimes lead to other places as well. The great achievement of Humphreys' research has been in laying bare the conditions of the tearoom trade, the social classes who engage in such activities and the appalling idiocy and brutality of society's (police) efforts to cope with the situation. Moreover, he has, relative to some of his professional colleagues, answered the question Which side are you on? with uncharacteristic candor, while at the same time he has conducted himself in the best tradition of professional sociology.

The only interesting issue raised by von Hoffman is one that he cannot, being a moralizer, do justice to. It is whether the work one does is good, and whether the good it does outweighs the bad. "No information," he writes, "is valuable enough to obtain by nipping away at personal liberty. . . ." It remains to be proven that Humphreys did in fact nip away at anyone's liberty; so far we have only von Hoffman's assertion that he did and Humphreys' assurance that he did not. But no amount of self-righteous dogmatizing can still the uneasy and troublesome thought that what we have here is not a conflict between nasty snoopers and the right to privacy, but a conflict between two goods: the right to privacy and the right to know.

What is required is a distinction between the responsibilities of social scientists to seek and to obtain greater knowledge and the responsibilities of the legal system to seek and obtain maximum security for the private rights of private citizens. Nothing is more insidious or dangerous than the over-professionalization of a trade. But for social scientists to play at being lawyers, at settling what the law is only now beginning to give attention to, is clearly not a sound way of solving the problems raised.

LIBERAL CONTRADICTIONS

It is certainly not that sociologists should deliberately violate any laws of the land, only that they should leave to the courtrooms and to the legislatures just what interpretation of these laws governing the protection of private citizens is to be made. Would the refusal of a family to disclose information to the Census Bureau on the grounds of the right to privacy take precedence over the United States government's right to knowledge in order to make budgetary allocations and legislation concerning these people? The really tough moral problem is that the idea of an inviolable right of privacy may move counter to the belief that society is obligated to secure the other rights and welfare of its citizenry. Indeed one might say that this is a key contradiction in the contemporary position of the liberal: he wants to protect the rights of private citizens, but at the same time he wants to develop a welfare system that could hardly function without at least some knowledge about these citizens. Von Hoffman's strident defense of the right to privacy is laudable; we are all behind him. What is inexcusable in someone of his intelligence is that he will not see that the issues he raises pose a moral dilemma that cannot be resolved in the abstract, only in the particular case. He may think that Humphreys' research is the moral equivalent of John Mitchell's FBI. We don't, and we have tried to explain why.

Several other minor points in the von Hoffman article require at least brief recollection. First, *Trans*-action has made no statement until this time on the ethics of the kind of research conducted by Laud Humphreys. Indeed, our editorial statements have always emphasized the right to privacy of the researcher over and against the wishes of established authority. To say that *Trans*-action has defended this piece in terms of "priority of motive" is an error of fact. The intent of *Trans*-action is to present the best available social science research, and we believe Humphreys' work admirably fits that description.

PUBLIC RIGHTS AND PRIVATE AGONY

Finally, von Hoffman's gratuitous linkage of the "conservatives over at the Justice Department" and the "liberals over at the sociology department" makes for a pleasant balance of syntax, but it makes no sense in real life terms. The political ideology of Laud Humphreys is first of all not an issue. At no point in the article or outside the article is the question of the political preference of the researcher raised.

We would suggest that von Hoffman is the real "liberal" in this argument, for it is he who is assuming the correctness of the classical liberal argument for the supremacy of the private person over and against the public commonweal. This assumption makes it appear that he is willing to suffer the consequences of the abuse of homosexuals by blackmailers, policemen or would-be participants, but that he is not willing to suffer the consequences of a research design or to try to change the situation by a factual understanding of the social sources of these problems.

Laud Humphreys has gone beyond the existing literature in sexual behavior and has proven once again, if indeed proof were ever needed, that ethnographic research is a powerful tool for social understanding and policymaking. And these are the criteria by which the research should finally be evaluated professionally. If the nonprofessional has other measurements of this type of research, let him present these objections in legal brief and do so explicitly. No such attempt to intimidate Humphreys for wrongdoing in any legal sense has been made, and none is forthcoming. The only indictment seems to be among those who are less concerned with the right to know than they are with the sublime desire to remain in ignorance. In other words, the issue is not liberalism vs. conservatism or privacy vs. publicity, but much more simply and to the point, the right of scientists to conduct their work as against the right of journalists to defend social mystery and private agony.

A Comment on Disguised
Observation in Sociology*

KAI T. ERIKSON

At the beginning of their excellent paper on the subject, Howard S. Becker and Blanche Geer define participant observation as "that method in which the observer participates in the daily life of the people under study, either openly in the role of researcher or covertly in some disguised role . . ."[1]

The purpose of this paper is to argue that the research strategy mentioned in the last few words of that description represents a significant ethical problem in the field of sociology. In point of sheer volume, of course, the problem is relatively small, for disguised participant observation is probably one of the rarest research techniques in use among sociologists. But in point of general importance, the problem is far more serious—partly because the use of disguises seems to attract a disproportionate amount of interest both inside and outside the field, and partly because it offers a natural starting point for dealing with other ethical issues in the profession.

In recent years, a handful of studies have been reported in the literature based on the work of observers who deliberately misrepresented their identity in order to enter an otherwise inaccessible social situation. Some of these studies have already provoked a good deal of comment—among them, for instance, the cases of the anthropologist who posed as a mental patient by complaining of symptoms he did not feel,[2] the sociologists who joined a gathering of religious mystics by professing convictions they did not share,[3] the Air Force officer who borrowed a new name, a new birth date, a new personal history, a new set of mannerisms and even a new physical appearance in order to impersonate an enlisted man,[4] and the group of graduate students who ventured into a meeting of Alcoholics Anonymous wearing

---

* Reprinted from *Social Problems,* 14 (Spring, 1967), pp. 366–373, by permission of the author and The Society for the Study of Social Problems, publisher.
1. Howard S. Becker and Blanche Geer, "Participant Observation and Interviewing: A Comparison," *Human Organization,* 16 (1957), pp. 28–32.
2. William C. Caudill *et al.,* "Social Structure and Interaction Processes on a Psychiatric Ward," *American Journal of Orthopsychiatry,* 22 (1952), pp. 314–334.
3. Leon Festinger, Henry W. Riecken, and Stanley Schacter, *When Prophecy Fails.* Minneapolis: University of Minnesota Press, 1956.
4. Mortimer A. Sullivan, Stuart A. Queen, and Ralph C. Patrick, Jr., "Participant Observation as Employed in the Study of a Military Training Program," *American Sociological Review,* 23 (1958), pp. 660–667.

the clothes of men from other social classes than their own and the facial expressions of men suffering from an unfortunate disability.[5]

In taking the position that this kind of masquerading is unethical, I am naturally going to say many things that are only matters of personal opinion; and thus the following remarks are apt to have a more editorial flavor than is usual for papers read at professional meetings. But a good deal more is at stake here than the sensitivities of any particular person, and my excuse for dealing with an issue that seems to have so many subjective overtones is that the use of disguises in social research affects the professional climate in which all of us work and raises a number of methodological questions that should be discussed more widely.

I am assuming here that "personal morality" and "professional ethics" are not the same thing. Personal morality has something to do with the way an individual conducts himself across the range of his human contacts; it is not local to a particular group of persons or to a particular set of occupational interests. Professional ethics, on the other hand, refer to the way a group of associates define their special responsibility to one another and to the rest of the social order in which they work. In this sense, professional ethics often deal with issues that are practical in their application and limited in their scope: they are the terms of a covenant among people gathered together into a given occupational group. For instance, it may or may not be ethical for an espionage agent or a journalist to represent himself as someone he is not in the course of gathering information, but it certainly does not follow that the conduct of a sociologist should be judged in the same terms; for the sociologist has a different relationship to the rest of the community, operates under a different warrant, and has a different set of professional and scientific interests to protect. In this sense, the ethics governing a particular discipline are in many ways local to the transactions that discipline has with the larger world.

The argument to be presented here, then, is that the practice of using masks in social research compromises both the people who wear them and the people for whom they are worn, and in doing so, violates the terms of a contract which the sociologist should be ready to honor in his dealings with others. There are many respects in which this is true, but I will be dealing here in particular with the relationship between the sociologist and a) the subjects of his research, b) the colleagues with whom he works, c) the students he agrees to teach, and d) the data he takes as his subject matter.

The first of these points has to do with the responsibilities a sociologist should accept toward other institutions and other people in the social order. It may seem a little cranky to insist that disguised observation constitutes an ugly invasion of privacy and is, on that ground alone, objectionable. But

---

5. John F. Lofland and Robert A. Lejeune, "Initial Interaction of Newcomers in Alcoholics Anonymous: A Field Experiment in Class Symbols and Socialization," *Social Problems*, 8 (1960), pp. 102–111.

it is a matter of cold calculation to point out that this particular research strategy can injure people in ways we can neither anticipate in advance nor compensate for afterward. For one thing, the sheer act of entering a human transaction on the basis of deliberate fraud may be painful to the people who are thereby misled; and even if that were not the case, there are countless ways in which a stranger who pretends to be something else can disturb others by failing to understand the conditions of intimacy that prevail in the group he has tried to invade. Nor does it matter very much how sympathetic the observer is toward the persons whose lives he is studying: the fact of the matter is that he does not *know* which of his actions are apt to hurt other people, and it is highly presumptuous of him to act as if he does—particulary when, as is ordinarily the case, he has elected to wear a disguise exactly because he is entering a social sphere so far from his own experience.

So the sheer act of wearing disguises in someone else's world may cause discomfort, no matter what we later write in our reports; and this possibility raises two questions. The first, of course, is whether we have the right to inflict pain at all when we are aware of these risks and the subjects of the study are not. The second, however, is perhaps more important from the narrow point of view of the profession itself: so long as we suspect that a method we use has at least *some* potential for harming others, we are in the extremely awkward position of having to weigh the scientific and social benefits of that procedure against its possible cost in human discomfort, and this is a difficult business under the best of circumstances. If we happen to harm people who have agreed to act as subjects, we can at least argue that they knew something of the risks involved and were willing to contribute to that vague program called the "advance of knowledge." But when we do so with people who have expressed no readiness to participate in our researches (indeed, people who would presumably have refused if asked directly), we are in very much the same ethical position as a physician who carries out medical experiments on human subjects without their consent. The only conceivable argument in favor of such experimentation is that the knowledge derived from it is worth the discomfort it may cause. And the difficulties here are that we do not know how to measure the value of the work we do or the methods we employ in this way, and, moreover, that we might be doing an extraordinary disservice to the idea of detached scholarship if we tried. Sociologists cannot protect their freedom of inquiry if they owe the rest of the community (not to mention themselves) an accounting for the distress they may have inadvertently imposed on people who have not volunteered to take that risk.

The second problem with disguised observation to be considered here has to do with the sociologist's responsibilities to his colleagues. It probably goes without saying that research of this sort is liable to damage the reputation of sociology in the larger society and close off promising areas of research for future investigators. This is true in the limited sense that a particular agency—say, for example, Alcoholics Anonymous—may decide that its integrity and perhaps even its effectiveness was violated by the appearance of sociologists pretending to be someone else and deny access to other students who propose to use an altogether different approach. And it is also true in the wider sense that any research tactic which attracts unfavorable notice may help diminish the general climate of trust toward sociology in the community as a whole. So long as this remains a serious possibility, the practice of disguised observation becomes a problem for everyone in the profession; and to this extent, it is wholly within the bounds of professional etiquette for one sociologist to challenge the work of another on this score.

This objection has been raised several times before, and the answer most often given to it is that the people who are studied in this fashion—alcoholics or spiritualists or mental patients, for example—are not likely to read what we say about them anyway. Now this argument has the advantage of being correct a good deal of the time, but this fact does not prevent it from being altogether irrelevant. To begin with, the experience of the past few years should surely have informed us that the press is more than ready to translate our technical reports into news copy, and this means that we can no longer provide shelter for other people behind the walls of our own anonymity. But even if that were not the case, it is a little absurd for us to claim that we derive some measure of protection from the narrowness of our audience when we devote so much time trying to broaden it. The fact is that we are increasingly reaching audiences whose confidence we cannot afford to jeopardize, and we have every right to be afraid that such people may close their doors to sociological research if they learn to become too suspicious of our methods and intentions.

The third objection to be raised here, if only as a note in passing, concerns the responsibilities the profession should accept toward its students. The division of labor in contemporary sociology is such that a considerable proportion of the data we use in our work is gathered by graduate students or other apprentices, and this proportion is even higher for research procedures that require the amount of energy and time necessary for participant observation. Of the dozen or more observers who took part in the studies I have cited, for example, all but one was a graduate student. Now a number of sociologists who have engaged in disguised observation have reported that it is apt to pose serious moral problems and a good deal of personal discomfort, and I think one might well argue that this is a heavy burden to place on any person who is, by our own explicit standards, not yet ready for professional life. I am not suggesting here that students are too immature to make a seasoned choice in the matter. I am suggesting that they should not be asked to make what one defender of the method has called "real and excruciating moral decisions" while they are still students and presumably protected from the various dilemmas and contentions which occupy us in meetings like this—particularly since they are so likely to be academically, economically, and even psychologically dependent upon those elders who ask them to choose.[6]

The fourth objection I would like to raise here about the use of undercover observation is probably the most important—and yet the most remote from what is usually meant by the term "ethics." It seems to me that any attempt to use masquerades in social research betrays an extraordinary disrespect for the complexities of human interaction, and for this reason can only lead to bad science. Perhaps the most important responsibility of any sociologist is to appreciate how little he really knows about his intricate and elusive subject matter. We have at best a poor understanding of the human mind, of the communication signals that link one mind to another, or the social structures that emerge from those linkages—and it is the most errant kind of over-simplification for us to think that we can assess the effect which a clever costume or a few studied gestures have on the social setting. The pose might "work" in the sense that the observer is admitted into the situation; but once this passage has been accomplished, how is he to judge his own influence on the lives of the people he is studying? This is a serious problem in every department of science, of course, and a good deal of time has been devoted to its solution. But the only way to cope with the problem in even a preliminary way is to have as clear a picture as possible of the social properties that the observer is introducing into the situation, and this is altogether impossible if we ourselves are not sure who he is. We can *impersonate* other modes of behavior with varying degrees of insight and skill, but we cannot *reproduce* them; and since this is the case, it seems a little irresponsible for a sociologist to assume that he can enter social life in any masquerade that suits his purpose without seriously disrupting the scene he hopes to study.

When people interact, they relate to one another at many different levels at once, and only a fraction of the messages communicated during that interchange are registered in the conscious mind of the participant. It may be possible for someone to mimic the conventional gestures of fear, but it is impossible for him to reproduce the small postural and chemical changes which go with it. It may be possible for a middle-class speaker to imitate the broader accents of lower-class speech, but his vocal equipment is simply not conditioned to do so without arousing at least a subliminal suspicion. It may be possible for a trained person to rearrange the slant of his body and re-set his facial muscles to approximate the bearing of someone else, but his performance will never be anything more than a rough imposture. Now we know that these various physiological, linguistic, and kinetic

---

6. To keep the record straight, I might add that I first became interested in these matters when I was a graduate student and applied for one of the observer posts mentioned here.

cues play an important part in the context of human interaction, but we have no idea how to simulate them—and what is probably more to the point, we never will. For one thing, we cannot expect to learn in a matter of hours what others have been practicing throughout a lifetime. For another, to imitate always means to parody, to caricature, to exaggerate certain details of behavior at the expense of others, and to that extent any person who selects a disguise will naturally emphasize those details which *he* assumes are most important to the character he is portraying. In doing so, of course, he is really only portraying a piece of himself. It is interesting to speculate, for example, why the Air Force lieutenant mentioned earlier thought he needed to present himself as a near-delinquent youth with a visible layer of personal problems in order to pose as an enlisted man. Whatever the reasoning behind this particular charade, it would certainly be reasonable for someone to suspect that it tells us more about the investigators' impression of enlisted men than it does about the men themselves—and since we have no way of learning whether this is true or not, we have lost rather than gained an edge of control over the situation we are hoping to understand. What the investigators had introduced into the situation was a creature of their own invention, and it would be hardly surprising if the results of their inquiry corresponded to some image they had in advance of the enlisted man's condition. (It is perhaps worth noting here that impersonation always seems easier for people looking down rather than up the status ladder. We find it reasonable to assume that officers "know how" to portray enlisted men or that sociologists have the technical capacity to pose as drunks or religious mystics, but it is not at all clear that the reverse would be equally true.)

This, then, is the problem. If we provide observers with special masks and coach them in the "ways" of the private world they are hoping to enter, how can we learn what is happening to the people who meet them in this disguise? What information is registered in the unconscious minds of the other people who live in that world? How does the social structure accommodate to this peculiar invasion?

It is clear, I think, that something happens—something over which we have no control. Let me relate two incidents drawn from the studies mentioned earlier. The first has to do with the Air Force officer who posed as an enlisted man. In their report of the study, the investigators used several pages of a short paper to describe the elaborate masquerade they had fashioned for the observer and the coaching he had received in the ways of the adolescent sub-culture. "So successful was the tutoring," reads the brief report, "that when the time for 'enlistment' arrived, the recruiting sergeant . . . suggested that the observer not be accepted by the Air Force because by all appearances he was a juvenile delinquent."[7] And later,

7. Sullivan, Queen, and Patrick, *op. cit.*, p. 663.

during an interview with a service psychologist, the observer was recommended for re-classification on the grounds that he appeared quite anxious over the death of his father. Now these events may indeed suggest that the pose was successful, for the observer *was* trying to look somewhat delinquent and *did* have a story memorized about the death of his father in an auto accident. But who would care to argue that the diagnosis of the sergeant and the psychologist were inaccurate? Surely something was wrong, and if they perceived an edge of uneasiness which reminded them of anxiety or detected a note of furtiveness which looked to them like delinquency, they may only have been responding to the presence of a real conflict between the observer and his mask. We may leave it to the psychoanalysts to ask whether vague anxieties about "killing" one's father are an unlikely impression for someone to leave behind when he is parading around with a new name, a new background, a new history, and, of course, a new set of parents. The authors of the article tell us that the observer "did have something of a problem to transform himself from a 27-year-old, college trained, commissioned officer into a 19-year-old, near-delinquent high school graduate," and this is certainly easy to believe.[8] What is more difficult to believe is that such a transformation is possible at all—and if it is not, we can have very little confidence in the information gathered by the observer. Since we do not know to what kind of creature the enlisted men were responding, we do not know what sense to make of what they said and did.

The second example comes from the study of the apocalyptic religious group. At one point in the study, two observers arrived at one of the group's meeting places under instructions to tell quite ordinary stories about their experience in spiritualism in order to create as little commotion as possible. A few days afterwards, however, the leader of the group was overheard explaining that the two observers had appeared upset, excited, confused, and unsure of their errand at the time of their original visit, all of which helped confirm her suspicion that they had somehow been "sent" from another planet. In one sense, of course, this incident offered the observers an intriguing view of the belief structure of the cult, but in another sense, the leader's assessment of the situation was very shrewd: after all, the observers *had* been sent from another world, if not another planet, and she may have been quite right to sense that they were a bit confused and unsure of their errand during their early moments in the new job. "In both cases," the report informs us, the visits of the observers "were given as illustrations that 'strange things are happening.' "[9] Indeed, strange things *were* happening; yet we have no idea how strange they really were. It is almost impossible to evaluate the reaction of the group to the appear-

---

8. Stuart A. Queen, "Comment," *American Sociological Review*, 24 (1959), pp. 399–400.
9. Festinger, Riecken, and Schacter, *op. cit.*, pp. 241–242.

ance of the pair of observers because we do not know whether they were seen as ordinary converts or as extraordinary beings. And it makes a difference, for in the first instance the investigators would be observing a response which fell within the normal range of the group's experience, while in the second instance they would be observing a response which would never have taken place had the life of the group been allowed to run its own course.

My point in raising these two examples, it should be clear, is not to insist on the accuracy of these or any other interpretations, but to point out that a wide variety of such interpretations is possible so long as one has no control over the effects introduced by the observer. A company of recruits with a disguised officer in its midst is simply a different kind of organization than one without the same ingredient; a group of spiritualists which numbers as many as eight observers among its twenty or so members has a wholly different character than one which does not—and so long as we remain unable to account for such differences, we cannot know the meaning of the information we collect.

In one of the most sensible pieces written on the subject, Julius Roth has reminded us that all social research is disguised in one respect or another and that the range of ethical questions which bear on the issue must be visualized as falling on a continuum.[10] Thus, it is all very well for someone to argue that deliberate disguises are improper for sociologists, but it is quite another matter for him to specify what varieties of research activity fall within the range of that principle. Every ethical statement seems to lose its crisp authority the moment it is carried over into marginal situations where the conditions governing research are not so clearly stipulated. For instance, some of the richest material in the social sciences has been gathered by sociologists who were true participants in the group under study but who did not announce to other members that they were employing this opportunity to collect research data. Sociologists live careers in which they occasionally become patients, occasionally take jobs as steel workers or taxi drivers, and frequently find themselves in social settings where their trained eye begins to look for data even though their presence in the situation was not engineered for that purpose. It would be absurd, then, to insist as a point of ethics that sociologists should always introduce themselves as investigators everywhere they go and should inform every person who figures in their thinking exactly what their research is all about.

But I do think we can find a place to begin. If disguised observation sits somewhere on a continuum and is not easily defined, this only suggests

---

10. Julius A. Roth, "Comments on 'Secret Observation,'" *Social Problems,* 9 (1962), pp. 283–284.

that we will have to seek further for a relevant ethic and recognize that any line we draw on that continuum will be a little artificial. What I propose, then, at least as a beginning, is the following: first, that it is unethical for a sociologist to *deliberately misrepresent* his identity for the purpose of entering a private domain *to which he is not otherwise eligible;* and second, that it is unethical for a sociologist to *deliberately misrepresent* the character of the research in which he is engaged. Now these negative sanctions leave us a good deal of leeway—more, perhaps, than we will eventually want. But they have the effect of establishing a stable point of reference in an otherwise hazy territory, and from such an anchored position as this we can move out into more important questions about invasion of privacy as an ethical issue.

In the meantime, the time has probably come for us to assume a general posture on the question of disguised participant observation even if we are not yet ready to state a specific ethic, and a logical first step in this direction would be to assess how most members of the profession feel about the matter. I am not suggesting that we poll one another on the merits of adopting a formal code, but that we take some kind of unofficial reading to learn what we can about the prevailing climate of opinion in the field. If we discover that a substantial number of sociologists are uncomfortable about the practice, then those who continue to employ it will at least know where they stand in respect to the "collective conscience" of their discipline. And if we discover that only a scattering of sociologists are concerned about the matter, we will at least have the satisfaction of knowing that the profession—as a profession—has accepted the responsibility of knowing its own mind.

[*Editor's Note:* In the appendix to his book *Tearoom Trade,* Humphreys took the time to analyze his research in terms of the two criteria for unethical behavior developed by Erikson. On the issue of deliberate misrepresentation of his identity Humphreys says: "Since one's identity within the interaction membrane of the tearoom is represented only in terms of the participant role he assumes, there was no misrepresentation on my part as an observer. . . . My role was primarily that of watchqueen, and that role I played well and faithfully. . . . Furthermore, my activities were intended to gain entrance not to a 'private domain' but to a public restroom." On the issue of the deliberate misrepresentation of his research purpose Humphreys' notes: "First, I gave less than full representation of what I was doing, though without giving false representation. I wore only one of two possible hats, rather than going in disguise. Second, I made multiple use of my data. It is unethical to use data that someone has gathered for purposes one of which is unknown to the respondent? With the employment of proper security precautions, I think such multiple use is quite ethical. . . ." Finally, Humphreys notes that he has carefully guarded the identities of his respondents, even going so far as allowing himself to be arrested to reduce the possibility of their identification. The reader is asked to judge whether these statements by Humphreys constitute an adequate rejoinder to those who feel his research methods were unethical.]

PART II

Social Processes

Chapter 3

Socialization and Social Control: How Much Control Does Society Have Over the Individual?

The famous article by Dennis Wrong which begins this section criticizes a pervasive theme in sociology: the control society has over the individual. Wrong takes the position (which is similar to the theme of this book) that sociology is characterized by necessary and interminable dialogue. What disturbs him is that this dialogue has ceased in sociology on the issues of socialization and social control. He attacks the two virtually unquestioned assumptions that have halted this dialogue. First, sociologists say that man is a conformist because he has internalized societal norms. Thus he carries society "around in his head" and conforms to its norms at all times. Second, sociologists see man as an acceptance-seeker who is generally trying to please those around him. Drawing on Freud (as have those who accept the preceding assumptions), Wrong points out that while man may internalize norms, this does not mean that he always conforms to them. In the Freudian view we violate norms with the result that our consciences may bother us, but nevertheless we do violate them. Wrong also contends that we do not always seek a positive image in the eyes of others. There are other drives such as materialism, sex and power which compete with the desire for approval. He concludes that while we are social, we are not entirely socialized. In other words, man is not totally a prisoner of society. He has some freedom, although Wrong does not tell us how much freedom we actually have.

In a reply to an entire school of thought of which Wrong is a member (other members are Erich Fromm, David Riesman and William H. Whyte), Everett K. Wilson defends the conformist. Man, in Wilson's view, must conform and it is in the process of conformity that he fulfills himself. By conforming to our culture we are freed from the necessity of making new decisions for each and every situation which arises. The power of the group ensures us of the order both the collectivity and the individual need in order to survive. Finally, it is only through conformity that we can fulfill ourselves. "Individual freedom in the sense of uncontrolled or unlimited behavior spells frustration, personal disorganization and is, in fact, no freedom." Conformity, to Wilson, is not only necessary, it is desirable. Wrong replies that those of his school of thought "are not protesting against conformity as such but against a kind of conformity that fails to allow for innovation, creativity and even personal eccentricity. Not 'nonconformity' but *individuality* is what they miss in American life." The kind of conformity Wrong is opposed to is "conformism," which he defines as "believing that one ought to try to be as much like other people as possible." Wrong certainly recognizes the need for conformity, but questions whether we need conformism. In another reply to Wilson, van den Haag wonders what it is he is supposed to conform to. Given the many contradictions we face, the conformity to one expectation means nonconformity to another expectation. Thus the important issue is *what* it is we conform to, not that we conform. Furthermore, Wilson's discussion of the necessity of conformity does not constitute an answer to the charge that in our society "there is too much unnecessary and detrimental conformity, and that our society promotes it."

In a concise follow-up study Herman Turk perceived an omission in Wrong's thinking on socialization. Wrong (and most other sociologists) have focused on the importance of socialization in man's self-control, but this ignores "the importance of his internalized social standards *in making him an agent in the social control of others.*" Turk feels that as a result of the latter conception of socialization there is greater consensus in society about what others should do than about how we should behave. He frames this in the form of an hypothesis and tests it in a study of thirty-eight Duke University students. The results confirm his hypothesis, and Turk concludes that socialization is more effective in determining what we expect others to do. As a result we directly sanction others who violate norms or support institutions which perform the same function for us.

The Oversocialized Conception of
Man in Modern Sociology*

Dennis H. Wrong

Gertrude Stein, bed-ridden with a fatal illness, is reported to have suddenly muttered, "What, then, is the answer?" Pausing, she raised her head, murmured, "But what is the question?" and died. Miss Stein presumably was pondering the ultimate meaning of human life, but her brief final soliloquy has a broader and humbler relevance. Its point is that answers are meaningless apart from questions. If we forget the questions, even while remembering the answers, our knowledge of them will subtly deteriorate, becoming rigid, formal, and catechistic as the sense of indeterminacy, of rival possibilities, implied by the very putting of a question is lost.

Social theory must be seen primarily as a set of answers to questions we ask of social reality. If the initiating questions are forgotten, we readily misconstrue the task of theory and the answers previous thinkers have given become narrowly confining conceptual prisons, degenerating into little more than a special, professional vocabulary applied to situations and events that can be described with equal or greater precision in ordinary language. Forgetfulness of the questions that are the starting points of inquiry leads us to ignore the substantive assumptions "buried" in our concepts and commits us to a one-sided view of reality.

Perhaps this is simply an elaborate way of saying that sociological theory can never afford to lose what is usually called a "sense of significance"; or, as it is sometimes put, that sociological theory must be "problem-conscious." I choose instead to speak of theory as a set of answers to questions because reference to "problems" may seem to suggest too close a linkage with social criticism or reform. My primary reason for insisting on the necessity of holding constantly in mind the questions that our concepts and theories are designed to answer is to preclude defining the goal of sociological theory as the creation of a formal body of knowledge satisfying the logical criteria of scientific theory set up by philosophers and methodologists of natural science. Needless to say, this is the way theory is often defined by contemporary sociologists.

Yet to speak of theory as interrogatory may suggest too self-sufficiently

* Reprinted from *American Sociological Review,* 26 (April, 1961), pp. 183–193, by permission of the author and publisher.

intellectual an enterprise. Cannot questions be satisfactorily answered and then forgotten, the answers becoming the assumptions from which we start in framing new questions? It may convey my view of theory more adequately to say that sociological theory concerns itself with questions arising out of problems that are inherent in the very existence of human societies and that cannot therefore be finally "solved" in the way that particular social problems perhaps can be. The "problems" theory concerns itself with are problems *for* human societies which, because of their universality, become intellectually problematic for sociological theorists.

Essentially, the historicist conception of sociological knowledge that is central to the thought of Max Weber and has recently been ably restated by Barrington Moore, Jr., and C. Wright Mills[1] is a sound one. The most fruitful questions for sociology are always questions referring to the realities of a particular historical situation. Yet both of these writers, especially Mills, have a tendency to underemphasize the degree to which we genuinely wish and seek answers to trans-historical and universal questions about the nature of man and society. I do not, let it be clear, have in mind the formalistic quest for social "laws" or "universal propositions," nor the even more formalistic effort to construct all-encompassing "conceptual schemes." Moore and Mills are rightly critical of such efforts. I am thinking of such questions as, "How are men capable of uniting to form enduring societies in the first place?"; "Why and to what degree is change inherent in human societies and what are the sources of change?"; "How is man's animal nature domesticated by society?"

Such questions—and they are existential as well as intellectual questions—are the *raison d'être* of social theory. They were asked by men long before the rise of sociology. Sociology itself is an effort, under new and unprecedented historical conditions, to find novel answers to them. They are not questions which lend themselves to successively more precise answers as a result of cumulative empirical research, for they remain eternally problematic. Social theory is necessarily an interminable dialogue. "True understanding," Hannah Arendt has written, "does not tire of interminable dialogue and 'vicious circles' because it trusts that imagination will eventually catch at least a glimpse of the always frightening light of truth."[2]

I wish briefly to review the answers modern sociological theory offers to one such question, or rather to one aspect of one question. The question may be variously phrased as, "What are the sources of social cohesion?"; or,

---

1. Barrington Moore, Jr., *Political Power and Social Theory*, Cambridge: Harvard University Press, 1958; C. Wright Mills, *The Sociological Imagination*, New York: Oxford University Press, 1959.
2. Hannah Arendt, "Understanding and Politics," *Partisan Review*, 20 (July–August, 1953), p. 392. For a view of social theory close to the one adumbrated in the present paper, see Theodore Abel, "The Present Status of Social Theory," *American Sociological Review*, 17 (April, 1952), pp. 156–164.

"How is social order possible?"; or, stated in social-psychological terms, "How is it that man becomes tractable to social discipline?" I shall call this question in its social-psychological aspect the "Hobbesian question" and in its more strictly sociological aspect the "Marxist question." The Hobbesian question asks how men are capable of the guidance by social norms and goals that makes possible an enduring society, while the Marxist question asks how, assuming this capability, complex societies manage to regulate and restrain destructive conflicts between groups. Much of our current theory offers an oversocialized view of man in answering the Hobbesian question and an overintegrated view of society in answering the Marxist question.

A number of writers have recently challenged the overintegrated view of society in contemporary theory. In addition to Moore and Mills, the names of Bendix, Coser, Dahrendorf, and Lockwood come to mind.[3] My intention, therefore, is to concentrate on the answers to the Hobbesian question in an effort to disclose the oversocialized view of man which they seem to imply.

Since my view of theory is obviously very different from that of Talcott Parsons and has, in fact, been developed in opposition to his, let me pay tribute to his recognition of the importance of the Hobbesian question—the "problem of order," as he calls it—at the very beginning of his first book *The Structure of Social Action*.[4] Parsons correctly credits Hobbes with being the first thinker to see the necessity of explaining why human society is not a "war of all against all"; why, if man is simply a gifted animal, men refrain from unlimited resort to fraud and violence in pursuit of their ends and maintain a stable society at all. There is even a sense in which, as Coser and Mills have both noted,[5] Parsons' entire work represents an effort to solve the Hobbesian problem of order. His solution, however, has tended to become precisely the kind of elaboration of a set of answers in abstraction from questions that is so characteristic of contemporary sociological theory.

We need not be greatly concerned with Hobbes' own solution to the problem of order he saw with such unsurpassed clarity. Whatever interest his famous theory of the origin of the state may still hold for political

---

3. Reinhard Bendix and Bennett Berger, "Images of Society and Problems of Concept Formation in Sociology," in Llewellyn Gross, editor, *Symposium on Sociological Theory*, Evanston, Ill.: Row, Petersen & Co., 1952, pp. 92–118; Lewis A. Coser, *The Functions of Social Conflict*, Glencoe, Ill.: The Free Press, 1956; Ralf Dahrendorf, "Out of Utopia: Towards a Re-Orientation of Sociological Analysis," *American Journal of Sociology*, 64 (September, 1958), pp. 115–127; and *Class and Class Conflict in Industrial Society*, Stanford, Calif.: Stanford University Press, 1959; David Lockwood, "Some Remarks on 'The Social System,'" *British Journal of Sociology*, 7 (June, 1956), pp. 134–146.
4. Talcott Parsons, *The Structure of Social Action*, New York: McGraw-Hill Book Co., 1937, pp. 89–94.
5. Coser, *op. cit.*, p. 21; Mills, *op. cit.*, p. 44.

scientists, it is clearly inadequate as an explanation of the origin of society. Yet the pattern as opposed to the details of Hobbes' thought bears closer examination.

The polar terms in Hobbes' theory are the state of nature, where the war of all against all prevails, and the authority of Leviathan, created by social contract. But the war of all against all is not simply effaced with the creation of political authority: it remains an ever-present potentiality in human society, at times quiescent, at times erupting into open violence. Whether Hobbes believed that the state of nature and the social contract were ever historical realities—and there is evidence that he was not that simple-minded and unsociological, even in the seventeenth century—is unimportant; the whole tenor of this thought is to see the war of all against all and Leviathan dialectically, as coexisting and interacting opposites.[6] As R. G. Collingwood has observed, "According to Hobbes . . . *a body politic is a dialectical thing,* a Heraclitean world in which at any given time there is a negative element."[7] The first secular social theorist in the history of Western thought, and one of the first clearly to discern and define the problem of order in human society long before Darwinism made awareness of it a commonplace, Hobbes was a dialectical thinker who refused to separate answers from questions, solutions to society's enduring problems from the conditions creating the problems.

What is the answer of contemporary sociological theory to the Hobbesian question? There are two main answers, each of which has come to be understood in a way that denies the reality and meaningfulness of the question. Together they constitute a model of human nature, sometimes clearly stated, more often implicit in accepted concepts, that pervades modern sociology. The first answer is summed up in the notion of the "internalization of social norms." The second, more commonly employed or assumed in empirical research, is the view that man is essentially motivated by the desire to achieve a positive image of self by winning acceptance or status in the eyes of others.

The following statement represents, briefly and broadly, what is probably the most influential contemporary sociological conception—and dismissal—of the Hobbesian problem: "To a modern sociologist imbued with the conception that action follows institutionalized patterns, opposition of individual and common interests has only a very limited relevance or is

6. A recent critic of Parsons follows Hobbes in seeing the relation between the normative order in society and what he calls "the sub-stratum of social action" and other sociologists have called the "factual order" as similar to the relation between war of all against all and the authority of the state. David Lockwood writes: "The existence of the normative order . . . is in one very important sense inextricably bound up with potential conflicts of interest over scarce resources . . . ; the very existence of a normative order mirrors the continual potentiality of conflict." Lockwood, *op. cit.,* p. 137.
7. R. G. Collingwood, *The New Leviathan,* Oxford: The Clarendon Press, 1942, p. 183.

thoroughly unsound."[8] From this writer's perspective, the problem is an unreal one: human conduct is totally shaped by common norms or "institutionalized patterns." Sheer ignorance must have led people who were unfortunate enough not to be modern sociologists to ask, "How is order possible?" A thoughtful bee or ant would never inquire, "How is the social order of the hive or ant-hill possible?" for the opposite of that order is unimaginable when the instinctive endowment of the insects ensures its stability and built-in harmony between "individual and common interests." Human society, we are assured, is not essentially different, although conformity and stability are there maintained by non-instinctive processes. Modern sociologists believe that they have understood these processes and that they have not merely answered but disposed of the Hobbesian question, showing that, far from expressing a valid intimation of the tensions and possibilities of social life, it can only be asked out of ignorance.

It would be hard to find a better illustration of what Collingwood, following Plato, calls *eristical* as opposed to dialectical thinking:[9] the answer destroys the question, or rather destroys the awareness of rival possibilities suggested by the question which accounts for its having been asked in the first place. A reversal of perspective now takes place and we are moved to ask the opposite question: "How is it that violence, conflict, revolution, and the individual's sense of coercion by society manage to exist at all, if this view is correct?"[10] Whenever a one-sided answer to a question compels us to raise the opposite question, we are caught up in a dialectic of concepts which reflects a dialectic in things. But let us examine the particular processes sociologists appeal to in order to account for the elimination from human society of the war of all against all.

---

8. Francis X. Sutton and others, *The American Business Creed,* Cambridge: Harvard University Press, 1956, p. 304. I have cited this study and, on several occasions, textbooks and fugitive articles rather than better-known and directly theoretical writings because I am just as concerned with what sociological concepts and theories are taken to mean when they are actually used in research, teaching, and introductory exposition as with their elaboration in more self-conscious and explicitly theoretical discourse. Since the model of human nature I am criticizing is partially implicit and "buried" in our concepts, cruder and less qualified illustrations are as relevant as the formulations of leading theorists. I am also aware that some older theorists, notably Cooley and MacIver, were shrewd and worldly-wise enough to reject the implication that man is ever fully socialized. Yet they failed to develop competing images of man which were concise and systematic enough to counter the appeal of the oversocialized models.

9. Collingwood, *op. cit.,* pp. 181–182.

10. *Cf.* Mills, *op. cit.,* pp. 32–33, 42. While Mills does not discuss the use of the concept of internalization by Parsonian theorists, I have argued elsewhere that his view of the relation between power and values is insufficiently dialectical. See Dennis H. Wrong, "The Failure of American Sociology," *Commentary,* 28 (November, 1959), p. 378.

THE CHANGING MEANING OF INTERNALIZATION

A well-known section of *The Structure of Social Action,* devoted to the interpretation of Durkheim's thought, is entitled "The Changing Meaning of Constraint."[11] Parsons argues that Durkheim originally conceived of society as controlling the individual from the outside by imposing constraints on him through sanctions, best illustrated by codes of law. But in Durkheim's later work he began to see that social rules do not "merely regulate 'externally' . . . they enter directly into the constitution of the actors' end themselves."[12] Constraint, therefore, is more than an environmental obstacle which the actor must take into account in pursuit of his goals in the same way that he takes into account physical laws: it becomes internal, psychological, and self-imposed as well. Parsons developed this view that social norms are constitutive rather than merely regulative of human nature before he was influenced by psychoanalytic theory, but Freud's theory of the superego has become the source and model for the conception of the internalization of social norms that today plays so important a part in sociological thinking. The use some sociologists have made of Freud's idea, however, might well inspire an essay entitled, "The Changing Meaning of Internalization," although, in contrast to the shift in Durkheim's view of constraint, this change has been a change for the worse.

What has happened is that internalization has imperceptibly been equated with "learning," or even with "habit-formation" in the simplest sense. Thus when a norm is said to have been "internalized" by an individual, what is frequently meant is that he habitually both affirms it and conforms to it in his conduct. The whole stress on inner conflict, on the tension between powerful impulses and superego controls the behavioral outcome of which cannot be prejudged, drops out of the picture. And it is this that is central to Freud's view, for in psychoanalytic terms to say that a norm has been internalized, or introjected to become part of the superego, is to say no more than that a person will suffer guilt-feelings if he fails to live up to it, not that he will in fact live up to it in his behavior.

The relation between internalization and conformity assumed by most sociologists is suggested by the following passage from a recent, highly-praised advanced textbook: "Conformity to institutionalized norms is, of course, 'normal.' The actor, having internalized the norms, feels something like a need to conform. His conscience would bother him if he did not."[13]

---

11. Parsons, *op. cit.,* pp. 378–390.
12. *Ibid.,* p. 382.
13. Harry M. Johnson, *Sociology: A Systematic Introduction,* New York: Harcourt, Brace and Co., 1960, p. 22.

What is overlooked here is that the person who conforms may be even more "bothered," that is, subject to guilt and neurosis, than the person who violates what are not only society's norms but his own as well. To Freud, it is precisely the man with the strictest superego, he who has most thoroughly internalized and conformed to the norms of his society, who is most wracked with guilt and anxiety.[14]

Paul Kecskemeti, to whose discussion I owe initial recognition of the erroneous view of internalization held by sociologists, argues that the relations between social norms, the individual's selection from them, his conduct, and his feelings about his conduct are far from self-evident. "It is by no means true," he writes, "to say that acting counter to one's own norms always or almost always leads to neurosis. One might assume that neurosis develops even more easily in persons who *never* violate the moral code they recognize as valid but repress and frustrate some strong instinctual motive. A person who 'succumbs to temptation,' feels guilty, and then 'purges himself' of his guilt in some reliable way (e.g., by confession) may achieve in this way a better balance, and be less neurotic, than a person who never violates his 'norms' and never feels conscious guilt."[15]

Recent discussions of "deviant behavior" have been compelled to recognize these distinctions between social demands, personal attitudes towards them, and actual conduct, although they have done so in a laboriously taxonomic fashion.[16] They represent, however, largely the rediscovery of what was always central to the Freudian concept of the superego. The main explanatory function of the concept is to show how people repress themselves, imposing checks on their own desires and thus turning the inner life into a battlefield of conflicting motives, no matter which side "wins," by successfully dictating overt action. So far as behavior is concerned, the psychoanalytic view of man is less deterministic than the sociological. For psychoanalysis is primarily concerned with the inner life, not with overt behavior, and its most fundamental insight is that the wish, the emotion, and the fantasy are as important as the act in man's experience.

Sociologists have appropriated the superego concept, but have separated it from any equivalent of the Freudian id. So long as most individuals are "socialized," that is, internalize the norms and conform to them in conduct, the Hobbesian problem is not even perceived as a latent reality.

14. Sigmund Freud, *Civilization and Its Discontents*, New York: Doubleday Anchor Books, 1958, pp. 80–81.
15. Paul Kecskemeti, *Meaning, Communication, and Value*, Chicago: University of Chicago Press, 1952, pp. 244–245.
16. Robert Dubin, "Deviant Behavior and Social Structure: Continuities in Social Theory," *American Sociological Review*, 24 (April, 1959), pp. 147–164; Robert K. Merton, "Social Conformity, Deviation, and Opportunity Structures: A Comment on the Contributions of Dubin and Cloward," *ibid.*, pp. 178–189.

Deviant behavior is accounted for by special circumstances: ambiguous norms, anomie, role conflict, or greater cultural stress on valued goals than on the approved means for attaining them. Tendencies to deviant behavior are not seen as dialectically related to conformity. The presence in man of motivational forces bucking against the hold social discipline has over him is denied.

Nor does the assumption that internalization of norms and roles is the essence of socialization allow for a sufficient range of motives underlying conformity. It fails to allow for variable "tonicity of the superego," in Kardiner's phrase.[17] The degree to which conformity is frequently the result of coercion rather than conviction is minimized.[18] Either someone has internalized the norms, or he is "unsocialized," a feral or socially isolated child, or a psychopath. Yet Freud recognized that many people, conceivably a majority, fail to acquire superegos. "Such people," he wrote, "habitually permit themselves to do any bad deed that procures them something they want, if only they are sure that no authority will discover it or make them suffer for it; their anxiety relates only to the possibility of detection. Present-day society has to take into account the prevalence of this state of mind."[19] The last sentence suggests that Freud was aware of the decline of "inner-direction," of the Protestant conscience, about which we have heard so much lately. So let us turn to the other elements of human nature that sociologists appeal to in order to explain, or rather explain away, the Hobbesian problem.

MAN THE ACCEPTANCE-SEEKER[20]

The superego concept is too inflexible, too bound to the past and to individual biography, to be of service in relating conduct to the pressures of the immediate situation in which it takes place. Sociologists rely more heavily therefore on an alternative notion, here stated—or, to be fair, overstated—in its baldest form: "People are so profoundly sensitive to the

17. Abram Kardiner, *The Individual and His Society,* New York: Columbia University Press, 1939, pp. 65, 72–75.
18. Mills, *op. cit.,* pp. 39–41; Dahrendorf, *Class and Class Conflict in Industrial Society,* pp. 157–165.
19. Freud, *op. cit.,* pp. 78–79.
20. In many ways I should prefer to use the neater, more alliterative phrase "status-seeker." However, it has acquired a narrower meaning than I intend, particularly since Vance Packard appropriated it, suggesting primarily efforts, which are often consciously deceptive, to give the appearance of personal achievements or qualities worthy of deference. "Status-seeking" in this sense is, as Veblen perceived, necessarily confined to relatively impersonal and segmental social relationships. "Acceptance" or "approval" convey more adequately what all men are held to seek in both intimate and impersonal relations according to the conception of the self and of motivation dominating contemporary sociology and social psychology. I have, nevertheless, been unable to resist the occasional temptation to use the term "status" in this broader sense.

expectations of others that all action is inevitably guided by these expectations."[21]

Parsons' model of the "complementarity of expectations," the view that in social interaction men mutually seek approval from one another by conforming to shared norms, is a formalized version of what has tended to become a distinctive sociological perspective on human motivation. Ralph Linton states it in explicit psychological terms: "The need for eliciting favorable responses from others is an almost constant component of [personality]. Indeed, it is not too much to say that there is very little organized human behavior which is not directed toward its satisfaction in at least some degree."[22]

The insistence of sociologists on the importance of "social factors" easily leads them to stress the priority of such socialized or socializing motives in human behavior.[23] It is frequently the task of the sociologist to

---

21. Sutton and others, *op. cit.,* p. 264. Robert Cooley Angell, in *Free Society and Moral Crisis,* Ann Arbor: University of Michigan Press, 1958, p. 34, points out the ambiguity of the term "expectations." It is used, he notes, to mean both a factual prediction and a moral imperative, e.g. "England expects every man to do his duty." But this very ambiguity is instructive, for it suggests the process by which behavior that is non-normative and perhaps even "deviant" but nevertheless "expected" in the sense of being predictable acquires over time a normative aura and becomes "expected" in the second sense of being socially approved or demanded. Thus Parsons' "interaction paradigm" provides leads to the understanding of social change and need not be confined, as in his use of it, to the explanation of conformity and stability. But this is the subject of another paper I hope to complete shortly.

22. Ralph Linton, *The Cultural Background of Personality,* New York: Appleton-Century Co., 1945, p. 91.

23. When values are "inferred" from this emphasis and then popularized, it becomes the basis of the ideology of "groupism" extolling the virtues of "togetherness" and "belongingness" that have been attacked and satirized so savagely in recent social criticism. David Riesman and W. H. Whyte, the pioneers of this current of criticism in its contemporary guise, are both aware, as their imitators and epigoni usually are not, of the extent to which the social phenomenon they have described is the result of the diffusion and popularization of sociology itself. See on this point Robert Gutman and Dennis H. Wrong, "Riesman's Typology of Character" (forthcoming in a symposium on Riesman's work to be edited by Leo Lowenthal and Seymour Martin Lipset), and William H. Whyte, *The Organization Man,* New York: Simon and Schuster, 1956, Chapters 3–5. As a matter of fact, Riesman's "inner-direction" and "other-direction" correspond rather closely to the notions of "internalization" and "acceptance-seeking" in contemporary sociology as I have described them. Riesman even refers to his concepts initially as characterizations of "modes of conformity," although he then makes the mistake, as Robert Gutman and I have argued, of calling them character types. But his view that all men are to some degree both inner-directed and other-directed, a qualification that has been somewhat neglected by critics who have understandably concentrated on his empirical and historical use of his typology, suggests the more generalized conception of forces making for conformity found in current theory. See David Riesman, Nathan Glazer, and Reuel Denny, *The Lonely Crowd,* New York: Doubleday Anchor Books, 1953, pp. 17 ff. However, as Gutman and I have observed: "In some respects Riesman's conception of character is Freudian rather than neo-Freudian: character is defined by superego mechanisms and, like Freud in *Civilization and Its Discontents,* the socialized individual is defined by what is forbidden him rather than by what society stimulates him to do. Thus in spite of Riesman's generally sanguine attitude towards modern America, implicit in his typology

call attention to the intensity with which men desire and strive for the good opinion of their immediate associates in a variety of situations, particularly those where received theories or ideologies have unduly emphasized other motives such as financial gain, commitment to ideals, or the effects on energies and aspirations of arduous physical conditions. Thus sociologists have shown that factory workers are more sensitive to the attitudes of their fellow-workers than to purely economic incentives; that voters are more influenced by the preferences of their relatives and friends than by campaign debates on the "issues"; that soldiers, whatever their ideological commitment to their nation's cause, fight more bravely when their platoons are intact and they stand side by side with their "buddies."

It is certainly not my intention to criticize the findings of such studies. My objection is that their particular selective emphasis is generalized—explicitly or, more often, implicitly—to provide apparent empirical support for an extremely one-sided view of human nature. Although sociologists have criticized past efforts to single out one fundamental motive in human conduct, the desire to achieve a favorable self-image by winning approval from others frequently occupies such a position in their own thinking. The following "theorem" has been, in fact, openly put forward by Hans Zetterberg as "a strong contender for the position as the major Motivational Theorem in sociology"[24]:

> An actor's actions have a tendency to become dispositions that are related to the occurence [*sic*] of favored uniform evaluations of the actor and-or his actions in his action system.[25]

Now Zetterberg is not necessarily maintaining that this theorem is an accurate factual statement of the basic psychological roots of social behavior. He is, characteristically, far too self-conscious about the logic of theorizing and "concept formation" for that. He goes on to remark that "the maximization of favorable attitudes from others would thus be the counterpart in sociological theory to the maximization of profit in economic theory."[26] If by this it is meant that the theorem is to be understood as a heuristic rather than an empirical assumption, that sociology has a selective point of view which is just as abstract and partial as that of economics and the other social sciences, and if his view of theory as a set of logically connected formal propositions is granted provisional acceptance, I am in

is a view of society as the enemy both of individuality and of basic drive gratification, a view that contrasts with the at least potentially benign role assigned it by neo-Freudian thinkers like Fromm and Horney." Gutman and Wrong, "Riesman's Typology of Character," p. 4 (typescript).

24. Hans L. Zetterberg, "Compliant Actions," *Acta Sociologica,* 2 (1957), p. 189.
25. *Ibid.,* p. 188.
26. *Ibid.,* p. 189.

agreement. (Actually, the view of the theory suggested at the beginning of this paper is a quite different one.)

But there is a further point to be made. Ralf Dahrendorf has observed that structural-functional theorists do not "claim that order *is based on* a general consensus of values, but that it *can be conceived of in terms of* such consensus and that, if it is conceived of in these terms, certain propositions follow which are subject to the test of specific observations."[27] The same may be said of the assumption that people seek to maximize favorable evaluations by others; indeed this assumption has already fathered such additional concepts as "reference group" and "circle of significant others." Yet the question must be raised as to whether we really wish to, in effect, define sociology by such partial perspectives. The assumption of the maximization of approval from others is the psychological complement to the sociological assumption of a general value consensus. And the former is as selective and one-sided a way of looking at motivation as Dahrendorf and others have argued the latter to be when it determines our way of looking at social structure. The oversocialized view of man of the one is a counterpart to the overintegrated view of society of the other.

Modern sociology, after all, originated as a protest against the partial views of man contained in such doctrines as utilitarianism, classical economics, social Darwinism, and vulgar Marxism. All of the great nineteenth and early twentieth century sociologists[28] saw it as one of their major tasks to expose the unreality of such abstractions as economic man, the gain-seeker of the classical economists; political man, the power-seeker of the Machiavellian tradition in political science; self-preserving man, the security-seeker of Hobbes and Darwin; sexual or libidinal man, the pleasure-seeker of doctrinaire Freudianism; and even religious man, the God-seeker of the theologians. It would be ironical if it should turn out that they have merely contributed to the creation of yet another reified abstraction in socialized man, the status-seeker of our contemporary sociologists.

Of course, such an image of man is, like all the others mentioned, valuable for limited purposes so long as it is not taken for the whole truth. What are some of its deficiencies? To begin with, it neglects the other half

---

27. Dahrendorf, *Class and Class Conflict in Industrial Society*, p. 158.
28. Much of the work of Thorstein Veblen, now generally regarded as a sociologist (perhaps the greatest America has yet produced), was, of course, a polemic against the rational, calculating *homo economicus* of classical economics and a documentation of the importance in economic life of the quest for status measured by conformity to arbitrary and shifting conventional standards. Early in his first and most famous book Veblen made an observation on human nature resembling that which looms so large in contemporary sociological thinking: "The usual basis of self-respect," he wrote, "is the respect accorded by one's neighbors. Only individuals with an aberrant temperament can in the long run retain their self-esteem in the face of the disesteem of their fellows." *The Theory of the Leisure Class*, New York: Mentor Books, 1953, p. 38. Whatever the inadequacies of his psychological assumptions, Veblen did not, however, overlook other motivations to which he frequently gave equal or greater weight.

of the model of human nature presupposed by current theory: moral man, guided by his built-in superego and beckoning ego-ideal.[29] In recent years sociologists have been less interested than they once were in culture and national character as backgrounds to conduct, partly because stress on the concept of "role" as the crucial link between the individual and the social structure has directed their attention to the immediate situation in which social interaction takes place. Man is increasingly seen as a "role-playing" creature, responding eagerly or anxiously to the expectations of other role-players in the multiple group settings in which he finds himself. Such an approach, while valuable in helping us grasp the complexity of a highly differentiated social structure such as our own, is far too often generalized to serve as a kind of *ad hoc* social psychology, easily adaptable to particular sociological purposes.

But it is not enough to concede that men often pursue "internalized values" remaining indifferent to what others think of them, particularly when, as I have previously argued, the idea of internalization has been "hollowed out" to make it more useful as an explanation of conformity. What of desire for material and sensual satisfactions? Can we really dispense with the venerable notion of material "interests" and invariably replace it with the blander, more integrative "social values"? And what of striving for power, not necessarily for its own sake—that may be rare and pathological—but as a means by which men are able to *impose* a normative definition of reality on others? That material interests, sexual drives, and the quest for power have often been over-estimated as human motives is no reason to deny their reality. To do so is to suppress one term of the dialectic between conformity and rebellion, social norms and their violation, man and social order, as completely as the other term is suppressed by those who deny the reality of man's "normative orientation" or reduce it to the effect of coercion, rational calculation, or mechanical conditioning.

The view that man is invariably pushed by internalized norms or pulled by the lure of self-validation by others ignores—to speak archaically for a moment—both the highest and the lowest, both beast and angel, in his nature. Durkheim, from whom so much of the modern sociological point of view derives, recognized that the very existence of a social norm implies and even creates the possibility of its violation. This is the meaning of his famous dictum that crime is a "normal phenomenon." He maintained that "for the originality of the idealist whose dreams transcend his century to find expression, it is necessary that the originality of the crimi-

---

29. Robin M. Williams, Jr., writes: "At the present time, the literature of sociology and social psychology contains many references to 'Conformity'—conforming to norms, 'yielding to social pressure,' or 'adjusting to the requirements of the reference group.' . . . ; the implication is easily drawn that the actors in question are *motivated* solely in terms of conformity or non-conformity, rather than in terms of 'expressing' or 'affirming' internalized values . . . ." (his italics). "Continuity and Change in Sociological Study," *American Sociological Review,* 23 (December, 1958), p. 630.

nal, who is below the level of his time, shall also be possible. One does not occur without the other."[30] Yet Durkheim lacked an adequate psychology and formulated his insight in terms of the actor's cognitive awareness rather than in motivational terms. We do not have Durkheim's excuse for falling back on what Homans has called a "social mold theory" of human nature.[31]

SOCIAL BUT NOT ENTIRELY SOCIALIZED

I have referred to forces in man that are resistant to socialization. It is not my purpose to explore the nature of these forces or to suggest how we ought best conceive of them as sociologists—that would be a most ambitious undertaking. A few remarks will have to suffice. I think we must start with the recognition that *in the beginning there is the body.* As soon as the body is mentioned the specter of "biological determinism" raises its head and sociologists draw back in fright. And certainly their view of man is sufficiently disembodied and non-materialistic to satisfy Bishop Berkeley, as well as being de-sexualized enough to please Mrs. Grundy.

Am I, then, urging us to return to the older view of a human nature divided between a "social man" and a "natural man" who is either benevolent, Rousseau's Noble Savage, or sinister and destructive, as Hobbes regarded him? Freud is usually represented, or misrepresented, as the chief modern proponent of this dualistic conception which assigns to the social order the purely negative role of blocking and re-directing man's "imperious biological drives."[32] I say "misrepresented" because, although Freud often said things supporting such an interpretation, other and more fundamental strains in his thinking suggest a different conclusion. John Dollard, certainly not a writer who is oblivious to social and cultural "factors," saw this twenty-five years ago: "It is quite clear," he wrote, ". . . that he (Freud) does not regard the instincts as having a fixed social goal; rather, indeed, in the case of the sexual instinct he has stressed the vague but powerful and impulsive nature of the drive and has emphasized that its proper social object is not picked out in advance. His seems to be a drive concept which is not at variance with our knowledge from comparative

---

30. Emile Durkheim, *The Rules of Sociological Method,* Chicago: University of Chicago Press, 1938, p. 71.
31. George C. Homans, *The Human Group,* New York: Harcourt, Brace and Company, 1950, pp. 317–319.
32. Robert K. Merton, *Social Theory and Social Structure,* Revised and Enlarged Edition, Glencoe, Ill.: The Free Press, 1957, p. 131. Merton's view is representative of that of most contemporary sociologists. See also Hans Gerth and C. Wright Mills, *Character and Social Structure,* New York: Harcourt, Brace and Company, 1953, pp. 112–113. For a similar view by a "neo-Freudian," see Erich Fromm, *The Sane Society,* New York: Rinehart and Company, 1955, pp. 74–77.

cultural studies, since his theory does not demand that the 'instinct' work itself out with mechanical certainty alike in every varying culture."[33]

So much for Freud's "imperious biological drives!" When Freud defined psychoanalysis as the study of the "vicissitudes of the instincts," he was confirming, not denying, the "plasticity" of human nature insisted on by social scientists. The drives of "instincts" of psychoanalysis, far from being fixed dispositions to behave in a particular way, are utterly subject to social channelling and transformation and could not even reveal themselves in behavior without social molding any more than our vocal chords can produce articulate speech if we have not learned a language. To psychoanalysis man is indeed a social animal; his social nature is profoundly reflected in his bodily structure.[34]

But there is a difference between the Freudian view on the one hand and both sociological and neo-Freudian conceptions of man on the other. To Freud man is a *social* animal without being entirely a *socialized* animal. His very social nature is the source of conflicts and antagonisms that create resistance to socialization by the norms of any of the societies which have existed in the course of human history. "Socialization" may mean two quite distinct things; when they are confused an oversocialized view of man is the result. On the one hand socialization means the "transmission of the culture," the particular culture of the society an individual enters at birth; on the other hand the term is used to mean the "process of becoming human," of acquiring uniquely human attributes from interaction with others.[35] All men are socialized in the latter sense, but this does not mean that they have been completely molded by the particular norms and values of their culture. All cultures, as Freud contended, do violence to man's socialized bodily drives, but this in no sense means that men could possibly exist without culture or independently of society.[36] From such a stand-

---

33. John Dollard, *Criteria for the Life History*, New Haven: Yale University Press, 1935, p. 120. This valuable book has been neglected, presumably because it appears to be a purely methodological effort to set up standards for judging the adequacy of biographical and autobiographical data. Actually, the standards serve as well to evaluate the adequacy of general theories of personality or human nature and even to prescribe in part what a sound theory ought to include.

34. One of the few attempts by a social scientist to relate systematically man's anatomical structure and biological history to his social nature and his unique cultural creativity is Weston La Barre's *The Human Animal*, Chicago: University of Chicago Press, 1954. See especially Chapters 4–6, but the entire book is relevant. It is one of the few exceptions to Paul Goodman's observation that anthropologists nowadays "commence with a chapter on Physical Anthropology and then forget the whole topic and go on to Culture." See his "Growing up Absurd," *Dissent*, 7 (Spring, 1960), p. 121.

35. Paul Goodman has developed a similar distinction. *Op. cit.*, pp. 123–125.

36. Whether it might be possible to create a society that does not repress the bodily drives is a separate question. See Herbert Marcuse, *Eros and Civilization*, Boston: The Beacon Press, 1955; and Norman O. Brown, *Life Against Death*, New York: Random House, Modern Library Paperbacks, 1960. Neither Marcuse nor Brown are guilty in their brilliant, provocative, and visionary books of assuming a "natural man" who

point, man may properly be called as Norman Brown has called him, the "neurotic" or the "discontented" animal and repression may be seen as the main characteristic of human nature as we have known it in history.[37]

But isn't this psychology and haven't sociologists been taught to foreswear psychology, to look with suspicion on what are called "psychological variables" in contradistinction to the institutional and historical forces with which they are properly concerned? There is, indeed, as recent critics have complained, too much "psychologism" in contemporary sociology, largely, I think, because of the bias inherent in our favored research techniques. But I do not see how, at the level of theory, sociologists can fail to make assumptions about human nature.[38] If our assumptions are left implicit, we will inevitably presuppose of a view of man that is tailor-made to our special needs; when our sociological theory over-stresses the stability and integration of society we will end up imagining that man is the disembodied, conscience-driven, status-seeking phantom of current theory. We must do better if we really wish to win credit outside of our ranks for special understanding of man, that plausible creature[39] whose wagging tongue so often hides the despair and darkness in his heart.

Conformity Revisited*

Everett K. Wilson

I come not to bury conformity but to praise it.

Conformity is a dirty word—nowhere so much as in my own college of Antioch. To promote nonconformity at Antioch is to propose virtue to a saint. Nevertheless, I hope to clean up that dirty word.

This takes a bit of doing since in the past few years it has become very

---

awaits liberation from social bonds. They differ from such sociological Utopians as Fromm, *op. cit.,* in their lack of sympathy for the de-sexualized man of the neo-Freudians. For the more traditional Freudian view, see Walter A. Weisskopf, "The 'Socialization' of Psychoanalysis in Contemporary America," in Benjamin Nelson, editor, *Psychoanalysis and the Future,* New York: National Psychological Association For Psychoanalysis, 1957, pp. 51–56; Hans Meyerhoff, "Freud and the Ambiguity of Culture," *Partisan Review,* 24 (Winter, 1957), pp. 117–130.

37. Brown, *op. cit.,* pp. 3–19.

38. "I would assert that very little sociological analysis is ever done without using at least an implicit psychological theory." Alex Inkeles, "Personality and Social Structure," in Robert K. Merton and others, editors, *Sociology Today,* New York: Basic Books, 1959, p. 250.

39. Harry Stack Sullivan once remarked that the most outstanding characteristic of human beings was their "plausibility."

fashionable to assert that we are escaping from the freedom of self-determination to cower in the security provided by a dead-level, mass society. Erich Fromm, David Riesman, and William H. Whyte have fulminated publicly and profitably against mass man, the anxious other-directed nothing, the organization man. Other, less effective voices provide an antiphonal chorus from the wings. Fromm sturdily, virtuously, and nonsensically asserts that "man is not a thing." People cannot be pigeon-holed. Yet these writers who abhor categorizing make easy generalizations about "the careful young men" of this generation.

Beyond college, they say, observe the specimens in the 30 to 40 age category. The stern, strong-willed, self-disciplined, inner-directed father of Clarence Day's household has now become the organization man, wallowing in belongingness and togetherness. His children get into trouble permissively, are disciplined understandingly, and learn their school lessons fluently. God has become a benevolent scout leader; and Uncle Sam is a cross between Big Brother and Santa Claus.

The current brouhaha about conformity is surprising when one considers that the issue is not really a current one. The to-do about conformity is the latest version of the ancient and largely futile discussion of the individual versus society.

Nonetheless, there has been insistent clamor. A covey of writers descry a new thing in history, an unprecedented combination of external pressure and personal compliance:

A dull uniformity or equality is implied which affronts our self-conception as unique individuals.
Conformity implies a calculating approach to human beings which damps out the life of the spirit, those ineffable human qualities which make for romance and mystery and delight.
Conformity implies manipulation by others; and Big Brothers are for the birds.
Conformity implies softness, decadence, an unwillingness to fight, a retreat from the challenges of freedom.
Conformity means mediocrity, a dead-level convergence in vulgarity.

CHARGE: CONFORMITY IMPLIES EQUALITY, UNIFORMITY;
THIS DEROGATES INDIVIDUALITY

The dignity of the individual, respect for the individual, self-determination—these are Yankee-doodle phrases. The Judeo-Christian tradition and the American heritage stress the immeasurable worth of the individual. Even the simplest person feels in his bones that he stands at the center of a unique network of relationships, experiences, influences. He is different and he knows it. But the determination of destiny through the accident of birth has been progressively qualified. If adventitious circumstances promoting inequalities are reduced, then we should expect more apparent equality and uniformity, less individuality.

But the conformity-criers would certainly not wish to accept the progressive fulfillment of man's nature as the reason for the alleged uniformities among men. They are concerned about the lowering of the top quality rather than the upward inching of the illiterate and depressed.

It could be argued that the fact of increased numbers alone would lead to the suppression of individuality. Big government, big industry, big unions, big military, big classes suggest the impossibility of dealing with the person as an individual. Our powers of discrimination and understanding are too limited. Beyond the first few units we commence to classify, to pigeonhole, to categorize. This is one of the unsavory aspects of collectivism; yet there it is.

Our numbers suggest the extent to which we are treated as equal and interchangeable units and stripped of individuality. Often the only relevant aspect of a relationship is that represented by a number: we are one in a host of numbers standing for insurance risks, or automobile owners, or a fraternity of coerced savers (for old age). Excluding numbered warranties on all kinds of household appliances, I have no trouble listing 25 numbers which are, severally, the chief identifying marks in my relationships with other persons and agencies.

CHARGE: CONFORMITY IMPLIES MANIPULATION

But limitation we are told is a far, far lesser evil than *manipulation* of choice. When we conform, we conform *to* something; and we may not do it willingly, or even consciously. There are Bossmen and Massmen, as J. B. Priestley puts it; and the placid—not to say flaccid—conformity of the Massmen is because they are manipulated, witlessly or willingly, by the Bossmen. Of course, the most sinister development along these lines is motivation research by advertisers. This is one of Fromm's complaints: psychology has been prostituted. Once it was employed to fulfill the good Socratic injunction, "Know thyself." It has now been transformed to read: "Know thy customer, the better to manipulate him." The time-motion studies of Taylor and Bedeaux were often criticized for making automata out of men in the sheerly physical aspect of work; psychologists are now attempting to control matters of choice, preference, the emotions. And, according to Fromm, even beyond that:

> (from) the manipulation of the customer and the worker, the uses of psychology have spread to the manipulation of everybody, to politics . . .
> practice of democracy becomes more and more distorted by the same

methods of manipulation which were first developed in market research and "human relations."

Note, however, that if we substitute the softer word "coordinate" for manipulate the results are about the same. Increasingly the behavior of each person is vested with a public interest. Man has always been implicated in a social system—a system of interlocking roles. But never have they been so diverse, never have so many sub-systems been linked with one another so that the faintest tremor in one part sends repercussions throughout the whole. Hence the need for coordination. You remember the chain reaction in the Mother Goose rhyme about the house that Jack built. It involved the farmer who kept a cock which waked the priest who married the man who kissed "the maiden all forlorn, that milked the cow with the crumpled horn," and the rest of it.

Contrast the rugged individualism, the sturdy independence and isolation of a Daniel Boone with the immobility of a New Yorker when the Motormen's Benevolent Association pulled a subway strike at Christmastime.

We are "coordinated"—even "manipulated"—because a complex and interdependent system requires it. The result is inevitably an increase in conformity. And of course war, with the survival of the whole nation at stake, brings in new extremes in conformity and makes them virtues.

Charge: Conformity Damps Out the Life of Impulse and Emotion

The uniform treatment of people as equivalent units in a given category and the suspicion of manipulation relate to a third indictment: the ascendance of mind over heart, of cool calculation over impulse, of intellect over emotion, the Apollonian mode over the Dionysian. Human beings are transformed into producing and consuming units. Social objects become physical objects. Beings become things. The mass society is a cold and mechanized society.

In mass society man is reckoned like a number quantitatively assessed. Detailed job descriptions specify expected behavior. Time-motion studies evaluate performance. Market researchers appraise buying patterns. Students in the tens of thousands are pre-tested, classified, go through the stipulated procedures, are graded, ranked, released. The probabilities of death and illness and unemployment are carefully calculated.

This much is true enough: there is a cold rationality which, by taking thought, increases efficiency and protects us against the unknown and unanticipated, but adds not a jot or a tittle to our *joie de vivre*.

Charge: Conformity Implies Softness

Another recurrent theme in the indictment is that of decadence. For the red pottage of collective security we have surrendered the birthright of individualism. Conformity is a coward's escape from the challenge of freedom. Our way of life has sapped our self-reliance.

But the great tragedy, the indictment states, is that we think this new deal is a good deal. Smug satisfaction in our well-feathered nests is the great seduction. It is not rabid right nor loony left-wingers who threaten our heritage of individualism. It is the more subtle influence of lush living which lulls us into complacency. The American is threatened not so much by toxins as by self-administered tranquillizers. He rarely has the perspicacity to ask, as the Progressive School youngster asked his teacher: "Do I have to do what I want to do today?" Ordinarily we never question whether our wants are in fact our own. We believe we *want* to be organization men.

Charge: Conformity Means Mediocrity

The final indictment is that the range of living is being restricted. We are converging on dead center. It is no golden mean: it's leaden mediocrity.

The range of life experiences is being foreshortened. We're developing a standard size for American families. Education is providing a uniform, thin, gray gruel for more of us: and the distance between the worst and the best educated is not, on the average, as great as it once was. Local and even regional differences are suppressed, national standards emphasized. The contrasts between Republicans and Democrats are scarcely visible to the naked eye when the only contest is over who hates tyranny and treachery more, whose concern for farmer and worker is greater, or even over whose corruption is less.

Exhortations to piety are not clearly distinguishable from the prudential morality of the Chamber of Commerce which asserts that "honesty is good business." Business has become philanthropic, and philanthropies must be businesslike. The blacks and whites are disappearing, giving way to the featureless uniformity of a company of men in gray-flannel suits.

All these casual observations about conformity suffer from this shortcoming—they are invariably wrong: The first error is overstatement—the joy of the wild, wild hyperbole and the cosmic generalization. The second error is the very partial character of casual observation—*we blindly fondle the tail and call the elephant a snake.*

But allegations about conformity do come from better sources than these. Let me give a few examples.

Data collected by Muzafer Sherif and Solomon Asch, studying perceptions of physical objects, suggest that a person tends to shape his judgment to fit that of others, even about something as clear and noncontroversial as the length of two lines. The judgment of others may be clearly wrong—Asch's experiments included some in which a majority of subjects were stooges deliberately instructed to give wrong answers—*but one-third of the others were willing to disbelieve their own eyes, apparently, in order to conform.* (For further reading on these experiments see Muzafer Sherif in *Readings in Social Psychology,* edited by T. M. Newcomb and E. L. Hartley, and *Social Psychology* by Solomon Asch.)

The primitive assumption underlying inquiry into any system of phenomena—physical, biological or social—is the assumption of order. It would clearly be fruitless to undertake a study of human behavior if it were assumed to be random. And it is a very slight step, the mere addition of an *ed*, from order to order*ed.* Let us be altogether candid about it. The student of human behavior does make the assumption of ordering, of determinacy.

Under specified conditions people respond in anticipated fashion. That is to say, they conform to our expectations in a predictable manner.

And so the results of research certainly confirm that we are conformists. But this is surely not the critical issue. The important questions are:

Are we as much more slavish in our conformity as the current alarms would indicate?
What kinds of conformity are either necessary or good?

Is there any reliable evidence that we are more conformist than our predecessors? Than the good people of Salem Village in 18th century Massachusetts were, for instance? Than Horace Mann's contemporaries in the 19th? Has a single point of view a monopoly over men's minds as in Medieval Europe, or 13th century Spain?

Are we more conformist than the Ifugao in the Philippines? The Hutterites in the Dakotas? We do not and cannot know. Conformity is a fuzzy, fighting word seldom if ever clearly specified. Even were the term a usable one, the data are lacking from the past and from contemporaries elsewhere.

A Definition of Conformity

Conformity is sanctioned conduct required of all persons falling in a given category. Certain rewards and punishments require doctors, teachers, parents, students, citizens, criminals to conform to a fairly narrow range within the spectrum of conduct. Everyone is restricted in his conduct by others' conceptions of propriety; and by the differing outcomes of alternative modes of conduct. It is not proper for the doctor or the teacher to become so emotionally involved with patient or student as to impair their technical efficiency or their equal concern for all their charges. We deem it proper to require that decisions be made through democratic processes; and to condemn those non-conformists who would circumvent or subvert such processes. It is proper—and good—to insist upon giving men "equal opportunities"—that is, to treat men equally in order to discover and use their inequalities. Thus it is proper to require people to conform to the Supreme Court mandate on integration. We think it legitimate to require that all citizens recognize and abide by the Bill of Rights.

Obviously, there are many *kinds* of conformity. If some are bad, some should be preserved at all costs. Some nonconformities are license rather than liberation—futile and destructive rather than purposeful and creative. "The effect of liberty to individuals is that they may do as they please," said Edmund Burke. "We ought to see what it will please them to do before we risk congratulations."

It seems to me that conformity is good when it involves those conventional forms, those niceties of conduct which are the customary cues to our respect for one another. They are the signs of reciprocity of consideration in human affairs. However trivial conventional greetings might seem, for instance, they carry some slight intimation of the Golden Rule.

Conformity is good, above all, when it applies to the political and scientific rules for making rules. *To rule on an issue politically we insist on free and open discussion,* encouragement of diverse views, decisions based on majority judgment, and impartial execution and respect for that decision, even if we disagree with it—until we can change it.

But conformity must rest upon conformity to the canons of science. That is, what we conform to must bring better results than other methods.

Equally, non-conformity is acceptable only when its results, morally and practically, are superior to its alternatives. Be it noted, however, that there is no such thing as pure nonconformity. The gentlemen who write and speak against conformity do it so well because they conformed to the necessities and routines of learning the basic tools and background of communication and education—much more so, in fact, and better and longer, than most. Even nonconformity must be built on a great deal of conformity.

CONFORMITY: NECESSARY AND DESIRABLE

"Must we conform?" Of course. And in the process, far from ceasing to be men, we fulfill ourselves. The great error perpetrated by the diatribes against conformity and the lofty celebrations of individualism is to obscure the fact that we are essentially, necessarily and fortunately social creatures. A few of those currently campaigning against conformity acknowledge the ambivalent implications of man's social nature. William H. Whyte, in a tardy acknowledgement, says, "The group is a tyrant; so also is it a friend, and *it is both at once.*" There is a measure of good fortune in being subject to the coercive and conformity-inducing influence of the group.

We are creatures of a culture which provides the categories of thought enabling us to deal with the infinite complexities of our worlds; and frees us from the need of dealing *de novo* and endlessly with the issues of life.

The limits imposed by group life guarantee that order without which neither group nor individual life would be possible.

The group, with all its constraints and conformities, is the agency of self-realization.

First, man has a heritage which, while it imposes serious restrictions, is both inescapable (polyandry or Zoroastrianism are really not live options for most Americans) and desirable. Man is not like the lowly ass, without pride of ancestry or hope of posterity. He has both; and he builds the latter upon the former.

The past, our ancestry, sometimes seems oppressive. The crust of custom imposes irksome conformity. Yet even the language and ideas in which we express our resentment of these cultural impositions are themselves derived from this heritage. Personality is the subjective aspect of culture. No child in the human family receives quite the same cultural legacy as another, but conformity is the necessary result of a common culture and provides the indispensable foundation of personality. Who can fail to acknowledge that he was largely created in other times and other places?

But aside from the *content* of our heritage (our religion, science, art, literature, philosophy, customs) our culture has formal aspects that both limit and liberate. To be able to think, to be free to solve problems, we rely chiefly on the thought-tools available in a society. Conformity to these categories of thought and feeling is the alternative to drivelling idiocy. Without them we could not handle our world—it would be a "big, buzzing, booming confusion." All of us—and everything we deal with—are parts of categories; and our society has labeled and classified them.

For so many of the details of life the answers are already given. Thus conformity emancipates us from the need to contrive, daily, new solutions. Of course, some solutions are bad; and probably none is as good as it might be. From this point of view we *should* be concerned with new and better solutions. But many are adequate; and not having to occupy ourselves with X we are free to tackle Y. How shall we solve the problem of old age? Individual savings from hard work and thrift is one answer. Another is

Social Security, Old Age and Survivor's Insurance, a major aspect of what some have been pleased to call "creeping socialism." It is possible that such collective solutions, binding on all, mortgaging the future and cutting out a range of individual decisions, may nevertheless have a liberal effect. If we sacrifice the privilege of personal and private solutions to the uncertainties and threats of the environing physical and social world, we may gain not merely a sort of narcotic security, but the possibility of creative expression in other (and possibly more significant) realms. If we admire the pioneer and patriarch subduing their refractory physical worlds, it would seem equally legitimate to admire the men at Harwell whose victories in the intellectual realm do not seem to be impeded by the security provided by parliamentary socialism in Great Britain. It is at least possible that the aesthetic sensibilities of the French have been improved rather than compromised by nationalization of the Comédie Française. In suburban Park Forest, William H. Whyte, Jr. (in *The Organization Man*) found a vigorous civic life, the emergence of vociferous minority groups, an active, often turbulent community. He disregarded this in favor of the evidence supporting his indictment of the servile, other-directed organization man. But doesn't this notion at least merit consideration: that such strong expression of variant views might be in part the outcome of collectively contrived security which emancipated these people from an exclusive preoccupation with matters of physical existence? Some conformities are both necessary *and* liberating.

Social relationships are necessary. The evidence suggests that outside of that system of human relationships we call a group, we find only sub-human behavior. Removed from social intercourse, the individual never becomes a person; worse, he can suffer traumatic collapse of what person-ality he has.

We have a social relationship when, among two or more people, there is a high probability that a given gesture on the part of one will elicit a predicted response on the part of the other. If to a given stimulus—like "Good morning" or "Can you tell me what time it is?"—any response is equally likely, from coitus to combat, a social relationship does not, could not exist. We would live—and promptly die—in a chaotic world. Human behavior is not random. It is predictable within a given range. And in order to elicit certain responses from others *we act in appropriate ways*. Which is to say, heaven help us, we manipulate others. We control their conduct. This is fundamental to the nature of social relationships. And so when Whyte suggests that man extends the range of his freedom when he applies science to control the physical, but *limits* his freedom when he applies science to control the social, he speaks a partial truth which is likely to convey total nonsense. For man achieves his freedoms only through the social relationships which require manipulation, control, prediction—in a word, conformity.

Human relationships, since they involve obligation, are intrinsically moral relationships. They rest upon mutually understood, pre-established rules which eliminate arbitrary or idiosyncratic action. They guarantee continuity. This is one feature of morality: it is a recurrent and dependable thing. Furthermore, a rule is general. It applies to all members of a given category of persons.

Three aspects of morality therefore apply to human relationships: rules are general, they are imposed, they are coercive—and they are constant or regular. Which is to say again that human relationships are of necessity constraining and conformity-inducing.

But the requirement of conformity built into human relationships is not desirable alone because it supports the social system. It is also desirable, paradoxically, because it implies personal limits. Individual freedom in the sense of uncontrolled or unlimited behavior spells frustration, personal disorganization and is, in fact, no freedom.

Thus a human relationship is basically a moral one, implying predictability, constancy, constraint—conformity. And this is not merely necessary: it is desirable.

We do not know who we are directly, but indirectly. A person becomes an object to himself through the responses of others. From the vantage point of others, he is able to get a fix on his position. As others act toward him, as he estimates the judgments of him implied in their actions, his self-conception, at first wavering and uncertain, crystallizes. George Herbert Mead says, "A self can arise only where there is a social process within which this self has had its (origin)."

Self-knowledge, then, is a gift of the group—and no small beneficence at that. It is only when we know who we are that the personal meaning of various choices can be assessed. Only after we acquire a self does the capacity for thought and choice emerge.

In short the attributes of man we most esteem are intimately linked to the group with all its coercive impact. Conformity of a very basic sort is the price of self-realization—even of non-conformity. Our cultural legacy, the very existence of a social order, personal stability, the development of a unique self with a capacity for thought and choice, grow out of the conformities of group life.

We have been fed a half-baked critique of conformity, noble in intent but shallow in analysis. Conformity is sometimes bad, of course. Conformity is sometimes good, certainly. But first of all, conformity *is*.

Reply to Wilson*

DENNIS H. WRONG

Everett Wilson's article produces in me a strange sense of vertigo. For in rebuttal of the critics of "conformity" he invokes precisely those commonplaces of contemporary sociology that, illegitimately converted into an ethic of conduct, were the source of the attitudes and values the critics were questioning. If these critics are simply ignoramuses easily refuted by citing the most elementary generalizations of the introductory sociology course, then Wilson has indeed taken their measure. But he at least owes us an explanation of why so many learned men have been so perversely misguided and why their errors have had such resonance on the Antioch campus and elsewhere.

Freud once remarked that if a man seriously maintained that the moon was full of jam, we would wish to examine not the interior of the moon but the inside of the man's head in order to discover how he could possibly have arrived at so bizarre a conclusion. Wilson tells us that the critics of conformity have asserted the sociological equivalent of claiming the moon to be full of jam, but he never bothers to tell us how they got such an idea or why so many have accepted their notions as true reflections of the quality of American life at midcentury. Surely a sociologist owes us no less than this.

I agree with Wilson that the view that we live in a "mass society" in which men are increasingly manipulated by others and regarded as interchangeable units in a huge and impersonal social system is often overstated and reduced to caricature. But one does not dispose of such a view by merely reiterating a few obvious truths about our dependence on a cultural heritage received from others or the need for some consensus on rules of conduct if we are to have a society at all. All views of social reality become distorted and sloganized when they pass from the writings of thoughtful scholars and intellectuals into popular parlance—something that happens very quickly nowadays. The critic is obliged to distinguish between their original and their—in the literal sense of the word—vulgar form, whether he is concerned with Christian theology, classical economic theory, Marxism, psychoanalysis, the theory of mass society, or the root ideas of modern sociology. Wilson's schoolmasterly admonitions include no recognition that the critics of conformity were originally challenging debased versions of the very ideas he solemnly affirms in rejecting similarly debased versions of the anti-conformity thesis. Someone is chasing his own tail and I do not think it is Riesman and company, who scarcely need to be reminded that when they write they conform to the rules of grammar and syntax and make use of "thought tools" they have acquired from others.

Let us examine Wilson's argument more closely. To begin with, he charges Riesman, Fromm, and Whyte with lauding "nonconformity," although none of the three makes use of this particular term as the "good" counterconcept to the "bad" conformity that is allegedly rejected. Riesman compares the "other-direction" he sees as spreading in modern society with "inner-direction" and "tradition-direction," and, lo and behold, he explicitly calls all three "modes of conformity!" Whyte contrasts the "social ethic" of organization men with the "Protestant ethic" of the past and regards both as culturally transmitted sets of values. A central contention of Fromm's is that men possess a common "social character" shaped by early experience in the family and by all the other groups and institutions that sociologists refer to as "agencies of socialization." All three writers, in short, make it plain that they are not, as Wilson suggests, pitting the individual against a separate and distinct entity called society. In effect, Riesman, Fromm, and Whyte are not protesting against conformity as such but against a kind of conformity that fails to allow for innovation, creativity and even personal eccentricity. Not "nonconformity" but *individuality* is what they miss in American life.

Of course, it is nonsense to extol nonconformity over conformity in all-or-none terms without any reference to particular standards to which people may or may not conform. The ultimate or absolute nonconformist is obviously the psychotic. The fallacy of nonconformity for its own sake has been most effectively pointed out not by a sociologist but by the poet, W. H. Auden:

> Yours you say were parents to avoid, avoid then
>   if you please—
> Do the reverse on all occasions till you catch
>   the same disease.

But Auden, unlike Wilson, makes it perfectly plain in the stanza preceding the above that we possess alternatives to imitating slavishly the models of conduct presented by others:

> Perfect pater. Marvelous mater. Knock the critic
>   down who dares—
> Very well, believe it, copy, till your hair is
>   white as theirs.

Wilson, however, does not content himself with scoring an easy victory over the straw man of nonconformity. He proceeds to list five specific charges that he considers central to the argument of the anti-conformists. It is hard to tell whether in stating the charges he also means to criticize them, for although he concludes that the charges are "invariably wrong" he never subjects them to detailed refutation. In general, he seems to accept them as true but with a shrug or a "so what?" implying that things can't help but be this way in our kind of society or that this is the price we have to pay for realizing other values.

Mr. Wilson argues, for example, that the elimination of hereditary inequalities is bound to produce more uniformity and less individuality. The claim is questionable. Greater equality of opportunity will certainly reduce differences between *groups* in society, but one of the chief reasons for favoring it has always been that it will increase the saliency and importance of *individual* differences, whether genetic or rooted in acquired character, by eliminating the rigid social categorization of individuals according to the accident of their having been born to parents of a given social class or ethnic group.

To the charge that conformity is based on manipulation, Wilson responds with a bit of word magic: if we call manipulation "coordination" it doesn't sound so bad. Moreover, our society is so complex and intricate that the planned coordination of individual activities is unavoidable. Also, success in war depends on national unity. Wilson dismisses the other charges in a like manner. He quickly tempers his initial judgment that they are simply wrong with the far more moderate claim that they are overstated and tell us only part of the truth about contemporary society. But he never provides us with the rest of the truth, unless his occasional references to our material comforts are meant to fill this bill. The critics of conformity, however, have explicitly defined their task as that of assessing the "costs of abundance" or "affluence."

To be sure, the anti-conformists have been unable to suggest any convincing ways of overcoming the conditions they describe. In *Liberalism and the Retreat from Politics,* William J. Newman accuses them of providing a "counsel of despair" as far as hopeful social change is concerned. Riesman suggests that personal autonomy may be found only in the interstices between rival social pressures. Whyte concedes that big bureaucracy is here to stay and can suggest only that we fight it by giving false answers on the questionnaires it requires us to fill out. Fromm draws an attractive picture of a communitarian socialist order but provides no clues as to how we might achieve such a total reversal of the dominant trends of our time.

Yet it is surely the task of the intellectual as social critic to say that the shoe pinches even if he is unable to provide us with a better-fitting pair of shoes. Wilson apparently believes that to explain why our society is driven to treat people as abstract functions is to dispose of any complaints about such treatment. In making the canons of empirical science his ultimate value, he is unable to imagine any other attitude toward the facts of contemporary society than placid acceptance of their necessity and desirability. But one can use sociological knowledge to gain an awareness of the social constraints on our conduct that partially frees us from these constraints. One can study society in order to change it or to free ourselves from it, as opposed to studying it in order to abase ourselves before its prevailing forms.

I am unable to see that the remainder of Wilson's essay has any relevance at all to the themes of contemporary social criticism that he is attacking. He cites some psychological experiments showing that people are influenced by the judgments of others and some opinion polls more than a decade old showing that "tolerance of nonconformists" varies somewhat among different categories of Americans; he then delivers what reads like the combination of an opening lecture in an introductory sociology course with an editorial against Barry Goldwater. Since the critics of conformity were talking in thoroughly specific terms about modern society, all these generalizations about man's dependence on group life, the necessity of social relationships, and the shaping of one's self-conception by the responses of others have nothing to do with the issues raised by the critics. Nor does Wilson's implied defense of parliamentary socialism in Britain and nationalized theatre in France.

CONFORMITY VS. FREEDOM

What, essentially, are the critics of conformity saying? The anticonformist or mass society thesis involves two major contentions. First, there are the central structural facts about modern society: the trend toward large-scale bureaucratic organization in all spheres of life, the centralization of decision-making and the consequent increase in the administrative and commercial manipulation (or "coordination") of individual responses. In describing how these trends restrict personal freedom, the writers quoted by Wilson stand in an intellectual tradition going back to Max Weber, Karl Mannheim and, in somewhat different form, Alexis de Tocqueville.

But there is a second line of argument that is more closely associated with Riesman, Whyte, and the social critics of the 1950's. This is the contention that an ethic or ideology of conformism has become increasingly prevalent in America today. It is conformism rather than the ubiquitous and inescapable facts of conformity to others recited by Wilson that the critics are attacking. Conformism is the extension of the dictum "when in Rome, do as the Romans do" to all social conduct and to thinking and feeling as well as to overt "doing." Wilson is quite correct in suggesting that there may be less behavioral conformity in contemporary society than in past eras or in small preliterate and agrarian communities. But this is not the point. People have conformed to rules of conduct because they could imagine no others owing to cultural isolation, because they reversed the authority of the "eternal yesterdays" of their ancestors, because they regarded the social norms of their society as God-given, or because they viewed the norms as "right" and their violation as "wrong" according to the dictates of an absolute code of morality. All these grounds of conformity differ from the belief that one should strive to do what others do, and to think and feel what they think and feel, for no other reason except that they in fact act, think and feel as they do. Conformism is *not* being like other people, but believing that one ought to try to be as much like other people as possible. Only this belief, when elevated into a principle of conduct, constitutes conformism.

What the social critics are saying is that conformism in this sense is highly prevalent in modern society and that it is promoted and sustained by major structural trends. They also suggest that to make a virtue out of patterning oneself totally on others is to undervalue individuality and to leave far less room for creative innovation and for a rich and uniquely personal inner life than is possible even when one's overt behavior is regulated by narrow traditions, weighty religious commandments, or absolute moral injunctions, as has so often been the case in the past. In addition, the social critics recognize that the doctrine of conformism owes much to the increasing self-consciousness about the ways in which we are shaped by others that we have acquired from modern social science. Sociology teaches us that our characters are molded by the social groups we belong to; conformism urges us to regard our group identities as our most important attributes and to seek out new groups in which we can find the security of collective solutions to all problems. Wilson's use of the facts of sociology to defend and uphold conformism merely suggests the continuing relevance of the position he thinks he is refuting.

Reply to Wilson*

ERNEST VAN DEN HAAG

Everett Wilson complains that "conformity" is a fuzzy term, but every time he seems about to define and clarify it, he hurries on to something else instead. This tantalizing tactic enables him to be "for" conformity (just as others are "against" it) by elaborating the obvious and the trivial which he

* Copyright © November/December, 1964, by *Trans*-action, Inc., New Brunswick, N.J. Vol. 2, No. 1.

does rather too thoroughly. Nonetheless, after reading Wilson I know no better what he wants me to conform to, how, and when, than I did before. Am I to conform always? and to everything? A tall order even for a dedicated conformist. Am I to conform to Goldwater or to Johnson? the Birchers or the anti-Birchers? the temperance league or the drunkards' society? Mr. Justice Black's views or those of Mr. Justice White? What troubles me is that it is impossible to conform to one without nonconforming to the other—which makes it hard to understand, let alone conform to, Wilson's advice.

Wilson treats "conformity" as though it were an opinion, a factual assertion, a logical conclusion, a rule, or a specific preference that one can be "for" or "against." But certainly "to conform" in general means no more than to agree or to comply, in thought or action, with an opinion, conclusion, action, rule, or preference. What sense does it make to advise people to conform (or not to) with opinions, conclusions, etc., without stating what they are? I'm opposed to conforming to communism, in favor of conforming to the rules of democracy. Whether I am right or wrong depends on what one thinks of communism and democracy, not, certainly, on whether one is for or against "conforming." By conforming to one set of ideas or rules, I nonconform to the other. And which ideas or rules are to be complied with should depend on *their* merits—not on the merits of "conformity." This calls for an analysis that Wilson has not undertaken.

Wilson points out that people usually conform to some rules and expectations, mostly the prevailing ones, and that this is necessary in any human society. Indeed, else rules and expectations would be pointless; and, certainly, the prevailing ones are, by definition, those most conformed to. Wilson accuses a number of straw men labelled Fromm, Riesman, et al., of denying so elementary a commonplace. But nobody—not even Paul Goodman—is for the kind of nonconformity Wilson opposes, or regards as impossible.

There are, however, some other definitions which give a specific meaning to "conformity." And these are the definitions that Fromm, Riesman, et al., implied. One may think, for instance, that fewer people dissent from some prevailing views than would if people were more reflective or courageous; that too many follow the majority when it is not obligatory to do so, even though doubting that the majority is right; or that too many people fail to analyze issues themselves and instead accept the views of others blindly. In all these cases conformity is a rather infelicitous expression for abdication of one's power to think and act independently whether agreeing (conforming) or disagreeing (nonconforming) with the powers that be, or the majority. To be sure, one who independently agrees with the majority is not a conformist; but one who agrees because it is the majority, or because he feels that it is easier to agree than to think independently or to oppose, is a conformist. And Riesman, et al., maintain that we have too many such conformists.

Another definition of conforming is "to agree with the status quo"—usually in specific, often political and social, respects. The merits of such a position, and of its opposite, can be determined only by discussing specific issues, never by discussing "conformity" in general.

However, Wilson might have pointed out that those who oppose the status quo often resort to a somewhat unfair rhetorical trick when they attribute to those who favor it the motive of "conformity"—as though one could not favor the status quo out of conviction rather than cowardice or intellectual laziness. Such "nonconformists" are often fanatic enough to convince themselves that their opponents must be fools or cowards, or to use a more fashionable expression, "neurotic." (Fromm certainly has at times used this trick. Perhaps he didn't know what he was doing, but that only makes it worse.) I think the status quo may well be preferable to what most "nonconformists" of my acquaintance advocate—and I am yet to be persuaded that I think so only because I am intellectually lazy, a coward, or neurotic—although I may be all of these.

PSYCHOLOGICAL CONFORMITY

Still another definition of "conformity" refers to a psychological attitude. A conformist thus may be a personality type who does not feel comfortable unless he shares the prevailing views, and acts according to the prevailing customs. A nonconformist is one who does not feel comfortable unless he dissents, opposes, and stands out. Both types may exist in mild and extreme, voluntary and compulsive editions. It seems to be about as silly to be "for" (or against) either, as it is to be "for" (or against) redheads. Neither Fromm nor Riesman advocate, as far as I know, the nonconforming character type as here described though they defend it as a useful antidote, or leaven, on occasion. Both advocate an autonomous personality type capable of conforming or nonconforming decisions without being driven by inner compulsion or by external pressure.

Thus if Fromm, Riesman, et al., maintain that people are too conformist, they argue that people too often unnecessarily abdicate their right to think and act independently and instead blindly accept prefabricated ideas, or submit to manipulation or to rules they ought and could not submit to; and that there is unnecessary manipulation which is not in the social interest. The indictment, to be sure, is not altogether clear; yet it is not half as obscure as Wilson makes it. At any rate, his retort strikes me as odd. He says that, after all, the Ifugaos might be more conformist. Or that in our own past we might have been more conformist. This is obviously irrelevant: if the Ifugaos are, and we were, more conformist in the past than we are now, it does not follow that we must be as conformist as we are now or that it is good to be a conformist.

Wilson goes on to tell his opponents that sometimes and to some extent it is good to obey rules—as though they had denied that. Finally, he seems to say that modern society after all requires more conformity because of its complexity—without realizing that this is precisely what his opponents have argued, except that they did not accept Wilson's logical fallacy of assuming that when something has a function (is necessary or, as he puts it, inevitable) it therefore becomes good.

Not so. What is unavoidable is not necessarily good, and unfortunately, what is good is not necessarily unavoidable. The defeat of Germany in the last war was, in my opinion, good, but not necessarily unavoidable. On the other hand, had Nazism been truly the "wave of the future" (or if communism were), this would not convince me that it is, or was, good. If conformity were unavoidable, that would not make it good—only unavoidable.

However, I do not think Wilson has shown that it is, except in the obviously irrelevant sense of social order in general; his opponents, taking that for granted, argue about what kind of social order and how much conformity. Actually, the greater complexity of society may make it possible for us to have less conformity—unlike primitive tribes. Riesman is certainly right in exploring why there is so much unnecessary conformity—conformity which is not required for the functioning of a reasonable society. Such conformity, as Riesman points out (and Wilson feebly echoes him), has a psychological explanation and function. Wilson, however, confuses explanation with justification and offers his own rather vague explanation of conformity as though it were a justification. (One might as well offer an explanation of the criminal's motives as a justification of his crime.)

Riesman is opposed to much of the status quo and, therefore, opposes conforming to it. I do not share Riesman's viewpoint on the status quo. But Riesman also makes the psychological point that people are manipulated into conforming and have internalized an attitude of conforming for the sake of conforming. This point must be dealt with on its own merits—whether one agrees with what people conform to or not. Wilson has not come to grips with those who deplore "conformity" (except, perhaps, for their most silly journalistic hangers-on). To explain that conformity is sometimes useful, sometimes necessary, and has always existed, does not constitute an answer to the objection that there is too much unnecessary and detrimental conformity, and that our society promotes it.

An Inquiry into the Undersocialized Conception of Man*

HERMAN TURK

A recent article cautioned against an "oversocialized conception of man." In it Dennis Wrong noted a tendency of current theory to confuse norms with motives, thereby ignoring the uneasy truce which exists in the individual between his bodily drives and the "process of becoming human."[1] Such neglect, he suggested, has resulted in failure to account for violence, conflict, and the individual's sense of coercion by society. Whether such phenomena result from the Freudian battle between id and superego, or whether they occur because societies contain, and individuals introject, *competing norms* need not concern us; since *either* approach paints an incomplete picture of the social function of internalized norms.

Both of these models, as well as other current conceptions of social man, seem to pay systematic attention only to the individual as *an agent of self-control,* thereby slighting—or perhaps viewing as non-problematic— the importance of his internalized social standards *in making him an agent in the social control of others.* In short, one can receive the impression that the norms which people internalize are socially more eufunctional when these people are *Egos* than when they are *Alters.* That *the opposite* may well be the case is the theme of the discussion to follow.

Whether people gladly conform to the mandates of groups or societies or whether they feel coerced into conforming, these mandates are still *mediated or enforced* by some or all of a set of individuals who have internalized them. In other words, the culture, be it benign or hostile to the individual, is applied by other individuals, acting either singly or in concert.[2] Indeed the application of internalized norms to others may be the principal source of order in society.

* Reprinted from *Social Forces,* 43 (May, 1965), pp. 518–521, by permission of the author and publisher. Thanks are extended to Alan P. Bates for his helpful comments on an earlier draft.
1. Dennis H. Wrong, "The Oversocialized Conception of Man in Modern Sociology," *American Sociological Review,* 26 (April 1961), pp. 183–193.
2. Groups and individuals are not only sources of social approval but also have the capacity of affording or withholding a wide variety of need satisfactions, both social and subsocial. In restricting his discussion of social pressure largely to the application of approval or disapproval, Wrong (*ibid.*) has underestimated the power that individuals and groups hold over other individuals. Experiments and field studies have demonstrated the awesome effect on the individual of complete, uncontradicted, group harmony.

It is quite likely that in deciding how he should act in any given social system, each individual resolves his internal conflicts between drives and norms, or among several sets of norms, in some manner that is unique. How, then, can there be any consensus, *any normative system at all*, if its content is some sort of population total of "how I should behave." If, however, the neglected function of internalized norms is considered, the possibility of consensus is more apparent. When we decide *how another should behave*, our bodily drives are less relevant, as are the norms of social systems other than the subsystem which ties us to him. It follows that we find it easier to agree among ourselves about what another should do, than about what each of us should do himself. Thus we should be able to control "deviation" in others more easily than we can control it in ourselves.

Stating one aspect of this argument more formally, the following hypothesis could be subjected to experimental test:

Several members of a given social system will be in greater agreement regarding what another member should do than regarding what each should do himself.

The Experiment

The author's introductory sociology class of 20 undergraduates yielded several members of the Duke University student community. These were employed as experimental subjects at a time when they could still be considered to have been sociologically naive. Three weeks later a professional colleague replicated the experiment in his own introductory sociology class of 18 additional Duke undergraduate students.[3]

The teaching staff had often remarked at the positive valuation of scholastic performance and at a somewhat inhibitive classroom etiquette which existed within the student body. Thus the existence of norms surrounding the use of classroom time could reasonably be expected. Asking the student to place an upper proscriptive limit on the use of such time appeared to be in keeping with the students' hesitance to be either verbose or argumentative. The use of time as the content of responses also had the tactical advantage of providing numerical data, which could easily be processed. Finally, asking each student what *should* be, coupled with the guarantee of his anonymity, was felt to assure the expression of *internal* standards.

In both the initial experiment and in its replication, the student's occupancy of an odd numbered or an even numbered position in the seating plan governed which of the following two questions he was asked in group-administered paper and pencil format:

---

3. Thanks are extended to Howard S. Gall for his generous cooperation in this respect.

If you were to express a lengthy opinion in a regular one-period class at Duke,[4] what is the longest you should take so that class time will not be monopolized? ———— minutes and ———— seconds.

If a classmate were to express a lengthy opinion in a regular one-period class at Duke, what is the longest he should take so that class time will not be monopolized? ———— minutes and ———— seconds.

TABLE 1.   *Distributions of Maximum Time Allowed Self and Classmate in Expressing an Opinion in Class*

	Time Allowed Self				Time Allowed Classmate			
	Initial		Replication		Initial		Replication	
Summary Measure	min.	sec.	min.	sec.	min.	sec.	min.	sec.
	1	30	2	0	2	0	3	20
	2	0	3	30	2	0	4	37
	2	30	4	0	3	0	5	0
	4	30	4	40	4	0	5	0
	5	0	5	0	5	0	5	0
	8	30	5	0	5	0	5	0
	10	0	14	20	5	0	10	0
	12	30	15	0	5	0	14	59
	25	0	24	0	5	0	15	15
	50	0			10	0		
Number of Respondents	10		9		10		9	
Mean Time (Min.)	12.15		8.61		4.60		7.55	
Variance in Time	266.11		55.39		5.16		21.14	

The variance of the time periods which were named by the respondents was adopted as the measure of disagreement. In terms of the hypothesis, the variance was expected to be greater among responses to the first question than among responses to the second one.

RESULTS AND DISCUSSION

The four arrays of responses which were obtained to the two questions and their respective replications are shown on Table 1. In both administrations of the experiment the variance was greater among persons who were asked to set standards for themselves than it was among those who set standards for a classmate. These differences are in the predicted direction. Using the exact distribution of each of the two variance ratios as the basis

---

4. Class periods were 50 minutes in length.

for assessing the significance of such differences,[5] the probabilities for the initial experiment and its replication were $<.02$ and $<.17$, respectively. Combining these two values by Fisher's method yielded the overall result of $P<.01$.[6]

Though not at acceptable levels of significance, students were some what more likely to apply fractions of a minute to themselves than to the classmate and tended to allocate the conventional "five minutes" to the latter.

Both the differences between variances and the latter suggestions in the data were sharper in the original experiment than in its replication. Why this was so cannot be said with certainty. It might simply have been a consequence of sampling fluctuation, but there is also some slight evidence that the two sets of research subjects held different orientations *toward the experiment itself*. The second group was less naive at the time of testing, and guesses about experimental purpose may have intruded on the responses. It was also the impression of the second investigator that some of his students dealt facetiously with the problem, perhaps as a result of tension produced by the imminence of their first sociology examination. The initial group, however, displayed considerable seriousness, both during the testing and in the subsequent discussion of the experiment. Even the man who had allowed himself the full 50 minutes revealed his identity and indicated the sincerity of his response by saying that he might someday know more than his instructor on a given subject. It is also possible that, contrary to request, some of the first set of students described the experiment to some of those in the second set. Despite these possibilities, the hypothesis was confirmed when both trials of the experiment were considered together.

A further problem of interpretation arose when it was noted that, both in the original study and in its replication, persons tended to allow themselves more time than others allowed the classmate. These differences in mean time allowed were not significant $(P>.10$ and $>.72$, combined $P > .25)$. However, the direction of differences was such as to restrict the variance of time allowed the classmate, since such time could not be less than zero. Thus the exact probability of each of the two variance ratios was computed separately (a) for mean differences as great as the one observed or greater, and (b) for mean differences less than that observed. The probabilities were (a) $<.16$ and $<.21$ and (b) $<.004$ and $<.05$. Combining probabilities over the two experiments yielded $P<.08$ and

---

5. A computer program was developed which permitted computation of these and other probabilities reported in the article, through enumeration of all possible combinations of the tabled observations. See Herman Turk and Theresa G. Turk, "IBM FORTRAN Program for the Exact Probability of Different Means and Variances in the 2-Sample Case," *Behavioral Science*, 9 (July 1964), pp. 291–292.
6. See Frederick Mosteller and Robert R. Bush, "Selected Quantitative Techniques," in Gardner Lindsey (ed.), *Handbook of Social Psychology*, Vol. 1, pp. 328–331.

P<.001, respectively. Thus taking the direction of the mean differences into account did not disturb the original findings. The hypothesis may be accepted as confirmed.

CONCLUSIONS

These findings suggest the necessity of distinguishing between the function of internalized norms and values for self-control and their function for the control of others. In the former case they combine with other aspects of the person to produce unique expectations; in the latter case they are operative in less contested fashion. Thus men are more likely to demand that others conform to any given norm than they are likely to make such demands of themselves.

In internalizing culture, the individual not only acquires a personal morality but he also becomes a *component of the collective conscience*. It is this latter, neglected function of internalization which permits a tentative leap to the institutional level of inquiry. Social sanctions, to be sure, are often applied by specialized agencies rather than through the informal actions of one or more persons. Nonetheless, the activities of such agencies require legitimation by consensus; and, in terms of the findings of this study, such consensus rests most often on what people feel *others* should do and on what should happen *to others* if they do not meet these expectations.

Socialization theory, then, should take into account not only our Freudian feelings of guilt when we violate certain social dictates, but also our Durkheimian "passionate reaction" when such dictates are violated by others.[7] Indeed, the Freudian mechanism *projection* of guilt would let the first of these feelings lend support to the second.

---

7. One is tempted to observe that what appears to be "frustration-aggression" may often be "deviance—social-control."

Chapter 4

Deviance: Is It an Act or a Label?

Early work on deviance focused on the individual, contending that there was something inherently deviant in him or his actions. Kitsuse is arguing against this traditional view in the lead article in this section. Instead of looking at the deviant we must, according to Kitsuse, focus on the "processes by which persons come to be defined as deviants by others." Deviance is a process by which members of a group, community or society interpret behavior as deviant; define people who so behave as certain types of deviants; and accord them the treatment considered appropriate to such deviants. This view in various forms has been picked up by a number of theorists and has come to be called "labelling theory." To the labelling theorists it is not the act that is important, but rather the label and the labelling process.

Gibbs summarizes the older conceptions of deviance which focused on the actor and his acts, as well as the newer labelling perspective. While Gibbs is not happy with the older conceptions, he is not satisfied with labelling theory either. He summarizes a number of the problems with the labelling approach and concludes by pointing out a number of unanswered questions in it: "First, what elements in the scheme are intended to be definitions rather than substantive theory? Second, is the ultimate goal to explain deviant behavior or to explain reactions to it? Third, is deviant behavior to be identified exclusively in terms of reaction to it? Fourth, exactly what kind of reaction identifies behavior as deviant?"

In a later article Akers takes the position that we must not be concerned with accounting for either behavior or the reaction, *but with both*. In studying *deviant behavior* we must be able to account for group and structural variations in rates of deviance *and* describe and explain the process by which individuals come to commit acts labelled as deviant. In studying *labelling* we must find out who applies the deviant label to whom, whose rules prevail, the circumstances which determine whether a label will be successfully applied and how the community decides which kinds of acts will be singled out.

Thus Kitsuse has pointed out a neglected dimension in the study of deviance (labelling), Gibbs has outlined some of the problems with the new conception and Akers has told us that we must integrate this new idea with our older conceptions of deviance.

Societal Reaction to Deviant Behavior: Problems of Theory and Method*

JOHN I. KITSUSE

Sociological theory and research in the area traditionally known as "social pathology" have been concerned primarily with the classification and analysis of *deviant forms of behavior* and relatively little attention has been given to societal reactions to deviance.[1] In a recent paper, Merton has noted this lack of a "systematic *classification* of the responses of the conventional or conforming members of a group to deviant behavior."[2] Similarly, Cohen has observed that "a sociology of deviant behavior-conformity will have to devise ways of conceptualizing responses to deviant behavior from the standpoint of their relevance to the production or extinction of deviant behavior."[3] In this paper, I shall discuss some of the theoretical and methodological issues posed by the problem of societal reactions to

---

* Reprinted from *Social Problems*, 9, No. 3 (Winter, 1962), pp. 247–256, by permission of the author and The Society for the Study of Social Problems, publisher. An earlier form of this paper was read at the meetings of the American Sociological Association, 1960. I have profited from the critical comments and suggestions of Herbert R. Barringer, Aaron V. Cicourel, Sheldon L. Messinger, and H. Jay Shaffer. Troy S. Duster's valuable assistance in the analysis of the data is gratefully acknowledged.
1. A notable exception is the work of Edwin M. Lemert who systematically incorporates the concept of societal reaction in his theory of sociopathic behavior. See *Social Pathology*, McGraw-Hill, New York: 1951.
2. Robert K. Merton, "Social Conformity, Deviation, and Opportunity-Structures: A Comment on the Contributions of Dubin and Cloward," *American Sociological Review*, 24 (1959), pp. 177–189.
3. Albert K. Cohen, "The Study of Social Disorganization and Deviant Behavior," in *Sociology Today*, R. Merton, L. Broom, and L. Cottrell, eds., Basic Books: New York, 1959, pp. 465–466.

deviant behavior and report on a preliminary attempt to formulate a re-search design which specifically takes them into account.

I propose to shift the focus of theory and research from the forms of deviant behavior to the *processes by which persons come to be defined as deviant by others*. Such a shift requires that the sociologist view as problematic what he generally assumes as given—namely, that certain forms of behavior are *per se* deviant and are so defined by the "conventional or conforming members of a group." This assumption is frequently called into question on empirical grounds when the societal reaction to behaviors defined as deviant by the sociologist is non-existent, indifferent, or at most mildly disapproving. For example, in his discussion of "ritualism" as a form of deviant behavior, Merton states that it is not that such behavior is treated by others as deviant which identifies it as deviant "since the overt behavior is institutionally permitted, though not culturally prescribed."[4] Rather, the behavior is deviant because it "clearly represents a departure from the cultural model in which men are obliged to move onward and upward in the social hierarchy."[5] The discrepancy between the theoretically hypothesized and empirically observable societal reaction is also noted by Lemert: "It is fairly easy to think of situations in which serious offenses against laws commanding public respect have only mild penalty or have gone entirely unpunished. Conversely, cases are easily discovered in which a somewhat minor violation of legal rules has provoked surprisingly stringent penalties."[6]

Clearly, the forms of behavior *per se* do not activate the processes of societal reaction which sociologically differentiate deviants from non-deviants. Thus, a central problem for theory and research in the sociology of deviance may be stated as follows: What are the behaviors which are defined by members of the group, community, or society as deviant, and how do those definitions organize and activate the societal reactions by which persons come to be differentiated and treated as deviants? In formulating the problem in this way, the point of view of those who interpret and define behavior as deviant must explicitly be incorporated into a sociological definition of deviance. Accordingly, deviance may be conceived as a process by which the members of a group, community, or society (1) interpret behavior as deviant, (2) define persons who so behave as a certain kind of deviant, and (3) accord them the treatment considered appropriate to such deviants. In the following pages, this conception of deviance and societal reaction will be applied to the processes by which persons come to be defined and treated as homosexuals.

---

4. Robert K. Merton, *Social Theory and Social Structure*, revised, Free Press: Glencoe, 1957, p. 150.
5. *Ibid.*, p. 150.
6. *Op. cit.*, p. 55.

Societal Reactions to "Homosexual Behavior"

As a form of deviant behavior, homosexuality presents a strategically important theoretical and empirical problem for the study of deviance. In the sociological and anthropological literature[7] homosexual behavior and the societal reactions to it are conceptualized within the framework of ascribed sex statuses and the socialization of individuals to those statuses. The ascription of sex statuses is presumed to provide a complex of culturally prescribed roles and behaviors which individuals are expected to learn and perform. Homosexual roles and behaviors are conceived to be "inappropriate" to the individual's ascribed sex status, and thus theoretically they are defined as deviant.

With reference to American society, Allison Davis states: "Sex-typing of behavior and privileges is even more rigid and lasting in our society than is age-typing. Indeed, sexual status and color-caste status are the only life-long forms of rank. In our society, one can escape them in approved fashion only by death. Whereas sexual mobility is somewhat less rare today than formerly, sex-inappropriate behavior, social or physical, is still one of the most severely punished infractions of our social code."[8] In Lemert's terminology, norms concerning sex-appropriate behavior have a high degree of "compulsiveness" and social disapproval of violations is stringent and effective.[9] Homosexuals themselves appear to share this conception of the societal reaction to their behavior, activities, and subculture.[10]

Such a view of homosexuality would lead one to hypothesize that "sex appropriate" (and conversely "sex-inappropriate") behaviors are unambiguously prescribed, deviations from those prescriptions are invariably interpreted as immoral, and the reactions of the conventional and conforming members of the society to such deviations are uniformly severe and effective. The evidence which apparently supports this hypothesis is not difficult to find, particularly with reference to the definition and treatment of male homosexuals. Individuals who are publicly identified as homo-

---

7. For examples, see Talcott Parsons and Robert F. Bales, *Family Socialization and Interaction Process*, Free Press: Glencoe, 1955, pp. 103–105; Ruth Benedict, "Continuities and Discontinuities in Cultural Conditioning," *Psychiatry*, 1 (1938), pp. 161–167; Abram Kardiner and Associates, *Psychological Frontiers of Society*, Columbia University Press: New York, 1945, pp. 57, 88, etc.; Clifford Kirkpatrick, *The Family*, Ronald Press: New York, 1955, pp. 57–58; Margaret Mead, *Sex and Temperament*, William Morrow: New York, 1955.
8. Allison Davis, "American Status Systems and the Socialization of the Child," *American Sociological Review*, 6 (1941), p. 350.
9. *Op. cit.*, Chapter 4.
10. Evelyn Hooker, "Sequences in Homosexual Identification," read at the meetings of the American Sociological Association, 1960; Donald Webster Cory, *The Homosexual in America*, Greenburg: New York, 1951, esp. Part I.

sexuals are frequently denied the social, economic, and legal rights of "normal" males. Socially they may be treated as objects of amusement, ridicule, scorn, and often fear; economically they may be summarily dismissed from employment; legally they are frequently subject to interrogation and harassment by police.

In citing such evidence, however, it is important to note that the societal reaction to and the differentiation of homosexuals from the "normal" population is a consequence of the fact that the former are "known" to be homosexuals by some individuals, groups or agencies. Thus, within the framework of the present formulation of homosexuality as a form of deviant behavior, the processes by which individuals come to be "known" and treated as sexually deviant will be viewed as problematic and a problem for empirical investigation. I shall not be concerned here with the so-called "latent homosexual," unless he is so defined by others and differentially treated as a consequence of that definition. Nor will I be concerned with the variety of "internal" conflicts which may form the "clinical" picture of the homosexual except insofar as such conflicts are manifested in behavior leading others to conceive of him as a homosexual. In short, I shall proceed on the principle that it is only when individuals are defined and identified by others as homosexuals and accorded the treatment considered "appropriate" for individuals so defined that a homosexual "population" is produced for sociological investigation.[11] With reference to homosexuality, then, the empirical questions are: What forms of behavior do persons in the social system consider to be "sex-inappropriate," how do they interpret such behaviors, and what are the consequences of those interpretations for their reactions to individuals who are perceived to manifest such behaviors?

In a preliminary attempt to investigate these questions, an interview schedule was constructed[12] and administered to approximately seven hundred individuals, most of whom were college undergraduates. The sample was neither random nor representative of any specified population, and the generalizability of the interview materials is limited except insofar as they are relevant to the previously noted hypothesis that homosexual behavior is uniformly defined, interpreted, and negatively sanctioned. The interview materials will therefore be used for the purpose of illustrating the theory and method of the present conception of deviance and societal reaction.

The objectives of the interview were threefold: It attempted to document (1) the behavior forms which are interpreted as deviant, (2) the processes by which persons who manifest such behaviors are defined and (3)

---

11. This principle has been suggested by Harold Garfinkel. See "Some Sociological Concepts and Methods for Psychiatrists," *Psychiatric Research Reports,* 6 (1956), pp. 181–195.
12. The interview schedule and methods were conceived and constructed in consultation with Aaron V. Cicourel.

treated as deviant. Thus, in the construction of the interview schedule, what the interviewees considered to be "deviant" behavior, the interpretations of such behavior, and the actions of subjects toward those perceived as deviant were addressed as empirical questions. Labels such as alcoholic, illiterate, illegitimate child, and ex-convict were assumed to be categories employed by persons in everyday life to classify deviants, but the behavioral forms by which they identify individuals as deviants were treated as problematic. "Sexual deviant" was one of ten categories of deviants about which subjects were questioned in the interview. Among the more than seven hundred subjects interviewed, seventy-five stated they had "known" a homosexual and responded to questions concerning their experiences with such individuals. The data presented below are drawn from the protocols of interviews with this group of subjects.

The interview proceeded as follows:

The subject was asked "Have you ever known anyone who was a sexual deviant?" If he questioned the meaning of "deviant," the subject was asked to consider the question using his own meaning of "sexual deviant."

When the subject stated he had known a sexual deviant—a homosexual in this case—as he defined the term, he was asked to think about the most recent incident involving him in an encounter with such a person. He was then asked "When was the first time you noticed (found out) that this person was a homosexual?" followed by "What was the situation? What did you notice about him? How did he behave?" This line of questioning was focused on the interaction between the subject and the alleged deviant to obtain a detailed description of the situation which led the subject to define the person as homosexual. The subject's description of the person's behavior was systematically probed to clarify the term of his description, particularly those which were interpretive rather than descriptive.

EVIDENCE OF HOMOSEXUALITY

Responses to the question "When was the first time you noticed (found out) that this person was homosexual?" and the related probes suggest that an individual's sexual "normality" may be called into question with reference to two broad categories of evidence. (a) *Indirect evidence* in the form of a rumor, an acquaintance's experience with the individual in question subsequently communicated to the subject, or general reputational information concerning the individual's behavior, associates, and sexual predilections may be the occasion for suspecting him to be "different." Many subjects reported that they first "found out" or "knew" that the individuals in question were homosexuals through the reports of others or by "reputation." Such information was generally accepted by the subjects without independent verification. Indeed, the information provided a new perspective for their retrospective as well as prospective observations and interpretations of the individuals' behaviors. An example of how hearsay organizes observation and interpretation is the following statement by a 35-year-old male (a draftsman):

I: Then this lieutenant was a homosexual?
S: Yes.
I: How did you find out about it?
S: The guy he approached told me. After that, I watched him. Our company was small and we had a bar for both enlisted men and officers. He would come in and try to be friendly with one or two of the guys.
I: Weren't the other officers friendly?
S: Sure, they would come in for an occasional drink; some of them had been with the company for three years and they would sometimes slap you on the back, but he tried to get over friendly.
I: What do you mean "over friendly"?
S: He had only been there a week. He would try to push himself on a couple of guys—he spent more time with the enlisted personnel than is expected from an officer.

(b) *Direct observation* by the subject of the individual's behavior may be the basis for calling the latter's sexual "normality" into question. The descriptions of behavior which subjects took to be indicative of homosexuality varied widely and were often vague. Most frequently the behaviors cited were those *"which everyone knows"* are indications of homosexuality. For example, a 20-year-old male subject reports an encounter with a stranger at a bar:

I: What happened during your conversation?
S: He asked me if I went to college and I said I did. Then he asked me what I was studying. When I told him psychology he appeared very interested.
I: What do you mean "interested"?
S: Well, you know queers really go for this psychology stuff.
I: Then what happened?
S: Ah, let's see. I'm not exactly sure, but somehow we got into an argument about psychology and to prove my point I told him to pick an area of study. Well, he appeared to be very pensive and after a great thought he said, "Okay, let's take homosexuality."
I: What did you make of that?
S: Well, by now I figured the guy was queer so I got the hell outta there.

The responses of other subjects suggest that an individual is particularly suspect when he is observed to behave in a manner which deviates from the *behaviors-held-in-common* among members of the group to which he belongs. For example, a behavior which is presumed to be held-in-common among sailors in the U.S. Navy is intense and active sexual activity. When a sailor does not affirm, at least verbally, his interest in such activity, his competence as a "male" may be called into question. A 22-year-old engineer, recently discharged from the Navy, responds to the "how did you first know" question as follows:

> All of a sudden you just get suspicious of something. I began to wonder about him. He didn't go in for leave activities that most sailors go for. You know, girls and high times. He just never was interested and when you have been out at sea for a month or two, you're interested. That just wasn't Navy, and he was a career man.

Although the responses of our subjects indicate there are many behavioral gestures which "everyone knows" are indicators of homosexuality in males, they are relatively few such gestures that lead persons to suspect females of homosexuality. Following is an excerpt from a 21-year-old college co-ed whose remarks illustrate this lack of definite indicators *prior* to her labeling of an acquaintance as a homosexual:

I: When was the first time you noticed she was a deviant?
S: I didn't notice it. I thought she had a masculine appearance when I first saw her anyway.
I: What do you mean?
S: Oh, her haircut, her heavy eyebrows. She had a rather husky build.
I: Exactly when did you think she had a masculine appearance?
S: It was long after [the first meeting] that I found out that she was "one."
I: How do you define it?
S: Well, a lesbian. I don't know too much about them. It was ———— who told me about her.
I: Did you notice anything else about her [at the first meeting]?
S: No, because you really don't know unless you're looking for those things.

Unlike "effeminate" appearance and gestures in males, "masculine" appearance in females is apparently less likely to be immediately linked to the suspicion or imputation of homosexuality. The statements of the subject quoted above indicate that although "masculine appearance" is an important element in her conception of a lesbian, its significance did not become apparent to her until a third person told her the girl was homosexual. The remarks of other subjects in our sample who state they have "known" female homosexuals reveal a similar ambiguity in their interpretations of what they describe as indicators of sexual deviance.

A third form of evidence by direct observation is behaviors which the subjects interpreted to be *overt sexual propositions*. Descriptions of such propositions ranged from what the subjects considered to be unmistakable evidence of the person's sexual deviance to ambiguous gestures which they did not attempt to question in the situation. The following is an excerpt from an interview with a 24-year-old male school teacher who recounts an experience in a Korean Army barrack:

I: What questions did he [the alleged homosexual] ask?
S: "How long have you been in Korea?" I told him. "What do you think of these Korean girls?" which I answered, "Not too much because they are dirty." I thought he was probably homesick and wanted someone to talk to. I do not remember what he said then until he said, "How much do you have?" I answered him by saying, "I don't know, about average I guess." Then he said, "Can I feel it just once?" To this I responded with, "Get the hell out of here," and I gave him a shove when he reached for me as he asked the question.

In a number of interviews, the subjects' statements indicate that they interpreted the sequence of the alleged deviants' behavior as progressively inappropriate or peculiar in the course of their interaction with them. The link between such behavior and their judgment that a sexual proposition was being made was frequently established by the subjects' growing realization of its deviant character. A 21-year-old male subject recalls the following experience involving his high school tennis coach who had invited him to dinner:

S: Anyway, when I get there he served dinner, and as I think back on it —I didn't notice it at the time—but I remember that he did act sort of effeminate. Finally he got up to change a record and picked up some of my English themes. Then he brought them over and sat down beside me. He began to explain some of my mistakes in my themes, and in the meantime he slipped his arms around me.
I: Would you say that this was done in a friendly manner or with an intent of hugging you or something?
S: Well, no, it was just a friendly gesture of putting his arm around my shoulder. At that time, I didn't think anything of it, but as he continued to explain my mistakes, he started to rub my back. Then he asked me if I wanted a back rub. So I said, "No! I don't need one." At this time, I began thinking something was funny anyway. So I said that I had to go. . . .

THE IMPUTATION OF HOMOSEXUALITY

When a detailed description of the subject's evidence concerning the alleged homosexual was obtained, he was asked, "What did you make of that?" to elicit information about how he interpreted the person's observed or reported behavior. This line of questioning yielded data on the inferential process by which the subject linked his information about the individual to the deviant category "homosexual."

A general pattern revealed by the subjects' responses to this section of the interview schedule is that when an individual's sexual "normality" is called into question, by whatever form of evidence, the imputation of homosexuality is documented by *retrospective interpretations* of the deviant's behavior, a process by which the subject re-interprets the individuals' past behavior in the light of the new information concerning his sexual deviance. This process is particularly evident in cases where the prior relationship between the subject and the alleged homosexual was more than a chance encounter or casual acquaintanceship. The subjects indicate that they reviewed their past interactions with the individuals in question, searching for subtle cues and nuances of behavior which might give further evidence of the alleged deviance. This retrospective reading generally provided the subjects with just such evidence to support the conclusion that "this is what was going on all the time."

Some of the subjects who were interviewed were themselves aware of their retrospective interpretations in defining individuals as sexually deviant. For example, a 23-year-old female graduate student states:

I: Will you tell me more about the situation?
S: Well, their relationship was a continuous one, although I think that it is a friendship now as I don't see them together as I used to; I don't think it is still homosexual. When I see them together, they don't seem to be displaying the affection openly as they did when I first realized the situation.
I: How do you mean "openly"?
S: Well, they would hold each other's hand in public places.
I: And what did you make of this?
S: Well, I really don't know, because I like to hold people's hands, too! I guess I actually didn't see this as directly connected with the situation. What I mean is that, if I hadn't seen that other incident [she had observed the two girls in bed together] I probably wouldn't have thought of it [i.e., hand-holding] very much. . . . Well, actually, there were a few things that I questioned later on that I hadn't thought really very much about. . . . I can remember her being quite affectionate towards me several times when we were in our room together, like putting her arm around my shoulder. Or I remember one time specifically when she asked me for a kiss. I was shocked at the time, but I laughed it off jokingly.

The Interactional Contexts of Societal Reactions

When the description of the alleged deviant's behavior and the subject's interpretations of that behavior were recorded, the subject was asked "What did you do then?" This question was directed toward documenting societal reactions to deviant behavior. Forms of behavior *per se* do not differentiate deviants from non-deviants; it is the responses of the conventional and comforming members of the society who identify and interpret behavior as deviant which sociologically transform persons into deviants. Thus, in the formulation of deviance proposed here, if the subject observes an individual's behavior and defines it as deviant but does not accord him differential treatment as a consequence of that definition, the individual is not sociologically deviant.

The reactions of the subjects to individuals they defined as homosexuals ranged from immediate withdrawal from the scene of interaction and avoidance of further encounters with the alleged deviants to the maintenance of the prior relationship virtually unaltered by the imputation of deviance. The following reponses to the question "What did you do then?" illustrate the variation in sanctions directed toward persons defined as homosexuals.

Explicit disapproval and immediate withdrawal: The most negatively toned and clearly articulated reaction reported by our subjects is that of the previously quoted Korean War veteran. It is interesting to note that extreme physical punishment as a reaction to persons defined as homosexuals, a reaction which is commonly verbalized by "normal" males as proper treatment of "queers," is not reported by any of the subjects. When physical force is used, it is invariably in response to the deviant's direct physical overtures, and even then it is relatively mild, e.g., "I gave him a shove when he reached for me."

Explicit disapproval and subsequent withdrawal: In the following excerpt, a 20-year-old male college student describes an encounter with a man whom he met in a coffee shop. In the course of their conversation, the man admitted his homosexuality to the subject. The two left the coffee shop and walked together to the subway station.

> I: What happened then?
> S: We got to the subway whereupon he suggested that he hail a cab and take me up to Times Square—a distance of almost 40 blocks.
> I: Did you agree, and what did you think?
> S: Yes, I thought he was just being very nice and I had no qualms about getting in a cab with a homosexual since I was quite sure I could protect myself against any advances in a cab.
> I: What happened then?
> S: When we had ridden a little distance, he put his hand on my knee, and I promptly removed it saying that it just wasn't right and that I wanted nothing of it. However, after a while, he put his hand back. This time I didn't take it away for a while because I was interested in what he would do. It was the funniest thing—he rubbed and caressed my knee the same way in which I would have done this to a girl. This time I took his hand and hit him across the chest with it, telling him to "cut it out." Finally, we got to Times Square, and I got out.

This example and that provided by the Korean War veteran's reaction to behavior interpreted as overt sexual propositions suggest the possibility that responses to persons suspected of homosexuality or defined as homosexuals on the basis of more indirect evidence of appearance, "confessions," hearsay, reputation, or association will vary within an even wider range of applied sanctions. Indeed, the statements of subjects concerning their responses to persons alleged to be deviant on such evidence indicate that the modal reaction is disapproval, implicitly rather than explicitly communicated, and a restriction of interaction through partial withdrawal and avoidance. It should be noted further that although the subject's silent withdrawal from an established relationship with an alleged deviant may represent a stronger disapproval than an explicitly communicated, physically enforced sanction against a stranger, moral indignation or revulsion is not necessarily communicated to the deviant. The subject's prior relationship with the alleged deviant and the demands of propriety in subsequent interactions with him qualify the form and intensity of the sanctions which are applied. Thus, when the organization of the subject's day-to-day activities "forces" him into interaction with the deviant, expressions of disapproval are frequently constrained and diffused by the rules of deference and demeanor.[13] The following excerpts provide illustrations:

Implicit disapproval and partial withdrawal: A 20-year-old co-ed's reaction to a girl she concluded was a homosexual was expressed as follows:

"Well, I didn't want to be alone with X [the homosexual] because the four of us had two connecting rooms and I was in the room with X. As much as I liked the girl and felt sorry for her, I knew she could really wring me through the wringer. So the rest decided that I should tell her that if she and Y wanted to be homos, to do it somewhere else and not in the room."

No disapproval and relationship sustained: The "live and let live" response to homosexuals, which is implied in the preceding reaction, was not uncommon among the subjects. Some subjects not only affirmed the right of the homosexual to "live his own life" but also reported that their knowledge of the deviance has had little or no effect upon their subsequent relationships with the deviants. In this regard, the mildest reaction, so mild that it might be considered no reaction at all, was that of a 19-year-old male college student:

I: What was your reaction to him?
S: My reactions to him have always been friendly because he seems like a very friendly person. Uh, and he has a very nice sense of humor and I've never been repelled by anything he's said. For one thing, I

---

13. Erving Goffman, "The Nature of Deference and Demeanor," *American Anthropologist,* 58 (1956), pp. 473–502.

think he's tremendously interesting because he seems to have such a
wide range for background. . . .

I: When was the last time you saw this person?

S: Last night. . . . I was sitting in a restaurant and he walked in with
some friends . . . he just stopped in and said hello, and was his usual
friendly self.

I: What in particular happened after that?

S: Actually, nothing. He sat down with his friends and we exchanged a
few words about the records that were playing on the juke box. But
nothing, actually. . . .

The theoretical significance of these data for the conception of deviance and societal reaction presented here is not that the subjects' information is of dubious accuracy or questionable relevance as evidence of
homosexuality. Nor is it that the subjects' interpretations of them are
unreasonable, unjustifiable, or spurious. They suggest rather that the concepts of persons in everyday life concerning "sex-appropriate" or "sex-
inappropriate" behavior may lead them to interpret a variety of behavioral
forms as indications of the same deviation, and the "same" behavioral forms
as indications of a variety of deviant as well as "normal" behavior. An
individual's sexual "normality" may be made problematic by the interpretations and re-interpretations of his behavior by others, and the interpretive
process may be activated by a wide range of situational behaviors which
lend new significance to the individual's past and present behavior. His
behavior with respect to speech, interests, dress, dating, or relations with
other males are not *per se* significant in the deviant-defining process. The
data suggest that the critical feature of the deviant-defining process is not
the behavior of individuals who are defined as deviant, but rather the
interpretations others make of their behaviors, whatever those behaviors
may be.

With specific reference to homosexuality as a form of deviant behavior, the interview materials suggest that while reactions toward persons
defined as homosexuals tend to be negatively toned, they are far from homogeneous as to the forms of intensity of the sanctions invoked and applied.
Indeed, reactions which may appear to the sociological observer or to the
deviant himself as negative sanctions, such as withdrawal or avoidance,
may be expressions of embarrassment, a reluctance to share the burden of
the deviant's problems, fear of the deviant, etc., as well as moral indignation
or revulsion. In none of the interviews does the subject react with extreme
violence, explicitly define or directly accuse the deviant of being a "queer,"
"fairy," or other terms of opprobrium, nor did any of them initiate legal
action against the deviant. In view of the extreme negative sanctions against
homosexuality which are posited on theoretical grounds, the generally mild
reactions of our subjects are striking.

The relative absence of extreme and overtly expressed negative sanctions against homosexuals among our subjects may, of course, reflect the higher than average educational level of the sample. A sample of subjects less biased toward the highly educated middle-class segment of the population than was interviewed in this preliminary study may be expected to reflect a more definite pattern with reference to such negative reactions. We must, therefore, be cautious in generalizing the range of reactions among our subjects to the general population. It it equally important to note, however, that these data do indicate that reactions to homosexuals in American society are not *societal* in the sense of being uniform within a narrow range; rather, they are significantly conditioned by sub-cultural as well as situational factors. Thus, not only are the processes by which persons come to be defined as homosexuals contingent upon the interpretations of their behavior by others, but also the sanctions imposed and the treatment they are accorded as a consequence of that definition vary widely among conventional members of various sub-cultural groups.

The larger implications of these data are that a sociological theory of deviance must explicitly take into account the variety and range of conceptions held by persons, groups, and agencies within the society concerning any form of behavior. The increasing differentiation of groups, institutions, and subcultures in modern society generates a continually changing range of alternatives and tolerance for the expression of sexual as well as other forms of behavior. Consequently, it is difficult if not impossible to theoretically derive a set of *specific behavioral prescriptions* which will in fact be normatively supported, uniformly practiced, and socially enforced by more than a segment of the total population. Under such conditions it is not the fact that individuals engage in behaviors which diverge from some theoretically posited "institutionalized expectations" or even that such behaviors are defined as deviant by the conventional and conforming members of the society which is of primary significance for the study of deviance. A sociological theory of deviance must focus specifically upon the interactions which not only define behaviors as deviant but also organize and activate the application of sanctions by individuals, groups, or agencies. For in modern society, the socially significant differentiation of deviants from the non-deviant population is increasingly contingent upon circumstances of situation, place, social and personal biography, and the bureaucratically organized activities of agencies of control.[14]

---

14. For a discussion of such contingencies, see Edwin M. Lemert, *op. cit.*, Chapter 4, and Erving Goffman, "The Moral Career of the Mental Patient," *Psychiatry*, 22 (1959), pp. 123–142.

Conceptions of Deviant Behavior: The Old and the New*

JACK P. GIBBS

The ultimate end of substantive theory in any science is the formulation of empirical relations among classes of phenomena, e.g., X varies directly with Y, X is present if and only if Y is present. However, unless such propositions are arrived at by crude induction or sheer intuition, there is a crucial step before the formulation of a relational statement. This step can be described as the way the investigator comes to perceive or "think about" the phenomena under consideration. Another way to put it is the development of a "conception."

There is no clear-cut distinction between, on the one hand, a conception of a class of phenomena and, on the other, formal definitions and substantive theory. Since a conception emphasizes the predominant feature of a phenomenon, it is not entirely divorced from a definition of it; but the former is not identical with the latter. Thus, for example, the notion of exploitation looms large in the Marxian conception of relations among social classes; but exploitation is or may be only one feature of class relations, and it does not serve as a formal definition of them. Further, in certain fields, particularly the social sciences, a conception often not only precedes but also gives rise to operational definitions. As the case in point, if an operational definition of social class relies on the use of "reputational technique," the investigator's conception of social class is in all probability non-Marxian.

What has been said of the distinction between definitions and conceptions holds also for the relation between the latter and substantive theory. A conception may generate a particular theory, but it is not identical with it. For one thing, a conception contains definitional elements and is therefore partially tautological, which means that in itself a conception is never a clear-cut empirical proposition. Apart from its tautological character, a conception is too general to constitute a testable idea. Nonetheless, a conception may generate substantive theory, and it is certainly true that theories reflect conceptions. Durkheim's work is a classic illustration. His theory on suicide clearly reflects his view of society and social life generally.

In a field without consensus as to operational definitions and little in

---

* Reprinted from *Pacific Sociological Review,* 9 (Spring, 1966), pp. 9–14, by permission of the author and publisher.

the way of systematic substantive theory, conceptions necessarily occupy a central position. This condition prevails in most of the social sciences. There, what purports to be definitions of classes of phenomena are typically general and inconsistent to the point of lacking empirical applicability (certainly in the operational sense of the word). Moreover, what passes for a substantive theory in the social sciences is more often than not actually a loosely formulated conception. These observations are not intended to deride the social sciences for lack of progress. All fields probably go through a "conceptions" stage; it is only more apparent in some than in others.

Of the social sciences, there is perhaps no better clear-cut illustration of the importance of conceptions than in the field identified as criminology and the study of deviant behavior. As we shall see, the history of the field can be described best in terms of changing conceptions of crime, criminals, deviants, and deviation. But the purpose of this paper is not an historical account of major trends in the field. If it is true that conceptions give rise to formal definitions and substantive theory, then a critical appraisal of conceptions is important in its own right. This is all the more true in the case of criminology and the study of deviant behavior, where conceptions are frequently confused with substantive theories, and the latter so clearly reflect the former.

OLDER CONCEPTIONS

In recent years there has been a significant change in the prevailing conception of deviant behavior and deviants. Prior to what is designated here as the "new perspective," it commonly was assumed that there is something inherent in deviants which distinguishes them from non-deviants.[1] Thus, from Lombroso to Sheldon, criminals were viewed as biologically distinctive in one way or another.[2] The inadequacies of this conception are now obvious. After decades of research, no biological characteristic which distinguishes criminals has been discovered, and this generalization applies even to particular types of criminals (e.g., murderers, bigamists, etc.). Consequently, few theorists now even toy with the notion that all criminals are atavistic, mentally defective, constitutionally inferior. But the rejection of the biological conception of crime stems from more than research findings. Even casual observation and mild logic cast doubt on the

---

1. Throughout this paper crime is treated as a sub-class of deviant behavior. Particular issues may be discussed with reference to crime, but on the whole the observations apply to deviant behavior generally.
2. Although not essential to the argument, it is perhaps significant that the alleged biological differentiae of criminals have been consistently viewed as "pathological" in one sense or another.

idea. Since legislators are not geneticists, it is difficult to see how they can pass laws in such a way as to create "born criminals." Equally important, since most if not all "normal" persons have violated a law at one time or another,[3] the assertion that criminals are so by heredity now appears most questionable.

Although the biological conception generally has been rejected, what is here designated as the analytic conception of criminal acts largely has escaped criticism. Rather than view criminal acts as nothing more or less than behavior contrary to legal norms, the acts are construed as somehow injurious to society. The shift from the biological to the analytical conception is thus from the actors to the characteristics of their acts, with the idea being that some acts are inherently "criminal" or at least that criminal acts share intrinsic characteristics in common.

The analytical conception is certainly more defensible than the biological view, but it is by no means free of criticism. Above all, the "injurious" quality of some deviant acts is by no means conspicuous, as witness Durkheim's observation:

. . . there are many acts which have been and still are regarded as criminal without in themselves being harmful to society. What social danger is there in touching a tabooed object, an impure animal or man, in letting the sacred fire die down, in eating certain meats, in failure to make the traditional sacrifice over the grave of parents, in not exactly pronouncing the ritual formula, in not celebrating holidays, etc.?[4]

Only a radical functionalism would interpret the acts noted by Durkheim as literally injuring society in any reasonable sense of the word. The crucial point is that, far from actually injuring society or sharing some intrinsic feature in common, acts may be criminal or deviant because and only because they are proscribed legally and/or socially. The proscription may be irrational in that members of the society cannot explain it, but it is real nonetheless. Similarly, a law may be "arbitrary" in that it is imposed by a powerful minority and, as a consequence, lacks popular support and is actively opposed. But if the law is consistently enforced (i.e., sanctions are imposed regularly on violators), it is difficult to see how it is not "real."

The fact that laws may appear to be irrational and arbitrary has prompted attempts to define crime independently of legal criteria, i.e., analytically. The first step in this direction was Garofalo's concept of natural crime—acts which violate prevailing sentiments of pity and probity.[5] Garofalo's endeavor accomplished very little. Just as there is probably

3. See Edwin H. Sutherland and Donald R. Cressey, *Principles of Criminology,* 6th ed., Chicago: J. B. Lippincott, 1960, p. 39.
4. Emile Durkheim, *The Division of Labor in Society,* trans. George Simpson, Glencoe, Illinois: The Free Press, 1949, p. 72.
5. Raffaele Garofalo, *Criminology,* Boston: Little, Brown, and Co., 1914, Chapter I.

no act which is contrary to law universally, it is equally true that no act violates sentiments of pity and probity in all societies. In other words, cultural relativity defeats any attempt to compile a list of acts which are crimes universally. Also, it is hard to see why the violation of a rigorously enforced traffic regulation is not a crime even though unrelated to sentiments of pity and probity. If it is not a crime, what is it?

The search for an analytic identification of crime continued in Sellin's proposal to abandon legal criteria altogether in preference for "conduct norms."[6] The rationale for the proposal is simple. Because laws vary and may be "arbitrary" in any one society, a purely legal definition of crime is not suited for scientific study. But Sellin's observations on the arbitrariness of laws apply in much the same way to conduct norms. Just as the content of criminal law varies from one society to the next and from time to time, so does the content of extra-legal norms. Further, the latter may be just as arbitrary as criminal laws. Even in a highly urbanized society such as the United States, there is evidently no rationale or utilitarian reason for all of the norms pertaining to mode of dress. Sure, there may be much greater conformity to conduct norms than to some laws, but the degree of conformity is hardly an adequate criterion of the "reality" of norms, legal or extra-legal. If any credence whatever can be placed in the Kinsey report, sexual taboos may be violated frequently and yet remain as taboos. As a case in point, even if adultery is now common in the United States, it is significant that the participants typically attempt to conceal their acts. In brief, just as laws may be violated frequently and are "unreal" in that sense, the same applies to some conduct norms; but in neither case do they cease to be norms. They would cease to be norms if and only if one defines deviation in terms of statistical regularities in behavior, but not even Sellin would subscribe to the notion that normative phenomena can or should be defined in statistical terms.

In summary, however capricious and irrational legal and extra-legal norms may appear to be, the inescapable conclusion is that some acts are criminal or deviant for the very simple reason that they are proscribed.

THE NEW CONCEPTION

Whereas both the pathological and the analytical conception of deviation assume that some intrinsic feature characterizes deviants and/or deviant acts, an emerging perspective in sociology flatly rejects any such assumption. Indeed, as witness the following statements by Kitsuse, Becker, and Erikson, exactly the opposite position is taken.

---

6. Thorsten Sellin, *Culture Conflict and Crime*, New York: Social Science Research Council, Bulletin 41, 1938.

Kitsuse:

Forms of behavior *per se* do not differentiate deviants from non-deviants; it is the responses of the conventional and conforming members of the society who identify and interpret behavior as deviant which sociologically transform persons into deviants.[7]

Erikson:

From a sociological standpoint, deviance can be defined as conduct which is generally thought to require the attention of social control agencies—that is conduct about which "something should be done." Deviance is not a property *inherent in* certain forms of behavior; it is a property *conferred upon* these forms by the audiences which directly or indirectly witness them. Sociologically, then, the critical variable in the study of deviance is the social *audience* rather than individual *person,* since it is the audience which eventually decides whether or not any given action or actions will become a visible case of deviation.[8]

Becker:

From this point of view, deviance is *not* a quality of the act a person commits, but rather a consequence of the application by others of rules and sanctions to an "offender." The deviant is one to whom that label has successfully been applied; deviant behavior is behavior that people so label.[9]

The common assertion in the above statements is that acts can be identified as deviant or criminal only by reference to the character of reaction to them by the public or by the official agents of a politically organized society. Put simply, if the reaction is of a certain kind, then and only then is the act deviant. The crucial point is that the essential feature of a deviant or deviant act is *external* to the actor and the act. Further, even if the act or actors share some feature in common other than social reactions to them, the feature neither defines nor completely explains deviation. To take the extreme case, even if Lombroso had been correct in his assertion that criminals are biologically distinctive, the biological factor neither identifies the criminal nor explains criminality. Purely biological variables may explain why some persons commit certain acts, but they do not explain why the acts are crimes. Consequently, since criminal law is spatially and temporally relative, it is impossible to distinguish criminals from non-criminals (assuming that the latter do exist, which is questionable) in terms of biological characteristics. To illustrate, if act X is a crime in society A but not a crime in society B, it follows that, even assuming

7. John I. Kitsuse, "Societal Reaction to Deviant Behavior: Problems of Theory and Method," *Social Problems,* 9 (Winter, 1962), p. 253.
8. Kai T. Erikson, "Notes on the Sociology of Deviance," *Social Problems,* 9 (Spring, 1962), p. 308.
9. Howard S. Becker, *Outsiders,* New York: The Free Press of Glencoe, 1963, p. 9.

Lombroso to have been correct, the anatomical features which distinguish the criminal in society A may characterize the non-criminal in society B. In both societies some persons may be genetically predisposed to commit act X, but the act is a crime in one society and not in the other. Accordingly, the generalization that all persons with certain anatomical features are criminals would be, in this instance, false. True, one may assert that the "born criminal" is predisposed to violate the laws of his own society, but this assumes either that "the genes" know what the law is or that the members of the legislature are geneticists (i.e., they deliberately enact laws in such a way that the "born criminal" will violate them). Either assumption taxes credulity.

The new perspective of deviant behavior contradicts not only the biological but also the analytical conception. Whereas the latter seeks to find something intrinsic in deviant or, more specifically, criminal acts, the new conception denies any such characterization. True, the acts share a common denominator—they are identified by the character of reaction to them—but this does not mean that the acts are "injurious" to society or that they are in any way inherently abnormal. The new conception eschews the notion that some acts are deviant or criminal in all societies. For that matter, the reaction which identifies a deviant act may not be the same from one society or social group to the next. In general, then, the new conception of deviant behavior is relativistic in the extreme.

CRITICISM OF THE NEW PERSPECTIVE

The new perspective of deviant behavior is much more consistent not only with what is known about deviant behavior but also with contemporary sociological principles generally. However, while containing a fundamentally sound idea, the new perspective leaves some crucial questions unanswered. For one thing, it is not clear whether the perspective is intended to be a "substantive theory" of deviant behavior (i.e., an explanation of the phenomenon) or a conceptual treatment of it. Consider, again, statements by Becker, Kitsuse, and Erikson:

Becker:
    . . . *social groups create deviance by making the rules whose infraction constitute deviance,* and by applying those rules to particular people and labeling them as outsiders.[10]

Kitsuse and Cicourel:
    . . . *rates of deviant behavior* are produced by *the actions taken by*

---

10. *Op. cit.,* p. 9.

persons in the social system which define, classify and record certain behaviors as deviant.[11]

Erikson:

> . . . transactions taking place between deviant persons on the one side and agencies of control on the other are boundary maintaining mechanisms. They mark the outside limits of the area in which the norm has jurisdiction, and in this way assert how much diversity and variability can be contained within the system before it begins to lose its distinct structure, its unique shape.[12]

Now these statements appear to be something more than definitions. However, if regarded as explanations of deviant behavior, these and other similar observations do not provide adequate answers to three major questions: (1) Why does the incidence of a particular act vary from one population to the next? (2) Why do some persons commit the act while others do not? (3) Why is the act in question considered deviant and/or criminal in some societies but not in others?

The assertion that deviation is created or produced by the character of reactions to behavior (see statements by Becker and Kitsuse above) implies an answer to the question on incidence. But are we to conclude that the incidence of a given act is in fact a constant in all populations and that the only difference is in the quality of reactions to the act? Specifically, given two populations with the same kind of reaction to a particular type of act, can the new perspective explain why the incidence of the act is greater in one population than in the other? Not at all! On the contrary, even if two populations have the same legal and social definition of armed robbery and even if instances of the crime are reacted to in exactly the same way, it is still possible for the armed robbery rate to be much higher in one population than in the other. Reaction to deviation may influence the rate of deviation in that certain kinds of reaction may have a deterrent effect, but the deterrent quality of reaction has not been examined systematically by Becker, Kitsuse, or Erikson, primarily because they view reaction in terms of *identifying* deviant behavior. Actually, apart from identifying deviation, the new conception presents a sophisticated framework for the study of deterrence as an aspect of reaction to deviant behavior. All three of the advocates are sensitive to the importance of the deviant's response to reaction, and it would not be inconsistent for them to devote more attention to the possibility that some kinds of reaction have consequences beyond identifying behavior as deviant.

---

11. John J. Kitsuse and Aaron Cicourel, "A Note on the Uses of Official Statistics," *Social Problems,* 11 (Fall, 1963), p. 135.
12. *Op. cit.,* p. 310.

What has been said of the new perspective with regard to explaining variation in the incidence of deviant acts also applies to the second major question: Why do some persons commit a given act while others do not? The point is that the new perspective does not generate an answer to this question. For example, the fact that the reaction to armed robbery may involve incarceration hardly explains why some but not all persons commit the act. Again, the quality of reaction (or the probability of reaction) may have a differential deterrent effect, a possibility which is relevant in attempting to answer the question; but, as noted before, the new perspective exhibits little concern not only with deterrence but also with etiological factors generally. The lack of concern with etiological factors suggests that Becker, Erikson, and Kitsuse actually are seeking a theory not about deviant behavior *per se* but rather about reactions to deviant behavior (i.e., why does the quality of reaction vary from place to place and time to time?). In any event, the three persons closely associated with the perspective have not explicitly stated that they are seeking such a theory.

It is not at all clear whether Becker is pursuing a theory about deviant behavior or a theory about reactions to deviation. If it is the latter, then his focus on deviants rather than reactors is puzzling. Kitsuse is concerned with reaction to deviant behavior as a process, but he views reaction not only as a criterion of deviant behavior but also (evidently) as the decisive factor in relation to incidence. As such, he is apparently seeking a theory about deviant behavior and not reactions to it. Erikson's "functionalist" position could be construed as a theory about deviant behavior, or reactions, or both. However, even if reactions to deviation do serve a "function"—boundary maintenance—a functional interpretation hardly explains why the quality of reaction varies from one society to the next. Further, with reference to incidence, are we to conclude that social boundaries are maintained or demarcated if and only if the rate of deviant behavior is high?

Even if deviant acts are defined in terms of reactions to behavior, the identification does not and cannot explain why a given act is considered deviant and/or criminal in some but not all societies (the third major question). After all, a certain kind of reaction may identify behavior as deviant, but it obviously does not explain why the behavior is deviant.

The danger in evaluating the work of Becker, Erikson, and Kitsuse is that of prematurely rejecting what is a most promising approach to the study of deviant behavior. The danger can be avoided if it is clearly understood that they have formulated what is essentially a conception. As such, it contains both definitions and elements of substantive theory, and the development of the latter would be furthered considerably by making the distinction explicit. Finally, since a conception precedes substantive theory, it would be most unrealistic to demand testable empirical propositions at this stage. The only justifiable criticism on this point is that the three men have not specified their goal adequately, i.e., whether they are seeking an explanation of deviant behavior or of reaction to it. The fact that it may be both testifies to the fertility of the conception, but it is all the more reason to treat the distinction seriously.

REACTION AS A CRITERION OF DEVIATION

The point stressed continually by the new perspective is that acts are identified as deviant by the character of reactions to them. Whatever the merits of this position, it is not free of criticism. For one thing, Becker, Erikson, and Kitsuse have never specified exactly what kind of reaction identifies deviant acts. Becker constantly refers to deviants as persons labelled as "outsiders," but this term is Becker's, not that of the man on the street. For that matter, the public may be more familiar with the meaning of the term "deviant" than with "outsider."

When we turn to concrete cases of reactions supposedly indicative of deviant acts, there are some rather curious results. Kitsuse, for example, found reactions of students to persons identified by the students as homo-sexuals to be "generally mild."[13] These reactions may or may not be representative of the public generally; nonetheless, two significant questions are posed. First, are we to conclude, because of the mildness of the reaction, that homosexuals are not deviants after all? Second, how "harsh" must the reaction be before the behavior is to be construed as deviant? More generally, since "mild" and "harsh" are subjective terms, exactly what "kind" of reaction identifies deviant acts or deviance? Some of Becker's observations are puzzling in this connection. As a case in point: "Whether an act is deviant, then, depends on how other people react to it. You can commit clan incest and suffer no more than gossip as long as no one makes a public accusation. . . ."[14] Why is it that gossip does not qualify as a reaction which identifies deviant behavior?

The failure of Becker, Erikson, and Kitsuse to specify the kind of reactions which identify deviation is further complicated by the contradictions in their own position. The contradictions stem from the fact that a deviant act can be defined as behavior *which is contrary to a norm or rule.* One type of norm is simply what the members of a social unit think conduct "ought" or "ought not" be. For example, on this basis it is probably true that the act of joining the Communist party is "deviant" in American society, even though the quality of reaction to it in a particular instance may be problematical. This conception of deviation enables one to treat deviant acts and reactions to them as conceptually distinct. But this is not so from the viewpoint of Becker, Erikson, and Kitsuse, because deviant

---

13. *Op. cit.,* p. 256.
14. *Op. cit.,* p. 11.

behavior for them *is defined in terms of reactions to it.* On the other hand, while advocates of the new perspective do recognize the "norm" conception of deviation, they do not consistently reject it. Witness, for example:

Becker:
An even more interesting kind of case is found at the other extreme of *secret deviance.* Here an improper act is committed, yet no one notices it or reacts to it as a violation of the rules.[15]

Kituse and Cicourel:
We wish to state explicitly that the interpretation of official statistics proposed here *does not* imply that the forms of behavior which the sociologist might define and categorize as deviant (e.g., Merton's modes of adaptation) have no factual basis or theoretical importance.[16]

Erikson:
There are societies in which deviance is considered a natural pursuit for the young, an activity which they can easily abandon when they move through defined ceremonies into adulthood. There are societies which give license to large groups of persons to engage in deviant behavior for certain seasons or on certain days of the year. And there are societies in which special groups are formed to act in ways 'contrary' to the normal expectations of the culture.[17]

Now all of these statements admit, in one way or another, that deviant behavior can be identified in terms of norms, but the authors do not come to grips with the problem and take a consistent stand on the issue. Thus, if deviant behavior is defined in terms of reactions to it, then Becker cannot speak properly of "secret deviance." If behavior defined as deviant by sociologists in reference to the prevailing social norms is "real," then in what sense can one maintain, as Kitsuse does elsewhere, that behavior is deviant if and only if there is a certain kind of reaction to it. Finally, in the case of Erikson, how can the behavior of "large groups of persons" be identified as deviant when they have been given a "license" to engage in it? To be consistent, Becker, Kitsuse, and Erikson would have to insist that behavior which is contrary to a norm is not deviant unless it is discovered and there is a particular kind of reaction to it. Thus, if persons engage in adultery but their act is not discovered and reacted to in a certain way (by the members of the social unit), then it is not deviant! Similarly, if a person is erroneously thought to have engaged in a certain type of behavior and is reacted to "harshly" as a consequence, a deviant act has taken place!

The extreme position of Becker, Erikson, and Kitsuse is also apparent when attempting to explain why reaction to deviant behavior is not

15. *Op. cit.,* p. 20.
16. *Op. cit.,* pp. 138–139.
17. *Op. cit.,* p. 313.

purely random and idiosyncratic. One could argue that a satisfactory explanation cannot be given without making reference to norms, but this concept evidently is not altogether welcome in the new perspective. Finally, apart from the issue of norms, the new perspective negates a significant empirical question: Why do reactions to deviant behavior vary from place to place and time to time? An answer to this question from the new perspective necessarily would be at least partially tautological because deviant behavior is defined in terms of reactions to it.

As the tone of the above criticism suggests, this writer differs with Becker, *et al.,* on the issue of identifying deviant behavior. My preference is to identify deviant acts by reference to norms, and treat reaction to deviation as a contingent property. However, this preference reflects nothing more than opinion, and the ultimate evaluation of the new conception on this point must await an assessment of substantive theory generated by it. Accordingly, no claim is made that Becker, Erikson, and Kitsuse are "wrong." Rather, the criticism is that (1) they have not specified exactly what kind of reaction identifies behavior as deviant and (2) they have failed to take a consistent stand on a particular conceptual issue.

OVERVIEW

The major trend in the study of crime and deviant behavior has been in the direction of a distinctly "social" conception of the subject matter. Whereas Lombroso thought of criminals in biological terms and later positivists sought to discover intrinsic features of criminal acts, the new perspective conceives of both in terms of the quality of social reaction to behavior. Accordingly, whether or not a person or an act is criminal or deviant is a matter of the way in which the public and/or officials react.

The relativistic criterion of deviation introduced by the new perspective is in keeping with contemporary sociological principles. Further, a social conception of the phenomenon promises to generate substantive theories that are distinctly sociological in outlook. But the new conception has left at least four crucial questions unanswered. First, what elements in the scheme are intended to be definitions rather than substantive theory? Second, is the ultimate goal to explain deviant behavior or to explain reactions to deviation? Third, is deviant behavior to be identified exclusively in terms of reaction to it? Fourth, exactly what kind of reaction identifies behavior as deviant?

No claim is made that the advocates of the new conception are unable to answer the above questions, nor that their answers would be wrong. The only point is that the questions must be answered if the new conception is to develop and receive the constructive attention that it deserves.

Problems in the Sociology of Deviance:
Social Definitions and Behavior*

RONALD L. AKERS

The conflict criminologist, George Vold, reminded us some years ago that the phenomenon of crime involves two major dimensions—the behavioral and the definitional:

> There is, therefore, always a dual problem of explanation—that of accounting for the behavior *as behavior,* and equally important, accounting *for the definitions* by which specific behavior comes to be considered crime or non-crime.[1]

A growing number of criminologists have become aware of the two-sided nature of the problem and suggest that interest be turned increasingly to the study of and accounting for the contents of the criminal law. They have suggested that the legal norms defining certain behavior as crime be subjected to analysis and explanations sought for why some acts are defined as crime and others are not.[2] One has even suggested that this constitutes *the* problem in the sociology of crime.[3]

While directly traceable to a conflict orientation,[4] this newer empha-

* Reprinted from *Social Forces,* 46 (June, 1968), pp. 455–465, by permission of the author and publisher. Version of a paper read at the annual meeting of the Pacific Sociological Association, March, 1967.
1. George Vold, *Theoretical Criminology* (New York: Oxford University Press, 1958), p. vi.
2. Clarence R. Jeffrey, "The Structure of American Criminological Thinking," *Journal of Criminal Law, Criminology, and Police Science,* 46 (January–February 1956), pp. 670–672; "Crime, Law and Social Structure," *Journal of Criminal Law, Criminology, and Police Science,* 47 (November–December 1956), pp. 423–425; and "An Integrated Theory of Crime and Criminal Behavior," *Journal of Criminal Law, Criminology, and Police Science,* 49 (March–April 1959), pp. 441–552. See also Donald J. Newman, "Legal Norms and Criminological Definitions," in Joseph S. Roucek (ed.), *Sociology of Crime* (New York: Philosophical Library, 1961), pp. 56–60; and "Sociology, Criminology, and Criminal Law," *Social Problems,* 7 (Summer 1959), pp. 43–45; and Richard Quinney, "Crime in Political Perspective," *American Behavioral Scientist,* 8 (December 1964), p. 19; and "Is Criminal Behaviour Deviant Behaviour?" *British Journal of Criminology* (April 1965), pp. 137–139.
3. Austin Turk, "Prospects for Theories of Criminal Behavior," *Journal of Criminal Law, Criminology, and Police Science,* 55 (December 1964), pp. 454–455; and "Conflict and Criminality," *American Sociological Review,* 31 (June 1966), pp. 338–352.
4. Vold, *op. cit.,* pp. 203–241; Thorsten Sellin, *Culture Conflict and Crime* (New York: Social Science Research Council, 1938); and Richard C. Fuller, "Morals and

sis on studying the law itself has also received major impetus from the theoretical issues raised by an interest in white-collar crime. The very differences between the set of laws regulating occupational behavior and other statutes embodying legal proscriptions and sanctions have raised questions about how and why they were enacted—not just why they have been violated.[5] The study of white-collar crime, as Newman says, calls for the investigator ". . . to cast his analysis not only in the framework of those who *break* laws, but in the context of those who *make* laws as well."[6]

In a recent article, Gibbs notes that one of the major questions left unanswered by the "new" labelling conception of deviance is whether the ultimate goal is "to explain deviant behavior or to explain reactions to deviations?"[7] A re-reading of the literature expounding this approach would suggest that the goal is not to account for *either* the behavior *or* the reaction, but *both*. Thus, in a sense, the labellers have illuminated the twofold problem of explanation in the broader study of deviance just as conflict and white-collar crime perspectives have done in the narrower field of criminology.

These, then, are the two basic problems facing the sociology of deviance: How and/or why certain kinds of behavior and people get defined and labelled as deviant. How and/or why some people engage in deviant acts. Our research must provide data on and our theories should explain *both* social definitions and behavior. The purpose of this paper is to explore the meaning of these two problems, the *nature* of theories and research revolving around them, and their implications for the future direction of the sociology of deviance.

THE BEHAVIORAL QUESTIONS

The explanation of deviant behavior must address itself to two interrelated problems: (a) accounting for the group and structural variations in rates of deviancy, and (b) describing and explaining the process by which individuals come to commit acts labelled deviant. Cressey, following

the Criminal Law," *Journal of Criminal Law and Criminology,* 32 (1942), pp. 624–630.

5. Vilhelm Aubert, "White Collar Crime and Social Structure," *American Journal of Sociology,* 58 (1952), p. 264.

6. Donald J. Newman, "White Collar Crime," *Law and Contemporary Problems,* 23 (1958), p. 746. See also Frank Hartung, "White Collar Crime: Its Significance for Theory and Practice," *Federal Probation,* 17 (1953), p. 31; Donald Cressy, "Foreword" to Edwin H. Sutherland, *White Collar Crime* (New York: Holt, Rinehart & Winston, 1961), p. xiii; and Earl R. Quinney, "The Study of White Collar Crime: Toward a Reorientation in Theory and Research," *Journal of Criminal Law, Criminology, and Police Science,* 55 (June 1964), p. 214.

7. Jack P. Gibbs, "Conceptions of Deviant Behavior: The Old and the New," *Pacific Sociological Review,* 9 (Spring 1966), p. 14.

Sutherland, refers to them as the problems of epidemiology and individual conduct.[8] Other terms could be used, but I prefer to talk about structural and processual questions. Some want to speak of them as the sociological and psychological "levels" of explanations.[9] Reference to the two problems of behavioral explanation in these terms continues the old Durkheimian polemic designed to assure sociologists that they have a unique discipline. This polemic in intellectual imperialism is probably no longer meaningful or necessary; but if it is, it is not relevant to this distinction between structural and processual explanations of deviant behavior, for both can be sociological.[10]

The theoretical emphasis in the sociology of deviance has been on structural explanations, however, and we have some fairly sophisticated notions about the kinds of structures and environments which produce certain kinds of deviancy. But this emphasis should be balanced by an increased concern with the process by which these environments do so. Although there are excellent miniature theories of embezzlement, drug addiction, marihuana use, and check forgery, little recently has been done to reconstruct the process of coming to commit various kinds of deviant behavior.[11] Moreover, there have been virtually no efforts to locate the

8. Donald R. Cressey, "Epidemiology and Individual Conduct: A Case From Criminology," *Pacific Sociological Review,* 3 (Fall 1960), pp. 47–58.
9. Albert K. Cohen, "The Study of Social Disorganization and Deviant Behavior," in Robert K. Merton, et al. (eds.), *Sociology Today* (New York: Basic Books, 1959), p. 461; *Deviance and Control* (Englewood Cliffs, New Jersey: Prentice-Hall, 1966), pp. 41–47; and "Review of Hermann Mannheim, Comparative Criminology," *Social Forces,* 45 (December 1966), pp. 298–299.
10. Homans seems to think that the argument is meaningful although he offers a different answer from the "levels" solution. See George C. Homans, "Bringing Men Back In," *American Sociological Review,* 29 (December 1964), pp. 808–818. He resolves the issue by arguing that there are no general "sociological" propositions which cannot be derived from "psychological" principles. Thus, he feels that the two are not "levels" of independent analytic status. This is somewhat unenlightening, however, because by "psychological" Homans means simply propositions about men's observable behavior, and this is not what is usually meant by "psychological." The fact that Homans sees these propositions coming from the work of psychologists such as Skinner does not *ipso facto* make them psychological. Whether a theoretical framework be labelled sociological or psychological, then, is a definitional problem. I would agree with this concept: If the explanatory variables and processes in propositions about behavior are those contained in or arising out of social interaction (as contrasted, for instance, with intrapsychic, individual constitutional, personality, or unconscious variables) then one is justified in naming them sociological. If the independent variables are social-environmental, then we have a sociological theory, whether the dependent variables be individual or collective behavior. It is in this sense that both structural and processual theories can be sociological.
11. Donald Cressey, *Other People's Money* (Glencoe, Illinois: The Free Press, 1953); Alfred R. Lindesmith, *Opiate Addiction* (Bloomington, Indiana: Principia Press, 1947); Howard S. Becker, *Outsiders* (Glencoe, Illinois: The Free Press, 1963), Chaps. 3 and 4; and Edwin M. Lemert, "An Isolation and Closure Theory of Naive Check Forgery," *Journal of Criminal Law, Criminology, and Police Science,* 44 (September–October 1953), pp. 296–307. Quinney has presented a miniature "structural" theory of a form of white-collar crime. Earl R. Quinney, "Occupational

common elements in these separate explanations toward the end of testing or constructing a general processual theory.

Sutherland's differential association theory is notable for standing nearly alone as a general processual theory of criminal behavior.[12] Sutherland recognized that while theories addressed to structural and processual questions may be different, the two must be consistent.[13] Not only should they be consistent, but as Cressey notes, they should be integrated.[14] This integration is possible because in the final analysis both kinds of theory propose answers to the *same overall* question of why some people come to commit deviant acts and others do not. The structural theories contend that more people in certain groups, located in certain positions in, or encountering particular pressures created by the social structure, will engage in deviancy than those in other groups and locations.[15] In a sense, they explain between-group variations. But in so doing, they implicitly or explicitly posit processes by which these structural conditions produce higher probabilities of deviancy. Processual theories explain within-group variation. They say that the individual commits deviancy because he has encountered a particular life history. But in so doing, they are also saying something about the deviancy-producing groups, structures, and circum-

Structure and Criminal Behavior: Prescription Violations by Retail Pharmacists," *Social Problems*, 11 (Fall 1963), pp. 179–185.

12. Edwin H. Sutherland and Donald R. Cressey, *Principles of Criminology* (6th ed.; Philadelphia: J. B. Lippincott, Co., 1960), pp. 77–79.

13. *Ibid.*, p. 80.

14. Donald R. Cressey, "The Theory of Differential Association: An Introduction," *Social Problems*, 8 (Summer 1960), p. 5.

15. Most other sociological perspectives are primarily structural in emphasis. The ones that have exerted the most influence are disorganization-anomie and conflict theory. Although there are now a number of variations on the disorganization-anomie theme, they all derive ultimately from Durkheim. The following are among the more careful and systematic statements on variants of this approach: Robert K. Merton, *Social Theory and Social Structure* (Glencoe, Illinois: The Free Press, 1957), pp. 131–194; Albert K. Cohen, *Delinquent Boys* (Glencoe, Illinois: The Free Press, 1955); Richard Cloward and Lloyd Ohlin, "Illegitimate Means, Anomie, and Deviant Behavior," *American Sociological Review*, 24 (April 1959), pp. 164–177, and *Delinquency and Opportunity* (Glencoe, Illinois: The Free Press, 1961); Arnold Rose, *Theory and Method in the Social Sciences* (Minneapolis: University of Minnesota Press, 1954), chap. 1; Cohen, "Study of Social Disorganization and Deviant Behavior"; Albert Cohen, "The Sociology of the Deviant Act: Anomie Theory and Beyond," *American Sociological Review*, 30 (February 1965), pp. 9–14; Marshall B. Clinard (ed.), *Anomie and Deviant Behavior* (New York: The Free Press of Glencoe, 1964); Clifford Shaw and Henry D. McKay, *Juvenile Delinquency and Urban Areas* (Chicago: University of Chicago Press, 1942); and Bernard Lander, *Towards an Understanding of Juvenile Delinquency* (New York: Columbia University Press, 1954). For the most thorough analysis, critique, and modification of that variant of anomie theory which emphasizes delinquent subcultures, see David Downes, *The Delinquent Solution* (New York: The Free Press, 1966). Conflict theories are found in Vold, *op. cit.*; Sellin, *op. cit.*; and Solomon Kobrin, "The Conflict of Values in Delinquency Areas," *American Sociological Review*, 16 (October 1951), pp. 653–661.

stances he must encounter to increase the probability of his becoming and remaining deviant.[16]

The differential association-reinforcement theory formulated by Burgess and Akers avoids some of the problems of Sutherland's original formulation and describes the general process (consistently and integrally with a broader theory of behavior) of deviant behavior.[17] It is capable of identifying the common elements in the separate processual theories and provides the groundwork for integrating structural and processual explanations. By conceptualizing groups and social structure as learning environments which structure the patterns of associations and reinforcement, a long step is taken in the direction of bringing the two together. Differential association-reinforcement spells out the *mechanisms* by which environmental stimuli produce and maintain behavior and the structural theories explicate the type of *environments* most likely to sustain norm and law-violating behavior.

But before we will learn which theory or combination of theories turns out to be our best explanation of deviance, we must broaden our data-gathering technology beyond the traditional research strategies. Compared to those in other sociological specialties, students of deviancy have relatively ready access to regularly compiled data on behavior that has come to

---

16. Other theories which attempt to answer the essentially processual questions of why particular individuals commit deviancy, although the "process" is not explicit in each case, are self-concept and role-commitment theories. The self-concept theory of Reckless and his associates and students at Ohio State is essentially a social control theory containing both structural and individual components, but the burden of this perspective is borne by the conceptualization of one's self-image as an individual selective mechanism which accounts for differential response to environment. Walter Reckless, "A New Theory of Delinquency and Crime," *Federal Probation,* 25 (December 1961), pp. 42–46; "The Self Component in Potential Delinquency and Potential Non-Delinquency," *American Sociological Review,* 22 (October 1957), pp. 566–570; "Self Concept as an Insulator Against Delinquency," *American Sociological Review,* 21 (December 1956), pp. 744–746; and "The Good Boy in a High Delinquency Area," *Journal of Criminal Law, Criminology, and Police Science,* 48 (August 1960), pp. 18–26; Frank R. Scarpitti, et al., "Good Boy in a High Delinquency Area: Four Years Later," *American Sociological Review,* 25 (August 1960), pp. 555–558. Role commitment theories can be found in Howard S. Becker, "Notes on the Concept of Commitment," *American Journal of Sociology,* 66 (July 1960), pp. 32–40; David Matza, *Delinquency and Drift* (New York: John Wiley & Sons, 1964); Richard Korn and Lloyd W. McKorkle, *Criminology and Penology* (New York: Henry Holt Co., 1959), pp. 327–353; and Scott Briar and Irving Piliavin, "Delinquency, Situational Inducements, and Commitment to Conformity," *Social Problems,* 13 (Summer 1965), pp. 35–45. Of course, the impact of labelling conceptions also can be seen to be perspectives on role commitment. One should also view Short and Strodtbeck's conceptions of gang delinquency as explanations of individual actions. James F. Short, Jr., and Fred L. Strodtbeck, *Group Process and Gang Delinquency* (Chicago: University of Chicago Press, 1965). All of these are consistent with a general learning perspective. I omit multicausation, psychiatric, personal pathology, and other personality theories from discussion.
17. Robert L. Burgess and Ronald L. Akers, "A Differential Association-Reinforcement Theory of Criminal Behavior," *Social Problems,* 14 (Fall 1966), pp. 128–147.

the attention of official agencies. Nevertheless, we still do not know very much about even the official distribution and variations in rates of some kinds of deviancy and are practically ignorant of the true distribution of nearly every type of deviant behavior. To test theories adequately, we need to utilize as broad a range of research techniques and as representative data as possible. This means that we must be more imaginative in ferreting out other sources of data beyond the usual official statistics, records, and populations of apprehended offenders to get a better idea of the distribution of rates of deviant behavior. More precise knowledge of the behavioral process in deviancy not only awaits more systematic and extensive use of case histories and analytic inductive techniques, but requires greater utilization of laboratory experimentation.

Reliable and valid techniques of studying delinquency in representative samples of the general adolescent population are being developed, and these could be extended into other fields.[18] Of course, there is much yet to be done even in the restricted area of delinquency, and it could be argued that these techniques are simply inappropriate to some types of deviancy. But the spirit, if not the substance, of the developing technology of unofficial measures of delinquency could be applied to some adult violations. This could be combined with the utilization of official and semi-official compilations. We have not yet realized the full implications of the pioneer-

18. Of a 32-item bibliography of studies using unofficial measures of delinquency I have collected, the following are cited: Ronald L. Akers, "Socioeconomic Status and Delinquent Behavior: A Re-Test," *Journal of Research in Crime and Delinquency,* 1 (January 1964), pp. 38–46; John P. Clark and Eugene P. Wenninger, "Goal Orientations and Illegal Behavior Among Juveniles," *Social Forces,* 42 (October 1963), pp. 49–60; Robert A. Dentler and Lawrence J. Monroe, "Social Correlates of Early Adolescent Theft," *American Sociological Review,* 26 (October 1961), pp. 733–743; Maynard L. Erickson and LaMar T. Empey, "Court Records, Undetected Delinquency, and Decision-Making," *Journal of Criminal Law, Criminology, and Police Science,* 54 (December 1963), pp. 456–469; Martin Gold, "Undetected Delinquent Behavior," *Journal of Research in Crime and Delinquency,* 3 (January 1966), pp. 27–46; David E. Hunt and Robert H. Hardt, "Developmental Stage, Delinquency, and Differential Treatment," *Journal of Research in Crime and Delinquency,* 2 (January 1965), pp. 20–31; Jay Lowe, "Prediction of Delinquency with an Attitudinal Configuration Model," *Social Forces,* 45 (September 1966), pp. 106–113; F. Ivan Nye and James Short, "Scaling Delinquent Behavior," *American Sociological Review,* 22 (June 1957), pp. 326–331; Austin Porterfield, "Delinquency and Its Outcome in Court and College," *American Journal of Sociology,* 49 (September 1943), pp. 199–204; John Finley Scott, "Two Dimensions of Delinquent Behavior," *American Sociological Review,* 24 (April 1959), pp. 240–243; James F. Short, Jr., "Differential Association with Delinquent Friends and Delinquent Behavior," *Pacific Sociological Review,* 1 (Spring 1958), pp. 20–25; James F. Short, Jr., and F. Ivan Nye, "Extent of Unrecorded Delinquency: Tentative Conclusions," *Journal of Criminal Law, Criminology, and Police Science,* 49 (November–December 1958), pp. 296–302; James F. Short, Jr., Ray A. Tennyson, and Kenneth I. Howard, "Behavior Dimensions of Gang Delinquency," *American Sociological Review,* 28 (June 1963), pp. 411–428; and Harwin L. Voss, "Socioeconomic Status and Reported Delinquent Behavior," *Social Problems,* 13 (Winter 1966), pp. 314–324.

ing work of Sutherland, Clinard, and Hartung on white-collar offenses.[19] There is a whole class of research sites of which we have thus far little availed ourselves—the files and records of private police, detective, security and similar agencies, insurance and management consultant firms, and business and occupational control boards and commissions.[20] Also, we are just beginning to recognize the importance and potential impact on sociology of the very effective experimental technology developing in the operant conditioning tradition.[21]

SOCIAL DEFINITIONS

In the broadest sense, the problem of explaining social definitions is that of accounting for why people come to have the values and norms they do. But more specifically the problem is to learn how the prevailing conceptions of what behavior constitutes the major forms of deviancy in society have come to be established. This entails examining two related processes: (a) establishing the rules, definitions, norms, and laws the infraction of which constitutes deviance, and (b) reacting to people who have or are believed to have violated the norms by applying negative sanctions and labels to them (and applying deviant labels to others not because of their actions but because they possess some physical characteristic or disability). We are infinitely more knowledgeable about both the behavioral questions than either of these two aspects of the defining and labelling process.

Those criminologists who have given thought to the problem of why certain behavior is defined as criminal offer explanations that converge on a group-conflict theme—what becomes defined as illegal is related to the ability of certain groups in society to have their values, norms, and interests incorporated into or reflected in the law and its administration even against the interests of other groups and the general public.[22] Thus, they have

19. Sutherland, *op. cit.*; Marshall B. Clinard, *The Black Market* (New York: Rinehart Co., 1952); and Frank Hartung, "White Collar Offenses in the Wholesale Meat Market Industry in Detroit," *American Journal of Sociology*, 56 (November 1950), pp. 325–342.
20. Mary O. Cameron, *The Booster and the Snitch: Department Store* (Glencoe, Illinois: The Free Press, 1964), makes use of department store detective files. James E. Price utilizes insurance statistics in "A Test of the Accuracy of Crime Statistics," *Social Problems*, 14 (Fall 1966), pp. 214–221. An imaginative combination of interview data and data from the records of drug law enforcement agencies is found in Earl Quinney, "Occupational Structure and Criminal Behavior." In addition, see the rich, but unsystematically reported, cases taken from the files of his management consultant firm by Norman Jaspan, *The Thief in the White Collar* (Philadelphia: J. B. Lippincott Co., 1960).
21. Robert L. Burgess and Ronald L. Akers, "Prospects for an Experimental Analysis in Criminology," paper read at the annual meeting of the American Sociological Association, August 1966.
22. Richard Quinney, "Crime in Political Perspective," pp. 19–21; Vold; *op. cit.*, pp. 207–209; Sellin, *op. cit.*; Clinard, *The Black Market*, p. 153; and F. James Davis, *et al.*, *Society and the Law* (New York: The Free Press of Glencoe, 1962), pp. 69–71.

been led to recognize the political nature of crime and a well-documented observation concerning politics in democratic society: the passage and content of nearly all laws, the formulation of nearly all public policy, and nearly every public decision, including court decisions, are in some measure the outcome of the direct or indirect political influence of competing interest groups.[23]

Investigation of the political process by which the criminal label is established and applied remains a neglected area, however. What literature there is on this point has been largely suggestive and programmatic, with little in the way of research.[24] We will have to scrutinize more carefully the process by which the criminal law is formed and enforced in a search for those variables which determine what of the total range of behavior becomes prohibited and which of the total range of norms become a part of the law. Certainly these variables would include not only the activities of political-interest groups but also a range of factors in the changing social, economic, political, and normative structures of society, its historical development, legal traditions, governmental forms, and the general political process.

It is the politically dominant subunits of society that at any given time can see to it that public policy reflects their interests, whether these be whole classes or segments, major vested interests, more specialized private groups, or even agencies of the government itself which exert influence in the law-making and enforcing processes. However, the law reflects not only the interests of particular segments but also the changing needs and functions of the whole society. The extent to which public policy is the result of the victories, compromises, and resolutions of group conflict is an empirical question that must be answered for the specific form of deviancy in question. Empirical research on this question may take the form of longitudinal or current study of some policy-in-the-making or historical reconstruction of the way the policy came into being. Such research is

23. Of the vast literature that could be cited on this point, these are among the best: David Truman, *The Governmental Process* (8th ed.; New York: Alfred A. Knopf, 1962); Earl Latham, *The Group Basis of Politics* (New York: Octagon Books, 1965); Harmon Zeigler, *Interest Groups in American Society* (Englewood Cliffs, New Jersey: Prentice-Hall, 1964); V. O. Key, *Politics, Parties, and Pressure Groups* (New York: Thomas Y. Crowell, 1958), and *Public Opinion and American Democracy* (New York: Alfred A. Knopf, 1961), pp. 500–531; Henry W. Ehrmann (ed.), *Interest Groups on Four Continents* (Pittsburgh: University of Pittsburgh Press, 1958); Donald C. Blaisdell (ed.), *Unofficial Government: Pressure Groups and Lobbies,* Special Issue of *Annals of the American Academy of Political and Social Science,* 319 (September 1958); and Lester W. Milbrath, *The Washington Lobbyists* (Chicago: Rand McNally & Co., 1963).
24. Turk, "Prospects for . . . Criminal Behavior"; Richard Quinney, "Crime in Political Perspective," p. 19; Jeffery, "Structure of American Criminological Thinking," pp. 663–667; and Jeffery, "An Integral Theory of Crime and Criminal Behavior," p. 534.

already available on theft law,[25] vagrancy law,[26] public policy on drugs,[27] prohibition,[28] and legal regulation of certain professional practices.[29] But the surface has just been scratched. The field is wide open for sociological research in the process of legislation, the content of laws, and the operation of administrative agencies, courts, police,[30] and other agents of formal social control as well as the operation and function of private police and detectives as more informal enforcement agencies.

Conflict explanations and research into the degree to which group interests form a part of the total political process is only a start. If differences in the power of interest groups accounts for some differences in the laws and public policy, what makes for power?[31] What differentials in organizational and other group properties account for differential political influence? Sociological theory has been nearly mute and systematic research almost nonexistent on this problem.[32]

This type of research should be complemented by research into the variables operative in the defining and reacting to deviance by more informal social audiences than those connected with the formulation and implementation of the law. The significant theoretical problem here is the relationship between prevailing moral sentiments of the society and the normative stances incorporated into public policy. This concern with the overlap of current public opinion and the contents of the law is part of the old question of whether the law always flows from or can induce changes in the folkways and mores. The reasonable answer, of course, is that law is both an independent and dependent variable in society, but research and theoretical perspectives are needed which define when and under what conditions it is one or the other.[33] Some research has already been reported which utilizes survey data on public views of certain kinds of deviancy and public policy,[34] and "impact" studies have been conducted or

25. Jerome Hall, *Theft Law and Society* (Indianapolis: The Bobbs-Merrill Co., 1952).
26. William Chambliss, "A Sociological Analysis of the Law of Vagrancy," *Social Problems,* 12 (Summer 1964), pp. 67–77.
27. Becker, *Outsiders,* pp. 135–146; Alfred R. Lindesmith, "Federal Law and Drug Addiction," *Social Problems,* 7 (Summer 1959), pp. 48–57.
28. Peter Odegard, *Pressure Politics: The Story of the Anti-Saloon League* (New York: Columbia University Press, 1928).
29. Ronald L. Akers, "Professional Organization, Political Power, and Occupational Laws," unpublished Ph.D. dissertation, University of Kentucky, 1966.
30. Jerome Skolnick, *Justice Without Trial* (New York: John Wiley & Sons, 1966).
31. Truman, *op. cit.,* p. 13; Marian D. Irish and James W. Prothro, *The Politics of American Democracy* (Englewood Cliffs, New Jersey: Prentice-Hall, 1959), p. 336.
32. Akers, "Professional Organization, Political Power and Occupational Laws."
33. William M. Evan, "Law as an Instrument of Social Change," *Estudio de Sociologia,* 2 (1962), pp. 167–175.
34. John I. Kitsuse, "Societal Reaction to Deviant Behavior: Problems of Theory and Method," *Social Problems,* 9 (Winter 1962), pp. 247–256; Elizabeth A. Rooney and Don C. Gibbons, "Social Reactions to 'Crimes without Victims,'" *Social Problems,* 13 (Spring 1966), pp. 400–410; J. L. Simmons, "Public Stereotypes of

are underway in the sociology of law.[35] This sort of research could be combined with studies of the similarities in the norms of specialized groups and particular legal norms.[36] Research of this nature may not tell us anything about the basic process by which norms are formed and social control is exercised, however. We may have to have recourse to historical, cross-cultural, and small-group experimental studies to get at this question.[37]

LABELLING AND DEVIANT BEHAVIOR

The professors of the labelling perspective contend that the important questions concerning deviancy are: Who applies the deviant label to whom? Whose rules shall prevail? Under what circumstances is the label successfully and unsuccessfully applied? How does a community decide what forms of conduct should be singled out for this kind of attention?[38] These kinds of questions do not exclude a concern with deviant behavior, but they do give it secondary importance. One would expect, then, that this approach offers a valuable balance to exclusive concern with the causes of deviation and the characteristics of deviants. Indeed, some of the research alluded to above has been generated by this perspective. However, the theoretical contribution of this approach to the problem of social definitions has not been as great as its promise.

Today only the most unregenerate biological or constitutional determinist would quibble with the basic contention of this school that the deviant nature of acts resides not in the acts or the person committing them, but rather in group definitions and reactions. Certainly, it has been a

---

Deviants," *Social Problems,* 13 (Fall 1965), pp. 223–232; Donald J. Newman, "Public Attitudes Toward a Form of White Collar Crime," *Social Problems,* 4 (1957), pp. 228–232; Edwin M. Schur, "Attitudes Towards Addicts: Some General Observations and Comparative Findings," *American Journal of Orthopsychiatry,* 34 (January 1964), pp. 80–90; and Arnold Rose and Arthur E. Prell, "Does the Punishment Fit the Crime? A Study of Social Valuation," *American Journal of Sociology,* 24 (September 1955), pp. 247–259. For a historical treatment see Harris Isbell, "Historical Development of Attitudes Toward Opiate Addiction in the U. S.," in Seymour Farber and Roger Wilson (eds.), *Conflict and Creativity* (New York: McGraw-Hill Book Co., 1963), pp. 154–170.
35. Harry V. Ball, "Social Structure and Rent Control Violations," *American Journal of Sociology,* 65 (May 1960), pp. 598–604; Richard Lempert, "Strategies of Research Design in the Legal Impact Study," *Law and Society Review,* 1 (November 1966), pp. 111–132; and N. Walker and M. Argyle, "Does the Law Affect Moral Judgment?" *British Journal of Criminology,* 4 (October 1964), pp. 570–581.
36. Earl Quinney, "The Study of White Collar Crime," pp. 210–212.
37. See Paul Secord and Carl Backman, *Social Psychology* (New York: McGraw-Hill Book Co., 1964), pp. 323–351.
38. Becker, *Outsiders,* pp. 1–18; Howard S. Becker (ed.), *The Other Side* (New York: The Free Press of Glencoe, 1964), p. 3; Kai T. Erikson, "Notes on the Sociology of Deviance," in Becker, *The Other Side,* p. 12; Kitsuse, *op. cit.,* p. 247.

long time since sociologists have said otherwise. It is true that in the past we have sometimes forgotten the basically social nature of deviance, and in an effort to untangle the etiology, we have become overly concerned with the conditions and characteristics of the deviants themselves. But this is just another way of saying that we have devoted most of our energy to the behavioral question and have implicity accepted, as given, the established norms defining various kinds of behavior as deviant. Nonetheless, this in no way implies that sociologists thought that there was something inherently evil or deviant about the behavior itself. Not since Garofalo have we attempted to erect universal or natural categories of inherently criminal behavior, and certainly since Durkheim we have been cognizant of the centrality of social definitions to the conception of criminal and deviant behavior. Yet, much of the effort expended by the writers in the labelling tradition has been to exorcise this nonexistent fallacy.

The labelling approach does rightly emphasize, neither wholly originally nor uniquely, the importance of studying social definitions and the process by which acts and people get labelled as deviant. But when labelling theorists have attempted to answer questions about social definitions, they say little more than what conflict theorists have been saying for some time, i.e., the dominant groups in society will have their norms and values prevail, will successfully apply their conceptions of who are the deviants and become more or less official definers of deviancy.[39] In fact, the most sophisticated statement (going much beyond this) about the determinants of one type of labelling, "criminalization," is in a recent article written from an avowedly conflict perspective, not a stigma or labelling perspective.[40] Rather, although those of this school come dangerously close to saying that the actual behavior is unimportant, their contribution to the

---

39. Becker, *Outsiders,* pp. 15–18. One example of what more is said about social definitions is Eliot Friedson, "Disability as Social Deviance," in Marvin R. Sussman (ed.), *Sociology and Rehabilitation* (Washington, D.C.: American Sociological Association, 1966), pp. 71–99. Friedson addresses the difficult problems of illness, disability, and handicaps as bases for labelling as a deviant. He offers a framework that could be applied not only to mental illness which has long been of interest to students of deviance but also to physical illness which has not received much attention. No special mention of the problem of illness as deviance has been made here, but it should be evident that this is another area awaiting further investigation. One can be socially defined as sick but not all sick roles are stigmatized. Friedson suggests that the curability of the illness and the extent to which the ill person is believed responsible for his disability or illness need to be considered in connection with stigmatized and nonstigmatized sick roles. Thus, he opens the way for research into the relationships among these variables and the question of why some illnesses are stigmatized and others are not. Another area of research which should prove profitable is deviation from the expectations of the sick role itself. Certainly, being sick or handicapped may prevent one from fulfilling his other role expectations, but it is also an acceptable excuse for doing so and may forestall sanctions for deviations from other roles. The question is what kinds of deviations from the norms of sickness, or under what conditions such deviations, are stigmatized or negatively sanctioned whether or not the person is labelled as a deviant.
40. Turk, "Conflict and Criminality."

study of deviancy comes precisely in their conception of the impact of labelling on behavior. One sometimes gets the impression from reading this literature that people go about minding their own business, and then— "wham"—bad society comes along and slaps them with a stigmatized label. Forced into the role of deviant the individual has little choice but to be deviant. This is an exaggeration, of course, but such an image can be gained easily from an overemphasis on the impact of labelling. However, it is exactly this image, toned down and made reasonable, which is the central contribution of the labelling school to the sociology of deviance.

Thanks to this image, we are now more appreciative of the impact of norm enforcement in the furtherance of deviancy. Societal reaction may deter individuals from engaging in further deviant behavior, but it may not effectively reduce the behavior it was designed to combat. In fact, it may play a role in setting up conditions conducive to subsequent and other deviancy. The stigmatization of deviance may have an impact such that the deviant comes to view himself as irrevocably deviant, becomes more committed to a deviant role, or becomes involved in deviant groups; this influences his future deviance and may force him to participate in various kinds of secondary deviance.[41] This perspective has also generated some ideas about what kinds of deviancy are likely to be affected in this way.[42]

When carried too far, however, this insight serves as a blinder. The labelling creates the deviance, yes, and often operates to increase the probability that certain stigmatized persons will commit future deviancy, and to promote deviant behavior that might not have occurred otherwise. But the label does not create the behavior in the *first place*. People can and do commit deviant acts because of the particular contingencies and circumstances in their lives, quite apart from or in combination with the labels others apply to them.[43] The labelling process is not completely arbitrary

---

41. Becker, *Outsiders*, pp. 31–39; Edwin M. Lemert, *Social Pathology* (New York: McGraw-Hill Book Co., 1951); Edwin M. Schur, *Narcotic Addiction in Britain and America: The Impact of Public Policy* (Bloomington: Indiana University Press, 1962); Harold Garfinkel, "Successful Degradation Ceremonies," *American Journal of Sociology,* 61 (January 1956), pp. 420–424; Richard D. Schwartz and Jerome H. Skolnick, "Two Studies of Legal Stigma," in Becker, *The Other Side,* pp. 103–117; Marsh B. Ray, "The Cycle of Abstinence and Relapse," in Becker, *ibid.,* pp. 163–179; Erikson, *op. cit.,* pp. 16–17; Alfred R. Lindesmith and John Gagnon, "Anomie and Drug Addiction," in Clinard, *Anomie and Deviant Behavior,* pp. 158–188; and Edwin M. Schur, *Crimes Without Victims* (Englewood Cliffs, New Jersey: Prentice-Hall, 1965), pp. 1–7. For discussion of the impact of stigmatized physical characteristics on behavior of the stigmatized see Fred Davis, "Deviance Disavowal: The Management of Strained Interaction by the Visibly Handicapped," in Becker, *The Other Side,* pp. 119–138; and Erving Goffman, *Stigma* (Englewood Cliffs, New Jersey: Prentice-Hall, 1963).
42. Schur, *Crimes Without Victims.*
43. Lemert, of course, does recognize this point and consistently maintains the distinction between primary and secondary deviance. Edwin Lemert, *Human Deviance, Social Problems and Social Control* (Englewood Cliffs, New Jersey: Prentice-Hall, 1967), pp. 40–64.

and unrelated to the behavior of those detected and labelled. Although errors are made and criteria extraneous to behavior are used, we do not react to others as homosexuals unless they exhibit behavior believed to be indicative of homosexuality, and the courts do not stigmatize with the label of criminal until it has been legally determined that criminal acts have been committed. There were addicts loose in the land long before Anslinger and the Narcotics Bureau were let loose on the addicts. Obviously, the behavior is not itself deviant; it is only because others have defined it so. But once defined, aside from questions of secondary deviations, the behavior is prior to the labelling reaction. One may say that, in this sense, the behavior creates the label.

Such statements do not go far enough, however. Neither behavior nor its social definitions occur in a vacuum; they are mutually influencing. A given class of behaviors and those performing them may carry no particular stigma or at best be mildly disapproved by the norm-enforcing and conventional segments of society until such time as they become more widespread, visible, and offensive to extant notions of propriety. There is certainly some question about the deviancy of taking *LSD-25* and similar drugs until some and then many began this practice. Who, just a few months ago, would have condemned the smoking of the baked parts of the inside of banana skins? There surely were those who made regular use of certain drugs before that use became proscribed. But that use began to violate other norms regarding drug "abuse," became offensive to large parts of the population, partly because it was by those already considered deviant on other counts, and was stigmatized to some degree. Once the behavior was proscribed and deviant labels attached to those engaging in this behavior, these users became more committed deviants, subcultural support for the behavior evolved, and various forms of secondary deviancy emerged. This then evoked stronger prohibitions and more stigmatized and even criminal labels, which then turned some off and others on the drugs. The theoretical problem, then, becomes one of specifying the ways and under what conditions such an interactive process involving both behavior and definitions will take place. What determines when a behavior pattern not previously specifically stigmatized will become defined as deviant and when labelling increases or decreases the probability of further involvement in that behavior pattern?

Conclusions

The two major problems of accounting for behavior and definitions are of equal importance, but both criminology and the broader field of the sociology of deviance have tended to give short shrift to explaining social definitions of deviancy. We have tended to see our job nearly exclusively as the study of those who break the laws and violate the norms. The time is here for increased theoretical and research interest in the making and enforcing of the laws and norms. Conflict theorists, those criminologists interested in white-collar crime, and those in the labelling school of deviance have been more alert to the problem than have those operating from other perspectives. But we are in the beginning stage of mapping out the parameters and still know very little about the determining variables in the social defining and reacting process.

To give more complete answers to the questions about deviant behavior, increased attention needs to be turned to explicating the process by which individuals come to commit deviant acts, and eventually we must integrate processual and structural explanations. We are not likely to come up with a complete explanation of deviant behavior in general until we tie it into a general theory of social behavior. By the same token, the study of societal control of deviance must be tied to the larger study and theory of conflict, power, and norm formation and enforcement.

Finally, the ultimate goal should be to specify the interaction and integrate explanations of behavior and social definitions. Jeffery has attempted something similar to this regarding crime and the law.[44] His formulation is not entirely satisfactory as a broader solution, however, mainly because it is too narrowly concerned with these rather than the whole problem of behavior and social definitions. It should be said, by no means originally and at the risk of sounding trite and mouthing platitudes, that the solution will need to be general enough that the sociology of deviance becomes simply sociology. Patterned social behavior, both conforming and nonconforming, is the stuff of which society is made, and social definitions is just another term for normative and value patterns, i.e., culture. The study of society *and* culture, of course, is the stuff of which sociology is made.

---

44. Jeffery, "An Integrated Theory of Crime and Criminal Behavior."

Chapter
5

Collective Behavior and Social Change:
Toward a Theory of Revolution?

The study of the process of social change has been one of the preeminent concerns of sociologists. However, social change is not a simple process. It can occur at a variety of levels, in many ways, have multiple causes and have very different rates. Because it is so complex, there are innumerable controversies over the process of change. In this section the focus is on only one controversy—social change through revolution. As with every other debate in this book, the lead article is in itself engaged in a dialogue, this time with previous ideas on revolutionary change. Davies is (really) taking issue with Karl Marx's emphasis on the worsening conditions of the proletariat as the cause of revolution. Dissatisfied with this, Davies finds, embedded in Marx's (and de Tocqueville's) work, an alternative view which focuses on *improving* economic conditions of the proletariat which do not keep pace with the growing welfare of the capitalists. What Davies does is combine Marx's two ideas into a new "theory" or revolution: "Revolutions are most likely to occur when a prolonged period of objective economic and social development is followed by a short period of sharp reversal." It is this, rather than inadequate food, equality or liberty, which produces a "dissatisfied state of mind" which in turn provides the basis for a revolution. With this orientation in hand, Davies proceeds to demonstrate how a series of rebellions follows his principles. He does not, however, claim that *all* revolutions follow this pattern.

Spurred on by Davies' work, Geschwender offers a critique of, and some additions to, it. He notes that Davies seeks to explain only "progressive" revolutions, not those from *either* the right or the left. In addition, Geschwender criticizes Davies for not distinguishing between those things which dispose individuals to take part in a revolution and "those factors which produce a revolution at a particular time and place." The former require motivational explanations, the latter are explanations of why institutions are disrupted.

In Geschwender's view, Davies' focus on the "rise and drop hypothesis" has blinded him to alternative patterns which would produce the state of mind needed for a revolution. He suggests various other explanations of this precondition for revolution—the rising expectations, the relative deprivation, the downward mobility and the status inconsistency hypotheses. Geschwender contends that all of these hypotheses, as well as Davies' rise and drop hypothesis, can be subsumed under dissonance theory. He goes on to present a series of propositions "which predict the particular mode of dissonance reduction that will be attempted under certain sets of conditions, the direction of change attempts (revolutionary or reform), and the conditions under which change will not be attempted but hostile outbursts emerge or apathy and hopelessness set in." Thus Geschwender has greatly expanded on Davies' original formulation and put it in a broader theoretical perspective. More importantly, he has moved beyond a single factor theory of revolution and the explanation of only one kind of social movement—progressive revolution.

Toward a Theory of Revolution*

JAMES C. DAVIES

In exhorting proletarians of all nations to unite in revolution, because they had nothing to lose but their chains, Marx and Engels most succinctly presented that theory of revolution which is recognized as their brain child. But this most famed thesis, that progressive degradation of the industrial working class would finally reach the point of despair and inevitable revolt, is not the only one that Marx fathered. In at least one essay he gave life to a quite antithetical idea. He described, as a precondition of widespread unrest, not progressive degradation of the proletariat but rather an improvement in workers' economic condition which did not keep pace with the growing welfare of capitalists and therefore produced social tension.

* Reprinted from *American Sociological Review*, 27 (February, 1962), pp. 5–19, by permission of the author and publisher. Several people have made perceptive suggestions and generous comments on an earlier version of this paper. I wish particularly to thank Seymour Martin Lipset, Lucian W. Pye, John H. Schaar, Paul Seabury, and Dwight Waldo.

A noticeable increase in wages presupposes a rapid growth of productive capital. The rapid growth of productive capital brings about an equally rapid growth of wealth, luxury, social wants, social enjoyments. Thus, although the enjoyments of the workers have risen, the social satisfaction that they give has fallen in comparison with the increased enjoyments of the capitalist, which are inaccessible to the worker, in comparison with the state of development of society in general. Our desires and pleasures spring from society; we measure them, therefore, by society and not by the objects which serve for their satisfaction. Because they are of a social nature, they are of a relative nature.[1]

Marx's qualification here of his more frequent belief that degradation produces revolution is expressed as the main thesis by de Tocqueville in his study of the French Revolution. After a long review of economic and social decline in the seventeenth century and dynamic growth in the eighteenth, de Tocqueville concludes:

> So it would appear that the French found their condition the more unsupportable in proportion to its improvement. . . . Revolutions are not always brought about by a gradual decline from bad to worse. Nations that have endured patiently and almost unconsciously the most overwhelming oppression often burst into rebellion against the yoke the moment it begins to grow lighter. The regime which is destroyed by a revolution is almost always an improvement on its immediate predecessor. . . . Evils which are patiently endured when they seem inevitable become intolerable when once the idea of escape from them is suggested.[2]

On the basis of de Tocqueville and Marx, we can choose one of these ideas or the other, which makes it hard to decide just when revolutions are more likely to occur—when there has been social and economic progress or when there has been regress. It appears that both ideas have explanatory and possibly predictive value, if they are juxtaposed and put in the proper time sequence.

Revolutions are most likely to occur when a prolonged period of objective economic and social development is followed by a short period of

1. The *Communist Manifesto* of 1848 evidently antedates the opposing idea by about a year. See Edmund Wilson, *To the Finland Station* (Anchor Books edition), New York: Doubleday & Co. (n.d.), p. 157; Lewis S. Feuer, *Karl Marx and Friedrich Engels: Basic Writings on Politics and Philosophy*, N. Y.: Doubleday & Co., Inc., 1959, p. 1. The above quotation is from Karl Marx and Frederick Engels, "Wage Labour and Capital," *Selected Works in Two Volumes*, Moscow: Foreign Languages Publishing House, 1955, vol. 1, p. 94.
2. A. de Tocqueville, *The Old Regime and the French Revolution* (trans. by John Bonner), N. Y.: Harper & Bros., 1856, p. 214. The Stuart Gilbert translation, Garden City: Doubleday & Co., Inc., 1955, pp. 176–177, gives a somewhat less pungent version of the same comment. *L'Ancien régime* was first published in 1856.

sharp reversal.[3] The all-important effect on the minds of people in a particular society is to produce, during the former period, an expectation of continued ability to satisfy needs—which continue to rise—and, during the latter, a mental state of anxiety and frustration when manifest reality breaks away from anticipated reality. The actual state of socio-economic development is less significant than the expectation that past progress, now blocked, can and must continue in the future.

Political stability and instability are ultimately dependent on a state of mind, a mood, in a society. Satisfied or apathetic people who are poor in goods, status, and power can remain politically quiet and their opposites can revolt, just as, correlatively and more probably, dissatisfied poor can revolt and satisfied rich oppose revolution. It is the dissatisfied state of mind rather than the tangible provision of "adequate" or "inadequate" supplies of food, equality, or liberty which produces the revolution. In actuality, there must be a joining of forces between dissatisfied, frustrated people who differ in their degree of objective, tangible welfare and status. Well-fed, well-educated, high-status individuals who rebel in the face of apathy among the objectively deprived can accomplish at most a coup d'état. The objectively deprived, when faced with solid opposition of people of wealth,

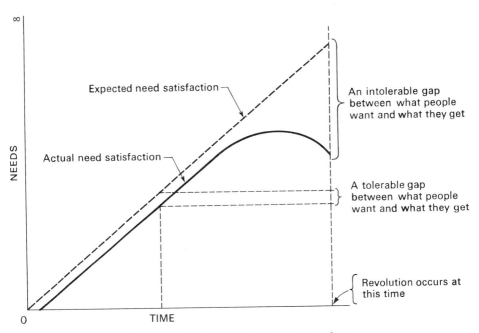

FIGURE 1. *Need Satisfaction and Revolution*

3. Revolutions are here defined as violent civil disturbances that cause the displacement of one ruling group by another that has a broader popular basis for support.

status, and power, will be smashed in their rebellion as were peasants and Anabaptists by German noblemen in 1525 and East Germans by the Communist élite in 1953.

Before appraising this general notion in light of a series of revolutions, a word is in order as to why revolutions ordinarily do not occur when a society is generally impoverished—when, as de Tocqueville put it, evils that seem inevitable are patiently endured. They are endured in the extreme case because the physical and mental energies of people are totally employed in the process of merely staying alive. The Minnesota starvation studies conducted during World War II[4] indicate clearly the constant preoccupation of very hungry individuals with fantasies and thoughts of food. In extremis, as the Minnesota research poignantly demonstrates, the individual withdraws into a life of his own, withdraws from society, withdraws from any significant kind of activity unrelated to staying alive. Reports of behavior in Nazi concentration camps indicate the same preoccupation.[5] In less extreme and barbarous circumstances, where minimal survival is possible but little more, the preoccupation of individuals with staying alive is only mitigated. Social action takes place for the most part on a local, face-to-face basis. In such circumstances the family is a—perhaps the major—solidary unit[6] and even the local community exists primarily to the extent families need to act together to secure their separate survival. Such was life on the American frontier in the sixteenth through nineteenth centuries. In very much attenuated form, but with a substantial degree of social isolation persisting, such evidently is rural life even today. This is clearly related to a relatively low level of political participation in elections.[7] As Zawadzki and Lazarsfeld have indicated,[8] preoccupation with physical survival, even in industrial areas, is a force strongly militating against the establishment of the community-sense and consensus on joint political action which are necessary to induce a revolutionary state of mind. Far from making people into revolutionaries, enduring poverty makes for concern with one's solitary self or solitary family at best and resignation or mute despair at worst. When it is a choice between losing their chains or

---

4. The full report is Ancel Keys *et al.*, *The Biology of Human Starvation*, Minneapolis: University of Minnesota Press, 1950. See J. Brozek, "Semi-starvation and Nutritional Rehabilitation," *Journal of Clinical Nutrition*, 1 (January, 1953), pp. 107–118, for a brief analysis.
5. E. A. Cohen, *Human Behavior in the Concentration Camp*, New York: W. W. Norton & Co., 1953, pp. 123–125, 131–140.
6. For community life in such poverty, in Mezzogiorno Italy, see E. C. Banfield, *The Moral Basis of a Backward Society*, Glencoe, Ill.: The Free Press, 1958. The author emphasizes that the nuclear family is a solidary, consensual, moral unit (see p. 85) but even within it, consensus appears to break down, in outbreaks of pure, individual amorality—notably between parents and children (see p. 117).
7. See Angus Campbell *et al.*, *The American Voter*, New York: John Wiley & Sons, 1960, Chap. 15, "Agrarian Political Behavior."
8. B. Zawadzki and P. F. Lazarsfeld, "The Psychological Consequences of Unemployment," *Journal of Social Psychology*, 6 (May, 1935), pp. 224–251.

their lives, people will mostly choose to keep their chains, a fact which Marx seems to have overlooked.[9]

It is when the chains have been loosened somewhat, so that they can be cast off without a high probability of losing life, that people are put in a condition of proto-rebelliousness. I use the term proto-rebelliousness because the mood of discontent may be dissipated before a violent outbreak occurs. The causes for such dissipation may be natural or social (including economic and political). A bad crop year that threatens a return to chronic hunger may be succeeded by a year of natural abundance. Recovery from sharp economic dislocation may take the steam from the boiler of rebellion.[10] The slow, grudging grant of reforms, which has been the political history of England since at least the Industrial Revolution, may effectively and continuously prevent the degree of frustration that produces revolt.

A revolutionary state of mind requires the continued, even habitual but dynamic expectation of greater opportunity to satisfy basic needs, which may range from merely physical (food, clothing, shelter, health, and safety from bodily harm) to social (the affectional ties of family and friends) to the need for equal dignity and justice. But the necessary additional ingredient is a persistent, unrelenting threat to the satisfaction of these needs: not a threat which actually returns people to a state of sheer survival but which puts them in the mental state where they believe they will not be able to satisfy one or more basic needs. Although physical deprivation in some degree may be threatened on the eve of all revolutions, it need not be the prime factor, as it surely was not in the American Revolution of 1775. The crucial factor is the vague or specific fear that ground gained over a long period of time will be quickly lost. This fear does not generate if there is continued opportunity to satisfy continually emerging needs; it generates when the existing government suppresses or is blamed for suppressing such opportunity.

Three rebellions or revolutions are given considerable attention in the sections that follow: Dorr's Rebellion of 1842, the Russian Revolution of 1917, and the Egyptian Revolution of 1952. Brief mention is then made of several other major civil disturbances, all of which appear to fit the J-curve pattern.[11] After considering these specific disturbances, some general theoretical and research problems are discussed.

---

9. A remarkable and awesome exception to this phenomenon occurred occasionally in some Nazi concentration camps, e.g., in a Buchenwald revolt against capricious rule by criminal prisoners. During this revolt, one hundred criminal prisoners were killed by political prisoners. See Cohen, *op. cit.,* p. 200.
10. See W. W. Rostow, "Business Cycles, Harvests, and Politics: 1790–1850," *Journal of Economic History,* 1 (November, 1941), pp. 206–221, for the relation between economic fluctuation and the activities of the Chartists in the 1830s and 1840s.
11. This curve is of course not to be confused with its prior and altogether different use by Floyd Allport in his study of social conformity. See F. H. Allport, "The J-Curve Hypothesis of Conforming Behavior," *Journal of Social Psychology,* 5 (May, 1934), pp. 141–183, reprinted in T. H. Newcomb & E. L. Hartley, *Readings in Social Psychology,* N.Y.: Henry Holt & Co., 1947, pp. 55–67.

No claim is made that all rebellions follow the pattern, but just that the ones here presented do. All of these are "progressive" revolutions in behalf of greater equality and liberty. The question is open whether the pattern occurs in such markedly retrogressive revolutions as Nazism in Germany or the 1861 Southern rebellion in the United States. It will surely be necessary to examine other progressive revolutions before one can judge how universal the J-curve is. And it will be necessary, in the interests of scientific validation, to examine cases of serious civil disturbance that fell short of producing profound revolution—such as the Sepoy Rebellion of 1857 in India, the Pullman Strike of 1894 in America, the Boxer Rebellion of 1900 in China, and the Great Depression of the 1920s and 1930s as it was experienced in Austria, France, Great Britain, and the United States. The explanation for such still-born rebellions—for revolutions that might have occurred—is inevitably more complicated than for those that come to term in the "normal" course of political gestation.

Dorr's Rebellion of 1842

Dorr's Rebellion[12] in nineteenth-century America was perhaps the first of many civil disturbances to occur in America as a consequence, in part, of the Industrial Revolution. It followed by three years an outbreak in England that had similar roots and a similar program—the Chartist agitation. A machine-operated textile industry was first established in Rhode Island in 1790 and grew rapidly as a consequence of domestic and international demand, notably during the Napoleonic Wars. Jefferson's Embargo Act of 1807, the War of 1812, and a high tariff in 1816 further stimulated American industry.

Rapid industrial growth meant the movement of people from farms to cities. In Massachusetts the practice developed of hiring mainly the wives and daughters of farmers, whose income was thereby supplemented but not displaced by wages. In Rhode Island whole families moved to the cities and became committed to the factory system. When times were good, industrialized families earned two or three times what they got from the soil; when the mills were idle, there was not enough money for bread.[13] From 1807 to 1815 textiles enjoyed great prosperity; from 1834 to 1842 they suffered depression, most severely from 1835 to 1840. Prosperity raised expectations and depression frustrated them, particularly when accompanied by stubborn resistance to suffrage demands that first stirred in 1790 and recurred in a wave-like pattern in 1811 and then in 1818 and 1820

---

12. I am indebted to Beryl L. Crowe for his extensive research on Dorr's Rebellion while he was a participant in my political behavior seminar at the University of California, Berkeley, Spring 1960.
13. Joseph Brennan, *Social Conditions in Industrial Rhode Island: 1820–1860*, Washington, D.C.: Catholic University of America, 1940, p. 33.

following suffrage extension in Connecticut and Massachusetts. The final crest was reached in 1841, when suffrage associations met and called for a constitutional convention.[14]

Against the will of the government, the suffragists held an election in which all adult males were eligible to vote, held a constitutional convention composed of delegates so elected and in December 1841 submitted the People's Constitution to the same electorate, which approved it and the call for an election of state officers the following April, to form a new government under this unconstitutional constitution.[15]

These actions joined the conflict with the established government. When asked—by the dissidents—the state supreme court rendered its private judgment in March 1842 that the new constitution was "of no binding force whatever" and any act "to carry it into effect by force will be treason against the state." The legislature passed what became known as the Algerian law, making it an offense punishable by a year in jail to vote in the April election, and by life imprisonment to hold office under the People's Constitution.

The rebels went stoutly ahead with the election, and on May 3, 1842, inaugurated the new government. The next day the People's legislature met and respectfully requested the sheriff to take possession of state buildings, which he failed to do. Violence broke out on the 17th of May in an attempt to take over a state arsenal with two British cannon left over from the Revolutionary War. When the cannon misfired, the People's government resigned. Sporadic violence continued for another month, resulting in the arrest of over 500 men, mostly textile workers, mechanics, and laborers. The official legislature called for a new constitutional convention, chosen by universal manhood suffrage, and a new constitution went into effect in January, 1843. Altogether only one person was killed in this little revolution, which experienced violence, failure, and then success within the space of nine months.

It is impossible altogether to separate the experience of rising expectations among people in Rhode Island from that among Americans generally. They all shared historically the struggle against a stubborn but ultimately rewarding frontier where their self-confidence gained strength not only in

---

14. The persistent demand for suffrage may be understood in light of election data for 1828 and 1840. In the former year, only 3600 votes were cast in Rhode Island, whose total population was about 94,000. (Of these votes, 23 per cent were cast for Jackson and 77 per cent for Adams, in contrast to a total national division of 56 per cent for Jackson and 44 per cent for Adams.) All votes cast in the 1828 election amount to 4 per cent of the total Rhode Island population and 11 per cent of the total U.S. population excluding slaves. In 1840, with a total population of 109,000 only 8300 votes—8 per cent—were cast in Rhode Island, in contrast to 17 per cent of the national population excluding slaves.
15. A. M. Mowry, *The Dorr War,* Providence, R.I.: Preston & Rounds Co., 1901, p. 114.

the daily process of tilling the soil and harvesting the crops but also by improving their skill at self-government. Winning their war of independence, Americans continued to press for more goods and more democracy. The pursuit of economic expectations was greatly facilitated by the growth of domestic and foreign trade and the gradual establishment of industry. Equalitarian expectations in politics were satisfied and without severe struggle—in most Northern states—by suffrage reforms.

In Rhode Island, these rising expectations—more goods, more equality, more self-rule—were countered by a series of containing forces which built up such a head of steam that the boiler cracked a little in 1842. The textile depression hit hard in 1835 and its consequences were aggravated by the Panic of 1837. In addition to the frustration of seeing their peers get

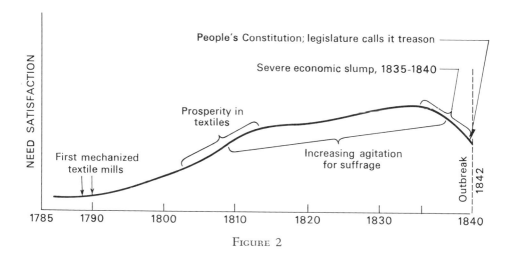

FIGURE 2

the right to vote in other states, poor people in Rhode Island were now beset by industrial dislocation in which the machines that brought them prosperity they had never before enjoyed now were bringing economic disaster. The machines could not be converted to produce food, and in Rhode Island the machine tenders could not go back to the farm.

When they had recovered from the preoccupation with staying alive, they turned in earnest to their demands for constitutional reform. But these were met first with indifference and then by a growing intransigence on the part of the government representing the propertied class. Hostile action by the state supreme court and then the legislature with its Algerian law proved just enough to break briefly the constitutional structure which in stable societies has the measure of power and resilience necessary to absorb social tension.

THE RUSSIAN REVOLUTION OF 1917

In Russia's tangled history it is hard to decide when began the final upsurge of expectations that, when frustrated, produced the cataclysmic events of 1917. One can truly say that the real beginning was the slow modernization process begun by Peter the Great over two hundred years before the revolution. And surely the rationalist currents from France that slowly penetrated Russian intellectual life during the reign of Catherine the Great a hundred years before the revolution were necessary, lineal antecedents of the 1917 revolution.

Without denying that there was an accumulation of forces over at least a 200-year period,[16] we may nonetheless date the final upsurge as beginning with the 1861 emancipation of serfs and reaching a crest in the 1905 revolution.

The chronic and growing unrest of serfs before their emancipation in 1861 is an ironic commentary on the Marxian notion that human beings are what social institutions make them. Although serfdom had been shaping their personality since 1647, peasants became increasingly restive in the second quarter of the nineteenth century.[17] The continued discontent of peasants after emancipation is an equally ironic commentary on the belief that relieving one profound frustration produces enduring contentment. Peasants rather quickly got over their joy at being untied from the soil after two hundred years. Instead of declining, rural violence increased.[18] Having gained freedom but not much free land, peasants now had to rent or buy land to survive: virtual personal slavery was exchanged for financial servitude. Land pressure grew, reflected in a doubling of land prices between 1868 and 1897.

It is hard thus to tell whether the economic plight of peasants was much lessened after emancipation. A 1903 government study indicated that even with a normal harvest, average food intake per peasant was 30 per cent below the minimum for health. The only sure contrary item of evidence is that the peasant population grew, indicating at least increased ability of the land to support life, as the following table shows.

---

16. There is an excellent summary in B. Brutzkus, "The Historical Peculiarities of the Social and Economic Development of Russia," in R. Bendix and S. M. Lipset, *Class, Status, and Power*, Glencoe, Ill.: The Free Press, 1953, pp. 517–540.

17. Jacqueries rose from an average of 8 per year in 1826–30 to 34 per year in 1845–49. T. G. Masaryk, *The Spirit of Russia*, London: Allen and Unwin, Ltd., 1919, vol. 1, p. 130. This long, careful, and rather neglected analysis was first published in German in 1913 under the title *Zur Russischen Geschichts– und Religionsphilosophie*.

18. Jacqueries averaged 350 per year for the first three years after emancipation. *Ibid.*, pp. 140–141.

TABLE 1.   *Population of European Russia (1480–1895)*

	Population in Millions	Increase in Millions	Average Annual Rate of Increase*
1480	2.1	—	—
1580	4.3	2.2	1.05%
1680	12.6	8.3	1.93%
1780	26.8	14.2	1.13%
1880	84.5	57.7	2.15%
1895	110.0	25.5	2.02%

* Computed as follows: dividing the increase by the number of years and then dividing this hypothetical annual increase by the population at the end of the preceding 100-year period.

    Source for gross population data: *Entsiklopedicheskii Slovar*, St. Petersburg, 1897, vol. 40, p. 631. Russia's population was about 97% rural in 1784, 91% in 1878, and 87% in 1897. See Masaryk, *op. cit.*, p. 162n.

The land-population pressure pushed people into towns and cities, where the rapid growth of industry truly afforded the chance for economic betterment. One estimate of net annual income for a peasant family of five in the rich blackearth area in the late nineteenth century was 82 rubles. In contrast, a "good" wage for a male factory worker was about 168 rubles per year. It was this difference in the degree of poverty that produced almost a doubling of the urban population between 1878 and 1897. The number of industrial workers increased almost as rapidly. The city and the factory gave new hope. Strikes in the 1880s were met with brutal suppression but also with the beginning of factory legislation, including the requirement that wages be paid regularly and the abolition of child labor. The burgeoning proletariat remained comparatively contented until the eve of the 1905 revolution.[19]

There is additional, non-economic evidence to support the view that 1861 to 1905 was the period of rising expectations that preceded the 1917 revolution. The administration of justice berfore the emancipation had largely been carried out by noblemen and landowners who embodied the law for their peasants. In 1864 justice was in principle no longer delegated to such private individuals. Trials became public, the jury system was

---

19. The proportion of workers who struck from 1895 through 1902 varied between 1.7 per cent and 4.0 per cent per year. In 1903 the proportion rose to 5.1 per cent but dropped a year later to 1.5 per cent. In 1905 the proportion rose to 163.8 per cent, indicating that the total working force struck, on the average, closer to twice than to once during that portentous year. In 1906 the proportion dropped to 65.8 per cent; in 1907 to 41.9 per cent; and by 1909 was down to a "normal" 3.5 per cent. *Ibid.*, p. 175n.

introduced, and judges got tenure. Corporal punishment was alleviated by the elimination of running the gauntlet, lashing, and branding; caning persisted until 1904. Public joy at these reforms was widespread. For the intelligentsia, there was increased opportunity to think and write and to criticize established institutions, even sacrosanct absolutism itself.

But Tsarist autocracy had not quite abandoned the scene. Having inclined but not bowed, in granting the inevitable emancipation as an act not of justice but grace, it sought to maintain its absolutist principle by conceding reform without accepting anything like democratic authority. Radical political and economic criticism surged higher. Some strong efforts to raise the somewhat lowered floodgates began as early as 1866, after an unsuccessful attempt was made on the life of Alexander II, in whose name serfs had just gained emancipation. When the attempt succeeded fifteen years later, there was increasing state action under Alexander III to limit constantly rising expectations. By suppression and concession, the last Alexander succeeded in dying naturally in 1894.

When it became apparent that Nicholas II shared his father's ideas but not his forcefulness, opposition of the intelligentsia to absolutism joined with the demands of peasants and workers, who remained loyal to the Tsar but demanded economic reforms. Starting in 1904, there developed a "League of Deliverance" that coordinated efforts of at least seventeen other revolutionary, proletarian, or nationalist groups within the empire. Consensus on the need for drastic reform, both political and economic, established a many-ringed circus of groups sharing the same tent. These groups were geographically distributed from Finland to Armenia and ideologically from liberal constitutionalists to revolutionaries made prudent by the contrast between their own small forces and the power of Tsardom.

Events of 1904–5 mark the general downward turning point of expectations, which people increasingly saw as frustrated by the continuation of Tsardom. Two major and related occurrences made 1905 the point of no return. The first took place on the Bloody Sunday of January 22, 1905, when peaceful proletarian petitioners marched on the St. Petersburg palace and were killed by the hundreds. The myth that the Tsar was the gracious protector of his subjects, however surrounded he might be by malicious advisers, was quite shattered. The reaction was immediate, bitter, and prolonged and was not at all confined to the working class. Employers, merchants, and white-collar officials joined in the burgeoning of strikes which brought the economy to a virtual standstill in October. Some employers even continued to pay wages to strikers. University students and faculties joined the revolution. After the great October strike, the peasants ominously sided with the workers and engaged in riots and assaults on landowners. Until peasants became involved, even some landowners had sided with the revolution.

The other major occurrence was the disastrous defeat of the Russian army and navy in the 1904–5 war with Japan. Fundamentally an imperialist venture aspiring to hegemony over the people of Asia, the war was not regarded as a people's but as a Tsar's war, to save and spread absolutism. The military defeat itself probably had less portent than the return of shattered soldiers from a fight that was not for them. Hundreds of thousands, wounded or not, returned from the war as a visible, vocal, and ugly reminder to the entire populace of the weakness and selfishness of Tsarist absolutism.

The years from 1905 to 1917 formed an almost relentless procession of increasing misery and despair. Promising at last a constitutional government, the Tsar, in October, 1905, issued from on high a proclamation renouncing absolutism, granting law-making power to a duma, and guaranteeing freedom of speech, assembly, and association. The first two dumas, of 1906 and 1907, were dissolved for recalcitrance. The third was made pliant by reduced representation of workers and peasants and by the prosecution and conviction of protestants in the first two. The brief period of a free press was succeeded in 1907 by a reinstatement of censorship and confiscation of prohibited publications. Trial of offenders against the Tsar was now conducted by courts martial. Whereas there had been only 26 executions of the death sentence, in the 13 years of Alexander II's firm rule (1881–94), there were 4,449 in the years 1905–10, in six years of Nicholas II's soft regimen.[20]

But this "white terror," which caused despair among the workers and intelligentsia in the cities, was not the only face of misery. For the peasants, there was a bad harvest in 1906 followed by continued crop failures in several areas in 1907. To forestall action by the dumas, Stolypin decreed a series of agrarian reforms designed to break up the power of the rural communes by individualizing land ownership. Between these acts of God and government, peasants were so preoccupied with hunger or self-aggrandizement as to be dulled in their sensitivity to the revolutionary appeals of radical organizers.

After more than five years of degrading terror and misery, in 1910 the country appeared to have reached a condition of exhaustion. Political strikes had fallen off to a new low. As the economy recovered, the insouciance of hopelessness set in. Amongst the intelligentsia the mood was hedonism, or despair that often ended in suicide. Industrialists aligned themselves with the government. Workers worked. But an upturn of expectations, inadequately quashed by the police, was evidenced by a recrudescence of political strikes which, in the first half of 1914—on the eve of war—approached the peak of 1905. They sharply diminished during

---

20. *Ibid.,* p. 189n.

1915 but grew again in 1916 and became a general strike in February 1917.[21]

Figure 3 indicates the lesser waves in the tidal wave whose first trough is at the end of serfdom in 1861 and whose second is at the end of Tsardom in 1917. This fifty-six year period appears to constitute a single long phase in which popular gratification at the termination of one institution (serfdom) rather quickly was replaced with rising expectations which resulted from intensified industrialization and which were incompatible with the continuation of the inequitable and capricious power structure of Tsarist society. The small trough of frustration during the repression that followed the assassination of Alexander II seems to have only briefly interrupted the rise in popular demand for more goods and more power. The trough in 1904 indicates the consequences of war with Japan. The 1905–6 trough reflects the repression of January 22, and after, and is followed by economic recovery. The final downturn, after the first year of war, was a consequence of the dislocations of the German attack on all kinds of concerted activities other than production for the prosecution of the war. Patriotism and governmental repression for a time smothered discontent. The inflation that developed in 1916 when goods, including food, became severely scarce began to make workers self-consciously discontented. The conduct of the war, including the growing brutality against reluctant, ill-provisioned troops, and the enormous loss of life, produced the same bitter frustration in the army.[22] When civilian discontent reached the breaking point in February, 1917, it did not take long for it to spread rapidly into the armed forces. Thus began the second phase of the revolution that really started in 1905 and ended in death to the Tsar and Tsardom—but not to absolutism—when the Bolsheviks gained ascendancy over the moderates in October. A centuries-long history of absolutism appears to have made this post-Tsarist phase of it tragically inevitable.

THE EGYPTIAN REVOLUTION OF 1952

The final slow upsurge of expectations in Egypt that culminated in the revolution began when that society became a nation in 1922, with the British grant of limited independence. British troops remained in Egypt to protect not only the Suez Canal but also, ostensibly, to prevent foreign aggression. The presence of foreign troops served only to heighten national-

---

21. In his *History of the Russian Revolution,* Leon Trotsky presents data on political strikes from 1903 to 1917. In his *Spirit of Russia,* Masaryk presents comparable data from 1905 through 1912. The figures are not identical but the reported yearly trends are consistent. Masaryk's figures are somewhat lower, except for 1912. Cf. Trotsky, *op. cit.,* Doubleday Anchor Books ed., 1959, p. 32, and Masaryk, *op. cit. supra,* p. 197n.
22. See Trotsky, *op. cit.,* pp. 18–21, for a vivid picture of rising discontent in the army.

ist expectations, which were excited by the Wafd, the political organization that formed public opinion on national rather than religious grounds and helped establish a fairly unified community—in striking contrast to late-nineteenth century Russia.

But nationalist aspirations were not the only rising expectations in Egypt of the 1920s and 1930s. World War I had spurred industrialization, which opened opportunities for peasants to improve, somewhat, their way of life by working for wages in the cities and also opened great opportunities for entrepreneurs to get rich. The moderately wealthy got immoderately so in commodity market speculation, finance, and manufacture, and the uprooted peasants who were now employed, or at any rate living, in cities were relieved of at least the notion that poverty and boredom must

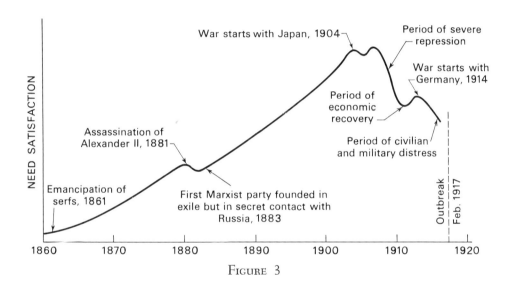

FIGURE 3

be the will of Allah. But the incongruity of a money-based modern semi-feudality that was like a chariot with a gasoline engine evidently escaped the attention of ordinary people. The generation of the 1930s could see more rapid progress, even for themselves, than their parents had even envisioned. If conditions remained poor, they could always be blamed on the British, whose economic and military power remained visible and strong.

Economic progress continued, though unevenly, during World War II. Conventional exports, mostly cotton, actually declined, not even reaching depression levels until 1945, but direct employment by Allied military forces reached a peak of over 200,000 during the most intense part of the African war. Exports after the war rose steadily until 1948, dipped, and then rose sharply to a peak in 1951 as a consequence of the Korean war. But in 1945 over 250,000 wage earners[23]—probably over a third of the working force—became jobless. The cost of living by 1945 had risen to three times the index of 1937.[24] Manual laborers were hit by unemployment; white collar workers and professionals probably more by inflation than unemployment. Meanwhile the number of millionaires in pounds sterling had increased eight times during the war.[25]

Frustrations, exacerbated during the war by German and thereafter by Soviet propaganda, were at first deflected against the British[26] but gradually shifted closer to home. Egyptian agitators began quoting the Koran in favor of a just, equalitarian society and against great differences in individual wealth. There was an ominous series of strikes, mostly in the textile mills, from 1946–8.

At least two factors stand out in the postponement of revolution. The first was the insatiable postwar world demand for cotton and textiles and the second was the surge of solidarity with king and country that followed the 1948 invasion of the new state of Israel. Israel now supplemented England as an object of deflected frustration. The disastrous defeat a year later, by a new nation with but a fifteenth of Egypt's population, was the beginning of the end. This little war had struck the peasant at his hearth, when a shortage of wheat and of oil for stoves provided a daily reminder of a weak and corrupt government. The defeat frustrated popular hopes for national glory and—with even more portent—humiliated the army and solidified it against the bureaucracy and the palace which had profiteered at the expense of national honor. In 1950 began for the first time a direct and open propaganda attack against the king himself. A series of peasant uprisings, even on the lands of the king, took place in 1951 along with some 49 strikes in the cities. The skyrocketing demand for cotton after the start of the Korean War in June, 1950 was followed by a collapse in March, 1952. The uncontrollable or uncontrolled riots in Cairo, on January 26, 1952, marked the fiery start of the revolution. The officers' coup in the early morning of July 23 only made it official.

---

23. C. Issawi, *Egypt at Mid-Century: An Economic Survey,* London: Oxford University Press, 1954, p. 262. J. & S. Lacouture in their *Egypt in Transition,* New York: Criterion Books, 1958, p. 100, give a figure of over 300,000. Sir R. Bullard, editor, *The Middle East: A Political and Economic Survey,* London: Oxford University Press, 1958, p. 221, estimates total employment in industry, transport, and commerce in 1957 to have been about 750,000.
24. International Monetary Fund, *International Financial Statistics,* Washington, D.C. See monthly issues of this report, 1950–53.
25. J. and S. Lacouture, *op. cit.,* p. 99.
26. England threatened to depose Farouk in February 1942, by force if necessary, if Egypt did not support the Allies. Capitulation by the government and the Wafd caused widespread popular disaffection. When Egypt finally declared war on the Axis in 1945, the prime minister was assassinated. See J. & S. Lacouture, *op. cit.,* pp. 97–98, and Issawi, *op. cit.,* p. 268.

Other Civil Disturbances

The J-curve of rising expectations followed by their effective frustration is applicable to other revolutions and rebellions than just the three already considered. Leisler's Rebellion in the royal colony of New York in 1689 was a brief dress-rehearsal for the American Revolution eighty-six years later. In an effort to make the colony serve the crown better, duties had been rasied and were being vigorously collected. The tanning of hides in the colony was forbidden, as was the distillation of liquor. An embargo was placed on unmilled grain, which hurt the farmers. After a long period of economic growth and substantial political autonomy, these new and burdensome regulations produced a popular rebellion that for a year displaced British sovereignty.[27]

The American Revolution itself fits the J-curve and deserves more than the brief mention here given. Again prolonged economic growth and political autonomy produced continually rising expectations. They became acutely frustrated when, following the French and Indian War (which had cost England so much and the colonies so little), England began a series of largely economic regulations having the same purpose as those directed against New York in the preceding century. From the 1763 Proclamation (closing to settlement land west of the Appalachians) to the Coercive Acts of April, 1774 (which among other things, in response to the December, 1773, Boston Tea Party, closed tight the port of Boston), Americans were beset with unaccustomed manifestations of British power and began to resist forcibly in 1775, on the Lexington-Concord road. A significant decline in trade with England in 1772[28] may have hastened the maturation of colonial rebelliousness.

The curve also fits the French Revolution, which again merits more mention than space here permits. Growing rural prosperity, marked by steadily rising land values in the eighteenth century, had progressed to the point where a third of French land was owned by peasant-proprietors. There were the beginnings of large-scale manufacture in the factory system. Constant pressure by the bourgeoisie against the state for reforms was met with considerable hospitality by a government already shifting from its old landed-aristocratic and clerical base to the growing middle class. Counter to these trends, which would *per se* avoid revolution, was the feudal reaction of the mid-eighteenth century, in which the dying nobility sought in numerous nagging ways to retain and reactivate its perquisites against a resentful peasantry and importunate bourgeoisie.

---

27. See J. R. Reich, *Leisler's Rebellion,* Chicago: University of Chicago Press, 1953.
28. See U.S. Bureau of the Census, *Historical Statistics of the United States, Colonial Times to 1957,* Washington, D.C., 1960, p. 757.

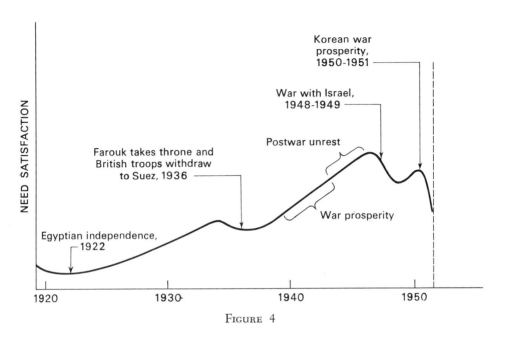

FIGURE 4

But expectations apparently continued rising until the growing opportunities and prosperity rather abruptly halted, about 1787. The fiscal crisis of the government is well known, much of it a consequence of a 1.5 billion livre deficit following intervention against Britain in the American war of independence. The threat to tax the nobility severely—after its virtual tax immunity—and the bourgeoisie more severely may indeed be said to have precipitated the revolution. But less well-known is the fact that 1787 was a bad harvest year and 1788 even worse; that by July, 1789 bread prices were higher than they had been in over 70 years; that an ill-timed trade treaty with England depressed the prices of French textiles; that a concurrent bumper grape crop depressed wine prices—all with the result of making desperate the plight of the large segment of the population now dependent on other producers for food. They had little money to buy even less bread. Nobles and bourgeoisie were alienated from the government by the threat of taxation; workers and some peasants by the threat of starvation. A long period of halting but real progress for virtually all segments of the population was now abruptly ended in consequence of the government's efforts to meet its deficit and of economic crisis resulting from poor crops and poor tariff policy.[29]

---

29. See G. Lefebvre, *The Coming of the French Revolution,* Princeton: Princeton University Press, 1947, pp. 101–109, 145–148, 196. G. Le Bon, *The Psychology of Revolution,* New York: G. Putnam's Sons, 1913, p. 143.

The draft riots that turned the city of New York upside down for five days in July, 1863, also follow the J-curve. This severe local disturbance began when conscription threatened the lives and fortunes of workingmen whose enjoyment of wartime prosperity was now frustrated not only by military service (which could be avoided by paying $300 or furnishing a substitute—neither means being available to poor people) but also by inflation.[30]

Even the riots in Nyasaland, in February and March, 1959, appear to follow the pattern of a period of frustration after expectations and satisfactions have risen. Nyasaland workers who had enjoyed the high wages they were paid during the construction of the Kariba dam in Rhodesia returned to their homes and to unemployment, or to jobs paying $5 per month at a time when $15 was considered a bare minimum wage.[31]

One negative case—of a revolution that did not occur—is the depression of the 1930s in the United States. It was severe enough, at least on economic grounds, to have produced a revolution. Total national private production income in 1932 reverted to what it had been in 1916. Farm income in the same year was as low as in 1900; manufacturing as low as in 1913. Construction had not been as low since 1908. Mining and quarrying was back at the 1909 level.[32] For much of the population, two decades of economic progress had been wiped out. There were more than sporadic demonstrations of unemployed, hunger marchers, and veterans. In New York City, at least 29 people died of starvation. Poor people could vividly contrast their own past condition with the present—and their own present condition with that of those who were not seriously suffering. There were clearly audible rumbles of revolt. Why, then, no revolution?

Several forces worked strongly against it. Among the most depressed, the mood was one of apathy and despair, like that observed in Austria by Zawadzki and Lazarsfeld. It was not until the 1936 election that there was an increased turnout in the national election. The great majority of the public shared a set of values which since 1776 had been official dogma— not the dissident program of an alienated intelligentsia. People by and large were in agreement, whether or not they had succeeded economically, in a belief in individual hard work, self-reliance, and the promise of success. (Among workers, this non-class orientation had greatly impeded the establishment of trade unions, for example.) Those least hit by the depression— the upper-middle class businessmen, clergymen, lawyers, and intellectuals—remained rather solidly committed not only to equalitarian values

---

30. The account by Irving Werstein, *July 1863*, New York: Julian Messner, Inc., 1957, is journalistic but to my knowledge the fullest yet available.
31. E. S. Munger, "The Tragedy of Nyasaland," American Universities Field Staff Reports Service, vol. 7, no. 4 (August 1, 1959), p. 9.
32. See U.S. Bureau of the Census, *Historical Statistics of the United States: 1789– 1945*, Washington, D.C.: 1949, p. 14.

and to the established economic system but also to constitutional processes. There was no such widespread or profound alienation as that which had cracked the loyalty of the nobility, clergy, bourgeoisie, armed forces, and intelligentsia in Russia. And the national political leadership that emerged had constitutionalism almost bred in its bones. The major threat to constitutionalism came in Louisiana; this leadership was unable to capture a national party organization, in part because Huey Long's arbitrariness and demagogy were mistrusted.

The major reason that revolution did not nonetheless develop probably remains the vigor with which the national government attacked the depression in 1933, when it became no longer possible to blame the government. The ambivalent popular hostility to the business community was contained by both the action of government against the depression and the government's practice of publicly and successfully eliciting the cooperation of businessmen during the crucial months of 1933. A failure then of cooperation could have intensified rather than lessened popular hostility to business. There was no longer an economic or a political class that could be the object of widespread intense hatred because of its indifference or hostility to the downtrodden. Had Roosevelt adopted a demagogic stance in the 1932 campaign and gained the loyalty to himself personally of the Army and the F.B.I., there might have been a Nazi-type "revolution," with a potpourri of equalitarian reform, nationalism, imperialism, and domestic scapegoats. Because of a conservatism in America stemming from strong and long attachment to a value system shared by all classes, an anticapitalist, leftist revolution in the 1930s is very difficult to imagine.

SOME CONCLUSIONS

The notion that revolutions need both a period of rising expectations and a succeeding period in which they are frustrated qualifies substantially the main Marxian notion that revolutions occur after progressive degradation and the de Tocqueville notion that they occur when conditions are improving. By putting de Tocqueville before Marx but without abandoning either theory, we are better able to plot the antecedents of at least the disturbances here described.

Half of the general, if not common, sense of this revised notion lies in the utter improbability of a revolution occurring in a society where there is the continued, unimpeded opportunity to satisfy new needs, new hopes, new expectations. Would Dorr's Rebellion have become such if the established electorate and government had readily acceded to the suffrage demands of the unpropertied? Would the Russian Revolution have taken place if the Tsarist autocracy had, quite out of character, truly granted the popular demands for constitutional democracy in 1905? Would the Cairo riots of January, 1952, and the subsequent coup actually have occurred if Britain had departed from Egypt and if the Egyptian monarchy had established an equitable tax system and in other ways alleviated the poverty of urban masses and the shame of the military?

The other half of the sense of the notion has to do with the improbability of revolution taking place where has been no hope, no period in which expectations have risen. Such a stability of expectations presupposes a static state of human aspirations that sometimes exists but is rare. Stability of expectations is not a stable social condition. Such was the case of American Indians (at least from our perspective) and perhaps Africans before white men with Bibles, guns, and other goods interrupted the stability of African society. Egypt was in such a condition, vis-à-vis modern aspirations, before Europe became interested in building a canal. Such stasis was the case in Nazi concentration camps, where conformism reached the point of inmates cooperating with guards even when the inmates were told to lie down so that they could be shot.[33] But in the latter case there was a society with externally induced complete despair, and even in these camps there were occasional rebellions of sheer desperation. It is of course true that in a society less regimented than concentration camps, the rise of expectations can be frustrated successfully, thereby defeating rebellion just as the satisfaction of expectations does. This, however, requires the uninhibited exercise of brute force as it was used in suppressing the Hungarian rebellion of 1956. Failing the continued ability and persistent will of a ruling power to use such force, there appears to be no sure way to avoid revolution short of an effective, affirmative, and continuous response on the part of established governments to the almost continuously emerging needs of the governed.

To be predictive, my notion requires the assessment of the state of mind—or more precisely, the mood—of a people. This is always difficult, even by techniques of systematic public opinion analysis. Respondents interviewed in a country with a repressive government are not likely to be responsive. But there has been considerable progress in gathering first-hand data about the state of mind of peoples in politically unstable circumstances. One instance of this involved interviewing in West Berlin, during and after the 1948 blockade, as reported by Buchanan and Cantril. They were able to ascertain, however crudely, the sense of security that people in Berlin felt. There was a significant increase in security after the blockade.[34]

Another instance comes out of the Middle Eastern study conducted by

---

33. Eugen Kogon, *The Theory and Practice of Hell,* New York: Farrar, Straus & Co., 1950, pp. 284–286.

34. W. Buchanan, "Mass Communication in Reverse," *International Social Science Bulletin,* 5 (1953), pp. 577–583, at p. 578. The full study is W. Buchanan and H. Cantril, *How Nations See Each Other,* Urbana: University of Illinois Press, 1953, esp. pp. 85–90.

the Columbia University Bureau of Applied Social Research and reported by Lerner.[35] By directly asking respondents whether they were happy or unhappy with the way things had turned out in their life, the interviewers turned up data indicating marked differences in the frequency of a sense of unhappiness between countries and between "traditional," "transitional," and "modern" individuals in these countries.[36] There is no technical reason why such comparisons could not be made chronologically as well as they have been geographically.

Other than interview data are available with which we can, from past experience, make reasonable inferences about the mood of a people. It was surely the sense for the relevance of such data that led Thomas Masaryk before the first World War to gather facts about peasant uprisings and industrial strikes and about the writings and actions of the intelligentsia in nineteenth-century Russia. In the present report, I have used not only such data—in the collection of which other social scientists have been less assiduous than Masaryk—but also such indexes as comparative size of vote as between Rhode Island and the United States, employment, exports, and cost of living. Some such indexes, like strikes and cost of living, may be rather closely related to the mood of a people; others, like value of exports, are much cruder indications. Lest we shy away from the gathering of crude data, we should bear in mind that Durkheim developed his remarkable insights into modern society in large part by his analysis of suicide rates. He was unable to rely on the interviewing technique. We need not always ask people whether they are grievously frustrated by their government; their actions can tell us as well and sometimes better.

In his *Anatomy of Revolution,* Crane Brinton describes "some tentative uniformities" that he discovered in the Puritan, American, French, and Russian revolutions.[37] The uniformities were: an economically advancing society, class antagonism, desertion of intellectuals, inefficient government, a ruling class that has lost self-confidence, financial failure of government, and the inept use of force against rebels. All but the last two of these are long-range phenomena that lend themselves to studies over extended time periods. The first two lend themselves to statistical analysis. If they serve the purpose, techniques of content analysis could be used to ascertain trends in alienation of intellectuals. Less rigorous methods would perhaps serve bettter to ascertain the effectiveness of government and the self-confidence of rulers. Because tensions and frustrations are present at all times in every society, what is most seriously needed are data that cover an

---

35. Daniel Lerner, *The Passing of Traditional Society,* Glencoe, Ill.: Free Press, 1958.
36. *Ibid.,* pp. 101–103. See also F. P. Kilpatrick & H. Cantril, "Self-Anchoring Scaling, A Measure of Individuals' Unique Reality Words," *Journal of Individual Psychology,* 16 (November, 1960), pp. 158–173.
37. See the revised edition of 1952 as reprinted by Vintage Books, Inc., 1957, pp. 264–275.

extended time period in a particular society, so that one can say there is evidence that tension is greater or less than it was N years or months previously.

We need also to know how long is a long cycle of rising expectations and how long is a brief cycle of frustration. We noted a brief period of frustration in Russia after the 1881 assassination of Alexander II and a longer period after the 1904 beginning of the Russo-Japanese War. Why did not the revolution occur at either of these times rather than in 1917? Had expectations before these two times not risen high enough? Had the subsequent decline not been sufficiently sharp and deep? Measuring techniques have not yet been devised to answer these questions. But their unavailability now does not forecast their eternal inaccessibility. Physicists devised useful temperature scales long before they came as close to absolute zero as they have recently in laboratory conditions. The far more complex problems of scaling in social science inescapably are harder to solve.

We therefore are still not at the point of being able to predict revolution, but the closer we can get to data indicating by inference the prevailing mood in a society, the closer we will be to understanding the change from gratification to frustration in people's minds. That is the part of the anatomy, we are forever being told with truth and futility, in which wars and revolutions always start. We should eventually be able to escape the embarrassment that may have come to Lenin six weeks after he made the statement in Switzerland, in January, 1917, that he doubted whether "we, the old [will] live to see the decisive battles of the coming revolution."[38]

Explorations in the Theory of Social Movements and Revolutions[*]

JAMES A. GESCHWENDER

James C. Davies made a first step toward formulating a theory of societal conditions which tend to produce revolutions.[1] His formulation is limited in two ways. First, Davies overly restricted himself by limiting his

38. Quoted in E. H. Carr, *A History of Soviet Russia,* vol. 1, *The Bolshevik Revolution: 1917–23,* London: Macmillan, 1950, p. 69.
* Reprinted from *Social Forces,* 46 (June, 1968), pp. 477–483, by permission of the author and publisher. I am indebted to Frederick B. Waisanen for the hours of discussion which gave rise to many of the ideas included herein. I am also indebted to William A. Rushing, Lewis M. Killian, and Leland Axelson for the careful reading of an earlier version and the useful suggestions which they made.
1. James C. Davies, "Toward a Theory of Revolution," *American Sociological Review,* 27 (February 1962), pp. 5–18.

concern to "progressive" revolutions rather than analyzing the preconditions for revolutions of either a leftist or rightist direction. As a result, he formulated a statement of a set of preconditions which may be a special case of a more general set which would produce revolutions of either type.

The second limitation arises from his failure to distinguish between two separate but related problems. One may attempt to ascertain those factors which dispose specific individuals or types of individuals to take part in revolutionary activity or one may attempt to ascertain those factors which produce a revolution at a particular time and place. These two problems require different types of information. The former requires a theory of motivation which predicts that individuals experiencing certain specified conditions will manifest the behavioral response of revolutionary activity. It would further require the ability to document the existence of instantiations or examples of the classes of preconditions called for in the motivational theory.

The second problem requires an explanation in terms of conditions which disrupt the normal societal or institutional processes operating at a given time. One may tie the two problems together by assuming that revolutions occurring at a particular time and place are the final product of intra- and inter-individual expressions of revolutionary activity of sufficient intensity. If one makes this assumption, it follows that *conditions which produce a revolution are no different in principle from those which produce a smaller or even an unsuccessful protest movement.* The major difference between the two would be in the numbers of individuals aroused to revolutionary activity and in those processes which develop after the protest movement has begun. The present analysis will parallel Davies as it will be limited to the initial conditions producing a movement.

The Rise and Drop Hypothesis

Let us examine the structure of the argument put forth by Davies. He explicitly focused on the problem of specification of conditions that produce a revolution at a particular time and place. But the structure of his reasoning is focused upon the manner in which specific sets of objective conditions impinge upon individuals or types of individuals and motivate them to take part in revolutionary activities. He states his reasoning as follows:

> Revolutions are most likely to occur when a prolonged period of objective economic and social development is followed by a short period of sharp reversal. The all-important effect on the minds of people in a particular society is to produce, during the former period, an expectation of con-

tinued ability to satisfy needs—which continue to rise—and, during the latter, a mental state of anxiety and frustration when manifest reality breaks away from anticipated reality. *The actual state of socioeconomic development is less significant than the expectation that past progress, now blocked, can and must continue in the future.*[2]

The conclusion that actual conditions of deprivation are less important than the development of a particular state of mind wherein one believes that he is unjustly deprived relative to another possible state of affairs is consistent with the earlier writings of L. P. Edwards[3] and Crane Brinton.[4] The suggestion that this state of mind may be produced by a period of progress followed by a sharp reversal is well documented in Davies' analysis of Dorr's Rebellion, the Russian Revolution, the Egyptian Revolution, and numerous other civil disorders. However, Davies' preoccupation with the point at which revolution begins led to overlooking the fact that his own data suggest the existence of other patterns which would also produce this state of mind.

ALTERNATIVE PATTERNS: THE RISING EXPECTATIONS HYPOTHESIS

Davies included a diagram of the period preceding Dorr's Rebellion.[5] This illustrates the fact that the rebellion broke out in 1842 after just such an improvement and decline in socio-economic conditions as predicted. However, the earlier period is of considerable interest. Davies labeled the period from about 1812 to about 1838 as a period of increased agitation for suffrage. This period of increased agitation represents a period of protest— the beginning of a protest movement—which results from the same state of mind that produces revolutionary activity. The individuals who are engaged in protest and agitation are doing so because they perceive an intolerable gap between a state of affairs believed possible and desirable and a state of affairs actually existing. This perception of an intolerable gap did not result from the curve of economic development proposed by Davies but rather from a simple decline in the rate of social and economic progress. The diagram shows a continued increase in the level of need satisfaction from 1812 to 1835 but at a slower rate of increase than had occurred from 1790 to 1810. In short, the mere decline in the rate of improvement in the

---

2. *Ibid.*, p. 6 (italics added for emphasis).
3. Lyford P. Edwards, *The Natural History of Revolution* (Chicago: University of Chicago Press, 1927).
4. Crane Brinton, *The Anatomy of Revolution* (New York: W. W. Norton & Co., 1938).
5. Davies, *op. cit.*, p. 9.

level of need satisfaction was sufficient to produce a gap between expectations and experience great enough to be considered intolerable by some.

This pattern of development of a gap between level of need satisfaction and expected level of need satisfaction appears to be a slight variant of the pattern suggested for the French Revolution by de Tocqueville,[6] and also suggested by Edwards,[7] and Crane Brinton[8] in their studies of commonalities in the Puritan, French, Russian, and American revolutions. They state that the experiencing of a period of improvement yields the expectation of, and desire for, further improvements. When these come too slowly, rebellion follows.

It seems that this scheme could be used to account for a portion of the protest activities on the part of Negroes in American society today. One could say that the improvement in general social conditions as evidenced by a certain amount of school integration, improved opportunities to vote, etc., have led many American Negroes to believe that progress is possible. They have experienced some acceptance into American life and expect to receive more. Once given this hope of full participation they become dissatisfied with the rather slow rate of change which may be observed. They see school integration, but only on a token basis; they see the loosening of many restrictions, but in such a slow rate that they become concerned that their shackles will never be completely thrown off. As they become increasingly impatient with the rate of improvement in social conditions, they begin to resort more and more to direct action, to sit-ins, wade-ins, etc.[9]

THE RELATIVE DEPRIVATION HYPOTHESIS

Marx suggested that workers become restless and eventually revolt after experiencing a similar improvement in the material conditions of their lives.[10] He suggested that workers develop the standards for their desired and expected level of need satisfaction from the level that they see prevailing throughout society. Their desired level of need satisfaction rises at a pace equivalent to the rate of improved living standards for the rest of society so that, despite an improvement in the objective level of need satisfactions, there is an increasing gap between what the workers feel they should get and what they actually receive. This gap grows until the workers revolt. In this case, the level of expected need satisfaction derives from perception of the level of need satisfaction experienced by a reference group.

---

6. Cited in *ibid.,* pp. 5–6.
7. Edwards, *op. cit.,* pp. 34–35.
8. Brinton, *op. cit.,* p. 286 and pp. 78–79.
9. Cf. Dan Wakefield, *Revolt in the South* (New York: Grove Press, 1960).
10. Cited in Davies, *op. cit.,* p. 5.

The current Negro revolt has been explained in terms of relative deprivation.[11] Many Negroes believe that Negroes are improving their objective position in American society but they are not gaining relative to whites. They use the metaphor of a train starting from New York to California and say that while they have reached Chicago they are still riding in the caboose and maybe the train has grown longer. In other words, the Negro today is better off than his grandfather but so is the white, and possibly the gap between Negro and white has increased. Thus, dissatisfaction results and leads to protest activities.

THE DOWNWARD MOBILITY HYPOTHESIS

While he did not study social revolutions, implications regarding the nature of the process of development of discrepancies between aspirations and need satisfactions may be drawn from Durkheim's classic study of suicide.[12] Durkheim's analysis of the development of anomie revolved around the relationship between needs (goals) and means of satisfying these needs. He assumed that satisfaction is a result of balance between needs and means of need satisfaction. Dissatisfaction results whenever needs exceed the means of need satisfaction. These needs may be dichotomized into organic and nonorganic needs. The former are limited in an absolute sense, while the latter are unlimited by nature. One's position in the stratification system places a limit upon aspirations and therefore maintains a balance between needs and need satisfactions.

Durkheim contended that the individual is in trouble whenever anything happens to disrupt this balance between needs and satisfactions. He will be frustrated whenever his desires exceed his achievements. A sudden improvement in wealth or power of the type that is expected to precede revolutions stimulates aspirations causing them to grow beyond means of satisfaction.

But improvements in status were not the only means envisioned by Durkheim whereby the balance between needs (aspirations) and means of satisfaction would be upset. He also stated that economic disasters upset the balance. Disasters declassify individuals, forcing them into a lower state than their previous one. This necessitates the painful process of reducing aspirations or needs to the level of possible need fulfillment. This is just as painful and disorienting a process as that which results from sudden improvement in one's position. It seems that this particular type of imbalance could also be brought about through downward social mobility in either an absolute or a relative sense.

---

11. James A. Geschwender, "The Negro Revolt: An Examination of Some Hypotheses," *Social Forces,* 43 (December 1964), pp. 248–256.
12. Emile Durkheim, *Suicide* (Glencoe, Illinois: The Free Press, 1951).

Relative downward mobility refers to the felt loss of status experienced by a group which observes a previously inferior group closing the gap between them. Killian points out that southern whites who have migrated to Chicago feel a loss of status relative to Negroes despite the fact that they have experienced an objective improvement in economic conditions.[13] This type of imbalance between reality and desire is as likely to produce a social movement or revolution as the types discussed above.[14]

There are sufficient empirical data to support the notion that rebelliousness may grow out of a decline in one's objective material position. Lipset's analysis of the rise of the C.C.F. (an agrarian socialist political party) in Saskatchewan is a case in point.[15] Lipset interpreted the C.C.F. as the culmination of a class-conscious movement on the part of Canadian wheat farmers. He suggested that the C.C.F. received its earliest and most consistent support from those groups in the rural population who had the highest social and economic status. By this he meant that they had the largest farms and were least likely to be tenants. The poorer farmers were more difficult to organize during the Thirties. However, once they were organized they turned out to be the movement's staunchest supporters during the war years. The Thirties were times of severe depression and the war years were prosperous times for the wheat farmers.

It is possible to reanalyze Lipset's findings with a view toward determining what happened during the Depression and how this led to the development of the movement. Historically, wheat farmers have an insecure income. They fluctuate between good and bad times depending upon the price of wheat. All farmers are not equally affected by economic fluctuations, as is especially revealed by the Depression. "In the first period, 1929–31, the small farms had a net cash income but increases in the size of the farm were accompanied by a declining income until at 500 acres no Net Cash Income and increasingly larger operating losses resulted for the larger farms."[16]

The wealthier farmers during the Depression experienced a rapid and sharp decline in their economic position in both absolute terms and relative to the poorer farmers. This decline relative to their previous high position (which we may assume they preferred) led to their organization and participation in the C.C.F. The poorer farmers did not become strong supporters until they experienced a rapid improvement in their objective

---

13. Lewis M. Killian, "The Adjustment of Southern White Migrants to Northern Urban Norms," *Social Forces,* 32 (October 1953), p. 61.
14. For a discussion of such countermovements see Ralph H. Turner and Lewis M. Killian, *Collective Behavior* (Englewood Cliffs, New Jersey: Prentice-Hall, 1957), pp. 382–384; Lewis M. Killian, "The Purge of an Agitator," *Social Problems,* 7 (Fall 1959), pp. 152–156; and James W. Vander Zanden, "Resistance and Social Movements," *Social Forces,* 37 (May 1959), pp. 212–315.
15. Seymour M. Lipset, *Agrarian Socialism* (Berkeley: University of California Press, 1950).
16. *Ibid.,* p. 91, quoted from William Allen and E. C. Hope, *The Farm Outlook for Saskatchewan* (Saskatchewan: University of Saskatchewan, 1934), p. 2.

economic status. They engaged in protest activity only after it had been demonstrated that this type of activity could bring about objective improvements. They were responding not only to the improvements, but also to the example set by the wealthier wheat farmers. The wealthier farmers protested in response to a deteriorating objective state and, in turn, acted as agitators in stimulating unrest and protest activities in others.

The American Populist Movement seems to have been produced by the same type of situation that gave rise to the C.C.F. Draper described the Populists as, "property-conscious farmers threatened with debt and bankruptcy."[17] Kornhauser suggests that the Italian Fascist and German Nazi movements drew heavily from individuals who had undergone a decline in their objective economic position. It is not unreasonable to assume that they looked back to their former positions as desirable and proper.[18] Therefore, they perceived themselves as experiencing an "intolerable gap" between their proper level of need satisfaction and their actual level. This experience led them to participate in a revolutionary protest movement.

THE STATUS INCONSISTENCY HYPOTHESIS

All of the patterns of conditions likely to produce protest or revolution discussed above have had temporal change as an essential element. They all analyzed the manner in which changes in one's position over time give rise to a belief in the possibility and justice of an improvement in circumstances. The difference between desired and actual circumstances is what leads to revolutionary or protest activity. The concept of status consistency, developed by Lenski, makes possible the analysis of a nontemporal source of this discrepancy.[19]

Broom agreed that status inconsistents may make up the membership of a social movement and gives the concept special relevance for ethnic minorities.[20] He suggested that an aggregate with a low degree of stratum consistency, i.e., a number of persons having similar patterns of inconsistency, may develop ethnic-consciousness. He predicted that tension will be

---

17. Theodore Draper, *The Roots of American Communism* (New York: Viking Press, 1957), p. 37.
18. William Kornhauser, *The Politics of Mass Society* (Glencoe, Illinois: The Free Press, 1959), p. 181. For a similar interpretation see also Emile Benoit-Smullyan, "Status, Status Types, and Status Interrelations," *American Sociological Review*, 9 (April 1944), pp. 353–359.
19. Gerhard Lenski, "Status Crystallization: A Non-Vertical Dimension of Social Status," *American Sociological Review*, 19 (August 1954), pp. 405–413. For a summary of some of the literature on the relationship between status inconsistency and participation in social movements see James A. Geschwender, "Continuities in Theories of Status Consistency and Cognitive Dissonance," *Social Forces*, 46 (December 1967), pp. 165–167.
20. Leonard Broom, "Social Differentiation and Stratification," in Robert K. Merton, Leonard Broom, and Leonard S. Cottrell (eds.), *Sociology Today* (New York: Basic Books, 1959), pp. 429–441.

positively associated with low attribute consistency. This is based on the assumption that an erratic profile will reflect areas of blockage of mobility opportunities. If a group's mobility were strictly determined by the abilities and initiative of its individual members, it would be expected to move up in all status hierarchies at corresponding rates. If their mobility in one dimension lags behind others it indicates the existence of impediments to free mobility. These impediments tend to create tensions which could produce protest activity. Status inconsistent members of minority groups have been found to participate in social movements, such as the N.A.A.C.P., Europe Socialist parties, and the C.C.F. in Canada.[21]

Sorokin used the concept of "multibonded stratification" to analyze the relation between status inconsistency and revolutionary behavior.[22] He considered stratification in terms of a number of status dimensions that are bonded or welded together to form affine or disaffine strata. Affine strata are defined as those groups whose multiple bonds are mutually congenial and lead the members of such groups to the same type of behavior or mentality. Disaffine strata are those whose bonds are innerly contradictory. This would include groups who are high occupationally but low racially or ethnically, or high on the racial ethnic dimension but low in economic status, as well as other combinations. Sorokin emphasized that these disaffine strata are not rare or exotic. They tend to appear quite frequently, though less frequently than affine strata. He further states that the disaffine strata are unstable and tend to decompose rapidly to be replaced by a new affine coalescence of the stratifying bonds.

The simultaneous appearance in a population of two double disaffine groups is a symptom which portends revolutionary change. Sorokin stated that the French Revolution was a perfect example of this. The nobility was a politically powerful group which had little economic wealth, while the third estate was a wealthy group virtually powerless in the political arena. The French Revolution was the decomposition of these two double disaffine strata and the creation of two new affine strata. Sorokin claimed that similar sets of circumstances prevailed in the case of the Russian Revolution of 1905, the Communist Revolution, and numerous other examples.

TOWARD A GENERAL THEORY OF SOCIAL MOVEMENTS

The empirical relationship between status inconsistency and propensity toward revolutionary or protest activities is documented above. However, each of the temporal hypotheses included a rationale which accounted for

---

21. Cf. E. Franklin Frazier, *Black Bourgeoisie* (Glencoe, Illinois: The Free Press, 1959), pp. 98–104; Robert Michels, *Political Parties* (New York: Dover Publications, 1959), pp. 260–261; and Lipset, *op. cit.*, p. 191.
22. Pitirim A. Sorokin, *Society, Culture and Personality* (New York: Harper & Brothers, 1947), pp. 289–294.

the development of individual dissatisfaction sufficiently intense to produce protest. This is lacking in the preceding discussion of status consistency. This gap has been filled through an integration of the status consistency literature, Homan's Theory of Distributive Justice,[23] and Festinger's Theory of Cognitive Dissonance,[24] into an expanded theory.[25]

This integrated theory includes seven assumptions. The following are the relevant portions for an analysis of social movements and revolutions:

1. All individuals hold sets of cognitions which include some that are reality-based, some that are definitional, and some that are normative.

2. Any set of cognitions may stand in a relation of dissonance, consonance, or irrelevance, depending upon the internal relations which hold among reality-based and normative cognitions. If the conjunction of a reality-based and a normative cognition implies the negation of another reality-based cognition, then a state of dissonance exists.

3. Reality-based cognitions will include perceptions of one's status in the educational, occupational, income, and ethnic hierarchies. Definitional cognitions will include the definition of ethnicity as an ascribed investment, education as an achieved investment, occupation as a social reward, and income as a material reward. Normative cognitions will include the belief that rewards received should be proportional to investments.

4. Dissonance is an upsetting state and will produce tension for the individual. This tension will lead to an attempt to reduce dissonance by altering cognitions, adding new cognitions, or deleting old ones. Attempts to alter reality-based cognitions will involve attempting to change the real world.

5. Status inconsistents whose rewards received are less than believed to be proper for their investments will feel anger and inconsistents whose rewards exceed investments will feel guilt. Anger is a sharper form of dissonance than guilt. The intensity of dissonance-reducing behavior will be directly proportional to the sharpness of dissonance.

6. Dissonance-reducing attempts will take the form of coping responses, attempts to change the real world, when possible.

7. Dissonance-reducing attempts will move from the simple to the complex. The most complex form of attempting to change reality is attempting to alter society.

These assumptions allow the derivation of predictions of specific behavioral responses to specific profiles of status inconsistency. Included are a number of predictions regarding the manner in which status inconsistency may contribute to the origin of social movements. More will be said on this below. The addition of the following assumptions will permit the deriva-

23. George C. Homans, *Social Behavior: Its Elementary Forms* (New York: Harcourt, Brace & World, 1961).
24. Leon Festinger, *A Theory of Cognitive Dissonance* (Evanston, Illinois: Row, Peterson & Co., 1957).
25. Geschwender, "Continuities . . . ," pp. 160–171.

tion of predictions regarding the manner in which temporal changes in socioeconomic conditions may contribute to the origin of social movements:

8. Reality-based cognitions will include perceptions of present socioeconomic circumstances, past socioeconomic circumstances, and time lapse between the two. A higher level of socioeconomic circumstances will be defined as preferable to a lower level of socioeconomic circumstances.

9. Individuals whose present socioeconomic circumstances are at a higher level than past circumstances will be aware of the fact that they have experienced improvement and will define further improvement as possible and desirable. The discrepancy between anticipated future circumstances and present circumstances will produce dissonance. Anticipation of future rate of progress will be determined by rate of past progress (time lapse cognition).

10. Reality-based cognitions will include perceptions of present and past socioeconomic statuses of relevant reference groups. Comparisons will be made between rates of progress of self and relevant reference groups. Discrepancies between perceived rates of progress will produce dissonance.

11. Individuals whose present socioeconomic circumstances are at a lower level than past circumstances will be aware that they have experienced a worsening of conditions and will be fearful of further deterioration. A comparison of present circumstances and past circumstances will produce dissonance.

12. Attempts to reduce dissonance will take the form of attempting to change society when it is believed that sufficient power is, or can be, harnessed to bring this about. They will take a rightist direction when present circumstances are at a lower level than past circumstances and a leftist direction when present circumstances are at a higher level than past circumstances.

13. The intensity of dissonance experienced will be inversely proportional to the time span during which the discrepancies developed and will be directly proportional to the size of the discrepancies. The intensity of change attempts will be directly proportional to the intensity of dissonance.

14. Change-oriented, dissonance-reducing attempts on the part of status inconsistents will take a rightist orientation when high ethnic status is combined with lower levels of occupation or income; they will take a leftist orientation when high educational status is combined with a lower level of occupation or income.

DISCUSSION

All of the patterns of temporal change which produce revolutionary activities may be explained within dissonance theory. Changes in objective conditions produce a state of mind in which individuals believe that they are unjustly deprived of a better way of life. First, they develop the image of a state of affairs which is possible of attainment. Second, they develop the belief that they are entitled to that state of affairs. Third, they know that they are not enjoying that state of affairs. The simultaneous possession of these three cognitions produces a state of dissonance. Dissonance is not comfortable and it produces pressures toward dissonance reduction. One means of reducing this dissonance is to alter the environment so as to produce the desired state of affairs. Therefore, dissonance-reducing activities often take the form of social protest or revolutionary behavior.

The fact that different individuals may experience different intensities of dissonance (or may have different levels of tolerance for dissonance) would lead to their engaging in protest activities at different points in time. It is conceivable that attempts to reduce dissonance (protest activities) on the part of the earliest and most severely affected will help to create dissonance in others similarly situated. Thus, the former group acts as agitators in helping to stir the latter to revolt.

It is also possible to predict the direction and intensity of the protest response with the aid of dissonance theory. It is reasonable to assume that the intensity of the response will be proportional to the intensity of dissonance experience. Certain of the patterns would be likely to produce a more intense state of dissonance than others. Davies' "rise and drop" hypothesis describes a set of circumstances which produces a large discrepancy between expected level of need satisfaction and actual level of need satisfaction. This discrepancy should be much smaller for those sets of circumstances described by the "rising expectations" hypothesis. The former might then be expected to produce a more intense form of dissonance, and, consequently, a more intense form of dissonance-reducing behavior (e.g., revolutionary rather than reform movements).

This can be illustrated by two types of Negro protest movements. The relationship between the "rising expectations" hypothesis and civil rights protest has been discussed above. The more extreme reaction to the "rise and drop" hypothesis can be illustrated with the Universal Negro Improvement Association of Marcus Garvey.[26]

Garvey had been actively, but unsuccessfully, attempting to recruit supporters prior to World War I. During the war opportunities for Negroes improved dramatically. As whites went into the armed services and defense needs expanded, many jobs were opened to Negroes for the first time. Other Negroes went into the service, and some went to Europe and saw that conditions prevailing in the United States were not necessarily inevitable. Their accounts were printed in Negro newspapers throughout the country. These circumstances produced an anticipation of, and a desire for, better conditions of life than those prevailing prior to the war. When

---

26. Gunnar Myrdal, *An American Dilemma* (New York: Harper & Row, 1962), pp. 745–749.

the war ended whites returned from the armed services and defense spending was sharply curtailed. Negroes lost jobs gained during the war. Riots occurred all over the country to "put the Negro back in his place." The "rise and drop" circumstances had been experienced and Marcus Garvey found his recruits. The growth of the movement, until it was crushed, is history.

It is conceivable that the growth of the Nation of Islam after World War II and of Black Nationalism after the federal government's recent retreat on civil rights is the result of a similar "rise and drop" experience. This would illustrate the fact that different segments of the Negro community differentially experience the same societal changes. Middle-class Negroes have experienced a continual improvement in life circumstances and may be reacting in terms of the "rising expectations" hypothesis. Lower-class Negroes have had their aspirations raised simply to find the doors closed as tightly as ever. They may be reacting in terms of the "rise and drop" hypothesis.

Similarly, we would expect that those sets of circumstances described by the "relative deprivation" hypothesis and the "downward mobility" hypothesis would vary in the intensity of dissonance created, and in intensity of dissonance-reducing behavior, according to the degree of relative deprivation and the rate of downward mobility. The set of circumstances described by the "status inconsistency" hypothesis would produce varying intensities of dissonance and dissonance-reducing behavior according to the degree of discrepancy between relevant status dimensions.

The "rise and drop" hypothesis, the "rising expectations" hypothesis, and the "relative deprivation" hypothesis all describe sets of circumstances in which dissatisfaction results from a comparison of actual conditions with anticipated conditions. It involves a future orientation on the part of those affected. This future orientation is represented by a desire to bring about a better state of affairs—one which has never existed in reality. Thus, it may be predicted that protest movements and revolutions resulting from these sets of conditions are likely to be "progressive" or leftist in character.

The "downward mobility" hypothesis, whether absolute or relative mobility, describes a set of circumstances in which dissatisfaction is created by comparing present conditions with conditions which existed in the past. Thus, it may be predicted that dissonance reduction would take the form of a "regressive" or rightist protest movement.

The direction taken by movements resulting from circumstances described in the "status inconsistency" hypothesis would depend upon the nature of the inconsistency involved. Individuals who experience status inconsistency resulting from greater educational investments than income and/or occupational rewards will likely attempt to reduce dissonance in one of two ways. They may attempt to bring about consonance through individual mobility. If this is not possible and they shift to protest activities, it is likely to be in the direction of creating an equalitarian society in which rewards are based upon universalistic criteria—a "progressive" or leftist movement.

Those individuals who experience dissonance resulting from their ethnic investment being greater than their income and/or occupational rewards are not likely to select either of these modes of dissonance reduction. Individual mobility is not possible without education, and rewards distributed upon the basis of universalistic criteria will not help. They are much more prone to support a movement emphasizing rewards based upon particularistic criteria—a "regressive" or rightist movement.

Just as not all revolutionary attempts succeed, Festinger acknowledged that not all attempts to reduce dissonance will be successful. If an attempted revolution or protest movement fails, the dissonant individuals will be forced to attempt to reduce dissonance by altering one of their cognitions (such as that of the desired state of affairs or the proper relation between investments and rewards), or by adding new cognitions (such as their lack of ability to bring about the desired state). This could produce the apathetic, disinterested, nonprotesting type of fatalistic behavior that we find among the severely downtrodden.

One of the assumptions presented above stated that social change would be perceived as a means of reducing dissonance if it is believed that sufficient power is, or could be, harnessed. It is also possible that the required intensity of dissonance may be present but the required perception of power absent. This combination cannot be expected to produce social movements or revolutions. However, the dissonance that has been generated will not simply dissipate and may not be reduced by cognitive reorganization. It is possible that this combination may produce hostile outbursts such as the ghetto riots currently occurring throughout the country.

Civil rights legislation, the "war on poverty," VISTA, and other governmental actions may lead ghetto-dwelling Negroes to drastically raise their levels of aspirations and expectations. The failure of these measures to bring about significant improvements may lead to disillusionment. The discrepancy between expectation and reality creates dissonance. No improvement is actually experienced; only hopes are raised. Thus, intense dissonance is combined with feelings of powerlessness that typify the ghetto dweller, and riots or explosions emerge.

CONCLUSIONS

It has been shown that the particular sequence of temporal changes described by Davies is only one of several sequences which produce in individuals the state of mind that tends to be expressed in revolutionary or other protest activities. The experiencing of status inconsistency is a non-temporal condition which also produces this same state of mind. Dissonance theory is capable of explaining the manner in which this state of mind is produced by these diverse sets of conditions and the manner in which it finds its expression in protest activities.

Hypotheses have been derived which predict the particular mode of dissonance reduction that will be attempted under certain sets of conditions, the direction of change attempts (rightist or leftist movements), the intensity of change attempts (revolutionary or reform), and the conditions under which change will not be attempted but hostile outbursts emerge or apathy and hopelessness set in. Research is needed to test these hypotheses and to detail the relationship between these and other possible sets of preconditions of revolutionary activity. Davies has taken a major step in the development of a theory of revolution and the present paper has helped to place this contribution into a more general context.

PART **III**

Social Organization

Social Stratification:

Is Stratification Necessary?

The debate over the necessity of social stratification is one of the longest and most acrimonious in all of sociology. It all began in 1945 with an innocently titled article "Some Principles of Stratification," by Kingsley Davis and Wilbert Moore. That famous article opens this section on stratification. The most controversial part of their argument is the contention that since stratification (defined by them as a system of positions) is universal, it is a functional necessity (not good or bad, but necessary) for motivating people to occupy, and placing them in, functionally important positions. In order to get people to occupy more responsible positions, they must be offered greater rewards.

The Davis-Moore article is followed by one by George Huaco, in which he summarizes the history of the controversy over that work. He goes through each of the critiques of the Davis-Moore position as well as the replies by the original authors. He not only underscores each of the major points, but he also offers the reader critical commentary as he goes along. In the end Huaco sorts out for us those aspects of the Davis-Moore theory which seem to have been destroyed by the critics as well as those which have stood up well in spite of the attacks. Huaco concludes: "Two decades of controversy seem to have effectively sorted out the metaphysical postulate and questionable assumptions from the more valuable ingredients. These ingredients contain considerable insight, but by themselves they do not add up to a fully adequate theory of social inequality, mobility, and ascription, much less of stratification." Thus the Davis-Moore controversy stands as a model for all sociological controversies. Over the years many things have become clarified about social stratification as some elements of their theory have been retained and others discarded.

Some Principles of Stratification*

Kingsley Davis and Wilbert E. Moore

In a previous paper some concepts for handling the phenomena of social inequality were presented.[1] In the present paper a further step in stratification theory is undertaken—an attempt to show the relationship between stratification and the rest of the social order.[2] Starting from the proposition that no society is "classless," or unstratified, an effort is made to explain, in functional terms, the universal necessity which calls forth stratification in any social system. Next, an attempt is made to explain the roughly uniform distribution of prestige as between the major types of positions in every society. Since, however, there occur between one society and another great differences in the degree and kind of stratification, some attention is also given to the varieties of social inequality and the variable factors that give rise to them.

Clearly, the present task requires two different lines of analysis—one to understand the universal, the other to understand the variable features of stratification. Naturally each line of inquiry aids the other and is indispensable, and in the treatment that follows the two will be interwoven, although, because of space limitations, the emphasis will be on the universals.

Throughout, it will be necessary to keep in mind one thing—namely, that the discussion relates to the system of positions, not to the individuals occupying those positions. It is one thing to ask why different positions carry different degrees of prestige, and quite another to ask how certain individuals get into those positions. Although, as the argument will try to show, both questions are related, it is essential to keep them separate in our thinking. Most of the literature on stratification has tried to answer the second question (particularly with regard to the ease or difficulty of mobility between strata) without tackling the first. The first question,

---

* Reprinted from *American Sociological Review*, 10 (April, 1945), pp. 242–249, by permission of the authors and publisher.

1. Kingsley Davis, "A Conceptual Analysis of Stratification," *American Sociological Review*, VII (June, 1942), 309–321.
2. The writers regret (and beg indulgence) that the present essay, a condensation of a longer study, covers so much in such short space that adequate evidence and qualification cannot be given and that as a result what is actually very tentative is presented in an unfortunately dogmatic manner.

however, is logically prior and, in the case of any particular individual or group, factually prior.

THE FUNCTIONAL NECESSITY OF STRATIFICATION

Curiously, however, the main functional necessity explaining the universal presence of stratification is precisely the requirement faced by any society of placing and motivating individuals in the social structure. As a functioning mechanism a society must somehow distribute its members in social positions and induce them to perform the duties of these positions. It must thus concern itself with motivation at two different levels: to instill in the proper individuals the desire to fill certain positions, and, once in these positions, the desire to perform the duties attached to them. Even though the social order may be relatively static in form, there is a continuous process of metabolism as new individuals are born into it, shift with age, and die off. Their absorption into the positional system must somehow be arranged and motivated. This is true whether the system is competitive or non-competitive. A competitive system gives greater importance to the motivation to achieve positions, whereas a non-competitive system gives perhaps greater importance to the motivation to perform the duties of the positions; but in any system both types of motivation are required.

If the duties associated with the various positions were all equally pleasant to the human organism, all equally important to societal survival, and all equally in need of the same ability or talent, it would make no difference who got into which positions, and the problem of social placement would be greatly reduced. But actually it does make a great deal of difference who gets into which positions, not only because some positions are inherently more agreeable than others, but also because some require special talents or training and some are functionally more important than others. Also, it is essential that the duties of the positions be performed with the diligence that their importance requires. Inevitably, then, a society must have, first, some kind of rewards that it can use as inducements, and second, some way of distributing these rewards differentially according to positions. The rewards and their distribution become a part of the social order, and thus give rise to stratification.

One may ask what kind of rewards a society has at its disposal in distributing its personnel and securing essential services. It has, first of all, the things that contribute to sustenance and comfort. It has, second, the things that contribute to humor and diversion. And it has, finally, the things that contribute to self-respect and ego expansion. The last, because of the peculiarly social character of the self, is largely a function of the opinion of others, but it nonetheless ranks in importance with the first two. In any social system three kinds of rewards must be dispensed differentially according to positions.

In a sense the rewards are "built into" the position. They consist in the "rights" associated with the position, plus what may be called its accompaniments or perquisites. Often the rights, and sometimes the accompaniments, are functionally related to the duties of the position. (Rights as viewed by the incumbent are usually duties as viewed by other members of the community.) However, there may be a host of subsidiary rights and perquisites that are not essential to the function of the position and have only an indirect and symbolic connection with its duties, but which still may be of considerable importance in inducing people to seek the positions and fulfil the essential duties.

If the rights and perquisites of different positions in a society must be unequal, then the society must be stratified, because that is precisely what stratification means. Social inequality is thus an unconsciously evolved device by which societies insure that the most important positions are conscientiously filled by the most qualified persons. Hence every society, no matter how simple or complex, must differentiate persons in terms of both prestige and esteem, and must therefore possess a certain amount of institutionalized inequality.

It does not follow that the amount or type of inequality need be the same in all societies. This is largely a function of factors that will be discussed presently.

THE TWO DETERMINANTS OF POSITIONAL RANK

Granting the general function that inequality subserves, one can specify the two factors that determine the relative rank of different positions. In general those positions convey the best reward, and hence have the highest rank, which (a) have the greatest importance for the society and (b) require the greatest training or talent. The first factor concerns function and is a matter of relative significance; the second concerns means and is a matter of scarcity.

DIFFERENTIAL FUNCTIONAL IMPORTANCE

Actually a society does not need to reward positions in proportion to their functional importance. It merely needs to give sufficient reward to them to insure that they will be filled competently. In other words, it must see that less essential positions do not compete successfully with more essential ones. If a position is easily filled, it need not be heavily rewarded, even though important. On the other hand, if it is important but hard to fill, the reward must be high enough to get it filled anyway. Functional importance is therefore a necessary but not a sufficient cause of high rank being assigned to a position.[3]

DIFFERENTIAL SCARCITY OF PERSONNEL

Practically all positions, no matter how acquired, require some form of skill or capacity for performance. This is implicit in the very notion of position, which implies that the incumbent must, by virtue of his incumbency, accomplish certain things.

There are, ultimately, only two ways in which a person's qualifications come about: through inherent capacity or through training. Obviously, in concrete activities both are always necessary, but from a practical standpoint the scarcity may lie primarily in one or the other, as well as in both. Some positions require innate talents of such high degree that persons who fill them are bound to be rare. In many cases, however, talent is fairly abundant in the population but the training process is so long, costly, and elaborate that relatively few can qualify. Modern medicine, for example, is within the mental capacity of most individuals, but a medical education is so burdensome and expensive that virtually none would undertake it if the position of the M.D. did not carry a reward commensurate with the sacrifice.

If the talents required for a position are abundant and the training easy, the method of acquiring the position may have little to do with its duties. There may be, in fact, a virtually accidental relationship. But if the skills required are scarce by reason of the rarity of talent or the costliness of training, the position, if functionally important, must have an attractive power that will draw the necessary skills in competition with other positions. This means, in effect, that the position must be high in the social scale—must command great prestige, high salary, ample leisure, and the like.

---

3. Unfortunately, functional importance is difficult to establish. To use the position's prestige to establish it, as is often unconsciously done, constitutes circular reasoning from our point of view. There are, however, two independent clues: (1) the degree to which a position is functionally unique, there being no other positions that can perform the same function satisfactorily; (2) the degree to which other positions are dependent on the one in question. Both clues are best exemplified in organized systems of positions built around one major function. Thus, in most complex societies the religious, political, economic, and educational functions are handled by distinct structures not easily interchangeable. In addition, each structure possesses many different positions, some clearly dependent on, if not subordinate to, others. In sum, when an institutional nucleus becomes differential around one main function, and at the same time organizes a large portion of the population into its relationships, the *key* positions in it are of the highest functional importance. The absence of such specialization does not prove functional unimportance, for the whole society may be relatively unspecialized; but it is safe to assume that the more important functions receive the first and clearest structural differentiation.

HOW VARIATIONS ARE TO BE UNDERSTOOD

In so far as there is a difference between one system of stratification and another, it is attributable to whatever factors affect the two determinants of differential reward—namely, functional importance and scarcity of personnel. Positions important in one society may not be important in another, because the conditions faced by the societies, or their degree of internal development, may be different. The same conditions, in turn, may affect the question of scarcity; for in some societies the stage of development, or the external situation, may wholly obviate the necessity of certain kinds of skill or talent. Any particular system of stratification, then, can be understood as a product of the special conditions affecting the two aforementioned grounds of differential reward.

Major Societal Functions and Stratification

RELIGION

The reason why religion is necessary is apparently to be found in the fact that human society achieves its unity primarily through the possession by its members of certain ultimate values and ends in common. Although these values and ends are subjective, they influence behavior, and their integration enables the society to operate as a system. Derived neither from inherited nor from external nature, they have evolved as a part of culture by communication and moral pressure. They must, however, appear to the members of the society to have some reality, and it is the role of religious belief and ritual to supply and reinforce this appearance of reality. Through belief and ritual the common ends and values are connected with an imaginary world symbolized by concrete sacred objects, which world in turn is related in a meaningful way to the facts and trials of the individual's life. Through the worship of the sacred objects and the beings they symbolize, and the acceptance of supernatural prescriptions that are at the same time codes of behavior, a powerful control over human conduct is exercised, guiding it along lines sustaining the institutional structure and conforming to the ultimate ends and values.

If this conception of the role of religion is true, one can understand why in every known society the religious activities tend to be under the charge of particular persons, who tend thereby to enjoy greater rewards than the ordinary societal member. Certain of the rewards and special privileges may attach to only the highest religious functionaries, but others usually apply, if such exists, to the entire sacerdotal class.

Moreover, there is a peculiar relation between the duties of the religious official and the special privileges he enjoys. If the supernatural world governs the destinies of men more ultimately than does the real world, its earthly representative, the person through whom one may communicate with the supernatural, must be a powerful individual. He is a keeper of sacred tradition, a skilled performer of the ritual, and an interpreter of lore and myth. He is in such close contact with the gods that he is viewed as possessing some of their characteristics. He is, in short, a bit sacred, and hence free from some of the more vulgar necessities and controls.

It is no accident, therefore, that religious functionaries have been associated with the very highest positions of power, as in theocratic regimes. Indeed, looking at it from this point of view, one may wonder why it is that they do not get *entire* control over their societies. The factors that prevent this are worthy of note.

In the first place, the amount of technical competence necessary for the performance of religious duties is small. Scientific or artistic capacity is not required. Anyone can set himself up as enjoying an intimate relation with deities, and nobody can successfully dispute him. Therefore, the factor of scarcity of personnel does not operate in the technical sense.

One may assert, on the other hand, that religious ritual is often elaborate and religious lore abstruse, and that priestly ministrations require tact, if not intelligence. This is true, but the technical requirements of the profession are for the most part adventitious, not related to the end in the same way that science is related to air travel. The priest can never be free from competition, since the criteria of whether or not one has genuine contact with the supernatural are never strictly clear. It is this competition that debases the priestly position below what might be expected at first glance. That is why priestly prestige is highest in those societies where membership in the profession is rigidly controlled by the priestly guild itself. That is why, in part at least, elaborate devices are utilized to stress the identification of the person with his office—spectacular costume, abnormal conduct, special diet, segregated residence, celibacy, conspicuous leisure, and the like. In fact, the priest is always in danger of becoming somewhat discredited—as happens in a secularized society—because in a world of stubborn fact, ritual and sacred knowledge alone will not grow crops or build houses. Furthermore, unless he is protected by a professional guild, the priest's identification with the supernatural tends to preclude his acquisition of abundant worldly goods.

As between one society and another it seems that the highest general position awarded the priest occurs in the medieval type of social order. Here there is enough economic production to afford a surplus, which can be used to support a numerous and highly organized priesthood; and yet the populace is unlettered and therefore credulous to a high degree. Perhaps the most extreme example is to be found in the Buddhism of Tibet, but others are encountered in the Catholicism of feudal Europe, the Inca regime of Peru, the Brahminism of India, and the Mayan priesthood of Yucatan. On the other hand, if the society is so crude as to have no surplus and little differentiation, so that every priest must be also a cultivator or hunter, the separation of the priestly status from the others has hardly gone far enough for priestly prestige to mean much. When the priest actually has high prestige under these circumstances, it is because he also performs other important functions (usually political and medical).

In an extremely advanced society built on scientific technology, the priesthood tends to lose status, because sacred tradition and supernaturalism drop into the background. The ultimate values and common ends of the society tend to be expressed in less anthropomorphic ways, by officials who occupy fundamentally political, economic, or educational rather than religious positions. Nevertheless, it is easily possible for intellectuals to exaggerate the degree to which the priesthood in a presumably secular milieu has lost prestige. When the matter is closely examined the urban proletariat, as well as the rural citizenry, proves to be surprisingly god-fearing and priest-ridden. No society has become so completely secularized as to liquidate entirely the belief in transcendental ends and supernatural entities. Even in a secularized society some system must exist for the integration of ultimate values, for their ritualistic expression, and for the emotional adjustments required by disappointment, death, and disaster.

GOVERNMENT

Like religion, government plays a unique and indispensable part in society. But in contrast to religion, which provides integration in terms of sentiments, beliefs, and rituals, it organizes the society in terms of law and authority. Furthermore, it orients the society to the actual rather than the unseen world.

The main functions of government are, internally, the ultimate enforcement of norms, the final arbitration of conflicting interests, and the overall planning and direction of society; and externally, the handling of war and diplomacy. To carry out these functions it acts as the agent of the entire people, enjoys a monopoly of force, and controls all individuals within its territory.

Political action, by definition, implies authority. An official can command because he has authority, and the citizen must obey because he is subject to that authority. For this reason stratification is inherent in the nature of political relationships.

So clear is the power embodied in political position that political inequality is sometimes thought to comprise all inequality. But it can be shown that there are other bases of stratification, that the following controls operate in practice to keep political power from becoming complete:

1. The fact that the actual holders of political office, and especially those de-termining top policy must necessarily be few in number compared to the total population.
2. The fact that the rulers represent the interest of the group rather than of themselves, and are therefore restricted in their behavior by rules and mores designed to enforce this limitation of interest.
3. The fact that the holder of political office has his authority by virtue of his office and nothing else, and therefore any special knowledge, talent, or capacity he may claim is purely incidental, so that he often has to depend upon others for technical assistance.

In view of these limiting factors, it is not strange that the rulers often have less power and prestige than a literal enumeration of their formal rights would lead one to expect.

WEALTH, PROPERTY, AND LABOR

Every position that secures for its incumbent a livelihood is, by defini-tion, economically rewarded. For this reason there is an economic aspect to those positions (i.e., political and religious) the main function of which is not economic. It therefore becomes convenient for the society to use unequal economic returns as a principal means of controlling the entrance of persons into positions and stimulating the performance of their duties. The amount of the economic return therefore becomes one of the main indices of social status.

It should be stressed, however, that a position does not bring power and prestige *because* it draws a high income. Rather, it draws a high income because it is functionally important and the available personnel is for one reason or another scarce. It is therefore superficial and erroneous to regard high income as the cause of a man's power and prestige, just as it is erroneous to think that a man's fever is the cause of his disease.[4]

The economic source of power and prestige is not income primarily, but the ownership of capital goods (including patents, good will, and professional reputation). Such ownership should be distinguished from the possession of consumers' goods, which is an index rather than a cause of social standing. In other words, the ownership of producers' goods is properly speaking, a source of income like other positions, the income itself remaining an index. Even in situations where social values are widely commercialized and earnings are the readiest method of judging social position, income does not confer prestige on a position so much as it induces people to compete for the position. It is true that a man who has a high income as a result of one position may find this money helpful in

---

4. The symbolic rather than intrinsic role of income in social stratification has been succinctly summarized by Talcott Parsons, "An Analytical Approach to the Theory of Social Stratification," *American Journal of Sociology*, XLV (May, 1940), 841–862.

climbing into another position as well, but this again reflects the effect of his initial, economically advantageous status, which exercises its influence through the medium of money.

In a system of private property in productive enterprise, an income above what an individual spends can give rise to possession of capital wealth. Presumably such possession is a reward for the proper management of one's finances originally and of the productive enterprise later. But as social differentiation becomes highly advanced and yet the institution of inheritance persists, the phenomenon of pure ownership, and reward for pure ownership, emerges. In such a case it is difficult to prove that the position is functionally important or that the scarcity involved is anything other than extrinsic and accidental. It is for this reason, doubtless, that the institution of private property in productive goods becomes more subject to criticism as social development proceeds toward industrialization. It is only this pure, that is, strictly legal and functionless ownership, however, that is open to attack; for some form of active ownership, whether private or public, is indispensable.

One kind of ownership of production goods consists in rights over the labor of others. The most extremely concentrated and exclusive of such rights are found in slavery, but the essential principle remains in serfdom, peonage, encomienda, and indenture. Naturally this kind of ownership has the greatest significance for stratification, because it necessarily entails an unequal relationship.

But property in capital goods inevitably introduces a compulsive element even into the nominally free contractual relationship. Indeed, in some respects the authority of the contractual employer is greater than that of the feudal landlord, inasmuch as the latter is more limited by traditional reciprocities. Even the classical economics recognized that competitors would fare unequally, but it did not pursue this fact to its necessary conclusion that, however it might be acquired, unequal control of goods and services must give unequal advantage to the parties to a contract.

TECHNICAL KNOWLEDGE

The function of finding means to single goals, without any concern with the choice between goals, is the exclusively technical sphere. The explanation of why positions requiring great technical skill receive fairly high rewards is easy to see, for it is the simplest case of the rewards being so distributed as to draw talent and motivate training. Why they seldom if ever receive the highest rewards is also clear: the importance of technical knowledge from a societal point of view is never so great as the integration of goals, which takes place on the religious, political, and economic levels. Since the technological level is concerned solely with means, a purely technical position must ultimately be subordinate to other positions that are religious, political, or economic in character.

Nevertheless, the distinction between expert and layman in any social order is fundamental, and cannot be entirely reduced to other terms. Methods of recruitment, as well as of reward, sometimes lead to the erroneous interpretation that technical positions are economically determined. Actually, however, the acquisition of knowledge and skill cannot be accomplished by purchase, although the opportunity to learn may be. The control of the avenues of training may inhere as a sort of property right in certain families or classes, giving them power and prestige in consequence. Such a situation adds an artificial scarcity to the natural scarcity of skills and talents. On the other hand, it is possible for an opposite situation to arise. The rewards of technical position may be so great that a condition of excess supply is created, leading to at least temporary devaluation of the rewards. Thus "unemployment in the learned professions" may result in a debasement of the prestige of those positions. Such adjustments and readjustments are constantly occurring in changing societies; and it is always well to bear in mind that the efficiency of a stratified structure may be affected by the modes of recruitment for positions. The social order itself, however, sets limits to the inflation or deflation of the prestige of experts: an over-supply tends to debase the rewards and discourage recruitment or produce revolution, whereas an under-supply tends to increase the rewards or weaken the society in competition with other societies.

Particular systems of stratification show a wide range with respect to the exact position of technically competent persons. This range is perhaps most evident in the degree of specialization. Extreme division of labor tends to create many specialists without high prestige since the training is short and the required native capacity relatively small. On the other hand it also tends to accentuate the high position of the true experts—scientists, engineers, and administrators—by increasing their authority relative to other functionally important positions. But the idea of a technocratic social order or a government or priesthood of engineers or social scientists neglects the limitations of knowledge and skills as a basic for performing social functions. To the extent that the social structure is truly specialized the prestige of the technical person must also be circumscribed.

Variation in Stratified Systems

The generalized principles of stratification here suggested form a necessary preliminary to a consideration of types of stratified systems, because it is in terms of these principles that the types must be described. This can be seen by trying to delineate types according to certain modes of variation. For instance, some of the most important modes (together with the polar types in terms of them) seem to be as follows:

(A) THE DEGREE OF SPECIALIZATION

The degree of specialization affects the fineness and multiplicity of the gradations in power and prestige. It also influences the extent to which particular functions may be emphasized in the invidious system, since a given function cannot receive much emphasis in the hierarchy until it has achieved structural separation from the other functions. Finally, the amount of specialization influences the bases of selection. Polar types: *Specialized, Unspecialized.*

(B) THE NATURE OF THE FUNCTIONAL EMPHASIS

In general when emphasis is put on sacred matters, a rigidity is introduced that tends to limit specialization and hence the development of technology. In addition, a brake is placed on social mobility, and on the development of bureaucracy. When the preoccupation with the sacred is withdrawn, leaving greater scope for purely secular preoccupations, a great development, and rise in status, of economic and technological positions seemingly takes place. Curiously, a concomitant rise in political position is not likely, because it has usually been allied with the religious and stands to gain little by the decline of the latter. It is also possible for a society to emphasize family functions—as in relatively undifferentiated societies where high mortality requires high fertility and kinship forms the main basis of social organization. Main types: *Familistic, Authoritarian (Theocratic* or sacred, and *Totalitarian* or secular), *Capitalistic.*

(C) THE MAGNITUDE OF INVIDIOUS DIFFERENCES

What may be called the amount of social distance between positions, taking into account the entire scale, is something that should lend itself to quantitative measurement. Considerable differences apparently exist between different societies in this regard, and also between parts of the same society. Polar types: *Equalitarian, Inequalitarian.*

(D) THE DEGREE OF OPPORTUNITY

The familiar question of the amount of mobility is different from the question of the comparative equality or inequality of rewards posed above, because the two criteria may vary independently up to a point. For instance, the tremendous divergences in monetary income in the United

States are far greater than those found in primitive societies, yet the equality of opportunity to move from one rung to the other in the social scale may also be greater in the United States than in a hereditary tribal kingdom. Polar types: *Mobile* (open), *Immobile* (closed).

(E) THE DEGREE OF STRATUM SOLIDARITY

Again, the degree of "class solidarity" (or the presence of specific organizations to promote class interests) may vary to some extent independently of the other criteria, and hence is an important principle in classifying systems of stratification. Polar types: *Class organized, Class unorganized.*

EXTERNAL CONDITIONS

What state any particular system of stratification is in with reference to each of these modes of variation depends on two things: (1) its state with reference to the other ranges of variation, and (2) the conditions outside the system of stratification which nevertheless influence that system. Among the latter are the following:

(A) THE STAGE OF CULTURAL DEVELOPMENT

As the cultural heritage grows, increased specialization becomes necessary, which in turn contributes to the enhancement of mobility, a decline of stratum solidarity, and a change of functional emphasis.

(B) SITUATION WITH RESPECT TO OTHER SOCIETIES

The presence or absence of open conflict with other societies, of free trade relations or cultural diffusion, all influence the class structure to some extent. A chronic state of warfare tends to place emphasis upon the military functions, especially when the opponents are more or less equal. Free trade, on the other hand, strengthens the hand of the trader at the expense of the warrior and priest. Free movement of ideas generally has an equalitarian effect. Migration and conquest create special circumstances.

(C) SIZE OF THE SOCIETY

A small society limits the degree to which functional specialization can go, the degree of segregation of different strata, and the magnitude of inequality.

COMPOSITE TYPES

Much of the literature on stratification has attempted to classify concrete systems into a certain number of types. This task is deceptively simple, however, and should come at the end of an analysis of elements and principles, rather than at the beginning. If the preceding discussion has any validity, it indicates that there are a number of modes of variation between different systems, and that any one system is a composite of the society's status with reference to all these modes of variation. The danger of trying to classify whole societies under such rubrics as *caste, feudal,* or *open class* is that one or two criteria are selected and others ignored, the result being an unsatisfactory solution to the problem posed. The present discussion has been offered as a possible approach to the more systematic classification of composite types.

The Functionalist Theory of Stratification: Two Decades of Controversy*

GEORGE A. HUACO

Long after Functionalism is discarded as a pseudo-explanation, Kingsley Davis and Wilbert E. Moore's attempts to explain stratification will be remembered as a brilliant effort. What is known as the Davis and Moore theory of stratification was first put forth in April, 1945. The authors argued that there is a "universal necessity which calls forth stratification in any social system." On the one hand, different positions have different degrees of functional importance for societal preservation or survival. On the other hand, the amount of talent and training available in the population is scarce. So the system attaches greater rewards to the functionally more important positions in order to insure that the individuals with greatest talent and training occupy these positions. Although the authors warned that due to space limitations they were emphasizing the universal aspects of stratification (and conversely, not giving much attention to variable features found in different systems), some peculiar consequences seemed to follow from this analysis. In the first place, Davis and Moore seemed to be describing all stratification systems as if they were

* Reprinted from *Inquiry* (Oslo, Norway), Vol. 9 (1966), pp. 215–240, by permission of the author and publisher.

pure achievement systems. In the second place, our authors seemed to suggest that the rich, powerful, and prestigious were not only the more talented and better trained but also the incumbents of roles which made a greater contribution to societal preservation and survival. These rather philistine implications aroused much opposition, and as we shall see, this opposition appears as the general background of the controversy that followed.

In his 1945 textbook, *Human Society*, Kingsley Davis added a major modification to the original theory:

> One may object to the foregoing explanation of stratification on the ground that it fits a competitive order but does not fit a non-competitive one. For instance, in a caste system it seems that people do not get their positions because of talent or training but rather because of birth. This criticism raises a crucial problem and forces an addition to the theory. . . . The necessity of having a social organization—the family—for the reproduction and socialization of children requires that stratification be somehow accommodated to this organization. Such accommodation takes the form of status ascription.[1]

In the new 1948 version, Davis conceptualized stratification in terms of a polarity:

> At one theoretical pole is the type which we might call absolutely closed, at the other pole the type which we might call absolutely open. The first would be one in which inheritance of the parental status (and hence the influence of the family) is complete; the second would be one in which there is no inheritance of the parental status and hence no family influence. Obviously, neither pole has ever been realized in practice. It is impossible to eliminate all competition for status, just as it is impossible to eliminate all ascription of status. In other words the role of the family in this matter is never absolute, nor is it ever nil. Thus the stratified systems we actually find in human society are mixed types.[2]

The addition of the ascriptive dimension results in a sizeable modification. We can now examine briefly the logical structure of the theory as a whole.

THE 1945 VERSION

a. Different positions have different degrees of functional importance (i.e. make different contributions to societal preservation or survival).

b. Adequate performance of different positions requires different amounts of talent and training.

1. Kingsley Davis, *Human Society* (New York: The Macmillan Company, 1948), pp. 369–70.
2. *Ibid.*, pp. 388–89.

c. Personnel with adequate amounts of talent and training is scarce.

d. Societies exhibit "stratification"; here defined as "unequal rewards attached to different positions." *Causal account:* (a) on the one hand, and (b) and (c) on the other, determine (d) in the following manner: greater rewards are attached to those positions which have greater functional importance and greater requirements of talent and training. In turn, (d) determines or "insures" (e):

e. The mobility of the more talented and trained individuals into the more highly rewarded positions.

Basic assumption: The achievement of condition (e) makes for societal preservation or survival (with the implication that the cause of (e), namely "stratification," also contributes to societal preservation or survival).

The 1948 Modification

A. Condition (e) describes an analytically pure achievement order.

B. In all societies the achievement of condition (e) is prevented partially or almost fully by status ascription.

C. The cause of status ascription is the family.

Before going on to the controversy a few initial comments are in order:

I. Items (b), (c), and (d) are fairly straightforward empirical generalizations.

II. The status of item (a) is unclear. It must be either a directly verifiable empirical generalization or an indirectly testable explanatory postulate, but it seems to be neither. It is not an empirical generalization, because degrees of differential functional importance are not part of the observable social universe. It is not a valid explanatory postulate, because it lacks the logical derivations or deductions which alone would make it indirectly testable.

III. The causal account contains two minor assumptions: (1) that those positions with greatest functional importance tend to require the greatest amounts of talent and training; and (2) that those positions with greatest functional importance tend to receive the highest rewards. The validity of these two assumptions is as questionable as the validity of item (a). Furthermore, their very existence rules out the use of talent, training, or rewards as either indicators or measures of differential functional importance.

IV. In terms of historical evidence the basic assumption is probably false: societies which approach the achievement of condition (e) might be more rational and more just, but there is as yet no evidence that they are either stronger or survive longer than the more ascriptive traditional societies.

V. Since the functionalist aspects of the theory consist precisely of item (a) together with the basic assumption, it follows that it is precisely the functionalist character of this theory which is most in question.

The critical controversy proper began in August, 1953, with Melvin M. Tumin's "Some Principles of Stratification: A Critical Analysis."[3] Tumin questioned the logical status of the notion of differential functional importance as being unmeasurable and intuitive. Further, he suggested that the derivation of differential functional importance from so-called societal functions is a useless tautology since "any *status quo* to any given moment is nothing more and nothing less than everything present in the *status quo*." Next, Tumin questioned differential scarcity of personnel as an adequate determinant of stratification. He argued that in practice most stratification systems artificially restrict the development of whatever potential talent and skill may exist in the population; "and the more rigidly stratified a society is, the less chance does that society have of discovering any new facts about the talents of its members." Next Tumin raised the issue of the possible existence of "functional equivalents" or alternatives to unequal rewards. He suggested two possible alternatives: intrinsic job satisfaction, and social service, as adequate motivations "for seeking one's appropriate position and fulfilling it conscientiously." At the linguistic level Tumin questioned the appropriateness of using the term "sacrifice" to describe the situation of those individuals who postpone joining the labor force by undergoing a lengthy period of specialized training. His second linguistic objection suggested that it would be more appropriate to speak of unequal "resources" rather than of unequal "rewards." Finally, he suggested that different positions have attached to them "certain highly morally-toned evaluations of their importance for the society," and implied that these evaluations stem from scarce and unequally distributed goods and services (and not from differential functional importance). Tumin also said that some of the vocabulary of analysis used by Davis and Moore came close to being "a direct reflection of the rationalizations offered by the more fortunate members of a society, of the rightness of their occupancy of privileged positions."[4]

Kingsley Davis replied that Tumin had examined the original 1945 version but ignored the modified 1948 version of the theory. He agreed that "differential functional importance" is difficult to measure, but protested that Tumin had not bothered to examine the "two independent clues" mentioned in the 1945 version. He added that:

> Rough measures of functional importance are in fact applied in practice. In wartime, for example, decisions are made as to which industries and occupations will have priority in capital equipment, labor recruitment, raw materials, etc. In totalitarian countries the same is done in peacetime, as also in underdeveloped areas attempting to maximize their social and

---

3. Melvin M. Tumin, "Some Principles of Stratification: A Critical Analysis," *American Sociological Review*, XVIII (August, 1953), 387–94.
4. *Ibid.*, p. 389.

economic modernization. Individual firms must constantly decide which positions are essential and which are not.[5]

Next, Davis agreed that in practice stratification systems often artificially restrict the manifestation of talent and training in the population, but argued that the 1948 version of the theory had already met this objection by explaining ascription in terms of the role of the family. Also, and quite correctly, he pointed out that Tumin had used the term "stratification" in a manner different from that of Davis and Moore (1945) and Davis (1948): Tumin's use of the term included "inheritance of class status"; while Davis and Moore's use of the term was limited to "unequal rewards attached to different positions." On the issue of possible "functional equivalents" to unequal rewards, Davis argued that intrinsic job satisfaction and social service "are supplementary rather than alternative to the positional reward mechanism." Davis rejected the notion that the theory was either evaluative or justificatory, and suggested that Tumin was being Utopian and "not so much interested in understanding institutionalized inequality as in getting rid of it"; and stated that the Davis and Moore theory explains how the individual pursuit of self-interest actually coincides with social interest.[6]

In his brief "Reply to Kingsley Davis,"[7] Tumin took issue with still another aspect of the Davis-Moore theory: he challenged the suggestion that the universality of stratification is any evidence for its alleged "necessity." On the issue of possible "functional equivalents" to unequal rewards, he quite correctly pointed out that their feasibility cannot be ruled out on *a priori* grounds; and that if Davis and Moore want to argue that alternatives are impossible, they have to present some evidence to that effect. In summary, in this first exchange between critic and defenders, the critic succeeded in challenging two major aspects of the Davis and Moore theory: first, Tumin succeeded in questioning the scientific validity of the notion of "differential functional importance" by suggesting that it might be nothing more than a set of hidden tautologies. Second, Tumin succeeded in questioning the necessity of "unequal rewards" by suggesting the feasibility of "functional equivalents." The real weight of this second challenge lies in the fact that the admission of equivalents or alternatives effectively destroys the theory's predictive power.

In August, 1955, Richard Schwartz's "Functional Alternatives to Inequality"[8] challenged the explanatory and predictive aspects of the Davis and Moore theory on the basis of a year's study of stratification phenomena

5. Kingsley Davis, "Reply," *American Sociological Review*, XVIII (August, 1953), 395.
6. *Ibid.*, p. 396.
7. Melvin M. Tumin, "Reply to Kingsley Davis," *American Sociological Review*, XVIII (December, 1953), 672.
8. Richard D. Schwartz, "Functional Alternatives to Inequality," *American Sociological Review*, XX (August, 1955), 424–30.

in two Israeli settlements: a bureaucratic and collectivistic kibbutz called Orah, and an individualistic Moshav co-op called Tamin. Schwartz described how the collectivistic and bureaucratic kibbutz developed what might be described as a compensatory informal pattern of positions and positional changes. This informal pattern, which included such things as relatively greater mechanization of routine tasks, job rotation, and individualistic outside jobs, contributed to job satisfaction by offsetting the dominant pattern of the group. Likewise, in the individualistic small-landowner's co-op, the development of a collectivistic informal pattern, which included such things as sharing scientific agricultural information and a process of collective decision-making, tended to increase job satisfaction by offsetting the dominant group pattern. Schwartz described how the populations of these two settlements had been self-elected in the sense that those individuals with a more collectivistic orientation chose to join the kibbutz and those with a more individualistic orientation joined the co-op. Further, he showed that this process of a population changing to fit the positional pattern received a powerful impetus from child socialization: the kibbutz children were socialized in a collectivistic direction, the co-op children were trained toward individual decision-making. Both settlements had a pattern of unequal rewards attached to different positions.

On the basis of this study Schwartz argued that "inequality as analyzed by Davis and Moore has functional alternatives";[9] or more specifically, that changes in the positional structure as well as changes in the characteristics of the population could be considered as feasible functional equivalents or alternatives to unequal rewards. The trouble here is that while Davis and Moore argued that unequal rewards insure that qualified individuals occupy positions with different requirements of talent and training, Schwartz argued that changes in positional structure and changes in population characteristics were adequate ways of promoting job satisfaction and role performance by position incumbents. But mobility into positions is not the same as job satisfaction or adequacy of role performance within positions; and thus Schwartz failed to prove what he was trying to prove. Nevertheless, and at a purely logical level, the Schwartz critique reemphasized the previous criticism of Tumin to the effect that Davis and Moore had failed to deal adequately with the possibility of functional alternatives to inequality of rewards.

In December, 1956, Richard L. Simpson's "A Modification of the Functional Theory of Social Stratification" made a new attack on several aspects of the Davis and Moore 1945 version:

> The adequacy of this theory and its assumptions can be questioned on several grounds: (1) the importance of a position is difficult if not impossible to evaluate. (2) Some positions exist and are rewarded which do

---

9. *Ibid.,* p. 424.

not seem to contribute to society at large; for example, the valet or the kept woman. (3) Some positions are given greater rewards than appears warranted by either their importance to society or the difficulty of training for them; for example, motion picture stars. (4) The theory implies an assumption that any scheme of stratification is somehow the best that could be had, that the prevailing distribution of rewards comes into being somehow because it is "functionally necessary."[10]

Objections (2) and (3) are irrelevant, because the identification of highly rewarded yet parasitical roles in no way challenges the Davis and Moore theory: economic contribution and degree of functional importance are not identical notions. Objection (4) is technically incorrect (despite Davis's remark to the effect that stratification systems are so arranged that the pursuit of individual self-interest coincides with social interest). Objection (1) alone is relevant, and here Simpson has tried to examine the two "clues" given by Davis and Moore, namely, "uniqueness" and "degree to which other positions are dependent on the one in question."

> Now, it may be admitted that a position which is uniquely capable of performing an essential function is important, but this statement still begs the question of how essential a given function is. Is public entertainment an essential function? If so, is only a movie star capable of performing it, or could a juggler or a bowling alley proprietor meet this social need equally well? The important criterion in imputing uniqueness of this sort would seem to be whether the public *thinks* that a given position or its incumbent is unique or important, not whether a sociologist considers that society could manage without the position or a given incumbent of it.[11]

Now this is very confused. The notion of "differential functional importance" presumably refers to an objective state of affairs; namely, the extent to which a given position contributes to the preservation or survival of the society. This is not the same as the opinion of a given sociologist or the opinion of the public. Furthermore, Davis has expressly rejected using "the position's prestige" as an indicator of functional importance, because this "constitutes circular reasoning." Simpson goes on:

> Let us consider the positions of janitor and garbage collector. These positions are presumably about equal in functional uniqueness and in the extent to which other positions depend on them. Yet we might feel that the garbage collector is more important, since uncollected refuse presents a more serious problem to society than unswept floors. Granting this, it is probable that the garbageman's prestige is lower than that of the janitor, as is the intrinsic pleasantness of his work, while their pay may be about

---

10. Richard L. Simpson, "A Modification of the Functional Theory of Stratification," *Social Forces,* XXXV (December, 1956), 132.
11. *Ibid.*

equal. Thus the rewards of the positions are inversely related to their importance, and their importance cannot be explained by Davis' and Moore's clues.[12]

The trouble with this exercise in uncontrolled speculation is that it goes too far, and in so doing, fails to establish contact with the Davis and Moore claim. Our theorists have argued that positions will *tend* to be rewarded in some manner commensurate with their degree of functional importance, *not* that there is a one-to-one correspondence between degree of functional importance and unequal rewards. Furthermore, differential functional importance is only one of the alleged determinants of unequal rewards attached to different positions, the other determinant being differential scarcity of personnel. Given this rather flexible apparatus, it would be very simple for Davis and Moore to say in answer to Simpson something to the effect that the apparent non-correspondence between functional importance and rewards (in the above example) is due to differential scarcity of personnel.

Simpson completes his critique by examining the attempt to derive differential functional importance from so-called "functional prerequisites."

> Some might claim that the importance of a position can be judged by seeing whether it contributes to the fulfillment of a "functional prerequisite" or "universal need" of the society. . . . Any investigator is free to invent his own list, and no one can gainsay him, for no one has found a way to test the validity of such a list. . . . Furthermore, the reasoning with regard to these universal social needs is often circular. Positions are said to be important because they meet one of the needs, but one suspects that some of the needs have been invented to account for the existence of the positions.[13]

Here Simpson repeats the earlier charge by Tumin to the effect that the claim that positions have different degrees of functional importance rests on nothing more than a set of hidden tautologies.

Two years later, in August, 1958, Walter Buckley's "Social Stratification and the Functional Theory of Social Differentiation" attacked Davis and Moore on both ideological and linguistic grounds. After reviewing the objections of Tumin, Schwartz, and Simpson, Buckley argued that the Davis-Moore theory

> accepts outmoded concepts and assumptions of classical economics, such as "inherent scarcity" of social ends and the inviolability of competition, all of which results in a picture of theoretical necessity and reproduces with remarkable faithfulness a culturally circumscribed ideology. . . . The

12. *Ibid.,* p. 133.
13. *Ibid.*

manner in which the functionalists present the stratification system as actually operating is rather the way in which many persons desire and believe that it would work in contemporary society if only the class structure did not exist to hinder it.[14]

This critique of the ideological implications of the Davis-Moore theory focuses on the understandable feelings of outrage aroused in some critics by a theory whose original version, in effect, tells us that those members of our society who have the greater amounts of wealth, power, and prestige are also the ones who make (thanks to their positions) the greatest contributions to the preservation or survival of the society. It is also obvious that however applicable this critique might be to the Davis-Moore 1945 version (which did not attempt to explain status ascription), it is not applicable to the Davis 1948 version (which attempted to explain ascription in terms of the family). The Davis 1948 version, in effect, suggests that if the family did not exist, and if society were organized as a pure achievement order, then the positions with greater rewards would also be the ones that make the greater contribution to the preservation and survival of the society, but that since the family does exist, and since all societies exhibit different mixtures of achievement and ascription, this correspondence between high rewards and high functional importance is no longer the case.

Buckley's second criticism concerns the Davis and Moore use of the term "stratification."

> The Davis-Moore theory specifies the central defining criterion of the concept of stratification as follows: "If the rights and prerequisites of different positions in a society must be unequal, then the society must be stratified, because that is precisely what stratification means." We shall argue, however, that this is not precisely what stratification has meant to most students. It is (or was) rather firmly imbedded in usage that stratification involved the existence of *strata,* generally agreed to refer to specifiable collectivities or subgroups that *continue through several generations* to occupy the same relative positions and to receive the same relative amounts of material ends, prestige, and power. The statement quoted above, on the other hand, refers only to the fact of the differentiation of social positions as seen at any one point in time, and implies nothing about the existence of strata, which, to extend our above definition, implies groupings of individuals with biological and social continuity whose movements into the differentiated positions can be predicted to some degree (if only statistically).[15]

Buckley's criticism is twofold: (a) that the Davis-Moore use of "stratification" is much too *abstract* (in that it refers to unequal rewards attached to

---

14. Walter Buckley, "Social Stratification and the Functional Theory of Social Differentiation," *American Sociological Review,* XXIII (August, 1958), 369–73.
15. *Ibid.,* p. 370.

positions and not to specific *strata*); and (b) that it fails to include the notion of *ascription* (in that it does not refer to "groupings of individuals with biological and social continuity"). And both of these criticisms seem to be in error. It is a commonplace that scientific theories require a fairly high level of abstraction; and if this abstraction makes possible an increase in analytical precision, then the desirability of abstraction is beyond question. As to the second criticism, it is applicable to the Davis and Moore 1945 version, but inapplicable to the Davis 1948 version.

Kingsley Davis's "The Abominable Heresy: Reply to Dr. Buckley" was an emotional and sarcastic counterattack. Davis affirmed his right to define "stratification" in a manner different from Buckley, and added that:

> the most significant thing about Dr. Buckley's paper is that he himself proposes no alternative theory of positional inequality or, for that matter, of what he calls stratification. If he had any specific curiosity about the subject one would expect him not only to refute an existing theory but to supply another in its place. Instead he falls back on a tenet of Marxian faith. "For an explanation of its ubiquity," he writes, "we must turn . . . to the sociocultural dynamics of particular times and places. . . ." The real heresy in the Davis-Moore article . . . is rather the sin of believing that *any* scientific explanation of social inequality can be found.
>
> The Davis-Moore theory of social inequality can certainly be improved upon. Along with others I have tried to do so in writings that my critic conveniently ignores. Improvement in the theory will come, however, by modification and extension rather than by all-out attack without replacement. The fact remains, of course, that the more the theory is improved as a scientific explanation, the more intransigent will be the attacks on it as a heresy.[16]

The scientific import of this reply is questionable, and it seems a bit absurd to castigate a critic for limiting his role to making a negative contribution.

In December, 1959, Dennis H. Wrong's "The Functional Theory of Stratification: Some Neglected Considerations" attempted to mediate between theory and its critics:

> The functional theory of stratification advanced by Davis and Moore attempts to explain the universality and necessity of inequality in societies with a complex division of labor, a task that is independent of efforts to explain the division of labor itself or the intergenerational perpetuation of inequalities along family lines. The theory is so general, however, that it excludes none of the Utopian models of "classless societies" proposed by Western thinkers and, its critics to the contrary notwithstanding, says nothing whatsoever about the range of inequality and the determinants of

---

16. Kingsley Davis, "The Abominable Heresy: A Reply to Dr. Buckley," *American Sociological Review*, XXIV (February, 1959), 83.

that range in concrete societies. The theory appears to understate the degree to which positions are inherited by failing to view societies in long range historical perspective. In common with the arguments of its critics, it also ignores the possible disruptive consequences of mobility and equality of opportunity, a theme notably neglected by American sociologists.[17]

Here the opening formulation is incorrect. Davis and Moore do not attempt "to explain the universality and necessity of inequality," but attempt to explain the universality of inequality by its alleged necessity. This aspect of the Davis-Moore theory, in effect, exemplifies the typical functionalist maneuver of explaining a cultural universal by claiming that it is necessary for the preservation or survival of a system. The observation that the Davis and Moore theory neglects "the power element in stratification," and is "lacking a truly historical perspective,"[18] is quite accurate.

In 1960, Tumin's "Competing Status Systems," a contribution to Arnold S. Feldman and Wilbert E. Moore's *Labor Commitment and Social Change in Developing Areas,* repeated Tumin's earlier contention that "there is nothing inevitable at all about the need for unequal rewards for unequal work."[19] The following year, in his book *Social Class and Social Change in Puerto Rico,* Tumin argued that:

> We must conclude that the actual shape of any reward system or any system of inducement and recruitment into tasks will be a function of the relevant powers of the sectors who hold differing judgments about the respective importance of tasks. Stratification, then, to the extent to which, as some have suggested, it can be defined by the system of unequal allocation of scarce, valued goods and services, is something very different from an unconsciously evolved device by which societies insure that the most competent persons will be induced to take on the tasks considered most functionally important to the society. It is rather an outcome, specified partly by social reward distributions, which is a function of the competition among variable definitions of what is important to the respective powers available to the competing sectors to implement their decision [the passage is italicized in the original].[20]

Since "the actual shape of any reward system" refers to the range of inequality, Tumin is here suggesting that the actual configuration of power is a crucial determinant of the range of unequal rewards attached to different

---

17. Dennis H. Wrong, "The Functionalist Theory of Stratification: Some Neglected Considerations," *American Sociological Review,* XXIV (December, 1959), 772.
18. *Ibid.,* pp. 774–78.
19. Melvin M. Tumin, "Competing Status Systems," in Arnold S. Feldman and Wilbert E. Moore, eds., *Labor Commitment and Social Change in Developing Areas* (New York: Social Science Research Council, 1960), p. 279.
20. Melvin M. Tumin with Arnold S. Feldman, *Social Class and Social Change in Puerto Rico* (Princeton, N.J.: Princeton University Press, 1961), p. 491.

positions. He is also suggesting that the effective power of relevant sectors implements their evaluation of which positions are more important than others by the allocation of greater rewards to these positions.

> It seems quite possible, however, to account for the universal presence of ranking and evaluation systems, and for the presence of inequalities in scarce, valued goods and services in nearly all societies, without relying upon some very restricted notion of the conditions under which actors will be induced to take up certain roles and perform them conscientiously. It would be equally reasonable to imagine an earlier historical condition where differences in age and strength made it possible for some members of groups to seize what they wanted when they wanted them, and to proceed to institutionalize their power over others by allocating the goods and services as they saw fit. Once in control of the socialization of the young, it is not much of a trick to teach certain patterns of deference which no longer require differences in physical strength to maintain.[21]

This formulation seems to involve some confusion. Tumin is unquestionably correct in taking power as a major determinant of role *ascription;* and a power explanation goes a long way in accounting for why the present incumbents of high-reward positions are who they are. But can a power explanation be equally effective in accounting for the inequality of rewards attached to positions? The difference can perhaps be made clear by appealing to a well-known historical example. The Aryan invasion is said to have been the historical origin of the Hindu caste system. This power event explains why the high-reward positions of priest and warrior were occupied exclusively by members of the conqueror group. It does *not* explain why both the conquerors and the conquered alike (together with many other similar traditional societies) should have regarded the roles of priest and warrior as high-reward positions.

In February, 1963, Wilbert E. Moore's "But Some Are More Equal than Others" answered Tumin and made a re-appraisal of the original Davis-Moore 1945 version.

> My current view is that the Davis-Moore position was incomplete, resulting in some overstatement (as noted by Simpson) and some neglect of dysfunctions. These criticisms have already been noted by Davis. In addition, I should specifically reject any stable equilibrium version of "functionalism" as both incorrect and extrinsic to the position that social inequality is a necessary feature of any social system. . . . The "functional theory of stratification" maintained only that positions of unequal importance would be unequally rewarded, and was silent, regrettably but not criminally, on the subject of systemic changes. . . . Although Davis and Moore were fairly explicit in equating "social stratification" with un-

---

21. *Ibid.,* p. 508.

equal rewards, that now appears unfortunate. I have some sympathy for Buckley's criticism on this point.[22]

After these modifications Moore turned to re-affirm the original thesis of the 1945 version:

> The single issue to which the present remarks are addressed is whether social inequality is a necessary feature of social systems. . . . The explanation presented here reiterates the thesis that "functional differentiation" of positions will inevitably entail unequal rewards—and adds the thesis that differences in performance must be expected to be and will be differentially valued.[23]

Here Moore reviews the many ways in which "inequality" can arise from the social valuation of "performances, qualities, and achievements," but this misses the point, because neither Tumin nor anyone has argued for the viability of a completely egalitarian order: the issue concerns only the possibility and feasibility of "equivalents" or "alternatives" to "unequal rewards"; namely, whether or not something other than unequal rewards can motivate individuals to occupy the different positions. Moore does not think so.

> Unless intrinsic task equalization is accomplished, it would seem extremely unlikely that equality of rewards—or rather, permitting only esteem rewards—would be institutionalized by any conceivable system of socialization. This would require a somewhat greater extension of martyrdom than any religious system has yet achieved—and religious martyrs expect future rewards. I believe that Tumin has become entrapped by an ideological position that I see no reason to accept: namely that equality is intrinsically more equitable than inequality.[24]

On the causes of "stratification" (unequal rewards attached to different positions), Moore repeated the 1945 formulation and rejected Tumin's modification:

> The Davis-Moore "functional" interpretation of inequality rested on the unequal functional importance of positions and the unequal supply of talents for filling them. That interpretation, unlike most functional analyses, was explicitly evolutionary, and like many had possible rationalistic overtones. Tumin essentially skirts the issues of importance and talents but rejects the evolutionary explanation, for which he substitutes

---

22. Wilbert E. Moore, "But Some Are More Equal than Others," *American Sociological Review*, XXVIII (February, 1963), 14–15.
23. *Ibid.*, p. 15.
24. *Ibid.*, p. 16.

the view that stratification is an anachronistic survival maintained by self-perpetuating power. (That revolutionary polities establish new modes of social stratification escapes his attention.)[25]

This account of Tumin's views is not quite accurate. Although Tumin did not discuss revolutionary polities, their existence does not constitute a counter-example to his argument. Tumin suggested that the values of relevant power sectors constitute a decisive determinant of "the actual shape of any reward system." And as we saw when we analyzed his argument with the aid of a concrete historical example, power is most certainly a decisive determinant of positional ascription, but it is questionable whether power can explain why within a given socio-historical setting some positions are given high rewards and not others.

Moore argued that the class system of industrial societies exhibits "fragmentation of even nominally singular statuses into comparable analytical subsystems," and that:

> Tumin's position here is compounded of several empirical errors: (1) a class system "really exists"; (2) it is posited upon only one dominant "phase" of social life, the economic, which is associated with (the cause of?) prestige and power; (3) other worthwhile human endeavors are given something less than their "due" because the economy had "invaded" other institutional areas. Not only does this entail an exaggeration of status comparability in industrial societies, but it leads to a perception of status anxieties more pervasive than any evidence indicates.[26]

Moore's formulation, in turn, would seem to rest on an exaggeration. If no class system "really exists" in industrial society because the "analytical subsystems" are really "incomparable," then it would seem to follow that most theories of stratification, including the Davis and Moore theory, are either irrelevant or inapplicable.

In "On Inequality," his reply to Moore, Melvin Tumin argued that the range of social inequality is much greater than that which is institutionalized in unequal rewards.

> Any of the diverse inequalities found in society can become subject to stratification. These inequalities arise from: (1) role specification; (2) ranking according to characteristics intrinsic to the role; (3) ranking according to moral conformity; (4) ranking according to contribution to (a) value and moral ideals and (b) functionally important tasks; (5) diffusion and transfer. Types (1), (2), and (4) have higher likelihood of being

---

25. Moore, *loc. cit.*
26. *Ibid.,* p. 17.

taken up into the stratification system, but none *need* so result. Considerable inequality can therefore coexist with little or no stratification.[27]

Here Tumin's main point represents a harmonious addition to the Davis and Moore theory. Tumin's secondary claim that some types of inequality "seem unavoidable as system features for survival of a society over two generations" is more complex and seems to involve disparate elements. First, Tumin is referring to parent-child, man-woman role differentiations (which Davis has explicitly ruled out as possible bases for stratification). Second, Tumin is referring to the universality of invidious valuations: "Everywhere men tend to make comparisons as to who is taller, or prettier, or quicker" (but need he follow the arbitrary functionalist maneuver of translating a cultural universal into an alleged functional necessity?). Third, Tumin is referring to "ranking by functional contribution," which he divides into two major analytical sub-types: (a) "Ranking according to contribution to or exemplification of ideals"; and (b) "Ranking according to functional contribution to desired social goals." In connection with the latter he says:

> Current theory attaches the greatest significance to differential functional importance as a basis of social stratification. It is argued that every society must make judgments about unequal functional importance and must allocate its scarce and desired goods at least partly in line with such judgments.[28]

As an account of what Davis and Moore claim this is surely in error. Once again, it must be emphatically pointed out that differential functional importance is not the same as the judgments or valuations of a given society. Differential functional importance is, presumably, the degree of contribution which each position makes to the preservation or survival of the society.

In his "Rejoinder" to Tumin, Wilbert E. Moore agreed that social inequality and unequal rewards are definitionally different, but he argued that they are empirically closer than Tumin allows. He questioned Tumin's "extremely relativistic view of cultural values and social institutions," and suggested that there is an underlying pattern of necessary functions:

> As I read the evidence, the evaluation of functionally differentiated positions is by no means as randomly variable as his discussion asserts or implies. I suggest that behavior relevant to the maintenance of order, the provision of economic support, the protection of the society, and the ex-

---

27. Melvin M. Tumin, "On Inequality," *American Sociological Review*, XXVIII (February, 1963), 18.
28. *Ibid.*, p. 23.

emplifications of religious and aesthetic values *always* involves differential positional as well as merely personal valuation.[29]

To say that positions in these general areas involve differential valuation is not very enlightening, since presumably all positions in a given society have some degree of positive or negative valuation. Furthermore, and as is the case with all lists of so-called functional prerequisites, the general areas listed by Moore add up to a fairly standard definition of society. It follows from this that the claim that these positions "always" involve valuation is little more than a tautology.

In October, 1963, Arthur L. Stinchcombe's "Some Empirical Consequences of the Davis-Moore Theory of Stratification" attempted to demonstrate that differential functional importance really exists and can be tested. With explicit reference to the Davis-Moore 1945 version, Stinchcombe argued that:

> Davis and Moore's basic argument is that unequal rewards tend to accrue to positions of great importance to society, provided that the talents needed for such positions are scarce. "Society" (i.e., people strongly identified with the collective fate) insures that these functions are properly performed by rewarding the talented people for undertaking these tasks. This implies that the greater the importance of positions, the less likely they are to be filled by ascriptive recruitment. (Footnote: The theory holds that the most important positions, if they require unusual talents, will recruit people who otherwise would not take them, by offering high rewards to talent. This result would take place if one assumed a perfectly achievement-based stratification system. Some have asserted that Davis and Moore's argument "assumes" such a perfectly open system, and hence is obviously inadequate to the facts. Since the relevant results will be obtained if a system recruits more talented people to its "important" positions but ascribes all others, and since this postulate is not obviously false as is the free market assumption, we will assume the weaker postulate here. It seems unlikely that Davis and Moore ever assumed the stronger, obviously false, postulate.)[30]

This seems to be very confused. First, Davis and Moore (1945) argued that high rewards (not "unequal rewards") "tend to accrue" to positions of high functional importance and high but scarce requirements of talent and training. Second, nothing in this proposition, or in the entire 1945 version, permits anyone to draw any inferences about "ascriptive recruitment." The reason for this is obvious: the 1945 version did not discuss ascription and the 1948 version attempted to remedy this lack by introducing the role of

---

29. Wilbert E. Moore, "Rejoinder," *American Sociological Review*, XXVIII (February, 1963), 27.
30. Arthur L. Stinchcombe, "Some Empirical Consequences of the Davis-Moore Theory," *American Sociological Review*, XXVIII (October, 1963), 805.

the family as the explanation of ascription. Furthermore, the 1948 version accounted for concrete stratification systems as approximations to two theoretical extremes: a complete achievement order versus a completely ascriptive one. Nothing in this formulation allows Stinchcombe to infer an inverse relationship between functional importance and ascription. Finally the assertion that "a system recruits more talented people to its 'important' positions but ascribes all others," implies a dichotomy between important and nonimportant positions; and this is clearly at variance with the usage of Davis and Moore, for whom, presumably, *every* position within the system has a *different degree* of functional importance.

Next, Stinchcombe gives us his first concrete example of what he regards as differential functional importance.

> It is quite difficult to rank tasks or roles according to their relative importance. But certain tasks are unquestionably more important at one time than at another, or more important in one group than another. For instance, generals are more important in wartime than in peacetime.[31]

But this is simply a misunderstanding. Here the position "general" is compared to itself in two different time periods (wartime versus peacetime), but the notion of differential functional importance in Davis and Moore refers to a comparison of different positions in the same time period. But then can we not say that in wartime the position "general" makes a greater contribution to societal survival than, say, the position "housewife"? In one obvious sense this is true, but this is not the sense involved in Davis and Moore's differential functional importance. A nation at war involves the co-ordination of social resources for the pursuit of a system-goal. This co-ordination involves the temporary and dichotomous classification of all system-positions into two categories: (a) those positions which are necessary or essential for the pursuit of the war (e.g., general, arms manufacturer, nuclear scientist, etc.), and (b) those positions which are not necessary or essential for the pursuit of the war (e.g., housewife, luxury-goods manufacturer, artist, etc.). Our improved version of Stinchcombe's example will not do for at least three good reasons: (1) differential functional importance involves, presumably, different *degrees* of contribution to societal survival attached to the various positions (and a dichotomy is useless for this purpose); (2) the example is set in wartime, and this involves a system whose positions are coordinated as means for the pursuit of a system-goal, and this is not the usual condition of social systems throughout history (in other words, even if this example of differential functional importance were a valid one, which it is not, the possibility of generalizing to peacetime would still be in question); (3) the assertion that

---

31. *Ibid.*

generals, foot soldiers, arms manufacturers (or any war specialists) are "necessary" for the pursuit of war is not an empirical statement but a tautology.

Stinchcombe's second example of differential functional importance involves changes in the position "king."

> The kingship in West European democratic monarchies has consistently declined in political importance as the powers of parliament have increased. . . . Their rewards have also changed, emphasizing more ceremonial deference and expressions of sentiment, less wealth and power. . . . Changes in the nature of the role-requirements and of the rewards indicate a shift of functions. At the least these changes indicate that some ceremonial functions of the kingship have declined much less in importance than the political functions. But to have a nonpolitical function in a political structure is probably to be less important in the eyes of the people.[32]

In the first place, this example is open to the same criticisms made of the last example: the position "king" is compared to itself over two or more time periods, but differential functional importance involves the comparison of different positions among themselves within one time period. In the second place, what does "to be less important in the eyes of the people" have to do with differential functional importance? What degree of contribution to societal survival was made by the position "king" before the rise of parliament? After the rise of parliament?

Stinchcombe's third example is a bit confused in that it is unclear whether it is intended as an example of differential functional importance, differential talent of personnel, or both.

> In some industries individual talent is clearly a *complementary* factor of production, in the sense that it makes other factors much more productive; in others, it is more nearly *additive*. To take an extreme case of complementarity, when Alec Guinness is "mixed" with a stupid plot, routine supporting actors, ordinary production costs, plus perhaps a thousand dollars for extra makeup, the result is a commercially very successful movie; perhaps Guinness increases the value of the movie to twice as much by being three times as good as the alternative actor. But if an equally talented housepainter (three times as good as the alternative) is "mixed" with a crew of 100 average men, the value of the total production goes to approximately 103 per cent. Relatively speaking then, individual role performance is much more "important" in the first kind of enterprise.[33]

"Much more important" here means "makes a greater contribution to the economic or commercial value of the product." All speculation apart, the

---

32. *Ibid.*, p. 806.
33. *Ibid.*

film example is unfortunate because in the case of Guinness his commercial value resides in his role as a film star and not in his role as a dramatic actor, and the two are not the same (in fact, in Hollywood they come close to being inversely related). Therefore it is very questionable whether it is the dramatic talent of Guinness which is the complementary input into the "commercially very successful movie." But beyond all this, what sense does it make to compare special creative talent and ordinary skill? And if the sense of the comparison is to tell us that creative talent generally receives greater rewards than ordinary skill, don't we know this already? Stinchcombe goes on to make up two lists of "enterprises" in which talent is said to be primarily complementary and primarily additive.

Talent Complementary Factor
Research
  Universities
Entertainment
Management
Teams in athletics and other "winner take all" structures
Violin Concertos

Talent Nearly Additive
Teaching
  Undergraduate colleges
  High Schools
Manufacturing
Manual Work
Groups involved in ordinary competition in which the rewards are divided
  among the meritorious
Symphonies.[34]

Now a simple inspection of the activities grouped under these two lists reveals that the first contains an appreciably greater proportion of high reward activities, and also of activities which involve special creative talents. Stinchcombe "predicts" that this will be the case. He again "predicts" that activities in the second list will involve a greater amount of ascription by age, time-in-grade, and seniority. It is difficult to see what is proved by these two lists beyond the well known fact that in the United States (the lists are culture-specific) role incumbents with special creative talents will generally receive greater rewards than those with ordinary skills (and that the latter will be more prone to seek the compensatory security of devices such as seniority).

In October, 1963, Walter Buckley's "On Equitable Inequality" replied to some of the points raised by Wilbert E. Moore's February, 1963, article. Buckley argued that the Davis-Moore theory involves a "competitive

---

34. *Ibid.*

differential surplus of personnel. This was the situation of Russia in 1917 with its highly educated and underemployed intelligentsia; and it is also the situation of many colonial societies where the colonial administration fosters the simultaneous education and underemployment of a native intelligentsia.

What remains of the Davis and Moore functionalist theory of stratification? Two decades of controversy seem to have effectively sorted out the metaphysical postulate and questionable assumptions from the more valuable ingredients. These ingredients contain considerable insight, but by themselves they do not add up to a fully adequate theory of social inequality, mobility, and ascription, much less of stratification.

| Chapter 7 | Minority Groups: What is the Relationship Between Race and Intelligence? |

One of the most exciting controversies in recent years began in 1969, with the publication of an article by Arthur Jensen dealing with the relationship between IQ, compensatory education, race and social class. This section opens with a brief summary by Jensen of the position he took in that article. He found that compensatory education had not significantly improved the measured intelligence or academic performance of its target population—"disadvantaged children." Recognizing that IQ is only one portion of mental ability, Jensen concluded that IQ is largely inherited, is inversely related to social class and that blacks typically have lower IQs than whites. He contends that it is reasonable to *hypothesize* that the causes of the racial differences are genetic *as well as* environmental. Further, since lower class blacks have a higher reproduction rate than middle class blacks, Jensen sees the possibility of a lowering of the IQ level in the black community and a widening of the gap between blacks and whites. Turning to other aspects of mental ability, Jensen found that there were negligible differences between classes and races on associative-learning abilities. Given this lack of significant differences, Jensen asks other social scientists to delineate other types of mental abilities. Basically Jensen is saying that compensatory education has failed in the black community because it is aimed at the raising of mental ability (IQ), which is largely genetically determined. Hence these efforts are doomed to failure. He asserts that there are other kinds of mental abilities, and that these must be delineated so that the kind of education program can be tailored to a given child's pattern of abilities.

Jensen's work caused an avalanche of criticism, and a sampling of those critiques is reprinted in this section. Bernstein and Giaquinta take issue with Jensen's contention that compensatory education has failed. They feel that Jensen's conclusions are based on three unwarranted assumptions. First, he assumed that such compensatory programs could compensate for social inequities. Second, Jensen assumed that these programs have been adequately implemented in the majority of the schools in which they have been introduced. Finally, Jensen contended that traditional public schooling is effective for children with the basic ability to learn. The bulk of Bernstein and Giacquinta's reply is concerned with documenting why these assumptions are unwarranted.

In another critique Anderson notes that blacks and whites are not distinctly different populations because race is socially defined—there is much passing and a great deal of cross-mating. Since scientific measures of heritability were developed to be used on "true" populations, they were incorrectly used by Jensen in his analysis. Anderson also underscores the fact that we are not sure what IQ measures and that a large number of situational factors can radically affect an IQ score. Finally, Anderson points out how small the difference between whites and blacks really is (about eleven IQ points) and concludes that this is strong evidence that there are no significant IQ differences between whites and blacks. In closing, Anderson raises the interesting point that the publication of Jensen's article and the exaggerated publicity which followed can serve only to fan racial tensions. Implicitly, Anderson is claiming that Jensen should not have published his article because of its adverse effect on race relations in the United States.

The political implications of Jensen's article are the theme of the reply by the Black Student Union of the Harvard Graduate School of Education. They feel that the editors of the *Harvard Educational Review* (which published Jensen's article) gave tacit support to the idea that blacks are genetically inferior. Roy L. Brown also responds in political terms, viewing Jensen's work as a "vain attempt to get blacks, and other deprived people, to quit fighting for equal opportunity and believe in the *Santa Claus* of automatic justice." Eckland is concerned with Jensen's belief that "no holds barred research" is the best way to conduct scientific inquiry. He rhetorically asks what the result would be if blacks were to be "proven" genetically inferior intellectually, and answers that it would be another piece of information which would serve to increase racism. Finally, eighteen members of the Society for the Psychological Study of Social Issues enter a plea for open inquiry, but in the process list the reasons why Jensen is wrong. Why, one may ask, is a group which is in favor of open inquiry in such a rush to prove Jensen wrong?

Race, Class and Intelligence*

Arthur R. Jensen

More than one year ago the Board of Editors of the *Harvard Educational Review* solicited from me an article for their Winter 1969 issue on the general topic "How Much Can We Boost I.Q. and Scholastic Achievement?" Their letter of solicitation outlined the main points to be discussed in the article, with particular reference to the contribution of heredity and environment to intelligence and scholastic performance, an evaluation of efforts to raise I.Q. and scholastic performance of disadvantaged children, my position on social class and racial differences in intelligence, and my own research on the triple interaction among the variables intelligence, associative learning ability, and socioeconomic status. The resulting article of 123 pages—the longest ever published by the *Harvard Educational Review*—discussed each of these topics in considerable detail. Here, very briefly, is the gist of what I said on each topic.

Compensatory Education

First, I reviewed the conclusions of a nationwide survey and evaluation of the large Federally funded compensatory education programs, an evaluation by the United States Commission on Civil Rights, which concluded that these special programs had produced no significant improvement in the measured intelligence or scholastic performance of the disadvantaged children whose educational achievements these programs were specially intended to raise. The evidence presented by the U.S. Commission on Civil Rights suggests to me that merely applying more of the same approach to compensatory education on a larger scale is not likely to lead to the desired results, namely increasing the benefits of public education to the disadvantaged. The well-documented fruitlessness of these well-intentioned large-scale compensatory programs indicates the importance of now questioning the assumptions, theories and practices on which they were based. I point out, also, that some small-scale experimental intervention programs have shown more promise of beneficial results. I do *not* advocate abandoning efforts to improve the education of the disadvan-

* Reprinted from *Psychology Today*, October, 1969. Copyright © Communications/Research/Machines, Inc.

taged. I urge increased emphasis on these efforts, in the spirit of experimentation, expanding the diversity of approaches and improving the rigor of evaluation in order to boost our chances of discovering the methods that will work best.

THE NATURE OF INTELLIGENCE

I point out that I.Q. tests evolved to predict scholastic performance in largely European and North American middle-class populations around the turn of the century. They evolved to measure those particular abilities most relevant to a particular curriculum and type of instruction, which in turn were shaped by the particular pattern of abilities of the children the schools were then intended to serve. I.Q. or abstract-reasoning ability is thus a selection of just one portion of the total spectrum of human mental abilities. This aspect of mental abilities measured by I.Q. tests is very important in our society, but is not the only set of educationally or occupationally relevant abilities. Other mental abilities have not yet been adequately measured; their distributions in various segments of the population have not been adequately determined; and their educational relevance has not been fully explored. I believe that a much broader assessment of the spectrum of abilities and potentials, and the investigation of their utilization for educational achievement, will be an essential aspect of improving the education of children called disadvantaged.

INHERITANCE OF INTELLIGENCE

Much of my paper is a review of the methods and evidence that lead me to the conclusion that individual differences in intelligence—that is, I.Q.—are predominantly attributable to genetic differences, with environmental factors contributing a minor portion of the variance among individuals in I.Q. The heritability of the I.Q.—that is, the percentage of individual differences variance attributable to genetic factors—comes out to about 80%, which is the average value obtained in all the relevant studies now reported in the literature, with values extending over a range from about 60% to 90%. These estimates of heritability are based on tests administered to European and North American populations and cannot properly be generalized to other populations. I believe we need similar heritability studies in minority populations if we are to increase our understanding of what our tests measure in these populations and how these abilities can be most effectively used in the educational process.

SOCIAL-CLASS DIFFERENCES

Although the full range of I.Q. and other abilities is found among children in every socioeconomic stratum in our population, it is well established that the I.Q. differs on the average among children from different social-class backgrounds. The evidence, some of which I refer to in my article, indicates to me that some of this I.Q. difference is attributable to environmental differences and some of it is attributable to genetic differences between social classes—largely as a result of differential selection of the parent generations for different patterns of ability. I have not yet met or read a modern geneticist who disputes this interpretation of the evidence. The geneticist C. O. Carter remarked, "Sociologists who doubt this show more ingenuity than judgment." I have also read at least three prominent sociologists who are students of this problem—Pitirim Sorokin, Bruce Eckland, and Otis Dudley Duncan—and all agree that selective factors in social mobility and assortative mating have resulted in a genetic component in social-class intelligence differences. As Eckland points out, this conclusion holds *within* socially defined racial groups but cannot properly be generalized *between* racial groups since barriers to upward social mobility have undoubtedly been quite different for various racial groups.

RACE DIFFERENCES

I have always advocated dealing with persons as individuals, each in terms of his own merits and characteristics. I am opposed to according any treatment to persons solely on the basis of their race, color, national origin, or social-class background. But I am also opposed to ignoring or refusing to investigate the causes of the well-established differences among racial groups in the distribution of educationally relevant traits, particularly I.Q.

I believe that the cause of the observed differences in I.Q. and scholastic performance among different ethnic groups is scientifically still an open question, an important question, and a researchable question. I believe that official statements, apparently accepted without question by some social scientists, such as "It is a demonstrable fact that the talent pool in any one ethnic group is substantially the same as in any other ethnic group" (U.S. Office of Education, 1966) and "Intelligence potential is distributed among Negro infants in the same proportion and pattern as among Icelanders or Chinese, or any other group" (Dept. of Labor, 1965) are without scientific merit. They lack any factual basis and must be regarded only as hypotheses. It would require a full article just to describe the ugly personal and professional consequences of challenging this prevailing hypothesis of genetic equality by suggesting alternative hypotheses that invoke genetic as well as environmental factors as being among the causes of the observed differences in patterns of mental ability between racial groups. The fact that different racial groups in this country have widely separated geographic origins and have had quite different histories which have subjected them to different selective social and economic pressures make it highly likely that their gene pools differ for some genetically conditioned behavioral characteristics, including intelligence or abstract-reasoning ability. Nearly every anatomical, physiological and biochemical system investigated shows racial differences. Why should the brain be an exception? The reasonableness of the hypothesis that there are racial differences in genetically conditioned behavioral characteristics, including mental abilities, is not confined to the poorly informed, but has been expressed in writings and public statements by such eminent geneticists as Kenneth Mather, C. D. Darlington, R. A. Fisher, and Francis Crick, to name but a few.

I indicated several lines of evidence that support my assertion that a genetic hypothesis is not unwarranted. The fact that we still have only inconclusive conclusions with respect to this hypothesis does not mean that the opposite of the hypothesis is true. Yet some social scientists speak as if this were the case and have even publicly censured me for suggesting an alternative to purely environmental hypotheses of intelligence differences. Scientific investigation proceeds most effectively by means of what Platt has called "strong inference," which means pitting against one another alternative hypotheses that lead to different predictions, and then putting these predictions to an empirical test.

DYSGENIC TRENDS

More important than the issue of racial differences *per se* is the probability, explicated in my article, of dysgenic trends in our urban slums, as suggested by census data showing markedly higher birth rates among the poorest segments of the Negro population than among successful, middle-class Negroes. This social-class differential in birth rate appears to be much greater in the Negro than in the white population. That is, the least able among Negroes have a higher reproductive rate than their white counterparts in ability, and the educationally and occupationally most able segment of the Negro population has a lower reproductive rate than their white counterparts. If social-class intelligence differences within the Negro population have a genetic component, as in the white population, the condition I have described could create and widen the genetic intelligence difference between Negroes and whites. The social and educational implications of this trend, if it exists and persists, are enormous. The problem obviously deserves thorough investigation by social scientists and geneti-

fallacy" because it interprets stratification in all societies in terms of an atypical case: "the competitive-achievement syndrome of contemporary industrial societies." He repeated Tumin's point (granted by Moore) that stratification limits or restricts the development of potential talent. He accused Moore of confusing "inequality" with "inequity" (or with using "inequality" in such a way that the meaning of the term shifts from "objective differences" to "inequity"). He argues that the real task of stratification studies should be to determine the minimum range of unequal rewards compatible with an industrial order. Finally, Buckley pointed out that Moore's claim that a class system does not really exist is an artifact created by an artificially restricted definition of "stratum"; and that to adopt Moore's usage would force us to say that "no known society is or has ever been stratified."[35]

In October, 1963, George A. Huaco's "A Logical Analysis of the Davis-Moore Theory of Stratification" attempted a detailed analysis of the notion of differential functional importance.

> The postulate of unequal functional importance means that for any given society, the performance of some roles contributes more to the preservation of survival of that society than the performance of other roles. For this statement we need an independent definition of survival. We also need criteria to measure how much a given role contributes to survival vis-à-vis any other role. Davis mentions the following examples of such criteria.
>
> "Rough measures of functional importance are in fact applied in practice. In wartime, for example, decisions are made as to which industries and occupations will have priority in capital equipment, labor recruitment, raw materials, etc. In totalitarian countries the same is done in peacetime, as also in underdeveloped areas attempting to maximize their social and economic modernization. Individual firms must constantly decide which positions are essential and which are not."[36]
>
> The difficulties with these examples are twofold:
>
> a. Each of them provides a dichotomous (essential/nonessential) criterion which seems to be tautologically derived from an over-all system goal. But what we need is criteria that permit us to measure the *degree* of contribution to societal survival of any role vis-à-vis any other role; in short, we need ranking criteria.
>
> b. Each of these examples is drawn from a partially or totally planned economic system, and as such, useless for drawing inferences applicable to unplanned systems (and most societies throughout history have been unplanned).[37]

---

35. Walter Buckley, "On Equitable Inequality," *American Sociological Review*, XXVIII (October, 1963), 800.

36. Davis, "Reply," *op. cit.*, p. 395.

37. George A. Huaco, "A Logical Analysis of the Davis-Moore Theory of Stratification," *American Sociological Review*, XXVIII (October, 1963), 803.

Huaco examined the two "clues" mentioned in the Davis and Moore 1945 version (role uniqueness, and degree to which other positions are dependent on the one in question). He pointed out that there is absolutely no empirical basis for admitting uniqueness and dependency as indicators of anything beyond themselves. Next he examined a claim made by Davis in both the 1945 and 1948 versions. Davis wrote:

> Owing to the universal necessity of certain functions in society, which require social organization for their performance, there is an underlying similarity in the kind of positions put at the top, the kind put at the middle, and the kind put at the bottom of the scale. . . . For this purpose we shall select religion, government, economic activity, and technology.[38]

Huaco remarked that this selection of four "necessary" societal "functions" is not only familiar, but it is also in the right order. And that:

> As described by Davis, the selected "functions" roughly correspond to the four analytical levels of a well-known model of society:
>
> | Davis | Marx |
> |---|---|
> | Religion | Upper layer of superstructure |
> | Government | Lower layer of superstructure |
> | Economic Activity | Relations of production |
> | Technology | Forces of production |
>
> The sole purpose of this comparison is to suggest that Davis and Moore's "universal" and "necessary" societal "functions" are really the various analytical parts of their implicit model of society, or are derived by a series of hidden tautologies from such an implicit model. The "necessity" involved is clearly analytical or logical necessity. It follows from this that Davis' claim that what he has selected are four "universal" and "necessary" societal "functions" is simply a tautology.[39]

Huaco concluded that differential functional importance is "a complete unknown," and that "it cannot serve as a legitimate explanation for unequal rewards."

In Retrospect

Now let us return to our initial analysis of the logical structure of the Davis and Moore theory to try and sort out those portions which have been destroyed by the critics from the more solid and promising fragments. In

---

38. Davis, *Human Society, op. cit.,* p. 371.
39. Huaco, *op. cit.,* p. 804.

the first place, it is fairly obvious that the basic concept of the theory, the postulate of differential functional importance, is a fallacy. There is not a shred of evidence that different positions make different degrees of contribution to societal preservation or survival. In the second place, it is also obvious that the assumption to the effect that societies whose stratification systems approach a pure achievement order have greater survival or endurance than more ascriptive societies is not only unwarranted, but probably false. Nevertheless, the remaining fragments of the theory seem to hold considerable promise.

I. *Unequal rewards attached to different positions are a cause of the mobility of individuals into positions.* Despite the technical issue of possible "alternatives," it now seems fairly certain that this is one of the most solid portions of the theory. Evidence for this is indirect, but impressive, and it comes from the area of experimental psychology known as learning theory. Very briefly, Davis and Moore's comprehensive definition of "rewards" corresponds to the psychological notion of "reinforcement." The notion of "high rewards" corresponds to "positive reinforcement" and "low rewards" to "negative reinforcement." Learning theorists have considerable experimental evidence that both animals and humans learn and act in response to the manipulation of positive and negative reinforcements.

II. *The existence and operation of the institution of the family is cause of status ascription.* That the particularistic character of kinship bonds tends to generate status ascription is probably self-evident. It is also evident that the existence of the family is an insufficient or incomplete explanation of ascription. We can set up a conceptual model in which the ascriptive propensities of the family are held in abeyance and in which a sizeable amount of status ascription is nevertheless generated. The Norman conquest of England will do as a point of departure: we know that the Norman conquerors reserved for themselves most high reward positions, and limited the conquered Saxons to low reward positions. We know that both societies had extensive family ascription; but the point is that similar ascriptive results would have followed a similar conquest even if both societies had been completely achievement oriented. The explanation of why the conquering Normans reserved for themselves most high reward positions cannot be found in the Norman family, but must be traced to the conquest itself, that is to say to the phenomenon of power.

III. *Differential scarcity of qualified personnel is a cause of "stratification" (unequal rewards attached to different positions).* Let us modify the statement to read: differential scarcity of qualified personnel is a cause of *the range* of unequal rewards attached to different positions. This interesting notion deserves to be developed beyond its brief formulation by Davis and Moore. It seems that we can posit variation along two different dimensions: on the one hand the positional structure of a given society may have high or low requirements for talent and training, on the other hand the population of the same society may have high or low amounts of effective talent and training. A state of relative differential scarcity of personnel can be said to exist whenever there is a sizeable gap between the amount of effective talent and training available in the population and the amount of talent and training required by the positional structure of the society. We can now set up a fourfold table and examine the various possibilities:

		Amount of Talent and Training Required by the Positional Structure of the Society	
		High	Low
Amount of Talent and Training Available in the Population	High	Mature Industrial Society	Pre-Revolutionary Society
	Low	Industrializing Society	Traditional Society

1. *Traditional Society:* Here the amount of talent and training required by the positional structure of the society is low and the amount of effective talent and training available in the population is also low. Here it makes little or no sense to speak of a differential scarcity of personnel; and whatever may be the range of unequal rewards, the scope of this range must be explained in terms of other (as yet unidentified) factors.

2. *Industrializing Society:* Here the amount of talent and training required by the positional structure of the society is high but the amount of effective talent and training available in the population remains low. Here there is a differential scarcity of personnel, and the hypothesis would predict that the range of unequal rewards would tend to increase. Historically speaking, this would seem very much to be the case. The period of early West European industrialization, the nineteenth-century American experience, and the period of Soviet industrialization all seem to exhibit an increased range of unequal rewards.

3. *Mature Industrial Society:* Here the amount of talent and training required by positional structure of the society is high, and the amount of effective talent and training available in the population also tends to become high. With a gradual diminution of differential scarcity of personnel, we can predict that mature industrial societies will exhibit a trend toward a gradual shortening of the range of unequal rewards. Again, the historical evidence seems to support this prediction.

4. *Pre-Revolutionary Society:* Here the amount of talent and training required by the positional structure of the society is relatively low but the amount of effective talent and training available in the population becomes relatively high. Instead of a differential scarcity of personnel we have a

differential surplus of personnel. This was the situation of Russia in 1917 with its highly educated and underemployed intelligentsia; and it is also the situation of many colonial societies where the colonial administration fosters the simultaneous education and underemployment of a native intelligentsia.

What remains of the Davis and Moore functionalist theory of stratification? Two decades of controversy seem to have effectively sorted out the metaphysical postulate and questionable assumptions from the more valuable ingredients. These ingredients contain considerable insight, but by themselves they do not add up to a fully adequate theory of social inequality, mobility, and ascription, much less of stratification.

Chapter 7

Minority Groups:
What is the Relationship
Between Race and Intelligence?

One of the most exciting controversies in recent years began in 1969, with the publication of an article by Arthur Jensen dealing with the relationship between IQ, compensatory education, race and social class. This section opens with a brief summary by Jensen of the position he took in that article. He found that compensatory education had not significantly improved the measured intelligence or academic performance of its target population—"disadvantaged children." Recognizing that IQ is only one portion of mental ability, Jensen concluded that IQ is largely inherited, is inversely related to social class and that blacks typically have lower IQs than whites. He contends that it is reasonable to *hypothesize* that the causes of the racial differences are genetic *as well as* environmental. Further, since lower class blacks have a higher reproduction rate than middle class blacks, Jensen sees the possibility of a lowering of the IQ level in the black community and a widening of the gap between blacks and whites. Turning to other aspects of mental ability, Jensen found that there were negligible differences between classes and races on associative-learning abilities. Given this lack of significant differences, Jensen asks other social scientists to delineate other types of mental abilities. Basically Jensen is saying that compensatory education has failed in the black community because it is aimed at the raising of mental ability (IQ), which is largely genetically determined. Hence these efforts are doomed to failure. He asserts that there are other kinds of mental abilities, and that these must be delineated so that the kind of education program can be tailored to a given child's pattern of abilities.

Jensen's work caused an avalanche of criticism, and a sampling of those critiques is reprinted in this section. Bernstein and Giaquinta take issue with Jensen's contention that compensatory education has failed. They feel that Jensen's conclusions are based on three unwarranted assumptions. First, he assumed that such compensatory programs could compensate for social inequities. Second, Jensen assumed that these programs have been adequately implemented in the majority of the schools in which they have been introduced. Finally, Jensen contended that traditional public schooling is effective for children with the basic ability to learn. The bulk of Bernstein and Giacquinta's reply is concerned with documenting why these assumptions are unwarranted.

In another critique Anderson notes that blacks and whites are not distinctly different populations because race is socially defined—there is much passing and a great deal of cross-mating. Since scientific measures of heritability were developed to be used on "true" populations, they were incorrectly used by Jensen in his analysis. Anderson also underscores the fact that we are not sure what IQ measures and that a large number of situational factors can radically affect an IQ score. Finally, Anderson points out how small the difference between whites and blacks really is (about eleven IQ points) and concludes that this is strong evidence that there are no significant IQ differences between blacks and whites. In closing, Anderson raises the interesting point that the publication of Jensen's article and the exaggerated publicity which followed can serve only to fan racial tensions. Implicitly, Anderson is claiming that Jensen should not have published his article because of its adverse effect on race relations in the United States.

The political implications of Jensen's article are the theme of the reply by the Black Student Union of the Harvard Graduate School of Education. They feel that the editors of the *Harvard Educational Review* (which published Jensen's article) gave tacit support to the idea that blacks are genetically inferior. Roy L. Brown also responds in political terms, viewing Jensen's work as a "vain attempt to get blacks, and other deprived people, to quit fighting for equal opportunity and believe in the *Santa Claus* of automatic justice." Eckland is concerned with Jensen's belief that "no holds barred research" is the best way to conduct scientific inquiry. He rhetorically asks what the result would be if blacks were to be "proven" genetically inferior intellectually, and answers that it would be another piece of information which would serve to increase racism. Finally, eighteen members of the Society for the Psychological Study of Social Issues enter a plea for open inquiry, but in the process list the reasons why Jensen is wrong. Why, one may ask, is a group which is in favor of open inquiry in such a rush to prove Jensen wrong?

Race, Class and Intelligence*

Arthur R. Jensen

More than one year ago the Board of Editors of the *Harvard Educational Review* solicited from me an article for their Winter 1969 issue on the general topic "How Much Can We Boost I.Q. and Scholastic Achievement?" Their letter of solicitation outlined the main points to be discussed in the article, with particular reference to the contribution of heredity and environment to intelligence and scholastic performance, an evaluation of efforts to raise I.Q. and scholastic performance of disadvantaged children, my position on social class and racial differences in intelligence, and my own research on the triple interaction among the variables intelligence, associative learning ability, and socioeconomic status. The resulting article of 123 pages—the longest ever published by the *Harvard Educational Review*—discussed each of these topics in considerable detail. Here, very briefly, is the gist of what I said on each topic.

Compensatory Education

First, I reviewed the conclusions of a nationwide survey and evaluation of the large Federally funded compensatory education programs, an evaluation by the United States Commission on Civil Rights, which concluded that these special programs had produced no significant improvement in the measured intelligence or scholastic performance of the disadvantaged children whose educational achievements these programs were specially intended to raise. The evidence presented by the U.S. Commission on Civil Rights suggests to me that merely applying more of the same approach to compensatory education on a larger scale is not likely to lead to the desired results, namely increasing the benefits of public education to the disadvantaged. The well-documented fruitlessness of these well-intentioned large-scale compensatory programs indicates the importance of now questioning the assumptions, theories and practices on which they were based. I point out, also, that some small-scale experimental intervention programs have shown more promise of beneficial results. I do *not* advocate abandoning efforts to improve the education of the disadvan-

* Reprinted from *Psychology Today*, October, 1969. Copyright © Communications/ Research/Machines, Inc.

taged. I urge increased emphasis on these efforts, in the spirit of experimentation, expanding the diversity of approaches and improving the rigor of evaluation in order to boost our chances of discovering the methods that will work best.

THE NATURE OF INTELLIGENCE

I point out that I.Q. tests evolved to predict scholastic performance in largely European and North American middle-class populations around the turn of the century. They evolved to measure those particular abilities most relevant to a particular curriculum and type of instruction, which in turn were shaped by the particular pattern of abilities of the children the schools were then intended to serve. I.Q. or abstract-reasoning ability is thus a selection of just one portion of the total spectrum of human mental abilities. This aspect of mental abilities measured by I.Q. tests is very important in our society, but is not the only set of educationally or occupationally relevant abilities. Other mental abilities have not yet been adequately measured; their distributions in various segments of the population have not been adequately determined; and their educational relevance has not been fully explored. I believe that a much broader assessment of the spectrum of abilities and potentials, and the investigation of their utilization for educational achievement, will be an essential aspect of improving the education of children called disadvantaged.

INHERITANCE OF INTELLIGENCE

Much of my paper is a review of the methods and evidence that lead me to the conclusion that individual differences in intelligence—that is, I.Q.—are predominantly attributable to genetic differences, with environmental factors contributing a minor portion of the variance among individuals in I.Q. The heritability of the I.Q.—that is, the percentage of individual differences variance attributable to genetic factors—comes out to about 80%, which is the average value obtained in all the relevant studies now reported in the literature, with values extending over a range from about 60% to 90%. These estimates of heritability are based on tests administered to European and North American populations and cannot properly be generalized to other populations. I believe we need similar heritability studies in minority populations if we are to increase our understanding of what our tests measure in these populations and how these abilities can be most effectively used in the educational process.

cists. The problem should not be ignored or superficially dismissed out of motives of well-meaning wishful thinking. The possible consequences of our failure seriously to study these questions may well be viewed by future generations as our society's greatest injustice to Negro Americans.

LEARNING ABILITY AND I.Q.

The last part of my paper deals with my theory of two broad categories of mental abilities which I call intelligence (or abstract-reasoning ability) and associative-learning ability. These types of ability appear to be distributed differently in various social classes and racial groups. While large racial and social-class differences are found for intelligence, there are practically negligible differences among these groups in associative-learning abilities, such as memory span and serial and paired-associate rote learning. Research should be directed at delineating still other types of abilities and at discovering how the particular strengths in each individual's *pattern* of abilities can be most effectively brought to bear on school learning and on the attainment of occupational skills. By pursuing this path, I believe that we can discover the means by which the reality of individual differences need not mean educational rewards for some children and utter frustration and defeat for others.

My article in the *Harvard Educational Review* has widely provoked serious thought and discussion among leaders in genetics, psychology, sociology and education who are concerned with these important fundamental issues and their implications for public education. I expect that my work will stimulate further relevant research as well as efforts to apply the knowledge gained thereby to educationally and socially beneficial purposes. The whole society will benefit most if scientists and educators treat these problems in the spirit of scientific inquiry rather than as a battlefield upon which one or another preordained ideology may seemingly triumph.

Misunderstanding Compensatory Education*

MARILYN BERNSTEIN AND JOSEPH GIACQUINTA

In the first pages of his lengthy article Arthur R. Jensen concludes that compensatory education has been tried and apparently has failed; this conclusion plays an important part in his overall analysis of the problem of

---

* Reprinted from *Harvard Educational Review,* 39 (Summer, 1969), pp. 587–590.

Negro underachievement in traditional public school settings. It provides him with a justification for arguing in favor of a much more non-environmental (genetic) explanation of the differences between black and white IQ and achievement than is currently acceptable to most educators and social scientists. This conclusion is also necessary in order to help validate his argument that *environmental* conditions are *not* at the center of the differences found between average achievement rates of children from each race.

Jensen fails, however, to demonstrate the validity of this conclusion inasmuch as he reaches it by an analysis containing, in our estimation, at least three untenable assumptions: (1) that most of the educational programs up to now offered as "compensatory" could in fact *compensate* for the social inequities causing the underachievement; (2) that these "compensatory programs," putting aside the issue of their potential redemptive powers for the moment, have indeed been *adequately implemented* in most of the schools in which they have been introduced and upon which assessments of their effects have been based; and (3) that the traditional structure of public schooling *is* effective for children exposed to it when they have the basic ability to learn.

Since we believe that a great deal of what follows in the article rests on these unwarranted postulates, we would like to discuss several aspects of them to explain our reservations.

First, based on the citations found in the article, Jensen relies on the Civil Rights Commission's conclusion about the *effects* of compensatory education. Apparently his eagerness to accept the Commission's conclusion did not permit him to raise fundamental questions regarding *its* logic and "findings." A far more rigorous and dispassionate review of "compensatory education" programs done by Gordon and Wilkerson,[1] which also found that compensatory education programs have had little effect, presented a very different interpretation, namely that, given the nature of the problem, these programs are not really compensatory.[2] In the words of the authors:

> Weaknesses and limitations in these programs have been stressed in order to call attention to the fact that we have not yet found answers to many of the pressing educational problems of the disadvantaged. To assume that we have the answer is to subject multitudes of children to less than optimal development. More seriously, to settle for the beginning effort now mounted is to lay the basis for the conclusion that children of low economic, ethnic, or social status cannot be educated to the same levels

---

1. E. W. Gordon and D. A. Wilkerson, *Compensatory Education for the Disadvantaged* (New York: College Entrance Examination Board, 1966).
2. On page 108 Jensen does acknowledge this excellent review, quoting from it in a way that *he* maintains support his "genetic" perspective. He fails to note, however, the following, central part of the authors' critical appraisal of compensatory education programs, which runs counter to his argument.

as other children in the society. This conclusion could be drawn because despite all of our current efforts tremendous gains are not yet being achieved in upgrading educational achievement in socially disadvantaged children. We are probably failing because we have not yet found the right answers to the problem. To act as if the answers were in is to insure against further progress. (pp. 178–79)

Most of the programs, if one gives them careful scrutiny, involve the specification *on paper* of various combinations of the following activities: spending money on new educational hardware, adding teachers with special training to conduct special classes such as remedial reading, developing after-school enrichment programs in the arts such as poetry and creative dancing, and including parents to attend their children's schools on a regular basis by developing a series of parental programs. If the basic causes of lower achievement were environmental, could such specific programs as these really overcome the obstacles? Although a discussion of the probable environmental causes is too complex to present in this brief statement, we maintain that one must question, as do Gordon and Wilkerson, whether this type of "compensatory" program could in fact ever overcome the effects of the historical oppression and continuing overwhelmingly negative *environmental* conditions to which these children are exposed. In short, whereas Jensen's argument assumes at face value the potential effectiveness of these programs, given the proposed causes upon which they are based, we think this assumption must be questioned.

Second, no matter how promising these compensatory education programs are on paper, the measurement of how well they operate in producing the desired rise in achievement rate is contingent upon how adequately they are implemented *at the school level*. We maintain, furthermore, that the proposal and acceptance of a program as it is spelled out on paper, the allocation of necessary funds, and the busy activities and pronouncements of school personnel must not be equated with adequate implementation of the desired changes embodied in the program. Thus, before one can argue that the program *itself* is no good, one must demonstrate that it has been adequately implemented.

Once more, careful scrutiny of program assessments strongly suggests that neither the *assessments* of the programs' effects, nor the Racial Isolation Commission's *review* of these assessments, nor Jensen's *analysis* of the Commission's review, nor even the Gordon and Wilkerson appraisal of compensatory education programs consider the possibility that in general these programs were ineffective because in general they were inadequately or inappropriately implemented. (None of the basic assessments measure with any accuracy the degree to which necessary implementation occurred.) However, Jensen's analysis assumes that adequate implementation did take place. Given the growing literature on the problems of successfully implementing organizational innovations, we think that Jensen's assumption is the epitome of naiveté in organizational analysis. Therefore, we question at this time the validity of his conclusion that these programs have not worked because of genetic conditions found within the children.

Third, in connection with the issue of program effectiveness, it is curious that Jensen does acknowledge in a footnote that evaluations suggest that Project Headstart did have noteworthy effects, but that these effects were lost after the children entered the traditional patterns of schooling in the first grade. Yet he fails to interpret this finding. He maintains that the traditional form of schooling is basically effective: "The interesting fact is that, despite all the criticisms that can easily be leveled at the educational system, the traditional forms of instruction have actually worked quite well for the majority of children." Jensen might have argued that the Headstart evaluation demonstrates something is inherently wrong with the underlying nature of these students, since even after they have been given an initial injection, they fail to achieve in the traditional school setting, which works for the majority of children.

What evidence is there that the *traditional form* of instruction acts as the prime determinant of how well children achieve in school? Indeed, available research tends to support an opposite interpretation, namely that without the presence of other conditions usually associated with family SES, the traditional form of instruction is basically ineffective in producing adequate cognitive achievement in children. In our estimation, this interpretation supports an environmental, not a genetic explanation for why disadvantaged children exposed to temporary compensatory education programs such as Headstart lose the initial gains in IQ and achievement when they are shuttled back to the traditional school setting. We believe that Jensen's conception that traditional schooling is effective does not permit him to reason along this line, one which we feel is more relevant, given the data available at this time.

In sum, we believe that Jensen's analysis falls short of its mark because it fails to deal with some very fundamental, perhaps sociological, issues. Are most compensatory programs really compensatory? Have "compensatory" education programs been implemented adequately and for a long enough time to permit one to look elsewhere for an explanation of why they are ineffective? Is it the traditional form that schooling takes which accounts for why the majority of children achieve "according to their capacities"?

Before Mr. Jensen suggests that we move on to a more genetic explanation of differential achievement and IQ, we believe that he must provide us with convincing answers to at least these prior questions.

The Social Factors Have Been Ignored*

E. N. Anderson, Jr.

Certain rather sensationalistic accounts in the popular press directed my attention to Arthur Jensen's article. The article will no doubt receive comments from persons more qualified than I in psychology, testing, and education. However, as an anthropologist, I can raise some points that may not be mentioned by other workers.

Jensen's work is based on two assumptions: 1) IQ tests are a valid measure of inherited intelligence; 2) blacks and whites represent biologically different races—each more or less homogeneous within itself—in the United States. The second is more obviously debatable, yet Jensen does not discuss it.

In any biological sense of the word "population," blacks and whites do not constitute separate populations in the United States. Insofar as they can be called "races," the term is being used either in a purely socially defined way, or to refer to certain superficial features (notably skin color, nose shape, hair) which may or may not relate to other hereditary entities. A biological population, on the other hand, is defined by breeding: its members interbreed with each other more frequently than they breed outside the group, and there is some sort of boundary—usually geographic—separating them from the out-group. Therefore the members of a population tend to share genes with each other more than they do with outsiders. Essential to defining a population is some measure of who mates with whom. Discussion of hereditary statistical differences is meaningful only in the context of well-defined populations.

Blacks and whites do not represent different populations in the United States—nor do poor whites and rich whites—because they do not fulfill these conditions. The social labels are not based on allocation to a gene pool. Many individuals have been classed as "black" at some time in their lives and as "white" at some other time (as when moving from an area of light-skinned people to an area of darker-skinned ones). The frequency of "passing" is high; it has been calculated that most Americans with some African ancestry are defined as "white."[1] More to the point, a mating

---

* Reprinted from *Harvard Educational Review*, 39 (Summer, 1969), pp. 581–585. Copyright © 1969 by President and Fellows of Harvard College.
1. Robert P. Stuckert, "Race Mixture: The African Ancestry of White Americans," in *Physical Anthropology and Archeology: Selected Readings*, ed. by Peter Hammond (New York: Macmillan, 1964).

between a black of one area and a white of the same area is usually more probable than a mating between persons of the same "race" but of widely different geographic residence. (Claims have been made that blacks and whites do not often interbreed. This is clearly wrong. In part it may be based on some confusion between local marriage norms and actual behavior patterns.) Therefore, to the extent that IQ is inherited, it will be inherited within the New York population or the Central Los Angeles population or whatever the genetically defined pool may be—not within the black or white races as Jensen uses the terms. The fact that individuals in city X have a low IQ has very little relevance (if any) to individuals of the same "race" in city Y, *whether or not the IQ scores are due to heredity,* unless there is extremely frequent and regular gene flow between the cities. The policy implication is that if IQ is indeed shown to be primarily inherited then we must determine IQs city by city, area by area, population by population, and educate accordingly.

Some other things follow from Jensen's use of socially or culturally defined groups as pseudo-populations. Scientific measures of heritability cannot be meaningfully used, since they are developed for use on true populations. If a pseudo-population is defined by reference to cultural traits X, Y, and Z, then a measure of heritability will always turn up the fact that traits X, Y, and Z are inherited, because parents teach children. Language and dialect, bicycle riding, drinking behavior, political party affiliation all correlate quite well between parents and children. Jensen's misuse of heritability measures would allow us to conclude that any and all of these are inherited. I suspect that identical twins raised apart speak the same language in almost all cases, since adoption agencies and other placing bodies very rarely place twins in two different linguistic groups. I suspect that there is a much better case for inheritance of language than for inheritance of IQ scores. (A test experiment is needed.) Yet no one, to my knowledge, believes languages are inherited as specific traits. Siblings in the same family also have a way of speaking the same language, down to peculiar turns of phrase not used outside the family.

This is relevant to Jensen's first assumption, namely, that IQ tests measure something called "intelligence" that is somehow inherited (without reference to biological populations). Let us gloss over, as Jensen does, the fact that Jensen begins his article by saying that intelligence is a unitary thing, *g,* and ends by saying that it is at least two things, "cognitive" and "associative" learning ability. The IQ tests measure *something.* What they measure is a point of question. By Jensen's own admission, they measure familiarity with the test and test situation; he caused a rise of 5 or 10 IQ points in an hour or so by allowing children to relax and play around between tests. IQ tests also measure fluency in the dialect the test is written in (or that the directions are spoken in, if the test is nonverbal). On arrival from Finland, as a child, the girl who is now my wife was given an

IQ test in English. A few years later she was given another similar test. Her score on the second was some 100 points better than on the first. I have been present at classrooms in which IQ tests in English were administered to monolingual English speakers and nearly-monolingual Spanish speakers—and the results treated as comparable. The southern dialects spoken by blacks in most cities are so different from general American English that a black and a northern white have real trouble communicating. To my knowledge, little attempt has been made to test speakers of southern dialect in tests written in their own dialect. (Note that southern whites score low on IQ tests.)

IQ tests also measure motivation. Under what conditions of motivation were the IQ tests cited by Jensen and Shuey administered? The middle-class white child is taught that his whole life depends on his doing the best he can on standardized tests; he becomes highly motivated, and often test-wise as well. The lower-class child rarely is so convinced. He is also apt to be in poorer health and nutritional state. Thus one expects class correlation with IQ scores, especially when class and skin color are both against the testee. One may ask whether the IQ tests cited were given under conditions controlled for health; if they were given by sympathetic blacks or by overtly hostile whites; if they were made to seem important to all students equally. These are legitimate questions that are not answered by Jensen. I have seen IQ tests administered in school contexts in which it was clear to me and to students I talked to that the examiner was not impartial. I propose experiments as follows: 1) extensive testing AFTER students are controlled for motivation and state of health; 2) testing students—black and white together—by an openly racist white, a neutral (stranger) white, and a black man (or perhaps a neutral black and an openly anti-white one); 3) testing under different situations: in a middle-class white preserve (public schools are usually believed to be so by black pupils), on neutral ground (if there is any left), and on a ghetto street. In the last case, non-ghetto residents might be at a considerable disadvantage.

Finally, I am struck by the very small size of the difference that is finally produced: "When gross socio-economic level is controlled, the average difference reduces to about 11 IQ points (Shuey, 1966, p. 519), which, it should be recalled, is about the same spread as the average difference between siblings in the same family" (Jensen, p. 81). It is also well within the percentage of IQ variation that Jensen allows the environment to control! It is also, on Jensen's own showing, only a very few points more than the difference between identical (monozygotic) twins reared apart! And this without even controlling for any but "gross" factors! I feel that Jensen has made an excellent case for the lack of any significant difference between blacks and whites in IQ.

I am also interested in the fact that Jensen is explicit about blacks, but says nothing about other races, except for a passing reference to Amer-indians. Orientals—even with language-barrier problems—do amazingly well on IQ tests in California. One misses a discussion of this, to say nothing of the differences between blacks of different cities and of different parts of given cities. Given these differences, it seems quite possible to me that IQ, including whatever heredity it may have, varies between populations. But populations are not races, nor are they at all close to races as defined in Jensen's work. Furthermore, policy implications of any difference that may be found are much less than Jensen seems to think. An average difference is not an absolute difference. Individuals vary so widely in IQ that the vast overlap is more conspicuous than the slight average difference. What of the millions of individuals assigned to the overlap section of Jensen's own bell curves? Would he consign them to the ash-heap?

A final consideration regarding Jensen's article comes from social-anthropological concerns. I feel that anthropologists know enough of cultural operations to be able to predict the effect of Jensen's article. It was published in a prestigious journal, easily available to the public. Quite predictably, the press seized on the article, exaggerated the racialist claims and played them up out of context and out of proportion, and failed to pay attention to refutations. The next step will be political; certain groups will use these press stories to bolster their political and social messages. This will involve further exaggeration. The public, poorly trained in genetics, will be swayed; I believe that major segments of the population will be convinced that "science" has "proved" that blacks are innately inferior to whites. Meanwhile, the blacks will not allow Jensen's article to go unchallenged, and in the current inflammatory racial situation this could have fearful results. Berkeley militants have already taken up the cry "Fire Jensen!" The outcome will be an escalation in the current racial conflict. It seems to me that responsibility for this escalation will fall on the author and publishers of Jensen's article.

Black Student Union Statement*

BLACK STUDENT UNION OF THE HARVARD
GRADUATE SCHOOL OF EDUCATION

In publishing the article by Arthur Jensen, the Editorial Board of the *Harvard Educational Review* gave tacit support, whether intended or not, to the argument that Black Americans are genetically inferior. This ques-

---

* Reprinted from *Harvard Educational Review*, 39 (Summer, 1969), p. 590. Copyright © 1969 by President and Fellows of Harvard College.

tion is, of course, far more political than scientific. The *Harvard Educational Review* Board either failed to recognize the need for consulting Black students or faculty on this article, or deliberately excluded them.

In a recent edition of the *Review,* an article on computers by Professor Oettinger drew apparently solicited responses that were included in the same issue. Evidently the Editorial Board went to considerable greater effort to provide a fair presentation on this far less controversial issue than it did on the question of racial inferiority.

The B.S.U. seriously doubts that the question of Jewish inferiority, Irish inferiority, or any other racist-inspired argument would have been thrust so arrogantly into prominence by the current Editorial Board.

We strongly oppose the license which the Editorial Board has exhibited in this matter and we demand the right to respond at an appropriate time of our own choosing to the Jensen article and to institute safeguards within the existing structure which will prevent the future printing of racist literature that is directed at maligning Black people in this country and/or abroad under the aegis of the Harvard Graduate School of Education.

Who's Being "Reasonable" Now?*

Roy L. Brown

It just isn't so—"Shock waves are rolling through the U.S. educational community over a frank and startling reappraisal of differences in classroom performance between Whites and Negroes" (taken from *U.S. News & World Report,* March 10th, 1969).

The great majority of white teachers already had preconceived notions about white genetic superiority.

There is nothing—absolutely nothing!—new or shocking about the genetic claims of embattled privilege; the claims are as old as men's inhumanity to men.

All through history, dominant and privileged groups—no matter what their color, race, religion, nationality, class, occupational level, or what have you—have claimed biological superiority; even the claim of moral superiority has genetic implications.

And all that stale nonsense about cognitive learning and abstract reasoning!

If Jensen were "intellectually honest" enough to research he could find

---

* Reprinted from *Harvard Educational Review,* 39 (Summer, 1969), pp. 591–594. Copyright © 1969 by President and Fellows of Harvard College.

hundreds of blacks throughout our 400 years of existence in America who were, or are, intellectually equal and even "superior" to many racists.

To name a few: Frederick Douglass, the great black abolitionist and leader; an "ex slave" with no formal education, his ability to conceptualize and reason abstractly would put most current white college graduates to shame. His 4th of July speech at Rochester, N.Y., in 1852, has the quality of intellectual genius.

And W. E. B. DuBois, who was the intellectual superior of almost every white man that America has produced; Carter G. Woodson, the black historian; Dr. Daniel Hale Williams, who performed the *first* heart operation; Dr. Howard Drew, the discoverer of blood plasma.

And James Baldwin, Malcolm X, and two black psychiatrists, Price M. Cobbs and William H. Grier—the list continues.

As always, environment is talked about, but almost nothing is done about "equal opportunity"—which is the valid and realistic battle cry of all oppressed groups.

It might interest racists that at *no* time in history have oppressed minorities been worried about the false claims of superiority of embattled privilege; what really agitates them is that superior freedom, superior rights (both legal and otherwise) and "superior" opportunities are projected as genetic superiority.

What happens to their genes when they fall from power? The Anglo-Saxon British aristocracy, for instance?

Aristotle was saying, some 2200 years ago, that some are "born" masters and some slave. He was talking about white men! One of the causes of the French Revolution was the upper-class claim of genetic superiority (they didn't use the term, but that is what they meant); i.e., that white men at the top of the social ladder were born to rule and exploit white men at the bottom of the social ladder, and those in between.

For well over 100 years white capitalists claimed that they were "here" and white workers "there" because of genetic inferiority. They still do.

To move back in time, there would be no Marxism if white capitalists had not ruthlessly exploited those whom they felt were their biological inferiors: the unorganized white workers; or, at least that was the fraudu-lent justifying principle—prejudice—or secondary reaction and "after-thought"—for their actions.

Jensen says: ". . . because the possible importance of genetic fac-tors . . . has been greatly ignored, almost to the point of being a tabooed subject." Garbage!

He has become merely the latest high-priest of racism. What about Arthur Gobineau, Madison Grant, Houston Chamberlain, Lothard Stod-dard, H. W. Odum, C. C. Brigham, McDougall, Nathaniel Weyl [*The Negro in American Civilization,* 1960], and Hitler?

Instead of science, this "exaggerated" genetics is better described as a neurotic—or is it paranoid?—vain attempt to get blacks, and other deprived people, to quit fighting for equal opportunity and believe in the *Santa Claus* of automatic justice.

How does the capacity for abstract reasoning and conceptual learning solve the problem of white injustice, lynching, burning, murder, denial of equal opportunity, and the most barbaric intimidation the world has ever seen?

Blacks have enough reasoning power not to accept all the nonsense and jazz that racists tell them is the cure for the Jim Crow system; i.e., *patience, education, be nice, Christian charity,* wait for the "good will" of the master, etc.

Blacks "know" that no privileged group in all history ever gave up its superior advantages, gracefully. Reason, education, and the ability to deal with abstractions are meaningless (were the Jews under Hitler lacking in intellectual ability?) unless the oppressed are willing to struggle, fight, defend, and die!

If blacks get justice—and they will!—it is because reason enables them to see through all the deception, pretense, hypocrisy, and make-believe.

Jensen says: "Heredity . . . plays some role in the heavy representation of Negroes in America's lower socio-economic groups."

That statement is unbelievable, when one considers the fact that absolutely nothing is said about the extreme deprivation that blacks have endured—300 years of the cruelest slavery known to mankind; 100 years of barbaric servitude, murder, lynching, burning, and intimidation, superimposed with an arrogant, savage con game. There was literally no intention of treating blacks as human beings; but, rather, they were to be exploited and kept in servitude by any and all means, legal and illegal.

The most hypocritical part of Jensen's statement is about individual qualities and merits: most whites regard blacks not as individuals, but as an undifferentiated mass, and he knows this.

Every sophisticated black knows that most whites have a vested interest in the Jim Crow system, and this need to defend privileges determines the motivation for biased research; it selects the methods of study; and it makes it predictable that the conclusions will be the ideology of racism.

As for being reasonable, it is, literally, impossible for most white men to be reasonable about racism: they are locked in the terrible contradiction of, first, deceiving themselves, and, then, futilely attempting to deceive blacks that they want them to have equal opportunity—while simultaneously handicapping them so that whites can be privileged.

Blacks will accept absolutely nothing—let's repeat: nothing!—as proof or evidence but complete equal opportunity.

What blacks need is not the white man's genes, but more and more of the spirit of rebellion against racism and injustice.

Is No-holds-barred Research Possible?*

BRUCE K. ECKLAND

Jensen's article is the most scholarly, comprehensive, and contemporary review on the genetics of intelligence that has ever been published. Because it is so well done and raises so many significant questions of both an empirical and practical nature, it is very likely to stand as a basic point of reference for many years to come.

Some reviewers, though, are almost certain to select one or more specific aspects of Jensen's lengthy thesis for special criticism and thereby appear to take exception to the whole argument. No doubt, too, some may even find a reporting error or two, as I have myself.[1] It indeed would be unfortunate, however, if readers were to make a final judgment about this work influenced solely by the kinds of uncertainties which may be found in virtually all forms of scientific inquiry, without weighing *all* the evidence.

Although social scientists admittedly tend to overlook the inheritance of intelligence, the idea itself certainly does not violate the senses of most people. One recent survey, for example, clearly demonstrates that the vast majority of adults, parents, school teachers, counselors, and even school children believe that intelligence tests measure, to a greater or lesser degree, what a person is born with, although at the same time they recognize that learned knowledge makes a difference, too.[2] Jensen is not saying anything essentially different. The contrary notion that "all children have similar potential at birth" is *not* widely shared, probably not even among psychologists and sociologists.

Jensen's discussion of race and intelligence obviously is a far more sensitive issue. Yet, he keeps the dialogue, as one should, on a scientifically "neutral" plane. He does *not* conclude, and this needs repeating, that the average difference between Negro and white distributions on intelligence is

---

* Reprinted from *Harvard Educational Review*, 39 (Summer, 1969), pp. 596–598. Copyright © 1969 by President and Fellows of Harvard College.
1. E.g., see the first sentence of the last paragraph on p. 76 where the correlations between SES and IQ (under two years of age) and between SES and IQ (beyond two years of age) are given as positive and negative, respectively. The data from which this conclusion is drawn, however, indicate just the opposite and it is reasonably clear that the author actually interpreted the data correctly but inadvertently reversed the labels.
2. David A. Goslin, *Teachers and Testing* (New York: Russell Sage Foundation, 1967).

the result of heredity. Rather, he only *hypothesizes* that genetic factors may play a *part* in the determination of the difference, then presents some rather convincing evidence indicating that the hypothesis is at least "reasonable" and concludes that "we need more appropriate research for putting it to the test" and that "such definitive research is entirely possible *but has not yet been done*" (italics added).

Nevertheless, despite these disclaimers, Jensen will be misread, misinterpreted, and misquoted (e.g., see *Newsweek*, March 31, 1969, p. 84). This is unfortunate for a variety of reasons but in part because it places a much heavier burden upon social and biological scientists who are just beginning to design collaborative studies which could provide answers to some of the important research issues the author has raised. If reviewers insist upon interpreting this paper as creating a "holy war between hereditarians and environmentalists" (as if such pure types actually exist), then we may wait still another generation for the kind of synthesis between the biological and social sciences that the answers to these issues undoubtedly require.[3]

I would like to comment on the implications of Jensen's point that " 'No holds barred' is the best formula for scientific inquiry." While I would like to believe that he is correct, I am not at all certain that he is. Yet, the "search for truth" probably is such a compelling force that the scientific community is not likely to stop prodding until it has more answers. What then is the danger in seeking the truth, particularly if inherited differences in cognitive learning actually are found between Negroes and whites and more specifically if these differences are very marked in the lower and upper ranges of intelligence? There is, I believe, a very real danger. Why?

Virtually all readers would agree with Jensen that persons should be treated on the basis of their individual capacities and performance and not on the basis of "irrelevant" criteria. Societies, however, simply never have been, are not now, and are not likely to be in the very near future, organized in just this manner. Although the tendency is much less pronounced when individuals have developed a close personal relationship with one another, in a great variety of situations people normally tend to respond to each other on the basis of "secondary cues"—a person's speech, his mannerisms, his dress, or his age—as well as, in many cases, the color of his skin. Such characteristics quickly convey, more or less faithfully, specific meanings to the "actors" and thereby tend to govern the outcome of their interaction.

---

3. I am actually more disturbed about the potentially destructive responses that two other articles on the genetics of race and intelligence are likely to receive than I am about Jensen's article. Both are soon to be published in leading academic journals with which I am familiar—one written by a qualified geneticist, the other by a self-educated physicist, i.e., "self-educated" with respect to the issue.

Given these propositions, which may be found in any introductory textbook in sociology, if Negroes, on the average, are actually *proven* to be genetically "inferior" in intelligence to any marked degree, it is almost a certainty that this "bit" of information will be added to the general catalogue of items of knowledge which each of us regularly stores away as useful guidelines in our daily conduct. Unhappily, no amount of extolling humanitarian and egalitarian virtues or referring to the "overlap" in IQ distributions could completely protect those "blacks" who do *not* fit the stereotype.[4]

Nor can sociologists probably find much comfort in the recommendations which Jensen and others have put forward that all we need to do is devise an educational system and occupational structure sufficiently diverse to provide for the development and utilization of all forms of human talent, plus a system of social rewards which does not discriminate one kind of talent from another. The assumptions upon which such false hopes are built are strikingly similar to those the Bolsheviks borrowed from the works of Karl Marx in planning a utopian, classless society. Social scientists and the Soviets alike have since discarded them.

First, it should be noted that it is the state of technology which largely determines the kinds of human talent that at any particular point in time a society finds useful to employ, and not the other way around. Second, in any free society which relies upon incentives rather than coercion to motivate and control human behavior, social rewards in the form of prestige, power, and wealth are going to be unevenly distributed. Consequently, those persons in positions that are more "functionally important" to a society and that require more in the way of one kind of talent than another are usually in greater demand. Being more highly valued commodities, they may even be called "superior." I frankly see no solution to this problem in the long run, except to consider more seriously than we have in the past some form of biological engineering *or* to prove Jensen's hypothesis wrong.[5]

---

4. For an excellent discussion of the potential social consequences of a hypothetical situation in which science were to "prove" Negroes intellectually inferior, see Marvin Bressler, "Sociology, Biology, and Ideology," in *Genetics,* ed. by David C. Glass (New York: Rockefeller University Press and Russell Sage Foundation, 1968), pp. 178–210.
5. E.g., see Frederick Osborn, *The Future of Human Heredity* (New York: Weybright and Talley, 1968).

The SPSSI Statement*

George W. Albee, Kurt W. Back, Launor F. Carter, Robert Chin, Kenneth B. Clark, Martin Deutsch, William A. Gamson, Harold B. Gerard, Kenneth R. Hammond, Robert Hefner, Edwin P. Hollander, Robert Kahn, Nathan Maccoby, Thomas F. Pettigrew, Harold Proshansky, M. Brewster Smith, Ralph K. White, and Philip G. Zimbardo (For the Society for the Psychological Study of Social Issues)

As behavioral scientists, we believe that statements specifying the hereditary components of intelligence are unwarranted by the present state of scientific knowledge. As members of the Council of the Society for the Psychological Study of Social Issues, we believe that such statements may be seriously misinterpreted, particularly in their applications to social policy.

The evidence of four decades of research on this problem can be readily summarized. There are marked differences in intelligence test scores when one compares a random sample of whites and Negroes. What is equally clear is that little definitive evidence exists that leads to the conclusion that such differences are innate. The evidence points overwhelmingly to the fact that when one compares Negroes and whites of comparable cultural and educational background, differences in intelligence test scores diminish markedly; the more comparable the background, the less the difference. There is no direct evidence that supports the view that there is an innate difference between members of different racial groups.

We believe that a more accurate understanding of the contribution of heredity to intelligence will be possible only when social conditions for all races are equal and when this situation has existed for several generations. We maintain that the racism and discrimination in our country impose an immeasurable burden upon the black person. Social inequalities deprive large numbers of black people of social, economic, and educational advantages available to a great majority of the white population. The existing social structures prevent black and white people even of the same social class from leading comparable lives. In light of these conditions, it is obvious that no scientific discussion of racial differences can exclude an

---

* Reprinted from *Harvard Educational Review*, 39 (Summer, 1969), pp. 625–627. Copyright © 1969 by President and Fellows of Harvard College.

examination of political, historic, economic, and psychological factors which are inextricably related to racial differences.

One of our most serious objections to Jensen's article is to his vigorous assertion that compensatory education has apparently failed. The major failure in so-called compensatory education has been in the planning, size, and scope of the programs. We maintain that a variety of programs planned to teach specific skills has been effective and that a few well-designed programs which teach problem-solving and thinking have also been successful. The results from these programs strongly suggest that continuous and carefully planned intervention procedures can have a substantially positive influence on the performance of disadvantaged children.

We point out that a number of Jensen's key assumptions and conclusions are seriously questioned by many psychologists and geneticists.

The question of the relative contributions of heredity and environment to human development and behavior has a long history of controversy within psychology. Recent research indicates that environmental factors play a role from the moment of the child's conception. The unborn child develops as a result of a complex, little understood, interaction between hereditary and environmental factors; this interaction continues throughout life. To construct questions about complex behavior in terms of heredity *versus* environment is to over-simplify the essence and nature of human development and behavior.

In an examination of Jensen's data, we find that observed racial differences in intelligence can be attributed to environmental factors. Thus, identical twins reared in different environments can show differences in intelligence test scores which are fully comparable to the differences found between racial groups.

We must also recognize the limitations of present day intelligence tests. Largely developed and standardized on white middle-class children, these tests tend to be biased against black children to an unknown degree. While IQ tests do predict school achievement, we cannot demonstrate that they are accurate as measures of innate endowment. Any generalizations about the ability of black or white children are very much limited by the nature of existing IQ tests.

We also draw attention to the fact that the concept of race is most frequently defined "socially," by skin color, but that genetic race differences are very difficult to determine. Many of the studies cited by Jensen have employed a social definition of race, rather than the more rigorous genetic definition. Conclusions about the genetic basis for racial differences are obviously dependent on the accuracy of the definition of race employed.

The Council of the Society for the Psychological Study of Social Issues reaffirms its long-held position of support for open inquiry on all aspects of human behavior. We are concerned with establishing high standards of scientific inquiry and of scientific responsibility. Included in these standards must be careful interpretation of research findings, with rigorous attention to alternative explanations. In no area of science are these principles more important than in the study of human behavior, where a variety of social factors may have large and far-reaching effects. When research has bearing on social issues and public policy, the scientist must examine the competing explanations for his findings and must exercise the greatest care in his interpretation. Only in this way can he minimize the possibility that others will overgeneralize or misunderstand the social implications of his work.

Organizations:

Are Bureaucracies Characterized by

Rationality and Competence?

This section opens with a brief excerpt from the work of Max Weber on bureaucracies. As with many controversies in sociology (including the one on religion in this book), the starting point is Weber's seminal ideas. Weber believed bureaucracy to be the most efficient form of organization in terms of precision, speed and other factors. The bulk of Weber's work is concerned with the distinctive rationality of the Western world, and bureaucracy represented to Weber one of the most rational manifestations of a society dominated by rationality. The bureaucrat is a specialist who learns more and more about his particular task. He carries out his business objectively according to calculable rules and without regard for personalities.

Many people have attacked Weber for emphasizing rationality and efficiency and deemphasizing irrationality and inefficiency, but the bulk of these criticisms are unfair. Weber clearly states, in a footnote in the excerpt included here, that he recognizes some of the "obstacles" to bureaucratic work but hasn't the time to go into them. Further, Weber was creating one of his famous ideal types, and an ideal type is not supposed to fit any particular case in the real world.

One of the major critiques of Weber's work was Robert Merton's essay on the bureaucratic personality. That article is not included here, but a follow-up study by Harry Cohen appears in its place. Cohen begins by summarizing Merton's ideas on the inflexibility of the bureaucrat and the reasons for that inflexibility. Summarizing his own research and that of his mentor, Peter Blau (whose mentor was Merton), Cohen finds "case after case" of bureaucratic flexibility. He then tries to reconcile his view of the bureaucrat (flexible) with Merton's view (inflexible). In part, both are correct. The bureaucrat is flexible in some instances and inflexible in others. Yet, this does not help reconcile Merton's view that bureaucratic inflexibility has given bureaucracies a bad name with Cohen's view that the cause is flexibility. The reconciliation here is that both flexibility and inflexibility have given bureaucracies a bad name because they have had the same effect—they have worked to the detriment of the client.

This section concludes with a popular and humorous analysis of those who work in bureaucracies, entitled *The Peter Principle*. In his summary of *The Peter Principle* Hull makes the same point that has been made in rather staid academic books—the inefficiency and irrationality of bureaucrats and bureaucracies. The cause for Hull lies in the principle that: "In a hierarchy every employee tends to rise to his level of incompetence." Bureaucracies irrationally promote people who have done well on one level to the next level, but there is no reason to believe that good performance on one level has anything to do with the ability to handle the next position up in the hierarchy. This process is repeated until everyone has reached his level of incompetence. Thus the only real work in an organization is done by those who have not *yet* reached their level of incompetence.

Technical Advantages of Bureaucratic Organization*

MAX WEBER

The decisive reason for the advance of bureaucratic organization has always been its purely technical superiority over any other form of organization. The fully developed bureaucratic mechanism compares with other organizations exactly as does the machine with the non-mechanical modes of production.

Precision, speed, unambiguity, knowledge of the files, continuity, discretion, unity, strict subordination, reduction of friction and of material and personal costs—these are raised to the optimum point in the strictly bureaucratic administration, and especially in its monocratic form. As compared with all collegiate, honorific, and avocational forms of administration, trained bureaucracy is superior on all these points. And as far as complicated tasks are concerned, paid bureaucratic work is not only more precise

* From *From Max Weber: Essays in Sociology,* edited and translated by H. H. Gerth and C. Wright Mills. Copyright 1946 by Oxford University Press, Inc. Reprinted by permission.

but, in the last analysis, it is often cheaper than even formally unremunerated honorific service.

Honorific arrangements make administrative work an avocation and, for this reason alone, honorific service normally functions more slowly; being less bound to schemata and being more formless. Hence it is less precise and less unified than bureaucratic work because it is less dependent upon superiors and because the establishment and exploitation of the apparatus of subordinate officials and filing services are almost unavoidably less economical. Honorific service is less continuous than bureaucratic and frequently quite expensive. This is especially the case if one thinks not only of the money costs to the public treasury—costs which bureaucratic administration, in comparison with administration by notables, usually substantially increases—but also of the frequent economic losses of the governed caused by delays and lack of precision. The possibility of administration by notables normally and permanently exists only where official management can be satisfactorily discharged as an avocation. With the qualitative increase of tasks the administration has to face, administration by notables reaches its limits—today, even in England. Work organized by collegiate bodies causes friction and delay and requires compromises between colliding interests and views. The administration, therefore, runs less precisely and is more independent of superiors; hence, it is less unified and slower. All advances of the Prussian administrative organization have been and will in the future be advances of the bureaucratic, and especially of the monocratic, principle.

Today, it is primarily the capitalist market economy which demands that the official business of the administration be discharged precisely, unambiguously, continuously, and with as much speed as possible. Normally, the very large, modern capitalist enterprises are themselves unequalled models of strict bureaucratic organization. Business management throughout rests on increasing precision, steadiness, and, above all, the speed of operations. This, in turn, is determined by the peculiar nature of the modern means of communication, including, among other things, the news service of the press. The extraordinary increase in the speed by which public announcements, as well as economic and political facts, are transmitted exerts a steady and sharp pressure in the direction of speeding up the tempo of administrative reaction towards various situations. The optimum of such reaction time is normally attained only by a strictly bureaucratic organization.*

Bureaucratization offers above all the optimum possibility for carrying through the principle of specializing administrative functions according to purely objective considerations. Individual performances are allocated to

---

* Here we cannot discuss in detail how the bureaucratic apparatus may, and actually does, produce definite obstacles to the discharge of business in a manner suitable for the single case.

functionaries who have specialized training and who by constant practice learn more and more. The "objective" discharge of business primarily means a discharge of business according to *calculable rules* and "without regard for persons."

"Without regard for persons" is also the watchword of the "market" and, in general, of all pursuits of naked economic interests. A consistent execution of bureaucratic domination means the leveling of status "honor." Hence, if the principle of the free-market is not at the same time restricted, it means the universal domination of the "class situation." That this consequence of bureaucratic domination has not set in everywhere, parallel to the extent of bureaucratization, is due to the differences among possible principles by which polities may meet their demands.

The second element mentioned, "calculable rules," also is of paramount importance for modern bureaucracy. The peculiarity of modern culture, and specifically of its technical and economic basis, demands this very "calculability" of results. When fully developed, bureaucracy also stands, in a specific sense, under the principle of *sine ira ac studio*. Its specific nature, which is welcomed by capitalism, develops the more perfectly the more the bureaucracy is "dehumanized," the more completely it succeeds in eliminating from official business love, hatred, and all purely personal, irrational, and emotional elements which escape calculation. This is the specific nature of bureaucracy and it is appraised as its special virtue.

The more complicated and specialized modern culture becomes, the more its external supporting apparatus demands the personally detached and strictly "objective" *expert*, in lieu of the master of older social structures, who was moved by personal sympathy and favor, by grace and gratitude. Bureaucracy offers the attitudes demanded by the external apparatus of modern culture in the most favorable combination. As a rule, only bureaucracy has established the foundation for the administration of a rational law conceptually systematized on the basis of such enactments as the latter Roman imperial period first created with a high degree of technical perfection. During the Middle Ages, this law was received along with the bureaucratization of legal administration, that is to say, with the displacement of the old trial procedure which was bound to tradition or to irrational presuppositions, by the rationally trained and specialized expert.

Bureaucratic Flexibility: Some Comments on Robert Merton's "Bureaucratic Structure and Personality"*

Harry Cohen

Introduction

Robert K. Merton wrote a now classic study of bureaucracy and bureaucrats entitled *Bureaucratic Structure and Personality*.[1] In it he analysed the relationship of bureaucratic structure, personality and bureaucratic inefficiency. Here I re-examine Professor Merton's analysis in the light of some additional evidence drawn from case studies of two government employment agencies, the first studied in 1949 and analysed by Peter Blau in the well-known book, *The Dynamics of Bureaucracy*,[2] and the second, an agency in the same city as, performing the same function as, and related bureaucratically to the one analysed by Professor Blau, studied ten years later by the writer and reported in the book, *The Demonics of Bureaucracy*.[3]

Theoretical Background

Many years ago Max Weber presented an "ideal-type" construction which listed characteristics of bureaucracy. One of these characteristics is: "Systematic and general rules which define procedure, and which are followed."[4]

Merton takes Weber's characteristic above and other of the latter's

---

* From *British Journal of Sociology*, Vol. XXI, No. 4 (December, 1970), pp. 390–399. Reprinted by permission.

1. In Robert K. Merton, *Social Theory and Social Structure*, Glencoe: The Free Press, rev. ed., 1957, pp. 195–206.
2. Peter M. Blau, *The Dynamics of Bureaucracy*, Chicago: University of Chicago Press, rev. ed., 1963.
3. Harry Cohen, *The Demonics of Bureaucracy*, Ames: Iowa State University Press, 1965.
4. Roy G. Francis and Robert C. Stone, *Service and Procedure in Bureaucracy*, Minneapolis: University of Minnesota Press, 1956, p. 5. This characteristic has been abstracted by Francis and Stone from H. H. Gerth's and C. Wright Mills' translation of Weber's work in their *From Max Weber: Essays in Sociology*, New York: Galaxy; Oxford University Press, 1958, pp. 196–8. Francis and Stone cite the earlier 1946 edition.

ideal-type constructions about bureaucracy another step further. He tells us that Weber is almost exclusively concerned with what the bureaucratic structure attains: precision, reliability and efficiency.[5] Yet, Merton correctly tells us that there is disagreement between the ideal conception and the actual public conception of the bureaucrat and of bureaucracy. On the theoretical or ideal level bureaucratic organization shows positive characteristics and functions; however, the community at large very obviously emphasizes the opposite, the imperfections of bureaucracy, "as is suggested by the fact that the 'horrid hybrid,' bureaucrat, has become an epithet, a *Schimpfwort.*"[6]

Merton then applies Thorstein Veblen's concept of "trained incapacity," which provides a transition to a study of such negative aspects of bureaucracy:

> Trained incapacity refers to that state of affairs in which one's abilities function as inadequacies or blind spots. Actions based upon training and skills which have been successfully applied in the past may result in inappropriate responses *under changed conditions.*[7]

Merton at this point leads directly to his major thesis, showing structural sources of trained incapacity and of overconformity:

> Such inadequacies in orientation which involve trained incapacity clearly derive from structural sources. The process may be briefly . . . [summarized]. (1) An effective bureaucracy demands reliability of response and strict devotion to regulations. (2) Such devotion to the rules leads to their transformation into absolutes; they are no longer conceived as relative to a set of purposes. (3) This interferes with ready adaptation under special conditions not clearly envisaged by those who drew up the general rules. (4) Thus, the very elements which conduce toward efficiency in general produce inefficiency in specific instances.[8]
>
> Adherence to the rules, originally conceived as a means, becomes transformed into an end-in-itself; there occurs the familiar process of *displacement of goals* whereby "an instrumental value becomes a terminal value."[9]

According to Merton's analysis clients then are faced with bureaucracies ostensibly established for their good, but often with a structure which, and practitioners who emphasize the rules first and the service second, to the detriment of the client. Such behaviour leads to a poor

5. Merton, op. cit., p. 198.
6. Ibid., p. 197.
7. Ibid., p. 198. Italics in the original.
8. Ibid., p. 200.
9. Ibid., p. 199.

public conception of bureaucracy and bureaucrats. Would you feel complimented if someone called you a bureaucrat? However, the word bureaucrat signifies, theoretically and on the ideal level at least, nothing more than a highly trained, specialized practitioner in a formal organization set up in a hierarchical fashion for the purposes of precise, reliable, fair, efficient, specialized service.

To summarize, among other processes, Professor Merton essentially lays the blame for bureaucratic "inefficiency" and the popular steretotype of the bureaucrat as inefficient and troublesome to rigidity, to the *overconformity* of bureaucrats to rules, where the rules as instrumental values (toward the attainment of the institutional mission) become terminal values, to the detriment and dismay of clients and the general public. Let us now look at some empirical data to see how Merton's theoretical approach to the problem of bureaucracy stands up when applied to actual conditions at two bureaucratically-organized government agencies.[10]

SOME EMPIRICAL FINDINGS IN RELATION TO MERTON'S THESIS

Peter Blau in his study of a government employment agency, reported in *The Dynamics of Bureaucracy* (originally a dissertation sponsored by Professor Merton himself), found case after case of flexibility on the part of the bureaucrats and bureaucracy, as is reflected even in the title of his book. Blau aptly showed that bureaucracy (at least the one he studied) is dynamic. Procedures at the government agency were adjusted, amplified and redefined in response to operating needs. For example, officials did not rigidly follow rules and procedures of the bureaucracy when assigning "due-dates" for clients to return to the agency. They interpreted procedure liberally and used discretion in relation to specific cases.

My own study of and experience in a related government agency from 1956–59, based on Blau's earlier (1949) study, corroborates Blau's findings of dynamism. Many illustrations may be given; however, only a few can be presented here.[11]

First, officials frequently modified due-date procedure and interviewing procedure to meet desires of some clients to avoid work and at the same time to remain on unemployment benefit rolls. Some such clients were sent home without interviews even when jobs were available in the files. However, according to organizational procedure and law, they should have been interviewed for referral to jobs. Second, statistical production records

---

10. Francis and Stone (op. cit.) also comment on issues somewhat, although not completely similar to those to be discussed in the following sections of this paper. See their pp. 9–11, 30–3 and 142ff.
11. See *The Demonics of Bureaucracy*, op. cit., for a full discussion of such cases and illustrations and much more data bearing on the point of bureaucratic changes.

of interviewer performance were frequently manipulated and fabricated by the officials, often to an extraordinary degree, reminiscent of George Orwell's novel *1984* where an official of a bureaucracy called the Ministry of Plenty realizes, as he readjusts the figures, that it is not even forgery, but merely "the substitution of one piece of nonsense for another." Records were modified and fabricated so often at the agency studied that comparable to the Ministry of Plenty in *1984* it might be said that "Statistics were just as much a fantasy in their original version as in their rectified version. A great deal of the time you were expected to make them up out of your head."[12] Third, visits to employers were formally required at the bureaucracy. Officials met special constraints of such required visits to employers by drastically modifying procedure and by performing these visits in only minutes when an entire afternoon had been set aside for them. Fourth, agency officials on operating and other levels were found to frequently violate the spirit and letter of the State Antidiscrimination Law. It is interesting to note that this government agency was duty-bound to help uphold the law by reporting violating private employers to the State Anti-discrimination Commission. A state-wide scandal came about when news-papers determined and reported such agency discriminatory practices against minority group members and the practice of many agency employ-ees of avoiding the reporting of cases of employment discrimination on the basis of race, contrary to the rules which specified that such reports were to be filed. The public scandal and resultant public furore led to a later formal reaffirmation by upper levels of agency responsibility to the law and retraining of officials; yet there was evidence of continued informal modification of procedure dealing with the State Antidiscrimination Law. A case occurring even after the scandal and formal reaffirmation of agency responsibility to the Antidiscrimination Law provides a good example of flexible modifications by bureaucrats.

An employer (one type of agency client) did not hire an applicant (another kind of client) referred by the agency, and indicated to a government official during a telephone conversation that the client was not hired because she was a Negro. Rules and procedure required the official to fill out a report on this issue. This action was taken. Procedure then required that a personal visit be made by an agency official to the em-ployer to determine the full facts of the case, and to attempt, in a face-to-face relationship, to explain the requirements of the law to the employer. This was in an attempt to have him relax the discriminatory hiring specifications in an effort to avoid further such occurrences and the penalty of possible litigation should the Antidiscrimination Commission press charges given his persistent deviation from state law. Another official

---

12. George Orwell, *1984*, New York: Harcourt, Brace and Co., 1949, pp. 41–2.

visited the employer, and the employer explained that he feared protest resignations of other white employees if a black were hired. The official then *modified* procedure and violated the law in order to meet the employer's problem. (Note lack of rigid application of rules and law here by the bureaucrat.) This occurred when the official told the employer how he might violate the law in the future without risk of official sanctions being applied. The employer was advised never to tell an official that he did not hire a non-white because of race, but only to indicate that the applicant did not have the required experience or qualifications. Thus he could discriminate but by lying would not get into trouble with governmental regulatory agencies. The official thus met the employer's needs and desires by not rigidly demanding adherence to the law and did not himself rigidly follow formal procedure.

There are many more examples of this kind that can be given as evidence for flexibility in the bureaucratic situation studied.

A Problem in Merton's Argument?

Professor Merton is certainly aware that bureaucrats do change rules and modify their behaviour, sometimes to ill-effect.[13] However, a major brunt of his article and a major thesis in it is that inflexibility born of the original necessity for rules to govern a large, bureaucratic structure leads to a displacement of goals where the rules, really a means to the end of better and fairer service to clients, become ends in themselves. Rules are emphasized. Rather than bending rules to fit special cases, they are strictly applied, even to the detriment of legitimate service to clients.

Cases of this type occurred at the agency studied; however, scores of opposite types of cases did too where rules were repeatedly modified and broken under daily operating constraints. Professor Merton is not saying that rigidity or displacement of goals in bureaucracy is an absolute, nor am I saying that change is an absolute either; rather, we are speaking of tendencies. In any case there is still a discrepancy since he speaks of a tendency in one direction whereas results of my study show a tendency in another. How can these opposing views be reconciled?

To complicate matters, I too, as does Merton, agree that the popular conception of bureaucracy is that of inefficiency and has become a word with foul connotations, a *Schimpfwort*. Merton attributes this mainly to a tendency towards rigid rule-following. I attribute such an ill-flavoured and ill-favoured conception to a tendency towards modifications of rules. Can such a discrepancy also be reconciled? My response is in the affirmative.

---

13. See Merton, op. cit., pp. 204–5.

A RECONCILIATION WITH MERTON

Clients, employers and job applicants alike at the agency I studied had an ill-conception of the bureaucracy and officials associated with it; however, recall that the agents were frequently modifying rules. The theory of the *demonics of bureaucracy* explains how flexibility can yield the same negative opinion as rigidity.

Bureaucrats modified rules at the government employment agency so often that often the agency deviated so far from its original aims that clients were frequently forgotten in the shuffle. This is the same process as that involved in rigidity. In such over-flexibility there is a displacement of goals; the same occurs with rigidity. The result is a negative opinion of bureaucracy in either case when the public often cannot get from the bureaucracy what it ostensibly promises.

For example, many clients were temporarily unemployed, but were required to report to the agency to prove their readiness, willingness and ability to work before they were allowed to collect unemployment compensation. Rules were modified in several ways to permit interviewers to claim referral and then placement credit when sending such clients back to their former employers, thus avoiding the strain, time-waste and bad public relations involved in sending unwilling clients to temporary jobs, even as the law required. At the same time officials were able to determine, by checking with the employer, that the client would be, and eventually was indeed, recalled to work by her former employer and was not a liar or malingerer. The great number of such clients reporting to this agency, the case of "referring" a person to the former employer as contrasted with the oftentimes difficult task of matching a fully unemployed client with a new job, pressures of statistical recording procedure (a type of displacement of goals of such procedure) and other constraints led the bureaucrats to spend some fifty per cent of their time on such work, thereby leaving many fully unemployed clients in the lurch because there was not always time enough for them. Often many of the temporarily unemployed clients were embittered at having to sit at the office, waiting their turn to be interviewed, sometimes for hours, only to be "referred" to their former employers who they *knew* would rehire them anyway. Thus these rule shifts caused many people to become disenchanted with the bureaucracy. If a newspaper reporter "discovered" the fifty per cent time-waste on such work and wrote it up for the local press there would have been another hue and cry and another scandal, again leading to a bad conception, not only of these bureaucrats and of this bureaucracy, but by extension to all others of its genre, especially when repeated reports in the press and by word of mouth reached the public of comparable cases at other agencies.

Here the dynamics of bureaucracy, i.e., flexibility, led to the *demonics of bureaucracy*, really changed towards devilish or dysfunctional ends, as original goals of rules, procedures and even of the agency itself were subverted, only to lead to client and public outrage. Rule modifications can thus be demonic. Flexibility can go too far and in the improper directions. Thus those who are angered at bureaucratic rigidity and who see salvation in bureaucratic flexibility ought to realize that the flexibility must be directed towards the aim of greater client service. Flexibility in itself does not necessarily decrease the dysfunctional aspects of bureaucracy. By the same token rule-following in itself is not bad, provided it leads to greater client service and greater attainment of organizational goals. However, even here the issue is confounded further. A Hitlerian organization maintaining rules *or* flexibility towards more efficient satisfaction of organizational goals, or even towards more efficient client "service" still is a horror as evaluated by humanistic standards. The point is that it is too simple to demand flexibility and rule changes on the part of bureaucracy and bureaucrats as a panacea to the ills of bureaucratic forms of organization; such flexibility can still lead to devilish ends. In a like manner, when the community is outraged at the time cases of excessive rule-breaking and deviation from organizational goals are brought to light, the cry of more rigidity and rule following will yield no panacea either, even if adopted by the bureaucracies in question. Rule-following, rule modifications, goal maintenance and goal deviation all must be evaluated not only in a bureaucratic context, but also in a societal context, and in addition on a humanistic basis too. What is efficient for a bureaucracy is not necessarily efficient for a society or its citizens, and what is efficient for a society does not necessarily make it good as evaluated on a moral or humanistic basis.

Another rule modification which led to poor conceptions of the bureaucracy is that of the racial discrimination case discussed earlier. When the public determined that the officials did not follow procedures relating to the control of racial discrimination an outcry was heard that reverberated around the area for weeks. Here flexibility made for a bad reputation of the bureaucracy. But note that modern bureaucracies often have multiple publics with different desires, needs and demands. If the bureaucrats had followed antidiscrimination procedures to the letter they would have alienated hundreds of discriminatory employers upon whom they were dependent for job orders.

A case of this type was that of the employer who told a visiting official that he harboured no ill-feelings against non-whites but that he was dependent upon skilled and scarce employees for his business-survival who did, and who he expected would react by resigning if he followed the law and hired a non-white. An official who followed procedure, who refused to bend the rules to this special case, and who reported the employer, would have been seen as rigid by the employer who would have reacted with outrage. There was flexibility when the official reported that the employer promised not to discriminate any further, a lie, and told the employer to only tell officials in the future that a non-white was not hired, not because of race, but because of lack of skill, a statement difficult to disprove given the multiple variations of skills and job demands. The bureaucrat pleased the employer and his biased employees. But he outrages non-whites who might learn of his behaviour, as well as liberal peoples of all races. In one case rigidity infuriates one client (the discriminatory employer); flexibility, the opposite, infuriates other sets of clients (non-whites and other publics). The bureaucrat in such cases is *damned if he does and damned if he doesn't*. The bureaucrat is seen negatively by many because rigidity bothers specific clients at some times and flexibility at others, depending on their particular desires and situations. Is it any wonder that the common stereotype of the bureaucrat is a foul one?

At the agency studied participants (employers, job-hunters and other unemployed clients) frequently pressed the bureaucrats for diverse actions in the form of deviation from established rules and procedures. These special local conditions pressed the bureaucrats into flexible deviation from rules and procedure in response which led to deviation from the organizational goals and missions. Here flexibility (rule changes) often became dysfunctional (as evaluated by deviation from the organizational mission); rigidity however often would have better met organizational goals and state law, and in some cases would have better protected disadvantaged classes of citizens such as non-whites, although truly it might have troubled other clients.

At other bureaucracies where client desires and demands tend to meet organizational goals and missions it would be hypothesized that bureaucrats would be pressed by such local conditions (to which my study showed bureaucrats were extremely responsive) to follow rules meeting these goals. It is in cases such as these that I would expect Merton's thesis to really apply to a significant degree. The clients desire service in line with the institutional mission (unlike many situations at the agency I studied) and the bureaucracy in response to such conditions thus tends towards rule-following and towards maintenance of the organizational goals. However, in such cases the *over*-conformist, the "bureaucratic virtuoso, who never forgets a single rule binding his action and hence is unable to assist many of his clients,"[14] deviates by his rigid behaviour from service goals of the bureaucracy and leads the client to dismay. (This did occur in relation to some clients at the agency who desired service in line with the institutional mission.) There is "inefficiency." The *flexible* bureaucrat is "efficient" where clients desire service in line with the organizational goals because he does

---

14. Ibid., pp. 199–200. Merton cites Karl Mannheim, *Ideology and Utopia,* New York: Harcourt, Brace and Co., 1936, p. 106.

not let rules interfere with the special conditions of unique cases. But where clients desire illegal action or action deviating from the mission of the bureaucracy the *flexible* bureaucrat (e.g., the interviewer discussed who told an employer how to break the Antidiscrimination Law without the risk of sanctions being applied) subverts the institutional mission. In the case of the agency studied, a "bureaucratic virtuoso" assigned to work with the discriminatory employer would probably have still reported the employer and, following procedure, would have advised the employer of the rigid Antidiscrimination Law, asking him to bring his employee's threats to resign to the Antidiscrimination Commisson for mediation under established procedure, hence maintaining the institutional mission. The "bureaucratic virtuoso," dysfunctional in one case, is functional in another, at least in reference to organizational goals which, it should be recalled, are not necessarily humane just because they are codified as part of a bureaucratic structure. But then one cannot call the rule follower who *leads to the attainment* of the institutional mission an *over*conformist, even if he irritates clients who demand something the law or bureaucracy does not allow and he should no longer be called a "bureaucratic virtuoso" in derogatory tone; his virtuosity is virtuous and he should be crowned with a halo and not with barbs.

Conclusions

This analysis shows that bureaucratic tendencies towards rigidity is only one cause of negative conceptions of bureaucracy; oddly enough, the opposite, flexibility, at least in the cases studied, yields the same. But this still leaves the need to reconcile Merton's emphasis on tendencies towards rigidity in bureaucracy with Blau's and my own findings of flexibility, although in my case towards "demonic" ends. First, different bureaucracies might vary, as do bureaucracies on a rigidity-flexibility continuum. The cases studied by Blau and I show tendencies towards flexibility while others for special reasons might show tendencies towards rigidity. In any case, I wish to emphasize that in both situations, in cases of rigidity and of flexibility, the bureaucrat often is seen in an unfavourable light for reasons stated earlier. This is not to speak of the distaste for bureaucracy the public might hold for other reasons, such as misunderstandings about the operations of and goals of such agencies, and other such problems.

In addition, flexibility in itself may be seen as rigidity; it is often only a matter of viewpoint and usage of words. For example, tendencies at the employment agency studied to repeatedly modify the Antidiscrimination Law and procedures on the one hand may be seen as flexibility, but on the other as *persistently and rigidly* changing rules to violate principles and procedures of the agency and law. In other words, persistent tendencies towards change of rules away from the law in itself shows rigidity. This is a rigidity of the bureaucrats involved in their not being able to *stop* modifying, and a rigidity evidenced in their lack of desire or inability to change their behaviour to meet the provisions of the law, instead of persistently succumbing to local pressures to neglect it.

In summary, Professor Merton's classic analysis of rigid bureaucratic structure and rigid personality has been reviewed. To it there has been added a discussion of processes of flexibility and how such dynamism can also lead to demonic results and ill-conceptions of bureaucracy. In addition, Merton's analysis and the opposite findings of two case-studies of bureaucracy have been reconciled.

Ours is a bureaucratically organized society. We are born in bureaucracies and die in them (hospitals); learn in them (schools and universities); fight in them and for them (armies and such); worship in them (churches); and work in them, and are thus highly dependent upon them. Their influence upon us is ubiquitous. If most people must be bureaucrat-specialists in large organizations in their work but are hated by others for being such; if we are dependent upon bureaucracy and bureaucrats for meeting our daily needs but hate, or at least hold ill-conceptions of these, is it any wonder, when added to other problems of our day, that *alienation* is the catchword of our time? The study of, popular understanding of, and control of the processes discussed here are thus scholarly and practical undertakings of great social and personal importance.

The Peter Principle*

RAYMOND HULL

Bunglers are always with us and always have been. Winston Churchill tells us, in his history of World War II, that in August, 1940, he had to take charge personally of the Armed Forces' Joint Planning Committee because, after almost twelve months of war, the Committee had not originated a single plan.

In the 1948 Presidential election, the advance public-opinion polls awarded an easy victory to Thomas E. Dewey. In the Fifties, there was the Edsel bungle. In 1965, Houston's domed baseball stadium opened and was so ill-suited to baseball that, on sunny days, fielders could not see fly balls against the blinding glare from the skylights.

We have come to expect incompetence as a necessary feature of

* From *Esquire*, Vol. 62, No. 1 (January, 1967), pp. 76–77. Reprinted by permission of Esquire Magazine. © 1966 by Esquire, Inc.

civilization. We may be irked, but we are no longer amazed, when our bosses make idiotic decisions, when automobile makers take back thousands of new cars for repairs, when store clerks are insolent, when law reforms fail to check crime, when moon rockets can't get off the ground, when widely used medicines are found to be poisons, when universities must teach freshmen to read, or when a hundred-ton airliner is brought down by a duck.

We see these malpractices and mishaps as unconnected accidents, inevitable results of human fallibility.

But one man says, "These occurrences are not accidents; they are simply the fruits of a system which, as I have shown, *develops, perpetuates and rewards incompetence.*"

The Newton of incompetence theory is a burly, black-haired, slow-spoken Canadian philosopher and iconoclast, Dr. Laurence J. Peter, who made his living as Assistant Professor of Education at the University of British Columbia until recently, when he moved down the coast to become a Professor of Education at the University of Southern California.

There is nothing incompetent about Dr. Peter. He is a successful author: his *Prescriptive Teaching* is a widely used text on the education of problem children. He built a house with his own hands, makes his own wine, is an expert cook, a skilled woodcarver, and an inventor. (He created a new tool rack for school woodwork shops and perfected an apparatus for marking fifty exam papers at once.) Yet his chief claim to fame may be his founding of the science of hierarchiology.

"Hierarchiology," he says, "is the study of hierarchies. 'Hierarchy' originally meant 'church government by clergy graded into ranks.' The term now includes any organization whose members or employees are arranged by rank or grade.

"Early in life, I faced the problem of occupational incompetence. As a young schoolteacher I was shocked, baffled, to see so many knotheads as principals, inspectors and superintendents.

"I questioned older teachers. All I could find was that the knotheads, earlier in their careers, had been capable, and that was why they had been promoted.

"Eventually I realized that the same phenomena occurs in all trades and professions, because the same basic role governs the climb through every hierarchy. A competent employee is eligible for promotion, but incompetence is a bar to promotion. So an employee's final position must be one for which he is incompetent!

"Suppose you own a drug-manufacturing firm, Perfect Pill Incorporated. Your foreman pill-roller dies of a perforated ulcer; you seek a replacement among the rank-and-file pill-rollers. Miss Cylinder, Mrs. Ellipse and Mr. Cube are variously incompetent and so don't qualify. You pick the best pill roller, Mr. Sphere, and promote him to foreman. Suppose Sphere proves highly competent in this new job: later, when deputy-works-manager Legree moves up one step, Sphere will take his place.

"But if Sphere is incompetent as foreman, he won't be promoted again. He has reached what I call his *level of incompetence* and there he will stay till he retires."

An employee may, like Mr. Cube, reach his level of incompetence at the lowest rank: he is never promoted. It may take one promotion to place him at his level of incompetence; it may take a dozen. But, sooner or later, he does attain it.

Dr. Peter cites the case of the late General A. Jacks.* "His hearty manner, informal dress, scorn for petty regulations and disregard for personal safety made him the idol of his men. He led them from victory to victory.

"Had the war ended sooner, Jacks might have retired, covered in glory. But he was promoted to the rank of field marshal. Now he had to deal, not with fighting men, but with politicians of his own country and with two punctilious Allied field marshals.

"He quarreled with them all and took to spending whole days drunk, sulking in his trailer. The conduct of the war slipped out of his hands and into those of his subordinates.

"The final promotion had brought him from doing what he *could* do, to attempting what he could not do. He had reached his level of incompetence."

The Jacks case exemplifies the Peter Principle, the basic theorem of hierarchiology. *In a hierarchy each employee tends to rise to his level of incompetence: every post tends to be occupied by an employee incompetent to execute its duties.*

How is it, then, that any work is done at all? Peter says, "Work is done by people who have not yet attained final placement at their level of incompetence."

And how is it that we occasionally see a competent person at the very top of a hierarchy? "Simply because there are not enough ranks for him to have reached his level of incompetence: in other words, *in that hierarchy* there is no task beyond his abilities.

"As a rule, such a prodigy of competence eventually sidesteps into another hierarchy—say from the Armed Forces into industry, from law to politics, from business to government—and there finds his level of incompetence. A well-known example is Macbeth, a successful general, but an incompetent king."

In an unpublished monograph, *The Pathology Of Success: Morbidity and Mortality at the Level of Incompetence,* Peter expands his theory to take in matters of health.

"Certain physical conditions are associated with final placement:

---

* It is Dr. Peter's usual practice to employ fictitious names in his case histories.

peptic ulcers, high blood pressure, nervous disorders, migraine headaches, alcoholism, insomnia, obesity and cardiovascular complaint. Obviously such symptoms indicate the patient's constitutional incompetence for his level of responsibility.

"Edgar Allen Poe, a highly competent writer, proved incompetent when raised to the rank of editor. He became 'nervous in a very unusual degree,' took to drink and then to drugs in a vain search for relief."

Such ailments, usually appearing two or more together, constitute the Final Placement Syndrome.

"Medication and surgery are often prescribed for F.P.S. patients, but they miss the root cause of the condition. Psychoanalysis fails for the same reason. The analyst is probing into the patient's subconscious for Oedipus complex, castration-complex, penis-envy or whatnot, when the trouble really lies outside, in the patient's hierarchal placement."

Is there no escape? Must every worker reach his level of incompetence, suffer the miseries of Final Placement Syndrome and become a laughingstock for his behavioral or temperamental symptoms?

Peter describes two escape routes. The first is for a man who realizes that he has reached his level of incompetence, yet still wants to preserve health, self-respect and sanity.

"Many an employee adjusts to final placement by the process of Substitution. Instead of executing his proper duties, he substitutes a set of irrelevant duties, and these self-imposed tasks he carries out to perfection.

"A. L. Tredwell, assistant principal of a secondary school, was intellectually competent and maintained good relationships with teachers, students and parents. He was promoted to principal. Soon it became clear that he lacked the finesse to deal with newspaper reporters, school-board members and the district superintendent. He fell out of favor with the officials, and his school lost community support. Realizing consciously or subconsciously —it doesn't matter which—that he was incompetent for the proper duties of a principal, Tredwell *Substituted.* He developed an obsessive concern with the movement of students and staff about the school.

"He drew complex plans of traffic-flow, had white lines painted on floors and arrows on walls, spent hours prowling the building looking for violations of his rules, and bombarded professional journals with articles about his scheme.

"Tredwell's Substitution is a great success. He is active and contented now, and shows no sign of the Final Placement Syndrome."

Peter's alternate escape route is for the employee who is capably and happily doing his work and who wants to avoid ever reaching his level of incompetence.

Merely to *refuse* promotion seldom leads to happiness. It annoys one's superiors, rouses suspicion among one's peers, and shames one's wife and children. Few people can endure all that. So one must contrive never to be *offered* promotion.

The first step is to avoid asking, or seeming to ask, for it. The oft-heard complaint, "My job lacks challenge," is usually understood as showing desire for promotion. So don't give voice to such complaints!

The second step is described by Peter in his lecture, Creative Incompetence: "I have found some employees who are contented in their work, and who seem to be using effective means of maintaining their position.

"Adam Greenaway, a gardener, happily tends the landscaped grounds of the Ideal Trivet Company. He is competent in all aspects of his work but one: He keeps losing delivery slips for goods received. He gives vague explanations such as 'I must have planted the papers with the shrubs.' Most important, he concealed the fact that he wanted to avoid promotion.

"Lack of delivery slips so upsets the accounting department that, when a new maintenance foreman was needed, Greenaway was not considered for the post.

"Thus he could stay indefinitely at a level of competence and enjoy the keen personal satisfaction of regularly accomplishing useful work. Surely this offers as great a challenge as the traditional drive for higher rank!"

By his Darwinian Extension Theorem, Peter applies his Principle to the whole human race. Man may go the way of the dinosaur and the sabre tooth tiger. Those beasts were destroyed by excessive development of the qualities—bulk and fangs—that had originally favored their survival. Man's cleverness was originally a survival characteristic, but now he has become clever enough to destroy himself. If he takes that step, he will achieve his ultimate level of incompetence, in proving himself unfit to live.

"Man's one hope," says Peter, "lies in hierarchiology. I feel that it will soon be recognized as the supreme science. Earlier sociological studies have insufficiently recognized man's hierarchal nature.

"A knowledge of the Peter Principle becomes more and more important as hierarchal systems become stronger. Government and education are prime examples. Both already swollen, both expanding their demands for money and manpower, both extending their influence as more people stay longer in school, and as government controls more functions of life. Even industry, once a stronghold of individualism, is largely an aggregation of hierarchies. My point is that man ought to be using the hierarchal system for his benefit. But he can't possibly use it unless he understands it, and to do that he must understand the Peter Principle. Failing such understanding, the system will destroy the individuals who comprise it."

Many people accept the Peter Principle on first hearing. It sounds so obvious, so like common sense; it explains so aptly a group of hitherto mystifying phenomena.

In academic circles, however, the Principle has made little impression. A few of Peter's subordinates when he was at the University of British

Columbia grasped it, but none of his superiors. Some of them saw it as a humorous trifle, others as sociological heresy. Said Peter at the time: "I'm neither primarily funny nor unfunny. I study society scientifically because I must live in it. I present my findings to you because they describe the world you live in.

"Anyway, I'm too busy to worry much about what others think of me. I teach future schoolteachers how to work with handicapped and disturbed children. I'm pursuing two fascinating lines of research: into autism, a profound emotional disorder in which children have no sense of self, and no ability to learn by experience; and into developmental dyslexia, an inability to recognize printed words that often, tragically, pins a 'mentally retarded' label on a genuinely intelligent child. It's all deeply satisfying: I'm about as happy in my work as anyone I know."

The thought then occurred that Peter's hierarchiology might, just might, be *his* form of Creative Incompetence—a means of making himself slightly suspect, and so avoiding an unwanted academic promotion.

"No, no! Of course not!" said the doctor. "But even if it were, of course I wouldn't admit it!"

Chapter	Urban:
9	*Is There an Urban Crisis?*

The issue in this controversy is whether or not there is an urban crisis. For a long time sociologists, politicians and the press have been warning us of a deepening crisis in our cities. We have been prone to accept these warnings somewhat uncritically—that is, until the publication of Edward Banfield's controversial book *The Unheavenly City*. The first chapter of that book is reprinted here. Whatever the merits of his argument, Banfield has performed the vital function of calling into question one of our basic assumptions. He finds many urban problems not very serious, since they could be solved, but we are not willing to pay the price. Those problems which he agrees are serious (poverty, ignorance, racial injustice) do not make for an urban crisis, since they affect only a small minority of the urban population, occur in only parts of the city and are more prevalent in nonurban areas. In Banfield's view the biggest urban problem is simply the sheer number of people who live in a relatively small area and represent a "tinderbox" which may explode at any time. Thus the city, according to Banfield, is not in as bad a shape as many contend and does not require much of the help it gets. This is particularly true when one realizes that much of that help from the government really goes for the comfort and convenience of the "haves," not the needs of the "have nots." In fact, much of the so-called help only serves to make things worse for those at the bottom of the social heap.

If things aren't really so bad in the cities, then why all the fuss? Banfield's reply: "The answer is that improvements in performance, great as they have been, have not kept pace with rising expectations." We haven't failed to progress, we've failed to progress as fast as many would like. Thus the reason for the urban crisis lies in the minds of those who complain about conditions in the city.

Such a position, as you might expect, has not been well received. It tells blacks, for example, that *they* are to blame for their problems—and not institutional racism. Yet, not everyone has attacked Banfield's thesis, as is indicated by the essay by Robert Nisbet. Nisbet's writing is included for two reasons. For one thing, it warns us not to dismiss Banfield's ideas simply because we don't like them. Secondly, it underscores the attack on the American drive to do *something, anything,* about virtually *everything.* Although the motives may (or may not) be noble, it should be made clear that we often tinker with things we really do not understand and this tinkering frequently has negative consequences (e.g., urban renewal). Thus Nisbet criticizes the dictum, "DON'T JUST SIT THERE. DO SOMETHING." and substitutes his own, "DON'T JUST DO SOME-THING, SIT THERE."

Finally, there is William Ryan's acid critique of *The Unheavenly City.* Ryan's point of view is fairly representative of many reviews I have seen of Banfield's work. The reasons for his distaste are clear, and need not be repeated here.

The Unheavenly City*

Edward C. Banfield

That we face an urban crisis of utmost seriousness has in recent years come to be part of the conventional wisdom. We are told on all sides that the cities are uninhabitable, that they must be torn down and rebuilt or new ones must be built from the ground up, that something drastic must be done—and soon—or else.

On the face of it this "crisis" view has a certain plausibility. One need not walk more than a few blocks in any city to see much that is wrong and in crying need of improvement. It is anomalous that in a society as technologically advanced and as affluent as ours there should be many square miles of slums and even more miles of dreary blight and chaotic sprawl. And when one considers that as many as 60 million more people may live in metropolitan areas in 1980 than lived there in 1960, it seems clear that unless something drastic is done things are bound to get worse.

There is, however, another side to the matter. The plain fact is that the overwhelming majority of city dwellers live more comfortably and conveniently than ever before. They have more and better housing, more and better schools, more and better transportation, and so on. By any conceivable measure of material welfare the present generation of urban Americans is, on the whole, better off than any other large group of people has ever been anywhere. What is more, there is every reason to expect that the general level of comfort and convenience will continue to rise at an even more rapid rate through the foreseeable future.

It is true that many people do not share, or do not share fully, this general prosperity, some because they are the victims of racial prejudice and others for other reasons that are equally beyond their control. If the chorus of complaint about the city arose mainly from these disadvantaged people or on behalf of them, it would be entirely understandable, especially if their numbers were increasing and their plight were getting worse. But the fact is that until very recently most of the talk about the urban crisis has had to do with the comfort, convenience, and business advantage of the well-off white majority and not the more serious problems of the poor, the Negro, and others who stand outside the charmed circle. And the fact also is that the number of those standing outside the circle is decreasing, as is the relative disadvantage that they suffer. There is still much poverty and much racial discrimination. But there is less of both than ever before.

The question arises, therefore, not of whether we are faced with an urban crisis, but rather, *in what sense* we are faced with one. Whose interest and what interests are involved? How deeply? What should be done? Given the political and other realities of the situation, what *can* be done?

The first need is to clear away some semantic confusions. Consider the statement, so frequently used to alarm luncheon groups, that 70 percent of the population now lives in urban places and that this number may increase to 80 percent in the next two decades if present trends continue. Such figures give the impression of standing room only in the city, but what exactly do they mean?

When we are told that the population of the United States is rapidly becoming overwhelmingly urban, we probably suppose this to mean that most people are coming to live in the big cities. This is true in one sense but false in another. It is true that most people live closer physically and psychologically to a big city than ever before; rural occupations and a rural style of life are no longer widespread. On the other hand, the percentage of the population living in cities of 250,000 or more (there are only fifty-one of them) is about the same now as it was in 1920. In Census terminology an "urban place" is any settlement having a population of 2,500 or more; obviously places of 2,500 are not what we have in mind when we use words like "urban" and "city." It is somewhat misleading to say that the country is becoming more urban, when what is meant is that more people are living in places like White River Junction, Vermont (pop. 2,546), and fewer in places like Boston, Massachusetts (pop. 697,197). But it is not altogether misleading, for most of the small urban places are now close to large cities and part of a metropolitan complex. White River Junction, for example, is now close enough to Boston to be very much influenced by it.

A great many so-called urban problems are really conditions that we either cannot change or do not want to incur the disadvantages of changing. Consider the "problem of congestion." The presence of a great many people in one place is a cause of inconvenience, to say the least. But the advantage of having so many people in one place far outweigh these inconveniences, and we cannot possibly have the advantages without the disadvantages. To "eliminate congestion" in the city must mean eliminating the city's reason for being. Congestion in the city is a "problem" only in the sense that congestion in Times Square on New Year's Eve is one; in fact, of course, people come to the city, just as they do to Times Square, precisely *because* it is congested. If it were not congested, it would not be worth coming to.

Strictly speaking, a problem exists only as we should want something different from what we do want or as by better management we could get a larger total of what we want. If we think it a good thing that many people have the satisfaction of driving their cars in and out of the city, and if we see no way of arranging the situation to get them in and out more conveniently that does not entail more than offsetting disadvantages for them or others, then we ought not to speak of a "traffic congestion problem." By the same token, urban sprawl is a "problem," as opposed to an "unpleasant condition," only if (1) fewer people should have the satisfaction of living in the low-density fringe of the city, or (2) we might, by better planning, build homes in the fringe without destroying so much landscape and without incurring costs (for example, higher per-unit construction costs) or foregoing benefits (for example, a larger number of low-income families who can have the satisfaction of living in the low-density area) of greater value than the saving in landscape.

Few problems, in this strict sense, are anywhere near as big as they seem. The amount of urban sprawl that could be eliminated simply by better planning—that is, without the sacrifice of other ends that are also wanted, such as giving the satisfaction of owning a house and yard to many low-income people—is probably trivial as compared to the total urban sprawl (that is, to the "problem" defined simplemindedly as "a condition that is unpleasant").

Most so-called urban problems are more characteristic of rural and small-town places than of cities. We have been conditioned to associate "slums" with "cities," but in 1960 74 percent of all deteriorating and 81 percent of all dilapidated housing was *outside* cities of 100,000 or more population, and about 60 percent of all families in substandard housing lived outside metropolitan areas. The situation is similar in other matters. "Low verbal ability," Sloan R. Wayland of Columbia Teachers College has written, "is described as though it could only happen in an urban slum." Actually, he points out, all but a very small fraction of mankind has always been "culturally deprived," and the task of formal education has always been to attack such conditions.

Most of the "problems" that are generally supposed to constitute "the urban crisis" could not conceivably lead to disaster. They are—some of them—important in the sense that a bad cold is important, but they are not serious in the sense that a cancer is serious. They have to do with comfort, convenience, amenity, and business advantage, all of which are important, but they do not affect either the essential welfare of individuals or what may be called the good health of the society.

Consider, for example, an item that often appears near the top of the list of complaints about the city—the journey to work. It takes the average worker in a metropolitan area about half an hour to get to work, and only about 15 percent of workers spend more than three-quarters of an hour getting there. It would, of course, be very nice if the journey to work were much shorter. No one can suppose, however, that the essential welfare of many people would be much affected even if it were fifteen minutes longer. Certainly its being longer or shorter would not make the difference between a good society and a bad.

Another matter causing widespread alarm is the decline of the central business district, by which is meant the loss of patronage to downtown department stores, theaters, restaurants, museums, and so on, which has resulted from the movement of many well-off people to suburbs. Clearly, the movement of good customers from one place to another involves inconvenience and business loss to many people, especially to the owners of real estate that is no longer in so great demand. These losses, however, are essentially no different from those that occur from other causes—say, a shift of consumers' tastes that suddenly renders a once-valuable patent valueless. Moreover, though some lose by the change, others gain by it: the overall gain of wealth by building in the suburbs may more than offset the loss of it caused by letting the downtown deteriorate.

There are those who claim that cultural and intellectual activity flourishes only in big cities and that therefore the decline of the downtown business districts and the replacement of cities by suburbs threatens the very survival of civilization. This claim is farfetched, to say the very least, if it means that we cannot have good music and good theater (not to mention philosophy, literature, and science) unless customers do their shopping in the downtown districts of Oakland, St. Louis, Nashville, Boston, and so on, rather than in the suburbs around them. Public efforts to preserve the downtown districts of these and other cities may perhaps be worth what they cost; the return, however, will be in terms of comfort, convenience, and business advantage—the comfort, convenience, and business advantage of the relatively well-off—and not in terms of anyone's essential welfare.

The same can be said about efforts to "beautify" the cities. That for the most part the cities are dreary and depressing if not offensively ugly may be granted: the desirability of improving their appearance, even if only a little, cannot be questioned. It is very doubtful, however, that people are dehumanized (to use a favorite word of those who complain about the cities) by the ugliness of the city or that they would be in any sense humanized by its being made beautiful. (If they were humanized, they would doubtless build beautiful cities, but that is an entirely different matter. One has only to read Machiavelli's history of Florence to see that living in a beautiful city is not in itself enough to bring out the best in one. So far as their humanity is concerned, the people of, say, Jersey City compare very favorably to the Florentines of the era of that city's greatest glory.) At worst, the American city's ugliness—or, more, its lack of splendor or charm—occasions loss of visual pleasure. This loss is an important one (it is surely much larger than most people realize), but it cannot lead to any kind of disaster either for the individual or for the society.

Air pollution comes closer than any of these problems to threatening essential welfare, as opposed to comfort, convenience, amenity, and business advantage. Some people die early because of it and many more suffer various degrees of bad health; there is also some possibility (no one knows how much) that a meteorological coincidence (an "air inversion") over a large city might suddenly kill thousands or even tens of thousands. Important as it is, however, the air pollution problem is rather minor as compared to other threats to health and welfare not generally regarded as "crises." According to the U.S. Public Health Service, the most polluted air is nowhere near as dangerous as cigarette smoke.

Many of the "problems" that are supposed to constitute the "crisis" could be quickly and easily solved, or much alleviated, by the application of well-known measures that lie right at hand. In some instances, the money cost of these measures would be very small. For example, the rush-hour traffic problem in the central cities (which, incidentally, is almost the whole of the traffic problem in these cities) could be much reduced and in some cases eliminated entirely just by staggering working hours in the largest offices and factories. Manhattan presents the hardest case of all, but even there, an elaborate study showed, rush-hour crowding could be reduced by 25 percent, enough to make the strap-hanger reasonably comfortable. Another quick and easy way of improving urban transportation in most cities would be to eliminate a mass of archaic regulations on the granting of public transit and taxi franchises. At present, the cities are in effect going out of their way to place obstacles in the paths of those who might offer the public better transportation.

The "price" of solving, or alleviating, some much-talked-about urban problems is largely political. The proposal to reduce transit jams in Manhattan by staggering work hours was quickly and quietly killed by the city administration because the business community preferred the traditional nine-to-five pattern.

If the rush-hour traffic problem is basically political, so is the revenue problem. A great part of the wealth of our country is in the cities. When a mayor says that his city is on the verge of bankruptcy, he really means that when the time comes to run for reelection he wants to be able to claim credit for straightening out a mess that was left him by his predecessor. What a mayor means when he says that his city *must* have state or federal aid to finance some improvements is (1) the taxpayers of the city (or some important group of them) would rather go without the improvement than pay for it themselves; or (2) although they would pay for it themselves if they had to, they would much prefer to have some other taxpayers pay for it. Rarely if ever does a mayor who makes such a statement mean (1) that for the city to pay for the improvement would necessarily force some taxpayers into poverty; or (2) that the city could not raise the money even if it were willing to force some of its taxpayers into poverty. In short, the "revenue crisis" mainly reflects the fact that people hate to pay taxes and that they think that by crying poverty they can shift some of the bill to someone else.

To some extent, also, the revenue problem of the cities arises from the way jurisdictional boundaries are drawn or, more precisely, from what are considered to be inequities resulting from the movement of taxable wealth from one side of a boundary line to another. When many large taxpayers move to the suburbs, the central city must tax those who remain at a higher rate if it is to maintain the same level of services. The "problem" in this case is not that the taxpayers who remain are absolutely unable to pay the increased taxes; rather, it is that they do not want to pay them and that they consider it unfair that they should have to pay more simply because other people have moved away. The simple and costless solution (in all but a political sense) would be to charge nonresidents for services that they receive from the city or, failing that, to redraw the boundary lines so that everyone in the metropolitan area would be taxed on the same basis.

That we have not yet been willing to pay the price of solving, or alleviating, such "problems" even when the price is a very small one suggests that they are not really as serious as they have been made out to be. Indeed, one might say that, by definition, a serious problem is one that people are willing to pay a considerable price to have solved.

With regard to these problems for which solutions are at hand, we will know that a real crisis impends when we see the solutions actually being applied. The solution, that is, will be applied when—and only when—the inconvenience or other disadvantage of allowing the problem to continue unabated is judged to have become greater than that of taking the necessary measures to abate it. In other words, a bad-but-not-quite-critical problem is one that it would almost-but-not-quite pay us to do something about.

If some real disaster impends in the city, it is not because parking spaces are hard to find, because architecture is bad, because department store sales are declining, or even because taxes are rising. If there is a genuine crisis, it has to do with the essential welfare of individuals or with the good health of the society, not merely with comfort, convenience, amenity, and business advantage, important as these are. It is not necessary here to try to define "essential welfare" rigorously: it is enough to say that whatever may cause people to die before their time, to suffer serious impairment of their health or of their powers, to waste their lives, to be deeply unhappy or happy in a way that is less than human affects their essential welfare. It is harder to indicate in a sentence or two what is meant by the "good health" of the society. The ability of the society to maintain itself as a going concern is certainly a primary consideration; so is its free and democratic character. In the last analysis, however, the quality of a society must be judged by its tendency to produce desirable human types; the healthy society, then, is one that not only stays alive but also moves in the direction of giving greater scope and expression to what is distinctively human. In general, of course, what serves the essential welfare of individuals also promotes the good health of the society; there are occasions, however, when the two goals conflict. In such cases, the essential welfare of individuals must be sacrificed for the good health of the society. This happens on a very large scale when there is a war, but it may happen at other times as well. The conditions about which we should be most concerned, therefore, are those that affect, or may affect, the good health of the society. If there is an urban crisis in any ultimate sense, it must be constituted of these conditions.

It is a good deal easier to say what matters are not serious (that is, do not affect either the essential welfare of individuals or the good health of the society) than it is to say what ones are. It is clear, however, that poverty, ignorance, and racial (and other) injustices are among the most important of the general conditions affecting the essential welfare of individuals. It is plausible, too, to suppose that these conditions have a very direct bearing upon the good health of the society, although in this connection other factors that are much harder to guess about—for example, the nature and strength of the consensual bonds that hold the society together—may be much more important. To begin with, anyway, it seems reasonable to look in these general directions for what may be called the serious problems of the cities.

It is clear at the outset that serious problems directly affect only a rather small minority of the whole urban population. In the relatively new residential suburbs and in the better residential neighborhoods in the outlying parts of the central cities and in the older, larger, suburbs, the over-whelming majority of people are safely above the poverty line, have at least a high school education, and do not suffer from racial discrimination. For something like two-thirds of all city dwellers, the urban problems that touch them directly have to do with comfort, convenience, amenity, and business advantage. In the terminology used here, these are "important" problems but not "serious" ones. In a great many cases, these problems cannot even fairly be called important; a considerable part of the urban population—those who reside in the "nicer" suburbs—lives under material conditions that will be hard to improve upon.

The serious problems are to be found in all large cities and in most small ones. But they affect only parts of these cities (and only a minority of the city populations). In the central cities and the larger, older suburbs the affected parts are usually adjacent to the central business district and spreading out from it. If these inner districts, which probably comprise somewhere between 10 and 20 percent of the total area classified as urban by the Census, were suddenly to disappear, along with the people who live in them, there would be no serious urban problems worth talking about. If what really matters is the essential welfare of individuals and the good health of the society as opposed to comfort, convenience, amenity, and business advantage, then what we have is not an "urban problem" but an "inner-central-city-and-larger-older-suburb" one.

The serious problems of these places, it should be stressed, are in most instances not caused by the conditions of urban life as such and are less characteristic of the city than of small-town and farm areas. Poverty, ignorance, and racial injustice are more widespread outside the cities than inside them.

One problem that is both serious and unique to the large cities is the existence of huge enclaves of people (many, but not all of them, Negro) of low skill, low income, and low status. In his book *Dark Ghetto,* Kenneth B. Clark presents Census data showing that eight cities—New York, Los Angeles, Baltimore, Washington, Cleveland, St. Louis, New Orleans, and Chicago—contain a total of sixteen areas, all of at least 15,000 population and five of more than 100,000, that are exclusively (more than 94 percent) Negro. There are smaller Negro enclaves in many other cities, and there are large Puerto Rican and large Mexican ones in a few cities. Whether these places can properly be called ghettoes is open to some doubt, as will be explained later. However, there is no question but that they are largely cut off both physically and psychologically from the rest of the city. What-ever may be the effect of this separation on the essential welfare of the individual (and it is arguable that it is trivial), it is clear that the existence of huge enclaves of people who are in some degree alienated from it constitutes a kind of hazard not only to the present peace and safety but also to the long-run health of the society. The problems of individual welfare that these people present are no greater by virtue of the fact that they live together in huge enclaves rather than in isolation on farms, or in small neighborhoods in towns and cities (the problem of individual welfare *appears* greater when they live in huge enclaves, but that is because in this form it is too conspicuous to be ignored). The problem that they present to the good health of the society, on the other hand, is very different and vastly greater solely by virtue of the fact that they live in huge enclaves. Unlike those who live on farms and in small towns, disaffected people who live in huge enclaves may develop a collective consciousness and sense of identity. From many standpoints it is highly desirable that they do so. In the short run, however, they represent a threat to peace and order, and it must be admitted that even in the long run the accommodation that takes place may produce a politics that is less democratic, less mindful of individual rights, and less able to act effectively in the common interest than that which we have now.

This political danger in the presence of great concentrations of people who feel little attachment to the society has long been regarded by some as *the* serious problem of the cities—the one problem that might conceivably produce a disaster that would destroy the quality of the society. "The dark ghettoes," Dr. Clark has written, "now represent a nuclear stockpile which can annihilate the very foundations of America." These words bring up-to-date apprehensions that were expressed by some of the Founding Fathers and that Tocqueville set forth in a famous passage of *Democracy in America:*

> The United States has no metropolis, but it already contains several very large cities. Philadelphia reckoned 161,000 inhabitants, and New York 202,000, in the year 1830. The lower ranks which inhabit these cities constitute a rabble even more formidable than the populace of European towns. They consist of freed blacks, in the first place, who are condemned by the laws and by public opinion to a hereditary state of misery and degradation. They also contain a multitude of Europeans who have been driven to the shores of the New World by their misfortunes or their misconduct; and they bring to the United States all our great vices, without any of those interests which counteract their baneful influence. As inhabitants of a country where they have no civil rights, they are ready to turn all the passions which agitate the community to their own advantage; thus, within the last few months, serious riots have broken out in Philadelphia and New York. Disturbances of this kind are unknown in the rest of the country, which is not alarmed by them, because the population of the cities has hitherto exercised neither power nor influence over the rural districts.
>
> Nevertheless, I look upon the size of certain American cities, and

especially on the nature of their population, as a real danger which threatens the future security of the democratic republics of the New World; and I venture to predict that they will perish from this circumstance, unless the government succeeds in creating an armed force which, while it remains under the control of the majority of the nation, will be independent of the town population and able to repress its excesses.

Strange as it may seem, the mammoth government programs to aid the cities are directed mainly toward the problems of comfort, convenience, amenity, and business advantage. Insofar as they have any effect on the serious problems, it is, on the whole, to aggravate them.

Two programs account for approximately 90 percent of federal government expenditure for the improvement of the cities (as opposed to the maintenance of more or less routine functions). Neither is intended to deal with the serious problems. Both make them worse.

The improvement of transportation is one program. The urban portions of the national expressway system are expected to cost about $18 billion. Their main effect will be to enable suburbanites to move about the metropolitan area more conveniently, to open up some areas for business and residential expansion, and to bring a few more customers from the suburbs downtown to shop. These are all worthy objects when considered by themselves; in context, however, their justification is doubtful, for their principal effect will be to encourage—in effect to subsidize—further movement of industry, commerce, and relatively well-off residents (mostly white) from the inner city. This, of course, will make matters worse for the poor by reducing the number of jobs for them and by making neighborhoods, schools, and other community facilities still more segregated. These injuries will be only partially offset by allowing a certain number of the inner-city poor to commute to jobs in the suburbs.

The huge expenditure being made for improvement of mass transit facilities (it may amount to $10 billion over a decade) may be justifiable for the contribution that it will make to comfort, convenience, and business advantage. It will not, however, make any contribution to the solution of the serious problems of the city. Even if every city had a subway as fancy as Moscow's, all these problems would remain.

The second great federal urban program concerns housing and renewal. Since the creation in 1934 of the Federal Housing Authority (FHA), the government has subsidized home building on a vast scale by insuring mortgages that are written on easy terms and, in the case of the Veterans Administration (VA), by guaranteeing mortgages. Most of the mortgages have been for the purchase of *new* homes. (This was partly because FHA wanted gilt-edged collateral behind the mortgages that it insured, but it was also because it shared the American predilection for newness.) It was cheaper to build on vacant land, but there was little such land left in the central cities and in their larger, older suburbs; therefore, most of the new homes were built in new suburbs. These were almost always zoned so as to exclude the relatively few Negroes and other "undesirables" who could afford to build new houses. In effect, then, the FHA and VA programs have subsidized the movement of the white middle class out of the central cities and older suburbs while at the same time penalizing investment in the rehabilitation of the run-down neighborhoods of these older cities. The poor—especially the Negro poor—have not received any direct benefit from these programs. (They have, however, received a very substantial unintended and indirect benefit, as will be explained later, because the departure of the white middle class has made more housing available to them.) After the appointment of Robert C. Weaver as head of the Housing and Home Finance Agency, FHA changed its regulations to encourage the rehabilitation of existing houses and neighborhoods. Very few such loans have been made, however.

Urban renewal has also turned out to be mainly for the advantage of the well-off—indeed, of the rich—and to do the poor more harm than good. The purpose of the federal housing program was declared by Congress to be "the realization as soon as feasible of the goal of a decent home and a suitable living environment for every American family." In practice, however, the principal objectives of the renewal program have been to attract the middle class back into the central city (as well as to slow its exodus out of the city) and to stabilize and restore the central business districts. Unfortunately, these objectives can be served only at the expense of the poor. Hundreds of thousands of low-income people have been forced out of low-cost housing, by no means all of it substandard, in order to make way for luxury apartments, office buildings, hotels, civic centers, industrial parks, and the like. Insofar as renewal has involved the "conversation" or "rehabilitation" of residential areas, its effect has been to keep the poorest of the poor out of these neighborhoods—that is, to keep them in the highest-density slums. "At a cost of more than three billion dollars," sociologist Scott Greer wrote in 1965, "the Urban Renewal Agency (URA) has succeeded in materially reducing the supply of low-cost housing in American cities."

The injury to the poor inflicted by renewal has not been offset by benefits to them in the form of public housing (that is, housing owned by public bodies and rented by them to families deemed eligible on income and other grounds). With the important exception of New York and the less important ones of some Southern cities, such housing is not a significant part of the total supply. Moreover, the poorest of the poor are usually, for one reason or another, ineligible for public housing.

Obviously, these government programs work at cross-purposes, one undoing (or trying to undo) what the other does (or tries to do). The expressway program and the FHA and VA mortgage insurance and guarantee programs in effect pay the middle-class white to leave the central city for the suburbs. At the same time, the urban renewal and mass transit programs pay him to stay in the central city or to move back to it.

In at least one respect, however, these government programs are consistent: they aim at problems of comfort, convenience, amenity, and business advantage, not at ones involving the essential welfare of individuals or the good health of the society. Indeed, on the contrary, they all sacrifice these latter, more important interests for the sake of the former, less important ones. In this the urban programs are no different from a great many other government programs. Price production programs in agriculture, Theodore Schultz has remarked, take up almost all the time of the Department of Agriculture, the agricultural committees of Congress, and the farm organizations, and exhaust the influence of farm people. But these programs, he says, "do not improve the schooling of farm children, they do not reduce the inequalities in personal distribution of wealth and income, they do not remove the causes of poverty in agriculture, nor do they alleviate it. On the contrary, they worsen the personal distribution of income within agriculture."

It is widely supposed that the serious problems of the cities are unprecedented both in kind and in magnitude. Between 1950 and 1960 there occurred the greatest population increase in the nation's history. At the same time, a considerable part of the white middle class moved to the newer suburbs, and its place in the central cities and older suburbs was taken by Negroes (and in New York by Puerto Ricans as well). These and other events—especially the civil rights revolution—are widely supposed to have changed completely the character of "the urban problem."

If the present situation is indeed radically different from previous ones, then we have nothing to go on in judging what is likely to happen next. At the very least, we face a crisis of uncertainty.

In a real sense, of course, *every* situation is unique. Even in making statistical probability judgments, one must decide on more or less subjective grounds whether it is reasonable to treat certain events as if they were the "same." The National Safety Council, for example, must decide whether cars, highways, and drivers this year are enough like those of past years to justify predicting future experience from past. From a logical standpoint, it is no more possible to decide this question in a purely objective way than it is to decide, for example, whether the composition of the urban population is now so different from what it was that nothing can be inferred from the past about the future. Karl and Alma Taeuber are both right and wrong when they write that we do not know enough about immigrant and Negro assimilation patterns to be able to compare the two and that "such evidence as we could compile indicates that it is more likely to be misleading than instructive to make such comparisons." They are certainly right in saying that one can only guess whether the pattern of Negro assimilation will resemble that of the immigrant. But they are wrong to imply that we can avoid making guesses and still compare things that are not known to be alike in all respects except one. (What, after all, would be the point of comparing immigrant and Negro assimilation patterns if we knew that the only difference between the two was, say, skin color?) They are also wrong in suggesting that the evidence indicates anything about what is likely to be instructive. If there were enough evidence to indicate that, there would be enough to indicate what is likely to happen; indeed, a judgment as to what is likely to be instructive is inseparable from one as to what is likely to happen. Strictly speaking, the Taeubers' statement expresses *their* guess as to what the evidence indicates.

The facts by no means compel one to take the view that the serious problems of the cities are unprecedented either in kind or in magnitude. That population growth in absolute numbers was greater in the decade 1950 to 1960 than ever before need not hold much significance from the present standpoint: American cities have frequently grown at fantastic rates (consider the growth of Chicago from a prairie village of 4,470 in 1840 to a metropolis of more than a million in fifty years). In any case, the population growth of the 1950's was not in the largest cities; most of them actually lost population in that decade. So far as numbers go, the migration of rural and small-town Negroes and Puerto Ricans to the large Northern cities in the 1950's was about equal to immigration from Italy in its peak decade. (In New York, Chicago, and many other cities in 1910, two out of every three schoolchildren were the sons and daughters of immigrants.) When one takes into account the vastly greater size and wealth of the cities now as compared to half a century or more ago, it is obvious that by the only relevant measure—namely, the number of immigrants relative to the capacity of the cities to provide for them and to absorb them—the movement in the 1950's from the South and from Puerto Rico was not large but small.

In many important respects, conditions in the large cities have been getting better. There is less poverty in the cities now than there has ever been. Housing, including that of the poor, is improving rapidly: one study predicts that substandard housing will have been eliminated by 1980. In the last decade alone the improvement in housing has been marked. At the turn of the century only one child in fifteen went beyond elementary school; now most children finish high school. The treatment of racial and other minority groups is conspicuously better than it was. When, in 1964, a carefully drawn sample of Negroes was asked whether, in general, things were getting better or worse for Negroes in this country approximately eight out of ten respondents said "better."

If the situation is improving, why, it may be asked, is there so much talk of an urban crisis? The answer is that the improvements in performance, great as they have been, have not kept pace with rising expectations. In other words, although things have been getting better absolutely, they have been getting worse *relative to what we think they should be.*

And this is because, as a people, we seem to act on the advice of the old jingle:

> *Good, better, best,*
> *Never let it rest*
> *Until your good is better*
> *And your better best.*

Consider the poverty problem, for example. Irving Kristol has pointed out that for nearly a century all studies, in all countries, have concluded that a third, a fourth, or a fifth of the nation in question is below the poverty line. "Obviously" he remarks, "if one defines the poverty line as that which places one-fifth of the nation below it, then one-fifth of the nation will always be below the poverty line." The point is that even if everyone is better off there will be as much poverty as ever, provided that the line is redefined upward. Kristol notes that whereas in the depths of the Depression, F.D.R. found only one-third of the nation "ill-housed, ill-clad, ill-nourished," Leon Keyserling, a former head of the Council of Economic Advisers, in 1962 published a book called *Poverty and Deprivation in the U.S.—the Plight of Two-Fifths of a Nation.*

Much the same thing has happened with respect to most urban problems. Police brutality, for example, would be a rather minor problem if we judged it by a fixed standard; it is a growing problem because we judge it by an ever more exacting standard. A generation ago the term meant hitting someone on the head with a nightstick. Now it often means something quite different:

> What the Negro community is presently complaining about when it cries "police brutality" is the more subtle attack on personal dignity that manifests itself in unexplainable questionings and searches, in hostile and insolent attitudes toward groups of young Negroes on the street, or in cars, and in the use of disrespectful and sometimes racist language. . . .

Following Kristol, one can say that if the "police brutality line" is defined as that which places one-fifth of all police behavior below it, then one-fifth of all police behavior will always be brutal.

The school dropout problem is an even more striking example. At the turn of the century, when almost everyone was a "dropout," the term and the "problem" did not exist. It was not until the 1960's, when for the first time a majority of boys and girls were graduating from high school and practically all had at least some high school training, that the "dropout problem" became acute. Then, although the dropout rate was still declining, various cities developed at least fifty-five separate programs to deal with the problem. Hundreds of articles on it were published in professional journals, the National Education Association established a special action project to deal with it, and the Commissioner of Education, the Secretary of Labor, and the President all made public statements on it. Obviously, if one defines the "inadequate amount of schooling line" as that which places one-fifth of all boys and girls below it, then one-fifth of all boys and girls will always be receiving an inadequate amount of schooling.

Whatever our educational standards are today, Wayland writes, they will be higher tomorrow. He summarizes the received doctrine in these words:

> Start the child in school earlier; keep him in school more and more months of the year; retain all who start to school for twelve to fourteen years; expect him to learn more and more during this period, in wider and wider areas of human experience, under the guidance of a teacher, who has had more and more training, and who is assisted by more and more specialists, who provide an ever-expanding range of services, with access to more and more detailed personal records, based on more and more carefully validated tests.

To a large extent, then, our urban problems are like the mechanical rabbit at the racetrack, which is set to keep just ahead of the dogs no matter how fast they may run. Our performance is better and better, but because we set our standards and expectations to keep ahead of performance, the problems are never any nearer to solution. Indeed, if standards and expectations rise *faster* than performance, the problems may get (relatively) worse as they get (absolutely) better.

Some may say that since almost everything about the city can stand improvement (to put it mildly), this mechanical rabbit effect is a good thing in that it spurs us on to make constant progress. No doubt this is true to some extent. On the other hand, there is danger that we may mistake failure to progress as fast as we would like for failure to progress at all and, in panic, rush into ill-considered measures that will only make matters worse. After all, an "urban crisis" that results largely from rising standards and expectations is not the sort of crisis that, unless something drastic is done, is bound to lead to disaster. To treat it as if it were might be a very serious mistake.

This danger is greatest in matters where our standards are unreasonably high. The effect of too-high standards cannot be to spur us on to reach the prescribed level of performance sooner than we otherwise would, for that level is by definition impossible of attainment. At the same time, these standards may cause us to adopt measures that are wasteful and injurious and, in the long run, to conclude from the inevitable failure of these measures that there is something fundamentally wrong with our society. Consider the school dropout problem, for example. The dropout rate can never be cut to zero: there will always be some boys and girls who simply do not have whatever it takes to finish high school. If we continue to make a great hue and cry about the dropout problem after we have reached the point where all those who can reasonably be expected to finish high school are doing so, we shall accomplish nothing constructive. Instead, we shall, at considerable cost to ourselves, injure the boys and girls who cannot finish (the propaganda against being a dropout both hurts the morale of such a youngster and reduces his or her job opportunities) while creating in ourselves and in others the impression that our society is morally or otherwise incapable of meeting its obligations.

In a certain sense, then, the urban crisis may be real. By treating a spurious crisis as if it were real, we may unwittingly make it so.

The Urban Crisis Revisited*

Robert Nisbet

Once in a great while there comes along a book that is radical in the true and intellectual sense of the word; one that shows us how to break categories of conventional wisdom rather than classroom windows, to uproot the stale flowers of secular piety rather than the flowers in the president's garden. *The Unheavenly City* is such a book. It is also a book that offers a vast amount of insight into that most obsessive of current national interests, the city and its future in American polity.

Edward Banfield is Henry Lee Shattuck Professor of American Government at Harvard University. He is the deeply respected author of nearly a dozen books and monographs on cities—their problems, their processes, and the policies through which we seek to deal with cities in this country. He is, finally, one of that still very small number of top flight social scientists in this country engaged in relentless examination of, not the conventional wisdom of, say, the Middle Ages, but the conventional wisdom of the social sciences and social policy-makers of the twentieth century. This makes him a possibly dangerous, certainly heretical man. It makes him a wonderfully valuable man, and even if his body lights up the sky as the result of Inquisitorial condemnation at 1970 meetings of the social science associations, I predict that he will prove to be a wonderful candle by which we find our way into the future.

Professor Banfield is much more modest. He predicts, in the Preface, that he is most likely to be thought an ill-tempered, mean-spirited fellow. Well, in these times, I like to think one could do much worse than be thought ill-tempered and mean-spirited. One doesn't come upon that rare type very often in our mass-middle class society composed so largely of the bland and the boneless, incessantly in quest of preening by peers—at least

* Reprinted with permission, from *The Intercollegiate Review*, Vol. 7, No. 1-2, © 1970, by the Intercollegiate Studies Institute, Inc., 14 S. Bryn Mawr Ave., Bryn Mawr, Penn. 19010.

in the academic world. Even so, I don't think the author is as likely to be thought mean and ill-tempered as he is to be thought the product of original sin and invincible ignorance—as these terms are currently defined in the lay theology of contemporary political science, sociology, and related academic disciplines.

The majority of readers will fall, I think, into two camps, at first unequally sized. The first camp will be, almost certainly, quite large in the beginning. Its inhabitants will be all the social scientists, policy-makers, and minions of Service Forever, Inc., who, after one horrified look at the book's conclusions and, worse, of the solid evidence that documents the conclusions, will either ignore it (probable) or else sweep it under a footnote as the sad example of a once fine mind corrupted by lurking penchant for the sociologically wicked.

The second camp, I make bold to predict, will be small at the outset, but it will grow—steadily and substantially. The book could even become —such is my stout optimism in these matters, despite all depressing evidence to the contrary in the social sciences—a classic. Certainly *The Unheavenly City* has the attributes of a classic: imagination united with immense and precise knowledge, profundity as well as brilliance of insight, a subject that is not likely to disappear, either in fact or in popular interest; and also *style;* style in the good and full sense of that often abused word. The style is Banfield; more accurately, Banfield's knowledge of the urban age as distilled through an incessantly experiencing mind. *Rem tene, verba sequentur,* wrote the elder Cato. Well, Edward Banfield has grasped his subject and the words have duly followed; very good words indeed.

What follows in this review will be scarcely more than selective paraphrase of the book. I am grateful for this. One grows weary from the anger that must be repressed or else dressed up in Sunday clothes when one ordinarily reviews books these days. Reading *The Unheavenly City,* and writing about it, come as welcome respite. I like the book, I concur with it so completely that any expression of differences would be no more than idle hair-splitting, and I want very much to see a large number of people read the book. Why, then, pretend otherwise or seek to interpose reviewer's own conceits between book and its forthcoming audience.

Since I have described *The Unheavenly City* as a radical assault on conventional wisdom in the social sciences and on secular piety in the burgeoning sphere of a middle class Service, it is well to single out, as background for our appreciation of the book, the major pillars on which this conventional wisdom and this piety rest. They are three.

The first pillar has to do with the universally undoubted belief that our large American cities have deteriorated in all important respects and may today be described—in words given us by Robert Dahl, political scientist at Yale—as "anti-cities: mean, ugly, gross, banal, inconvenient, hazardous, formless, incoherent, unfit for human living." Believe me, those words are about average for reigning wisdom and piety alike.

The second pillar, depending upon the first, declares that our cities are seething cauldrons of repressed revolt because—I repeat, *because*—cities are mean, ugly, gross, etc., and also because within these sinks of inconvenience and squalor, problems of poverty, schooling, police protection, medical services, and housing become more crisis-ridden all the time. As we shall see, these problems *are* crisis-ridden in many respects but for reasons very different from those assigned by conventional wisdom and secular piety.

The third pillar of conventional wisdom, dependent upon both the first two, declares that only through massive political action of direct type, chiefly Federal, supplemented by the efforts of innumerable Urban Coalitions spread out in a vast network across the country, financed by hundreds of billions of dollars (I do not exaggerate) can we hope to make even a faint beginning in our mastery of what is called by everyone "the urban crisis." The fact that political onslaught after onslaught has failed, or else has worsened the problem, or else has fattened the riches of the already rich in the cities, leaving the poor relatively poorer, has no effect upon this crisis-based mentality in politics. Neither does the fact that the present Urban Coalition is in large part a failure; worse, has left in many a community a substantial residue of bitterness and frustration. There must be *more* political forms of direct action, *more* Urban Coalitions.

Now, I do not think I have exaggerated in the foregoing paragraph. In fact, as I reflect on some recent dispatches from John Gardner's Urban Coalition and related agencies in Washington, I think I have been commendably restrained. I have wanted to be, for it is not necessary to enhance or caricature the central propositions of conventional wisdom on the city in America. It suffices merely to state them if we are to appreciate the radical character of Edward Banfield's book.

For the book may be best viewed as a learned and perceptive reply, by one of our foremost social scientists, precisely to these three propositions. From Professor Banfield's engaging of each conventional proposition emerges a radical conclusion. Taken together, his three conclusions—assuming, that is, that they are read and pondered in the right places, chiefly in the minds of voting citizens—could well lead to the kind of reappraisal of the city, the reformulation of values, that Irving Kristol has suggested in his recent inaugural lecture as Henry R. Luce Professor of Urban Values at New York University.[1]

---

1. "Urban Civilization and Its Discontents," printed as the lead article in *Commentary*, July, 1970. Along with Banfield, Kristol is one of the tiny number that has seen the fallacies of the conventional wisdom in the social sciences regarding the city, poverty, and other idols of secular diabolism in our time.

Let me turn now, with this necessary background briefly sketched, to the three major conclusions that I am able to draw from the dozen, research-rooted, closely argued, superbly lucid chapters that form *The Unheavenly City*.

First, the city in America, far from being the metropolitan jungle, the setting of unprecedented material deprivation and ethical ugliness, is in fact a very good place for most persons to live. Admittedly not good by criteria which any bush league disciple of Service could summon up in an instant out of his infinite knowledge of the Neverland of utopian dream. But good when assessed by any standards, past and present, American and foreign, that a *scholar* might work with. Bear in mind too that when Banfield writes of the city he is dealing, overwhelmingly, not with the tiny locality of 2,500 persons that for some reason I shall never understand is the Census Bureau's notion of the dividing line between rural and urban. Banfield is writing about New York, Chicago, Los Angeles, and others comparable. Moreover he reminds us occasionally that for the worst of the urban jungle so-called in contemporary America one would do better to visit some of the localities which come close to Census Bureau dividing line. No matter by what realistic standard of life and service we choose to assess these no longer rural, not yet truly urban scenes, they come out rather badly alongside the Chicagos, Clevelands, San Franciscos, and New Yorks of our time. These, not the "cities" of five and ten thousand inhabitants, are the places Banfield has chiefly in mind when he writes the following passage:

There is less poverty in the cities now than there has ever been. Housing, including that of the poor, is improving rapidly; one study predicts that substandard housing will have been eliminated by 1980. In the last decade alone the improvement in housing has been marked. At the turn of the century only one child in fifteen went beyond elementary school; now most children finish high school. The treatment of racial and other minority groups is conspicuously better than it was. When, in 1964, a carefully drawn sample of Negroes was asked whether in general things were getting better or worse for Negroes in this country, approximately eight out of ten respondents said "better."

Add to the measurable, verifiable improvement within the city itself the presence of large and increasing numbers of newly arrived inhabitants from certain rural areas of America whose condition in a Chicago, Los Angeles, Cleveland, or New York is much better than it was, or stood any likelihood of becoming, in the rural areas from which these individuals have come. Not only, in short, are conditions better in the city, compared with conditions in the same city fifty or twenty years ago, an even larger factor of improvement of condition may be seen in the lives of large numbers of people who have only just arrived.

The plain fact is that the overwhelming majority of city dwellers live more comfortably and conveniently than ever before. They have more and better housing, more and better schools, more and better transportation, and so on. By any conceivable measure of material welfare the present generation of urban Americans is, on the whole, better off than any large group of people has ever been anywhere. What is more, there is every reason to expect that the general level of comfort and convenience will continue to rise at an even more rapid rate through the foreseeable future.

So much for the first conclusion. And should there be a reader of this review in slight doubt that Professor Banfield can back up these bold—nay, mind-boggling—statements, I invite him to the several chapters of the book and to the voluminous notes and references which may be found unobtrusively collected at the end of the book. Not only will the reader find the conclusion just stated well anchored in official records, he will find them confirmed in the studies of the city done by other social scientists—many of whom will, as I have suggested, shrink from their implications when set forth as Banfield sets them forth.

What is the second major conclusion of *The Unheavenly City?* It is this. *Because of the conspicuous improvement in the American city,* metropolis included, the tensions, conflicts, frustrations, and overall revolt against the city will continue to make the city what it now is, a scene of distinct crisis. I repeat: *because of,* not despite, the absolute improvement of material conditions, including housing, medical service, and schooling. Why should this be? The answer is a vital one to any person interested in the ferment and revolution-tinctured nature of, not merely urban America, but American society as a whole.

"The answer is that the improvements in performance, great as they have been, have not kept pace with rising expectations. In other words, although things have been getting better absolutely, they have been getting worse *relative to what we think they should be.* And this is because, as a people, we seem to act on the advice of the old jingle:

> *Good, better, best,*
> *Never let it rest*
> *Until your good is better*
> *And your better best."*

Consider poverty. Manifestly, with but the fewest exceptions, even the worst off in American cities are in a substantially better condition than their poverty-stricken predecessors were at the beginning of the century. Studies show that around 40 percent of those below what is called the "poverty line" own automobiles, and the overwhelming majority have television sets. More important, schooling opportunities, medical services, and straight economic relief, through welfare payments and other means, are far more numerous than they were even fifty years ago.

But as Irving Kristol reminded us—and he is quoted at appropriate places by Banfield—several years ago in a now historic piece, so long as we hold the concept at all of "poverty line" there cannot fail to be a one-fourth, one-third, or one-fifth of the nation officially—or at least politically—pronounced in poverty. No matter how well off a population may be, if one defines poverty as that condition in which the lowest fifth exists, there cannot help but be officially regarded poverty.

Precisely the same holds with respect to the school dropout problem. Not very many decades ago almost everyone was a "dropout" but the "problem" didn't exist. But by the 1960's, when for the first time in history a majority of boys and girls were graduating from high school and practically all had at least some high school training, the "dropout problem" became acute. "Then, although the dropout rate was still declining, various cities developed at least fifty-five separate programs to deal with the problem." As Banfield concludes, if we follow the splendid insight Irving Kristol earlier gave us into poverty, as officially dealt with, then there cannot help but be, forever and ever, an educational dropout problem even if we have pushed the "dropout line" up to the Master's degree.

So too with police brutality. Once this meant, incontestably, physical beating, usually with police clubs, or confinement without charge, of the helpless. Today the "brutality line" has been pushed up to the point where a sharp word or look, especially when directed toward those belonging to a politically sensitive ethnic minority, can be charged with "brutality."

Now the point of all this—whether in Professor Banfield's book or in my review—is emphatically *not* to denigrate problems, to seek to remove them by rhetorical deprecation. Problems *are* as problems are *perceived*—seen, felt, heard, endured. If I feel aggrieved in economic position it does no good to be reminded that I am still better off than the greatest of scholar-teachers may have been five hundred years ago, or even five. Professor Banfield is not saying that statistics prove the lowest fifth are in fact "well off," as this complex phrase tends to be defined by all of us. He is saying something very different indeed; something profound, something Tocquevillian, and also something very depressing.

What he is saying is this: A new and seemingly unmanageable phenomenon is present in our society, one foreseen by Tocqueville, one that, once created, feeds on itself. And this phenomenon is the dynamic tension provided by American middle class *expectations*. I cannot blame the following formulation on Banfield, but it seems to me an appropriate corollary of the famous Malthusian law of food supply and population. I put my corollary thus: Whereas material benefits can rise in a social order only at arithmetical rate, expectations tend to rise geometrically. That is, in a middle class society where expectations have been, as Tocqueville showed us masterfully a century and a half ago, the very substructure of American society. It was Tocqueville who first put into systematic form the proposition that the greatest agonies over the problem of equality would be experienced precisely in those countries, such as the United States, where the work of equality has been carried the farthest, where substantive inequalities become ever finer to the eye.

What we have, then, in Banfield's phrasing of the whole matter, is a new kind of dismal science, or rather a new dimension to the dismal science of Malthus and Ricardo. What he seems to be saying, in effect, is that urban problems, including poverty, schooling, medical service, housing, and employment income, in fact, the whole complex we call "urban crisis," is not likely to be dealt with in such a way as to remove present tensions and sense of impending conflict, for the reason that while affluence does indeed rise, *the sense of relative deprivation* rises also, and at faster rate. The same middle class values that drive hundreds of thousands of middle class citizens into incessant uplift work—into what Banfield calls Service—lead to the implanting of these values among those minorities who are the recipients of the uplift work. The consequence is seemingly an iron one. It can be described as comparable to the mechanical rabbit at the racetrack, which is set to keep just ahead of the dogs, no matter how fast they run.

We come now to the third major conclusion that can be drawn from *The Unheavenly City*. It falls in the vast area of political action of direct uplift and reform, of civic service that is by now almost indistinguishable from middle class life in America. The conclusion is this: Although a turning to political action—and to related forms, such as quasi-political service—is almost a predictable response to the kinds of problems and strains we encounter in the city today, the actual consequences of such action and service tend, in the overwhelming majority of cases, to worsen, not help, the problems and the strains. Banfield writes: "Government seems to have a perverse tendency to choose measures that are the very opposites of those which would be recommended on the basis of analysis in the preceding chapters. The reasons for this perversity may be found *in the nature of American political institutions* and, especially, in the influence on public opinion of the upper-class cultural ideal of 'service' and 'responsibility to the community.' " (Italics added)

I would offer the following larger, more general, proposition:[2] From the time the political habit of mind became deeply entrenched in the West, which was not much before the nineteenth century, though with

---

2. See my "The Grand Illusion: Politics; An Appreciation of Jacques Ellul" in *Commentary*, August, 1970.

the aid of concepts going back earlier, there has been profound affinity between political power or action on the one hand and, on the other, problems such as those contained in the contemporary city in which manifest improvement of popular condition is accompanied by *perceptions of worsening of condition,* of, in short, *relative deprivation.* And, with the rarest of exceptions, it has been, and continues to be on ever-widening scale, the fate of such political action to worsen the problems, by cutting off whatever adaptive responses to them might otherwise have taken place in the behavior of those closest to the conditions.

Two or three examples of my proposition will suffice—and perhaps give useful background to Professor Banfield's brilliant arguments. I think it can fairly be established that a reasonably good balance of pluralism and homogeneity was being worked out in Western society prior to the excited discovery, by political intellectuals—largely those trained in Roman Law but unable to get jobs—of something called "feudalism." By endowing this freshly coined word and concept with all kinds of sinister meanings the work of political centralization was brought through its first major phase. Later, despite the legacy of Hobbes, it would have been possible (I am, admittedly, speculating here; I cannot "prove" statements of this sort), I think, to have worked out a useful balance of private enterprise and public service in the West. Unhappily "capitalism" was invented by certain intellectuals, promptly endowed with meanings every bit as sinister in the nineteenth and early twentieth centuries as those earlier intellectuals had given to "feudalism," and the work of modern political centralization was carried an even longer step forward. Worse, the mind of the middle class Westerner was permanently stamped by the goodness of the political and the lurking evil of the economic—or, in our day, the *technological,* for it is the weasel concept of "technology" that slithers rhetorically among the dense thickets of the American intellectual mind, leading to ever more massive political responses to its intellectually endowed evils.

What Professor Banfield shows us so convincingly is the degree to which the city—"the urban crisis"—parallels technology, succeeding, as I have suggested here, "capitalism" and before it "feudalism" as the handy fulcrum on which the mighty level of political action can rest. Just as some sixteenth century political intellectuals (who called themselves *les politiques*) found a "feudal crisis," so to speak, and some nineteenth century political intellectuals, with Marxists chief among them, a "capitalist crisis," and as each of these "crises" led to a massive increase in the political structure of society, so do intellectuals in our midst find a technological crisis or, as Banfield shows us so valuably, an urban crisis, each the means of providing fresh fodder to hungry politicians, miserable intellectuals, and the unrequited masses of middle class Americans who have found pleasure no longer tolerable unless it surmounts, or joins with, Service. On the walls of all these individuals hang, as Banfield notes wickedly, homely

Edgar Guest-like apothegms: DON'T JUST SIT THERE. DO SOME-
THING! and DO GOOD! (The only good thing I can say for Jeremy
Bentham, the devotee of Good who did so much harm in the world, is an
essay he once wrote on the harm that good men do.)

> The politician, like the TV commentators, must always have some-
> thing to say even when nothing urgently needs to be said. If he lived in
> a society without problems, he would have to invent some (and, of course,
> "solutions" along with them) in order to attract attention and to kindle
> the interest and enthusiasm needed to carry him into office and enable
> him, once there, to levy taxes and do the other unpopular things of which
> governing largely consists. Although in the society that actually exists
> there are many problems, there are still not enough—enough about which
> anyone can say or do anything very helpful—to meet his constant need
> for program material. . . .

As I suggested above, one can construct an understanding of the
whole history of political thought on the basis of an insight such as that
contained in Banfield's words. Add to that passage some delicious passages
in the book on the subject of middle and upper class consecration to Service, the incessant and endless projects by which people seemingly incapable of being alone for more than a few moments without tortured feelings
of helpless isolation pass the time and work off feelings of affluence-bred
guilt, and you have a Banfieldian portrait of America that, *mutatis
mutandis,* should hang in the National Gallery.

Incessant Politics and Perpetual Service would not be other than
quaint aberrations of the mass-middle class mind were it not for the very
real harm that is done so many others in society—the working class, for
example, more accustomed to doing for itself, and, not least, a great many
who belong to ethnic minorities. For, as Banfield's book makes evident—to
me, at least, and I think I am a careful reader—there are two major, built-
in consequences of the benign and oblivious work of the devotee of Politics
and of Service.

In the first place, the mere act of *doing* for others, especially when
armed with the might and wealth of the democratic state, cannot help but
destroy, or set back grievously, processes of an adaptive nature *in the areas,
and within the communities* that—too late—we learn, and relearn and
relearn, so often made for, or would clearly have made for, a *socially*
superior form of life to what the Federal bulldozer wreaks. To do *for* is to
do *to.* To cut into the social bond for allegedly therapeutic reasons is
generally more harmful than to cut into it for outrightly exploitative reasons. The attention of the members of the community, usually self-protec-
tive, is lulled into passivity when the act is called therapeutic rather than
exploitative.

The second great, and equally built-in, penalty of incessant political action and Service is that, given the idol-like status each of these has in our time, more and more well-meaning, bumbling, lonely, and mission-oriented members of the middle class are brought into the act—whether in the roles of the Paid or the Unpaid—and this cannot help but result in, through what we may properly call Banfield's Law, an ever larger number of issues, problems, crises-that-cannot-possibly-be-longer-endured-without-disaster-to-the-world, and so on. As the philosopher Ortega y Gasset once wrote, people do not come together to *be* together; they come together to *do something* together. And if the joys of middle class family life, the church, *kaffee klatsch,* and country club pall, if the experience of being alone in a room for two hours (Pascal once wrote that most of the evil in the world has been done by individuals incapable of being alone for more than an hour) becomes utterly painful, if you've read all the good books, are tired of movies and vacations at the seashore or in the mountains, why what else is there to do but go out and find PROBLEMS: problems which, virtually by definition, *must* be met, and immediately, if we are to prosper, to survive, etc. etc.

In short, given the nature of our politically-driven, morality-obsessed middle class society, its by now seemingly unrequitable passion for direct ACTION, at all levels, it follows that the more persons there are who are dedicated to solving problems, the more problems there have to be. Situations that would not have drawn passing glance five years ago from the most pious of uplifters are compared in newspaper editorials to the Black Hole of Calcutta. Problems breed, in other words, at geometric rate, not through parthenogenesis but through incessant fertilization by American middle class eagerness for large families of problems to fill its spare time.[3] Or so it might seem.

On first thought after reading *The Unheavenly City,* one may feel depressed. The analysis and the conclusions *do* seem pessimistic. Second thought may produce rather different feelings. One may find a certain tentative optimism coming over him; instead of pessimistic, the analysis Professor Banfield gives us may seem optimistic. It depends in large degree upon whether one believes—as I do—that occasionally the smashing of accepted categories of thinking is the prelude to reaching new ones, new categories of thought that are themselves the bases of new perspectives of

---

3. Banfield's discussion suggests a new conception of the springs of power in certain types of personality; one based on inability of a person to see even the most unruffled situation other than in terms of "problems." The individual I have personally known who did the greatest harm to a very large organization, over which he presided for some years prior to recent disaster, was of this type: gentle, service-dedicated, action-compelled, and his every third or fourth word was "problems." Where others saw only use and wont he saw cancer-like problems requiring immense dosages of direct action.

life, new conceptions of the desirable and the feasible by increasing numbers of persons. We know such mutations of mind and action have taken place before, though admittedly rarely, in the history of thought.

Daniel P. Moynihan, to whom as much is owing, it seems to me, as to Banfield and a very few others, for capacity to see old data in new and fertilizing ways, has recently written: "The social sciences are in a very early stage of finding out that most of the things we thought were so aren't so." Splendid! For all the heavy pall of conventional wisdom in the social sciences, I am myself struck by the number of social scientists—still pathetically small, I concede—for whom the secular pieties and mores of even a decade ago are today unacceptable. Some of these, with unusual courage, are trying to reach new perspectives of understanding, perspectives unbeholden to spirit of direct Service that has generated so many political follies and disasters in the twentieth century. Edward Banfield is one of these social scientists. Who knows, as one of the long term consequences of *The Unheavenly City,* we may yet have a new genus of electable, appointable politician and administrator on whose walls hangs the not-so-homely apothegm: DON'T JUST DO SOMETHING. SIT THERE!

Is Banfield Serious?*

WILLIAM RYAN

In *The Unheavenly City,* Edward Banfield has produced a marvelously funny book, perhaps the most brilliant satire since *Catch-22* (which it resembles in many ways). With near-perfect control of tone and style, the author sets forth what purports to be a series of pompous academic lectures, delivered by an addled professor, outlining a ridiculously insensitive and perverse view of the social problems of American cities. Displaying an unerring ear for the bitchy vocabulary and smart-aleck syntax that characterize this kind of shoddy social science, Banfield pushes his mindless discussion of each separate problem to the very edge of sanity and credibility. Occasionally, he loses his sure grip and slides over into broad burlesque; but, all in all, it is a virtuoso performance.

The author relies, of course, on tried and true methods; and his debt to old masters—notably Voltaire, Carroll, Heller, and Swift—is evident. One is reminded of Pangloss, for example, as Banfield's Professor keeps

* From *Social Policy,* Vol. I, No. 4 (November/December, 1970), pp. 74–76. Reprinted by permission of *Social Policy,* published by International Arts and Science Press, Inc., 901 North Broadway, White Plains, N.Y. 10603.

insisting that life in the city grows better day by day (". . . the present generation of urban Americans is, on the whole, better off than any other large group of people has ever been anywhere. . . . The general level of comfort and convenience will continue to rise at an even more rapid rate. . . ." and ". . . our urban problems are like the mechanical rabbit at the racetrack . . . our performance is better and better, but because we set our standards and expectations to keep ahead of performance, the problems are never any nearer to solution"). Equally Panglossian are the Professor's stoic and reasonable explanations of why whatever is (whether slums, lopsidedly unequal distribution of income, or the distaste that he and others from the "normal culture" feel for those tainted with "lower class culture") is natural and inevitable. He says that "some" of these problems are "important in the sense that a bad cold is important, but they are not serious in the sense that a cancer is serious."

The most outstanding successful satirical devices in *The Unheavenly City* are those that make use of the mad, circular illogic that characterizes the best passages of Lewis Carroll and Joseph Heller. It is pure *Alice in Wonderland* when Banfield solemnly explains why raising the income of the poor to any substantial extent would "do more harm than good." ("Giving them income, even in rather large amounts, is unlikely to reduce and may even increase their poverty. . . . Mrs. H. would be able to go to the dog races, leaving the children alone, and Mr. H. could devote more time to his bottle and T.V. set.") He warns against talking about white racism on the grounds that Blacks might overhear and be tempted to believe that their problems are the result of prejudice and discrimination, thereby neglecting their real trouble, which is their own (lower-class) characteristics. He carefully points out that ". . . lower class education is a contradiction in terms; lower class culture is the attitudes and behavior patterns of people who have not been educated at all." He systematically nails down this point by reminding us that a major distinction between those who come from "lower class culture" and those who come from "normal culture" is that the latter are educable, whereas the former are not. He asserts that poverty is, in fact, a grossly exaggerated issue since the poor lie about their income in the first place. He redefines the slum problem as essentially a fashion issue. (". . . there was ample housing of a sort for most of those seeking it. . . . All that was wrong with much of it was that it was out-of-date, esthetically and otherwise, by the standards of the well-off. . . .") It is all extremely well done, and all delicious.

It is when Banfield turns to Swift for inspiration that the results become perhaps a trifle bizarre and grisly. For example, he advances the idea of custodial institutionalization for "nonlearners" too young to work, and for the "semicompetent" poor ("the hardest cases among the lower class"). For the problem of crime, he proposes the solutions of "curbstone justice" and long-term preventive detention and abridgment of civil rights for those lower-class young men who might be identified as likely to commit some misdemeanors.

His most chilling Swiftian conceit is the idea of gradually liquidating the lower class by encouraging the poor to auction off their children. (He would guard against greedy procreation for profit by requiring the sellers to accept sterilization.)

Some of his solutions, however, are gay and whimsical, rather than gruesome. One of the zaniest is that we should overcome unemployment and youthful crime by repealing minimum-wage, child-labor, and school-attendance laws, thereby freeing employers to hire the poor and juvenile delinquents at wages equivalent to their worth—fifty cents or a dollar an hour.

As might have been anticipated from several of the quotations, the central thesis of *The Unheavenly City* is a brilliantly cockeyed redefinition of social stratification. In a mocking parody of those social scientists who deal with this issue by ignoring money and power and concentrating on "culture" and "life-style," Banfield has his Professor equate class position with time perspective—the lower class is "present-oriented"; the "normals" (middle and upper classes) are "future-minded." (". . . a person who is poor, unschooled, and of low status may be upper class; indeed he *is* upper class if he is psychologically capable of providing for a distant future. By the same token, one who is rich and a member of 'the 400' may be lower class. . . .") He then plays out the hilarious consequences of the cuckoo definition. It follows, of course, that "people who are capable of providing for a distant future tend . . . to get education . . . and with it wealth, status, and power." We can also deduce that many of our social problems can be attributed to immigration from countries (mostly Catholic, of course) with "present-oriented cultures." And so forth, and so forth.

With a stroke of satirical genius, Banfield turns the class struggle upside down, attributing a great deal of our urban crisis to the *upper* classes—but for a very different reason than might be supposed. The truth is that they are too altruistic and community-minded and keep trying fruitlessly to raise the lower classes from the degradation that they *prefer*—we are dealing with "people who would live in squalor and misery even if their incomes were doubled or tripled." Such constant attention, it seems, tends to persuade the poor that they are victims of injustice rather than simple slobs.

As the author of a forthcoming book on these very topics (entitled *Blaming the Victim*), I must confess to a certain envy of Banfield's technique. Whereas I try to analyze and refute the ideology of finding the cause of society's problems in the characteristics of society's victims, Banfield exposes this ideology by pushing it to ridiculous extremes: "Extreme present-mindedness, not lack of income or wealth, is the principal cause of poverty." The major cause of crime is the "unremitting search for sex and for relief from boredom" that is the hallmark of the lower-class life-style. "There seems to have been a marked increase since the civil rights revolution began in the amount of crime by Negroes." The cause of educational failure, as we have seen, is the fact that the lower-class child is not "educable." It is a sustained, wild performance, a real *tour de force.*

The one real problem with the book is that it is *too* cleverly done; it is so *believable* that it might be taken seriously, as, for example, Swift's *Modest Proposal* was taken seriously. There have already been several reviews that have treated the book with a straight face rather than as the great joke it in fact is. This is rather surprising since Banfield takes great pains to keep his satire consistent by including an ample amount of incompetent scholarship and outrageous misstatements of fact that should have tipped off any reasonably informed reviewer. (Black residents of an urban renewal neighborhood in Boston could have moved to white neighborhoods if they so wished: "There was nothing to stop them from doing so." "The poor in the cities receive as many visits from physicians as do the well-off. . . . They are somewhat less likely than the well-off to suffer from chronic conditions." Ghetto riots are caused, in part, by *predictions* of riots by Black militants, by television coverage of other riots, and by the fact that "it was well known, too, that the police would not use their guns.")

As illustrated by the last point, Banfield's taste is occasionally questionable. I am not sure how really funny it is to say that police would not use their guns in riots—although, I suppose, one could go further and say that this is a principle of which the Black citizens shot to death in Detroit, Watts, and Newark should have reminded the policeman who murdered them.

In a sense, to review this book seriously would be to insult Professor Banfield, to accuse the Henry Lee Shattuck Professor of Urban Government at *Harvard* of being a social science Strangelove, an advocate of virtual genocide of the poor. If *The Unheavenly City* were intended to be a serious book, it would, of course, impose a moral obligation on every decent social scientist in America to repudiate, refute, and denounce it.

Chapter	Community:
10	Who Rules?

One of the central concerns of those sociologists who study community has been the discovery of who wields the power. There have been numerous studies of this phenomenon, and two of them are included here. The first, by Robert O. Schulze, begins with a critique of past community studies because they have been ahistorical in their analysis of power. He seeks to correct this omission by focusing on the changing position of "economic dominants" in the town he calls "Cibola." Cibola has a population of 20,000 people and is located thirty miles from a large midwestern city. Schulze hypothesized that as the relationship between the town and the larger society changed, there would be changes in its internal structure; in particular, in the position of the economic dominants. What he found was that between 1823 and 1955 the earlier control of Cibola by economic leaders had bifurcated, and in later years there was a separation between economic dominants and sociopolitical leaders. Among the causes of this change were the growing influence of the nearby metropolitan area and increasing absentee ownership of the businesses which were once locally owned.

Clelland and Form sought to replicate Schulze's study in "Wheelsburg," a city of 100,000 (dominating a metropolitan area of 180,000) about sixty miles west of Cibola. Their research tends to support some of Schulze's findings and to contradict others. For example, although they too found a sharp decline in the number of economic dominants holding office, they did not find two distinct power bases. In collecting lists of economic and public leaders they found that 31 percent of the names appeared on both lists. Further, economic dominants were more involved in community issues in Wheelsburg than in Cibola. They account for the differences in the two studies in terms of differences between the two cities. For example, the firms in Wheelsburg were more stable, the city was less influenced by the growth of a large competing metropolis and fewer of the economic dominants lived out of town.

The Role of Economic Dominants in Community Power Structure*

ROBERT O. SCHULZE

That persons occupying positions of economic importance are among the key wielders of local influence and control has long been one of the most commonplace assumptions of American sociologists and one of the most consistent findings of research concerned with American communities and community power structure.[1] With very few exceptions, however, most studies relevant to the role of economic dominants in community control structures have focused on current power configurations. Relatively little research attention has yet been devoted to historical shifts in local power structures associated with the metropolitan and bureaucratic drift of American life.[2] Likewise, while most relevant studies have indicated that a considerable number of persons of significant local influence are men of economic substance, they have not revealed the pattern of community involvement (nor changes in that pattern) of the economically most-powerful considered as a category. Thus, we have heard a good deal about the activities and influence of the "X" family and its equivalents in American communities, but rather less about the "Y" families, and almost

* Reprinted from *American Sociological Review*, 23 (February, 1958), pp. 3–9, by permission of the author and publisher.
    Expanded version of paper read at the annual meeting of the American Sociological Society, August, 1957. I wish to thank Morris Janowitz and Melvin Reichler, both of the University of Michigan, for their helpful comments on this paper.
1. In addition to the well-known works of the Lynds, Warner, Hollingshead, Mills, and Hunter, see: Roland J. Pellegrin and Charles H. Coates, "Absentee-Owned Corporations and Community Power Structure," *American Journal of Sociology*, LXI, 5 (March, 1956), pp. 413–419; George Belknap and Ralph Smuckler, "Political Power Relations in a Mid-West City," *Public Opinion Quarterly*, XX, 1 (Spring, 1956), pp. 73–81; A. Alexander Fanelli, "A Typology of Community Leadership Based on Influence and Interaction Within the Leader Subsystem," *Social Forces*, 34, 4 (May, 1956), pp. 332–338; Robert E. Agger, "Power Attributions in the Local Community," *ibid.*, pp. 322–331; Peter Rossi, "Historical Trends in the Politics of an Industrial Community," paper presented at the 51st annual meeting of the American Sociological Society, September, 1956.
2. Rossi's study is a notable exception.

nothing at all about the ration of "Xs" to "Ys" either currently or over time.

This paper reports some findings of an investigation of the power structure of a middle-sized American community—findings concerned primarily with the historical role of the economic dominants in that community's power structure.[3] Although the study has among its numerous limitations those inevitable in any piece of single-community research, it is hoped that it might be theoretically and methodologically suggestive for research in other communities, especially those which—like the subject of this study—have become satellites in a society increasingly dominated by giant metropolitan centers and large national corporations.

The rudimentary theory underlying this research may be briefly summarized. The basic assumption was that as the functional relationship of the community to the larger society changes, so does the nature and form of its control structure, and so, too, does the role of its economic dominants in that structure.

It was hypothesized that in the community *relatively* self-contained and uninvolved in the larger social and economic system, the community with few and scattered commitments beyond its borders, local power would tend to be structured as a pyramid and heavily concentrated at the apex. More specifically, it was surmised that those persons who exercised major control over the community's economic system would tend to be the same persons who exercised preponderant control over its socio-political system, and that this latter control would be reflected, at least in part, by their active leadership and participation in the political and civic life of the community.

With increasing urbanization and as the community passed beyond what Lloyd Warner has called "the period of local capitalism,"[4] however, it was suggested that the economic dominants would begin to withdraw their interest and active attention from the local socio-political system. Although the major economic units would have grown in size and potential influence, it was hypothesized that several factors would militate against the effective exercise, the actual "cashing-in" of their power in the community. The most significant of these would be the fact that the local community would have become ever less important to the survival and prosperity of its dominant economic units. As the activities of these units became increasingly directed toward—and by—populations and groups other than the local ones, the relevance of local community organizations and the impact of local political influences on the major economic units would accordingly

---

3. Robert O. Schulze, *Economic Dominance and Public Leadership: A Study of the Structure and Process of Power in an Urban Community*, microfilmed Ph.D. dissertation, University of Michigan, 1956. (University Microfilms, Publication No. 21,359.)

4. W. Lloyd Warner and J. O. Low, "The Factory in the Community," in William Foote Whyte (ed.), *Industry and Society*, New York: McGraw-Hill, 1946, p. 35.

diminish. As this occurred, the local power structure would, in effect, bifurcate—with those who exercised primary direction over its socio-political system no longer being essentially the same set of persons who exercised primary control over its economic system.[5]

An effort was made to test this general theory in Cibola, a Midwestern industrial community of some 20,000 inhabitants, located approximately 30 miles from Metro City, one of the nation's largest metropolitan centers. Founded in 1823, Cibola grew rather slowly until World War II. Between 1940 and 1950, however, its population increased over 50 per cent, a shift symptomatic of countless other changes to which the community has lately been subject. One of the principal changes has been the gradual absorption of its major industrial plants by large, absentee-owned corporations, a trend sharply accelerated during the World War II period.

In our research, we attempted to reconstruct Cibola's economic dominants from the time of its founding in 1823 until 1955, and to determine the general nature and extent of their overt involvement in the political and civic life of the community.

The economic dominants for the various historical periods were operationally-defined as those persons who: (a) occupied the top formal roles in the largest industries and banks in the community; or (b) were members of the boards of directors of two or more of these industries and banks, thus serving formally to "interlock" the dominant economic units; or (c) were the largest property-owners in the community.[6]

---

5. It is not suggested that the decline in the economic dominants' leadership and participation in community decision-making processes stems wholly from their diminishing concern with local affairs. With their attenuation of local involvement, it is obvious that effective contact and meaningful communication between economic dominants and diverse elements of the community population are likewise reduced, contributing to what has been referred to as the loss of "multi-class leadership" by the top business groups in American communities. In such a situation, economic dominants—when they occasionally may want to influence community decisions—may find that their local leadership base has so shrunken that their effectiveness is impaired. Somewhat illustrative of this was the case of Cal Lamkin, the general manager of a large industrial plant in the community studied. Long inactive in local political and voluntary associational affairs, Lamkin was eventually prevailed upon to stand for election to the board of directors of the local Chamber of Commerce. To the considerable embarrassment of the Chamber's officials, however, Lamkin failed to muster sufficient votes to win a seat on the board. Cf. Wilbert E. Moore, *Industrial Relations and the Social Order*, New York: The Macmillan Company, 1951, pp. 547–553. Although presented in causal terms somewhat different from those suggested in this paper, the best known and perhaps most sanguine statement of the American business elites' loss of multi-group leadership is contained in Kenneth Galbraith, *American Capitalism and the Concept of Countervailing Power*, Boston: Houghton Mifflin, 1952.

6. Specific criteria for classification as an economic dominant in each historical period were based on such measures as number of employees (industries), capital worth (banks), and assessed valuation of holdings (property-owners). Various source data were utilized in the determination of these measures, including county tax records, city directories and histories, newspapers, records of individual companies and of the Chamber of Commerce and the State Historical Collections, plus such standard references as *Poor's Register of Directors and Executives* and *Polk's Bank Directory*.

Insofar as local involvement was reflected by occupancy of formal offices in the political and civic organizations in the community, the research tended clearly to support the basic hypothesis. *The historical drift has been characterized by the withdrawal of the economic dominants from active and overt participation in the public life of Cibola.* Tables 1, 3,. and 4 are presented to illustrate this withdrawal.

TABLE 1.   *Number and Per cent of Economic Dominants in Public Office, 1823–1954 Periods*

Period	Number of Economic Dominants	Number of Economic Dominants in Public Office	Per Cent of Economic Dominants in Public Office
1823–1860	12	10	83
1860–1900	21	17	81
1900–1940	43	12	28
1940–1954	31	7	23

Table 1 indicates that prior to the turn of the century, fully four-fifths of Cibola's economic dominants held public office in the community, while since 1900, the proportion has declined to approximately one-quarter.[7] Likewise, as shown in Table 3, the proportion of economic dominants who have held the top political office in Cibola has sharply diminished. Not indicated in either of these two tables is the fact that *none* of the most recent type of economic dominant—the managers of the absentee-owned

TABLE 2.   *Changes in Number of Economic Dominants and Number of Available Offices, 1823–1954 Periods*

Period	Percentage Change in Number of Economic Dominants	Percentage Change in number of Public Offices in City Government
From 1823–1860 to 1860–1900 periods	plus 75	plus 80
From 1860–1900 to 1900–1940 periods	plus 105	plus 183
From 1900–1940 to 1940–1954 periods	minus 28	minus 30

7. It might be suggested that the declining proportion of economic dominants in public office was a function of the fact that the number of dominants increased at a greater rate than the number of available offices, and therefore, that the declining proportions are spurious. This was not the case. Changes in the number of economic dominants throughout the four periods were very closely paralleled by proportionately similar changes in the number of available public offices. (See Table 2.)

TABLE 3.   *Number and Per Cent of Economic Dominants in Office
of Village President or Mayor, 1823–1954 Periods*

Period	Number of Dominants in Office of Village President or Mayor	Per Cent of Dominants in Office of Village President or Mayor	Per Cent of "Politically-Active" Dominants in Office of Village President or Mayor*
1823–1860	5	42	50
1860–1900	7	33	41
1900–1940	2	5	17
1940–1954	1	3	14

* "Politically-Active": All those economic dominants who had held *any* public office.

corporations—has held any public office (elective or appointive) in the community.

There was some evidence that in the early decades of this century the arena of active local involvement of Cibola's economic dominants shifted from politics to the important voluntary associations. Even in this area, however, an appreciable subsequent diminution of active participation has been apparent—perhaps best reflected by the declining number of dominants holding responsible office in the community's most influential association, the local Chamber of Commerce.

TABLE 4.   *Number of Economic Dominants in Offices of the
Chamber of Commerce, 1920–1955**

Period	Median Number of Memberships per Year on Board of Directors	Number Serving as President
1920–1927	6	3
1927–1934	3	2
1934–1941	3	0
1941–1948	2	1
1948–1955	1	0

* The Cibola Chamber of Commerce was founded in 1920. From that date until 1953, the number of directors was fifteen; in the latter year, the number was increased to eighteen. Directors serve two-year terms and are eligible for reelection.

It is suggested that the withdrawal of the economic dominants was primarily a consequence of the changing relationship of the community's economic system to that of the larger society. Prior to about 1900, three aspects of Cibola's economic life were especially notable: (a) all of its economic dominants were local residents; (b) all of its dominant economic units were locally-owned; and (c) the majority of its dominants were associated in extensive economic networks *within* the community.

Our research established that in the pre-1900 period, almost 70 per cent of the economic dominants had known business or financial ties—as partners, co-officers or co-directors—with other dominants in the community. Thus, throughout most of Cibola's history, its "average" economic dominant was not only a local resident, or merely the head of a single major economic unit; he was also directly and indirectly linked with a considerable number of other major economic units and dominants within the community.

Combined, these factors provided most economic dominants with deep, branching roots in Cibola. The business and financial links, in particular, afforded many of them a basis for shared concern in the local community. The economic networks served to weld together blocs of dominants, giving them frequent and specific occasion for interpersonal contact. By the same token, the very diversity of the "average" dominant's local economic commitments meant that there was always a variety of areas and methods in which local political considerations could impinge upon his pecuniary and related interests. The evidence suggests that these considerations were closely associated with the high incidence of involvement by economic dominants in the socio-political system of the community.

The period since 1900, and more particularly, since 1930, has been marked by the increasing absorption of the local economic system into the larger industrial complex, especially that of Metro City. While several complex social factors were patently involved, the following three seem most closely related to the eventual withdrawal of the economic dominants from active participation in the political-civic life of Cibola: (a) the establishment by a growing number of locally-owned industrial units of direct supplier relationships with a small number of large, non-local manufacturing plants; (b) the subsequent introduction into the local economic system of an increasing number of branch plants of large, absentee-owned corporations; and (c) the concomitant dissolution of the extensive networks of inter-locking director and officerships which had formerly served to link significant numbers of local economic dominants within the community.

Consequently, the overt direction of the political and civic life of Cibola has passed almost wholly into the hands of a group of middle-class business and professional men, almost none of whom occupies a position of economic dominance in the community. That this has in fact been the case was suggested in another aspect of our research by the finding that only two of Cibola's seventeen current economic dominants were perceived by the local voluntary association heads to have been among the eighteen most influential leaders in the community.[8] And both of these two, by the way, were heads of relatively small, locally-owned economic units.

Patently, these data reveal changes only in the level of overt and manifest involvement of the economic dominants in the local power structure. It may be suggested, of course, that covertly—"behind-the-scenes"— the economic dominants continue to exercise considerable direction and control of community affairs. However, the findings of another part of our research strongly suggest that things may, in fact, be what they seem.

In an effort to view the community power structure "in action," we endeavored to determine the patterns and processes of local decision-making in a series of recent community episodes (including a successful campaign to change the structure of municipal government from a mayor-aldermen to a city manager form, and an ambitious but unsuccessful annexation effort).[9] Our findings in this aspect of the research forced us to conclude that the recent economic dominants—and especially those representing the growing number of large, absentee-owned corporations—appear indeed to have dissociated themselves from active involvement in Cibola's power structure.

These episodes reflected a growing adherence on the part of the absentee-owned corporations in Cibola to a "hands-off" position with regard to local political decision-making. And while it cannot be conclusively documented within the limits of the present paper, this evolving policy is graphically suggested by presenting excerpts from interviews with several executives in the larger economic units.

The general manager of the second largest manufacturing plant in the community, commenting on our findings that but two of the top ten officials in his plant actually resided in Cibola, stated:

> That's a sore spot with me. I've always felt that if I'm going to work in a town, I ought to live there. But there's no consensus on that by a long ways. It's been discussed at the highest levels in our corporation—I know because I've been on the company's community relations committee ever since it was set up. The company has decided that it won't encourage its executives to live in the communities where they work if

---

8. The heads of 143 voluntary associations in Cibola were asked a series of five questions intended to elicit their perceptions of the most influential leaders in the community. On the basis of their total "nominations," the eighteen most-frequently cited persons were designated as the "public leaders" of Cibola. See Robert O. Schulze and Leonard U. Blumberg, "The Determination of Local Power Elites," *American Journal of Sociology*, 63, 3 (November, 1957), pp. 290–296.

9. In these reconstructions, a variety of source materials was utilized, including intensive interviews with the seventeen current economic dominants, the eighteen persons perceived by the 143 local voluntary association heads as the community's most influential leaders, and a selected number of informants. In addition, relevant newspaper files, Chamber of Commerce records and reports, and city council minutes were reviewed.

they don't already or if they don't want to. . . . The company doesn't feel its people—at least its executives—have to live in a town in order to have good community relations. Just about the opposite, as a matter of fact. You're always subject to a hell of a lot of local pressures if you're there. If they know where you are, you're always a target. So maybe it's better not to be in a position to be asked to do something than to have to say, "No."

In discussing the paucity of both formal and informal contacts between corporation officials and local leaders, the assistant general manager of the largest industrial plant in Cibola said:

No, I've almost never gone downtown for lunch "with the boys." I sometimes get my hair cut in [Cibola], but outside of that I don't show my face any more than I feel I absolutely have to. . . . The people at the Chamber of Commerce seem to fall all over themselves trying to do anything we want—but the point is, we don't really *want* anything there except for the people to have a good opinion of us. But mostly due to this placating attitude of the town's leaders, I'm afraid to say much or be around much.

The corporations were interested, to be sure (as the title of one company's "kit for divisional executives" indicated), in "Making Friends for [U.S. Motors] in the Local Community," but a growing number of them were coming to regard "making friends" and "getting involved" as inconsonant. The general manager of another large plant summed up his attitude:

One sure way to give [our firm] a black eye would be for me to get myself into things so deeply in town that no matter what I did, I'd end up alienating a lot of people.

And another:

You've got to remember that what I do doesn't affect us just here. The guy who represents our company in this area could affect our reputation a lot of other places as well. . . . Why, if I went out and got myself [involved] in local politics, you'd see a new boy in these shoes so damned fast it'd make your head swim.

Meaningful participation in the decision-making processes of a community such as Cibola was mainly regarded by these corporations as entailing risks to their operations and to their positions in the larger social system—risks which could not be offset by any palpable advantages which might accrue to them through playing significant roles in the local power structure. They were clearly cognizant, for example, of the possibility that involvement by their executives in local affairs might induce conflicting loyalties. Likewise, their executives recognized that decisive involvement in critical community decisions posed the threat of alienating significant superiors and publics at the extra-community level, thus endangering their larger occupational and public relations objectives. It seems tenable that it was the very sensitivity of the large corporations to socio-political determinations at the regional and national levels which militated against their involvement in these matters at the level of the local community.

The central finding of the Cibola study—the bifurcation of the community's power structure, stemming from the withdrawal of the economic dominants from active direction of the political and civic life of the community—appears quite generally to corroborate the investigation of Peter Rossi and his associates of the changing patterns of political participation in a middle-sized industrial community in New England.[10] Likewise, our findings seem to be consistent with C. Wright Mills' observations regarding the altered position of large economic units in the power structures of local communities.[11] On the other hand, the Cibola findings do not appear consistent with Hunter's research in Regional City, nor, especially, with that of Pellegrin and Coates in Bigtown.[12]

In addition to the obvious and perhaps significant differences in the sizes of the several communities involved, it will be noted that Hunter and Pellegrin and Coates studied the structures and dynamics of community power in Southern Cities, while Rossi's and the present research concern New England and Midwestern communities, respectively. In correspondence with the writer, Pellegrin has suggested that the disparate findings may be largely the function of regional differences: the historical tradition of paternalism being perhaps stronger in the South than in the North. It has also been suggested that economic dominants may become involved in community power structures independent of the desires of their economic units to guide or influence local decision-making. Thus, for example, to the extent that economic dominants represent the wealthier interests in the community and are a major source of voluntary donations to local charities and similar activities, they may be coopted into decision structures by those actively "in charge" in order to reinforce the latter's control positions and to guarantee a continued source of contributions. Likewise, to the extent that the economic dominants represent the upper prestige levels in a community, they may be drawn into the control structure by the active community leaders in an effort by the latter to legitimize their own prestige positions.

It should be noted, however, that both of the foregoing hypothetical

10. Rossi, *op. cit.*
11. C. Wright Mills, *The Power Elite,* New York: Oxford University Press, 1956.
12. Floyd Hunter, *Community Power Structure,* Chapel Hill: University of North Carolina Press, 1953; Pellegrin and Coates, *op. cit.*

instances cast the economic dominants in the role of rather reluctant participants in local power structures. In such situations, it would be *other* members of the community, not the economic dominants nor the dominant economic units themselves, who would have most stake in the latters' local involvement. And this, in turn, would have, perhaps, significant ramifications for the kinds of roles which the economic dominants played in community power structures and for the degree of interest and local concern with which they acted out these roles.

Whatever the reasons for the apparent differences in the nature and extent of economic dominant involvement in local power structures—and the delineation of these reasons should certainly be one objective of future research—the Cibola study appears to document the absence of any neat, constant, and direct relationship between *power as a potential for determinative action,* and *power as determinative action,* itself. It suggests, likewise, the need to re-examine the role of economic dominance in community power structures in view of the continued drift of American society, on the one hand, toward the concentration of population in suburban and satellite communities, and, on the other, toward the continuing expansion of huge economic bureaucracies.

Economic Dominants and Community Power: A Comparative Analysis[*][1]

DONALD A. CLELLAND
AND
WILLIAM H. FORM

INTRODUCTION

Three avenues to the study of American community power structure have received widest attention during the last decade. The earliest approach studied a single set of community influentials who allegedly made the major community decisions.[2] Adherents of this method have generally

* From *American Journal of Sociology,* Vol. 69 (March, 1964), pp. 511–521. Reprinted by permission of The University of Chicago Press, publisher.
1. We are grateful to Professor James B. McKee for a critical reading of the manuscript.
2. The tradition of Robert S. Lynd and Helen Merrill Lynd, *Middletown in Transition* (New York: Harcourt, Brace & Co., 1937); C. Wright Mills, *The Power Elite* (New York: Oxford University Press, 1956); Floyd Hunter, *Community Power Structure* (Chapel Hill: University of North Carolina Press, 1953), and many others.

concluded that business leaders are the "ruling elite" or at least *primi inter pares* in the community power structure. The second method discerned the power structure by examining how specific persons and groups behaved in specific community issues and decisions.[3] Those using this technique have generally found a pluralistic system of decision-making. The third avenue has investigated the forces changing the character of persons holding positions of potential power.[4] Irrespective of approach, an ideological question has been persistent—whether the community is governed informally by an economic elite or whether the dominant pattern is political pluralism, a situation where decision-makers represent groups with differing interests.

One instructive way of posing this controversy is to ask what types of relationships characterize the stratification orders in American communities in the past and in the present.[5] More specifically, the sociological question is: To what extent has private economic power been translated directly into community or public power? Although R. O. Schulze did not formally place his research within the Weberian framework, operationally he did study the question we have posed by tracing historically the place of economically powerful figures in the public life of Cibola.[6] The study reported here attempts to replicate his investigation in a different type of community, which we shall call "Wheelsburg."

Schulze's findings upheld his hypothesis that as a city grows from an isolated, self-contained entity to an urbanized community "increasingly involved and interrelated in the large social complex," its sociopolitical power structure changes from a monolithic one dominated by persons possessing great economic power to a bifurcated structure comprising "two crucial and relatively discrete power sets, the economic dominants and the public leaders."[7] Economic dominants were defined as "those persons who

---

3. E.g., Robert A. Dahl, "Equality and Power in American Society," in *Power and Democracy in America,* ed. William V. D'Antonio and Howard J. Ehrlich (Notre Dame, Ind.: University of Notre Dame Press, 1961); Nelson W. Polsby, "The Sociology of Community Power: A Reassessment," *Social Forces,* XXXVII (March, 1959), 232–36; Linton C. Freeman *et al.,* "Local Community Leadership," *Syracuse College Paper No. 15* (Syracuse, N.Y.: Syracuse University, 1960); and Edward C. Banfield, *Political Influence* (New York: Free Press of Glencoe, 1961); and many others.
4. Robert A. Dahl, *Who Governs?* (New Haven, Conn.: Yale University Press, 1961); Constance Green, *Holyoke, Massachusetts* (New Haven, Conn.: Yale University Press, 1939); Thorstein Veblen, *Absentee Ownership* (New York: Viking Press, 1939); and the works of R. O. Schulze cited in n. 6.
5. In the framework of Max Weber as explicated in "Class, Status and Power," in *From Max Weber: Essays in Sociology,* ed. and trans. Hans H. Gerth and C. Wright Mills (New York: Oxford University Press, 1946).
6. Schulze, Robert O. "Economic Dominance and Public Leadership: A Study of the Structure and Process of Power in an Urban Community" (microfilmed Ph.D. dissertation, University of Michigan, 1956); "The Role of Economic Dominants in Community Power Structure," *American Sociological Review,* XXIII (February, 1958), 3–9; "The Bifurcation of Power in a Satellite City," in *Community Political Systems,* ed. Morris Janowitz (Glencoe, Ill.: Free Press, 1961), pp. 19–80.
7. "The Bifurcation of Power . . . ," *op. cit.,* pp. 21–22.

occupy the top formal statuses in the major economic units within the community area,"[8] and public leaders (or top influentials) as those who, in the opinion of community "knowledgeables," exercise major influence and leadership in community affairs.[9]

Schulze tentatively explained the dissociation of economic dominants from local political-civic affairs by the following three trends:

(a) the establishment by a growing number of locally-owned industrial units of direct supplier relationships with a small number of large, non-local manufacturing plants; (b) the subsequent introduction into the local economic system of an increasing number of branch plants of large, absentee-owned corporations; and (c) the concomitant dissolution of the extensive networks of interlocking directorates and officerships which had formerly served to link significant numbers of local economic dominants within the community.[10]

These trends have also occurred in Wheelsburg, but to a more limited degree. The greatest variation between Cibola and Wheelsburg is in the first factor, because in Wheelsburg many local supply plants were established to serve the local automobile firms.

COMPARISON OF THE COMMUNITIES

The two communities differ significantly in a number of ways. For most of its history Cibola was a small independent town. It is now a satellite city of approximately 20,000 inhabitants located just beyond the

---

8. *Ibid.*, p. 21. For Schulze's operational criteria for determining economic dominants and public leaders see *ibid.*, Appendixes A and B, pp. 73–75. Essentially the same criteria were utilized to identify the dominant economic units (and consequently economic dominants themselves) in the two cities. Number of employees, capital worth, and assessed valuation were used as measures. However, since Wheelsburg is a much larger city than Cibola, the minimum figures for cutoff points were necessarily larger. In Cibola the only dominant economic units were manufacturing plants, banks, and savings and loan companies. In Wheelsburg a wider variety of economic units was included in the dominant group, e.g., department stores, utilities, and insurance companies. In addition to the heads of the major economic units, all who were on the board of directors of two or more of the major economic units were also identified as economic dominants.
9. As suggested by Hunter, *op. cit.* The "knowledgeables" who were interviewed in the two studies differed somewhat. Schulze's knowledgeables were the heads of local voluntary associations. This research relied on the nominations of fourteen high-ranking officials from seven institutional sectors of the community (mass communication, business, union, welfare, education, government, religion). David A. Booth and Charles A. Adrian compared the results of the method used by Schulze with the simpler method we employed, and found almost identical results (see their "Simplifying the Discovery of Elites," *American Behavioral Scientist*, V [October, 1961], 14–16).
10. Schulze, "The Role of Economic Dominants . . .," *op. cit.*, p. 6.

Standard Metropolitan Area of a large midwest industrial center containing more than 3,000,000 people. The five largest of its eight major industrial plants were absentee-controlled. Cibola is an extreme example of a city that "has felt the full impact of the metropolitan drift of American life."[11] A period of rapid expansion began during World War II with the establishment just outside the city's boundaries of a gigantic war-production plant which employed over 40,000 workers at its peak. After the war the economic instability of absentee-owned companies occupying this plant caused wide and rapid fluctuations in the local labor force. Consequently, during the 1940's the community experienced rapid fluctuation and high turnover in population. At the time of Schulze's study employment at the main plant had leveled off at 9,500 as it became tied securely to the motor vehicle industry.

Wheelsburg is located about 60 miles west of Cibola. It is an independent city of over 100,000 dominating a metropolitan area with a population of approximately 180,000. Like Cibola, its economy is based primarily on motor vehicle production. In fact, the same motor vehicle company is the largest single employer in both communities. In Wheelsburg the company employs nearly 15,000 workers. However, significant sections of Wheelsburg's labor force are employed in state government and in a nearby state university. Wheelsburg's period of most rapid industrial and population growth occurred earlier than Cibola's, between 1900 and 1920. This growth largely reflected the success of locally owned automobile and supplier plants. Since 1920 Wheelsburg's growth has been moderate and steady even with the large invasion of absentee-owned companies. Such companies came earlier to Wheelsburg, but entered and grew more gradually than in Cibola.

Currently, thirteen of the twenty non-financial dominant economic units are absentee-controlled.[12] Unlike Cibola, (a) Wheelsburg's major firms have been fairly stable operations, (b) the vast majority of its labor force has always been employed within the city limits, (c) very few of its economic dominants have lived beyond the city's contiguous suburbs, and (d) the city is removed from the influence of a large competing metropolis. Wheelsburg, then, is a much more stable and "normal" type of community setting in which to test Schulze's hypothesis.

Following Schulze's method closely, we tested his main hypothesis by (1) reconstructing the formal participation patterns of economic dominants

---

11. Schulze, "The Bifurcation of Power . . . ," *op. cit.*, p. 24.
12. An absentee-controlled company is defined as one having a majority of its board of directors living outside of the local community. In both Cibola and Wheelsburg, slightly less than 50 per cent of the dominant economic units were absentee-controlled —five of eleven units in Cibola and thirteen of twenty-seven units in Wheelsburg. In both cities, all of the financial units (three and seven, respectively) were locally owned.

over the past century in the political and civic activities of the community; (2) ascertaining the representation of current economic dominants among public leaders, that is, in the "reputational" power structure; and (3) analyzing the role of current economic dominants in specific community issues and programs.

ECONOMIC DOMINANTS AS POLITICAL AND CIVIC LEADERS

In Wheelsburg, as in Cibola, the proportion of economic dominants who occupied high local governmental offices declined dramatically over the century. Data in Tables 1 and 2 reveal that in both communities prior to 1900 the economic dominants were highly represented in local government. The comparable percentages in each table are virtually identical. Although the twentieth century ushered in a sharp decline in the proportion of economic dominants holding public office in both communities, this decline was sharper in Wheelsburg than in Cibola. Moreover, in both cities, but especially in Wheelsburg, the offices held by economic dominants have been increasingly appointive rather than elective. Indeed, no economic dominant has served as mayor since 1899, or as councilman since 1932.

TABLE 1.   *Economic Dominants Serving in Public Office in Wheelsburg and Cibola*

		Per Cent			
Period	No. of Economic Dominants	In Public Office	In Elective Office	On Governing Body	In Highest Public Office
1823–60:					
Wheelsburg	*				
Cibola	12	83	83	75	50
1860–1900:					
Wheelsburg	44	73	64	57	30
Cibola	21	81	67	57	33
1900–1940:					
Wheelsburg	80	25	11	4	0
Cibola	43	26	16	12	5
1940–59:					
Wheelsburg	71	14	0	0	0
Cibola	31	23	13	10	3

* Wheelsburg was not incorporated until 1859.
Source: Cibola data, see Schulze, "The Bifurcation of Power . . .," *op. cit.*, pp. 37–38.

TABLE 2.   *Offices Held by Politically Active Economic Dominants in Wheelsburg and Cibola**

	No. of Politically Active Economic Dominants	Per Cent		
Period		In Elective Office	On Govern-ing Body	In Highest Public Office
1823–1860:				
Wheelsburg				
Cibola	10	100	90	60
1860–1900:				
Wheelsburg	32	88	78	41
Cibola	17	88	71	41
1900–1940:				
Wheelsburg	20	45	15	0
Cibola	12	64	45	18
1940–1959:				
Wheelsburg	10	0	0	0
Cibola	7	57	43	14

* "Politically active" refers to economic dominants holding any appointive or elective office.
Source: Cibola data, see Schulze, "The Bifurcation of Power . . .," *op. cit.,* pp. 37–38.

The trend of these developments in Wheelsburg may be seen more clearly by examining the data in terms of twenty-year periods. A precipitous decline in public officeholding by economic dominants occurred in the 1900–1920 period, with relatively little change thereafter. However, there has been a continuing change in the type of office held. In each succeeding twenty-year period, fewer of the economic dominants who held office were elected. Increasingly, they have come to hold advisory and honorary positions in local government. Since it is probably fair to assume that the power potential of appointive offices is less than that of elective offices, the shift of economic dominants from the latter may be taken as evidence of continuing loss of formal political power.

Schulze suggests that after 1900 the arena of local involvement of the economic dominants shifted from politics to voluntary associations. The Wheelsburg data confirm his observation. Thus data in Table 3 show that at the beginning the economic dominants were highly represented among the members and officers of the Chamber of Commerce, and that their representation declined at a later era. Apparently the Wheelsburg economic dominants were even more powerful in the Chamber than their Cibola counterparts, for one of their number was president during nine-

TABLE 3. *Economic Dominants as Board Members of Chamber of Commerce*

	Median No. of Memberships per Year on Board of Directors*		No. Serving as President	
Period	Wheelsburg	Cibola	Wheelsburg	Cibola
1901–6	8		3	
1906–13	9		4	
1913–20	9		4	
1920–27	10	6	3	3
1927–34	9	3	2	2
1934–41	9	3	2	0
1941–48	4	2	0	1
1948–55	3	1	3	0
1955–59	5		0	

* The number of directors varied from 15 to 18 in Cibola and from 15 to 21 in Wheelsburg.
Source: Cibola data, Schulze, "The Bifurcation of Power . . .," *op. cit.*, p. 49. Since the Cibola Chamber was founded in 1920, there are no data for earlier periods.

teen of the first twenty years of the organization's existence. During the past two decades their representation in the Chamber has declined, but not so sharply as in Cibola. An historical analysis of the proportion of officerships held by Wheelsburg economic dominants in other civic organizations (major service clubs, community chest, and the board of trustees of the leading local hospital) reveals patterns of withdrawal similar to that evident in Table 3. While it is difficult to estimate the power potential of these officerships, current public leaders or top influentials regard the Chamber of Commerce as the single most influential organization in the city. Yet, as indicated above, direct control of this organization by economic dominants has probably declined over the years.

In both Wheelsburg and Cibola economic dominants reduced their incumbency in public offices at the turn of the century. A similar withdrawal from civil leadership positions began about 1940.[13] A comparative analysis of the economic development of the two communities corroborates some of Schulze's explanations and contradicts others. The evidence fails to support Schulze's position that the growth of absentee ownership and the dissolution of local business ties (interlocking directorates) among the

---

13. "Withdrawal" is probably an apt phrase, because no evidence is available to suggest that there was community pressure on the economic dominants to reduce their community involvement. However, individual economic dominants were constantly changing. Their withdrawal consisted not so much in dropping civic leadership positions as in the failure of new economic dominants to seek such positions.

economic dominants account for their withdrawal from public office. In both communities these phenomena occurred *after* the withdrawal; in Cibola, the first absentee-controlled plant was established in 1932, and in Wheelsburg as late as 1940 two-thirds of the major economic units were locally owned. Moreover, 80 per cent of the Wheelsburg economic dominants maintained local business ties with other economic dominants as late as 1940. A third factor which Schulze associated with withdrawal, namely, the growth of direct supplier relationships to non-local industries by locally owned plants, must also be discarded, for in Wheelsburg no such growth took place and yet the pattern of withdrawal was similar to that of Cibola. Moreover, in Wheelsburg this withdrawal does not seem to have been forced by the growing political power of ethnic groups as was the case in many American cities.[14] There has never been a large ethnic proletariat in Wheelsburg, nor have local politics ever been heavily based on ethnic lines or class conflict.

What factors, then, are associated with the sharp decline in political participation by economic dominants (i.e., the bifurcation of political and economic power structure) since the turn of the century? At the broadest level of explanation, the increased involvement of the community and its economic units in state and nationwide social economic systems was, no doubt, an important factor. More specifically, in Wheelsburg, the end of the period in which political and economic power tended to coincide was marked by the rise of a new breed of economic elite, namely, managers and owners of the new automobile and supply plants. Younger, wealthier, operating larger businesses, more directly involved in the day-to-day operation of their businesses, introducing a wide variety of new products, these men did not participate in local politics probably largely because they lacked the time and because they probably found that business was much more exciting. A growing separation of wealth and social honor may have been a second factor, but the new economic elite was partly based on old local wealth and the majority were entrepreneurs rather than simply managers of companies financed by non-local capital. However, in the absence of ethnic and class cleavage in the community, it is doubtful that the new economic dominants, many of whom were classed Horatio Alger success models, lacked the popularity needed for election. They probably did not choose to run.

On the other hand, later withdrawal from civic leadership positions seems to be associated with the introduction of absentee-owned plants and

---

14. E.g., in New Haven, from the late nineteenth century until recently, local politics were controlled primarily by "ex-plebes," individuals on the rise from the ethnic proletariat, who gained office through "the skills of ethnic politics." From 1842 to 1898, New Haven politics were dominated by the leading entrepreneurs. It may be significant that the period of dominance by economic dominants is almost identical in New Haven, Wheelsburg, and Cibola (see Dahl, *Who Governs?* chap. iii and iv).

the related decrease in common local business ties (interlocking directorates) among the economic dominants. The importance of the latter factor is underscored in Wheelsburg where economic dominants not only have more local economic linkages but also comprise a larger proportion of the local civic leaders.[15]

The so-called pattern of withdrawal needs to be interpreted within a broad context of the local participation. In Wheelsburg, the historical pattern has been for the economic dominants to become officers of new organizations as they emerged in the community, then to retain membership, and later to withdraw from active participation. Thus when the Chamber of Commerce was created, dominants were its earliest officers; when the service clubs arose they again became officers; when the Community Chest arrived they became its sponsors and officers; and they sponsored the largest hospital and dominated its board. This pattern of domination and later "withdrawal" is subject to various interpretations. We are inclined to believe that it demonstrates two related phenomena: (*a*) assumption of officerships in new organizations validated not only their importance to the community but the power and status of the original officers, namely, the economic dominants, and (*b*) the policies, direction, and administration of the new organizations were set and institutionalized by the original officers. After this initial period the organizations needed only informal and non-official guidance from the dominants and not their active officeholding. In other words, a change in officers did not necessarily mean a change in policy or loss of power and control by dominants.[16]

COMMUNITY INFLUENCE OF ECONOMIC DOMINANTS

In order to assess the community influence of current economic dominants in Wheelsburg, two procedures were used. First, their reputational influence was investigated by assessing their representation in the list of public leaders (community influentials as determined by the method outlined in n. 9). Second, their "actual" influence was probed by examining their role in a number of community issues or projects.

In 1958–59, thirty-nine individuals were found to be economic dominants, and coincidentally, thirty-nine people were designated as public leaders. The names of twelve persons (31 per cent) appeared on both lists. This overlap is considerably higher than that found in Cibola where only

---

15. Sixty-five per cent of the economic dominants in the 1940–59 period were associated as officers, partners, or directors in at least one other business with other economic dominants.

16. Lest the concentration on "withdrawal" be overwhelming, it should be noted that almost half the economic dominants in the 1940–59 period held civic leadership positions in Wheelsburg and that their participation in the Chamber of Commerce was increasing.

two of seventeen economic dominants were among the community's eighteen public leaders. Moreover, eight of the top fifteen public leaders in Wheelsburg, including the top four, as rated by the public leaders themselves, were economic dominants. Although major absentee-owned corporations were "underrepresented" among the economic dominants who were also public leaders, "U.S. Motors" (the absentee-owned industrial giant in the community) was represented by three executives (two of whom were not defined as economic dominants). From these observations we cannot conclude that two discrete power sets are found in Wheelsburg.

In order to substantiate the basic dissimilarities between the economic dominants and public leaders in Cibola, Schulze examined their patterns of political and civic participation. He found that the economic dominants had held only about half as many governmental offices as the public leaders. The same was true in Wheelsburg, although both groups were less active. Somewhat surprisingly, economic dominants were as well represented as the public leaders in the five most influential associations. Table 4 reveals a similar situation of high participation by both economic dominants and public leaders in Wheelsburg's most influential associations. However, the Cibola situation of wide differences between public leaders and economic dominants in the number of officerships held in these associations was not in evidence. Table 5 reveals that a higher proportion of economic dominants in Wheelsburg (from both locally and absentee-owned companies) have in the past held office in the five most influential organizations. Differences are small between the two communities in the proportions currently holding such offices. In short, both Tables 4 and 5 document no deep bifurcation in associational participation between Wheelsburg's economic dominants and public leaders. The relatively high rate of participation by absentee-owned corporation executives is especially notable.[17]

One of the reasons for the failure of economic dominants to participate in the civic life of Cibola was that they regarded the city mainly as the locus of their work life and not their community life.[18] Moreover, their private economic interests were primarily non-local. This may not be surprising since the city's largest economic units were absentee-owned and oriented toward a national market. However, Table 6 indicates that a much more extensive network of economic ties exists in Wheelsburg than

---

17. Although managers of the largest absentee-owned corporation did not dominate the local scene as extensively as in the case of Bigtown, they did have representatives on most of the local bodies to co ordinate knowledge of what was going on in the city. For data on Bigtown see Roland J. Pellegrin and Charles II. Coates, "Absentee-owned Corporations and Community Power Structure," *American Journal of Sociology,* LXI (March, 1956), 413–19.
18. A large proportion lived in other communities in the metropolitan area and may have participated in the associational life of these other communities.

TABLE 4.   *Membership of Current Public Leaders and Economic Dominants in the Most Influential Associations**

| | | Per Cent Belonging to Association | | |
| | | | Economic Dominants | | |
Association	Public Leaders	Local	Absentee	Total
Chamber of Commerce:				
Wheelsburg	87	96	100	97
Cibola	78	100	87	94
Rotary:				
Wheelsburg	49	38	40	38
Cibola	50	70	14	47
Kiwanis:				
Wheelsburg	18	13	7	10
Cibola	44	30	0	18
Lions:				
Wheelsburg	5	8	0	5
Cibola	11	0	0	0

* In Cibola the five most influential associations were determined by polling the voluntary association heads, public leaders, and economic dominants. The four associations listed above and the Junior Chamber of Commerce were named by all of the groupings questioned. These organizations were also designated by Wheelsburg public leaders as highly influential. Since few public leaders or economic dominants were young enough to be eligible for membership in the Junior Chamber of Commerce in either city, and none were members, this association was omitted from the table. Source for Cibola data: Schulze, "The Bifurcation . . . ," *op. cit.,* p. 47.

in Cibola.[19] Despite a high degree of absentee ownership in Wheelsburg, a fairly extensive network of economic ties unites the interests of the economic dominants and the public leaders. These ties may explain the higher rate of civic participation by its economic dominants and their closer social integration to public leaders.

As a final demonstration of the bifurcation of Cibola economic dominants and public leaders, Schulze analyzed the decision-making process on two important community issues. The economic dominants refused to become involved in resolving either of them, leaving the public leaders autonomous but perhaps without a solid power basis for community action.

In Wheelsburg, an analysis of eleven community issues[20] revealed

19. "Economic ties" are instances in which a pair of individuals serves as officers or directors of the same firm. Each pair is counted as one economic tie. For example, if four public leaders serve on the board of directors of a bank, there are six economic ties (pairs).
20. These issues were selected and recapitulated by the public leaders in interviews. They included hospital expansion drive, downtown development, establishment of a metropolitan planning agency, improvement of airport terminal facilities, establish-

TABLE 5. *Officerships of Public Leaders and Economic Dominants in Five Most Influential Community Associations*

| | Public Leaders | | Economic Dominants | | | | | |
| | | | Local | | Absentee | | Total | |
	Wheels-burg	Cibola	Wheels-burg	Cibola	Wheels-burg	Cibola	Wheels-burg	Cibola
Per cent having served as president of at least one of the five associations	31	61	25	20	20	0	23	12
No. of presidencies occupied in the five associations	17	14	8	2	3	0	11	2
Per cent *currently* serving as officer or board member in at least one of the five associations*	18	44	4	10	27	30	13	18
No. of officerships or board memberships *currently* held in the five associations	7	12	1	1	4	2	5	3

* "Currently" refers to the year of research: 1954 for Cibola, 1958–59 for Wheelsburg.
Source: Cibola data, Schulze, "The Bifurcation of Power . . .," *op. cit.*, p. 48.

TABLE 6.   *Number of Known Local Economic Ties among Public
Leaders and Economic Dominants*

| | | Economic Dominants | |
	Public Leaders	Local Firm	Absentee Firm
Public leaders:			
Wheelsburg	23	31	8
Cibola	4	3	2
Local-firm dominants:			
Wheelsburg		47	11
Cibola		15	0
Absentee-firm dominants:*			
Wheelsburg			2
Cibola			2

* In neither Wheelsburg nor Cibola were there any economic ties between absentee-firm dominants from *different* corporations. In the case of two absentee firms in Wheelsburg, a second person in addition to the general manager was defined as an economic dominant because he held a directorship in a local bank as well as an officership in the absentee-owned firm.
Source: Cibola data supplied by Robert O. Schulze in an unpublished manuscript.

that eight of the economic dominants who were also public leaders were among those mentioned as influential in initiating and resolving these issues. Economic dominants, including some representing absentee-owned corporations, either initiated or co-initiated programs of action for six of the eight issues in which they were involved. Although this evidence suggests that economic dominants have not withdrawn from community decision-making and that they are not just ceremonial leaders, apparently they do not form a monolithic power elite. Different individuals became involved in different issues, doing so in the process of playing their own "games."[21]

Not all of the broad community issues in which economic dominants were involved were controversial. Some of them may more properly be called "projects." The major issues in Cibola seemed to involve a higher degree of conflict in the political arena. Perhaps this conflict reflected the inertia of partisan party politics which existed in the community as late as

---

ment of a tricounty planning agency, annexation of a school district to the city, widening of a city street, ban on Sunday shopping, proposed shift of location of city hall, proposed sale of bonds by the city to finance construction of parking facilities, and proposed annexation of a suburban shopping center. Our inspection of newspapers and other documents reveals that these indeed represent the full range of community issues during the last five or six years. One or two others might be added by other local interests such as organized labor (see William H. Form and Warren L. Sauer, "Community and Labor Influentials: A Comparative Study of Participation and Imagery," *Industrial and Labor Relation Review,* XVII [October, 1963], 3–19).
21. Norton E. Long, "The Urban Community as an Ecology of Games," *American Journal of Sociology,* LXIV (November, 1958), 251–61.

1947. In addition, both of the major issues in Cibola—adoption of a new city charter and annexation—were the direct results of rapid urbanization and industrialization, processes which had occurred at a more gradual rate in Wheelsburg. There, political life seemed less marked by conflict, for local government not only was non-partisan but it traditionally and customarily responded to the needs of business.[22] It is highly probable that the lack of political conflict and the tendency for community decision-making to be channeled to the private rather than public sphere are interdependent. In Wheelsburg there was little evidence of basic differences in values among the economic dominants, the public leaders, and the elected officials. If representation of conflicting interests or values is chosen as the indicator of pluralism in the power structure, Wheelsburg (and most American communities) will be judged less pluralistic than if a weaker test of pluralism, such as the participation of separate individuals in different issues, is used.[23]

Thus, the social climate of the decision-making roles of the economic dominants in the two cities is not identical. Whether Wheelsburg dominants would become involved in highly conflictful issues should they arise is not known. Certainly they hesitated to publicize their involvement in controversial issues.[24] One large firm, for example, refused to become overtly involved in an annexation issue despite the fact that its economic interests were involved. However, it made its position known. What covert influence this might have had cannot be accurately appraised. Yet, since executives of the absentee-owned corporations were less likely to become involved in community decision-making than economic dominants from locally owned enterprises, possibly Wheelsburg's pattern of influence is evolving toward the type found in Cibola. On the other hand, both economic dominants and public leaders work hard to solve issues without conflict, and controversial issues probably arise less often in gradually expanding cities such as Wheelsburg than in cities which have grown very rapidly and have experienced extreme economic fluctuations, such as Cibola. Further research is required to determine the power roles of economic dominants in cities differing in size, social composition, economic composition, and economic history.

---

22. Form and Sauer, *op. cit.*
23. For a fuller discussion of this problem see Marshall N. Goldstein, "Absentee Ownership and Monolithic Power Structures: Two Questions for Community Studies," in *Current Trends in Comparative Community Studies,* ed. Bert E. Swanson (Kansas City, Mo.: Community Studies, Inc., 1962), pp. 49–59.
24. The same attitudes were revealed in interviews conducted by Rossi in Mediana. This does not mean that economic dominants had withdrawn from local influence systems because, as Rossi points out, "this is the age of community projects" (Peter H. Rossi, "The Organizational Structure of an American Community," in *Complete Organizations,* ed. Amitai Etzioni [New York: Holt, Rinehart & Winston, 1961], p. 301).

CONCLUSIONS

Comparative analysis of the roles of economic dominants in power structures of a satellite and an independent city reveals that in both communities the formal political and economic power structures which were once melded have tended to become bifurcated over time. This process seems to have paralleled the integration of local economic units into national markets and the process of governmental centralization. The economic dominants, once highly active leaders in civic associations, have tended to reduce their participation in this area, especially in the satellite community. This withdrawal coincided roughly with the rapid extension of absentee ownership in both cities. Currently, the nearly complete bifurcation of economic dominants and public leaders (top influentials) found in the satellite city was not as evident in the independent city, where an extensive network of economic ties bound the two groups together. Moreover, unlike the economic dominants in the satellite city, those in the independent city have not abandoned their decision-making role in community issues.

While the evidence cited in this research is not conclusive, it points to variable patterns of relations between economic dominants and public leaders in different types of communities. Apparently the absence of local party politics, a history of local industries becoming absentee-owned rather than the introduction of branch plants from outside the community, the institutionalization of local political controls, and the absence of ethnic, class, or other cleavages which contribute to partisan politics reduce the withdrawal rate of economic dominants from participation in community associations and local power arrangements. The time is ripe for many rapid comparative studies of a wide range of communities to determine more precisely the factors responsible for the bifurcation of persistence of ties between economic dominants, civic leaders, and community influentials.

	Population:
Chapter	*How Can We*
11	*Control Its Growth?*

Two articles are included in this section which take issue with some widely held beliefs about population control. In the first, Kingsley Davis attacks the idea that population growth and size can be reduced through "family planning" or the dissemination of contraceptives. Such a program focuses on reducing the birth rate, but it ignores two other factors which influence population size and growth—death rate and migration. Furthermore, family planning is not even crucial in affecting birth rates because it ignores "most of the determinants of reproductive performance." If this is so, why are so many countries pushing family planning programs? Davis sees the answer to this question in political terms. What is really needed is a major change in the social structure of a society, but this is opposed by a variety of entrenched interests which would be threatened by such changes. Thus countries do something (family planning), but they make sure that what they do is safe politically. What really needs to be done, in Davis' view, is to institute changes that will effect the motivation to have children, such as changing the structure of families, the position of women and sexual mores. However, these are far too radical for most governments, which prefer the safer (and far less effective) route of family planning. Davis feels that family planning is all right as a first step, but much more needs to be done. Among the other approaches Davis advocates is motivating people to marry later and have fewer children when they do marry.[1]

Judith Blake takes issue with a related program, but one which is restricted to the United States. The basis of the program "is that the

1. For an analysis of Davis' position see: Bernard Berelson, "Beyond Family Planning," *Science,* Vol. 163, February 7, 1969, pp. 533–543.

government should give highest priority to ghetto-oriented family-planning programs designed to 'deliver' birth-control services to the poor and uneducated, among whom, it is claimed, there are at least five million women who are 'in need' of such federally sponsored birth-control assistance." Blake's criticisms of the assumptions which underlie this program are extremely important because many blacks have attacked the efforts to limit population growth in the ghettos as an attempt at genocide by the white power structure. She concludes that what we must focus on is not just the poor, but all fecund Americans. Furthermore, like Davis, she feels that the attack on the population problem must be broader than simply a concern with contraception. Blake points out that our society is dominated by pressures to reproduce and that what we need to do is lift some of these pressures, rather than coerce people into being less productive. For example, it would help if we would lift the pressure on people to conform to their sex roles, thereby allowing life styles different from marriage and parenthood.[2] The implication that can be drawn from these two papers is that what is needed to control population size and growth are broad-scale social changes, and not mere palliatives.

Frank Notestein's article is a very recent response to the position taken by Davis and Blake. In the process of attacking their position, Notestein also takes pot shots at the advocates of Zero Population Growth and those ecologists who are making a career out of warning the populace about pollution. Most importantly, from the point of view of the controversy covered in this section, Notestein is an advocate of voluntary contraception in order to control population growth. Notestein favors voluntarism in this country as well as in the underdeveloped regions of the world. He is happier than his critics with the progress that has been made in population control, and he believes the kinds of broader efforts proposed by Davis and Blake will find little support in most countries. In summary, Notestein is far more optimistic than Davis and Blake, and opposed to the kind of motivational changes they suggest. Finally, we have Blake's acerbic response to Notestein. As you might guess, Blake has little sympathy for Notestein's position and tells him so in no uncertain terms.

---

2. For a critique of Judith Blake's position see Oscar Harkavy, Frederick S. Jaffe, and Samuel M. Wishik, "Family Planning and Public Policy: Who Is Misleading Whom?" *Science*, Vol. 165, July 25, 1969, pp. 367–373.

Population Policy: Will Current Programs Succeed?*

KINGSLEY DAVIS

Throughout history the growth of population has been identified with prosperity and strength. If today an increasing number of nations are seeking to curb rapid population growth by reducing their birth rates, they must be driven to do so by an urgent crisis. My purpose here is not to discuss the crisis itself but rather to assess the present and prospective measures used to meet it. Most observers are surprised by the swiftness with which concern over the population problem has turned from intellectual analysis and debate to policy and action. Such action is a welcome relief from the long opposition, or timidity, which seemed to block forever any governmental attempt to restrain population growth, but relief that "at last something is being done" is no guarantee that what is being done is adequate. On the face of it, one could hardly expect such a fundamental reorientation to be quickly and successfully implemented. I therefore propose to review the nature and (as I see them) limitations of the present policies and to suggest lines of possible improvement.

THE NATURE OF CURRENT POLICIES

With more than 30 nations now trying or planning to reduce population growth and with numerous private and international organizations helping, the degree of unanimity as to the kind of measures needed is impressive. The consensus can be summed up in the phrase "family planning." President Johnson declared in 1965 that the United States will "assist family planning programs in nations which request such help." The Prime Minister of India said a year later, "We must press forward with family planning. This is a programme of the highest importance." The Republic of Singapore created in 1966 the Singapore Family Planning and Population Board "to initiate and undertake population control programmes."[1]

---

* Reprinted from *Science,* 158 (November 10, 1967), pp. 730–739, by permission of the author and publisher. Copyright 1967 by the American Association for the Advancement of Science.
1. *Studies in Family Planning, No. 16* (1967).

As is well known, "family planning" is a euphemism for contraception. The family-planning approach to population limitation, therefore, concentrates on providing new and efficient contraceptives on a national basis through mass programs under public health auspices. The nature of these programs is shown by the following enthusiastic report from the Population Council[2]:

> No single year has seen so many forward steps in population control as 1965. Effective national programs have at last emerged, international organizations have decided to become engaged, a new contraceptive has proved its value in mass application, . . . and surveys have confirmed a popular desire for family limitation . . .
> An accounting of notable events must begin with Korea and Taiwan . . . Taiwan's program is not yet two years old, and already it has inserted one IUD [intrauterine device] for every 4–6 target women (those who are not pregnant, lactating, already sterile, already using contraceptives effectively, or desirous of more children). Korea has done almost as well . . . has put 2,200 full-time workers into the field, . . . has reached operational levels for a network of IUD quotas, supply lines, local manufacture of contraceptives, training of hundreds of M.D.'s and nurses, and mass propaganda . . .

Here one can see the implication that "population control" is being achieved through the dissemination of new contraceptives, and the fact that the "target women" exclude those who want more children. One can also note the technological emphasis and the medical orientation.

What is wrong with such programs? The answer is, "Nothing at all, if they work." Whether or not they work depends on what they are expected to do as well as on how they try to do it. Let us discuss the goal first, then the means.

GOALS

Curiously, it is hard to find in the population-policy movement any explicit discussion of long-range goals. By implication the policies seem to promise a great deal. This is shown by the use of expressions like *population control* and *population planning* (as in the passages quoted above). It is also shown by the characteristic style of reasoning. Expositions of current policy usually start off by lamenting the speed and the consequences of runaway population growth. This growth, it is then stated, must be curbed—by pursuing a vigorous family-planning program. That family planning can solve the problem of population growth seems to be taken as self-evident.

---

2. *Ibid.*, No. 9 (1966), p. 1.

For instance, the much-heralded statement by 12 heads of state, issued by Secretary-General U Thant on 10 December 1966 (a statement initiated by John D. Rockefeller III, Chairman of the Board of the Population Council), devotes half its space to discussing the harmfulness of population growth and the other half ·to recommending family planning.[3] A more succinct example of the typical reasoning is given in the Provisional Scheme for a Nationwide Family Planning Programme in Ceylon:[4]

> The population of Ceylon is fast increasing. . . . [The] figures reveal that a serious situation will be created within a few years. In order to cope with it a Family Planning programme on a nationwide scale should be launched by the Government.

The promised goal—to limit population growth so as to solve population problems—is a large order. One would expect it to be carefully analyzed, but it is left imprecise and taken for granted, as is the way in which family planning will achieve it.

When the terms *population control* and *population planning* are used, as they frequently are, as synonyms for current family-planning programs, they are misleading. Technically, they would mean deliberate influence over all attributes of a population, including its age-sex structure, geographical distribution, racial composition, genetic quality, and total size. No government attempts such full control. By tacit understanding, current population policies are concerned with only the *growth* and *size* of populations. These attributes, however, result from the death rate and migration as well as from the birth rate; their control would require deliberate influence over the factors giving rise to all three determinants. Actually, current policies labeled population control do not deal with mortality and migration, but deal only with the birth input. This is why another term, *fertility control,* is frequently used to describe current policies. But, as I show below, family planning (and hence current policy) does not undertake to influence most of the determinants of human reproduction. Thus the programs should not be referred to as population control or planning, because they do not attempt to influence the factors responsible for the attributes of human populations, taken generally; nor should they be called fertility control, because they do not try to affect most of the determinants of reproductive performance.

The ambiguity does not stop here, however. When one speaks of controlling population size, any inquiring person naturally asks, What is "control"? Who is to control whom? Precisely what population size, or what rate of population growth, is to be achieved? Do the policies aim to produce a growth rate that is nil, one that is very slight, or one that is like

---

3. The statement is given in *Studies in Family Planning* (I, p. 1), and in *Population Bull.* 23, 6 (1967).
4. The statement is quoted in *Studies in Family Planning* (I, p. 2).

that of the industrial nations? Unless such questions are dealt with and clarified, it is impossible to evaluate current population policies.

The actual programs seem to be aiming simply to achieve a reduction in the birth rate. Success is therefore interpreted as the accomplishment of such a reduction, on the assumption that the reduction will lessen population growth. In those rare cases where a specific demographic aim is stated, the goal is said to be a short-run decline within a given period. The Pakistan plan adopted in 1966[5] aims to reduce the birth rate from 50 to 40 per thousand by 1970; the Indian plan[6] aims to reduce the rate from 40 to 25 "as soon as possible"; and the Korean aim[7] is to cut population growth from 2.9 to 1.2 percent by 1980. A significant feature of such stated aims is the rapid population growth they would permit. Under conditions of modern mortality, a crude birth rate of 25 to 30 per thousand will represent such a multiplication of people as to make use of the term *population control* ironic. A rate of increase of 1.2 percent per year would allow South Korea's already dense population to double in less than 60 years.

One can of course defend the programs by saying that the present goals and measures are merely interim ones. A start must be made somewhere. But we do not find this answer in the population policy literature. Such a defense, if convincing, would require a presentation of the *next* steps, and these are not considered. One suspects that the entire question of goals is instinctively left vague because thorough limitation of population growth would run counter to national and group aspirations. A consideration of hypothetical goals throws further light on the matter.

Industrialized nations as the model. Since current policies are confined to family planning, their maximum demographic effect would be to give the underdeveloped countries the same level of reproductive performance that the industrial nations now have. The latter, long oriented toward family planning, provide a good yardstick for determining what the availability of contraceptives can do to population growth. Indeed, they provide more than a yardstick; they are actually the model which inspired the present population policies.

What does this goal mean in practice? Among the advanced nations there is considerable diversity in the level of fertility.[8] At one extreme are countries such as New Zealand, with an average gross reproduction rate (GRR) of 1.91 during the period 1960–64; at the other extreme are countries such as Hungary, with a rate of 0.91 during the same period. To a

5. *Hearings on S. 1676, U.S. Senate, Subcommittee on Foreign Aid Expenditures, 89th Congress, Second Session, April 7, 8, 11* (1966), pt. 4.
6. B. L. Raina, in *Family Planning and Population Programs*, B. Berelson, R. K. Anderson, O. Harkavy, G. Maier, W. P. Mauldin, S. G. Segal, Eds. (Univ. of Chicago Press, Chicago, 1966).
7. D. Kirk, *Ann. Amer. Acad. Polit. Soc. Sci.* 369, 53 (1967).
8. As used by English-speaking demographers, the word *fertility* designates actual reproductive performance, not a theoretical capacity.

considerable extent, however, such divergencies are matters of timing. The birth rates of most industrial nations have shown, since about 1940, a wavelike movement, with no secular trend. The average level of reproduction during this long period has been high enough to give these countries, with their low mortality, an extremely rapid population growth. If this level is maintained, their population will double in just over 50 years—a rate higher than that of world population growth at any time prior to 1950, at which time the growth in numbers of human beings was already considered fantastic. The advanced nations are suffering acutely from the effects of rapid population growth in combination with the production of ever more goods per person.[9] A rising share of their supposedly high per capita income, which itself draws increasingly upon the resources of the underdeveloped countries (who fall farther behind in relative economic position), is spent simply to meet the costs, and alleviate the nuisances, of the unrelenting production of more and more goods by more people. Such facts indicate that the industrial nations provide neither a suitable demographic model for the nonindustrial peoples to follow nor the leadership to plan and organize effective population-control policies for them.

Zero population growth as a goal. Most discussions of the population crisis lead logically to zero population growth as the ultimate goal, because *any* growth rate, if continued, will eventually use up the earth. Yet hardly ever do arguments for population policy consider such a goal, and current policies do not dream of it. Why not? The answer is evidently that zero population growth is unacceptable to most nations and to most religious and ethnic communities. To argue for this goal would be to alienate possible support for action programs.

Goal peculiarities inherent in family planning. Turning to the actual measures taken, we see that the very use of family planning as the means for implementing population policy poses serious but unacknowledged limits on the intended reduction in fertility. The family-planning movement, clearly devoted to the improvement and dissemination of contraceptive devices, states again and again that its purpose is that of enabling couples to have the number of children they want. "The opportunity to decide the number and spacing of children is a basic human right," say the 12 heads of state in the United Nations declaration. The 1965 Turkish Law Concerning Population Planning declares[10]:

> *Article 1.* Population Planning means that individuals can have as many children as they wish, whenever they want to. This can be ensured through preventive measures taken against pregnancy. . . .

9. K. Davis, *Rotarian* 94, 10 (1959); *Health Educ. Monographs* 9, 2 (1960); L. Day and A. Day, *Too Many Americans* (Houghton Mifflin, Boston, 1964); R. A. Piddington, *Limits of Mankind* (Wright, Bristol, England, 1956).
10. *Official Gazette* (15 Apr. 1965); quoted in *Studies in Family Planning* (*I*, p. 7).

Logically, it does not make sense to use *family* planning to provide *national* population control or planning. The "planning" in family planning is that of each separate couple. The only control they exercise is control over the size of *their* family. Obviously, couples do not plan the size of the nation's population, any more than they plan the growth of the national income or the form of the highway network. There is no reason to expect that the millions of decisions about family size made by couples in their own interest will automatically control population for the benefit of society. On the contrary, there are good reasons to think they will not do so. At most, family planning can reduce reproduction to the extent that unwanted births exceed wanted births. In industrial countries the balance is often negative—that is, people have fewer children as a rule than they would like to have. In underdeveloped countries the reverse is normally true, but the elimination of unwanted births would still leave an extremely high rate of multiplication.

Actually, the family-planning movement does not pursue even the limited goals it professes. It does not fully empower couples to have only the number of offspring they want because it either condemns or disregards certain tabooed but nevertheless effective means to this goal. One of its tenets is that "there shall be freedom of choice of method so that individuals can choose in accordance with the dictates of their consciences,"[11] but in practice this amounts to limiting the individual's choice, because the "conscience" dictating the method is usually not his but that of religious and governmental officials. Moreover, not every individual may choose: even the so-called recommended methods are ordinarily not offered to single women, or not all offered to women professing a given religious faith.

Thus, despite its emphasis on technology, current policy does not utilize all available means of contraception, much less all birth-control measures. The Indian government wasted valuable years in the early stages of its population-control program by experimenting exclusively with the "rhythm" method, long after this technique had been demonstrated to be one of the least effective. A greater limitation on means is the exclusive emphasis on contraception itself. Induced abortion, for example, is one of the surest means of controlling reproduction, and one that has been proved capable of reducing birth rates rapidly. It seems peculiarly suited to the threshold stage of a population-control program—the stage when new conditions of life first make large families disadvantageous. It was the principal factor in the halving of the Japanese birth rate, a major factor in the declines in birth rate of East-European satellite countries after legalization of abortions in the early 1950's, and an important factor in the reduc-

---

11. J. W. Gardner, Secretary of Health, Education, and Welfare, "Memorandum to Heads of Operating Agencies" (Jan. 1966), reproduced in *Hearings on S. 1676* (5), p. 783.

tion of fertility in industrializing nations from 1870 to the 1930's.[12] Today, according to *Studies in Family Plannning*,[13] "abortion is probably the foremost method of birth control throughout Latin America." Yet this method is rejected in nearly all national and international population-control programs. American foreign aid is used to help *stop* abortion.[14] The United Nations excludes abortion from family planning, and in fact justifies the latter by presenting it as a means of combating abortion.[15] Studies of abortion are being made in Latin America under the presumed auspices of population-control groups, not with the intention of legalizing it and thus making it safe, cheap, available, and hence more effective for population control, but with the avowed purpose of reducing it.[16]

Although few would prefer abortion to efficient contraception (other things being equal), the fact is that both permit a woman to control the size of her family. The main drawbacks to abortion arise from its illegality. When performed, as a legal procedure, by a skilled physician, it is safer than childbirth. It does not compete with contraception but serves as a backstop when the latter fails or when contraceptive devices or information are not available. As contraception becomes customary, the incidence of abortion recedes even without its being banned. If, therefore, abortions enable women to have only the number of children they want, and if family planners do not advocate—in fact decry—legalization of abortion, they are to that extent denying the central tenet of their own movement. The irony of anti-abortionism in family-planning circles is seen particularly in hair-splitting arguments over whether or not some contraceptive agent (for example, the IUD) is in reality an abortifacient. A Mexican leader in family planning writes[17]:

> One of the chief objectives of our program in Mexico is to prevent abortions. If we could be sure that the mode of action [of the IUD] was not interference with nidation, we could easily use the method in Mexico.

The questions of sterilization and unnatural forms of sexual intercourse usually meet with similar silent treatment or disapproval, although

12. C. Tietze, *Demography* 1, 119 (1964); *J. Chronic Diseases* 18, 1161 (1964); M. Muramatsu, *Milbank Mem. Fund Quart.* 38, 153 (1960); K. Davis, *Population Index* 29, 345 (1963); R. Armijo and T. Monreal, *J. Sex Res.* 1964, 143 (1964); Proceedings World Population Conference, Belgrade, 1965; Proceedings International Planned Parenthood Federation.
13. *Studies in Family Planning, No. 4* (1964), p. 3.
14. D. Bell (then administrator for Agency for International Development), in *Hearings on S. 1676* (5), p. 862.
15. *Asian Population Conference* (United Nations, New York, 1964), p. 30.
16. R. Armijo and T. Monreal, in *Components of Population Change in Latin America* (Milbank Fund, New York, 1965), p. 272; E. Rice-Wray, *Amer. J. Public Health* 54, 313 (1964).
17. E. Rice-Wray, in "Intra-Uterine Contraceptive Devices," *Excerpta Med. Intern. Congr. Ser. No. 54* (1962), p. 135.

nobody doubts the effectiveness of these measures in avoiding conception. Sterilization has proved popular in Puerto Rico and has had some vogue in India (where the new health minister hopes to make it compulsory for those with a certain number of children), but in both these areas it has been for the most part ignored or condemned by the family-planning movement.

On the side of goals, then, we see that a family-planning orientation limits the aims of current population policy. Despite reference to "population control" and "fertility control," which presumably mean determination of demographic results by and for the nation as a whole, the movement gives control only to couples, and does this only if they use "respectable" contraceptives.

THE NEGLECT OF MOTIVATION

By sanctifying the doctrine that each woman should have the number of children she wants, and by assuming that if she has only that number this will automatically curb population growth to the necessary degree, the leaders of current policies escape the necessity of asking why women desire so many children and how this desire can be influenced.[18, 19] Instead, they claim that satisfactory motivation is shown by the popular desire (shown by opinion surveys in all countries) to have the means of family limitation, and that therefore the problem is one of inventing and distributing the best possible contraceptive devices. Overlooked is the fact that a desire for availability of contraceptives is compatible with *high* fertility.

Given the best of means, there remain the questions of how many children couples want and of whether this is the requisite number from the standpoint of population size. That it is not is indicated by continued rapid population growth in industrial countries, and by the very surveys showing that people want contraception—for these show, too, that people also want numerous children.

The family planners do not ignore motivation. They are forever talking about "attitudes" and "needs." But they pose the issue in terms of the "acceptance" of birth control devices. At the most naive level, they assume that lack of acceptance is a function of the contraceptive device itself. This reduces the motive problem to a technological question. The task of population control then becomes simply the invention of a device that *will* be acceptable.[20] The plastic IUD is acclaimed because, once in place, it does

---

18. J. Blake, in *Public Health and Population Change,* M. C. Sheps and J. C. Ridley, Eds. (Univ. of Pittsburgh Press, Pittsburgh, 1965).
19. J. Blake and K. Davis, *Amer. Behavioral Scientist,* 5, 24 (1963).
20. See "Panel discussion on comparative acceptability of different methods of contraception," in *Research in Family Planning,* C. V. Kiser, Ed. (Princeton Univ. Press, Princeton, 1962), pp. 373–86.

not depend on repeated *acceptance* by the woman, and thus it "solves" the problem of motivation.[21]

But suppose a woman does not want to use *any* contraceptive until after she has had four children. This is the type of question that is seldom raised in the family-planning literature. In that literature, wanting a specific number of children is taken as complete motivation, for it implies a wish to control the size of one's family. The problem woman, from the standpoint of family planners, is the one who wants "as many as come," or "as many as God sends." Her attitude is construed as due to ignorance and "cultural values," and the policy deemed necessary to change it is "education." No compulsion can be used, because the movement is committed to free choice, but movie strips, posters, comic books, public lectures, interviews, and discussions are in order. These supply information and supposedly change values by discounting superstitions and showing that unrestrained procreation is harmful to both mother and children. The effort is considered successful when the woman decides she wants only a certain number of children and uses an effective contraceptive.

In viewing negative attitudes toward birth control as due to ignorance, apathy, and outworn tradition, and "mass-communication" as the solution to the motivation problem,[22] family planners tend to ignore the power and complexity of social life. If it were admitted that the creation and care of new human beings is socially motivated, like other forms of behavior, by being a part of the system of rewards and punishments that is built into human relationships, and thus is bound up with the individual's economic and personal interests, it would be apparent that the social structure and economy must be changed before a deliberate reduction in the birth rate can be achieved. As it is, reliance on family planning allows people to feel that "something is being done about the population problem" without the need for painful social changes.

Designation of population control as a medical or public health task leads to a similar evasion. This categorization assures popular support because it puts population policy in the hands of respected medical personnel, but, by the same token, it gives responsibility for leadership to people who think in terms of clinics and patients, of pills and IUDs, and who bring to the handling of economic and social phenomena a self-confident naiveté. The study of social organization is a technical field; an action program based on intuition is no more apt to succeed in the control of human beings

---

21. "From the point of view of the woman concerned, the whole problem of continuing motivation disappears, . . ." [D. Kirk, in *Population Dynamics,* M. Muramatsu and P. A. Harper, Eds. (Johns Hopkins Press, Baltimore, 1965)].

22. "For influencing family size norms, certainly the examples and statements of public figures are of great significance . . . also . . . use of mass-communication methods which help to legitimize the small-family style, to provoke conversation, and to establish a vocabulary for discussion of family planning." [M. W. Freymann, in *Population Dynamics,* M. Muramatsu and P. A. Harper, Eds. (Johns Hopkins Press, Baltimore, 1965)].

than it is in the area of bacterial or viral control. Moreover, to alter a social system, by deliberate policy, so as to regulate births in accord with the demands of the collective welfare would require political power, and this is not likely to inhere in public health officials, nurses, midwives, and social workers. To entrust population policy to them is "to take action," but not dangerous "effective action."

Similarly, the Janus-faced position on birth-control technology represents an escape from the necessity, and onus, of grappling with the social and economic determinants of reproductive behavior. On the one side, the rejection or avoidance of religiously tabooed but otherwise effective means of birth prevention enables the family-planning movement to avoid official condemnation. On the other side, an intense preoccupation with contraceptive technology (apart from the tabooed means) also helps the family planners to avoid censure. By implying that the only need is the invention and distribution of effective contraceptive devices, they allay fears, on the part of religious and governmental officials, that fundamental changes in social organization are contemplated. Changes basic enough to affect motivation for having children would be changes in the structure of the family, in the position of women, and in the sexual mores. Far from proposing such radicalism, spokesmen for family planning frequently state their purpose as "protection'" of the family—that is, closer observance of family norms. In addition, by concentration on *new* and scientific contraceptives, the movement escapes taboos attached to old ones (the Pope will hardly authorize the condom, but may sanction the pill) and allows family planning to be regarded as a branch of medicine: overpopulation becomes a disease, to be treated by a pill or a coil.

We thus see that the inadequacy of current population policies with respect to motivation is inherent in their overwhelmingly family-planning character. Since family-planning is by definition private planning, it eschews any societal control over motivation. It merely furnishes the means, and, among possible means, only the most respectable. Its leaders, in avoiding social complexities and seeking official favor, are obviously activated not solely by expediency but also by their own sentiments as members of society and by their background as persons attracted to the family-planning movement. Unacquainted for the most part with technical economics, sociology, and demography, they tend honestly and instinctively to believe that something they vaguely call population control can be achieved by making better contraceptives available.

THE EVIDENCE OF INEFFECTIVENESS

If this characterization is accurate, we can conclude that current programs will not enable a government to control population size. In countries where couples have numerous offspring that they do not want, such programs may possibly accelerate a birth-rate decline that would occur anyway, but the conditions that cause births to be wanted or unwanted are beyond the control of family planning, hence beyond the control of any nation which relies on family planning alone as its population policy.

This conclusion is confirmed by demographic facts. As I have noted above, the widespread use of family planning in industrial countries has not given their governments control over the birth rate. In backward countries today, taken as a whole, birth rates are rising, not falling; in those with population policies, there is no indication that the government is controlling the rate of reproduction. The main "successes" cited in the well-publicized policy literature are cases where a large number of contraceptives have been distributed or where the program has been accompanied by some decline in the birth rate. Popular enthusiasm for family planning is found mainly in the cities, or in advanced countries such as Japan and Taiwan, where the people would adopt contraception in any case, program or no program. It is difficult to prove that present population policies have even speeded up a lowering of the birth rate (the least that could have been expected), much less that they have provided national "fertility control."

Let us next briefly review the facts concerning the level and trend of population in underdeveloped nations generally, in order to understand the magnitude of the task of genuine control.

Rising Birth Rates in Underdeveloped Countries

In ten Latin-American countries, between 1940 and 1959,[23] the average birth rates (age-standardized), as estimated by our research office at the University of California, rose as follows: 1940–44, 43.4 annual births per 1000 population; 1945–49, 44.6; 1950–54, 46.4; 1955–59, 47.7.

In another study made in our office, in which estimating methods derived from the theory of quasi-stable populations were used, the recent trend was found to be upward in 27 underdeveloped countries, downward in six, and unchanged in one.[24] Some of the rises have been substantial, and most have occurred where the birth rate was already extremely high. For instance, the gross reproduction rate rose in Jamaica from 1.8 per thousand in 1947 to 2.7 in 1960; among the natives of Fiji, from 2.0 in 1951 to 2.4 in 1964; and in Albania, from 3.0 in the period 1950–54 to 3.4 in 1960.

The general rise in fertility in backward regions is evidently not due to failure of population-control efforts, because most of the countries either

---

23. O. A. Collver, *Birth Rates in Latin America* (International Population and Urban Research, Berkeley, Calif., 1965), pp. 27–28; the ten countries were Colombia, Costa Rica, El Salvador, Ecuador, Guatemala, Honduras, Mexico, Panama, Peru, and Venezuela.

24. J. R. Rele, *Fertility Analysis through Extension of Stable Population Concepts* (International Population and Urban Research, Berkeley, Calif., 1967).

have no such effort or have programs too new to show much effect. Instead, the rise is due, ironically, to the very circumstance that brought on the population crisis in the first place—to improved health and lowered mortality. Better health increases the probability that a woman will conceive and retain the fetus to term; lowered mortality raises the proportion of babies who survive to the age of reproduction and reduces the probability of widowhood during that age.[25] The significance of the general rise in fertility, in the context of this discussion, is that it is giving would-be population planners a harder task than many of them realize. Some of the upward pressure on birth rates is independent of what couples do about family planning, for it arises from the fact that, with lowered mortality, there are simply more couples.

UNDERDEVELOPED COUNTRIES WITH POPULATION POLICIES

In discussions of population policy there is often confusion as to which cases are relevant. Japan, for instance, has been widely praised for the effectiveness of its measures, but it is a very advanced industrial nation and, besides, its government policy had little or nothing to do with the decline in the birth rate, except unintentionally. It therefore offers no test of population policy under peasant-agrarian conditions. Another case of questionable relevance is that of Taiwan, because Taiwan is sufficiently developed to be placed in the urban-industrial class of nations. However, since Taiwan is offered as the main showpiece by the sponsors of current policies in underdeveloped areas, and since the data are excellent, it merits examination.

Taiwan is acclaimed as a showpiece because it has responded favorably to a highly organized program for distributing up-to-date contraceptives and has also had a rapidly dropping birth rate. Some observers have carelessly attributed the decline in the birth rate—from 50.0 in 1951 to 32.7 in 1965—to the family-planning campaign,[26] but the campaign began only in 1963 and could have affected only the end of the trend. Rather, the decline represents a response to modernization similar to that made by all countries that have become industrialized.[27] By 1950 over half of Taiwan's population was urban, and by 1964 nearly two-thirds were urban, with 29 percent of the population living in cities of 100,000 or more. The pace of economic development has been extremely rapid. Between 1951 and 1963, per capita income increased by 4.05 percent per year. Yet the island is closely packed, having 870 persons per square mile (a population density higher than that

---

25. J. C. Ridley, M. C. Sheps, J. W. Lingner, J. A. Menken, *Milbank Mem. Fund Quart.* 45, 77 (1967); E. Arriaga, unpublished paper.
26. "South Korea and Taiwan appear successfully to have checked population growth by the use of intrauterine contraceptive devices" [U. Borell, *Hearings on S. 1676* (5), p. 556].
27. K. Davis, *Population Index* 29, 345 (1963).

of Belgium). The combination of fast economic growth and rapid population increase in limited space has put parents of large families at a relative
disadvantage and has created a brisk demand for abortions and contraceptives. Thus the favorable response to the current campaign to encourage
use of the IUD is not a good example of what birth-control technology can
do for a genuinely backward country. In fact, when the program was
started, one reason for expecting receptivity was that the island was already
on its way to modernization and family planning.[28]

At most, the recent family-planning campaign—which reached significant proportions only in 1964, when some 46,000 IUDs were inserted
(in 1965 the number was 99,253, and in 1966, 111,242)[29, 30]—could have
caused the increase observable after 1963 in the rate of decline. Between
1951 and 1963 the average drop in the birth rate per 1000 women (see
Table 1) was 1.73 percent per year; in the period 1964–66 it was 4.35

TABLE 1. *Decline in Taiwan's Fertility Rate, 1951 through 1966*

Year	Registered Births per 1000 Women Aged 15–49	Change in Rate (Percent)*
1951	211	
1952	198	−5.6
1953	194	−2.2
1954	193	−0.5
1955	197	+2.1
1956	196	−0.4
1957	182	−7.1
1958	185	+1.3
1959	184	−0.1
1960	180	−2.5
1961	177	−1.5
1962	174	−1.5
1963	170	−2.6
1964	162	−4.9
1965	152	−6.0
1966	149	−2.1

* The percentages were calculated on unrounded figures. Source of data through
1965,*Taiwan* Demographic Fact Book (1964, 1965); for 1966, *Monthly Bulletin of
Population Registration Statistics of Taiwan* (1966, 1967).

28. R. Freedman, *ibid*. 31, 421 (1965).
29. Before 1964 the Family Planning Association had given advice to fewer than
60,000 wives in 10 years and a Pre-Pregnancy Health Program had reached some
10,000, and, in the current campaign, 3650 IUDs were inserted in 1965, in a total
population of 2½ million women of reproductive age. See *Studies in Family Planning,
No. 19* (1967), p. 4, and R. Freedman *et al., Population Studies* 16, 231 (1963).
30. R. W. Gillespie, *Family Planning on Taiwan* (Population Council, Taichung,
1965).

percent. But one hesitates to assign all of the acceleration in decline since 1963 to the family-planning campaign. The rapid economic development has been precisely of a type likely to accelerate a drop in reproduction. The rise in manufacturing has been much greater than the rise in either agriculture or construction. The agricultural labor force has thus been squeezed, and migration to the cities has skyrocketed.[31] Since housing has not kept pace, urban families have had to restrict reproduction in order to take advantage of career opportunities and avoid domestic inconvenience. Such conditions have historically tended to accelerate a decline in birth rate. The most rapid decline came late in the United States (1921–33) and in Japan (1947–55). A plot of the Japanese and Taiwanese birth rates (Fig. 1) shows marked similarity of the two curves, despite a

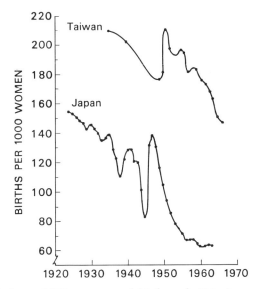

FIG. 1.   *Births per 1000 women aged 15 through 49 in Japan and Taiwan.*

difference in level. All told, one should not attribute all of the post-1963 acceleration in the decline of Taiwan's birth rate to the family-planning campaign.

The main evidence that *some* of this acceleration is due to the campaign comes from the fact that Taichung, the city in which the family-planning effort was first concentrated, showed subsequently a much faster

31. During the period 1950–60 the ratio of growth of the city to growth of the noncity population was 5:3; during the period 1960–64 the ratio was 5:2; these ratios are based on data of Shaohsing Chen, *J. Sociol. Taiwan* 1, 74 (1963) and data in the United Nations *Demographic Yearbooks*.

drop in fertility than other cities.[30, 32] But the campaign has not reached throughout the island. By the end of 1966, only 260,745 women had been fitted with an IUD under auspices of the campaign, whereas the women of reproductive age on the island numbered 2.86 million. Most of the reduction in fertility has therefore been a matter of individual initiative. To some extent the campaign may be simply substituting sponsored (and cheaper) services for those that would otherwise come through private and commercial channels. An island-wide survey in 1964 showed that over 150,000 women were already using the traditional Ota ring (a metallic intrauterine device popular in Japan); almost as many had been sterilized; about 40,000 were using foam tablets; some 50,000 admitted to having had at least one abortion; and many were using other methods of birth control.[30]

The important question, however, is not whether the present campaign is somewhat hastening the downward trend in the birth rate but whether, even if it is, it will provide population control for the nation. Actually, the campaign is not designed to provide such control and shows no sign of doing so. It takes for granted existing reproductive goals. Its aim is "to integrate, through education and information, the idea of family limitation *within the existing attitudes, values, and goals* of the people"[30] (italics mine). Its target is *married* women who do not want any more children; it ignores girls not yet married, and women married and wanting more children.

With such an approach, what is the maximum impact possible? It is the difference between the number of children women have been having and the number they want to have. A study in 1957 found a median figure of 3.75 for the number of children wanted by women aged 15 to 29 in Taipei, Taiwan's largest city; the corresponding figure for women from a satellite town was 3.93; for women from a fishing village, 4.90; and for women from a farming village, 5.03. Over 60 percent of the women in Taipei and over 90 percent of those in the farming village wanted 4 or more children.[33] In a sample of wives aged 25 to 29 in Taichung, a city of over 300,000, Freedman and his co-workers found the average number of children wanted was 4; only 9 percent wanted less than 3, 20 percent wanted 5 or more.[34] If, therefore, Taiwanese women used contraceptives that were 100-percent effective and had the number of children they desire, they would have about 4.5 each. The goal of the family-planning effort would be achieved. In the past the Taiwanese woman who married and lived through the reproductive period had, on the average, approximately 6.5 children; thus a figure of 4.5 would represent a substantial

32. R. Freedman, *Population Index* 31, 434 (1965). Taichung's rate of decline in 1963–64 was roughly double the average in four other cities, whereas just prior to the campaign its rate of decline had been much less than theirs.
33. S. H. Chen, *J. Soc. Sci. Taipei* 13, 72 (1963).
34. R. Freedman et al., *Population Studies* 16, 227 (1963); *ibid.*, p. 232.

decline in fertility. Since mortality would continue to decline, the population growth rate would decline somewhat less than individual reproduction would. With 4.5 births per woman and a life expectancy of 70 years, the rate of natural increase would be close to 3 percent per year.[35]

In the future, Taiwanese views concerning reproduction will doubtless change, in response to social change and economic modernization. But how far will they change? A good indication is the number of children desired by couples in an already modernized country long oriented toward family planning. In the United States in 1966, an average of 3.4 children was considered ideal by white women aged 21 or over.[36] This average number of births would give Taiwan, with only a slight decrease in mortality, a long-run rate of natural increase of 1.7 percent per year and a doubling of population in 41 years.

Detailed data confirm the interpretation that Taiwanese women are in the process of shifting from a "peasant-agrarian" to an "industrial" level of reproduction. They are, in typical fashion, cutting off higher-order births at age 30 and beyond.[37] Among young wives, fertility has risen, not fallen. In sum, the widely acclaimed family-planning program in Taiwan may, at most, have somewhat speeded the later phase of fertility decline which would have occurred anyway because of modernization.

Moving down the scale of modernization, to countries most in need of population control, one finds the family-planning approach even more inadequate. In South Korea, second only to Taiwan in the frequency with which it is cited as a model of current policy, a recent birth-rate decline of unknown extent is assumed by leaders to be due overwhelmingly to the government's family-planning program. However, it is just as plausible to say that the net effect of government involvement in population control has been, so far, to delay rather than hasten a decline in reproduction made inevitable by social and economic changes. Although the government is advocating vasectomies and providing IUDs and pills, it refuses to legalize abortions, despite the rapid rise in the rate of illegal abortions and despite the fact that, in a recent survey, 72 percent of the people who stated an opinion favored legalization. Also, the program is presented in the context of maternal and child health; it thus emphasizes motherhood and the family rather than alternative roles for women. Much is made of the fact that opinion surveys show an overwhelming majority of Koreans (89 percent in 1965) favoring contraception,[38] but this means only that Koreans

---

35. In 1964 the life expectancy at birth was already 66 years in Taiwan, as compared to 70 for the United States.
36. J. Blake, *Eugenics Quart.* 14, 68 (1967).
37. Women accepting IUDs in the family-planning program are typically 30 to 34 years old and have already had four children. [*Studies in Family Planning No. 19* (1967), p. 5.]
38. Y. K. Cha, in *Family Planning and Population Programs,* B. Berelson et al., Eds. (Univ. of Chicago Press, Chicago, 1966).

are like other people in wishing to have the means to get what they want. Unfortunately, they want sizable families: "The records indicate that the program appeals mainly to women in the 30–39 year age bracket who have four or more children, including at least two sons . . ."[38]

In areas less developed than Korea the degree of acceptance of contraception tends to be disappointing, especially among the rural majority. Faced with this discouragement, the leaders of current policy, instead of reexamining their assumptions, tend to redouble their efforts to find a contraceptive that will appeal to the most illiterate peasant, forgetting that he wants a good-sized family. In the rural Punjab, for example, "a disturbing feature . . . is that the females start to seek advice and adopt family planning techniques at the fag end of their reproductive period."[39] Among 5196 women coming to rural Punjabi family-planning centers, 38 percent were over 35 years old, 67 percent over 30. These women had married early, nearly a third of them before the age of 15;[40] some 14 percent had eight or more *living* children when they reached the clinic, 51 percent six or more.

A survey in Tunisia showed that 68 percent of the married couples were willing to use birth-control measures, but the average number of children they considered ideal was 4.3.[41] The corresponding averages for a village in eastern Java, a village near New Delhi, and a village in Mysore were 4.3, 4.0, and 4.2, respectively.[42,43] In the cities of these regions women are more ready to accept birth control and they want fewer children than village women do, but the number they consider desirable is still wholly unsatisfactory from the standpoint of population control. In an urban family-planning center in Tunisia, more than 600 of 900 women accepting contraceptives had four living children already.[44] In Bangalore, a city of nearly a million at the time (1952), the number of offspring desired by married women was 3.7 on the average; by married men, 4.1.[43] In the metropolitan area of San Salvador (350,000 inhabitants) a 1964 survey[45] showed the number desired by women of reproductive age to be

39. H. S. Ayalvi and S. S. Johl, *J. Family Welfare* 12, 60 (1965).
40. Sixty percent of the women had borne their first child before age 19. Early marriage is strongly supported by public opinion. Of couples polled in the Punjab, 48 percent said that girls *should* marry before age 16, and 94 percent said they should marry before age 20 (H. S. Ayalvi and S. S. Johl, *ibid.*, p. 57). A study of 2380 couples in 60 villages of Uttar Pradesh found that the women had consummated their marriage at an average age of 14.6 years [J. R. Rele, *Population Studies* 15, 268 (1962)].
41. J. Morsa, in *Family Planning and Population Programs*, B. Berelson *et al.*, Eds. (Univ. of Chicago Press, Chicago, 1966).
42. H. Gille and R. J. Pardoko, *ibid.*, p. 515; S. N. Agarwala, *Med. Dig. Bombay* 4, 653 (1961).
43. *Mysore Population Study* (United Nations, New York, 1961), p. 140.
44. A. Daly, in *Family Planning and Population Programs*, B. Berelson *et al.*, Eds. (Univ. of Chicago Press, Chicago, 1966).
45. C. J. Gómez, paper presented at the World Population Conference, Belgrade, 1965.

3.9, and in seven other capital cities of Latin America the number ranged from 2.7 to 4.2. If women in the cities of underdeveloped countries used birth-control measures with 100-percent efficiency, they still would have enough babies to expand city populations senselessly, quite apart from the added contribution of rural-urban migration. In many of the cities the difference between actual and ideal number of children is not great; for instance, in the seven Latin-American capitals mentioned above, the ideal was 3.4 whereas the actual births per woman in the age range 35 to 39 was 3.7.[46] Bombay City has had birth-control clinics for many years, yet its birth rate (standardized for age, sex, and marital distribution) is still 34 per 1000 inhabitants and is tending to rise rather than fall. Although this rate is about 13 percent lower than that for India generally, it has been about that much lower since at least 1951.[47]

Is FAMILY PLANNING THE "FIRST STEP"
IN POPULATION CONTROL?

To acknowledge that family planning does not achieve population control is not to impugn its value for other purposes. Freeing women from the need to have more children than they want is of great benefit to them and their children and to society at large. My argument is therefore directed not against family-planning programs as such but against the assumption that they are an effective means of controlling population growth.

But what difference does it make? Why not go along for a while with family planning as an initial approach to the problem of population control? The answer is that any policy on which millions of dollars are being spent should be designed to achieve the goal it purports to achieve. If it is only a first step, it should be so labeled, and its connection with the next step (and the nature of that next step) should be carefully examined. In the present case, since no "next step" seems ever to be mentioned, the question arises, Is reliance on family planning in fact a basis for dangerous postponement of effective steps? To continue to offer a remedy as a cure long after it has been shown merely to ameliorate the disease is either quackery or wishful thinking, and it thrives most where the need is greatest. Today the desire to solve the population problem is so intense that we are all ready to embrace any "action program" that promises relief. But postponement of effective measures allows the situation to worsen.

---

46. C. Miro, in *Family Planning and Population Programs,* B. Berelson *et al.,* Eds. (Univ. of Chicago Press, Chicago, 1966).
47. *Demographic Training and Research Centre (India) Newsletter* 20, 4 (Aug. 1966).

Unfortunately, the issue is confused by a matter of semantics. "Family *planning*" and "fertility *control*" suggest that reproduction is being regulated according to some rational plan. And so it is, but only from the standpoint of the individual couple, not from that of the community. What is rational in the light of a couple's situation may be totally irrational from the standpoint of society's welfare.

The need for societal regulation of individual behavior is readily recognized in other spheres—those of explosives, dangerous drugs, public property, natural resources. But in the sphere of reproduction, complete individual initiative is generally favored even by those liberal intellectuals who, in other spheres, most favor economic and social planning. Social reformers who would not hesitate to force all owners of rental property to rent to anyone who can pay, or to force all workers in an industry to join a union, balk at any suggestion that couples be permitted to have only a certain number of offspring. Invariably they interpret societal control of reproduction as meaning direct police supervision of individual behavior. Put the word *compulsory* in front of any term describing a means of limiting births—*compulsory sterilization, compulsory abortion, compulsory contraception*—and you guarantee violent opposition. Fortunately, such direct controls need not be invoked, but conservatives and radicals alike overlook this in their blind opposition to the idea of collective determination of a society's birth rate.

That the exclusive emphasis on family planning in current population policies is not a "first step" but an escape from the real issues is suggested by two facts. (i) No country has taken the "next step." The industrialized countries have had family planning for half a century without acquiring control over either the birth rate or population increase. (ii) Support and encouragement of research on population policy other than family planning is negligible. It is precisely this blocking of alternative thinking and experimentation that makes the emphasis on family planning a major obstacle to population control. The need is not to abandon family-planning programs but to put equal or greater resources into other approaches.

NEW DIRECTIONS IN POPULATION POLICY

In thinking about other approaches, one can start with known facts. In the past, all surviving societies had institutional incentives for marriage, procreation, and child care which were powerful enough to keep the birth rate equal to or in excess of a high death rate. Despite the drop in death rates during the last century and a half, the incentives tended to remain intact because the social structure (especially in regard to the family) changed little. At most, particularly in industrial societies, children became less productive and more expensive.[48] In present-day agrarian societies, where the drop in death rate has been more recent, precipitate, and independent of social change,[49] motivation for having children has changed little. Here, even more than in industrialized nations, the family has kept on producing abundant offspring, even though only a fraction of these children are now needed.

If excessive population growth is to be prevented, the obvious requirement is somehow to impose restraints on the family. However, because family roles are reinforced by society's system of rewards, punishments, sentiments, and norms, any proposal to demote the family is viewed as a threat by conservatives and liberals alike, and certainly by people with enough social responsibilty to work for population control. One is charged with trying to "abolish" the family, but what is required is selective restructuring of the family in relation to the rest of society.

The lines of such restructuring are suggested by two existing limitations on fertility. (i) Nearly all societies succeed in drastically discouraging reproduction among unmarried women. (ii) Advanced societies unintentionally reduce reproduction among married women when conditions worsen in such a way as to penalize childbearing more severely than it was penalized before. In both cases the causes are motivational and economic rather than technological.

It follows that population-control policy can de-emphaszie the family in two ways: (i) by keeping present controls over illegitimate childbirth yet making the most of factors that lead people to postpone or avoid marriage, and (ii) by instituting conditions that motivate those who do marry to keep their families small.

POSTPONEMENT OF MARRIAGE

Since the female reproductive span is short and generally more fecund in its first than in its second half, postponement of marriage to ages beyond 20 tends biologically to reduce births. Sociologically, it gives women time to get a better education, acquire interests unrelated to the family, and develop a cautious attitude toward pregnancy.[50] Individuals who have not married by the time they are in their late twenties often do not marry at all. For these reasons, for the world as a whole, the average age at marriage for women is negatively associated with the birth rate: a rising age at marriage is a frequent cause of declining fertility during the middle phase

---

48. K. Davis, *Population Index* 29, 345 (1963). For economic and sociological theory of motivation for having children, see J. Blake [Univ. of California (Berkeley)], in preparation.
49. K. Davis, *Amer. Economic Rev.* 46, 305 (1956); *Sci. Amer.* 209, 68 (1963).
50. J. Blake, *World Population Conference [Belgrade, 1965]* (United Nations, New York, 1967), vol. 2, pp. 132–36.

of the demographic transition; and, in the late phase, the "baby boom" is usually associated with a return to younger marriages.

Any suggestion that age at marriage be raised as a part of population policy is usually met with the argument that "even if a law were passed, it would not be obeyed." Interestingly, this objection implies that the only way to control the age at marriage is by direct legislation, but other factors govern the actual age. Roman Catholic countries generally follow canon law in stipulating 12 years as the minimum *legal* age at which girls may marry, but the actual average age at marriage in these countries (at least in Europe) is characteristically more like 25 to 28 years. The actual age is determined, not by law, but by social and ecomomic conditions. In agrarian societies, postponement of marriage (when postponement occurs) is apparently caused by difficulties in meeting the economic prerequisites for matrimony, as stipulated by custom and opinion. In industrial societies it is caused by housing shortages, unemployment, the requirement for overseas military service, high costs of education, and inadequacy of consumer services. Since almost no research has been devoted to the subject, it is difficult to assess the relative weight of the factors that govern the age at marriage.

ENCOURAGING LIMITATION OF BIRTHS WITHIN MARRIAGE

As a means of encouraging the limitation of reproduction within marriage, as well as postponement of marriage, a greater rewarding of nonfamilial than of familial roles would probably help. A simple way of accomplishing this would be to allow economic advantages to accrue to the single as opposed to the married individual, and to the small as opposed to the large family. For instance, the government could pay people to permit themselves to be sterilized;[51] all costs of abortion could be paid by the government; a substantial fee could be charged for a marriage license; a "child-tax"[52] could be levied; and there could be a requirement that illegitimate pregnancies be aborted. Less sensationally, governments could simply reverse some existing policies that encourage childbearing. They could, for example, cease taxing single persons more than married ones; stop giving parents special tax exemptions; abandon income-tax policy that discriminates against couples when the wife works; reduce paid maternity leaves; reduce family allowances;[53] stop awarding public housing on the

---

51. S. Enke, *Rev. Economics Statistics* 42, 175 (1960); ———, *Econ. Develop. Cult. Change* 8, 339 (1960); ———, *ibid.* 10, 427 (1962); A. O. Krueger and L. A. Sjaastad, *ibid.*, p. 423.
52. T. J. Samuel, *J. Family Welfare India* 13, 12 (1966).
53. Sixty-two countries, including 27 in Europe, give cash payments to people for having children [U.S. Social Security Administration, *Social Security Programs Throughout the World, 1967* (Government Printing Office, Washington, D.C., 1967), pp. xxvii–xxviii].

basis of family size; stop granting fellowships and other educational aids (including special allowances for wives and children) to married students; cease outlawing abortions and sterilizations; and relax rules that allow use of harmless contraceptives only with medical permission. Some of these policy reversals would be beneficial in other than demographic respects and some would be harmful unless special precautions were taken. The aim would be to reduce the number, not the quality, of the next generation.

A closely related method of de-emphasizing the family would be modification of the complementarity of the roles of men and women. Men are now able to participate in the wider world yet enjoy the satisfaction of having several children because the housework and childcare fall mainly on their wives. Women are impelled to seek this role by their idealized view of marriage and motherhood and by either the scarcity of alternative roles or the difficulty of combining them with family roles. To change this situation women could be required to work outside the home, or compelled by circumstances to do so. If, at the same time, women were paid as well as men and given equal educational and occupational opportunities, and if social life were organized around the place of work rather than around the home or neighborhood, many women would develop interests that would compete with family interests. Approximately this policy is now followed in several Communist countries, and even the less developed of these currently have extremely low birth rates.[54]

That inclusion of women in the labor force has a negative effect on reproduction is indicated by regional comparisons.[18, 55] But in most countries the wife's employment is subordinate, economically and emotionally, to her family role, and is readily sacrificed for the latter. No society has restructured both the occupational system and the domestic establishment to the point of permanently modifying the old division of labor by sex.

In any deliberate effort to control the birth rate along these lines, a government has two powerful instruments—its command over economic planning and its authority (real or potential) over education. The first determines (as far as policy can) the economic conditions and circumstances affecting the lives of all citizens; the second provides the knowledge and attitudes necessary to implement the plans. The economic system largely determines who shall work, what can be bought, what rearing children will cost, how much individuals can spend. The schools define family roles and develop vocational and recreational interests; they could, if it were desired, redefine the sex roles, develop interests that transcend the home, and transmit realistic (as opposed to moralistic) knowledge concern-

---

54. Average gross reproduction rates in the early 1960's were as follows: Hungary, 0.91; Bulgaria, 1.09; Romania, 1.15; Yugoslavia, 1.32.
55. O. A. Collver and E. Langlois, *Econ. Develop. Cult. Change* 10, 367 (1962); J. Weeks [Univ. of California (Berkeley)], unpublished paper.

ing marriage, sexual behavior, and population problems. When the problem is viewed in this light, it is clear that the ministries of economics and education, not the ministry of health, should be the source of population policy.

THE DILEMMA OF POPULATION POLICY

It should now be apparent why, despite strong anxiety over runaway population growth, the actual programs purporting to control it are limited to family planning and are therefore ineffective. (i) The goal of zero, or even slight, population growth is one that nations and groups find difficult to accept. (ii) The measures that would be required to implement such a goal, though not so revolutionary as a Brave New World or a Communist Utopia, nevertheless tend to offend most people reared in existing societies. As a consequence, the goal of so-called population control is implicit and vague; the method is only family planning. This method, far from de-emphasizing the family, is familistic. One of its stated goals is that of helping sterile couples to *have* children. It stresses parental aspirations and responsibilities. It goes along with most aspects of conventional morality, such as condemnation of abortion, disapproval of premarital intercourse, respect for religious teachings and cultural taboos, and obeisance to medical and clerical authority. It deflects hostility by refusing to recommend any change other than the one it stands for: availability of contraceptives.

The things that make family planning acceptable are the very things that make it ineffective for population control. By stressing the right of parents to have the number of children they want, it evades the basic question of population policy, which is how to give societies the number of children they need. By offering only the means for *couples* to control fertility, it neglects the means for societies to do so.

Because of the predominantly pro-family character of existing societies, individual interest ordinarily leads to the production of enough offspring to constitute rapid population growth under conditions of low mortality. Childless or single-child homes are considered indicative of personal failure, whereas having three to five living children gives a family a sense of continuity and substantiality.[56]

Given the existing desire to have moderate-sized rather than small families, the only countries in which fertility has been reduced to match reduction in mortality are advanced ones temporarily experiencing worsened economic conditions. In Sweden, for instance, the net reproduction rate (NRR) has been below replacement for 34 years (1930–63), if

---

56. Roman Catholic textbooks condemn the "small" family (one with fewer than four children) as being abnormal [J. Blake, *Population Studies* 20, 27 (1966)].

the period is taken as a whole, but this is because of the economic depression. The average replacement rate was below unity (NRR-0.81) for the period 1930–42, but from 1942 through 1963 it was above unity (NRR-1.08). Hardships that seem particularly conducive to deliberate lowering of the birth rate are (in managed economies) scarcity of housing and other consumer goods despite full employment, and required high participation of women in the labor force, or (in freer economies) a great deal of unemployment and economic insecurity. When conditions are good, any nation tends to have a growing population.

It follows that, in countries where contraception is used, a realistic proposal for a government policy of lowering the birth rate reads like a catalogue of horrors: squeeze consumers through taxation and inflation; make housing very scarce by limiting construction; force wives and mothers to work outside the home to offset the inadequacy of male wages, yet provide few childcare facilities; encourage migration to the city by paying low wages in the country and providing few rural jobs; increase congestion in cities by starving the transit system; increase personal insecurity by encouraging conditions that produce unemployment and by haphazard political arrests. No government will institute such hardships simply for the purpose of controlling population growth. Clearly, therefore, the task of contemporary population policy is to develop attractive substitutes for family interests, so as to avoid having to turn to hardship as a corrective. The specific measures required for developing such substitutes are not easy to determine in the absence of research on the question.

In short, the world's population problem cannot be solved by pretense and wishful thinking. The unthinking identification of family planning with population control is an ostrich-like approach in that it permits people to hide from themselves the enormity and unconventionality of the task. There is no reason to abandon family-planning programs; contraception is a valuable technological instrument. But such programs must be supplemented with equal or greater investments in research and experimentation to determine the required socioeconomic measures.[57]

---

57. Judith Blake's critical readings and discussions have greatly helped in the preparation of this article.

Population Policy for Americans:
Is the Government Being Misled?*

JUDITH BLAKE

Pressure on the federal government for "action" to limit population growth in the United States has intensified greatly during the past 10 years, and at present such action is virtually unchallenged as an official national goal. Given the goal, the question of means becomes crucial. Here I first evaluate the particular means being advocated and pursued in public policy, then I present alternative ways of possibly achieving the goal.

The prevailing view as to the best means is remarkably unanimous and abundantly documented. It is set forth in the 17 volumes of congressional hearings so far published on the "population crisis";[1] in "The Growth of U.S. Population," a report by the Committee on Population of the National Academy of Sciences[2]; in a statement made by an officer of the Ford Foundation who was asked by the Department of Health, Education, and Welfare to make suggestions;[3] and, finally, in the "Report of the President's Committee on Population and Family Planning," which was officially released this past January.[4] The essential recommendation throughout is that the government should give highest priority to ghetto-oriented family-planning programs designed to "deliver" birth-control services to the poor and uneducated, among whom, it is claimed, there are at least 5 million women who are "in need" of such federally sponsored birth-control assistance.

By what logic have the proponents of control moved from a concern with population growth to a recommendation favoring highest priority for poverty-oriented birth-control programs? First, they have assumed that

---

* Reprinted from *Science*, 164 (May 2, 1969), pp. 522–529, by permission of the author and publisher. Copyright 1969 by the American Association for the Advancement of Science.

1. *Hearings on S. 1676, U.S. Senate Subcommittee on Foreign Aid Expenditures* (the 1965 and 1966 Hearings each comprise seven volumes; the 1967–1968 Hearings, to date, comprise three volumes) (Government Printing Office, Washington, D.C.).
2. "The Growth of U.S. Population," *Nat. Acad. Sci.–Nat Res. Council Pub. 1279* (1965).
3. O. Harkavy, F. S. Jaffe, S. S. Wishik, "Implementing DHEW Policy on Family Planning and Population" (mimeographed, 1967; available from the Ford Foundation, New York).
4. "Report of the President's Committee on Population and Family Planning: The Transition from Concern to Action" (Government Printing Office, Washington, D.C., 1968).

fertility is the only component of population growth worthy of government attention. Second, they have taken it for granted that, to reduce fertility, one sponsors birth-control programs ("family planning"). Just why they have made this assumption is not clear, but its logical implication is that population growth is due to births that couples would have preferred to avoid. Furthermore, the reasoning confuses couple control over births with societal control over them.[5] Third, the proponents of the new policy have seized on the poor and uneducated as the "target" group for birth-control action because they see this group as the only remaining target for a program of voluntary family planning. The rest of the population is handling its family planning pretty well on its own: over 95 percent of fecund U.S. couples already either use birth-control methods or intend to do so. The poor, on the other hand—at least those who are fecund—have larger families than the advantaged; they not only use birth-control methods less but they use them less effectively. The family-planning movement's notion of "responsible parenthood" carries the implication that family size should be directly, not inversely, related to social and economic advantage, and the poor are seen as constituting the residual slack to be taken up by the movement's efforts. Why are the poor not conforming to the dictates of responsible parenthood? Given the movement's basic assumptions, there are only two answers: the poor are irresponsible, or they have not had the opportunity. Since present-day leaders would abhor labeling the poor irresponsible, they have chosen to blame lack of opportunity as the cause. Opportunity has been lacking, in their eyes, either because the poor have not been "educated" in family planning or because they have not been "reached" by family-planning services. In either case, as they see it, the poor have been deprived of their "rights."[2,6] This deprivation has allegedly been due to the prudery and hypocrisy of the affluent, who have overtly tabooed discussion of birth control and dissemination of birth-control materials while, themselves, covertly enjoying the benefits of family planning.[7]

So much for the logic underlying recent proposals for controlling population growth in the United States. But what is the evidence on which this argument is based? On what empirical grounds is the govern-

5. K. Davis, *Science* 158, 730 (1967); J. Blake, in *Public Health and Population Change,* M. C. Sheps and J. C. Ridley, Eds. (Univ. of Pittsburgh Press, Pittsburgh, Pa., 1965).
6. In the words of the Committee on Population, "The freedom to limit family size to the number of children wanted when they are wanted is, in our view, a basic human right . . . most Americans of higher income and better education exercise this right as a matter of course, but . . . many of the poor and uneducated are in fact deprived of the right."
7. W. J. Cohen, *Family Planning: One Aspect of Freedom to Choose* (Government Printing Office, Washington, D.C., 1966), p. 2. Cohen, former Secretary of Health, Education, and Welfare, says: "Until a few years ago, family planning and population problems were considered 'hush-hush' subjects. Public discussion was curtailed not only in polite society, but in the legislative and executive branches of the government as well."

ment being asked to embark on a high-priority program of providing contraceptive services to the poor? Moreover, what, if any, are some of the important public issues that the suggested policy raises—what are its social and political side effects? And, finally, is such a policy, even if appropriate for the poor and even if relatively unencumbered by public disapproval, relevant to the problem of population growth in America? If demographic curtailment is really the objective, must alternative policies be considered and possibly given highest priority?

Turning to the alleged need for government-sponsored birth-control services, one may ask whether birth control has in fact been a tabooed topic among the middle and upper classes, so that the less advantaged could be said to have suffered "deprivation" and consequently now to require government help. One may then question whether there is a mandate from the poor for the type of federally sponsored service that is now being urged, and whether as many as 5 million women are "in need" of such family-planning assistance.

Has Birth Control Been a Tabooed Topic?

The notion that the American public has only recently become willing to tolerate open discussion of birth control has been assiduously cultivated by congressmen and others concerned with government policy on population. For example, Senator Tydings credited Senators Gruening and Clark and President Johnson with having almost single-handedly changed American public attitudes toward birth control. In 1966 he read the following statement into the 28 February *Congressional Record*.[8]

> The time is ripe for positive action. Ten years ago, even five years ago, this was a politically delicate subject. Today the Nation has awakened to the need for Government action.
> This change in public attitude has come about through the efforts of men who had the courage to brook the tides of public opinion. Senator Clark is such a man. Senator Gruening is such a man. So is President Johnson. Because of their leadership it is no longer necessary for an elected official to speak with trepidation on this subject.

A year later, Senator Tydings reduced his estimate of the time required for the shift in public opinion to "3 or 4 years."[9, 10] Senator Gruening main-

---

8. *Hearings on S. 2993, U.S. Senate Subcommittee on Employment, Manpower, and Poverty,* 89th Congress, Second Session, May 10 (Government Printing Office, Washington, D.C., 1966), p. 31.
9. *Hearings on S. 1676, U.S. Senate Subcommittee on Foreign Aid Expenditures,* 90th Congress, First Session, November 2 (Government Printing Office, Washington, D.C., 1967), pt. 1.
10. Senator Tydings (D–Md.) said at the Hearings on S. 1676 (see 9): "As recently as 3 or 4 years ago, the idea that Federal, State or local governments should make

tained[11] that the "ninety-eight distinguished men and women" who testified at the public hearing on S. 1676 were "pioneers" whose "names comprise an important honor roll which historically bears an analogy to other famous lists: the signers of the Declaration of Independence, those who ratified the Constitution of the United States and others whose names were appended to and made possible some of the great turning points in history." Reasoning from the continued existence of old, and typically unenforced, laws concerning birth control (together with President Eisenhower's famous anti-birth-control statement), Stycos, in a recent article,[12] stated:

> The public reaction to family planning in the United States has varied between disgust and silent resignation to a necessary evil. At best it was viewed as so delicate and risky that it was a matter of "individual conscience." As such, it was a matter so totally private, so sacred (or profane), that no external agents, and certainly not the state, should have anything to do with it.

Does the evidence support such impressionistic claims? How did the general public regard government sponsorship of birth control long before it became a subject of congressional hearings, a National Academy report, and a Presidential Committee report? Fortunately, a question on this topic appeared in no less than 13 national polls and surveys conducted between 1937 and 1966. As part of a larger project concerned with public knowledge and opinions about demographic topics, I have gathered together the original data cards from these polls, prepared them for computer processing, and analyzed the results. The data are all from Gallup polls and are all from national samples of the white, adult population. Here I concentrate on adults under 45—that is, on adults in the childbearing age group.

The data of Table 1 contradict the notion that Americans have only recently ceased to regard birth control as a tabooed topic. As far back as 30 years ago, almost three-quarters of the women questioned in these surveys actively approved having the *government* make birth-control information available to the married. By the early 1960's, 80 percent or more of women approved overcoming legal barriers and allowing "anyone who wants it" to have birth-control information. The figures for men are similar. The

---

available family planning information and services to families who could not otherwise afford them was extremely controversial. But in a brief period of time there has been a substantial shift of opinion among the moral leadership of our country, brought about in large measure by the vigorous efforts of the distinguished Senator from Alaska, Ernest Gruening, the chairman of this subcommittee."
11. E. Gruening, "What the Federal Government is now Doing in the Field of Population Control and What is Needed," speech presented before the U.S. Senate, 3 May 1967.
12. J. M. Stycos, in *World Population and U.S. Government Policy and Programs,* F. T. Brayer, Ed. (Georgetown Univ. Press, Washington, D.C., 1968).

TABLE 1. *Percentages of White U.S. Men and Women Between the Ages of 21 and 44 Who, in Various National Polls and Surveys Made Between 1937 and 1964,* Expressed the Opinion That Birth-Control Information Should Be Made Available to Individuals Who Desired it.*

	Men		Women	
Year	%	N	%	N
1937	66	1038	70	734
1938	67	1111	72	548
1939	74	1101	73	630
1940	72	1127	75	618
1943	67	628	73	866
1945	64	714	70	879
1947	76	353	75	405
1959	78	301	79	394
1961	82	336	81	394
1962	85	288	80	381
1963	78	323	79	373
1964	89	324	86	410

* The questions asked of respondents concerning birth control were as follows. In 1937: Do you favor the birth control movement? In 1938, 1939, 1940, 1943, 1945, and 1947: Would you like to see a government agency (or "government health clinics") furnish birth-control information to married people who want it? In 1959, 1961, 1962, and 1963: In some places in the United States it is not legal to supply birth control information. How do you feel about this—do you think birth-control information should be available to anyone who wants it, or not? In 1964: Do you think birth-control information should be available to anyone who wants it, or not?

question asked in 1964 the one question in recent years that did not mention illegality—brought 86 percent of the women and 89 percent of the men into the category of those who approved availability of birth-control information for "anyone who wants it." Furthermore, in judging the level of disapproval, one should bear in mind that the remainder of the respondents, in all of these years, includes from 7 to 15 percent who claim that they have "no opinion" on the subject, not that they "disapprove."

An important difference of opinion corresponds to a difference in religious affiliation. Among non-Catholics (including those who have "no religion" and do not attend church) approval has been considerably higher than it has been among Catholics. Among non-Catholic women, over 80 percent approved as early as 1939, and among non-Catholic men the percentages were approximately the same. The 1964 poll showed that 90 percent of each sex approved. Among Catholics, in recent years about 60 percent have approved, and, in 1964, the question that mentioned neither the government nor legality brought opinions of approval from 77 percent of the women and 83 percent of the men.

Clearly, if birth-control information has in fact been unavailable to the poor, the cause has not been a generalized and pervasive attitude of prudery on the part of the American public. Although public officials may have misjudged American opinion (and may have mistakenly assumed that the Catholic Church "spoke for" a majority of Americans, or even for a majority of Catholics), most Americans of an age to be having children did not regard birth control as a subject that should be under a blanket of secrecy and, as far back as the 1930's, evinced a marked willingness to have their government make such information widely available. It seems unlikely, therefore, that poorer sectors of our population were "cut off" from birth-control knowledge primarily because informal channels of communication (the channels through which most people learn about birth control) were blocked by an upper- and middle-class conspiracy of silence.

What has happened, however, is that pressure groups for family planning, like the Catholic hierarchy they have been opposing, have been acting as self-designated spokesmen for "public opinion." By developing a cause as righteous as that of the Catholics (the "rights" of the poor as against the "rights" of a religious group), the family planners have used the American way of influencing official opinion. Now public officials appear to believe that publicly supported birth-control services are what the poor have always wanted and needed, just as, in the past, official opinion acceded to the notion that such services would have been "offensive" to certain groups. Nonetheless, the question remains of whether or not publicly supported services are actually appropriate to the attitudes and objectives of the poor and uneducated in matters of reproduction. Is the government responding to a mandate from the poor or to an ill-concealed mandate from the well-to-do? If there is no mandate from the poor, the provision of birth-control services may prove a convenience for certain women but is likely to have little effect on the reproductive performance of the poor in general. Let us look at the evidence.

Is There a Mandate from the Poor?

The notion that the poor have larger families than the affluent only because they have less access to birth-control information implies that the poor *desire* families as small as, or smaller than, those of the well-to-do. The poor are simply unable to realize this desire, the argument goes, because of lack of access to birth-control information. The National Academy of Sciences Committee on Population stated the argument very well.[2]

> The available evidence indicates that low-income families do not want more children than do families with higher incomes, but they have more because they do not have the information or the resources to plan their families effectively according to their own desires.

The committee, however, presents none of the "available evidence" that "low-income families do not want more children than do families with higher incomes." Actually, my data supply evidence that runs counter to the statement quoted above, both with respect to the desired or ideal number of children and with respect to attitudes toward birth control.

I shall begin with the preferred size of family. A number of national polls, conducted over some 25 years, provide data concerning opinions on ideal family size. In addition, I include tabulations of data from two national surveys on fertility (the "Growth of American Families Studies"), conducted in 1955 and 1960.[13,14] My detailed analyses of the results of these polls and surveys are given elsewhere [15] and are only briefly summarized here. Table 2 gives mean values for the family size considered ideal by white, non-Catholic women, according to education and economic status.

TABLE 2. *Mean Number of Children Considered Ideal by Non-Catholic Women, According to Education and Economic Status, for Selected Years Between 1943 and 1968.*

Date	Age Range	Level of Education* Col-lege	High School	Grade School	Income or Economic Status† 1	2	3	4	Total Respondents X̄	N
1943	20–34	2.8	2.6	2.6	2.9	2.7	2.7	2.5	2.7	1893
1952	21+	3.3	3.1	3.6	3.3		3.3	3.3	3.3	723
1955‡	18–39	3.1	3.2	3.7	3.2	3.1	3.2	3.5	3.3	1905
1955§	18–39	3.3	3.4	3.9	3.4	3.3	3.4	3.7	3.4	1905
1957	21+	3.4	3.2	3.6	3.3		3.2	3.5	3.3	448
1959	21+	3.5	3.4	3.9	3.5		3.5	3.6	3.5	472
1960‡	18–39	3.1	3.2	3.5	3.1	3.2	3.3	3.2	3.2	1728
1960§	18–39	3.2	3.4	3.6	3.2	3.3	3.5	3.4	3.4	1728
1963	21+	3.2	3.4	3.5	3.3	3.3	3.5	3.5	3.4	483
1966	21+	3.1	3.3	3.7	3.2	3.2	3.4	3.7	3.3	374
1967	21+	3.1	3.3	3.4	3.3	3.2	3.1	3.4	3.3	488
1968	21+	3.2	3.3	3.7	3.2	3.0	3.4	3.6	3.3	539

* Level of education is measured by the highest grade completed.
† Levels 1 to 4 for economic status range in order from "high" to "low."
‡ Minimum ideal (results from coding range answers to the lowest figure).
§ Maximum ideal (results from coding range answers to the highest figure).

13. R. Freedman, P. K. Whelpton, A. A. Campbell, *Family Planning, Sterility and Population Growth* (McGraw-Hill, New York, 1959).
14. P. K. Whelpton, A. A. Campbell, J. E. Patterson, *Fertility and Family Planning in the United States* (Princeton Univ. Press, Princeton, N.J., 1966).
15. J. Blake, *Demography* 3, 154 (1966); *Population Studies* 20, 27 (1966); *ibid*. 21, 159 (1967); *ibid*., p. 185; *ibid*. 22, 5 (1968).

The data lend little support to the hypothesis that the poor desire families as small as those desired by the middle and upper classes. Within both the educational and the economic categories, those on the lower rungs not only have larger families than those on the higher rungs (at least in the case of non-Catholics) but say they want larger families and consider them ideal. This differential has existed for as long as information on preferred family size in this country has been available, and it persists. It thus seems extremely hazardous to base a major governmental effort on the notion that, among individuals (white individuals, at least) at the lower social levels, there is a widespread and deeply held desire for families as small as, or smaller than, those desired by the well-to-do. No major survey shows this to be the case.

Not only do persons of lower socio-economic status prefer larger families than the more affluent do, they also generally favor birth control less. Tables 3 and 4 show the percentages of white men and women who expressed approval of birth control in surveys made between 1937 and 1964, by educational level and economic status, respectively.

Looking at the educational differential (Table 3), one finds that, in general, the proportion of those who approve birth control drops precipitately between the college and grade school levels. As far back as the early 1940's, over 80 percent of women and 75 percent of men with some or more college education approved government action on birth control. By 1964, over 90 percent of both sexes approved. By contrast, only 60 percent

TABLE 3.   *Percentages of White U.S. Men and Women Between the Ages of 21 and 44 Who, in Various National Polls Taken Between 1943 and 1964, Expressed the Opinion That Birth-Control Information Should Be Made Available to Individuals Who Desired It. The Percentages Are Given by Level of Education*; the Numbers in Parentheses Are Total Numbers of Respondents in Each Category.*

	Men			Women		
Year	College	High School	Grade School	College	High School	Grade School
1943	75 (184)	68 (284)	56 (157)	82 (216)	74 (442)	60 (207)
1945	74 (202)	62 (360)	58 (140)	83 (216)	68 (434)	56 (207)
1947	91 (84)	72 (199)	67 (66)	81 (89)	74 (228)	72 (81)
1959	88 (89)	76 (163)	65 (49)	91 (55)	79 (279)	68 (41)
1961	88 (102)	81 (188)	67 (46)	84 (81)	81 (265)	78 (50)
1962	91 (93)	85 (171)	61 (23)	84 (79)	82 (258)	66 (44)
1963	86 (105)	79 (178)	53 (40)	81 (80)	78 (251)	81 (42)
1964	92 (107)	88 (188)	83 (29)	94 (79)	86 (293)	74 (38)

* The level of education is measured by the last grade completed.

of men and women with an elementary school education approved in the 1940's, and, despite a rise in approval, there is still a differential. When non-Catholics alone are considered, the educational difference is even more pronounced in many cases.

Turning to economic or income status (Table 4), one generally finds the same results. The high proportions (close to 100 percent) of women in the highest and next-to-highest economic brackets who, in recent years, have approved birth-control efforts is noteworthy, as is the fact that approximately 80 percent of women in these brackets approved such efforts as far back as the 1930's. On the other hand, men and women in lower income brackets have been slower to approve birth-control policies.

Despite the inverse relationship just described, I may have over-emphasized the lesser approval of birth-control programs on the part of persons of lower economic and social status. After all, in recent years approval often has been high even among people at the lowest social levels. Among women with only a grade school education, the percentage of those favoring birth-control programs averaged 73 percent in polls taken between 1959 and 1964; among men at the lowest educational level, the corresponding average was 66 percent. Yet it is undeniably true that, throughout the period for which data are available, the people who needed birth-control information most, according to recent policy pronouncements, have been precisely the ones who were least in favor of a policy that would make it widely available.

The truth of this conclusion becomes more evident when we move to an analysis of a question asked on the 1966 Gallup poll: Do you think birth-control pills should be made available free to all women on relief who are of childbearing age? This question presents the public with the specific issue that is the focus of current policy—namely, birth control especially for the poor. A summary of the replies to this question is given in Table 5, together with average percentages of people who, in five surveys made between 1959 and 1964, replied that they approved birth control generally.

It is clear that the overall level of approval drops when specific reference to a poverty-oriented birth-control policy is introduced. The decline is from an average of approximately 80 percent for each sex during the period 1959–64 to 65 percent from men and 71 percent for women in 1966. Of most significance, however, is the fact that the largest proportionate drop in approval occurs among members of the "target" groups themselves—the poor and uneducated. In particular, there is a remarkable drop in approval among men at this socioeconomic level. There is a 42-percent decline in approval among men who have had only a grade school education and a 29-percent drop among those with a high school education. Among the college-educated men the drop in approval is only 6 percent. The results, by income, parallel those by education: there is a 47-percent drop for men in the lowest income group but only a 9-percent drop for those in the

TABLE 4. Percentages of White U.S. Men and Women Between the Ages of 21 and 44 Who, in Various National Polls Taken Between 1937 and 1964, Expressed the Opinion That Birth-Control Information Should Be Made Available to Individuals Who Desired It. The Percentages Are Given by Economic Status (Levels 1–4*); the Numbers in Parentheses Are Total Numbers of Respondents in Each Category.

	Men				Women			
Year	1	2	3	4	1	2	3	4
1937	78 (112)	70 (406)	61 (520)		67 (69)	78 (293)	64 (372)	
1938	65 (125)	74 (453)	62 (521)		80 (51)	73 (232)	70 (259)	
1939	78 (116)	75 (432)	73 (553)		71 (68)	77 (260)	71 (302)	
1940	79 (131)	75 (443)	68 (553)		80 (49)	78 (258)	71 (311)	
1943	76 (80)	72 (219)	62 (330)		80 (90)	79 (272)	68 (500)	
1945	73 (67)	66 (286)	62 (352)		83 (75)	77 (264)	64 (531)	
1947	86 (42)	77 (123)	72 (188)		92 (38)	71 (119)	73 (237)	
1959	83 (101)	76 (120)	73 (79)		83 (139)	82 (152)	72 (95)	
1961	93 (42)	85 (80)	87 (103)	69 (111)	88 (41)	80 (97)	80 (76)	81 (138)
1962	82 (45)	89 (71)	86 (94)	80 (74)	82 (51)	80 (75)	84 (110)	77 (140)
1963	88 (60)	84 (79)	76 (96)	61 (97)	87 (67)	79 (107)	79 (98)	75 (100)
1964	90 (67)	87 (26)	93 (82)	85 (79)	96 (90)	90 (87)	85 (104)	78 (120)

* Levels 1 to 4 for the years 1961–64 range from income of $10,000 and over down to incomes under $5000. Prior to 1961, levels 1 to 3 represent "upper," "middle," and "lower" income brackets.

386

TABLE 5. *Percentages of White U.S. Men and Women Between the Ages of 21 and 44 Who, in a 1966 Poll, Expressed Approval of Free Distribution of Birth-Control Pills for Women on Relief, and Average Percentages of Individuals in This Age Group Who, in Polls Taken Between 1959 and 1964, Expressed Approval of Birth Control. Percentages Approving and Numbers of Individuals Interviewed Are Given as Totals and Also By Education and Economic Status of the Respondents.*

	Men			Women		
	1966		1959–64	1966		1959–64
Item	%	N	(av. %)	%	N	(av. %)
Total	65	264	82	71	385	81
Education						
College	82	98	87	75	197	87
High school	58	142	82	70	392	81
Grade school	38	24	66	59	32	73
Economic status						
1	79	80	89	70	110	87
2	69	75	84	76	99	82
3	59	65	83	70	91	80
4	39	41	74	67	76	78

highest income bracket. Even if the tabulations are restricted to non-Catholics (data that are not presented here), the results are essentially the same.

If the ghetto-oriented birth-control policy urged on the federal government meets with limited public enthusiasm, how does the public view extension of that policy to teen-age girls? This question is of some importance because a notable aspect of the pressure for government-sponsored family-planning programs is advocacy of making birth-control information and materials available at the high school level.

The Committee on Population of the National Academy of Sciences urges early education in "family planning" in order to prevent illegitimacy.[2]

. . . government statistics show that the mothers of approximately 41 per cent of the 245,000 babies born illegitimately in the United States every year are women 19 years of age or younger. Thus a large proportion of all illegitimate children are progeny of teen-age mothers. To reduce the number of such children born to teen-age mothers, high-school education in family planning is essential.

Katherine B. Oettinger, Deputy Secretary for Family Planning of the Department of Health, Education, and Welfare, importunes us not to "demand the eligibility card of a first pregnancy before we admit vulnerable girls to family planning services."[16] The Harkavy report states:[3]

> Eligibility requirements should be liberal with respect to marital status. Such services should be made available to the unmarried as well as the married. . . . Eligibility requirements should be liberal with respect to the age of unmarried women seeking help. This will undoubtedly pose some problems, but they may not be insurmountable. Some publically supported programs are already facing them (for example, in Baltimore).

Representative Scheuer from New York has berated the federal government for not "bringing family planning into the schools." He has cited the "desperate need for family planning by unmarried 14-, 15-, and 16-year-old girls in school [which] is so transparently evident that it almost boggles the imagination to realize that nothing has been done. Virtually no leadership has come from the federal government."[9]

Obviously there is little recognition in these statements that such a policy might engender a negative public response. Yet such a possibility cannot be discounted. The results of the 1966 question "Do you think they [the pills] should be made available to teen-age girls?" suggest that a policy of pill distribution to female adolescents may be viewed by the public as involving more complex issues than the mere democratization of "medical" services. These results, tabulated by social level, are shown in Table 6.

It may be seen that, in general, a proposal for distribution of pills to teen-age girls meets with very little approval. There is more disapproval among women than among men. Even among women under the age of 30, only 17 percent approve; among men in this age group, 29 percent approve. At no age does feminine approval reach 20 percent, and in most cases it is below 15 percent. Furthermore, restriction of the results to non-Catholics does not raise the percentages of those who approve the policy. Most noteworthy is the socioeconomic gradient among men. Whereas 32 percent of college-educated men approve distribution of pills to young girls, only 13 percent of men with a grade school education do. Thirty-three percent of men in the highest income bracket approve, but only 13 percent in the lowest bracket do.

Clearly, the extension of "family planning" to poor, unmarried teen-agers is not regarded simply as "health care." Individuals may approve, in a general way, a wider availability of birth-control information without approving federal expenditure to facilitate a high level of sexual activity by teen-age girls. One suspects that explicit recognition and implied approval of such activity still comes hard to our population, and that it comes hardest to the group most involved in the problems of illegitimacy and premarital conception—namely, the poor and uneducated themselves. The

---

16. *Family Planner* 2, 3 (1968).

TABLE 6.   *Percentages of White U.S. Men and Women Who, in a 1966 Poll, Expressed Approval of Making Birth-Control Pills Available to Teen-Age Girls. Percentages Approving and Numbers of Individuals Interviewed Are Given by Age Group, by Education, and by Economic Status.*

| | All religions | | | | Non-Catholics | | | |
| | Men | | Women | | Men | | Women | |
Item	%	N	%	N	%	N	%	N
Age								
Under 30	29	86	17	149	34	65	19	102
30–44	19	172	8	238	20	133	7	169
Education								
College	32	98	15	100	36	75	13	71
High school	18	142	9	264	19	110	9	180
Grade school	13	24	11	35	6	17	14	28
Economic status								
1	33	80	11	113	35	58	11	75
2	20	75	13	105	24	58	14	72
3	19	65	7	94	18	50	5	64
4	13	41	16	82	15	33	14	66

extreme disapproval of a policy of pill distribution to teen-age girls that is found in lower-class groups (particularly among lower-class men) suggests that a double standard of sexual behavior is operative in these groups—a standard that does not allow open toleration of the idea that the ordinary teen-age girl requires the pill, or that a part of her junior high school and high school education should include instruction in its use.

CAN "FIVE MILLION WOMEN" BE WRONG?

The most widely publicized argument favoring federal birth-control programs, and apparently the one that elected officials find most persuasive, is the claim that there are approximately "five million" poor women "in need" of publicly subsidized birth-control help.[17] I list below some of the principal assumptions upon which this estimate is based—all of which introduce serious upward biases into the evidence.

1) It is claimed that women at the poverty and near-poverty levels desire families of 3.0 children. While this may be true of nonwhite wives at

---

17. The estimate (by Arthur A. Campbell) under discussion here may be found in the Harkavy report (see 3, attachment A, pp. 4–19). Another estimate has been circulated by the Planned Parenthood Federation in a brochure entitled *Five Million Women* (Planned Parenthood, New York).

this economic level, it is not true, as we have seen, of white women, who comprise a major share of the "target" group and who, on the average, desire a number of children closer to 4 (especially if Catholics are included, as they are in the "five million").

2) It is assumed by the estimators that 82 percent of all poor women aged 15 to 44 are at risk of conception (that is, exposed sexually), in spite of the fact that only 45 percent of poor women in this age group are married and living with their husbands. In arriving at the figure of 82 percent, the estimators assumed that all women in the "married" category (including those who were separated from their husbands and those whose husbands were absent) were sexually exposed regularly, and that half of the women in the "non-married" category—that is, single, widowed, and divorced women—were exposed regularly. Information is scarce concerning the sexual behavior of widows and divorced women, but Kinsey's data on premarital coitus leads one to believe that the assumption of 50 percent for single women may be high. Among the women with a grade school education in Kinsey's sample, 38 percent had had coitus at some time between the ages of 16 and 20, and 26 percent, at some time between the ages of 21 and 25. Moreover, as Kinsey emphasizes, these encounters were characteristically sporadic.[18]

3) The proportion of sterile women among the poor is assumed to be 13 percent, although the Scripps 1960 "Growth of American Families Study" showed the proportion among white women of grade school education to be 22 percent.[14]

4) No allowance is made for less than-normal fecundity, although the Scripps 1960 study[14] had indicated that, among women of grade school education, an additional 10 percent (over and above the 22 percent) were subnormal in their ability to reproduce.

5) It is taken for granted by the estimators that no Catholic women would object, on religious grounds, to the use of modern methods, and no allowance is made for objection by non-Catholics, on religious or other grounds. In other words, it is assumed that all women "want" the service. Yet, in response to a question concerning the desirability of limiting or spacing pregnancies, 29 percent of the wives with grade school education who were interviewed in the Scripps 1960 study said they were "against" such limitation or spacing.[14] Among the Catholic wives with grade school education, the proportion "against" was 48 percent, although half of these objectors were "for" the rhythm method. Similar objections among the disadvantaged have been revealed by many polls over a long period.

6) Perhaps most important, the estimate of 5 million women "wanting" and "in need of" birth-control information includes not only objectors

18. A. C. Kinsey, W. B. Pomeroy, C. E. Martin, P. B. Gebhard, *Sexual Behavior in the Human Female* (Saunders, Philadelphia, 1953), pp. 291 and 337.

but women who are already practicing birth control. Hence, in addition to all the other biases, the estimate represents a blanket decision by the estimators that the women require medical attention regarding birth control—particularly that they need the pill and the coil. In the words of the Harkavy report:[2]

> This may be considered a high estimate of the number of women who need to have family planning services made available to them in public clinics, because some of the couples among the poor and near poor are able to exercise satisfactory control over their fertility. However, even these couples do not have the same access as the non-poor to the more effective and acceptable methods of contraception, particularly the pill and the loop. So, simply in order to equalize the access of the poor and the near-poor to modern methods of contraception under medical supervision, it is appropriate to try to make contraceptive services available to all who may need and want them.

Yet the 1960 Scripps study found that, among fecund women of grade school education, 79 percent used contraceptives.[14] The 21 percent who did not included young women who were building families and said they wanted to get pregnant, as well as Catholics who objected to birth control on religious grounds. As for the methods that women currently are using, it seems gratuitous for the federal government to decide that only medically supervised methods—the pill and the coil—are suitable for lower-income couples, and that a mammoth "service" program is therefore required. In fact, the implications of such a decision border on the fantastic—the implications that we should substitute scarce medical and paramedical attention for all contraceptive methods now being used by poor couples.

In sum, the argument supporting a "need" for nationwide, publicly sustained birth-control programs does not stand up under empirical scrutiny. Most fecund lower-class couples now use birth-control methods when they want to prevent pregnancy; in the case of those who do not, the blame cannot simply be laid at the door of the affluent who have kept the subject of birth control under wraps, or of a government that has withheld services. As we have seen, opinion on birth control has been, and is, less favorable among the poor and the less well educated than among the well-to-do. In addition, the poor desire larger families. Although it may be argued that, at the public welfare level, birth control has, until recently, been taboo because of the "Catholic vote," most individuals at all social levels have learned about birth control *informally* and without medical attention. Furthermore, the most popular birth-control device, the condom, has long been as available as aspirin or cigarettes, and certainly has been used by men of all social classes. When one bears in mind the fact that the poor have no difficulty in gaining access to illegal narcotics (despite their obvious "unavailability"), and that the affluent had drastically reduced their fertility before present-day contraceptive methods were available, one must recognize and take into account a motivational component in nonuse and inefficient use of contraceptives. Indeed, were relative lack of demand on the part of the poor not a principal factor, it would be difficult to explain why such an important "market" for birth-control materials—legal or illegal—would have escaped the attention of enterprising businessmen or bootleggers. In any event, any estimate based on the assumption that all poor women in the reproductive group "want" birth-control information and materials and that virtually all "need" publicly supported services that will provide them—including women with impaired fecundity, women who have sexual intercourse rarely or not at all, women who object on religious grounds, and women who are already using birth-control methods—would seem to be seriously misleading as a guide for our government in its efforts to control population growth.

Moreover, the proposal for government sponsorship takes no account of the possible advantages of alternative means of reaching that part of the "market" that may not be optimally served at present. For example, competitive pricing, better marketing, and a program of advertising could make it possible for many groups in the population who are now being counted as "targets" for government efforts to purchase contraceptives of various kinds. When one bears in mind the fact that an important reason for nonuse or lack of access to contraceptives may be some sort of conflict situation (between husband and wife, adolescent child and parent, and so on), it becomes apparent that the impersonal and responsive marketplace is a far better agency for effecting smooth social change than is a far-flung national bureaucracy loaded with well-meaning but often blundering "health workers." The government could doubtless play an initial stimulating and facilitating role in relation to private industry, without duplicating, on a welfare basis, functions that might be more efficiently handled in the marketplace.

Would the Policy Have Side Effects?

The possible inadvisability of having the government become a direct purveyor of birth-control materials to poverty groups becomes more clear when we consider some of the risks involved in such a course of action.

Even if the goal of reducing family size were completely and widely accepted by the poorer and less well educated sectors of the population, we should not assume that the general public would necessarily view a policy concerned with the means and practice of birth control (in any social group) as it views ordinary medical care—that is, as being morally neutral and obviously "desirable." Birth control is related to sexual behavior, and, in all viable societies, sexual behavior is regulated by social institutions. It is thus an oversimplification to think that people will be unmindful of what are, for them at least, the moral implications of changes in the conditions under which sexual intercourse is possible, permissible, or likely. An issue such as distribution of pills to teen-age girls runs a collision course with norms about premarital relations for young girls—norms that, in turn, relate to the saliency of marriage and motherhood as a woman's principal career and to the consequent need for socially created restrictions on free sexual access if an important inducement to marriage is not to be lost. Only if viable careers alternative to marriage existed for women would the lessening of controls over sexual behavior outside of marriage be unrelated to women's lifetime opportunities, for such opportunities would be independent of the marriage market and, a fortiori, independent of sexual bargaining. But such independence clearly does not exist. Hence, when the government is told that it will be resolving a "medical" problem if it makes birth-control pills available to teen-agers, it is being misled into becoming the protagonist in a sociologically based conflict between short-run feminine impulses and long-run feminine interests—a conflict that is expressed both in relations between parents and children and in relations between the sexes. This sociological conflict far transcends the "medical" issue of whether or not birth-control services should be made widely available.

Actually, the issue of sexual morality is only one among many potentially explosive aspects of direct federal involvement in family-planning programs for the poor. Others come readily to mind, such as the possibility that the pill and other physiological methods could have long-run, serious side effects, or that racial organizations could seize on the existence of these programs as a prime example of "genocide." Eager promoters of the suggested programs tend to brush such problems aside as trivial, but the problems, like the issue of sexual morality, cannot be wished away, for they are quite patently there.[9] There *are* risks involved in all drug-taking, and it is recognized that many of the specific ones involved in long-term ingestion of the pill may not be discovered for many years. No one today can say that these are less than, equal to, or greater than the normal risks of pregnancy and childbirth. Equally, a class-directed birth-control program, whatever its intent, is open to charges of genocide that are difficult to refute. Such a program cannot fail to appear to single out the disadvantaged as the "goat," all the while implying that the very considerable "planned" fertility of most Americans inexplicably requires no government attention at all.

Population Policy for Americans

It seems clear that the suggested policy of poverty-oriented birth-control programs does not make sense as a welfare measure. It is also true that, as an inhibitor of population growth, it is inconsequential and trivial. It does not touch the principal cause of such growth in the United

States—namely, the reproductive behavior of the majority of Americans who, under present conditions, want families of more than three children and thereby generate a growth rate far in excess of that required for population stability. Indeed, for most Americans the "family planning" approach, concentrating as it does on the distribution of contraceptive materials and services, is irrelevant, because they already know about efficient contraception and are already "planning" their families. It is thus apparent that any policy designed to influence reproductive behavior must not only concern itself with all fecund Americans (rather than just the poor) but must, as well, relate to family-size goals (rather than just to contraceptive means). In addition, such a policy cannot be limited to matters affecting contraception (or even to matters affecting gestation and parturition, such as abortion), but must, additionally, take into account influences on the formation and dissolution of heterosexual unions.[19]

What kinds of reproductive policies can be pursued in an effort to reduce long-term population growth? The most important step toward developing such new policies is to recognize and understand the existing ones, for we already have influential and coercive policies regarding reproductive behavior. Furthermore, these existing policies relate not merely to proscriptions (legal or informal) regarding certain means of birth control (like abortion) but also to a definition of reproduction as a primary societal end and to an organization of social roles that draws most of the population into reproductive unions.

The existence of such pronatalist policies becomes apparent when we recall that, among human beings, population replacement would not occur at all were it not for the complex social organization and system of incentives that encourage mating, pregnancy, and the care, support, and rearing of children. These institutional mechanisms are the pronatalist "policies" evolved unconsciously over millennia to give societies a fertility sufficient to offset high mortality: The formation and implementation of antinatalist policies must be based, therefore, on an analysis and modification of the existing pronatalist policies. It follows, as well, that antinatalist policies will not necessarily involve the introduction of coercive measures. In fact, just the opposite is the case. Many of these policies will entail a *lifting* of pressures *to* reproduce, rather than an *imposition* of pressures *not* to do so. In order to understand this point let us consider briefly our present-day pronatalism.

It is convenient to start with the family, because pronatalism finds its most obvious expression in this social institution. The pronatalism of the family has many manifestations, but among the most influential and universal are two: the standardization of both the male and the female sexual roles in terms of reproductive functions, obligations, and activities, and the standardization of the occupational role of women—half of the popula-

19. K. Davis and J. Blake, *Econ. Develop. Cult. Change* 4, 211 (1956).

tion—in terms of child-bearing, child-rearing, and complementary activities. These two "policies" insure that just about everyone will be propelled into reproductive unions, and that half of the population will enter such unions as a "career"—a life's work. Each of the two "policies" is worth considering.

With regard to sex roles, it is generally recognized that potential human variability is greater than is normally permitted *within* each sex category. Existing societies have tended to suppress and extinguish such variability and to standardize sexual roles in ways that imply that all "normal" persons will attain the status of parents. This coercion takes many forms, including one-sided indoctrination in schools, legal barriers and penalties for deviation, and the threats of loneliness, ostracism, and ridicule that are implied in the unavailability of alternatives. Individuals who—by temperament, health, or constitution—do not fit the ideal sex-role pattern are nonetheless coerced into attempting to achieve it, and many of them do achieve it, at least to the extent of having demographic impact by becoming parents.

Therefore, a policy that sought out the ways in which coercion regarding sex roles is at present manifesting itself could find numerous avenues for relieving the coercion and for allowing life styles different from marriage and parenthood to find free and legitimatized expression. Such a policy would have an effect on the content of expectations regarding sex roles as presented and enforced in schools, on laws concerning sexual activity between consenting adults, on taxation with respect to marital status and number of children, on residential building policies, and on just about every facet of existence that is now organized so as exclusively to favor and reward a pattern of sex roles based on marriage and parenthood.

As for the occupational roles of women, existing pressures still attempt to make the reproductive and occupational roles coterminus for all women who elect to marry and have children. This rigid structuring of the wife-mother position builds into the entire motivational pattern of women's lives a tendency to want at least a moderate-size family. To understand this point one must recognize that the desired number of children relates not simply to the wish for a family of a particular size but relates as well to a need for more than one or two children if one is going to enjoy "family life" over a significant portion of one's lifetime. This need is increased rather than lessened by improved life expectancy. Insofar as women focus their energies and emotions on their families, one cannot expect that they will be satisfied to play their only important role for a diminishing fraction of their lives, or that they will readily regard make-work and dead-end jobs as a substitute for "mothering." The notion that most women will "see the error of their ways" and decide to have two-child families is naive, since few healthy and energetic women will be so misguided as to deprive themselves of most of the rewards society has to offer them and choose a situation that allows them neither a life's work outside the home nor one within it. Those who do deprive themselves in this fashion are, in effect, taking the brunt of the still existing maladjustment between the roles of women and the reproductive needs of society. In a society oriented around achievement and accomplishment, such women are exceptionally vulnerable to depression, frustration, and a sense of futility, because they are being blocked from a sense of fulfillment both at home and abroad.

In sum, the problem of inhibiting population growth in the United States cannot be dealt with in terms of "family-planning needs" because this country is well beyond the point of "needing" birth control methods. Indeed, even the poor seem not to be a last outpost for family-planning attention. If we wish to limit our growth, such a desire implies basic changes in the social organization of reproduction that will make nonmarriage, childlessness, and small (two-child) families far more prevalent than they are now. A new policy, to achieve such ends, can take advantage of the antinatalist tendencies that our present institutions have suppressed. This will involve the lifting of penalties for antinatalist behavior rather than the "creation" of new ways of life. This behavior already exists among us as part of our covert and deviant culture, on the one hand, and our elite and artistic culture, on the other. Such antinatalist tendencies have also found expression in feminism, which has been stifled in the United States by means of systematic legal, educational, and social pressures concerned with women's "obligations" to create and care for children. A fertility-control policy that does not take into account the need to alter the present structure of reproduction in these and other ways merely trivializes the problem of population control and misleads those who have the power to guide our country toward completing the vital revolution.[20]

Zero Population Growth*

FRANK W. NOTESTEIN

Zero population growth, a platitude, sales slogan or urgent goal, has caught the public by storm—and included in that public are many biologists and economists, as well as a considerable number of sociologists and demographers.

20. I make grateful acknowledgment to the Ford Foundation for support of the research presented in this article and to the National Institutes of Health (general research support grant 1501-TR-544104) for assistance to Statistical Services, School of Public Health, University of California, Berkeley. I am also indebted to Kingsley Davis, whose critical comments and helpful suggestions have greatly advanced my thinking. The Roper Center and the Gallup Poll kindly supplied me with polling data.
* Reprinted from *Population Index*, 36 (October/December, 1970), pp. 444–452, by permission of the publisher.

From one point of view, favoring zero population growth is somewhat like favoring the laws of motion. Anyone who knows how to use a table of logarithms must be aware that in the long run the average rate of population growth will approach zero as a limit. If, for example, the world's population had grown at its present rate since the beginning of the Christian era, the water content of the human race would fill a sphere having a radius more than ten times that of the earth. Zero growth is, then, not simply a desirable goal; it is the only possibility in a finite world. One cannot object to people who favor the inevitable.

There is another group that values zero population growth because it is a powerful sales slogan. They are willing to accept, even to promote, the slogan, despite its ambiguity, because of the energy and resources it brings to the subject of population. Some of these supporters foster the popular impression that population growth could be stopped quickly by acceptable means if only the public were alerted to the dangers of the situation; and a few of them advance this line despite their private opinions to the contrary. They justify this lack of candor on the grounds that egregious overstatement is necessary to arouse public interest. They seem to feel that it takes massive advertising to sell both soap and the ecological necessity for a prompt end to population growth. With that I am inclined to agree. But it is a sad day when we see professionally expert distortions of the truth peddled to the public under the highest scientific auspices, as if truth can be fostered best by untruth. When scientists become concerned with reform, as I think duty indeed requires, they will at their peril abandon the ardent respect for truth that lies at the basis of their professions. It is hard enough to stick to the truth when one tries. Fortunately, this huckstering group is only a small part of those who see zero population growth as a slogan that arouses interest in objectives perceived to be both timely and important. To this there can be no objection. It is our obligation to stick to the truth, but we are not compelled to be dull about it.

Many of its most earnest advocates obviously see zero population growth as more than a slogan, and more than a platitude about long-run objectives. They want, or at least some of them want, zero growth, if not yesterday, at least now. They want it, moreover, if not on any terms, at least with the sense of urgency that makes them willing to accept many second- and third-order effects without careful examination. It is to these questions that we must turn our most careful attention. This means that we must ask with what urgency it is necessary to seek zero growth under varying circumstances. What are the advantages and disadvantages of attaining the goal with varying speeds, and what are the advantages and disadvantages of using various methods for its attainment? The assessment of the means is quite as important as the assessment of the goal.

There may be different answers for the technologically more developed and less developed countries, because of differences in the severity of the problem as well as differences in the availability of means for their solution. Let us consider first the problem in developed countries, and particularly the United States.

ZPG in the Developed Regions

Here the ecologists take the hardest line. Some of them seem to be saying that we now stand in mortal danger if our population continues to grow; indeed, that we already have too much population and should start reducing the size. On matters of resources, energy, and ecology I am out-side of my professional field, but I have read some and listened more, and I find these ecologists' case wholly unpersuasive. There are no substantial limits in sight either in raw materials or in energy that alterations in the price structures, product substitution, anticipated gains in technology and pollution control cannot be expected to solve.[1] Subject to one condition, my statement seems to be in agreement with the overwhelming weight of professional opinion. The limitation arises from the fact that on the side of resources and technology we can look ahead only about a generation in terms of specific technology and known raw materials. Obviously our human interests run much farther into the future; but we cannot spell out the nature of a technology not yet developed. One can, however, on the assumption of an ordered world, reasonably predict immensely powerful developments based on cheap and virtually unlimited energy, and, thanks partly to that, on an enormously expanded availability of conventional and new raw materials.

Much of the pessimistic argument is based on the idea that there are nonrenewable resources in our finite world. This seems to me to miss the point. Basically resources are not material; they are socially defined. Coal did not become a resource until a few centuries ago. It is barely one hundred years since petroleum had any but medical and magical uses. Nuclear energy is only beginning to become a resource, although it has almost unlimited prospects. We talk of diminishing returns from non-renewable resources, but so far as I know almost all materials usually put in that category have declined in relative worth. Even with modern ma-chinery it no longer pays to clear land in the United States. Indeed, land has never been so abundant. The fact is that basically we have only one

---

1. The very extensive literature is summarized in a nutshell by R. Philip Hammond in a letter to *Science* 167(3924):1439, March 13, 1970, reading in part as follows: "Even 20 x 10⁹ people, each producing 20 kilowatts of heat (twice the U.S. average), would add only 1/300 of the present atmospheric heat load. This would raise the average temperature of the earth by about 0.25°. . . . At an energy budget of 20 kilowatts per person, we could maintain a worldwide living standard near the present U.S. level even when we have exhausted our high-grade mineral resources. We could do this without placing an impossible heat load on the earth for a very large popula-tion, but not for an 'unlimited' one."

nonrenewable resource, and that is space. Otherwise, mankind's basic resources are knowledge and skill, mainly of the organizational kind.

Nor do I share in that ocean of guilt now flooding the literature because our small fraction of the world's population consumes the lion's share of the world's resources. I hope our share becomes smaller as others gain, but I do not want a reduction of our per capita consumption. Thanks, indeed, to the high consumption of the developed world we have generated the knowledge and techniques that have greatly expanded both the supplies and the reserves of such raw materials in the world. There has often been outrageous waste but, on balance, our heavy use is expanding the world's resources, not diminishing them. We can get into intricate discussions about whether the more developed regions have paid enough for the raw materials they have purchased from the less developed regions,[2] but we cannot fail to see that substantial reductions of our purchases from those regions would bring them to economic chaos and greatly retard their development. Our sin is not use. Rather, it is the failure to pay the costs of use by avoiding pollution and by recycling minerals instead of further degrading them. I think it is time that social scientists look at resources in the same dynamic terms with which they have become accustomed recently to study population.

If we consider the evidence, not just the inchoate fears, there is not the slightest indication that per capita income in the United States would be consequentially different if we had 50 or 100 million more people than we have, or 50 or 100 million fewer people. At present, the costs of both energy and raw materials represent such a small proportion of our total costs that they could be drastically increased with a negligible effect on per capita income.

Moreover, the current excitement about the size of population as a cause of pollution is almost completely without merit, save in the sense that there can be no pollution without polluters. That there is severe pollution is all too evident; but it is equally evident that pollution is related almost exclusively to mismanagement and to our high standard of living. It is related negligibly to our numbers. If we had half the population and the same per capita income, we would have much the same kind of urban concentration and much the same local pollution. Australia is sparsely populated but has 80 per cent of its people concentrated in huge cities, and has much the same kind of smog and other pollution as do we.

Moreover, it is silly to suggest that reductions in population would drastically help in attacking pollution while we continue to raise our per capita incomes. There has been a vast increase in use of electricity in this country since World War II—a fact which has worried those concerned

2. By more developed regions, I mean Europe, the Soviet Union, Japan, Northern America, temperate South America, Australia and New Zealand. The remainder of the world comprises the less developed regions.

with heat and air pollution. But if we wished to achieve the per capita use of electricity of 1960 without increasing the total produced above the 1940 level, we would need to reduce our United States population below 25 million. Pollution control of all kinds will involve social and economic changes of considerable magnitude, but manipulation of the numbers of people in the society to solve this problem is probably not a realistically open option.

Nor, incidentally, does the exhortation that people should stop aspiring to lift their standards of living come gracefully from college professors, already sitting comfortably in the top ten per cent of the income distribution of the richest nation on earth. I doubt that we members of the international jet set will be very effective in telling others that they should not aspire to live half as well as we do, lest pollution destroy our narrowly balanced ecology.

In political terms, relating pollution to population may have done harm to a serious attack on both pollution and population growth. It weakens interest in the present by concentrating on a distant goal. The effective approach to pollution is to make the polluters pay, and to start doing so as soon as possible. This will cost all of us money, for we are all polluters. We also need research on a vastly increased scale. That, too, is expensive. Particularly, we need research in ecology. It is time for some solid information to replace the bad dreams of the enthusiasts, their yearnings for traditional biological equilibria, and their reasoning by analogy. It is a distraction from an immediate attack on pollution to concentrate attention on the importance of stopping population growth in, say, 20, 30 or 50 years. Similarly, it is a distraction from legitimate concern for the nation's population policy to base the attack on ecological ghost stories instead of the actual inhumanities of our reproductive process. The present population-pollution axis, by raising false issues, deters rather than helps realistic and urgently needed efforts in both fields.

My own interest in speeding the end of population growth in the United States is based on much less urgent problems than the constraints of dwindling resources and energy or the risk of insoluble ecological problems. It is clear that growth must stop sometime, both here and in the world as a whole. It does not seem that we are likely to grow in national effectiveness by virtue of increasing numbers. At least, I have difficulties thinking of any national need for which we do not have enough population to provide the economies of large-scale production. On esthetic grounds it seems to me that we should avoid becoming a highly crowded nation. Europe is much more densely settled, but we are a more mobile people, and more space will almost certainly add to our enjoyment. I would like to come to zero population growth, but with no great haste and without making important sacrifices in the process of accomplishing it.

It is also clear that some costs will be entailed if we come to an end of growth. I shall not detail them, because they are well set out in the prewar literature on stagnation. I doubt that the costs of stopping growth will be nearly as high as then envisioned. Much has since been learned about managing the level of economic activity. But some adjustments will have to be made. Our entire economy has developed in a period of population growth with the relatively young populations that high birth rates produce. Nevertheless, this is an adjustment that must be made sometime unless we start lifting the death rates of the oldsters drastically—a proposal with which I have an understandable lack of sympathy. In short, I would like to see population growth come to a gradual end in the United States. But my lack of a sense of great urgency makes me unwilling to accept drastic means such as those often proposed by the people to whom the problems of energy, resources, and ecological protection have high saliency.

I would be happy if, for example, we could reach replacement level of reproduction in 10 or 15 years and stay there until the end of the century. After that I would have no objection to an intrinsic rate of natural decrease of a quarter of one per cent for a time. If we did this, we would still come to a maximum population of something like 300 millions in some 70 to 90 years. These to me are acceptable goals as to numbers. They are not very important, however, compared to the means for their attainment.

The rates of population change and the factors determining them are very much more important than the size of the population. Family planning represents a new and important freedom in the world. It will surely be a happy day when parents can have and can avoid having children, as they see fit. We're coming close to realization of that goal—a goal that has given new dignity and new importance to the individual. We have not yet arrived at it. Larry Bumpass and Charles F. Westoff[3] have shown that the proportion of unwanted births was substantial in the first half of the 1960's. It was very much higher in the lower educational groups, in the lower income groups, and, partly as a consequence of this, among Negroes. It is a matter of major importance that this kind of new freedom to choose, now existing for the bulk of the population, be extended to its most disadvantaged parts. If it were extended, reproduction would be brought fairly close to the replacement level. However, I would advocate the right to choose even if I thought the demographic consequences would be highly adverse, because it will always remain possible to manipulate the environment in which the choice is made.

I happen also to favor the repeal of laws against abortion in the belief that parents should control the destiny of the nonviable products of their bodies. I do not favor it on demographic grounds, and hope that when

---

3. Larry Bumpass and Charles F. Westoff. The "perfect contraceptive" population: extent and implications of unwanted fertility in the United States are considered. Unpublished manuscript. [Editor's note: The paper was published in *Science* 169(3951):1177–1182. Sept. 18, 1970.]

abortion becomes legal, no one will advocate it as anything but the personal tragedy which it inevitably is. One may expect, however, that easy abortion will further reduce the birth rate.

It is not at all beyond belief that, with contraceptives of ever increasing efficiency and legal abortion, fertility may fall below the replacement level. And, of course, it also may not. But, lacking a sense of urgency in matters of population size and believing in the importance of voluntary parenthood as a human freedom, I hope we do not accept drastic proposals to reward or penalize reproduction. We should wait at least until all of the population has ready access to effective contraception, and we can see under these conditions how the trend is going.

It seems to me dangerous to endeavor to penalize reproduction by various economic constraints because almost certainly the political process would result in maximum pressures on the most defenseless sectors of the population. There is too often willingness on the part of the bulk of the population to blame its troubles on the poor and ignorant minorities. But economic sanctions taken against the poor to compel a reduction of fertility seldom work. Generally, fertility does not fall in response to the lash of poverty. The most fertile sectors of the population will reduce their fertility with maximum speed if they can have easy access to competent contraception and the kind of support that brings them into the mainstream of the economy and society. At least in the present temper of the times, I would rather accept growth than step up the constraints which we have reason to expect would fall most heavily on the poor and their children.

It must also be recognized that the actual adoption of drastic programs designed to restrict fertility would, if they were successful, contain the seeds of their early reversal. If we could imagine a program that would drop the crude birth rate to the crude death rate in five years, we would have to imagine, as Tomas Frejka[4] has shown, a net reproduction rate of less than 0.6—not a two-child, but a one-child family—which if maintained for a few years would evoke the specter of rapid population decline, cries of race suicide, and a turnabout. It is to be noted that no nation, however heavily populated and poor, has adopted a policy for population decline. At best they want to bring the rates of growth down to two or even one percent, and just possibly to become stationary in the long run. It is interesting to note that Japan is already talking of the dangers of slow growth, that Romania repealed its liberal abortion law because of plummeting birth rates, and that in Hong Kong one hears a great deal of talk about a labor shortage. Quickly successful policies of a drastic nature would certainly contain the seeds of their own reversal. I think there is every reason to believe that the quick way to a stationary population is the gentle

---

4. Tomas Frejka. Reflections on the demographic conditions needed to establish a U.S. stationary population growth. *Population Studies* 22(3):379–397. Nov. 1968.

one, both in action and in propaganda. And herein lies the weakness of the hucksters. Their line is successful until people realize that they have been misled. Then even sensible discussion suffers, for people once burned are twice cautious.

ZPG AND THE LESS DEVELOPED REGIONS

The situation of that two-thirds of the world's population living in the less developed regions contrasts sharply with that of the United States. In general, in the less developed regions the economy rests heavily on subsistence agriculture and other extractive industries; per capita income and literacy are very low, birth rates are very high, and death rates range from the world's highest to the world's lowest, as do the densities of population. Rates of growth vary from a little under two per cent to well over three per cent. Moreover, where the increase is relatively low, as in parts of Africa, it is clear that it will rise as soon as rudimentary health protection can be introduced.

It is evident that most of these populations are already too large to rise from poverty on the basis of a traditional subsistence agriculture. Their only hope of achieving reasonable per capita incomes, literacy, and health lies in the modernization of their economies. Such modernization entails heavy investment in productive equipment, transport, education, and health. Rapid progress in this direction is considerably deterred by the necessity of meeting the costs of rapid population growth at the same time. Indeed, I think that there is grave danger that population growth will so retard economic transformation and the improvement of living conditions that there will be a breakdown of civil order in a number of large countries. This risk gravely threatens the lives of tens, perhaps scores, of millions of people.

It seems difficult to exaggerate the importance of reducing the rate of population growth as soon as possible throughout most of the less developed regions. Indeed, even the areas now viewed as too sparsely populated might well benefit from the reduction of the rate of increase. In these circumstances, wisdom may enjoin favoring development at the expense of population growth where possible. This is not the place to discuss the issue, but it is my impression that there are extremely few places in the less developed regions that would not be aided in their struggle for modernization by a slower rate of population growth.

From my point of view, then, the need for slowing population growth is vastly greater in the less developed than in the more developed regions. A rapid decline of fertility for some decades until there is even a small negative rate of increase would be desirable. But zero growth, as a meaningful proposal in the near term, is idle talk. It could be achieved only by a rise in the death rate, which no one will accept as a goal of policy for his own people. During the next century, for theoretical purposes, zero growth is not low enough, and, for practical purposes, it is too low. Although the problems of the less developed regions are much greater, unfortunately the opportunities for relevant action are far fewer than in the rest of the world.

A rather large and growing number of countries in the less developed regions have national policies designed to foster the reduction of the birth rate and thereby a slowing of population growth. But even in these countries there would be minimal support for zero population growth. Policies in support of family planning have been widely adopted because the provision of services to the citizens who want them entails few political risks, and much of the top leadership realizes that the unprecedented speed of growth is blocking efforts at development. It is one thing to favor a reduction of the pace of population increase, and another thing to ask for a complete stop. When one begins to talk about growth rates of less than one per cent, attention quickly shifts to the rate of growth of the traditional enemy or rival. Israel's victories in the Six-Day War did much to devalue large populations as a source of power; but the rivalry of numbers remains. It is possible that, among small countries, Hong Kong and Singapore would be content to stop growing fairly soon; and, among large countries, India and Pakistan might accept the idea at the level of top leadership. I can think of no other countries where this position would be accepted. Even where leadership agreed on the long-run objective, it would almost certainly wish not to advertise that fact, because more limited objectives would be expected to attract more widespread political support and serve program needs as well.

A number of scholars have been critical of people of my persuasion who advocate voluntarism through family planning as a means of slowing population growth and who have concentrated efforts on contraceptive methods, information and service. They hold that since the difficulty lies in the lack of motivation for restriction, it makes little sense to concentrate on the means while failing to strengthen the motives.

Naturally, I think that my approach respresents the first and most effective step in strengthening the motivation for fertility restriction. Obviously, there are large numbers of people who are behaving in the traditional manner, governed by the values of the traditional society. But the number is larger in the minds of the leadership than it is in reality. Surveys, trials, and national experiences show that major proportions, often, indeed, a heavy majority, of the population express an interest in limiting their fertility. To be sure, they generally want more children than are needed to maintain a stationary population. To be sure, also, many aspects of their society still foster the ideal of the large family. I am aware that values influence behavior, but I am also aware that behavior influences values. It seems to me that the example of successful fertility limitation set by those now motivated is probably the most effective means of fostering both new values and innovative behavior. Moreover, I am greatly impressed by the speed with which the restrictive behavior has spread where family planning programs have been skillfully introduced.

I am happier than the critics with the progress that has been made, possibly for two reasons. On the one hand, I view the ultimate constraints to population growth as less narrowly drawn than they do. On the other hand, in the light of the situation a decade ago, I think there has been great and accelerating progress. By contrast, I am much less hopeful than are the critics of voluntarism about the feasibility of using more drastic measures to lift incentives for the restriction of fertility. The leadership would accept them in very few countries. Indeed, even in many of the countries having policies to foster family planning, the opposition in influential parts of the leadership group remains substantial—more substantial, I think, than among the people. In the near term more drastic means will be entirely unacceptable almost everywhere.

In the less developed regions, moreover, it would, simply for administrative reasons, be impossible to introduce even such measures as fiscal sanctions and rewards. Even now, weak administration is proving more of an obstacle to the spread of family planning than lack of public interest. Almost all of the governments are far too poor and weak to carry out a drastic program. Few of them can even count the number of their births and deaths, or have more than rudimentary medical services and facilities, or social security systems. It is hard to remember how poor they are. Canada, for example, with some 21 million people, has a larger national income and federal budget than the Government of India, with more than 500 million people. It is at best idle to talk of governments in this position drastically coercing their people's reproductive behavior. They are governments that can do something to educate and lead, but, save in the most primitive matters of public order, they cannot coerce.

The inability to coerce is perhaps fortunate in this field. I think we have reason to believe that voluntarism through education and service is the most direct route, as it is certainly the most civilized.

My own reaction to zero population growth, therefore, comes out about the same way for the less developed regions as for the more developed regions. The countries that could apply drastic constraints to human fertility do not need to; the countries that need drastic constraints cannot apply them; and in any case, the path of voluntarism through family planning is likely to be both more efficient and more civilized.

If zero population growth means the downgrading of voluntarism and the strident demand for a quick end to population growth, then it will do more harm than good. If, on the other hand, it is taken as an organizing focus for research and educational efforts concerning the importance of a worldwide trend to a stationary population and the means by which it is ultimately to be achieved, then it should be enthusiastically welcomed.

Reply to Notestein*

JUDITH BLAKE

Favoring zero population growth is platitudinous, according to Notestein, as "it is the only possibility in a finite world." By this reasoning, the
human effort to control the time and manner of all sorts of inevitabilities—
the effort expended on postponing death, maintaining houses, saving
money—is also pointless. The spokesmen for ZPG do not argue that a
stationary world population will never come about without a ZPG policy,
but rather that, without directed effort, zero growth will occur only after
human numbers have greatly increased over present levels, and perhaps
then by the mechanism of high mortality instead of fertility control.

Our choice lies in the timing and manner of accomplishing a stationary population. Since this choice will doubtless color our destiny as a
species, widespread interest in the problem should not, in my opinion, be
downgraded. As observers, demographers cannot, by definition, say what
human beings, as actors, should desire for themselves or for their children.
But we can certainly inform our fellow men of the probable consequences
of a ZPG sooner rather than later, and of the fact that the timing is not
beyond our control. Indeed, I learned a share of what I have just said as a
graduate student reading Professor Notestein's articles some 18 years ago. I
believe that he has now been goaded by the popularity of the Zero Population Growth movement into taking an unreasonable position against it.

Notestein characterizes ZPG as a "powerful sales slogan." He sees
"professionally expert distortions of the truth peddled to the public under
the highest scientific auspices." The ZPG *movement* is certainly open to
this criticism, but so are movements—like family planning—that are close
to Notestein's own door. Those who live by the slogan ("Five Million
Women," "Children by Choice," "Trouble Parking??? Support Planned
Parenthood"), must be prepared to die by shinier slogans. That's the way it
crumbles, hucksterwise.

With respect to timing, Notestein asks whether ZPG is as urgent a
goal as its supporters claim. Dealing first with developed countries, he
accuses the ecologists of stating that we are "in mortal danger," from
scarcity of resources, if our population continues to grow. In refutation, he
takes the traditional position that our principal limitation is not a shortage

---

* Reprinted from *Population Index,* 36 (October/December, 1970), pp. 456–459, by
permission of the publisher.

of resources but a want of imagination: we cannot envision what technological miracles lie ahead, nor what new resources will be discovered. However, in dismissing the urgency of ZPG for developed countries, I think he underestimates the intellectual sophistication of ecology. This discipline is a long way ahead of merely bemoaning the disappearance of nonrenewable resources. Rather, it deals with the *interrelation* among resources as itself an independent limitation. In effect, the limiting factor is not a resource, or a set of resources, but rather the set of conditions under which resources can be maintained as an interrelated system. Ecology is restating Malthus. Whereas Malthus saw a factor—land—as the limiting element, ecology sees the conditions supporting environmental balance and equilibrium as imposing limits to population growth. The *deus ex machina* —technology—has turned out to be far from cost-free. Ecologists may not always be able to pinpoint the costs of massive technological intervention, but they have alerted us to the principle involved. Only a crank would deny that technology can do wonderful things, but Notestein, inconsistently, would have us believe that it is a panacea for demographic folly.

Notestein says that the current argument about population as a cause of pollution is without merit. Pollution is due to "mismanagement" and our "high standard of living." When is management to be dubbed "mismanagement"? Since he relies on price structures and the market as mechanisms of control, perhaps he can explain why these mechanisms have allowed so much "mismanagement" of the pollution problem. Whence will come the mechanisms that manage it? How far will mismanagement go before enlightened self-interest puts a stop to it? In effect, Notestein is saying that if developed countries achieved greater control over economic activity, they could sustain a larger population without pollution. Since he offers no reason why economic activity should be under such constraint, while population is given free rein, his argument is unclear. The same is true of his criticism of the level of living of developed countries. To be sure our living levels cause pollution, but little will be gained by lowering them simply to accommodate more people. Nor is it true that, in the future, we will necessarily confine ourselves to an index of living levels based on the production of goods. Clean air and water, open spaces, privacy, and quiet will increasingly be in demand, and will probably be regulated and distributed by the market, as are other scarce goods in developed societies. A "high standard of living" may thus increasingly become one that insures, at high cost, the qualities of life that we used to think were free.

Notestein's bias in favor of individual reproductive freedom, at the expense of any other values and freedoms that might get in the way, is unexplained but persistent. He advocates the "right to choose" one's family size, even if "the demographic consequences would be highly adverse, because it will always remain possible to manipulate the environment in which the choice is made." It is, of course, his privilege, as an individual, to entertain any bias he chooses. But if he is speaking as a demographer, he should recognize that it is not his job to advocate one freedom over another, or to make unsubstantiated claims about unlimited environmental manipulation. As demographers, our contribution to public policy is not to air our opinions in fields outside our own, but to tell people about the tradeoffs available to them concerning population issues.

Notestein points out correctly that as countries approach zero population growth (and frequently experience reproduction rates below unity), they back off from population limitation. He believes that this is an argument for a "go-slow" policy regarding zero growth. From the point of view of the observer, however, international reluctance is not, in and of itself, an argument against ZPG. Such reluctance is simply one of the obstacles with which a ZPG policy has to deal. Obviously, there are innumerable obstacles to the achievement of zero growth. Were this not the case, we would have it. The question for us, as demographers, is *why* nations become so skittish when the reality of population limitation is borne in upon them. What are the political and military constraints (plus all the other intra-societal constraints) that set a floor under population growth?

Equally, ZPG's aging effect on population structure cannot be regarded as axiomatically baleful. To be sure, there are doubtless intrinsically undesirable features in having a high proportion aged, features rooted in man's physiological decline with age. However, many of the undesirable features are socially induced and, in any event, the problem remains one of tradeoffs, not absolutes. We cannot have low mortality and low fertility without an aging population, and we cannot have low mortality and moderate fertility without fairly rapid growth. That is the reality of the situation. If, as seems to be agreed, population limitation is desirable our scientific interest does not require reraising the issue of its desirability at every turn. Rather, we must apprise ourselves of the forces that induce individuals and nations to accept the undesirable side effects of the desired goal, and we must examine possible ways in which the side effects can be minimized.

Taking into account that, on the average, ZPG implies a mini-family, one can make an even stronger case than Notestein's for the potential unpopularity of a stationary population, other things being equal. Birth limitation to the levels required by ZPG will confine family life to a brief period and will require, therefore, a reorganization of our present interests, activities, and goals. Otherwise, ZPG will be experienced as a poignant deprivation. The problem will be increasingly to encourage the development of alternatives to life in families, because life without them will characterize more and more of our total existence as ZPG is established. A zero population growth policy will inevitably involve some redefinition of the choices available to individuals and some change in the rewards held out to them, just as present policy (albeit implicit) directs their current choices and manipulates their existing rewards. It is important to bear in mind, however, that an anti-natalist policy would not necessarily be less "voluntaristic" than a pro-natalist one. What would be altered is not the amount of social control, but the things for which people "volunteer." This is what we call social change, and we do not ordinarily regard it as a disaster.

Notestein's support for "voluntarism" in family planning seems to be a support for voluntarism under existing and unchanging pro-natalist incentives and coercions. His version of voluntarism is precisely what leads biologists and ecologists to make many of the coercive suggestions concerning fertility control that he regards as frightening and extreme. His theoretical model contains no clue as to how reproductive motivation can be changed. Hence, non-social scientists, who also have no clue, propose that we start knocking heads together. To our biological colleagues, this suggestion looks like business, *en finale*. To Notestein, it is apparently like being the protagonist in a Greek tragedy. To me, it is only a measure of my discipline's failure so far to see the problem clearly and outline the solution. The failure, I am afraid, is not that of the ecologist but that of demographers of the Notestein stamp.

As the *coup de grâce*, Notestein not only phrases population policy in terms of coercion, but states categorically that it will put maximum pressure on the poor, rather than on other sectors. To brand all possible anti-natalist policies—regardless of content—as having the poor as the butt is not only patently inaccurate but also subversive of the rational discussion that Notestein professes to desire. It stifles all discussion on the spot, for certainly no one in academic life, or in a rich foundation, or in government, wants anyone to be able even to hint that he harbored a thought that could conceivably be interpreted perhaps to mean that the poor could be induced to do anything—even in their own interest.

In short, in his pique with the ZPG movement, Notestein tries to put the Indian sign on important problems and to spook us into thinking that they are irrelevant, impractical, or illiberal. In fact, anything but the mindless distribution of contraception in ever wider concentric circles is a "no-no." In response, I feel constrained to tell him that our field is no longer waiting for signs from on high. We have moved into the public domain, and the problems to be discussed, together with the solutions to be offered, are not the ones he alone is to choose. The days when the charter members of the Population Association of America caucused to decide what should be discussed and researched in the field are over. Demographers and others are discussing and doing research. They are as individuals acting under their own steam and with support from diverse constituencies. And they have mass exposure. Such times separate the tyros from the pro—not by fiat, nor by the laying on of well manicured hands— but by intellectual challenge. To meet this challenge one has to deliver some goods. Simply telling the world what one approves and disapproves of will no longer succeed. It will take far more than Notestein's polite but empty derogation to exorcise Paul Ehrlich.

PART IV

Social Institutions

Chapter

12

The Family:

What Is Its Future?

Will the American family survive? If so, what form or forms will it take? Hobart opens this debate with the position that although the family is changing, it remains necessary for the "development and expression of humanity." He sees four basic changes taking place (although Edwards points out, in the last article in this section, that it is unclear whether these are *causes* of change or *consequences* of change): loss of functions, increase in personal mobility, decline in status ascription and increase in status achievement, and ascendance of materialistic values which are inconsistent with such familial values as loving and caring. Despite these changes and despite the fact that the family is no longer a necessary economic unit, Hobart finds America without the family to be unthinkable. Yet, the retention of the family in a modified form depends, according to Hobart, "upon a value revolution in American society—a displacement of the now pre-eminent success, efficiency, productivity, prosperity values by the human oriented being, knowing, caring, loving values." A key to such a revolution lies in a renewal of commitment to the family. The family of the future will be a flexible unit, allowing its members to express their individuality. Mates are to be chosen on the basis of who they are, not what they can do, and there will be a renewed emphasis on being rather than doing.

Following Hobart's article is a critique by Kephart and a reply by Hobart. The criticisms and the replies are clear, but one point needs to be underscored. Kephart assails Hobart for not specifying how the renewed commitment to the family is to come about. Although Hobart replies to the other criticisms, it is noteworthy that he fails to answer on this point. It would appear that it is easier to forecast that something will occur, but it is much more difficult to specify how.

Finally, an article by Edwards is included which constitutes a critique of Hobart's position and an expression of an alternate position. Edwards admits that the family has undergone the changes suggested by Hobart, but he questions whether these have led to family instability. For each of the changes, he points out some of the positive functions they have had for the family. Thus, in Edwards' view, we are not witnessing a growth in family instability. Nor does Edwards see any signs of, or need for, the value revolution Hobart discerns as so important. Instead, he argues that what is happening, and must continue to happen, is a trend toward bringing the family more in accord with the economic system. The economic system is based on tangible rewards, while the family continues (although it is changing) to be based on affective rewards. In Edwards' view both institutions must be based on tangible rewards. The family of the future will be based on reason (presumably economic reason) rather than on "the impulse of habit."

The battle lines are clear: Hobart sees the family of the future as being more affective. Edwards sees it as more rational.

Commitment, Value Conflict and the Future of the American Family*

CHARLES W. HOBART

There are many attempts to characterize the nature of modern society: the affluent society, the other-directed society, the managerial society, the mass society, the expert society, the pluralistic society, the achieving society, the insane society. Most of these characterizations share at least one underlying assumption, that as a society we tread where man has never trod before, that there are qualitative differences between our society and earlier ones which make extrapolation on the basis of earlier societal experience unreliable at best, and often completely invalid.

One consequence is that the continued utility of many features fundamental to earlier societies becomes problematic. Examples include the segregation of sex roles, homogeneity of culture, widespread status ascription. It is both important and difficult to speculate about what further structural modifications may be in the offing. So long as an institution provides functions prerequisite to the survival of any human social system

* Reprinted from *Journal of Marriage and the Family*, Vol. 25 (November, 1963), pp. 405–412, by permission of the author and publisher.

we must think in terms not of the disappearance of the institution but of the evolution of functional alternatives.

It is in this context that the following discussion of the future of the family is set. This paper deals first with the argument that the family as we know it is becoming obsolete, and with some recent changes in social structure which are contributing to this apparent obsolescence. Second there is a discussion of value conflicts and of future societal development given continued pre-eminence of materialistic values. Finally there is consideration of bases for anticipating a value revolution which would facilitate renewed commitment to family relationships.

There is no need to cite the varied evidence which seems to suggest the progressive obsolescence of the family as we know it. Some maintain that the family, no longer an economic necessity, is an inefficient, artificial, arbitrary, outmoded structuring of relationships. Barrington Moore, in his provocative "Thoughts of the Future of the Family" protests such "obsolete and barbaric features" as "the obligation to give affection as a duty to a particular set of persons on account of the accident of birth," "the exploitation of socially sanctioned demands for gratitude, when the existing social situation no longer generates any genuine feeling of warmth."[1] Moore concludes that "one fine day human society may realize that the part-time family, already a prominent part of our social landscape, has undergone a qualitative transformation into a system of mechanized and bureaucratized child rearing" since "an institutional environment can be . . . warmer than a family torn by obligations its members resent."[2]

In contradiction to this position, it is the thesis of this paper that though the family is from some value perspectives an outdated structural unit, defined in terms of responsibility and commitment it remains a necessary condition for the development and expression of humanity. Furthermore, if it in fact is such a necessary condition, concern for its effective survival should help to shape the course of the future development of society.

It must be admitted that the family is undergoing changes, both within itself and in relation to the rest of society which tend significantly to weaken its solidarity. At least four of these changes may be mentioned: 1) loss of functions; 2) increased personal mobility within society; 3) the decline of status ascription and the increase in status achievement; and 4) the ascendancy of materialistic values.

1. In regard to loss of family functions, note that not only has the emergence of separate and distinct institutions accomplished the functional depletion of the once omnifunctional family, but active family membership

---

1. Barrington Moore, "Thoughts on the Future of the Family," in Maurice R. Stein, Arthur J. Vidich and David M. White, Eds., *Identity and Anxiety,* Glencoe, Ill.: The Free Press, 1960, pp. 393–94.
2. *Ibid.,* p. 401.

has become optional in our day. Social status placement is primarily based on occupational achievement, rather than family ascription. There are now no imperious deterrents to a solitary family-alienated existence; all necessary services are available commercially. In fact, family responsibilities today distract and detract from single-minded pursuit of highly prized personal success in most occupations—scholarly, commercial, or professional.

Americans *are* getting married with greater frequency than ever before, a reflection, perhaps, of the increasing significance of companionship and emotional security within the family for people today. But if they marry for companionship and security, the high level of divorce rates[3] suggests that Americans seek divorce when they fail to attain these goals.

2. The rate of spatial mobility of Americans today is remarkable: in the last decade one half of all families in the States have moved every five years. Some consequences of this unprecedented movement have been 1) increase in the number and variety of readjustments which a family must make; 2) radical loss of support of the family by neighborhood, friendship, and kinship primary groups; and 3) weakened discouragement of separation and divorce by these groups. Thus increased mobility may be seen as 1) precipitating more crises and adjustment difficulties within the family, 2) stripping the family of external support at the very time of heightened stress, and 3) weakening the opposition to traditionally disapproved means of resolving difficulties, such as divorce.

Since mobility involves physical removal from the informal controls exercised by primary groups, Howard S. Becker's conceptualization of commitment becomes relevant to this discussion. Becker conceives of commitment as an act, consciously or unconsciously accomplished, whereby a person involves additional interests of his ("side bets") directly in action he is engaged in, which were originally extraneous to this action. Becker emphasizes that the process is relative to the values or valuables of the person.[4] I am emphasizing its relativity to the importance of the reference groups in whose eyes he stands to gain or lose on his "side bets."

In Becker's terms, then, commitment in marriage was once strengthened by making side bets involving staking one's reputation on one's trustworthiness, loyalty, fidelity in marriage. These bets were secured by the scrutiny of unchanging reference groups: close neighbors, fellow parishioners, occupational associates. The increasing speed of physical mobility as well as the growth of value confusion and of heterogeneous sub-cultures have tended to sharply depreciate the coin with which side bets to marital commitment were once made. This devaluation further weakens the stability of marriage.

---

3. See, for example, U.S. Bureau of the Census, *Statistical Abstract of the United States,* Washington, D.C., 1961, p. 48.
4. Howard S. Becker, "Notes on the Concept of Commitment," *American Journal of Sociology,* 66 (July, 1960), p. 35.

3. Another trend in American society which appears to have a powerful potential for further weakening the family is suggested by the phrases "proliferation of associations," "personality market," "individuation." These suggest a growing contrast with the recent past when most close relationships of people were traditionally defined ascribed relationships with mate and children, with other kin, with neighbors, with fellow parishioners. Today, more and more relationships are achieved. They are "cultivated" in school, at work, in voluntary associations; they are promoted through friends and professional or business contacts.

The significant point is that rather than being ascribed, and thus traditionally defined and delimited, relationships are now more often achieved and thus more idiosyncratic and potentially boundless. Herein lies their threat to the family, for they, like many other aspects of contemporary life, may readily infringe upon family claims, may alienate members from the family. Note that at one time only men, as sole bread winners of the family, were vulnerable to these possibilities, in work and voluntary association situations. Their colleagues in these situations were other men, thus posing no threat to devotion to the wife at home. But with the spectacular increase in the employment of married as well as unmarried women, both sexes are vulnerable, and increasingly their work and voluntary association relationships *may* endanger the marriage bond. With this bond under greater stress, the decline of the primary group discouragements to divorce becomes increasingly consequential.

The proliferation of achieved, and thus potentially unlimited relationships for both men and women is by no means exclusively dysfunctional. Restriction of "close" relationships to a small circle of sharply limited ascribed relationships tends to be delimiting as far as growth of the person is concerned. Mead and others have demonstrated that the personality is a social product, and personality growth can occur only in relationships. Hence a small circle of ascribed relationships tends to be stultifying in at least three ways. In the first place, since the limits of an ascribed relationship are traditionally defined in terms of convention and appropriateness, the personality potential in an ascribed relationship is far more limited than in the more open, uncircumscribed achieved relationship. Second, since the circle of ascribed relationships is more homogeneous than the range of possible achieved relationships, the latter may awaken a broader range of latent potentialities within the person. Third, the circle of ascribed relationships may soon be rather thoroughly explored and exhausted, especially given geographical immobility, early in life. By contrast, the opportunities for new achieved relationships may last until death and may be limited only by the activity and involvement of the person. Thus it seems that the increase in proportion of achieved relationships is a necessary condition for actualization of more human potential in society.

I noted above that any achieved relationship, particularly a cross sex one, may jeopardize the marriage bond and perhaps parental responsibilities. Yet, given extensive and rapid spatial and vertical mobility, almost all relationships tend to be shifting sand, lacking in dependability and security, providing no basis on which to build a life. The very impermanence of these manifold relationships heightens the need for *some* relationships which are dependable; which can be, invariably, counted on; which will not be weakened or destroyed by the incessant moving about of people. Such secure relationships can only be found, given the structural peculiarities for our society today, within the family. Actualization of this security within the family depends upon commitment, a commitment symbolized in the phrase "in sickness and in health, for better or for worse, for richer or for poorer, till death do you part."

4. A final source of instability within the family is the value confusion which appears to be one of the hallmarks of our age. The crucial significance of values depends upon the fact that man is a being who must *live* his life since it is not lived for him by imperious drives or instincts, as Fromm says.[5] Man, thus emancipated from the security of nature's control, needs human community to humanize him and to structure his choice between the alternatives which confront him. The basis for choice is a set of values, generated in society, in terms of which choice priorities may be assigned.

One linkage between values and the family lies in the fact that the original unit of human community and the universal humanizing unit of all societies is the family. It is in the family that many of the most important values, bases for choice, are learned. The family not only transmits values; it is predicated on, and in fact symbolizes some of the distinctively "human" values: tenderness, love, concern, loyalty.

Man's capacity for consistent and responsible action depends on his being able to orient himself and to act on the basis of commitment to values; thus a certain level of value consistency is important. But a prominent feature of American society today is a pervasive value conflict. The family depends upon and symbolizes "inefficient values" of being, knowing, caring, loving, unconditionally committing oneself. These values are incompatible with the urban industrial values of production, achievement, exchange, quantification, efficiency, success. Simultaneous unlimited commitment to people—in love and concern—and to achievement, success, prosperity, is impossible. The resultant tension in a society which pays uncritical lip-service to both sets of values is disruptive and potentially incapacitating. It tends toward resolution, in favor of the "inhuman" urban values. Fromm has noted that as a society we tend to *love things,* and *use people,* rather than the reverse. And Whyte has remarked that the "organization men" he interviewed seemed to prefer to sacrifice success in marriage to career success, if forced to choose between them.

---

5. Erich Fromm, *The Sane Society,* New York: Holt, Rinehart, and Winston, 1960, p. 24.

This value confusion is, of course, a source of instability within the American family. A family presumes unlimited commitment between family members: "till death do you part" between husband and wife, "all we can do for the kids" on the part of parents toward children. But the priority of these love and concern values is directly challenged by success and achievement values which may imply that status symbols are more important than babies; that what a child *achieves* is more important than what he *is;* that what we *own* is more important than what we *are.* Thus the stage is set for conflict between a success oriented husband and a child-people welfare oriented wife, or for a rather inhuman family which values things over people, and which may raise children who have difficulty living down this experience of worthlessness.

The question may be raised whether what one does versus what one is are polar characteristics, or is not what one does a part of what one is? Purely logically the latter is of course true. But social psychologically speaking there are significant differences in the way these two value emphases influence the process and consequences of parent-child interaction. Briefly, parents who emphasize *doing* respond to their children in terms of conditional love, and the child comes to feel that he is unacceptable unless he conforms, and also unless he meets certain "production quotas." By contrast, parents who emphasize *being* respond to their children in terms of unconditional love, and their children come to feel that they are intrinsically acceptable and love worthy. Successful performance is thus a matter of much more anxious preoccupation for the former than for the latter ideal type of child.

This review of some changes in family and society—loss of functions, increased mobility, increased status achievement, and ascendancy of materialistic values—has pointed out that some of these changes have functional as well as dysfunctional consequences. What are the likely prospects for the future? Which way will the value conflict be resolved? What are the preconditions, the prospects, and the probable consequences of more explicit self-conscious commitment to the family?

Let us look first at some further consequences of the value predicament in our society today. Consider the emerging character type in America. Torn from family commitments by the demands of urban living—dedication to efficiency, success, etc., modern man is often alienated from himself and from others.[6] To escape the anxious awareness of

6. A few recent titles in the growing literature on alienation in modern man include: *American Journal of Psychoanalysis,* A Symposium on Alienation and the Search for Identity, Vol. 21, no. 2, 1961; Eric and Mary Josephson, *Man Alone,* Alienation in Modern Society, New York: Dell Publishing Co., 1962; Robert Nisbet, *The Quest for Community,* New York: Oxford University Press, 1953; Fritz Pappenheim, *The Alienation of Modern Man,* New York: Monthly Review Press, 1959; Maurice Stein, *The Eclipse of Community,* Princeton: Princeton University Press, 1960; Maurice Stein, Arthur Vidich and David White, Eds., *Identity and Anxiety,* Survival of the Person in Mass Society, Glencoe, Ill.: Free Press, 1960; Allen Wheelis, *The Quest for Identity,* New York: W. W. Norton, 1958.

his inability to express his humanity and to relate to others through his role as a functionary in a bureaucratic system, he is tempted to identify with the system, becoming, in Mills' terms, a "cheerful robot."[7] In Riesman's terms he is the "other-directed,"[8] forever adapting to the demands of the situation, of the people at hand; in Fromm's terms he is the "personality package," an exchangeable commodity to be sold for success.[9]

The ecology of the American city likewise reflects this value pattern and has important consequences for the family. Most cities can be characterized as central places for the merchandizing of goods and credits. They are the center of great webs of communication and transportation through which our economy of exchange functions. The natural areas of the city are determined by land values: the allocation of people and facilities is in accord with who can pay. Thus it is not for the family that the city functions, and it is not in accord with the values foundational to the family that people and facilities are located. Because the city is not a livable habitat for family units, families have fled to the suburbs. Here children can play, but here too, mothers are often stranded, driven to distraction by childish babbling from which there is no escape, and fathers are missing, early and late, commuting.

From an institutional perspective the family is weakening, and again our value confusion is involved. No longer a necessary economic unit, the family continues to provide for the socialization of children and for companionship. Yet even in these two remaining areas the family is losing significance. Children have more and more been turned over to schools, and, in some instances, nursery schools and Sunday schools, for a major portion of their socialization, as parents occupy themselves with other activities. More significant than the time turned over to such institutional socialization of children is the responsibility that parents more than willingly relinquish or do not recognize as theirs. There appears to be little concern in America today that the shaping of a human life, a human personality, a future of happiness or hell, which is best accomplished in a primary group, is turned over ever earlier and for longer periods to secondary, impersonal, social agencies. In these agencies children can only be "handled" and manipulated in groups, rather than cared for as individuals.

Leisure time is used by some to cultivate companionship with wife and children. But for many it appears that what time is spent together is seldom spent primarily in *being* together, but rather in *doing* simultaneously: watching T.V., going someplace, being entertained. Leisure is thus

---

7. C. Wright Mills, *The Sociological Imagination*, New York: Oxford University Press, 1959, p. 171.
8. David Riesman, Nathan Glazer, Reuel Denny, *The Lonely Crowd*, New York: Doubleday Anchor Books, 1956.
9. Erich Fromm, *The Art of Loving*, New York: Harper and Bros., 1956, p. 3.

often an escape from the tension of urban life which pulls people in different directions, a distraction from "the great emptiness."[10]

The family persists because people want and need the family. The problem is that, having often lost the family in its meaningful sense as a primary commitment, people want a fantasy; they compulsively seek security. They get disillusionment.[11] Pulled apart by the value conflict of our society they want both personal loving involvement and social efficient achievement, and often they can commit themselves to neither. Thus straddling both ways of life, they can only distract themselves from their predicament.

This admittedly pessimistic overview forces us to confront a further question. What kind of a *future* is in store for our society? Will time tolerate the tension of values, will it tolerate the embarrassing persistence of the family? Some current trends suggest the resolution of the tension in favor of materialistic urban values which place a premium on man, the efficient doer.

To be more explicit, the character type of the future, according to some, will be the true functionary, the "cheerful robot." "Human engineering" seems determined to insuring that man is socialized into this mold, his human anxieties conditioned out. The power structure of the society will be even more centralized than the current structure. The city will rid itself of remaining small shops and other lingering evidences of human sentiment, so that where there is now variety and diversity, there will be functional monotony. With the rapid increase in urban population there is the prospect that the inefficiency of suburban living will be eliminated and people will be housed in compact apartments or even in some collective arrangement.

The family as we know it will be eliminated from this society, Moore has suggested,[12] and Skinner, in *Walden Two*,[13] agrees.[14] Children, housed separately, will not endanger the efficiency of adult activity. They will not be left to the haphazard care of their accidental parents but will be socialized by behavioral conditioning experts. Couples will have no use for lifelong commitments and will often tend to go their separate ways. Each man for himself by himself will escape into the mass of interchangeable associates. Such is the vision of the future that some foresee.

10. Robert MacIver, "The Great Emptiness," in Eric Larrabee and Rolf Meyersohn, Eds., *Mass Leisure*, Glencoe, Illinois: The Free Press, 1958, pp. 118–122.
11. Charles W. Hobart, "Disillusionment in Marriage and Romanticism," *Marriage and Family Living*, Vol. 20 (May, 1958), pp. 156–162.
12. Barrington Moore, *op. cit.*
13. B. F. Skinner, *Walden Two*, New York: The Macmillan Co., 1948.
14. But note that the evolution of child handling procedures in the Jewish communal Kibbutzim is in the direction of granting parents more access to their children and permitting children to spend more time in their parents' apartments. John Bowlby, *Maternal Care and Mental Health*, Geneva: World Health Organization, 1952, pp. 42–43.

But it seems undeniable that such a future would, in one sense, mean the end of human society. Human society is not an automatic process as are subhuman spheres of life. There is reason to believe that man, *as we know him*, has to care enough to carry on,[15] and to care enough he has to have a reason; life has to have some meaning. Without at least the illusion, the vision, of human ends that today's contradiction of values yet provides man, what would keep him going? Thus it seems impossible to conceive of the future of man in the above terms. Something more or less than man might emerge to carry on something more or less than human society, but such speculation is best left to science fiction writers.

But while the inhuman potential in current trends is not only sobering but frightening, the *human* possibilities are also unparalleled. An alternative future depends upon a value revolution in American society—not just the emergence of an unambiguous value hierarchy, but a displacement of the now pre-eminent success, efficiency, productivity, prosperity values by the more human oriented being, knowing, caring, loving values. This revolution is in fact overdue; it is prerequisite to our continued societal survival. It is heralded by Winston White's provocative discussion *Beyond Conformity* which maintains that we are even now undergoing "a shift from emphasis on the development of economic resources to the development of human resources—particularly the capacities of personalities."[16] A society of scarcity must encourage productivity and efficiency upon pain of greater scarcity, poverty and starvation. But in an affluent society, plagued not by *underproduction* but by *underconsumption*, production-increasing values *are in fact dysfunctional*, aggravating the chronic overproduction problem. In the affluent society, the implementation of "human" values is not only possible as it is not in a society of scarcity, it is also functional in the sense of diverting initiative and energy from the productive sphere, where they threaten to aggravate existing over-production, to other areas where they may serve to free people to be more themselves.

A key to this value change lies in renewed commitment to the family and in thus re-establishing the centrality of the commitment to inefficient, human values which the family relationship symbolizes. There are some who would try to solve the problems of our heterogeneous society in terms of restructuring (Fromm's work communities for example), of eliminating structurally some of the diversity and complexity of our society. But this is the kind of shortsightedness that tries to move forward by moving backward. To look wistfully at the beauty and relative simplicity of the rigidly structured life in a primitive society without at the same time realizing that

---

15. William H. R. Rivers, "The Psychological Factor," in W. H. R. Rivers, ed., *Essays on the Depopulation of Melanesia,* Cambridge, England: The University Press, 1922.
16. Winston White, *Beyond Conformity,* New York: The Free Press of Glencoe, Ill., 1961, p. 162.

our human potentialities are greater than would be realized in such a society is the kind of irresponsibility that evades the task at hand. This is the most significant point made in *Beyond Conformity*. White sees human personality as emancipated from ascriptive ties in contemporary society. Since man is no longer *determined* automatically by family, church, or occupation, greater individuality of personality is possible. In the absence of automatic structural determinants, man is "indeed, forced to be free," to become more individualistic.[17]

It follows from this that the family of the future must not be defined in terms of more structure, but in terms of less explicit structure. It must at once be flexible enough for increasingly individuated people, yet a stable basic unit for human life. The family as a commitment implies freedom in the definition of the marital relationship in order to meet the demands of the particular way of life of the two people involved. For its members, family relationships should be a part of a larger pattern of meaningful, involving relationships. Only thus, individually defined and not exclusive, can the family tie avoid being a trapping, arbitrarily binding, stultifying commitment for its members. Defined in this way, the family would be a sustaining, liberating, and humanizing influence since it would invest life in modern society with context, continuity, and direction. As a commitment, a limiting choice, an orienting value complex, it would permit a decisive stance in the urban sea of alternatives, not an artificial reduction of the alternatives.

Are there any alternative side bet possibilities in our day to shore up the marriage commitment, which have not suffered the erosion of effectiveness noted earlier in contemporary society? I think that the answer is yes. It is an answer which is not only compatible with, but dependent on the fact that since *doing* is inescapably becoming less important in contemporary society than *being*, husbands and wives are increasingly chosen because of the persons that they *are,* rather than what they can *do.* Increasingly mates may be known deeply and loved for what they are. To know and love the person in this way is to feel for and care for the person. Love in this sense, then, involves the inadvertent side bet of deeply feeling with and for and caring about this person. A risking of the marriage vows involves immediate apprehension of the pain this causes my mate, as my own pain. My empathy with and ego involvement with my mate guarantees a "side bet penalty" which is likely to be heavier than the attractiveness of what I stand to gain from my breach of commitment.

Here is a basis for a new, deeper commitment to the family, in so far as couple members dare to invest themselves to this extent, in each other. And in this deeper commitment, more of meaning in life would be discovered in the experience of human values, the intrinsic values of being,

---

17. *Ibid.,* p. 164.

becoming, knowing and being known, caring and being cared for, in contrast to the values of doing and achieving. And out of this profound experiencing of human values might come the basis for the slow revolution in values which would further facilitate deeper commitment to the family, and in time the reorientation of contemporary society.

The implications of such a changed significance of the family and such a value revolution for future society are many. The character type which could emerge in this kind of family setting would be neither the chameleon-like, other-directed nor the rigid, artificially dogmatic inner-directed, to use Riesman's terms. Instead there could emerge the autonomous individual who is able to see and consciously choose between the alternatives; who knows himself and can express himself in decisive, directed action; who retains his sense of identity discovered *beyond* role, in the various roles he must play. Not merely functioning, having sold his soul "true believer" fashion, not living oblivious of alternatives, he could consciously exercise the greatest sense of freedom and responsibility that man has ever known; he could live Winston White's vision.[18]

With renewed emphasis on *being* rather than on *doing*, the family and the concern with human relationships which it symbolizes could once again be an organizing principle in society. With less emphasis on over-efficiency our society could significantly cut down the length of the working day. Such a work schedule would make possible an enriched home life. While older children were in school both men and women could work, if they chose, and thus perhaps develop specialized interests. The specialization of their work could be balanced by the vocations of homemaking and greater involvement in parenthood for both men and women, and by the opportunity to develop other interests in their leisure time. A shorter work day would mean that children could once again be socialized more within the family primary group. The school could accomplish its distinctive function of transmitting knowledge in half a day, leaving the humanization responsibility to the home. Here the inefficient process of growing up could take place in a context where there is time for each child, and where each child is valued and known as an individual. In the home children need not be collectively handled, regimented and manipulated as they must be at school, but might be better freed to become, to find themselves, to develop their unique potentials.

In addition to assuming the responsibility for socializing children, such a family could provide meaningful and sustaining relationships which are a prerequisite to open, undefended, loving relationships with others. As I noted above, it is inevitable that most relationships in an urban society will be time-bound, that the demands of complex and highly mobile living will pull people apart, but the family can offer the element of permanence

---

18. Winston White, *op. cit.*

which other relationships cannot. And thus safe-guarded by their family-centered security against being left unbearably alone when the hour of separation came, people could dare to invest themselves in a number of invaluable but often short term relationships whose dissolution would otherwise be unbearable. Increased leisure time would enable individuals to develop these relationships both within and without the family.

The question arises, could people really bear to spend more time with their families than they now do? To this a number of things can be said. In the first place, people presumably would not have the same need that they do today to escape the emptiness of shallow, family-togetherness by constantly doing or being with different people. Time spent together could be on a more meaningful level than it can now be. Secondly, time would also be spent in other meaningful, involving relationships with non-family members which would mean that the family would not seem a trap and would not degenerate into a stagnating aggregate of individuals. The family would lose the compulsive exclusive security which makes it dull for those who spend most of their leisure time with their family and dare not do otherwise. Assuming a commitment of family members to each other more profound than any based merely on exclusion or external structure, family members could tolerate an element of genuine insecurity in their relationships which would not have to be evaded and would keep the relationship from being static and dull.

Finally young people, no longer stranded, disoriented, alienated from parents—as they often are now when neither adolescents nor parents know each other—would not have to escape compulsively, haphazardly into marriage. They could postpone marriage until they knew what they wanted, what they needed and what they were entering into.

There are a few shreds of evidence that the American family may in fact be evolving in the direction advocated in this paper. Hilsdale, in a rather sensitive interviewing study, sought to discover whether subjects entered marriage with an absolute commitment to marriage, or merely a commitment to trial of marriage. He found that 80% entered with an absolute commitment. This commitment was, significantly, associated with an "almost total absence of starry-eyed Hollywood-type 'romantic love.' "[19] Another finding of this study was the preoccupation of his subjects with communication: they felt that their marriage would last "because we can talk to each other, because we can discuss our problems together."[20] Hilsdale terms this faith "magical," but it can also be seen as a reaction to the fact that in an increasingly impersonal society, people cannot talk with each other. In this light it appears as both awareness by people of their need to really communicate with another, and a commitment to safeguard

---

19. Paul Hilsdale, "Marriage as a Personal Existential Commitment," *Marriage and Family Living,* 24 (May, 1962), p. 142.
20. *Ibid.,* p. 143.

this highly valued and important aspect of the marriage relationship. Moreover, there is evidence that communication is related to marital adjustment.[21]

In this paper I have argued that if an affluent society is to survive, it must undergo a value revolution which will make what we have called human values pre-eminent over production values. Such a society-wide evaluation would eliminate a major source of the compromised commitment, of the value conflict between and within the family members, and of the inadequate and distorting socialization of children, which exist in the American family today. There seems to be reason for hoping that such a value revolution may come out of the changing pattern of husband-wife relationship. If this should continue such that the family were restructured along the lines suggested by these values, people could find the security and sustenance which they need, but often cannot find, in today's world. The nature of contemporary urban society makes this increasingly necessary for a number of reasons. Earlier alternative bases of family solidarity are disappearing, and thus commitment is an increasingly crucial bond. Increasingly, the family is the only security base available to man today. Where commitment-based family security is dependably available to man, he will have a basis for relating fearlessly to the greater varieties of people available to him in a society organized in terms of achieved statuses, deepening and enriching himself and others in the process.

Discussion of Hobart's Position*

WILLIAM M. KEPHART

Professor Hobart suggests four large-scale changes in social structure which have "tended significantly to weaken family solidarity": loss of functions; ascendancy of materialistic values; increased spatial mobility; and decline in status ascription. He then posits a set of value changes, a key to which "lies in renewed commitment to the family." The author has thus ventured into a theoretical area all too seldom explored by family scholars. He has aimed high and deserves a hearing. There are, however, for better or worse, some unlooked for complexities in the formulation of etiological family theory, and it might be well to point out some specific examples.

21. Charles W. Hobart and William J. Kausner, "Some Social Interactional Correlates of Marital Role Disagreement and Marital Adjustment," *Marriage and Family Living,* 21 (Aug., 1959), p. 263.
* Reprinted from *Journal of Marriage and the Family,* Vol. 25 (November, 1963), pp. 412–413, by permission of the author and publisher.

Hobart contends that the decline in status ascription may have weakened the family institution. But when primitive and civilized societies are compared, a curious—and little recognized—truism emerges. Primitive groups, which by and large evidence a high level of status ascription, have a relatively high rate of marital breakup! Civilized societies, which tend to emphasize achieved rather than ascribed status, have a comparatively stable type of family organization.[1] It may well be that the concept of "ascribed and achieved status," as originally used by Linton, needs to be sharpened to meet the needs of the more sophisticated social theory currently on the drawing boards.

The author also maintains that the ascendancy of materialistic values has weakened the family. But if this is so, why is it that the middle and upper classes—where presumably materialism flourishes—have a much more stable type of family organization than that found in the lower socio-economic groups. (Virtually all the research studies are in agreement on this point, and there is no need to list the voluminous references.) On a cross-cultural basis, furthermore, could it really be shown that socialistic economies manifest a more stable family type than do capitalistic (materialistic) economies?

In discussing spatial mobility in terms of Becker's commitment process, Hobart states that increasing mobility reduces the so-called marital commitment. This is a logical inference, and yet a long range displacement-weighting factor may be operative. In a historical sense, that is, have there not always been social elements—perhaps more significant than mobility—which have impinged on the marital-familial commitment? Military service and chronic warfare, political change and revolution, conflict with the gods, serfdom, the woman's rights movement, tyranny, economic uncertainty—all of these and many more have, through the ages, in some ways reduced family commitment. As a reductive factor, mobility may simply be superseding one or more of these anti-commitment forces.

The question might also be raised as to why Hobart chose the particular four changes he did. Why these and not others? Could not an equally cogent case be made for the proposition that a decline in the institution of

---

1. The prevalence of family instability among primitive peoples was reported 60 years ago in George E. Howard's *History of Matrimonial Institution.* (Vol. I, University of Chicago Press, 1904.) Thirty years ago Goodsell reexamined the anthropological literature and reaffirmed that "Nothing appears more striking to the student of the primitive family than the instability of marriage." (Willystine Goodsell, *A History of Marriage and the Family,* N.Y., The Macmillan Company, 1934, p. 30.) In his cross-cultural survey of 1950, Murdock reported that in 60% of his sample of societies "the divorce rate manifestly exceeds that among ourselves." (George Murdock, "Family Stability in Non-European Cultures," *Annals of the American Academy of Political and Social Science,* November, 1950, pp. 196–197.) Ardener's major ethnographic study, published only last year, yields the same conclusions. (Edwin Ardener, *Divorce and Fertility: An African Study,* Oxford University Press, 1962.) In view of the long-range consistency of the findings, it is somewhat surprising that students of the family have generally avoided comment on the relative fragility of marriage among primitive peoples.

the family is associated with an increase in the acceptability of various forms of nonmarital sex activity, or with a decline in religiosity, or with a falling birth rate, and so on.

In brief, there are two major difficulties in the Hobart-type analysis: (1) Any social change (e.g., the weakening family) must be explained by another variation rather than by a constant, and in the long run the effects of institutional changes often tend to cancel each other in terms of the behavioral phenomenon under consideration. (2) There is an unmeasured parallax in focusing on certain changes at the exclusion of others.

In any case, the study of social causation is perhaps the most complex of all sociological and anthropological endeavors, and in this sense Hobart has made some telling observations.

The concept of commitment, as applied to family centrality, stands as a worthwhile applicatory contribution. The term is more definitive—and certainly more amenable to quantification and paradigm—than are, say, the typologies of LePlay, Sorokin, Spengler, Zimmerman, Bebel, and Engels.[2] All of these men have constructed theoretical subsumptions under which family systems are seen in terms of sequences or cycles. Yet these formulations are such that verification and replication, for the most part, remain methodologically unresolved. Engels, for example—to take a not-too-well-known illustration—held that the human family has passed through deterministic stages: the "no-family" stage, the consanguine family, the Punaluan family, and the monogamous family. But how to put Engels' theory to the empirical test? Within the lattice of family commitment, on the other hand, an imaginative researcher could set up criteria, indexes, and models on both a historical and cross-cultural basis, in addition to exploring variations within our own culture.

Hobart's analysis of the competitive relation between materialism and marriage is—in spite of my nominal criticism above—first rate, as is his over-all statement regarding value conflict, dabs of moralism notwithstanding.

The author states that "if an affluent society is to survive, it must undergo a value revolution which will make human values preeminent over production values." He is not, however, overly explicit as to just how this "renewed commitment to the family" will come about. One possibility would be to encourage family researchers to continue their investigation of the elusive elements involved effective mate selection. It is not enough to say that mates should "be known deeply and loved for what they are." To bring about this turn of events we will probably have to know a good deal more regarding need-satisfaction and the meshing (or grinding) of cross-sex personality traits.

---

2. For a discussion of these typologies within the family framework, see David Greenwood, *Essays in Human Relations,* Ch. IV, "Institutional Development of the Family," Washington, D.C., Public Affairs Press, 1956, pp. 36–47.

One final word. For some time now, it has been evident to those of us in the family field that there is a paucity of theoretical and socio-historical systematization. Hobart has had to start, if not from scratch, from a rather nebulous base line, and for this he is to be commended. Implicit in his paper, I believe, is a challenge to all of us: we cannot go on interminably gathering facts about family behavior without at some point taking the necessary time to sort out and "wrap up" the ones we already have, and to see whether we can really say something demonstrably worthwhile about the institution we purport to study.

Rejoinder to Kephart*

CHARLES W. HOBART

My discussion is predicated on some implications of Galbraith's conception of the Affluent Society. In the past there were many forms of waste of human resources, many sources of pain and suffering which were unavoidable because scarcity—of food, clothing, shelter, of education, health facilities, jobs—made it inevitable. Today these "scarcity evils" may be banished: such a day may be anticipated. However, there is the danger that a lagging, obsolete "folk wisdom" of scarcity may distort our response to abundance in such a way as to produce some entirely avoidable "evils of abundance."

Two polar possibilities in the situation of the United States today are expenditure of our abundance in such a way as to cultivate the potential of persons, or expenditure of our abundance in such a way as to maximize the materialism potential in our culture. There are other possibilities of course: militarism, the space-race, etc., but these do not seem to be so immanently likely.

In this paper I have not attempted a cross-cultural analysis. I am preoccupied with the situation of the United States today, with the "self realization" probabilities of the American people, and with the family in evolution, which *may* be rather pivotal to the future of American society and the futures of its individual members. I have considered only the situation of middle class people because increasingly the majority of Americans appear to be middle class in orientation if not in fact, and this appears to be the national class norm.

Kephart's comments suggest that three points foundational to my

* Reprinted from *Journal of Marriage and the Family,* Vol. 25 (November, 1963), pp. 413–414, by permission of the author and publisher.

discussion should be underscored. 1. Ours is a Gesellschaft type rather than a Gemeinschaft type of society; thus the experience of community is not to be found in the mere fact of societal membership. 2. The extreme heterogeneity of contemporary America means that the absence of cultural structuring of behavior imposes the obligation of more freedom and more choice on people. 3. I presume as a baseline for analysis the ideal situation of a couple who "know each other deeply and love each other for what they are." The values which I would seek to maximize are openness, freedom, trust.

The first point is relevant to Kephart's observation that "primitive groups have a higher rate of marital breakup" than civilized societies. It seems to me that this is as one would expect since the former are Gemeinschafts and the latter are Gesellschafts. For reasons which Homans has analyzed in *The Human Group,* the relationship between husbands and wives in simple societies is commonly distant, formal, impersonal, not intimate and sharing as is the relationship suggested by our companionate marital ideal. This contrast is even yet found between the traditional farm family and the newer urban family in the States. In such simple societies the experience of community is provided and the sustaining function is accomplished by the extended family and often by the community as a whole. Here the instrumental aspects of the marital relationship are more significant than the expressive aspects. Emotional involvement is more diffuse, more widely spread. Marrying and separating are more like hiring and firing a cook or a hired hand: there will be some emotional implications (as of course may hiring and firing) but the primary considerations are more likely to be those of convenience (although there are admittedly wide variations in different societies). Indeed the sternness of the survival struggle in many simple societies tends to place a premium on the ability of people to stifle emotional response. One consequence of our greater ability in this day to safeguard the survival of the weak and handicapped and to relieve suffering is, I suspect, a general increase in emotional responsiveness. Thus, I am arguing that in contrast to simple societies divorce in a complex society often takes place for entirely different reasons (barrenness is an infrequent reason in American divorce cases) and has different meanings and emotional significances.

I am not at all convinced that materialism flourishes particularly among the middle and the upper classes. The economic surplus of these groups, given the cultural heterogeneity noted above, forces them more often to confront the question of how this surplus is to be spent. But the greater liveliness of the materialism issue does not mean that these classes are more identified with materialism. The reason for the more frequent disorganization of lower class families must originate in large part in poverty and its consequences: exploitation, hardening, brutalization, etc. The middle class is spared most of this. But the marital ideal which prosperity makes more possible by banishing degrading poverty—is jeopardized anew by the materialistic preoccupation to which the middle class is now vulnerable.

I would agree that mobility may be only the latest of a long series of social elements, military service, revolution, serfdom, etc., which have divided allegiance to the family. But contemporary mobility does appear to be an especially pervasive threat because 1. such a large (and increasing) proportion of the population is being affected, and 2. it is a "triple threat," subjecting the family to increased stress, stripping it of supporting primary groups, and weakening the commitment of its members to unity. The act, and attitude, of commitment is a major safeguard to marital stability in this situation, I think. If the safeguard is in operation the self realization potentials intrinsic to greater mobility which I tried to suggest may be actualized with minimal risk.

Why did I choose the four changes whose impact on the family I have considered? The only honest answer is observation and intuition, explored and illuminated in many discussions with others. In response to Kephart's challenge, however, it occurs to me that the four which I considered are preeminently *sociological changes.* Loss of family functions, family activity, is related to sentiment and interaction, as Homans has convincingly suggested. The ascendancy of materialistic values in so far as it is associated with a decline in "people values" affects interpersonal relationships. The increase in spatial mobility tends to curtail primary relationships and to substitute for them more of secondary relationships. And the decline in status ascription has widespread and important consequences for interpersonal interaction. All of these affect the intrafamily and extrafamily relationships of people.

Two of the possibilities which Kephart suggests, increased nonmarital sexual activity and falling birth rate, lean somewhat toward biological reductionism. Although they certainly have interactional consequences their range of implications appear to me to be not so broad as those I have considered.

The religious sentiment has been linked to such a wide range of human interests that I have difficulty seeing this as a prime mover in family change. However, that we *are* dealing with a large and complexly interrelated system, in which there are second and third and higher order consequences, and that any or all of these may feed back to strengthen incipient changes in the family; to this I will readily agree. But such complexity does not absolve us from trying to ferret out the first order causes, to anticipate further changes, and to seek ways to maximize their functional and minimize the dysfunctional consequences.

The Future of the Family Revisited*

JOHN N. EDWARDS

Functional losses, increased mobility, declining status ascription, and the ascendency of materialistic values, cited either singly or in concert, are frequently the identified causal agents and results of familial change. A reexamination of these factors suggests, however, that there are severe limitations in employing them as explanations of change. It is contended, moreover, that the current value predicament in American society does not point to a revolution in family values which other analyses have indicated. Rather, the preponderance of evidence strongly suggests increased interpenetration and interdependence between the family and the economic sphere.

Familial change and institutional interpenetration are subjects which have attracted the continued but sporadic attention of sociologists and social scientists.[1] For the most part observers of the family, in essence, have considered the interchange between various institutional sectors and the family a one-sided affair. Familial change is perceived, in other words, as resulting from social changes in other institutional spheres with few, if any, reciprocal effects. A considerable amount of evidence has been and can be marshalled to substantiate this interpretation. Yet, one of the consequences of adopting this prevailing view is that it has frequently resulted in the formulation of a unifactorial "theory" or in the development of a theory of such a general nature that it has little heuristic and predictive

---

* Reprinted from *Journal of Marriage and the Family*, Vol. 29 (August, 1967), pp. 505–511, by permission of the author and publisher.
1. See, for example, William F. Ogburn, *Social Change*, New York: Viking Press, 1922; William F. Ogburn and Meyer F. Nimkoff, *Technology and the Changing Family*, New York: Houghton Mifflin, 1955; Pitirim A. Sorokin, *The Crisis of Our Age*, New York: E. P. Dutton, 1941; Carle C. Zimmerman, *Family and Civilization*, New York: Harper and Brothers, 1947; Margaret P. Redfield, "The American Family: Consensus and Freedom," *American Journal of Sociology*, 52 (November, 1946), pp. 175–183; Ernest Burgess, "The Family in a Changing Society," *American Journal of Sociology*, 53 (May, 1948), pp. 417–422; Lawrence K. Frank, "Social Change and the Family," *Annals of the American Academy of Political and Social Science*, 160 (March, 1932), pp. 94–102; Joseph K. Folsom, *The Family and Democratic Society*, New York: John Wiley and Sons, Inc., 1934; Ruth N. Anshen, "The Family in Transition," in *The Family: Its Function and Destiny*, ed. by Ruth N. Anshen, New York: Harper, 1959, pp. 3–19; Sidney M. Greenfield, "Industrialization and the Family in Sociological Theory," *American Journal of Sociology*, 67 (November, 1961), pp. 312–322; Meyer F. Nimkoff, "Biological Discoveries and the Future of the Family. A Reappraisal," *Social Forces*, 41 (December, 1962), pp. 121–127; and Reuben Hill, "The American Family of the Future," *Journal of Marriage and the Family*, 26 (February, 1964), pp. 20–28.

utility. Ogburn and Nimkoff's[2] citation of technological innovations as the determinants of functional losses typifies the unifactorial approach, while Burgess'[3] suggestion that familial changes are the consequences of alterations in economic conditions and societal ideology is indicative of the level of abstraction with which change has been treated.

In addition to their predilection for unifactorial and highly general formulations, it has been noted that our earlier analysts of the family and social change were far from dispassionate observers. Either by implication or explicitly, the majority of writers during the 1940's took a stance on our perennial, theoretical antistrophe between persistence and change.[4] With few exceptions, social and family change was treated as a unique and disturbing occurrence. The views of these sociologists were not only tainted with traditional nostalgia in the midst of generalized and rapid change but reflected an over-rigid model of society which was then current.

Despite an increased awareness of the limitations of prior discussions of changes in the American family, many of the issues recently have been raised anew. Hobart, in contending that the family serves as a humanizing influence in modern society, suggests four significant changes being undergone: functional losses, increased personal mobility, declining status ascription, and the continued ascendency of materialistic values.[5] Although there is a certain amount of confusion at times as to whether these are consequences or causes of change, all of these factors have been isolated as important explanatory variables by previous theorists of familial change. In combining these four factors, Hobart argues that they have led to a profound value predicament in which the primary commitment and meaning of the family are being lost. Material abundance and our present commitment to its expenditure, he maintains, threaten the centrality of "human" values and our prospects of "self-realization." Consequently, if the current trends persist, it is possible "that something more or less than man might emerge to carry on something more or less than human society."[6]

Within the limited compass of this paper, this interpretation of the variables will be examined and an attempt will be made to indicate, whenever appropriate, their limitations as explanations of change. In doing so, the efficacy of these variables as explanations of change, whether employed singly or in concert, will be evaluated. Secondly, an alternative interpretation of marriage and the family will be suggested as a base line for the development of future theories of change.

---

2. Ogburn and Nimkoff, *op. cit.*
3. Burgess, *op. cit.*
4. Sorokin and Zimmerman during this period were two outstanding proponents of the theme of family decay and deterioration.
5. Charles W. Hobart, "Commitment, Value Conflict and the Future of The American Family," *Marriage and Family Living,* 25 (November, 1963), pp. 405–412.
6. *Ibid.,* p. 409.

VARIABLES OF FAMILIAL CHANGE

1. LOSS OF FUNCTIONS

Hobart, in discussing the American family's loss of functions, points to the provision of companionship and emotional security as the basic function and reason for family formation today. Without question, many of the former functions such as economic production, education, protection, and recreation have been shifted to other institutional spheres or, at the very least, their content and form as they are carried out by the American family have been altered. Juxtaposed against this is evidence which suggests that the attractiveness of family formation has increased over the decades. However, Hobart's assertion that Americans seek divorce when they fail to attain a sufficient level of companionship and emotional security lacks empirical support. The precipitating influences in the initiation of divorce proceedings are, in fact, a matter of some debate. In making such an assertion, Hobart appears to be in accord with Ogburn that "the dilemma of the modern family is due to its loss of function"[7] and that family instability and disintegration are a consequence.

In the words of Barrington Moore, the American family today may have "obsolete and barbaric features,"[8] but family units have persisted and the vast majority continue to persist despite the ongoing loss of functions. Durkheim's classic proposition concerning social differentiation is most suggestive in this connection. Increasing specialization and differentiation, concomitants of societal complexity, Durkheim contended, lead to an increment in interdependence.[9] This is no less true of familial functions than it is of the division of labor. Our present family system, organized around whatever tasks, is more highly interdependent with other institutional sectors than previously. Even the various totalitarian experiments with the eradication of family functions, including those of childrearing and socialization, tentatively suggest the ultimate functionality of the family in societal maintenance, regardless of its specific structure and functions.[10] It thus would appear that the issue of functional losses as a

---

7. William F. Ogburn, "The Changing Functions of the Family," in *Selected Studies in Marriage and the Family*, ed. by Robert F. Winch, Robert McGinnis, and Herbert R. Barringer, New York: Holt, Rinehart, and Winston, 1962, pp. 159–163.
8. Barrington Moore, "Thoughts on the Future of the Family," in *Identity and Anxiety*, ed. by Maurice R. Stein, Arthur J. Vidich, and David M. White, New York: The Free Press, a division of the Macmillan Co., 1960, p. 394.
9. Emile Durkheim, *The Division of Labor in Society*, New York: The Free Press, a division of the Macmillan Co., 1947.
10. Nicholas S. Timasheff, "The Attempt to Abolish the Family in Russia," in *The Family*, ed. by Norman W. Bell and Ezra F. Vogel, New York: The Free Press, a division of the Macmillan Co., 1960, pp. 55–63. Reiss has argued that Timasheff's

source or indication of instability is a misleading one. It is indeed questionable if family instability (divorce and separation) can be eliminated or reduced however many or few functions the family performs. The issue for any theory of family change seems to be, rather, identification of the specific direction of interdependence and the concomitants which accompany and lead to increased interdependence.

2. INCREASED PERSONAL MOBILITY

The relatively high rate of spatial mobility within industrialized society, according to Hobart, affects the family in at least three ways: (1) it precipitates a larger amount of crises and adjustments, (2) it breaks the family from its external supports such as friendship and kinship groups, and (3) it weakens the proscriptions against divorce as a means of resolving family difficulties.[11] Increased personal or spatial mobility undoubtedly occasions the need for more adjustments. Generally such mobility is related to changes in work and, at times, to shifts in family status. The transitions attendant to these alterations are not to be underestimated. Yet, as the Rapoports indicate, conflicts and stresses are not necessarily multiplied by these transitions.[12] They may, in actuality, have desirable consequences. As a result of mobility, the functions of the family are by no means residual but become an inextricable background in the free choice of work and career. The prescriptions of work may allow, in turn, considerable latitude in the organization of family structure that was not formerly possible. The pursuit of higher education by women has enabled them to share occupational positions with their spouses and, in so doing, their involvement in the structuring of the family as well as in economic activities has been intensified.

The contention that the American family lacks external support during crisis periods is a corollary of the notion that the nuclear family is isolated in an urban situation. There are now a number of empirical indications which contradict or at least modify this view. Data from a Cleveland study, presented by Sussman, suggest that, in spite of extensive spatial mobility, nuclear families operate within a matrix of mutual kin assistance.[13] It is, in fact, during periods of crises that the aid of kin is

---

interpretation of the Russian failure to eradicate the family may be based on a logical fallacy. See Ira L. Reiss, "The Universality of the Family: A Conceptual Analysis," *Journal of Marriage and the Family,* 27 (November, 1965), pp. 443–453.

11. Hobart, *op. cit.,* p. 406.

12. Robert Rapoport and Rhona Rapoport, "Work and Family in Contemporary Society," *American Sociological Review,* 30 (June, 1965), pp. 381–394.

13. Marvin B. Sussman, "The Isolated Nuclear Family: Fact or Fiction?" *Social Problems,* 6 (Spring, 1959), pp. 333–340. Similar findings based on New Haven, Connecticut, data are contained in Marvin B. Sussman, "The Help Pattern in the Middle-Class Family," *American Sociological Review,* 18 (February, 1953), pp. 22–28.

most likely to be offered and accepted. Axelrod's research in Detroit indicates that relatives rather than non-relatives are the most important type of informal group association.[14] Babchuk and Bates, in a study of primary relations, also suggest that a large number of close friendships are maintained on a nonlocal and non-face-to-face basis.[15] On the whole, the evidence indicates that the high rate of annual movement by families has a relatively negligible effect on their external supports and does not, as often contended, weaken the informal controls of primary groups. It is patent that family transitions of one sort or another have always existed. The possibility that mobility as a crisis point in family life has merely superseded others is not to be discounted; but, if this is true, the impact of mobility on the family still remains to be demonstrated.

3. DECLINING ASCRIBED RELATIONSHIPS

In identifying the decline of traditionally defined or ascribed relationships as another element in the weakening of family bonds, Hobart concedes that the emphasis on achieved relationships fosters greater choice in establishing social relations. He argues, though, that the cross-sex contact, particularly in voluntary associations, subjects the marriage bond to greater stress.[16] To view voluntary organizations as potential agents for family dissolution is to over-simplify and distort the complexity of these organizations. Expressive voluntary groups (a dance club, for example) and those whose memberships are comprised of both sexes may serve to reinforce family relations. By their very nature, expressive associations are organized to supply immediate and personal gratification to their respective members. Their focus is, in other words, integrative at an individual level, while instrumental groups (such as the Chamber of Commerce) provide integration at a communal level. Particularly where expressive organizations are bisexual in composition, solidarity may be enhanced.[17]

It is, on the other hand, among those organizations which attract their constituencies from only one sex or the other that the probability of affiliation disturbing familial equilibrium is increased. In the one-sex groups, family members become geographically dispersed and may expend considerable amounts of time apart from one another. Even still, a number of

14. Morris Axelrod, "Urban Structure and Social Participation," *American Sociological Review*, 21 (February, 1956), pp. 13–18.

15. Nicholas Babchuk and Alan P. Bates, "The Primary Relations of Middle-Class Couples: A Study in Male Dominance," *American Sociological Review*, 28 (June, 1963), pp. 377–385.

16. Hobart, *op. cit.*, pp. 406–407.

17. The integrative impact of voluntary organizations is discussed at length in Nicholas Babchuk and John N. Edwards, "Voluntary Associations and the Integration Hypothesis," *Sociological Inquiry*, 35 (Spring, 1965), pp. 149–162.

relevant studies suggest that these are exceptional cases.[18] A sizeable proportion of the population are not affiliated with any type of voluntary association. Moreover, among those who do belong, their participation is neither extensive nor intensive. Americans, all folklore to the contrary, are not a nation of joiners, and it is thus difficult to perceive achieved relationships as a threat to family and marital solidarity.

In conceiving the proliferation of associations and achieved relationships as causes of dissolution and change, there is also an implicit assumption made about the nature of man. Basically, in positing cross-sex contact as a disruptive force, man is viewed as primarily a sexual being. Presumably, social control of the sexual drive is tenuous and exposure to the opposite sex is sufficient to deteriorate this control altogether. Since every society is interested in controlling sexual outlets to some extent, it is particularly imperative for an industrialized society which severely limits such outlets to segregate the sexes. This conception of man is not only incompatible with most sociological theories, but it is ultimately an untenable position. Even if we grant that adultery is a widespread experience, there remains the intricate, and as yet unaccomplished, task of sorting out extramarital involvement from other causes of instability.

4. ASCENDENCY OF MATERIALISTIC VALUES

Materialistic values are seen as fundamentally incongruous with the more important values of the family; therefore, value confusion and instability result. The resolution of the present value confusion, Hobart notes, is doubly important for the family in that it is one of the basic socializing agents and it symbolizes many of the more fundamental humane values. Either human values must become preeminent in American society or the values of success, efficiency, and prosperity will continue to alter the family institution and eventually erode it. Hobart suggests, in this regard, that a value revolution is essential for continued societal survival. Such a revolution, he argues, cannot be a mere emergence of a consistent value hierarchy but must be a total displacement of our now-prevailing economic values. Although current trends appear to make such a revolution remote, the position set forth by Hobart is in essence opimistic. As a key to renewed commitment to marriage, he suggests that, increasingly, indi-

18. For instance, see Charles Wright and Herbert Hyman, "Voluntary Association Memberships of American Adults: Evidence from National Sample Surveys," *American Sociological Review*, 23 (June, 1958), pp. 284–294; John Foskett, "Social Structure and Social Participation," *American Sociological Review*, 20 (August, 1955), pp. 431–438; Wendell Bell and Maryanne Force, "Urban Neighborhood Types and Participation in Formal Associations," *American Sociological Review*, 21 (February, 1956), pp. 25–34; and John Scott, Jr., "Membership and Participation in Voluntary Associations," *American Sociological Review*, 22 (June, 1957), pp. 315–326.

viduals in our affluent society are becoming more important for what they are, rather than for what they are capable of doing. Individuals are perceived and cared for in terms of their intrinsic value, rather than their extrinsic and utilitarian worth. Thus, despite the current prominence of utilitarian values, it is felt that the family is evolving in a new direction.[19]

THE FAMILY TODAY AND TOMORROW

To this juncture, I have attempted to point out several limitations in invoking functional loss, spatial mobility, and the emphasis on achieved relationships as explanations for familial change. I should like, at this point, to offer an alternative interpretation of contemporary marriage and family living as a base line for further analysis, since it is quite apparent with the data now at hand that there is some measure of disagreement. Specific alternative explanatory variables of change will not be indicated; it is equally important in the formulation of any future theories of change, however, that we avoid stereotyping our present situation as we have done with the rural family of the past. In offering this admittedly tentative and sketchy analysis, Hobart's excellent example is followed by focusing on value orientations.

A basic underlying theme of American culture, Jules Henry has noted, is a preoccupation with pecuniary worth or value that is a consequence of what he terms "technological driveness."[20] Though our institutional structure is highly interdependent, the point is that our economic system and its values have become so pervasive that American life can be characterized as being driven by the constant creation of new wants and desires. Each new want—with considerable impetus from advertising—aids in the destruction of self-denial and impulse control, both virtues of a previous era. Where an economic system has no ceiling or production limits, all hesitation to indulgence must be overcome. And overcome it is, as witnessed by the tremendous growth of the advertising industry.

The preoccupation with pecuniary worth appears to be a necessary complement to a social system dominated by its economic institutional sphere. The nature of an economy of such a social system is that rewards must be transferable and negotiable; hence, the institutionalization of a monetary system. Whether one is selling the products of his labors or his personality and training, tangible rewards are mandatory. No doubt the efficacy of religious thought has suffered for this reason. Eternal damnation is not sufficiently definite, nor the prospect of heaven sufficiently imminent, to normatively persuade many who exist in a society where most rewards

---

19. Hobart, *op. cit.,* pp. 407–412.
20. Jules Henry, *Culture Against Man,* New York: Random House, Inc., 1963.

are quantified. Quantified rewards and our nearly obsessive concern with them are not identical with status achievement which other writers have cited as a crucial factor in the dissolution of the family. Status achievement may take many forms, of which the accumulation of monetary rewards is only one manifestation. The point is, rather, that the prospect of quantified rewards has become so pervasive in our society that it permeates virtually all social relationships including that between husband and wife and the progeny. The non-rewarding character of unlimited procreation has partially contributed to the diminution of that function and family size. To speak of "human obsolescence" and to consider the treatment accorded the elderly in our society are also evidence of the importance attached to tangibly rewarded behavior. In many instances it is not too much of an overstatement to consider as objects those that have not yet developed exchangeable resources (the young) and those who have exhausted theirs (the elderly). Even those occupying the middle ground, however, are not necessarily in an enviable position, for their relationships often lack all but a vestige of emotional interchange.

Insofar as marriage and the family are concerned, the first difficulties arising from this emphasis on pecuniary rewards are encountered in the dating process. The emergence of the rating and dating complex, Waller suggested, has fostered exploitative relationships in dating.[21] In such a relationship each partner attempts to maximize his or her returns with the least amount of concessions. Control and therefore the maximization of rewards are vested in that individual who has the least investment in the situation. Were it not a serious matter, it would be ironical that low commitment should be so highly rewarded. Indeed it is significant and symptomatic of contemporary society that rewards from this type of relationship should be consciously and avidly pursued. The exploitative nature of dating, were it merely confined to dating, would be less problematic. Due to the lengthy dating period, ranging from the preteen years to the early twenties, this orientation becomes reinforced through repetition. It cannot fail, therefore, to have an impact on marital relationships, particularly in the first years of marriage, the period when couples are most vulnerable to divorce.

Marital relationships, ideally at least, are defined in our society as relationships involving mutual sacrifice, sharing, and giving. Magoun states in this regard: "Anyone going into marriage with the expectation of being thanked for bringing home the bacon—even against dismaying odds—or for shining the ancestral silver tea service till it glistens from the buffet in little pinwheels of light is headed for heartache."[22] And heartache is

21. Willard Waller and Reuben Hill, *The Family: A Dynamic Interpretation,* New York: Holt, Rinehart and Winston, 1951, pp. 131–157.
22. F. Alexander Magoun, *Love and Marriage,* New York: Harper and Brothers, 1956, p. 44.

precisely what a large proportion of marriages, not only those that termi-nate in divorce but also the so-called normal marriages, garner. With monotonous repetition we are conditioned, primarily as a result of the pervasiveness of our economic institutions, to react to situations in a manner designed to elicit rewards. When the potential of tangible rewards is absent, interaction tends to be halting and random. Through the condi-tioning of the economic system and the lengthy continuation of this basic orientation during the dating process, the newly married are grossly unpre-pared for the prescriptions of marriage.

Recent findings amply illustrate this trend. The marriages of what Cuber refers to as the "significant Americans" are predominantly utilitarian in nature. The partners of these marriages are primarily interested in what each derives from the relationship. There is little concern with mutual sacrifice and sharing other than that which is essential to the maintenance of the marital bond. Moreover, the types of rewards sought in these mar-riages are not psychic or emotional but those which enhance material security. In fact, these marriages are, as Cuber points out, characterized by continual conflict, passivity, and a lack of vitality. Only a minority of the marriages approximate the cultural ideal of an intimate, emotional attach-ment between partners that results in mutual concern and sharing; and it is these marriages which are most vulnerable to divorce.[23] Thus, it would appear that, like the devil, the family in contemporary, industrialized society must take the hindmost. As an institution it is unorganized and, therefore, lacks the influence that may be exercised by those institutions which are. Through necessity it must be flexible and adaptable; those that are not fail.[24]

A central proposition of functional analysis is that a change in one element of an integrated system leads to changes in other elements. The major impetus for social change in our society has been and continues to be our dynamic economic institutions, which seek to create ever new wants and markets for their products and services. Due to its decreasing size, the family's adaptability for change has kept pace. From many perspectives the various social alterations, such as the employment of women, have resulted in greater independence and increased potentialities for individual family members. In other respects, of course, the changes have been dysfunctional. As we have tried to indicate, the disparity that now exists between the ideal marriage and the real is considerable—just as considerable as it prob-ably was in the past. Future alterations are of a high order of probability, particularly adjustments pertaining to the normative emphasis on material rewards and the affective character of marriage. Still, the desinence of the

23. John F. Cuber and Peggy B. Harroff, The Significant Americans: A Study of Sexual Behavior Among the Affluent, New York: Appleton-Century, 1965.
24. Clark E. Vincent, "Familia Spongia: The Adaptive Function," Journal of Mar-riage and the Family, 28 (February, 1966), pp. 29–36.

family appears to be a phantasm born of the anxiety accompanying rapid social change.

If, indeed, contemporary marriages are based more on what the marital partners *are* rather than what they *do* as Hobart suggests, the major disjunctive feature of current family life is that what individuals *are* is primarily reward-seeking organisms. This commitment to economic values is logically incompatible with the values of family life, but it is not a source of major dislocation or dissolution of the family group.

Given this condition, what future has our present family system? Earlier industrialization has relieved a major proportion of our female population from the more onerous activities associated with household management. In spite of the unprecedented opportunity for experimentation, women in general have found it to be a frustrating era. Either they have found a combination of childrearing and outside activities unrewarding or they have felt that the channels for careers remain severely limited. Ongoing social change with respect to career expansion has been marked, nonetheless, and it is highly probable that the tempo will be increased.

This may have major significance for future marital relationships. The tremendous expansiveness of the insurance industry signifies, to some at least, the import attached to the economic aspects of marriage. This is again high-lighted by the frequency with which insurance enters into divorce suits. More importantly, it is clear that marriage for men is more desirable, if not perhaps more necessary, than it is for women. Bernard's study of remarriage adequately illustrates the greater dependence which men have on the marital relationship; women, especially those that are economically secure, are less likely to remarry.[25] With increased avenues for more satisfying gainful employment, women will be afforded an enhanced alternative to wedlock. The generalized societal expectations regarding the desirability of marriage for everyone is quite pervasive, to be sure. But marriage, to put it simply, has become a habit—a habit which many young women with attractive career alternatives are beginning to question, however.

Economic overabundance, it is submitted, in the long run will have a repressive effect on the rate of marriage. The recognition of alternatives to wedlock, as that concerning alternatives to premarital chastity, will not occasion sudden behavioral consequences. But change is overdue. When women, already imbued with the economic ethos, fully realize their equality in this sphere, much of the *raison d'être* of marriage will no longer be present. This is not to say, it should be emphasized, that family formation will precipitously decline; it is merely contended that the consequences of our reward-seeking orientation will become more evident, and this will be reflected in the marriage rate. In other words, one of the present structural

---

25. Jessie Bernard, *Remarriage,* New York: The Dryden Press, 1956, pp. 55, 62–63.

supports which buttresses the attractiveness of the marital relationship will cease to exist. Women will no longer find economic dependence a virtue and worthy byproduct of marriage, for, given the opportunity, they will succeed for themselves as ably as any male might.

Numerous other current trends support this contention. The availability of reliable contraceptive devices, the expectations regarding small family size, and the declining influence and authority of men all suggest that the supports for the marital bond are weakening. Educational opportunities for women and the impetus these provide for the pursuance of careers are another consideration. Universities and colleges will probably attract even larger numbers of women in the future, as they have done for each of the last seven decades. Although most of these women may anticipate marriage eventually, more equitable hiring practices and salaries guaranteed by the Civil Rights Act of 1964 will alter this to some extent. The current popularized literature on the single state also dramatizes the interest in alternatives to marriage.

As stated earlier, the family is not and is not likely to be a nonfunctional entity. The prominence of affective behavior in familial relationships as an ideal appears to be a central support for the continuance of these relationships. Still, just how important effective behavior will remain for individuals and how well these needs will be met in the family stand as primary issues in family research. It is illuminating that study after study to date has found that interaction among couples tends to be halting.[26] It is difficult to conceive of warm, intimate, and emotional relationships being maintained over time when vital interaction is almost non-existent. Perhaps even sporadic episodes of spontaneous communication are sufficient to sustain these relationships, but the accessibility of legal outlets suggests that, without these and other structural supports, many marriages will terminate in divorce.

Despite the many elements of organizational life that are incompatible with our more humane values, bureaucratic structures in many respects recognize the desirability of maintaining intimate familial relationships. W. H. Whyte has noted, in his inimitable analysis of bureaucracies, the attempt to integrate the wife into the organizational structure.[27] In many ways and in many corporations, of course, this is a defensive act. Even as a mechanism of defense, though, this maneuver implicitly recognizes the wife's role as a supportive agent. Regardless of corporate motivation, the attempted integration of wives into the system can have beneficial conse-

---

26. Robert S. Ort, "A Study of Role-Conflicts as Related to Happiness in Marriage," *Journal of Abnormal and Social Psychology*, 45 (October, 1950), pp. 691–699; Peter C. Pineo, "Disenchantment in the Later Years of Marriage," *Marriage and Family Living*, 23 (February, 1961), pp. 2–11; and Cuber and Haroff, *op. cit.*
27. William H. Whyte, Jr., *The Organization Man*, Garden City, New York: Doubleday and Company, Inc., 1957.

quences for the family. Where such an attempt is not made, the abyss between the economic and family group is only widened. Naturally, from the viewpoint of many individuals, this is not an ideal solution. It is, nonetheless, an alternative—an alternative upon which improvement may be made and, in view of increasing societal bureaucratization, one which demands attention.

A man and woman marrying today can contemplate, in the majority of cases, over 40 years' duration of the relationship, encompassing over one-half of their lives. In a society in which group membership is extremely transitory, this represents a significant departure. Because of its duration and its small size, the individual has no greater opportunity in influencing the character and quality of a group.

What we are presently witnessing, moreover, is not a revolution of societal values or the demise and increased instability of the American family. Rather, given the current preeminence of economic orientations in our value system, the marital union and family are becoming more highly interdependent with the economic sphere. Cross-culturally and historically, the family, irrespective of its particular structure and functions, has been and is primarily an instrumental group from a societal perspective. It is not accidental, therefore, that marriage in most societies is based on considerations other than an affective and human orientation. That this is less true in the United States is not an indication of incipient instability but intimates that we are engaged in a radical experiment of familism. It is an experiment in which we are seeking to integrate a new individualism with the other more highly organized institutions. Insofar as our value orientations are dominated by economic values, marriages and family formation in the future are more likely to be based on reason rather than the impulse of habit.

Chapter

13

Education:

A Radical Approach?

The first reading in this section (an excerpt from Erich Fromm's introduction to *Summerhill* by A. S. Neill) constitutes a summary of the basic principles of Summerhill, which is a devastating critique of the traditional educational system. Schools generally function to teach substantive areas (reading, writing, etc.) *and* to socialize the child to fit into society. The basic concepts which underlie Summerhill stand in stark opposition to both of these traditional functions. Neill (the founder of Summerhill, which is both a school and an ideology) is not interested in teaching basic subjects (unless his students express an interest in learning them) because he believes that "learning itself is not as important as personality and character." Thus education, according to Neill, should allow the child to be a child since he "is innately wise and realistic. If left to himself without adult suggestion of any kind, he will develop as far as he is capable of developing." This view of the child is very different from that of most educators, who believe that he must be molded. Based on this conception, the Summerhill school provides a free environment where a child can develop into a scientist or a laborer. In fact, Neill would prefer producing a happy laborer than a neurotic scientist.

Thus Summerhill does not focus on subject matter. Furthermore, Neill is not very much concerned with fitting his students into society. Traditional schools are organized autocratically and education is coercive, since this is their view of the way the world operates. Children are educated in this kind of environment because it is felt that it prepares them better for adulthood and life in an hierarchical and coercive society. In contrast, the Summerhill school is highly democratic and education is not coercive. What Neill is interested in is producing a free, creative child, not

445

one who fits well into a society of which he clearly disapproves. Yet, a free child is *not* a spoiled child. Summerhill students are free to do as they please as long as they do not infringe on the rights of others. They cannot destroy Neill's garden because that constitutes an infringement on his rights. Conversely, Neill must leave a five-year-old's room if he is requested to do so by the child.

It should come as no surprise that Summerhill has been attacked by many traditional educators. Max Rafferty's essay on Summerhill is included here because it is typical of that genre. Rafferty quaintly characterizes Neill's views as "twaddle." To Rafferty, contemporary society is an artificial construct and education, therefore, must also be an artificial process and not the natural one described by Neill. While happiness is Neill's goal, Rafferty's is "the equipping of the individual with the arsenal he will need throughout life in his combat against the forces of error." Rafferty also does not think that the school should be made to fit the child; he asks, "Will life in later years recast its iron imperatives to fit the individual?" Since society does not recast itself, schools must not either.

The crux of the controversy is whether the child should be made to fit into society. Neill feels that he can wait until adulthood, Rafferty contends that the child should be taught the "rules of the game." Neill wants a happy child, while Rafferty feels we are doing the child a cruel disservice if the rules are not inculcated at a young age and the child is not taught to think and act "in an orderly, disciplined manner."

The final selection in this section, by Goodwin Watson, is another analysis of Summerhill, but this time with a positive view. Watson outlines the basic principles of Summerhill, but the real significance of his article is his demonstration of the applicability of those principles to higher education.

Basic Principles of Summerhill*

Erich Fromm

A. S. Neill's system is a radical approach to child rearing. In my opinion, his book is of great importance because it represents the *true* principle of education without fear. In Summerhill School authority does not mask a system of manipulation.

---

* Reprinted from Part II of Erich Fromm's introduction to *Summerhill: A Radical Approach to Child Rearing,* by A. S. Neill, pp. xii–xv. Copyright 1960, Hart Publishing Co., Inc., New York City.

Summerhill does not expound a theory; it relates the actual experience of almost 40 years. The author contends that "freedom works."

The principles underlying Neill's system are presented in this book simply and unequivocally. They are these in summary.

1. Neill maintains a firm faith "in the goodness of the child." He believes that the average child is not born a cripple, a coward, or a soulless automaton, but has full potentialities to love life and to be interested in life.

2. The aim of education—in fact the aim of life—is to work joyfully and to find happiness. Happiness, according to Neill, means being interested in life; or as I would put it, responding to life not just with one's brain but with one's whole personality.

3. In education, intellectual development is not enough. Education must be both intellectual *and* emotional. In modern society we find an increasing separation between intellect and feeling. The experiences of man today are mainly experiences of thought rather than an immediate grasp of what his heart feels, his eyes see, and his ears hear. In fact, this separation between intellect and feeling has led modern man to a near schizoid state of mind in which he has become almost incapable of experiencing anything except in thought.

4. Education must be geared to the psychic needs and capacities of the child. The child is not an altruist. He does not yet love in the sense of the mature love of an adult. It is an error to expect something from a child which he can show only in a hypocritical way. Altruism develops *after* childhood.

5. Discipline, dogmatically imposed, and punishment create fear; and fear creates hostility. This hostility may not be conscious and overt, but it nevertheless paralyzes endeavor and authenticity of feeling. The extensive disciplining of children is harmful and thwarts sound psychic development.

6. *Freedom does not mean license.* This very important principle, emphasized by Neill, is that respect for the individual must be mutual. A teacher does not use force against a child, nor has a child the right to use force against a teacher. A child may not intrude upon an adult just because he is a child, nor may a child use pressure in the many ways in which a child can.

7. Closely related to this principle is the need for true sincerity on the part of the teacher. The author says that never in the 40 years of his work in Summerhill has he lied to a child. Anyone who reads this book will be convinced that this statement, which might sound like boasting, is the simple truth.

8. Healthy human development makes it necessary that a child eventually cut the primary ties which connect him with his father and mother, or with later substitutes in society, and that he become truly independent. He must learn to face the world as an individual. He must

learn to find his security not in any symbiotic attachment, but in his capacity to grasp the world intellectually, emotionally, artistically. He must use all his powers to find union with the world, rather than to find security through submission or domination.

9. Guilt feelings primarily have the function of binding the child to authority. Guilt feelings are an impediment to independence; they start a cycle which oscillates constantly between rebellion, repentance, submission, and new rebellion. Guilt, as it is felt by most people in our society, is not primarily a reaction to the voice of conscience, but essentially an awareness of disobedience against authority and fear of reprisal. It does not matter whether such punishment is physical or a withdrawal of love, or whether one simply is made to feel an outsider. All such guilt feelings create fear; and fear breeds hostility and hypocrisy.

10. Summerhill School does not offer religious education. This, however, does not mean that Summerhill is not concerned with what might be loosely called the basic humanistic values. Neill puts it succinctly: "The battle is not between believers in theology and nonbelievers in theology; it is between believers in human freedom and believers in the suppression of human freedom." The author continues, "Some day a new generation will not accept the obsolete religion and myths of today. When the new religion comes, it will refute the idea of man's being born in sin. A new religion will praise God by making men happy."

Neill is a critic of present-day society. He emphasizes that the kind of person we develop is a mass-man. "We are living in an insane society" and "most of our religious practices are sham." Quite logically, the author is an internationalist, and holds a firm and uncompromising position that readiness for war is a barbaric atavism of the human race.

Indeed, Neill does not try to educate children to fit well into the existing order, but endeavors to rear children who will become happy human beings, men and women whose values are not to *have* much, not to *use* much, but to *be* much. Neill is a realist; he can see that even though the children he educates will not necessarily be extremely successful in the worldly sense, they will have acquired a sense of genuineness which will effectually prevent their becoming misfits or starving beggars. The author has made a decision between full human development and full marketplace success—and he is uncompromisingly honest in the way he pursues the road to his chosen goal.

Analysis of Summerhill [Con]*

MAX RAFFERTY

Summerhill is old hat, you know. Not new. Not revolutionary. Not even shocking.

It's hard to pinpoint the first educational quack. I suppose the line of frauds goes back well beyond Jean-Jacques Rousseau, but that heartless mountebank will serve as a starting point.

Jean-Jacques was a real character. With an irresponsibility character-istic of his entire philosophy, he fathered several bastards and thoughtfully shunted them into foundling asylums for his more humdrum fellow-citizens to support. At various times he practiced voyeurism, exhibitionism, and masturbation with equally feverish enthusiasm, preserving himself from any legal unpleasantness by pleading softening of the brain. He fought viciously, if verbally, with every normal intellect in Europe, and died insane.

Rousseau spawned a frenetic theory of education which after two centuries of spasmodic laboring brought forth a by-blow in the form of A. S. Neill's neolithic version of the hallowed halls of academe: Summer-hill. According to the confused Frenchman, education was running, jump-ing, shouting, doing as one pleased. The first impulses of nature are always right. Keep the child's mind idle as long as you can. And suchlike rot.

This sort of guff is as old as the human race. The child is a Noble Savage, needing only to be let alone in order to insure his intellectual salvation. Don't inhibit him. Never cross him, lest he develop horrid neu-roses later on in life. The cave children of the Stone Age grew up happier, better adjusted, and less frustrated than do ours today, simply because they were in a blissful state of nature. So just leave the kids alone. They'll educate themselves.

Twaddle.

Schooling is not a natural process at all. It's highly artificial. No boy in his right mind ever wanted to study multiplication tables and historical dates when he could be out hunting rabbits or climbing trees. In the days when hunting and climbing contributed to the survival of *homo sapiens,* there was some sense in letting the kids do what comes naturally, but when man's future began to hang upon the systematic mastery of orderly subject

---

* Reprinted from *Summerhill: For and Against,* edited by Harold H. Hart, pp. 11–25. Copyright 1970, Hart Publishing Co., Inc., New York City.

matter, the primordial, happy-go-lucky, laissez-faire kind of learning had to go. Today it's part and parcel of whatever lost innocence we may ever have possessed. Long gone. A quaint anachronism.

Except at Summerhill.

The story of mankind is the rise of specialization with its highly artificial concomitants. Over the years, natural medicine gave way to anesthesia, antiseptics, and antibiotics. In the field of transportation, hiking sturdily along dim forest trails took a back seat to freeways, air routes, and eventually lunar orbits. And in the communications sector, old Stentor himself, brass lungs and all, couldn't compete today with radio and the telephone.

So it is with education. When writing was invented, "natural" education went down the drain of history. From then on, children were destined to learn artificially, just as men around the world were increasingly to live artificially. This is civilization—the name of the game. When Rousseau and his cave-dwelling modern imitators cry out against artificiality, they are in fact down on all fours, mopping and mowing, hurling twigs and dirt at civilization. For all civilization is artificial.

This brings us gently on to Summerhill.

Just as Rousseau was the engendering spirit of Romanticism two hundred years ago, so too is A. S. Neill the soul of Summerhill, if one can say this accurately of an institution which acknowledges neither soul nor God. Hear him intone his own hemi-decalog:

> "The aim of education is to work joyfully and find happiness."
> "Make the school fit the child."
> "The absence of fear is the finest thing that can happen to a child."
> "Lessons are optional. Children can go to them or stay away from them —for years if they want to."

and

> "Heterosexual play in childhood is the royal road to a healthy, balanced sex life."

Every one of these Devil's Dictionary definitions is seductive, specious, and spurious. Allow me to demonstrate:

(1) "The aim of education is to work joyfully and find happiness."

No it isn't.

The aim of education is to give young people the intellectual tools which the race over the centuries has found indispensable in the pursuit of truth. Working joyfully, finding happiness, making a million dollars, trapping a sexually attractive mate—all these consummations are, I suppose, devoutly to be wished and have in fact occupied a considerable fraction of human interest and ingenuity down the ages. But none of them has much to do with the main goal of education, which is the equipping of the individual with the arsenal he will need throughout life in his combat against the forces of error. Happiness is a byproduct of education, not its be-all and its end-all. Education does not guarantee happiness. It merely enables one to be more discriminating in his quest for that elusive butterfly.

(2) "Make the school fit the child."

But will life in later years recast its iron imperatives to fit the individual? And isn't the school supposed to be, in the large, divine and comfortable words of the Gospel according to St. John Dewey, a microcosm of life, or at the very least a preparation for it?

If we deceive the child into thinking that life is going to adapt itself to him through all the vexing decades ahead, then surely we are lying to him in the most cynical and scoundrelly fashion. More, we are sowing the dragon's teeth of disillusion and defeat for every youngster who goes through his formative years swaddled in a cotton-batting environment of sweetness and light, only to have the ugly face of reality thrust suddenly into his own at the age of eighteen.

Sooner or later, a human being must come to an arrangement with the world about him. Either he adjusts to it, or by dint of personality, intelligence and force of will he shapes a small corner of it more closely to his heart's desire. In either case, he will be ill-fitted for the task if his teachers have convinced him since infancy that the universe is going to accommodate itself to him.

The school must meet individual needs and differences, true enough. It should help the child in every possible way to prepare himself for life in a world diked and plowed by two hundred generations of men past. The school should be just. It should be kindly. It should by all means be as interesting as possible. But it should not and it cannot "fit" every child.

Mr. Neill conceives the school as Proteus. It isn't. It's Atlas, holding up the centuries of human thought. Somehow the children of each generation must come to terms with the titan.

(3) "The absence of fear is the finest thing that can happen to a child."

In Heaven, yes. On our imperfect earth, certainly not. It's one of the worst things which could possibly happen to a child.

One wiser than Neill has said, "The fear of the Lord is the beginning of wisdom." This is one kind of fear, and a necessary one for sheer salvation's sake. On another level altogether, children should be taught to fear all sorts of earthly evils, from ant paste to sex perverts, if they are to grow up at all. Survival is the password here.

Assuredly the school cannot be an updated version of Dotheboys Hall, with assorted Squeers-instructors wielding terror weapons against panicked pupils. Fear as a motivation for learning is little better than no motivation at all. But fear, as an ingredient of existence, is as necessary for the survival of the species as is pain. Like pain, too, it has been a fellow traveller with man since the very beginning. When man ceases to be healthily afraid, he will be extinct.

The *unnecessary* fears are those which the schools should war against unceasingly. Ghosts, werewolves, witches, broken mirrors, skin a different color from our own—these chimeras should indeed be exorcised instructionally. On the other hand, live wires, drunken drivers, venereal disease, atomic fallout—fears of these all-too-actual menaces had better be encouraged by the schools, not discouraged, or presently there will be no more pupils to instruct, nor schools to instruct them, for that matter.

As we shall point out more than once, Mr. Neill's blithe penchant for striking generalizations in his little book betrays him into postures which only the charity of the reviewer keeps him from describing as those of a perfect ass. This is one of those times.

(4) "Lessons are optional. Children can go to them or stay away from them—for years if they want to."

Here the Progressive Education strand which runs through the tapestry of Summerhill comes on strongly.

Subject matter is relatively unimportant.

What is learned is less significant than *how* it is learned.

Cooperation and in-groupness and togetherness are the main objectives of instruction.

And I am the Maharajah of Mysore . . .

Let's exercise a little rudimentary logic. If the lessons are important, they should be taught to everyone, or somebody isn't getting what his parents are paying for. Conversely, if the lessons are unimportant, why bother with them at all? There is, of course, a third alternative: the lessons may be important for some, but not for all. In that case, why not diversify the lessons, so that all can profit from attending them?

Nowhere in the Summerhill philosophy does there seem to be the merest hint that children should learn to think and act in an orderly, disciplined manner. Nowhere is there even the insinuation that in this life, this world, this universe there are some things which are important to be learned, simply because—like Everest—they are there. If a child is to grow up saying and doing just as he pleases, there is precious little use in spending money on his tuition. He can do this sort of thing at home, free.

A school is not a health resort, nor a recreation center, nor a psychiatric clinic. It's a place where the massed wisdom of the ages is passed from one generation to the next, and where youngsters are taught to think in a logical and systematic fashion. A school where lessons are unimportant is a school where education itself has become irrelevant.

Is it, then, impossible to learn except in an institution?

By no means. Hundreds of great men have proved that a school is not essential to one's becoming truly learned. The experience of the great mass of humanity over the centuries, however, has demonstrated that the easiest, most efficient, and most economical way to learn is in organized classes, from trained instructors with assigned lessons.

A school, therefore, is taking money under false pretenses when it offers education without lessons. It can masquerade as a frolic in the park, a daisy-picking foray, or an experiment in free love, but it isn't a school unless it offers organized knowledge in some systematic way.

And if it lets some of its immature charges amass the wisdom of the ages while it simultaneously permits others to go out and romp in the hay, it is simply short-changing kids who are too young to know the difference.

(5) "Heterosexual play in childhood is the royal road to a healthy, balanced sex life."

Note that Headmaster Neill never concerns himself with corny old ideas like good or evil. The concept of virginity leaves him not only cold, but convulsed with mocking merriment. Mutual masturbation, he admits, is quite often practiced by pupils under his genial supervision, and he gives the definite impression in his book that he wouldn't raise the slightest objection if his adolescent clients were to stage a love-in, a gang rape, or a Black Mass with Neill himself presiding as Master of the Revels, for that matter.

It seems superfluous to point out that a child who is taught in school that premarital sex is perfectly jolly, comfy and gung-ho is apt to continue to practice it in all its ramifications when he gets to be an adult. And since Western civilization is based very largely upon monogamy and the family unit, Summerhill is obviously not only uncivilized but also anti-civilized.

This is perhaps the understatement of the decade. Speaking as dispassionately as possible but with complete sincerity, I would as soon enroll a child of mine in a brothel as in Summerhill. I know of no research which indicates that encouraging uninhibited sexual activity in childhood does anything to produce a sexually decent and happy adult. Neither does indiscriminate sexual experimentation at an early age impel the individual in later life toward an avoidance of sexual immorality. It would make as much sense for Mr. Neill to teach his little friends to sandpaper their finger ends and manipulate tumblers in the dark, and then to claim that this would induce in them a healthier attitude toward safecracking. What the unkempt and sometimes terrifying generation of tomorrow quite obviously needs are more inhibitions, not fewer.

Judging from the amount of space the author devotes to the topic in his book, Summerhill must be the sexiest spot since Sybaris. This rather nasty facet of Mr. Neill's flawed diamond reminds me irresistibly of the comment Bentley made upon the publication of Pope's translation of the Iliad, "A fine poem, Mr. Pope, but you must not call it Homer."

Summerhill may be a very pretty and permissive piece of phallic paganism, Mr. Neill, but you mustn't call it school. You really mustn't.

* * * *

If time but permitted, a coldly logical analysis of a few other direct quotations from Mr. Neill would prove not only illuminating but positively enticing.

"Discipline creates fear, and fear creates hostility."
"Summerhill pupils don't stand room inspection, and no one picks up after them."
"My staff and I have a hearty hatred of all examinations."

and most revealingly

"Summerhill is a difficult place in which to study."

But alas! Temptation must be spurned by the resolute reviewer, no matter how juicily it may offer itself, and peripheral opportunities must be sternly set aside in order that we may come grimly to grips with the main body of Neill's folly.

It's not really the headmaster's statement of principles which bothers me so much as it is his obvious hypocrisy. He wrote his book apparently to prove that the example set by Summerhill can and should be practiced by education in general. Yet he admits that he takes only the children of the well-to-do: "We have never been able to take the children of the very poor."

This, of course, makes Summerhill an exercise in aristocratic futility. In America, we educate everybody. True, we do it under certain difficulties, and the results, to say the least, are somewhat mixed. But we don't just teach the children of wealthy atheists, as Mr. Neill confesses he does. Neither are we able to limit luxuriously our enrollment to 70, and then to employ a staff of seven or more to instruct them. A pupil-teacher ratio of ten to one is a little rich for our Yankee blood. Our American ratio is more like 30 to one.

Just as an aside, almost *any* educational philosophy can be implemented with fair results if the school is able to supply one teacher for every ten pupils. With that kind of tutorial staffing and with above-average intellects to educate, Neill should be able to teach his kids to do everything except levitate.

In his book, he brags that Summerhill graduates succeed in later life. But how could they fail? With their background, their wealth, and their brains, they would probably have done well if they had been educated in the Himalayas, with yaks as instructors. The test of a school or of an educational philosophy is how well it educates *all* kinds of children—rich, poor, smart, stupid, black, white. When Summerhill starts doing this, I'll be glad to stop back for a second look.

Another detestably hypocritical posture is to be found in one of the beaming headmaster's more sordid little anecdotes:

"Some years ago, we had two pupils arrive at the same time: a boy of seventeen and a girl of sixteen. They fell in love with one another, and were always together. I met them one night and stopped them.

"'I don't know what you two are doing,' I said, 'and morally I don't care, for it isn't a moral question at all. But economically I do care. If you, Kate, have a kid, my school will be ruined.'"

It doesn't matter one whit to Neill that the baby will be illegitimate. Like his bedraggled spiritual mentor, Rousseau, he would presumably clap the kid into an orphan asylum and forget about him. After all, what are the woes of one more miserable foundling compared to the joys of "let's-all-have-a-ball-and-to-hell-with-the-consequences?"

Nor does he worry about the chilling selfishness involved in premarital sex, the anguish guaranteed by sexual experimentation on the part of those least prepared to face the consequences, nor even the breakdown of our Western code of morality implicit in the spread of Neill's hedonism to the majority of the next generation.

No, he worries about none of these things. Morality be damned. Delinquency be hanged. Venereal disease? Pooh-pooh! The only thing which concerns him is whether his school will be ruined financially.

"Economically I do care . . ."

You'd better believe he does. Because his school is his livelihood, and if it begins to be a breeding ground for little bastards, even some of his probably incredulous and certainly incredible parents might come to have second thoughts and to pull their offspring out of this junior-grade Gomorrah. And this would hurt Neill's pocketbook.

Faugh! What kind of pandering Pied Piper have we here?

When Summerhill gets a student who is a crook, Neill tells him more ways to be a crook.

When a child smokes at Summerhill, as many do, Neill lets him. Never mind the ghastly threat of lung cancer looming somewhere up ahead. Live it up, kids. The present is the only time there is.

When mass sex play is indulged in by his charges, Neill smiles benevolently. After all, the kids like it, don't they? And shouldn't children be encouraged to do everything they like? He wants to assuage guilt feelings, he says. But as everyone realizes who reads the daily news, who watches television, or who dares to visit a college campus these days, the problem of the next generation is not too many guilt feelings, but too few.

A teacher who deliberately encourages vice in children who have been given into his care for good or ill, and who profits economically for so doing, is no teacher. Not in my book, anyway. He's an educational prostitute.

In my home state of California, some of us fighting under the banner of "Education in Depth" clashed shield to shield and helm to helm with Progressive Education years ago, and brought it crashing heavily to earth. Summerhill, half a world away, evokes memories of that old strife. For this is no wave of the future, this Fata Morgana which goes by the idyllic name of Summerhill. It is a return to old Rousseau, to the hoary clichés and the half-baked romanticism of the 18th century. It's a pastiche of the Isle of Boobies and Never-Never-Land, of Pantisocracy, and of "Lord of the Flies."

Summerhill is convinced that there are no absolutes, no eternal verities, no positive standards of good or evil. We who follow the standard of Education in Depth know that there are, and know that education exists to identify these lasting values and to seek after them as long as life itself shall last.

Summerhill stresses complete freedom in behavior as the main goal of the instructional process. Education in Depth holds that the teaching of organized, disciplined and systematic subject matter is the principal objective of the schools.

Summerhill feels that the curriculum should depend entirely upon the immediate interests of the individual. Education in Depth wants a curriculum to provide for the individual the tools and skills he needs to become a cultured and productive citizen.

Summerhill believes that education exists to make the individual joyful. Education in Depth exists to make him learned.

Summerhill advocates "experiencing" learning through as many sense avenues as practicable. Education in Depth thinks this is a ridiculous waste of precious time, and regards reading and recitative discussion as still the most effective and economical method of instruction.

Summerhill holds that the pupil should be encouraged to compete only with himself, or rather with his own previous best efforts. Education in Depth believes that the success of the individual in later life depends upon how well he is taught in school to hold his own in an increasingly competitive world.

However, let us let the English themselves have at least the next-to-the-last word on what is essentially an English phenomenon. Here's what

the Ministry of Education, with the masterful understatement typical of
the island race, had to say about Summerhill a few years back:

> "On the whole, the results of this system are unimpressive. It is true
> that the children work with a will and an interest that is most impressive,
> but their achievements are rather meager."

and

> "'To have created a situation in which academic education of the
> most intelligent kind could flourish is an achievement, but in fact it is
> not flourishing and a great opportunity is thus being lost."

I can only bow to the Ministry's ability to recognize a fraud when it
sees one. If only the purblind parents who turn their younglings over to
the perpetually permissive Mr. Neill would bother to read their own
Ministry's report!

But the very last word belongs traditionally to the reviewer himself,
and I herewith claim my rights. As I remarked ten years ago in "Suffer,
Little Children":

> "The educator should approach his class not as the chemist ap-
> praises his retorts nor the astronomer his nebulae but rather as the con-
> ductor confronts his symphony orchestra. From the breathless whispering
> of the strings, from the clarion peals of the brass, from the muted thunder
> of the percussions, the conductor will weave the very fabric of great music,
> threaded throughout with the polychromatic strands of his own genius.
> Even so will the teacher evoke from the myriad experiences and abilities
> of his pupils the chords which, laced and interwoven with something of
> himself, will ring grandly in the harmony of life. There is a mingling of
> moods, an elusive interplay of spiritual counterpoint implicit in the teach-
> ing process which marks the closest human approach to the phenomenon
> of symbiosis. In its highest form it approximates creation . . .
>
> "This is an eternal verity. It has always been true. It always will be.
> It had the same solid ring of reality in the days of Pericles that it will
> have for our remote descendants. We must train our teachers as a sculptor
> is trained, not as a physicist. They must think like poets, not like statis-
> ticians. For they are dealing not with things like the chemists, nor with
> bodies like the physicians, nor yet with minds alone like the psychologists.
> To them is reserved the splendid privilege of fashioning and nurturing
> those coruscating and iridescent entities called personalities, transient as
> glancing sunbeams but more lasting than the granite of our hills. It is at
> once the most precious and most dangerous duty entrusted by mankind
> to men."

That's why Summerhill is a dirty joke. It degrades true learning to
the status of a disorganized orgy. It turns a teacher into a sniggering

projectionist of a stag movie. It transforms a school into a cross between a bear garden and a boiler factory. It is a caricature of education.

Things certainly are learned at Summerhill. Things are also learned in pool halls, drag races, and discotheques. But we do not call these places schools.

Herein lies Summerhill's twin sin against the Holy Ghost of education. It lies, and it corrupts.

Worst of all, it does these things to children. I'll spare you the Biblical injunction about child harmers, millstones, and the depths of the sea. I think you will know what I mean. I think Mr. Neill will, too. And who knows? Scuba diving with weights about the neck may be his favorite sport. In which event the Hereafter may hold no terrors for him, after all.

Analysis of Summerhill [Pro]*

GOODWIN WATSON

Campuses from California to Maine and from Miami to Seattle have feared or experienced uprisings of frustrated students. A. S. Neill's pioneer experiment at Summerhill has demonstrated what freedom (not license) can do to transform the petty tyranny of most elementary and high school classrooms. Numerous schools for young children and a few secondary schools have ventured along similar paths. Are the same basic, underlying principles applicable to the undergraduate college and to the graduate school? Would they, if incorporated in the life of an institution of higher education, alleviate the current student distress? Would the institutions then be as educative as are the best of traditional colleges?

From reading Neill's books and articles, from a visit to Summerhill, and from several other talks with him, the writer ventures to distill five principles which differentiate Neill's work from that of most other schools.

1. Learning is self-motivated rather than imposed.

Neill assumes that it is natural for children to want to learn. The evidence from the behavior of pre-school children strongly supports this view. If, as they grow older, they cease to seek new knowledge and try to escape from school requirements, this changed behavior has been brought

---

* Reprinted from *Summerhill: For and Against,* edited by Harold H. Hart, pp. 175–192. Copyright 1970, Hart Publishing Co., Inc., New York City.

about by the bad procedures of formal education. It took some of the pupils at Summerhill many weeks of idleness before they could recover from the distorted school-nurtured perception of learning as inherently disagreeable. Consider the following quotations from this master-educator.

"The function of the child is to live his own life—not the life that his anxious parents think he should live, nor a life according to the purpose of the educator who thinks he knows what is best."[1]

"Love is being on the side of the other person. Love is approval. I know that children learn slowly that freedom is something totally different from license. But they can learn this truth and do learn it."[2]

"The method of freedom is almost sure with children under twelve, but children over twelve take a long time to develop from a spoon-fed education."[3]

Douglas McGregor in his book *The Human Side of Enterprise*[4] develops an analogous principle for the management of adult workers. If the manager follows "Theory X," he believes that workers are naturally lazy: they will work only if "motivated" by the stick of fear and the carrot of advancement in pay and prestige. He assumes that unless closely supervised, his workers will goof off. So he runs a tight ship. He treats the workmen as unable or unwilling to discipline themselves or to share in planning the work to be done. He drives the crews.

If his theory of motivation be, in contrast, "Theory Y," he believes that men enjoy devising work plans and carrying them out. He believes they can be trusted to share in decisions about what is to be done, by whom, when, and how. He believes that they will become more rather than less productive, if they are self-directing.

Now the fascinating, fact is that each theory is a self-fulfilling prophecy. The employer, using Theory X, can cite abundant evidence that his workers do try to shirk, to evade, and to deceive their supervisors. If he lets up on the pressures, the men do goof off. They have no apparent interest in helping to run the business; that job they leave to the boss. He can prove the necessity of his strict controls.

But likewise, the employer who relies on Theory Y can cite from his own experience instances which confirm his different expectations. Given opportunity to participate in finding better ways to do the job, the workers are interested, involved, creative and practical. Sensing that they are trusted, they become increasingly responsible and self-disciplined. They often go beyond job-definitions and requirements to meet unexpected

---

1. *Summerhill,* p. 12.
2. *Summerhill,* p. 293.
3. *Summerhill,* p. 293.
4. McGraw-Hill, N.Y., 1960.

emergencies. They turn out fewer defective parts when they are their own inspectors.

The educational situation is similar. Teachers who assume that pupils will try to do as little work as they can possibly get away with will behave in ways which make their expectations come true. The pupils will turn out to be apathetic, lazy, dependent, and in need of close direction by the teacher. The Summerhill type of teacher will have an opposite experience which confirms his predictions. Pupils given freedom to decide what they will do, when, and how, develop increasing independence, stronger interests, and better quality of work.

This is why arguments between traditional teachers and progressive facilitators are so unproductive. Each has first-hand evidence confirming his own assumptions.

There are some other truths underlying Neill's approach which also support freedom to learn rather than attempts to impose instruction. One is that what teachers think they are teaching by traditional methods does not correspond very closely to what pupils are actually learning. The teacher feels better if he has "covered the subject" (a ridiculous aspiration in this culture of accelerated explosion of knowledge) but he can easily discover that what pupils recall a week later is but a tiny fraction of what he had hoped to impart. What is learned is largely the result of the learner's own efforts. An energetic teacher may well reduce the effort which pupils feel called upon to make. So emerges the common predicament of a pupil who felt he understood the subject quite clearly while the teacher was explaining it, only to find, when tested later, that he is very confused and vague about the whole matter.

Still another truth about learning, which Summerhill took into account better than do the usual school procedures, is that there are different styles and rhythms of learning. Not all pupils in the first grade, the sixth grade or the twelfth grade are *ready* to learn the same thing at the same time. Some were ready long before the teacher got to the new material. Others got hung up by something days earlier, or weeks or even years earlier; and until this block is removed, they are not ready to move on to whatever comes next in the teacher's syllabus.

Even among those who are ready for a given act of learning, there are still important differences. Some will grasp the whole idea in a flash; others need the slower step-by-step approach. Some will learn better from their friends than from an adult teacher. Some require first-hand encounter with experience; others can use pictures; only a few learn best from print or from being told.

Intensity of learning effort normally rises and falls. Any adult writer or scholar or thinker or artist knows that for days at a time he may be unproductive, but then suddenly he finds himself taking hold, digging in, grappling with the problems and making extraordinary progress. The formal school takes no account of this natural rhythm in learning. It assumes that each morning when the bell rings, pupils will be able to put out the standard quota of learning effort required to progress at a standard rate through the standard curriculum. Everyone concerned with schools knows that this is factually untrue, but it is maintained as an assumption to rationalize present procedures.

Let us listen again for a moment to Neill's wisdom!

> "Let me emphasize again that a child must be left to grow at its own rate. Many parents make dreadful mistakes in trying to force the pace."[5]
> Q. What would you do with a child who won't stick to anything? He is interested in music for a short period, then he changes to dancing, and so on. A. I'd do nothing. Such is life. In my time I have changed from photography to bookbinding, then to woodwork, then brasswork. Life is full of fragments of interests. For many years I sketched in ink; when I realized I was a tenth-rate artist I gave it up.
> "A child is always eclectic in his tastes. He tries all things. That's how he learns. We never suggest that a child should finish his work; if his interest has gone, it is wrong to pressure him to finish it."[6]

Carl R. Rogers has helped many teachers to learn the basic truth that the best learning for personal growth occurs in a nonthreatening situation. A major distinction between Summerhill and all the other British boarding schools has been the absence of coercive threats in Neill's school. Because there is no need to impose and to threaten, the pupil can become more truly himself. He can learn to listen to his real feelings, and to be responsive to them. He is free to change and to grow. He does not need to use a large part of his energy to defend his autonomy or to evade those who would take freedom from him. Hence he can discover interests and concerns which lead to the kind of learning which is satisfying. There is no battle against the teacher or the curriculum. Learners and teachers become natural collaborators.

As Neill has said:

> "True freedom practiced in community living, as in Summerhill, seems to do for the many what psychoanalysis does for the individual. It releases what is hidden. It is a breath of fresh air blowing through the soul to cleanse it of self-hatred and hatred of others."[7]

2. Affective learning is even more important than cognitive acquisition.

Neill was concerned basically with the feelings of his pupils. He was central in their lives not because of his scholarship in some academic field but because of his ability to understand and to accept their actual feelings.

---

5. *Summerhill,* p. 362.
6. *Summerhill,* p. 361.
7. *Summerhill,* p. 297.

Again and again, in his case reports, he rejects the offered mask and calls forth the true reactions hidden beneath the "proper" surface. This he learned from psychoanalysis and his discussions with Wilhelm Reich. He concludes:

> "Knowledge in itself won't help unless a parent (or student) is emotionally ready to receive the knowledge and has the inner capacity to act on what new knowledge comes his way."[8]
>
> "When I lecture to students at teacher training colleges and universities I am often shocked at the ungrownupness of these lads and lasses stuffed with useless knowledge . . . They have been taught to know but have not been allowed to feel."[9]

Concern for feelings leads to greater awareness of the role of the body. The old dualism between mental and physical had no place in Neill's work. The "whole child" is now a trite expression, but it was a vital reality at Summerhill. Again, Neill found Reich congenial because Reich had pioneered insights into the way muscular tensions and other physiological changes revealed attitudes which might be verbally denied.

> "If you educate children in freedom, they will be more conscious of themselves, for freedom allows more and more of the unconscious to become conscious. That is why most Summerhill children have few doubts about life. They know what they want. And I guess they will get it, too."[10]

In the affective life, sex always plays a vital role. Our whole society has today moved far in the direction pioneered by Neill.

When Neill began his professional work it was in a culture which still retained the stiff standards of Puritanism and the prudery associated with Queen Victoria. As in the Vienna where Freud made his great discoveries, most neurotic behavior arose from forms of sexual repression. Immense changes have taken place during Neill's lifetime. The naughty four-letter words are commonplace in current periodicals. Nudity is no longer seen as intrinsically indecent and appears on the stage and in films.

One of Neill's important services to pupils and their parents was his early recognition of the corrupting effect of the prevailing prudishness. He shocked many by his open acceptance of normal sexual interests. This aspect of culture has changed so radically during the past generation or two, that it is hard today to realize that Neill's sensible attitude toward sex was once the basis for much hostile criticism. It seems fair to conclude that in today's freer world, Neill would have been even more outspoken. Granting all the progress that has been made, we must recognize that true sexual freedom has been attained by very few persons in our current society.

---

8. *Summerhill,* p. 355.
9. *Summerhill,* p. 25.
10. *Summerhill,* p. 348.

3. The quality of living in the here and now takes precedence over efforts to prepare for the future.

Here is perhaps the most basic contrast between the goals of Summerhill and those of schools which regard themselves as essentially "preparatory." The prep school exists to facilitate some future good. Any violation of the quality of life for pupils in the traditional school is defended on the ground that it is necessary as a preparation for entrance to the university or for securing a future job. Attendance at boring classes, reading of dull books, writing of required but distasteful papers, taking of acutely painful and humiliating tests—all these cruelties to children are rationalized as good preparation for some life to come.

This shift in values from some supposed future (viewed in a rather murky crystal ball) to the evident here-and-now was brought home to the writer when he talked one day with the mother and teacher of Harry, a seven year old child who suffered from a disease which would almost certainly lead to death within the next four or five years. What should be the "curriculum" for Harry? What requirements should he have to meet? Clearly, in his case, the right prescription was that every day should be made as satisfying as possible.

But would it really be so different for a child with normal life expectancy? Neill probably didn't study John Dewey's philosophy of education, but if he had done so, he would have met the idea that a good life today is the best possible preparation for tomorrow. Neill was more likely to have been influenced by Robert Louis Stevenson's observation that we would not compliment a hungry man who denied himself the main course of a meal so he could save all his appetite for the dessert, before he knew whether there was going to be any dessert or not.

In any case, Neill's pupils differed from those in other private schools of Britain, in that they were not as ambitious to "succeed" by current standards. They were more apt to carry away from school a quality of living which brought satisfaction in the present. More art, more music, more relaxed play, more friendly conversation!

The work of David McClelland on "Need to Achieve" has shown that the fantasies and activities of youth have a marked influence on this character trait. Summerhill pupils would probably rate much higher on need for joy and need for serenity and need for affection than on need to achieve.

4. A school should be education for creativity.

In a rapidly changing society the old answers are likely to be wrong answers. Neill's pupils studied the basic skills, not for their own sake, but as instruments useful in creative activity. He wrote:

"Creators learn what they want to learn in order to have the tools that their originality and genius demand. We do not know how much creation is killed in the classroom with its emphasis on learning."[11]

Neill contrasts his view with that of the prestigious "public schools" (really private and restricted) in England.

"The strict school carries on the tradition of keeping the child down, keeping him quiet, respectful, castrated. Moreover the school does excellent work only in treating the head of the child. It restrains his emotional life, his creative urge. It trains him to be obedient to all the dictators and bosses of life . . . The strict school demands only power—and the fearful parent is satisfied."

5. A school should be a democratic community.

At Summerhill town meetings each person—man, woman or child—director, teacher, household staff, or pupil—has one vote. Each has an equal right to attend or to stay away: to do his thing in his own way. It is not anarchy, for there are norms and rules. The rules are made by a legislative process in which the whole community participates. Each individual wins the respect and influence which others freely give. There are no uniforms or badges of status.

"Summerhill is a self-governing school, democratic in form. Everything connected with social, or group life, is settled by vote at the Saturday night General School Meeting. Each member of the teaching staff and each child, regardless of his age, has one vote. My vote carries the same weight as that of a seven-year-old."[12]

Neill's conception of the teaching staff in any good school reflects the same quality of human relations.

"Teachers would be taught to be the equal of pupils, not the superiors. They would retain no protective dignity, no sarcasm. They would inspire no fear. They would have to be men and women of infinite patience, able to see far ahead, willing to trust in ultimate results."[13]

The principles which underlie life at Summerhill can equally well be applied at the college level. They might well revolutionize higher education. It is a strange paradox that self-directed education has been attempted most often at the nursery school and kindergarten level. As the pupil grows

---

11. *Summerhill*, p. 26.
12. *Summerhill*, p. 45.
13. *Summerhill*, p. 287.

older and more competent, he is less and less likely to be trusted to make his own educational decisions.

Much of the student protest is directed at those aspects of contemporary campus life which contradict the Summerhill philosophy. Students resist imposed requirements. They want to pursue kinds of learning which seem to them interesting and relevant. They are infuriated by close supervision and want to run their own lives. They want to remove the threats of tests and grades. They seek for ecstasy as well as knowledge. They want joyful experiences in the here-and-now, and they refuse to climb the ladders set up by the Establishment. They want creative living. They want to be respected as equals and not derogated to the role portrayed in an oft-quoted paper entitled "The Student as Nigger." They want power to shape decisions which have a bearing on their own lives. A short summary of what the student activists are now demanding is that they want their colleges to be more like Summerhill!

Neill may well be pleased at the student demands. He once wrote:

> "I wish I could see a movement of rebellion among our younger teachers. Higher education and university degrees do not make a scrap of difference in confronting the evils of society."[14]

Some of the more experimental colleges already include features which, by Neill's principles, are sound. At Antioch, Goddard, and New College (Sarasota, Florida) it is possible for a student to propose a large part of his own educational program and to carry this out in whatever way he wants to. As at Summerhill, there are courses available if a student wants to learn that way. He may, however, do independent study while living on the campus, or he may go to a Field Center in this country or abroad where he can have experiences with a style of life quite different from those he has previously known at home or at college. He has a voice and vote in determining policies on his campus. Coeducational dormitories are accepted, and restrictive rules are few. Creativity is appreciated rather than repressed.

To extend such opportunities more widely, the Union for Research and Experimentation in Higher Education, a consortium of a dozen or more unusually progressive colleges,[15] has proposed the formation of a *University Without Walls*. Basic features have been listed as follows:

1. Admission: Persons 16–60 years of age, interested to learn.
2. Program for each student worked out individually to meet his needs and interests.

---

14. *Summerhill,* p. 28.
15. Antioch, Bard, Goddard, Hofstra, Loretto Heights, Monteith, Nasson, New College at Sarasota, Northeastern Illinois State, Sarah Lawrence, Shimer, Stephens.

3. An Inventory of Learning Resources, well-indexed (computer memory-bank?), will direct the learner to sources (print, tape, persons, laboratories, etc.) of knowledge he seeks.
4. Courses,, laboratories, studios, etc., in all the participating colleges will be open to qualified U.W.W. students, but most of the learning will be independent and self-directed, carried out by the students alone or with a small group of peers.
5. A student begins his work by attending for one quarter (10 weeks?) a center on or near the campus of one of the participating colleges. Here he meets his fellow students, a team of faculty representing different specialties, and with his advisor works out his personal learning program. He attends two groups during the first quarter—one directed to understanding self and other (L-group); the other toward improving basic learning skills.
6. From time to time, a student will again join a group of peers (with homogeneous or heterogeneous interests) at one of the campus centers.
7. At least one term will be spent in an off-campus field center; some students may live for a time in each of several different subcultures in the U.S.A. and abroad.
8. A dialogue is continuously maintained between each student and his advisor. This may be done face-to-face, or by letters, or telephone, or tapes, or records, or papers read and returned with comments. Communication between a student and other faculty and a student with his peers is also expected.
9. "Faculty" for the U.W.W. may include, in addition to persons teaching in one of the participating colleges, experts from any walk of life: agriculture, business, science, the arts, politics, etc.
10. Each student will complete at least one major project of excellent quality in his chosen field of work.
11. Each student keeps a cumulative record of his activities and learning. He may use standardized tests for his own guidance.
12. If a student wants a Bachelor of Arts degree he applies when he believes he is ready for it. No fixed Commencement dates. His achievements are reviewed by a committee of faculty and students, who recommend a degree or further study.

The name—*University Without Walls*—recalls Neill's statement about most school buildings:

"The classroom walls and prison-like buildings narrow the teacher's outlook and prevent him from seeing the true essentials of education."[16]

The Summerhillian principles suggest also a need for fundamental change in post-graduate education. In most universities today, Ph.D. programs are discipline-oriented with prescribed course requirements, certification examinations within the subject area, and research of a fairly standard

---

16. *Summerhill*, p. 28.

pattern. Yet the needs of students and of society would require a more flexible program which is person-oriented and problem-focused. Again the U.R.E.H.E. has come forward with a proposal.

The proposed Graduate School of U.R.E.H.E. will provide opportunity for capable students to go beyond the B.A. to a Ph.D. The design continues many features of the University Without Walls. Programs are designed to fit the needs of each individual student. Interdisciplinary work is encouraged. Any course in any university in the world may be included. Dialogue between student and a faculty committee is maintained. Students review their progress, from time to time, in a colloquium of fellow-candidates. Each student keeps a cumulative record of his progress. His graduate work culminates in a major project which may be research, or a book, or a work of art, or an achievement in social change, or may take other forms. The doctorate may be applied for, and on recommendation of faculty and peers, awarded at any time. The program will begin at several different geographic centers in 1970.

Summerhill was the creation of an earlier era, related to a different world from that in which we today struggle for survival. Without negating the valid view of personal development and the learning process which Neill developed, we are pressed to take more account of unsolved social problems. In the United States, extrication from the Viet Nam war and the prevention of similar allegedly anti-Communist military escapades in future years is of primary concern. So is the continuing battle against poverty and against white racism. Environmental pollution is another center of concern. The right of women and children to be fully respected as persons and not chattels has yet to be fully realized.

The specific grievances are contemporary but the basic concern that schools should make a difference in society was apparent in Neill's philosophy. He saw, as noted above, a clear connection between authoritarian control in the classroom and submission to dictatorship in the nation.

In another passage—anticipating the central thesis of Norman O. Brown's *Life Against Death*[17]—Neill wrote about society as well as school:

> "Pro-life equals fun, games, love, interesting work, hobbies, laughter, music, dance, consideration for others, and faith in men. Anti-life equals duty, obedience, profit and power. Throughout history anti-life has won, and will continue to win as long as youth is trained to fit into present-day adult conceptions."[18]

At a recent conference of innovative college faculty members and students (New College, Sarasota, Florida, June 30–July 12, 1969) the

---

17. *Life Against Death*, Norman O. Brown; New York, Vintage Books.
18. *Summerhill*, p. 344.

following statements were adopted almost unanimously and have been central to student protests in many colleges.

"This culture is oppressive.

"There is no human task more important than creating alternatives to our culture.

"Alternatives begin in self-liberation.

"A lack of trust infects American society and we cannot survive without trust.

"Our present structures and institutions are inept—frequently accelerate the malignancy in our society, rarely do anything to arrest it and are absolutely unable to cure it and prevent further recurrences.

"Urgent and critical problems which threaten the survival of life on this violent planet demand immediate attention."

These truths, if indeed they are valid, call for changes in education at every age level, from youngest children through to the elderly and retired adults. They call for a progressive advance which incorporates the wisdom of Neill of Summerhill, but which moves further to cope with the problems emerging in America and the world on the verge of the 21st Century.

Neill himself has provided a fitting close to this proposal for a Summerhill University.

"The future of Summerhill itself may be of little import. But the future of the Summerhill idea is of the greatest importance to humanity. New generations must be given the chance to grow in freedom. The bestowal of freedom is the bestowal of love. And only love can save the world."[19]

---

19. *Summerhill,* p. 92.

Chapter

14

Economy:
Is There a
Culture of Poverty?

The idea that there is a "culture of poverty" has caused a considerable stir in the social sciences. This section begins with an article by the man who is most frequently associated with that concept—Oscar Lewis. To most life in the lower classes seems disorganized and unstable, but to Lewis it is frequently patterned, fairly predictable and highly adaptive. He finds that these patterns transcend "national boundaries and regional and rural-urban differences within nations." Yet, not all poor people live in the culture of poverty, since such a culture can exist only in "a class-stratified, highly individuated, capitalistic society." The culture of poverty which develops in these societies "represents an effort to cope with feelings of hopelessness and despair that arise from the realization by members of the marginal communities in these societies of the improbability of their achieving success in terms of the prevailing values and goals." Lewis goes on to outline some seventy traits which characterize such a culture. Although these traits are adaptive, Lewis finds in them much "pathos, suffering and emptiness."

In his book (a summary of which follows Lewis' article) Charles Valentine attacks the idea of a culture of poverty and related concepts. Valentine contends that Lewis' ideas "are contradicted . . . by his own data, and his methods are inadequate to support his theory." Valentine accuses Lewis of placing the burden for reform on the poor and being concerned with doing away with a culture and not poverty. He presents an alternate model, which "portrays the poor as a heterogeneous series of subsocieties with variable and adaptable subcultures that are only partially and relatively distinct from American culture as a whole and locates the chief sources of deprivations suffered by poor people in their structural

469

position in the wider social system and in the actions and attitudes of the non-poor."

In his acid reply to Valentine, Lewis succeeds in clarifying many of his ideas about the culture of poverty. For example, he makes it clear that he recognizes it as a subculture and not a culture, and that he used the term "culture" only so that there would be no misunderstanding among his nonprofessional readers. He also notes that the culture of poverty is not isolated from that of the broader society. It would be impossible to enumerate all of the clarifications made by Lewis in his reply to Valentine. The reader is advised to pay careful attention to his reply because it contains many ideas which will add greatly to his understanding of the elusive concept of a culture of poverty. David Matza also defends himself from attacks by Valentine by making it clear that he does not hold the poor to blame for their plight, but rather the privileged elements in society. Yet, Matza does not think that the privileged groups will solve these problems. Rather, he implies that organization of the poor is the solution. Matza also attacks Valentine's propensity to romanticize the way of life of the poor.

This section ends with Valentine's reply to both Lewis and Matza. His remarks serve to show some points of convergence as well as some outstanding disagreements between these authors. The lingering disagreements should not surprise us—they are characteristic of all of the controversies in this book, as well as in all of the social sciences. If these disagreements were all resolved, this debate (and all others) would lose its dynamism and we would cease to gain an increasingly clear picture of the culture of poverty.

The Culture of Poverty*

OSCAR LEWIS

Poverty and the so-called war against it provide a principal theme for the domestic program of the present Administration. In the midst of a population that enjoys unexampled material well-being—with the average annual family income exceeding $7,000—it is officially acknowledged that some 18 million families, numbering more than 50 million individuals, live below the $3,000 "poverty line." Toward the improvement of the lot of these people some $1,600 million of Federal funds are directly allocated

* From *La Vida*, by Oscar Lewis. Copyright © 1965, 1966 by Oscar Lewis. Reprinted by permission of Martin Secker & Warburg Ltd., publishers, Random House, Inc., and Ruth M. Lewis.

through the Office of Economic Opportunity, and many hundreds of millions of additional dollars flow indirectly through expanded Federal expenditures in the fields of health, education, welfare and urban affairs.

Along with the increase in activity on behalf of the poor indicated by these figures there has come a parallel expansion of publication in the social sciences on the subject of poverty. The new writings advance the same two opposed evaluations of the poor that are to be found in literature, in proverbs and in popular sayings throughout recorded history. Just as the poor have been pronounced blessed, virtuous, upright, serene, independent, honest, kind and happy, so contemporary students stress their great and neglected capacity for self-help, leadership and community organization. Conversely, as the poor have been characterized as shiftless, mean, sordid, violent, evil and criminal, so other students point to the irreversibly destructive effects of poverty on individual character and emphasize the corresponding need to keep guidance and control of poverty projects in the hands of duly constituted authorities. This clash of viewpoints reflects in part the infighting for political control of the program between Federal and local officials. The confusion results also from the tendency to focus study and attention on the personality of the individual victim of poverty rather than on the slum community and family and from the consequent failure to distinguish between poverty and what I have called the culture of poverty.

The phrase is a catchy one and is used and misused with some frequency in the current literature. In my writings it is the label for a specific conceptual model that describes in positive terms a subculture of Western society with its own structure and rationale, a way of life handed on from generation to generation along family lines. The culture of poverty is not just a matter of deprivation or disorganization, a term signifying the absence of something. It is a culture in the traditional anthropological sense in that it provides human beings with a design for living, with a ready-made set of solutions for human problems, and so serves a significant adaptive function. This style of life transcends national boundaries and regional and rural-urban differences within nations. Wherever it occurs, its practitioners exhibit remarkable similarity in the structure of their families, in interpersonal relations, in spending habits, in their value systems and in their orientation in time.

Not nearly enough is known about this important complex of human behavior. My own concept of it has evolved as my work has progressed and remains subject to amendment by my own further work and that of others. The scarcity of literature on the culture of poverty is a measure of the gap in communication that exists between the very poor and the middle-class personnel—social scientists, social workers, teachers, physicians, priests and others—who bear the major responsibility for carrying out the antipoverty programs. Much of the behavior accepted in the culture of poverty goes counter to cherished ideals of the larger society. In writing about "multi-problem" families social scientists thus often stress their instability, their lack of order, direction and organization. Yet, as I have observed them, their behavior seems clearly patterned and reasonably predictable. I am more often struck by the inexorable repetitiousness and the iron entrenchment of their lifeways.

The concept of the culture of poverty may help to correct misapprehensions that have ascribed some behavior patterns of ethnic, national or regional groups as distinctive characteristics. For example, a high incidence of common-law marriage and of households headed by women has been thought to be distinctive of Negro family life in this country and has been attributed to the Negro's historical experience of slavery. In actuality it turns out that such households express essential traits of the culture of poverty and are found among diverse peoples in many parts of the world and among peoples that have had no history of slavery. Although it is now possible to assert such generalizations, there is still much to be learned about this difficult and affecting subject. The absence of intensive anthropological studies of poor families in a wide variety of national contexts—particularly the lack of such studies in socialist countries—remains a serious handicap to the formulation of dependable cross-cultural constants of the culture of poverty.

My studies of poverty and family life have centered largely in Mexico. On occasion some of my Mexican friends have suggested delicately that I turn to a study of poverty in my own country. As a first step in this direction I am currently engaged in a study of Puerto Rican families. Over the past three years my staff and I have been assembling data on 100 representative families in four slums of Greater San Juan and some 50 families of their relatives in New York City.

Our methods combine the traditional techniques of sociology, anthropology and psychology. This includes a battery of 19 questionnaires, the administration of which requires 12 hours per informant. They cover the residence and employment history of each adult; family relations; income and expenditure; complete inventory of household and personal possessions; friendship patterns, particularly the *compadrazgo*, or godparent, relationship that serves as a kind of informal social security for the children of these families and establishes special obligations among the adults; recreational patterns; health and medical history; politics; religion; world view and "cosmopolitanism." Open-end interviews and psychological tests (such as the thematic apperception test, the Rorschach test and the sentence-completion test) are administered to a sampling of this population.

All this work serves to establish the context for close-range study of a selected few families. Because the family is a small social system, it lends itself to the holistic approach of anthropology. Whole-family studies bridge the gap between the conceptual extremes of the culture at one pole and of the individual at the other, making possible observation of both culture and personality as they are interrelated in real life. In a large metropolis such as San Juan or New York the family is the natural unit of study.

Ideally our objective is the naturalistic observation of the life of "our" families, with a minimum of intervention. Such intensive study, however, necessarily involves the establishment of deep personal ties. My assistants include two Mexicans whose families I had studied; their "Mexican's-eye view" of the Puerto Rican slum has helped to point up the similarities and differences between the Mexican and Puerto Rican subcultures. We have spent many hours attending family parties, wakes and baptisms, responding to emergency calls, taking people to the hospital, getting them out of jail, filling out applications for them, hunting apartments with them, helping them to get jobs or to get on relief. With each member of these families we conduct tape-recorded interviews, taking down their life stories and their answers to questions on a wide variety of topics. For the ordering of our material we undertake to reconstruct, by close interrogation, the history of a week or more of consecutive days in the lives of each family, and we observe and record complete days as they unfold. The first volume to issue from this study is to be published next month under the title of *La Vida, a Puerto Rican Family in the Culture of Poverty—San Juan and New York* (Random House).

There are many poor people in the world. Indeed, the poverty of the two-thirds of the world's population who live in the underdeveloped countries has been rightly called "the problem of problems." But not all of them by any means live in the culture of poverty. For this way of life to come into being and flourish it seems clear that certain preconditions must be met.

The setting is a cash economy, with wage labor and production for profit and with a persistently high rate of unemployment and underemployment, at low wages, for unskilled labor. The society fails to provide social, political and economic organization, on either a voluntary basis or by government imposition, for the low-income population. There is a bilateral kinship system centered on the nuclear progenitive family, as distinguished from the unilateral extended kinship system of lineage and clan. The dominant class asserts a set of values that prizes thrift and the accumulation of wealth and property, stresses the possibility of upward mobility and explains low economic status as the result of individual personal inadequacy and inferiority.

Where these conditions prevail the way of life that develops among some of the poor is the culture of poverty. That is why I have described it as a subculture of the Western social order. It is both an adaptation and a reaction of the poor to their marginal position in a class-stratified, highly individuated, capitalistic society. It represents an effort to cope with feelings of hopelessness and despair that arise from the realization by the members of the marginal communities in these societies of the improbability of their achieving success in terms of the prevailing values and goals. Many of the traits of the culture of poverty can be viewed as local, spontaneous attempts to meet needs not served in the case of the poor by the institutions and agencies of the larger society because the poor are not eligible for such service, cannot afford it or are ignorant and suspicious.

Once the culture of poverty has come into existence it tends to perpetuate itself. By the time slum children are six or seven they have usually absorbed the basic attitudes and values of their subculture. Thereafter they are psychologically unready to take full advantage of changing conditions or improving opportunities that may develop in their lifetime.

My studies have identified some 70 traits that characterize the culture of poverty. The principal ones may be described in four dimensions of the system: the relationship between the subculture and the larger society; the nature of the slum community; the nature of the family; and the attitudes, values and character structure of the individual.

The disengagement, the nonintegration, of the poor with respect to the major institutions of society is a crucial element in the culture of poverty. It reflects the combined effect of a variety of factors including poverty, to begin with, but also segregation and discrimination, fear, suspicion and apathy and the development of alternative institutions and procedures in the slum community. The people do not belong to labor unions or political parties and make little use of banks, hospitals, department stores or museums. Such involvement as there is in the institutions of the larger society—in the jails, the army and the public welfare system—does little to suppress the traits of the culture of poverty. A relief system that barely keeps people alive perpetuates rather than eliminates poverty and the pervading sense of hopelessness.

People in a culture of poverty produce little wealth and receive little in return. Chronic unemployment and underemployment, low wages, lack of property, lack of savings, absence of food reserves in the home and chronic shortage of cash imprison the family and the individual in a vicious circle. Thus for lack of cash the slum householder makes frequent purchases of small quantities of food at higher prices. The slum economy turns inward; it shows a high incidence of pawning of personal goods, borrowing at usurious rates of interest, informal credit arrangements among neighbors, use of secondhand clothing and furniture.

There is awareness of middle-class values. People talk about them and even claim some of them as their own. On the whole, however, they do not live by them. They will declare that marriage by law, by the church or by both is the ideal form of marriage, but few will marry. For men who have no steady jobs, no property and no prospect of wealth to pass on to their children, who live in the present without expectations of the future, who want to avoid the expense and legal difficulties involved in marriage and divorce, a free union or consensual marriage makes good sense. The women, for their part, will turn down offers of marriage from men who are likely to be immature, punishing and generally unreliable. They feel that a consensual union gives them some of the freedom and flexibility men have. By not giving the fathers of their children legal status as husbands, the women have a stronger claim on the children. They also maintain exclusive rights to their own property.

Along with disengagement from the larger society, there is a hostility to the basic institutions of what are regarded as the dominant classes. There is hatred of the police, mistrust of government and of those in high positions and a cynicism that extends to the church. The culture of poverty thus holds a certain potential for protest and for entrainment in political movements aimed against the existing order.

With its poor housing and overcrowding, the community of the culture of poverty is high in gregariousness, but it has a minimum of organization beyond the nuclear and extended family. Occasionally slum dwellers come together in temporary informal groupings; neighborhood gangs that cut across slum settlements represent a considerable advance beyond the zero point of the continuum I have in mind. It is the low level of organization that gives the culture of poverty its marginal and anomalous quality in our highly organized society. Most primitive peoples have achieved a higher degree of sociocultural organization than contemporary urban slum dwellers. This is not to say that there may not be a sense of community and *esprit de corps* in a slum neighborhood. In fact, where slums are isolated from their surroundings by enclosing walls or other physical barriers, where rents are low and residence is stable and where the population constitutes a distinct ethnic, racial or language group, the sense of community may approach that of a village. In Mexico City and San Juan such territoriality is engendered by the scarcity of low-cost housing outside of established slum areas. In South Africa it is actively enforced by the *apartheid* that confines rural migrants to prescribed locations.

The family in the culture of poverty does not cherish childhood as a specially prolonged and protected stage in the life cycle. Initiation into sex comes early. With the instability of consensual marriage the family tends to be mother-centered and tied more closely to the mother's extended family. The female head of the house is given to authoritarian rule. In spite of much verbal emphasis on family solidarity, sibling rivalry for the limited supply of goods and maternal affection is intense. There is little privacy.

The individual who grows up in this culture has a strong feeling of fatalism, helplessness, dependence and inferiority. These traits, so often remarked in the current literature as characteristic of the American Negro, I found equally strong in slum dwellers of Mexico City and San Juan, who are not segregated or discriminated against as a distinct ethnic or racial group. Other traits include a high incidence of weak ego structure, orality and confusion of sexual identification, all reflecting maternal deprivation; a strong present-time orientation with relatively little disposition to defer gratification and plan for the future; and a high tolerance for psychological pathology of all kinds. There is widespread belief in male superiority and among the men a strong preoccupation with *machismo,* their masculinity.

Provincial and local in outlook, with little sense of history, these people know only their own neighborhood and their own way of life. Usually they do not have the knowledge, the vision or the ideology to see the similarities between their troubles and those of their counterparts elsewhere in the world. They are not class-conscious, although they are sensitive indeed to symbols of status.

The distinction between poverty and the culture of poverty is basic to the model described here. There are numerous examples of poor people whose way of life I would not characterize as belonging to this subculture. Many primitive and preliterate peoples that have been studied by anthropologists suffer dire poverty attributable to low technology or thin resources or both. Yet even the simplest of these peoples have a high degree of social organization and a relatively integrated, satisfying and self-sufficient culture.

In India the destitute lower-caste peoples—such as the Chamars, the leatherworkers, and the Bhangis, the sweepers—remain integrated in the larger society and have their own panchayat institutions of self-government. Their panchayats and their extended unilateral kinship systems, or clans, cut across village lines, giving them a strong sense of identity and continuity. In my studies of these peoples I found no culture of poverty to go with their poverty.

The Jews of eastern Europe were a poor urban people, often confined to ghettos. Yet they did not have many traits of the culture of poverty. They had a tradition of literacy that placed great value on learning; they formed many voluntary associations and adhered with devotion to the central community organization around the rabbi, and they had a religion that taught them they were the chosen people.

I would cite also a fourth, somewhat speculative example of poverty dissociated from the culture of poverty. On the basis of limited direct observation in one country—Cuba—and from indirect evidence, I am inclined to believe the culture of poverty does not exist in socialist countries. In 1947 I undertook a study of a slum in Havana. Recently I had an opportunity to revisit the same slum and some of the same families. The physical aspect of the place had changed little, except for a beautiful new nursery school. The people were as poor as before, but I was impressed to find much less of the feelings of despair and apathy, so symptomatic of the culture of poverty in the urban slums of the U.S. The slum was now highly organized, with block committees, educational committees, party committees. The people had found a new sense of power and importance in a doctrine that glorified the lower class as the hope of humanity, and they were armed. I was told by one Cuban official that the Castro government had practically eliminated delinquency by giving arms to the delinquents!

Evidently the Castro regime—revising Marx and Engels—did not write off the so-called *lumpenproletariat* as an inherently reactionary and antirevolutionary force but rather found in them a revolutionary potential and utilized it. Frantz Fanon, in his book *The Wretched of the Earth,* makes a similar evaluation of their role in the Algerian revolution: "It is within this mass of humanity, this people of the shantytowns, at the core of the *lumpenproletariat,* that the rebellion will find its urban spearhead. For the *lumpenproletariat,* that horde of starving men, uprooted from their tribe and from their clan, constitutes one of the most spontaneous and most radically revolutionary forces of a colonized people."

It is true that I have found little revolutionary spirit or radical ideology among low-income Puerto Ricans. Most of the families I studied were politically conservative, about half of them favoring the Statehood Republican Party, which provides opposition on the right to the Popular Democratic Party that dominates the politics of the commonwealth. It seems to me, therefore, that disposition for protest among people living in the culture of poverty will vary considerably according to the national context and historical circumstances. In contrast to Algeria, the independence movement in Puerto Rico has found little popular support. In Mexico, where the cause of independence carried long ago, there is no longer any such movement to stir the dwellers in the new and old slums of the capital city.

Yet it would seem that any movement—be it religious, pacifist or revolutionary—that organizes and gives hope to the poor and effectively promotes a sense of solidarity with larger groups must effectively destroy the psychological and social core of the culture of poverty. In this connection, I suspect that the civil rights movement among American Negroes has of itself done more to improve their self-image and self-respect than such economic gains as it has won although, without doubt, the two kinds of progress are mutually reinforcing. In the culture of poverty of the American Negro the additional disadvantage of racial discrimination has generated a potential for revolutionary protest and organization that is absent in the slums of San Juan and Mexico City and, for that matter, among the poor whites in the South.

If it is true, as I suspect, that the culture of poverty flourishes and is endemic to the free-enterprise, pre-welfare-state stage of capitalism, then it is also endemic in colonial societies. The most likely candidates for the culture of poverty would be the people who come from the lower strata of a rapidly changing society and who are already partially alienated from it.

Accordingly the subculture is likely to be found where imperial conquest has smashed the native social and economic structure and held the natives, perhaps for generations, in servile status, or where feudalism is yielding to capitalism in the latter evolution of a colonial economy. Landless rural workers who migrate to the cities, as in Latin America, can be expected to fall into this way of life more readily than migrants from stable peasant villages with a well-organized traditional culture, as in India. It remains to be seen, however, whether the culture of poverty has not already begun to develop in the slums of Bombay and Calcutta. Compared with Latin America also, the strong corporate nature of many African tribal societies may tend to inhibit or delay the formation of a full-blown culture of poverty in the new towns and cities of that continent. In South Africa the institutionalization of repression and discrimination under *apartheid* may also have begun to promote an immunizing sense of identity and group consciousness among the African Negroes.

One must therefore keep the dynamic aspects of human institutions forward in observing and assessing the evidence for the presence, the waxing or the waning of this subculture. Measured on the dimension of relationship to the larger society, some slum dwellers may have a warmer identification with their national tradition even though they suffer deeper poverty than members of a similar community in another country. In Mexico City a high percentage of our respondents, including those with little or no formal schooling, knew of Cuauhtémoc, Hidalgo, Father Morelos, Juárez, Díaz, Zapata, Carranza and Cárdenas. In San Juan the names of Rámon Power, José de Diego, Baldorioty de Castro, Rámon Betances, Nemesio Canales, Lloréns Torres rang no bell; a few could tell about the late Albizu Campos. For the lower-income Puerto Rican, however, history begins with Muñoz Rivera and ends with his son Muñoz Marín.

The national context can make a big difference in the play of the crucial traits of fatalism and hopelessness. Given the advanced technology, the high level of literacy, the all-pervasive reach of the media of mass communications and the relatively high aspirations of all sectors of the population, even the poorest and most marginal communities of the U.S. must aspire to a larger future than the slum dwellers of Ecuador and Peru, where the actual possibilities are more limited and where an authoritarian social order persists in city and country. Among the 50 million U.S. citizens now more or less officially certified as poor, I would guess that about 20 percent live in a culture of poverty. The largest numbers in this group are made up of Negroes, Puerto Ricans, Mexicans, American Indians and Southern poor whites. In these figures there is some reassurance for those concerned, because it is much more difficult to undo the culture of poverty than to cure poverty itself.

Middle-class people—this would certainly include most social scientists—tend to concentrate on the negative aspects of the culture of poverty. They attach a minus sign to such traits as present-time orientation and readiness to indulge impulses. I do not intend to idealize or romanticize the culture of poverty—"it is easier to praise poverty than to live in it." Yet the positive aspects of these traits must not be overlooked. Living in the present may develop a capacity for spontaneity, for the enjoyment of the sensual, which is often blunted in the middle-class, future-oriented man. Indeed, I am often struck by the analogies that can be drawn between the mores of the very rich—of the "jet set" and "café society"—and the culture of the very poor. Yet it is, on the whole, a comparatively superficial culture. There is in it much pathos, suffering and emptiness. It does not provide much support or satisfaction; its pervading mistrust magnifies individual helplessness and isolation. Indeed, poverty of culture is one of the crucial traits of the culture of poverty.

The concept of the culture of poverty provides a generalization that may help to unify and explain a number of phenomena hitherto viewed as peculiar to certain racial, national or regional groups. Problems we think of as being distinctively our own or distinctively Negro (or as typifying any other ethnic group) prove to be endemic in countries where there are no segregated ethnic minority groups. If it follows that the elimination of physical poverty may not by itself eliminate the culture of poverty, then an understanding of the subculture may contribute to the design of measures specific to that purpose.

What is the future of the culture of poverty? In considering this question one must distinguish between those countries in which it represents a relatively small segment of the population and those in which it constitutes a large one. In the U.S. the major solution proposed by social workers dealing with the "hard core" poor has been slowly to raise their level of living and incorporate them in the middle class. Wherever possible psychiatric treatment is prescribed.

In underdeveloped countries where great masses of people live in the culture of poverty, such a social-work solution does not seem feasible. The local psychiatrists have all they can do to care for their own growing middle class. In those countries the people with a culture of poverty may seek a more revolutionary solution. By creating basic structural changes in society, by redistributing wealth, by organizing the poor and giving them a sense of belonging, of power and of leadership, revolutions frequently succeed in abolishing some of the basic characteristics of the culture of poverty even when they do not succeed in curing poverty itself.

Culture and Poverty:
Critique and Counter-Proposals*

CHARLES A. VALENTINE

This is a critical study of ideas about poverty and the poor. Written from an anthropological viewpoint, it focuses on prominent contemporary writings about poverty by social scientists. Examination of crucial issues in this literature leads to proposals in four interdependent areas: (1) the theory of poverty; (2) research methods for validating the theory; (3) public policy to deal with the social problems of poverty; and (4) philosophical positions consistent with these proposals.

The discussion opens by clarifying the central concepts of culture and poverty as used throughout the book. The idea of culture is identified with the consensus that has grown up within anthropology as to the meaning of this term: The whole way of life created, followed, and passed on by human groups. Implications of this concept are briefly explored, including its relationship to ethnographic methodology, to humanist philosophy, and to humanitarian ideology. The essence of poverty is shown to be social inequality and relative deprivation in terms of culturally recognized values. The relevance of this definition of poverty for stratified complex societies with egalitarian ideologies is made explicit. The assertion is made that the twin concepts "culture of poverty" and "lower-class culture" constitute misunderstandings of the poor and contradictions of the idea of culture. Most of the book is devoted to supporting this assertion and proposing alternative ideas that are more useful or constructive.

An influential source of the sociological conception of "lower-class culture" in America is E. Franklin Frazier's several works portraying the urban Negro poor as utterly disorganized (Frazier 1932, 1939, 1957, 1966). From this background has grown a pejorative, moralistic tradition that has been cultivated by Nathan Glazer, Daniel P. Moynihan, and others (Glazer 1966; Glazer and Moynihan 1963; Moynihan 1965, 1966, 1967a, b). Weak in method and static in theory, this approach prominently displays the contention or implication that poverty is perpetuated primarily by defects in the lifeways of the poor. There is an associated tendency to confuse the ethnic group "Negro" with the stratification category "lower class." This school of thought produces policy which stresses

* Reprinted from *Current Anthropology*, 10 (April/June, 1969), pp. 181–182, by permission of the author and publisher.

"self-help" and offers for the most part token assistance. In effect, the position is taken that the poor cannot enjoy equality unless they adopt middle-class conventions. To solve associated social problems it is the poor who must be changed, not the society as a whole. The ideological implications of this tradition amount to a lightly veiled Social Darwinism.

The idea of a "culture of poverty" comes from the well-known work of Oscar Lewis, though it has been endlessly popularized and applied by others (Lewis 1959, 1961, 1966a, b; cf. CA 8: 480–500). These writings present serious and thoughtful attempts to develop new ethnographic methods and to adapt the culture concept to elucidating certain kinds of modern poverty. Moreover, Lewis is an avowed humanist with an explicitly humanitarian interest in the people he studies. His abstractions of the life of the poor are contradicted, however, by his own data, and his methods are inadequate to support his theory. While he describes his own work as an indictment of society—not of the poor—his policy proposals indicate that it is primarily the lifeways of poor people which he believes must be reformed. Focusing on disorganization and pathology in the ways of the poor, he insistently assigns first priority to doing away with the "*culture* of poverty," not poverty itself.

Thus, in effect and in implications, the notions of "lower-class culture" and "culture of poverty" are much the same. Along with a host of minor variants under different labels (e.g., "cultural deprivation"), these conceptions dominate virtually all public attention to the problems of poverty and clearly guide most governmental policies and programs dealing with the poor, pre-eminently the "war on poverty."

A few social scientists are pursuing a different line of thought. Clark (1965; also HARYOU 1964) points out that the "cult of cultural deprivation" serves to rationalize discrimination against the poor. Gladwin, beginning with early doubts about the scientific validity of the "culture of poverty" (1961), has come to believe (1967) that the "war on poverty," founded on that very conception, is a failure. Liebow (1967) documents the assertion that street-corner men—far from representing a separate culture—strive to live by standard American values but are continually met by externally imposed failure.

Working in part from clues in these and other sources, the author suggests a series of key methodological and conceptual clarifications (e.g., with regard to subculture and subsociety, ethnic group and social class). It is argued that we must build upon the developing anthropology of complex societies (Banton 1966; Eisenstadt 1961; Steward 1965, 1967) to revitalize ethnography as the prime instrument for delineating the cultures of the poor.

Three prominent formulations of poverty subcultures (Lewis 1966a, b; Miller 1958; Gans 1962, 1965) are presented as outlines of concrete propositions, together with alternative hypotheses, which can be tested by ethnographic fieldwork. A methodological appendix covers specific procedures for such research.

Three broad models are presented to summarize alternative views of the structural position of the poor in our society, the culture patterns associated with poverty, and related orientations with respect to public policy and social action. The model representing the tentative conclusions of the author portrays the poor as a heterogeneous series of subsocieties with variable and adaptable subcultures that are only partially and relatively distinct from American culture as a whole and locates the chief sources of the deprivations suffered by poor people in their structural position in the wider social system and in the actions and attitudes of the non-poor. The presentation of the models is followed by some imaginative projections of the immediate future, including attention to the part anthropology may play in understanding and dealing with poverty.

Finally, a postscript is devoted to a detailed plan for a federally sponsored and financed program to combat poverty by reducing inequality. The central purpose of this plan is to change radically the distribution of prime sociocultural resources (money, jobs, education) to serve directly the interests of the poor. The main operating principle of this program is to grant real, democratically managed power to the poor in order that they may enforce compulsory positive discrimination in favor of presently disadvantaged groups. It is suggested that only by peacefully instituting such a radical egalitarianism can we resolve the national crisis surrounding poverty without ever increasing bloodshed and destruction, probably accompanied by increasing totalitarianism.

Reply to Valentine*

Oscar Lewis

In the preface to his book, Valentine characterizes his work as "ambitious" and "presumptuous." This is not an idle disclaimer, but a candid and accurate appraisal which, I suspect, he arrived at belatedly after finishing his book. This interpretation is suggested by the difference in quality between the early portion of the book, where he is the overzealous critic, and the latter portion, where he tries to be constructive and presents his own rather uninspired views of what should be done about the poor. It is exasperating to find that some of his most belabored criticism in the early

* Reprinted from *Current Anthropology*, Vol. 10, No. 2–3 (April/June, 1969), pp. 189–192, by permission of Harold Ober Associates, Inc.

parts of the book is negated in the latter part, where he quietly incorporates as his own the very point of view he has earlier decried. It is at the same time reassuring, because it suggests some flexibility and capacity for growth. The ideas he has borrowed improve the quality of the book. Thus, his "Postscript: A Proposal for Empowering the Poor to Reduce Inequality" is a worthwhile and important statement. (On the other hand, his "Appendix: Toward an Ethnographic Research Design" is unexciting and reads like a graduate student's research outline.)

Valentine warns us that he has done no firsthand, systematic research among the poor and that his knowledge is based essentially on his reading and library research. He writes as an anthropologist and as a citizen concerned with problems of social justice and with the persistence of poverty. He also writes as a self-appointed defender of the image of the poor, whom he tends to idealize in a Rousseauean fashion.

Valentine believes that those of us who have some professional expertise in the study of poverty have had a "predominantly pernicious influence." He is critical of the work of most of the people he discusses. He examines, with varying degrees of superficiality, the writings of E. Franklin Frazier, Nathan Glazer, Daniel P. Moynihan, Walter Miller, David Matza, Oscar Lewis, Kenneth Clark, Charles Keil, Thomas Gladwin, Elliott Liebow, and Herbert Gans. Only Gans and Liebow come off relatively unscathed.

On the whole, I find Valentine's book tendentious, self-righteous, pedestrian, and downright irresponsible in its distortion of the views of others. Some of the criticism has a horsefly quality about it: it buzzes and irritates, but is lightweight and poses no serious threat. Nor does Valentine offer any new solutions. For all his aggressive rhetoric, he seems opposed to revolutionary solutions to the problems of the poor. He suggests no fundamental changes in the structure of the social and economic system beyond that of providing better jobs for the unemployed by a national policy of compensatory hiring. His own contribution to the subject consists essentially in saying that we need well-rounded, intensive anthropological studies of slum life, based upon the traditional methods of participation, observation, etc. While I would certainly agree that we need more studies of many kinds, this is hardly an original contribution.

Because so much of his criticism is directed to my own work, I should like to reply to some of the issues he raises, even though I find most of them spurious and unenlightening.[1] Valentine criticizes me for using the expression "culture of poverty" instead of "subculture of poverty." It should have been evident to any careful reader, but especially to an anthropologist, that I was describing a model of a subculture and not of a culture. I made this clear on several occasions:

---

1. For examples of more creative criticism, see Gans (1968) and Rainwater (1966).

Poverty becomes a dynamic factor which affects participation in the larger national culture and *creates a subculture of its own* (1959: 2, italics added).

The culture of poverty . . . is a dynamic factor which affects participation in the larger national culture and becomes a subculture of its own (1961: xxiv).

The culture or subculture of poverty comes into being in a variety of historical contexts (1961: xxv).

While the term "subculture of poverty" is technically more accurate, I have used "culture of poverty" as a shorter form (1966*b*: xxxix).

The subculture of poverty, as defined by these traits, is a statistical profile; that is, the frequency of distribution of the traits both singly and in clusters will be greater than in the rest of the population (1968: 11).

I decided to use the term culture of poverty because my books were intended for a wide audience. I believed that the concept of a subculture, difficult even for social scientists, would confuse the average reader and, like the term subhuman, might suggest inferiority. I hoped that the term "culture" would convey a sense of worth, dignity, and the existence of pattern in the lives of the poor despite the miserable conditions under which they live.

I believe that most of my colleagues understood my intention. For example, Herzog in her article, "Some assumptions about the poor," wrote (1963: 395):

To the extent that the word "culture" is appropriate, the culture of poverty should be thought of as a subculture rather than as a culture in itself—a distinction made, in fact, by Oscar Lewis. . . .

Actually, Valentine, too, understood my position. Unfortunately, this does not become apparent until late in the volume when he discusses some of the problems inherent in the conceptions of subsocieties and subcultures.

Valentine insistently attributes to me the idea that the people I am describing have a self-contained and self-sufficient way of life. This is absurd. I never suggested that people with a subculture of poverty are totally isolated from the institutions and values of the larger society. The marginality I described is obviously a relative matter and involves not isolation but the degree of effective participation (Lewis 1966*b*: xlv). If we were to devise a scale of participation, individuals and families with a subculture of poverty would receive lower scores than the rest of the population.

Valentine misunderstands the relationship between the autobiographical material in my recent books and the theoretical model of a subculture of poverty, and he is disturbed by the difficulties in relating these two distinct levels. This problem is inherent in all social science models, and the lack of perfect fit is in itself no proof of the inadequacy of the model, especially when it is an ideal-type model. However, I should like to make a few clarifications.

The idea of the model of the subculture of poverty did not grow out of my study of the Sánchez family alone. Rather, it developed out of my comparative analysis of two Mexican *vecindades,* one a large *vecindad* of 157 families, the other a small one of 14 families. In reviewing the findings on these 171 families and in comparing it with data on slums published by social scientists (and also with data from novels), I noted certain persistent patterned associations of traits among families with the lowest income level and the least education. It was the configuration of these traits which, for lack of a better term, I called the subculture of poverty.

I have recently explained in more detail some aspects of the subculture of poverty model (1968: 11–12):

> . . (1) The traits fall into a number of clusters and are functionally related within each cluster. (2) Many, but not all, of the traits of different clusters are also functionally related. For example, men who have low wages and suffer chronic unemployment develop a poor self-image, become irresponsible, abandon their wives and children, and take up with other women more frequently than do men with high incomes and steady jobs. (3) None of the traits, taken individually, is distinctive per se of the subculture of poverty. It is their conjunction, their function, and their patterning that define the subculture. (4) The subculture of poverty, as defined by these traits, is a statistical profile; that is, the frequency of distribution of the traits both singly and in clusters will be greater than in the rest of the population. In other words, more of the traits will occur in combination in families with a subculture of poverty than in stable working-class, middle-class, or upper-class families. Even within a single slum there will probably be a gradient from culture of poverty families to families without a culture of poverty. (5) The profiles of the subculture of poverty will probably differ in systematic ways with the difference in the national cultural contexts of which they are a part. It is expected that some new traits will become apparent with research in different nations. I have not yet worked out a system of weighting each of the traits, but this could probably be done and a scale could be set up for many of the traits. Traits that reflect lack of participation in the institutions of the larger society or an outright rejection—in practice, if not in theory—would be the crucial traits; for example, illiteracy, provincialism, free unions, abandonment of women and children, lack of membership in voluntary associations beyond the extended family.

I had no intention of equating an entire slum settlement with the subculture of poverty as Valentine erroneously does. In my experience, the people who live in slums, even in small ones, show a great deal of heterogeneity in income, literacy, education, political sentiments, and life styles.

Indeed, I claimed that for some characteristics my sample of 100 families from four San Juan slums was a good sample of the island as a whole (Lewis 1968: 21–23).

It should be clear to anyone who has read the Introduction to *La Vida* that the Ríos family was not intended to be an ideal representative of the subculture of poverty model. The income of the various members of the Ríos family living in separate households was well in the middle group of the La Esmeralda slum. Had I intended to illustrate the model in its purest form, I would have published a volume on a family with an annual income of less than $500.00 a year; 22% of the families in the slum were in this category in 1960. In his efforts to show that some of the characters in *La Vida* were less provincial and isolated than one might have expected from the ideal type, Valentine stacked the cards against the model by selecting as his examples individuals who had lived for many years in New York City and who had incomes many times higher than their relatives in San Juan! For example, Benedicto and Soledad together earned over $8,000 a year and Simplicio and his wife earned over $5,000. Moreover, Benedicto was a bilingual, literate, and sophisticated merchant seaman who had seen the world. Again, the Sánchez family was not presented as an ideal example of the subculture of poverty model. It seemed to me that the very wide range of types in this family would make that self-evident. Furthermore, I made it clear that they were in the middle-income group of the Casa Grande *vecindad*. Manuel Sánchez was relatively sophisticated, literate, and well-traveled compared to his younger sister Marta, and the contrast between Consuelo and Aunt Guadalupe was even more marked. Had my primary objective been to illustrate the model, I would have published an entire volume on Guadalupe and her husband, two minor characters in *The Children of Sánchez*.[2]

Since the model of the subculture of poverty was not derived from the Sánchez and Ríos families alone, it is pointless to seek a one-to-one correspondence between the model and the characters in these books. It would be more helpful to think of the subculture of poverty as the zero point on a continuum which leads to the working class and middle class; the various characters in *The Children of Sánchez* and in *La Vida* would then fall at different points on the continuum.

Many of the "contradictions" between the model and the data cited by Valentine are not contradictions at all. For example, he sees a contradiction between my statement about low level of organization and my description of La Esmeralda (and also of Casa Grande) as little communities. Simply to state that there is a community does not describe the level of organiza-

---

2. See my forthcoming book, *A Death in the Sánchez Family* (New York: Random House, September 1969).

tion. Furthermore, in the model I stipulated a range of level of organization for the subculture of poverty. In this connection I wrote (1966*b*: xlvii):

> In spite of the generally low level of organization there may be a sense of community and *esprit de corps* in urban slums and in slum neighborhoods. This can vary within a single city or from region to region or country to country. The major factors that influence this variation are the size of the slum, its location and physical characteristics, length of residence, incidence of homeownership and landownership (versus squatter rights), rentals, ethnicity, kinship ties, and freedom or lack of freedom of movement. When slums are separated from the surrounding area by enclosing walls or other physical barriers, when rents are low and fixed and stability of residence is great (twenty or thirty years), when the population constitutes a distinct ethnic, racial or language group or is bound by ties of kinship or *compadrazgo,* and when there are some internal voluntary associations, then the sense of local community approaches that of a village community. In many cases this combination of favorable conditions does not exist. However, even where internal organization and *esprit de corps* are at a bare minimum and people move around a great deal, a sense of territoriality develops that sets off the slum neighborhoods from the rest of the city. In Mexico City and San Juan this sense of territoriality results from the unavailability of low income housing outside of the slum areas. In South Africa the sense of territoriality grows out of the segregation enforced by the government, which confines the rural migrants to specific locations.

In his critique of my subculture of poverty model, Valentine manages to distort my position by omitting my discussion of the causes of the phenomenon, the conditions under which it arises, its adaptive functions, and the conditions under which it will probably disappear. He misses the significance of the difference between poverty and the subculture of poverty. In making this distinction I have tried to illustrate a broader generalization; namely, that it is a serious mistake to lump all poor people together, because the causes, the meaning, and the consequences of poverty vary considerably in different sociocultural contexts.

Valentine sometimes denies the existence of the subculture of poverty and at other times reluctantly accepts it. The issue is whether the way of life described in my books is simply an adaptation of the poor to the total social system (an adaptation which supposedly begins from scratch with each new generation!), or whether the very process of adaptation of the poor develops a set of values and norms which justify calling it a subculture. At one point he writes (p. 117),

> Evidence presented in the literature surveyed here seems to provide little basis for a clear choice between these interpretations. To conclude that the

two formulations are both valid but not mutually exclusive—that the two causal sequences may be coexistent and perhaps mutually reinforcing—is a position that may ultimately prove well founded.

In the light of this admission, one wonders why he attacks my proposition that once the subculture of poverty comes into existence as a result of the total social system, it is also in some measure internally self-perpetuating.

More serious is Valentine's insistence that I have given highest priority to the elimination of the culture of poverty as a way of life rather than to the elimination of poverty per se, and the related charge that I have put the onus of poverty on the character of the people rather than upon the larger society. This is patently false and flies in the face of my published statements, in which I have consistently considered it most urgent to eliminate economic poverty in the United States by creating new jobs, by paying people higher wages, by training unskilled workers, and by guaranteeing people a decent minimum annual income. My point, however, was that even if all this were done, there would still remain a large number of families with many social and psychological problems. It was in this connection that I have suggested special services in addition to income improvement. I mentioned this problem in my dialogue with the late Senator Robert Kennedy, published in *Redbook* (1967). For example, in response to Kennedy's question about the importance of better jobs and higher income, I replied (p. 104),

> Yes, it would make a difference and it should receive the highest priority in any case. Every American citizen deserves that as a minimum. How they run their lives is their business, if it doesn't hurt society as a whole. But we oversimplify the solution if we think it's just a question of money.

At one point Valentine charges that my concept of a culture of poverty was a guiding principle of the war against poverty and must, therefore, bear some responsibility for its failure. What a naïve and absurd conception of the power of social science in our society! It is not the concept of a culture or subculture of poverty which is responsible for the lack of success of the anti-poverty program, but rather (1) the failure of the President and the Congress of the United States to understand the degree of national commitment necessary to cope with the problem; and (2) the Vietnam war, which has been draining our economic and human resources.

Having attended Moynihan's year-long seminar on poverty and having heard some of the men who were directly responsible for formulating, organizing, and carrying out the war against poverty, I can testify that most of them had only the vaguest conception of the difference between poverty and the subculture of poverty. The anti-poverty program was correctly directed at economic poverty and not at the subculture of poverty (which, I believe, is found only in approximately 20% of the families who live below the poverty level).

What I find most disappointing in Valentine's treatment of my recent work is his failure to respond with sympathy and warmth to the people who tell of their lives in *Five Families, The Children of Sánchez, Pedro Martínez,* and *La Vida.* This is surprising in the light of his statement of his objectives (p. 148):

> If we can really regain the art of living with the natives [i.e., urban slum dwellers], . . . we should be able to see the world as it is from within the alien subsociety . . . for we shall know the people ourselves at firsthand. . . . It seems probable that the future ethnographer of the poor will have clear knowledge of what lower-class people want. . . .

This is what I have tried to do in my studies of slums in Mexico City, San Juan, and New York, and I have said so explicitly in each of the volumes discussed (e.g., Lewis 1961: xii; 1966b: xii). Valentine does not analyze the meaning of poverty and its political implications as seen in the rich data provided by the people themselves in these volumes. Instead, he brushes this data aside as "raw material" and concentrates on the more abstract issue of theoretical models and the culture of poverty, issues which were quite incidental to the major objectives of the books. As far as I am concerned, my formulation of a subculture of poverty is simply a challenging hypothesis which should be widely tested by empirical research.

I suspect that one of Valentine's problems is that he is so enamoured of traditional ethnography and community studies that he has developed resistance to data derived from any approach which tries to go beyond the traditional. He ignores the valuable insights one can get about the nature of institutions from the way in which they are experienced and reflected in the lives of individuals and families. His belief that a few good old-fashioned ethnographies of urban slums will open up entirely new horizons and almost automatically push ahead the war against poverty is naïve. To my knowledge, the many studies of tribal and peasant societies have rarely led to any marked improvement in the conditions under which these people live. Moreover, he fails to recognize some of the serious limitations of traditional ethnography and community studies. As an old practitioner of the art, I am sensitive to these limitations and have described them at various times.

Too often the generalizations which appear in ethnographic monographs about culture patterns are no more than good guesses based upon the reports of a few informants who may not represent the total range and variety of custom and behavior. Having done both community studies and family studies, I am convinced (and at some later time shall try to demonstrate) that, for all of my editing, selection, and organization, the data in my family studies is more precise, more valid, and more reliable than many generalizations in traditional ethnographic monographs.

I should like to make it clear for the record, however, that: (1) I have not abandoned community studies. (2) I consider them one of the basic research designs of anthropology. (3) It is certainly feasible to do community-like ethnographic studies of the kind Valentine yearns for in urban slums and shanty towns. Indeed, a number of such studies have already been done in Africa and in Latin America.[3] (4) I have never stated that "poor people living in cities cannot be studied by focusing on neighborhoods, localities, wards, or other sizeable social units within the urban complex," as is falsely charged by Valentine (p. 175). (He knows better, because he has cited my data on Casa Grande and La Esmeralda.) (5) I have never intended my family studies as a substitute for community studies, but rather as a complement to them. My last four books all began as part of community studies, and my decision to publish the family studies first was simply a matter of publication strategy. Indeed, *Pedro Martínez* (1964) combines a description of a community with full-length individual biographies. In the light of his criticism of my work, Valentine's failure to even mention this book reflects upon his sincerity and reliability as a scholar. Opler (1964), in his review of the book, has written:

> There are some who have argued that the autobiography is too personal and idiosyncratic to tell us much about a way of life. Others are just as sure that the usual ethnography or anthropological account of a culture is too divorced from specific human activity to be convincing. It is the merit of Lewis' effort to present both of these approaches together and, by providing a historical setting, to give a sense of direction to them as well.

Valentine misrepresents my work when he suggests that my focus on the family as a unit of study has led me to neglect or eliminate "evidence of life beyond the confines of the household" (p. 63). Can it be that he didn't read or doesn't remember the descriptions in *The Children of Sánchez* of jail scenes, police brutality, Army life, gang activities in the *vecindac*, work in the market, work in shops and factories, work in the fields as a *bracero* in California, impressions of life in the United States, etc.?

Throughout most of the early and middle portion of the book, Valentine consistently complains about the unduly negative images of the poor which emerge from the studies of professional social scientists. Speaking for myself, I should like to take sharp exception to his implication that I have exaggerated the pathology and weaknesses of the poor. It is curious

---

3. I am now preparing a work on "The Social Organization and Material Culture of a Mexico City Slum," as well as a series of volumes on La Esmeralda in San Juan.

and ironical that he should even make this charge. Some critics have complained that I have glorified the poor and that I have improved their language to give more beauty and profundity to it than they are capable of expressing. My own evaluation of the people in my books belies Valentine's charges (Lewis 1961: xii, 1966b: xxvii, xxviii).

Belatedly, Valentine acknowledges the relationship between culture and personality and, if I understand him correctly, affirms the self-perpetuating element in the subculture of poverty, an idea which had been anathema to him earlier in the book. He writes (p. 145),

> . . . there is certainly empirical evidence of pathology, incompetence, and other kinds of inadequacy among the people of the ghettos and slums, as there is in the rest of society. There can be no doubt that living in poverty has its own destructive effect on human capacities and that these impairments become part of the whole process perpetuating deprivation.

The crucial question from both the scientific and the political point of view is: How much weight is to be given to the internal, self-perpetuating factors in the subculture of poverty as compared to the external, societal factors? My own position is that in the long run the self-perpetuating factors are relatively minor and unimportant as compared to the basic structure of the larger society. However, to achieve rapid change and improvement with the minimum amount of trauma one must work on both the "external" and "internal" conditions. To ignore the internal factors is to ignore and distort the reality of people with a subculture of poverty. In effect, this is harmful to their interests because it plays down the extent of their special needs and the special programs which are necessary to make up for the deprivations and damage which they have suffered over many generations.

Reply to Valentine*

David Matza

In *Culture and Poverty*, Valentine develops a perspective on the phenomenon of poverty. His view differs sharply from that of most writers, and thus the main part of the volume is devoted to an assault on the literature. Being a minor exemplar of the perspective criticized by Valen-

---

* Reprinted from *Current Anthropology*, Vol. 10, No. 2–3 (April/June, 1969), pp. 192–194, by permission of the author and publisher.

tine, I suppose I ought to provide a defense and counter-attack. I intend to. But how defend a perspective against so wild a misreading; how attack a writer so steeped in unreality?

Valentine purports to an anthropological perspective. Mainly, this means he embraces the idea of cultural relativism with an avidity professors find refreshing when manifested by bright, suburban sophomores. Additionally, he seems to conceive himself a (C.W.) Millsian. Mainly, this means he proclaims empathy with the poor and a concern for solutions. Morally armed with such admirable postures, Valentine considers the question of poverty. Throughout, he seems guided by the premise that virtually everyone who has written on the subject is an enemy of the poor, misled by ethnocentric judgments, ordinary bigotry, or (Lord spare us!) plain old middle-class bias. To the list of recent writers considered by Valentine—all of whom agree that life among the poor generally speaking stinks—could be added such notable enemies of the working class as Engels, Marx, DuBois, and Bukharin. All have made the same mistake. Unaware, perhaps, of the revolutionary discoveries in cultural anthropology, writers from E. Franklin Frazier to Oscar Lewis have continued to conceive the poor as if in many ways they shared the general presumptions of American life—as if they actually were affected by some of the beliefs and aspirations existing all around them. Because of that basic misunderstanding, recent writers harbor a reactionary tendency, according to Valentine. Seeing only the negative side of being poor, they are led to hold the poor responsible for their own conditions.

I will come to the issue of perspective in a moment, but, first, I want to consider the simpler question: whether stressing the negative side of poverty implies holding the poor responsible for their condition. I would have thought such an association self-evidently absurd, but apparently it is not. Valentine's zeal in locating the reactionary tendency to hold the poor responsible is great. Thus, even when a writer tries to convey the view that property and its agencies—and not the poor—produce the oppressive conditions of poverty, Valentine can still find a way to glimpse reaction. He says (p. 47):

> Matza's historical interpretations clearly imply that masses of poor people were pauperized by the economic and political behavior of the non-poor. Yet he gives no hint that the privileged strata of today's society bear any responsibility for relieving the plight of the poor.

I must confess that after reading those two sentences, I felt a sudden sympathy with residents of mental institutions. Trapped, looped, I could see that there was no way of avoiding a self-assured accusation of error, sin, or worse. I am confident that most of the other authors considered by

Valentine will have much the same feeling. Only Frazier—who is looped two or three times—will escape it, but that is because he is dead.

As it happens, my interpretation of pauperization does not just "imply" that the main agency for its foul achievement is what Valentine rather blandly calls the "non-poor." That pauperization is the work of property and the state is explicitly a main point of the essay. The thesis is hardly novel—certainly not since Marx. Many writers—including most of those assaulted by Valentine—have held that the demoralization of being poor is created and produced by the oppressive weight of historical circumstance. Even those who have too greatly stressed the "culture" of poverty see it as resulting from an oppressive set of historical circumstances. More pertinent, however, than the genuine issue of whether a "culture" may reify the product of historical circumstance is the more immediate question: if one holds privilege responsible for creating the condition of poverty, should one address requests and plans for "relief" to it? I happen to think not—unless, of course, it's a dole Valentine is after. For genuine relief, something a bit more forceful is generally required—as the history of worker's organizations surely testifies.

It is for that reason that Valentine's recommendations for massive employment opportunities with compensatory training and hiring seem largely beside the point, worthy as they may be. To entertain the expectation that the current military and political economy in America will permit even the watered-down version of the A. Philip Randolph program promulgated by Valentine seems to me misleading. The meaningful question is not whether aynone's plan is intelligent, rational, or feasible, but, instead, whether black rebellion will become organized, whether the alliance between students and blacks can ever materialize, and, most of all, whether organized labor can conceivably be shaken from its established lethargy to ally with an unemployed underclass and return to its occasional militancy. If these things, or something like them, should happen, a program will be devised. If not, privilege will not be responsive—however "responsible" it may be. Instead of providing genuine relief, it will continue in its current response; the good citizens will shriek "law and order," further arm their police, and somnambulistically await a summer in which America's world mission of crushing revolution is finally brought home.

Finally, as to the perspective on poverty, the basic point at issue: here too, I am afraid, Valentine's radicalism and relativism prove disappointing. Wishing ardently to avoid giving offense to the poor, he falls heir to a charming infantilism. For him, despite the oppression of historic circumstance—for which we are to hold the "non-poor" responsible—the organization of social life among the poor remains largely undaunted and intact. Far from seeing the poor as stupefied or disorganized until they have mobilized and achieved consciousness—the classic view of writers since Marx—Valentine follows the romantic tradition in which the poor are merely different in their customs and arrangements. Family life is not threatened, despite its shaky survival, but simply pursued in a different and equally laudable way. Solidarity and organization are not thwarted by the surroundings, but simply defined differently. Being poor does not lead to a degradation and debasement of the potentialities of human personality; this is just something that is wrongly construed in that way by ethnocentric outsiders. One wonders, in light of such a perspective, why black Americans desperately risk their lives putting the torch to a ghetto that represents their "way of life." Is it perhaps, because—like Orientals—they place a different value on life than Caucasians; or is it a form of potlatch?

Parts of Valentine's unmitigated relativism read like a cruel joke. Perhaps the presentation of one glaring example is the best way to conclude. Valentine wishes to contrast the sweet fruits of relativism with the sour, judgmental conclusions of someone like Oscar Lewis. To do this, he frames some of Lewis' allegations in propositional form and suggests alternative formulations. Thus, for instance, "Proposition 1 a" (p. 130) represents Lewis' perspective:

> Patterned lack of participation in important aspects of the wider society is an internally perpetuated characteristic of the culture of the poor.

Valentine's "Alternative 1 a" is designed to rescue the poor from their judgmental detractors and to straighten the anthropological account. It releases the poor from a responsibility Lewis hardly assigned them and, then, goes on to the more important matter of transforming conditions that are worse into those that are different:

> Socioeconomically disadvantaged groups show strikingly differential participation in various specific institutional areas of the wider society; these contrasting patterns are imposed and perpetuated externally through institutional structures and processes, particularly recruitment avenues that are beyond local control.

So far, so good—but now comes the punch line. What are the specific institutional areas in which the poor are high and low participants? Valentine tells us:

> High participation: police-courts–prison complex, armed services, welfare system, primary public education. Low participation: stable employment, property ownership, political parties, labor unions, higher education.

When Anatole France made a similar point about a different sort of equality between rich and poor, his intention was to occasion bitter laughter. That remains my reaction to the cultural equality less humorously conjured by Charles Valentine.

Reply to Lewis and Matza*

CHARLES A. VALENTINE

Perhaps the basic difficulty between Oscar Lewis and myself is a failure of communication. I do not question his motives; rather, I declare my sympathy and respect for his intentions; yet he accuses me of insincerity and misrepresentation. I thought I was giving the people in Lewis' books more credit for their capacities and greater empathy with their situation than he did; yet what he finds "most disappointing" in my work is a "failure to respond with sympathy and warmth." I intended my analysis of his work to convey respect as well as criticism; this obviously did not get through to Lewis. Wherever I am responsible for these misunderstandings I apologize; I hope the communication failure will end here.

Lewis' remark that I have done "no firsthand, systematic research among the poor" directly contradicts the facts presented in my Preface and documented in the Bibliography. Characterizing my thoughts as "opposed to revolutionary solutions" is completely inconsistent with my discussion of Models 2 and 3 (pp. 142–47) as well as the Postscript, the latter being much more than a scheme for "compensatory hiring." Nor was my proposal "borrowed" from anywhere (see reply to Matza below).

On culture and subculture, the major issue is that, regardless of terminology, Lewis often writes about the subject as if he had a full culture in mind. This begins with his definition, "a culture in the traditional anthropological sense" (quoted more fully on p. 129), and continues throughout much theoretical discussion. Whether or not people are "totally isolated from . . . the larger society" is not the issue. Lewis says that "disengagement," "non-integration," "is a crucial element in the culture of poverty." This is what I question. We also disagree about "lack of fit." Lack of fit with the facts is *exactly* what makes a model unsatisfactory. *"Perfect fit"* is not the issue. The point is that Lewis' model, like all others, can be improved by posing alternatives and testing them empirically. This is the essence of what my book suggests on this topic.

The quotation from Lewis' new book on Slum Culture is certainly welcome. As he knows, of course, this was not available when I was writing. (I have since commented on it [Valentine 1968].) In any case, it does not change the essentials of the debate between us. If one has "no

* Reprinted from *Current Anthropology,* 10 (April/June, 1969), pp. 198–199, by permission of the author and publisher.

intention of equating an entire slum settlement" with a definite (sub)cultural design, why call it "slum culture"? If one does not believe certain (sub)cultural patterns typify most populations living in poverty, why use the phrase "culture of poverty"? A major question remains unanswered: How representative—and of what—are Lewis' family studies? If the presentation of data in these volumes did not have as the "primary objective . . . to illustrate the model," then what was the purpose? The very labels with which the books are titled or subtitled seem to me to contradict their author's disclaimers.

Lewis still sees no contradiction between his model and his description of La Esmeralda. His rebuttal on this point rests on "sense of community," "esprit de corps," and "sense of territoriality." This does not clear up the contradiction between "minimum of organization" in the model and the many structural or institutional features in the descriptive data. He feels I have distorted his position by "omitting" his discussion of causes, functions, and conditions for the disappearance of poverty. He should reread my book (especially pp. 67–77). I am confident he will find no omission and no distortion. As for his distinction between poverty and poverty culture, this is considered at more than one place in my book. It was not entirely clear earlier, and his present addition does not seem to me to clarify it any further.

On the issue of priorities for policy, I am most happy to have Lewis' clear, definite statement that doing away with poverty as such is more urgent than attacking the culture of the poor. I cannot agree, however, that my contention about his theory guiding the war on poverty is "naïve and absurd." In a forthcoming publication (Valentine 1969) this thesis is further developed and documented, using sources ranging from the direct link of Harrington's work (1962) to the insightful commentary of Gladwin (1967) and Rodman (1968). My point is not that there is any "special power of social science in our society," but rather that the idea of a poverty culture appealed to many powerful people who appropriated and developed it for their own purposes, using it to justify a series of pernicious policies. Bluntly stated, Lewis' ideas have been used for purposes which have nothing in common with his aims, particularly as he now states them. Obviously this happens to many of us and could happen to anyone, but we cannot evade some measure of responsibility for what others do with ideas we have made public property.

As for the failure of the war on poverty, my point is that anti-poverty programs based on widely current versions of the culture of poverty were bound to fail even without such immense additional handicaps as the irresponsibilities of the President and Congress, including the Viet Nam war. The basic failure was not the scale of the effort but rather the conceptions that underlay it, the nature of the resulting programs, and probably the real intentions of the most significant decision-makers. Thus Lewis' statement that "the anti-poverty program was correctly directed at economic poverty and not at the subculture of poverty" seems to me to fly in the face of the facts (cf., e.g., Gladwin 1967, Rodman 1968).

Lewis ascribes to me a "belief that [urban ethnography will] almost automatically push ahead the war against poverty." I don't believe this, nor did I say anything like it. He is quite right that generalizations in some ethnographies are "no more than good guesses based upon the reports of a few informants." If he read my sections on methodology, however, he knows that I am not the least bit interested in that kind of ethnography. I am glad we now agree on the need for and feasibility of community-oriented urban ethnography. Nevertheless, my remarks about his earlier stand on this issue are not a false charge. He will remember that he wrote: "city dwellers cannot be studied as members of little communities" (Lewis 1959: 17, quoted in my book, p. 49).

Lewis accuses me of "misrepresentation" and casts doubt on my "sincerity and reliability" because I don't give as much attention as he would like to all of his works, especially early ones. Actually I do cite much of his earlier work and comment on contrasts with later books. Nevertheless, my main concern is obviously with his recent works on the subculture of poverty. Here I think my strictures hold good. I claim no more than this, either here or in my book.

I am sorry that Lewis seems to have misunderstood me again as to my position on the alleged self-perpetuating quality of a poverty culture. I have said before and now repeat that this hypothesis must be examined and tested, not just proclaimed. When Lewis now says that the "self-perpetuating factors are relatively minor and unimportant compared to the basic structure of the larger society," I am glad we are closer to agreement than we were before. Again I hope Lewis will join me in ending our misunderstandings. If so, debate can prosper constructively.

My next critic, Matza, says writers from Frazier to Lewis "conceive the poor as if in many ways they shared the general presumptions of American life." On the contrary, this is one of the more important propositions about poor people which the relevant authors most often neglect, minimize, or deny. Much of my book is devoted to documenting and exploring this very point. Matza seems to misunderstand grossly both the book and the literature it criticizes.

Nowhere in my book is there anything resembling Matza's statement that "stressing the negative side of poverty implies holding the poor responsible for their condition." I do say that overemphasizing negative qualities of poor *people* often goes with blaming poverty on the poor—a quite different point. In either case, however, when the paired orientations appear together the combination has been constructed by individual thinkers. There is obviously no inherent logical connection between negative views either of poverty or of the poor and any particular belief about causes or responsibility.

Matza is entitled to his preference for such abstractions as "property" and "the state." I am equally entitled to translate these into more concrete terms of reference. I think that "economic and political behavior of the non-poor," though stylistically lackluster, is otherwise not a bad translation. Perhaps Matza's main objection to my translation is that it carries implications of ethical responsibility as distinct from the amoral casuality of his more abstract formulations. This objection has no force for me, because I do not pretend to be a value-free scholar. I believe that value-free social science is a myth.

Nothing in my book should convey the impression mentioned by Matza that I harbor an "expectation" that "relief" will be freely or easily granted by holders of power and privilege. That is why my several discussions of solutions are coupled with the contention that a radical and powerful social movement, launched by the poor themselves, will be necessary to eradicate poverty. The plan I proposed was intended to make available one utopian but concrete model of necessary changes. This was offered as an aid in the ongoing process of thinking through what kind of society should be built if a revolutionary social movement should emerge successfully. The proposal was deliberately designed to be an extension of already current reformist ideas, going beyond available plans but growing out of widespread notions. Today, only a few months after publication of the book, I would be inclined to revise that proposal in a more radical direction. It is an insulting travesty, however, to describe it as a "watered-down version of the A. Philip Randolph program." The principal contrast with the Randolph Freedom Budget is that my proposal demands a significant transfer of power to poor people. Because this is an inherently revolutionary demand, it may well require changes that cannot be accommodated within the existing political structure and processes of our society.

Matza judges me guilty of "romanticism" and "infantilism" with respect to the poor. Assuming misunderstanding rather than deliberate distortion, I ask the critic to read the book carefully and seriously. My book says nothing to the effect that the poor are "not threatened" or "not thwarted." I do feel, even more strongly today after further experience with poor people, that "being poor is not a degradation and debasement of the potentialities of human personality." Perhaps this is the nub of the disagreement. In contrast with some of my critics, I believe the poor have shown that their potentialities (and their achievements) are very great—precisely because they are not debased in spite of all oppression. As for black Americans taking great risks to burn down ghettos, I believe they do this precisely because the ghetto does *not* "represent their way of life." What they are burning down was imposed on them by external forces. More and more of them are declaring their total resistance to this imposed structure by risking their own destruction in trying to destroy what they experience as oppression.

Mead's statements that Lewis has not fallen into certain mistakes do not automatically make it so. A seriously argued critique commands respect; mere pronouncements, even when they come from deservedly eminent people, should not. My discussion of holism is not, of course, intended to deal with problems of part-societies and subcultures. These problems are dealt with in other parts of my book, and I would have welcomed attention to these sections. This is one of the problem areas in which my own work, as well as that of others, is most noticeably incomplete. It is disappointing that none of the more negative critics chose to respond constructively to the challenge of these problems.

Chapter	Religion:
15	What Is the Relationship between Protestantism and Capitalism?

The debate on the relationship between religion and capitalism is one of the longest and most fascinating in sociology. It began with Max Weber's *The Protestant Ethic and the Spirit of Capitalism,* an excerpt from which opens this portion of the book. Weber's basic thesis was that Protestantism was one of the basic causes of the growth of the spirit of capitalism, and ultimately of the rise of the capitalistic system. Weber's work, however, was not actually the beginning of the debate, since Weber was really taking issue with the earlier work of Karl Marx. Upset by Marx's economic determinism, Weber tried to expand Marxian theory by demonstrating the importance of ideas (in this case, religious ideas) in social change (in this case, the rise of capitalism). From the beginning, Weber's thesis was highly controversial and led to many theoretical attacks on it.[1] Although these critiques have cast doubt on the relationship between Protestantism and capitalism (for example, whether Protestantism caused the rise of capitalism, or whether it was capitalism which led to the rise of Protestantism), Weber's thesis that ideas are a factor in social change has emerged unscathed. I have chosen not to include in this section the theoretical debate on Weber's ideas, but instead an empirical piece which casts doubt on them.

The paper by Howard Schuman, which concludes this section, serves two purposes: it summarizes the results of the major empirical study (by Gerhard Lenski) of Weber's thesis, and it constitutes a replication of some aspects of that study. Basically, Lenski found support in his earlier study

---

1. For the positions of many of Weber's critics see: Robert W. Green (ed.), *Protestantism and Capitalism: The Weber Thesis and Its Critics.* Boston: D. C. Heath, 1955.

for Weber's thesis, but in his follow-up study Schuman casts doubt on many of Lenski's findings and, therefore, Weber's ideas. Yet, it should be pointed out that Weber contended that Protestantism was important to the beginnings of capitalism, and not that it would continue as a potent force today. If future studies support Schuman's findings, that is not really evidence that Weber was wrong about the origins of capitalism.

The Protestant Ethic and the Spirit of Capitalism*

Max Weber

A glance at the occupational statistics of any country of mixed religious composition brings to light with remarkable frequency a situation which has several times provoked discussion in the Catholic press and literature, and in Catholic congresses in Germany, namely, the fact that business leaders and owners of capital, as well as the higher grades of skilled labour, and even more the higher technically and commercially trained personnel of modern enterprises, are overwhelmingly Protestant. This is true not only in cases where the difference in religion coincides with one of nationality, and thus of cultural development, as in Eastern Germany between Germans and Poles. The same thing is shown in the figures of religious affiliation almost wherever capitalism, at the time of its great expansion, has had a free hand to alter the social distribution of the population in accordance with its needs, and to determine its occupational structure. The more freedom it has had, the more clearly is the effect shown. It is true that the greater relative participation of Protestants in the ownership of capital, in management, and the upper ranks of labour in great modern industrial and commercial enterprises, may in part be explained in terms of historical circumstances which extend far back into the past, and in which religious affiliation is not a cause of the economic conditions, but to a certain extent appears to be a result of them. Participation in the above economic functions usually involves some previous ownership of capital, and generally an expensive education; often both. These are to-day largely dependent on the possession of inherited wealth, or at least on a certain degree of material well-being. A number of those sections of the old Empire which were most highly developed economically

* Reprinted by permission of Charles Scribner's Sons from *The Protestant Ethic and the Spirit of Capitalism,* pages 35–46, by Max Weber, translated by Talcott Parsons. Used also by permission of George Allen & Unwin Ltd.

and most favoured by natural resources and situation, in particular a majority of the wealthy towns, went over to Protestantism in the sixteenth century. The results of that circumstance favour the Protestants even to-day in their struggle for economic existence. There arises thus the historical question: why were the districts of highest economic development at the same time particularly favourable to a revolution in the Church? The answer is by no means so simple as one might think.

The emancipation from economic traditionalism appears, no doubt, to be a factor which would greatly strengthen the tendency to doubt the sanctity of the religious tradition, as of all traditional authorities. But it is necessary to note, what has often been forgotten, that the Reformation meant not the elimination of the Church's control over everyday life, but rather the substitution of a new form of control for the previous one. It meant the repudiation of a control which was very lax, at that time scarcely perceptible in practice, and hardly more than formal, in favour of a regulation of the whole of conduct which, penetrating to all departments of private and public life, was infinitely burdensome and earnestly enforced. The rule of the Catholic Church, "punishing the heretic, but indulgent to the sinner," as it was in the past even more than to-day, is now tolerated by peoples of thoroughly modern economic character, and was borne by the richest and economically most advanced peoples on earth at about the turn of the fifteenth century. The rule of Calvinism, on the other hand, as it was enforced in the sixteenth century in Geneva and in Scotland, at the turn of the sixteenth and seventeenth centuries in large parts of the Netherlands, in the seventeenth in New England, and for a time in England itself, would be for us the most absolutely unbearable form of ecclesiastical control of the individual which could possibly exist. That was exactly what large numbers of the old commercial aristocracy of those times, in Geneva as well as in Holland and England, felt about it. And what the reformers complained of in those areas of high economic development was not too much supervision of life on the part of the Church, but too little. Now how does it happen that at that time those countries which were most advanced economically, and within them the rising bourgeois middle classes, not only failed to resist this unexampled tyranny of Puritanism, but even developed a heroism in its defence? For bourgeois classes as such have seldom before and never since displayed heroism. It was "the last of our heroisms," as Carlyle, not without reason, has said.

But further, and especially important: it may be, as has been claimed, that the greater participation of Protestants in the positions of ownership and management in modern economic life may to-day be understood, in part at least, simply as a result of the greater material wealth they have inherited. But there are certain other phenomena which cannot be explained in the same way. Thus, to mention only a few facts: there is a great difference discoverable in Baden, in Bavaria, in Hungary, in the type of higher education which Catholic parents, as opposed to Protestant, give their children. That the percentage of Catholics among the students and graduates of higher educational institutions in general lags behind their proportion of the total population, may, to be sure, be largely explicable in terms of inherited differences of wealth. But among the Catholic graduates themselves the percentage of those graduating from the institutions preparing, in particular, for technical studies and industrial and commercial occupations, but in general from those preparing for middle-class business life, lags still farther behind the percentage of Protestants. On the other hand, Catholics prefer the sort of training which the humanistic Gymnasium affords. That is a circumstance to which the above explanation does not apply, but which, on the contrary, is one reason why so few Catholics are engaged in capitalistic enterprise.

Even more striking is a fact which partly explains the smaller proportion of Catholics among the skilled labourers of modern industry. It is well known that the factory has taken its skilled labour to a large extent from young men in the handicrafts; but this is much more true of Protestant than of Catholic journeymen. Among journeymen, in other words, the Catholics show a stronger propensity to remain in their crafts, that is they more often become master craftsmen, whereas the Protestants are attracted to a larger extent into the factories in order to fill the upper ranks of skilled labour and administrative positions. The explanation of these cases is undoubtedly that the mental and spiritual peculiarities acquired from the environment, here the type of education favoured by the religious atmosphere of the home community and the parental home, have determined the choice of occupation, and through it the professional career.

The smaller participation of Catholics in the modern business life of Germany is all the more striking because it runs counter to a tendency which has been observed at all times including the present. National or religious minorities which are in a position of subordination to a group of rulers are likely, through their voluntary or involuntary exclusion from positions of political influence, to be driven with peculiar force into economic activity. Their ablest members seek to satisfy the desire for recognition of their abilities in this field, since there is no opportunity in the service of the State. This has undoubtedly been true of the Poles in Russia and Eastern Prussia, who have without question been undergoing a more rapid economic advance than in Galicia, where they have been in the ascendant. It has in earlier times been true of the Huguenots in France under Louis XIV, the Nonconformists and Quakers in England, and, last but not least, the Jew for two thousand years. But the Catholics in Germany have shown no striking evidence of such a result of their position. In the past they have, unlike the Protestants, undergone no particularly prominent economic development in the times when they were persecuted or only tolerated, either in Holland or in England. On the other hand, it is a fact that the Protestants (especially certain branches of the movement to be fully discussed later) both as ruling classes and as ruled, both as majority and as minority, have shown a special tendency to develop economic rationalism which cannot be observed to the same extent among Catholics either in the one situation or in the other. Thus the principal explanation of this difference must be sought in the permanent intrinsic character of their religious beliefs, and not only in their temporary external historico-political situations.

It will be our task to investigate these religions with a view to finding out what peculiarities they have or have had which might have resulted in the behaviour we have described. On superficial analysis, and on the basis of certain current impressions, one might be tempted to express the difference by saying that the greater other-worldliness of Catholicism, the ascetic character of its highest ideals, must have brought up its adherents to a greater indifference toward the good things of this world. Such an explanation fits the popular tendency in the judgment of both religions. On the Protestant side it is used as a basis of criticism of those (real or imagined) ascetic ideals of the Catholic way of life, while the Catholics answer with the accusation that materialism results from the secularization of all ideals through Protestantism. One recent writer has attempted to formulate the difference of their attitudes toward economic life in the following manner: "The Catholic is quieter, having less of the acquisitive impulse; he prefers a life of the greatest possible security, even with a smaller income, to a life of risk and excitement, even though it may bring the chance of gaining honour and riches. The proverb says jokingly, 'either eat well or sleep well.' In the present case the Protestant prefers to eat well, the Catholic to sleep undisturbed."

In fact, this desire to eat well may be a correct though incomplete characterization of the motives of many nominal Protestants in Germany at the present time. But things were very different in the past: the English, Dutch, and American Puritans were characterized by the exact opposite of the joy of living, a fact which is indeed, as we shall see, most important for our present study. Moreover, the French Protestants, among others, long retained, and retain to a certain extent up to the present, the characteristics which were impressed upon the Calvinistic Churches everywhere, especially under the cross in the time of the religious struggles. Nevertheless (or was it, perhaps, as we shall ask later, precisely on that account?) it is well known that these characteristics were one of the most important factors in the industrial and capitalistic development of France, and on the small scale permitted them by their persecution remained so. If we may call this seriousness and the strong predominance of religious interests in the whole conduct of life otherworldliness, then the French Calvinists were and still are at least as otherworldly as, for instance, the North German Catholics, to whom their Catholicism is undoubtedly as vital a matter as religion is to any other people in the world. Both differ from the predominant religious trends in their respective countries in much the same way. The Catholics of France are, in their lower ranks, greatly interested in the enjoyment of life, in the upper directly hostile to religion. Similarly, the Protestants of Germany are to-day absorbed in worldly economic life, and their upper ranks are most indifferent to religion. Hardly anything shows so clearly as this parallel that, with such vague ideas as that of the alleged otherworldliness of Catholicism, and the alleged materialistic joy of living of Protestantism, and others like them, nothing can be accomplished for our purpose. In such general terms the distinction does not even adequately fit the facts of to-day, and certainly not of the past. If, however, one wishes to make use of it at all, several other observations present themselves at once which, combined with the above remarks, suggest that the supposed conflict between otherworldliness, asceticism, and ecclesiastical piety on the one side, and participation in capitalistic acquisition on the other, might actually turn out to be an intimate relationship.

As a matter of fact it is surely remarkable, to begin with quite a superficial observation, how large is the number of representatives of the most spiritual forms of Christian piety who have sprung from commercial circles. In particular, very many of the most zealous adherents of Pietism are of this origin. It might be explained as a sort of reaction against mammonism on the part of sensitive natures not adapted to commercial life, and, as in the case of Francis of Assisi, many Pietists have themselves interpreted the process of their conversion in these terms. Similarly, the remarkable circumstance that so many of the greatest capitalistic entrepreneurs—down to Cecil Rhodes—have come from clergymen's families might be explained as a reaction against their ascetic upbringing. But this form of explanation fails where an extraordinary capitalistic business sense is combined in the same persons and groups with the most intensive forms of a piety which penetrates and dominates their whole lives. Such cases are not isolated, but these traits are characteristic of many of the most important Churches and sects in the history of Protestantism. Especially Calvinism, wherever it has appeared, has shown this combination. However little, in the time of the expansion of the Reformation, it (or any other Protestant belief) was bound up with any particular social class, it is characteristic and in a certain sense typical that in French Huguenot Churches monks and business men (merchants, craftsmen) were particularly numerous among the proselytes, especially at the time of the persecution. Even the Spaniards knew that heresy (i.e. the Calvinism of the Dutch) promoted trade, and this coincides with the opinions which Sir William Petty expressed in his discussion of the reasons for the capitalistic development of the Netherlands. Gothein rightly calls the Calvinistic diaspora the seed-bed of capitalistic economy. Even in this case one might consider the decisive factor to be the superiority of the French and Dutch economic cultures from which these communities sprang, or perhaps the immense influence of exile in the breakdown of traditional relationships. But in France the situation was, as we know from Colbert's struggles, the same even in the seventeenth century. Even Austria, not to speak of other countries, directly imported Protestant craftsmen.

But not all the Protestant denominations seem to have had an equally strong influence in this direction. That of Calvinism, even in Germany, was among the strongest, it seems, and the reformed faith more than the others seems to have promoted the development of the spirit of capitalism, in the Wupperthal as well as elsewhere. Much more so than Lutheranism, as comparison both in general and in particular instances, especially in the Wupperthal, seems to prove. For Scotland, Buckle, and among English poets, Keats, have emphasized these same relationships. Even more striking, as it is only necessary to mention, is the connection of a religious way of life with the most intensive development of business acumen among those sects whose otherworldliness is as proverbial as their wealth, especially the Quakers and the Mennonites. The part which the former have played in England and North America fell to the latter in Germany and the Netherlands. That in East Prussia Frederick William I tolerated the Mennonites as indispensable to industry, in spite of their absolute refusal to perform military service, is only one of the numerous well-known cases which illustrates the fact, though, considering the character of that monarch, it is one of the most striking. Finally, that this combination of intense piety with just as strong a development of business acumen, was also characteristic of the Pietists, is common knowledge.

It is only necessary to think of the Rhine country and of Calw. In this purely introductory discussion it is unnecessary to pile up more examples. For these few already all show one thing: that the spirit of hard work, of progress, or whatever else it may be called, the awakening of which one is inclined to ascribe to Protestantism, must not be understood, as there is a tendency to do, as joy of living nor in any other sense as connected with the Enlightenment. The old Protestantism of Luther, Calvin, Knox, Voet, had precious little to do with what today is called progress. To whole aspects of modern life which the most extreme religionist would not wish to suppress to-day, it was directly hostile. If any inner relationship between certain expressions of the old Protestant spirit and modern capitalistic culture is to be found, we must attempt to find it, for better or worse, not in its alleged more or less materialistic or at least anti-ascetic joy of living, but in its purely religious characteristics. Montesquieu says (*Esprit des Lois,* Book XX, chap. 7) of the English that they "had progressed the farthest of all peoples of the world in three important things: in piety, in commerce, and in freedom." Is it not possible that their commercial superiority and their adaptation to free political institutions are connected in some way with that record of piety which Montesquieu ascribes to them?

A large number of possible relationships, vaguely perceived, occur to us when we put the question in this way. It will now be our task to formulate what occurs to us confusedly as clearly as is possible, considering the inexhaustible diversity to be found in all historical material. But in order to do this it is necessary to leave behind the vague and general concepts with which we have dealt up to this point, and attempt to penetrate into the peculiar characteristics of and the differences between those great worlds of religious thought which have existed historically in the various branches of Christianity.

Before we can proceed to that, however, a few remarks are necessary, first on the peculiarities of the phenomenon of which we are seeking an historical explanation, then concerning the sense in which such an explanation is possible at all within the limits of these investigations.

The Religious Factor in Detroit: Review, Replication, and Reanalysis*†

Howard Schuman

The application of Weber's Protestant Ethic thesis to the United States has two aspects that go far to explain its attractiveness to many American sociologists. On the one hand, the tracing of economic attitudes and behavior to religious values and beliefs is a nonobvious but intuitively interesting linkage. As such, it seems to provide a persuasive instance where sociology has developed insights that are not apparent to the layman. At the same time, the primary application of the hypothesis to the United States makes this more than a purely theoretical exercise. The division of the American population into one quarter Catholic and three quarters Protestant, it is argued, must be taken into account if we are to understand such nonreligious features of American life as its stratification and mobility system, economic organization, and socialization practices.

The single, most influential writing on the Protestant Ethic hypothesis is probably Gerhard Lenski's *The Religious Factor* (1963).[1] As a

*Reprinted from *American Sociological Review*, 36 (February, 1971), pp. 30–48, by permission of the author and publisher.
† This investigation was carried out through the University of Michigan's Detroit Area Study. I am indebted to Edward O. Laumann with whom I collaborated in designing the 1966 Detroit Area Study. Many of the specific problems involved in replication and reanalysis were solved by James House and Paula Pelletier, who worked as research assistants on this part of the project. Gerhard Lenski kindly furnished advice on use of certain codes from his 1958 study.
1. The 1963 Anchor edition is not simply a reprint of the original 1961 Doubleday edition but contains important changes in analysis and writing. All references in this paper will be to the 1963 edition.

widely available and forcefully written book, Lenski's work has been frequently cited.[2] No doubt a major reason for its impact is that it reports strikingly positive findings and concludes that the Protestant Ethic thesis *is* relevant to contemporary America, that Protestant-Catholic differences in secular attitudes are both large and manifold (more so in fact than class differences), and that these indirect effects of religion in America seem to be on the increase rather than the decrease. One other characteristic of Lenski's work that distinguishes it from most other efforts in this area is its concern to measure social psychological attitudes and values that intervene between religious identification and larger macro-social processes such as occupational mobility.[3]

Despite its intriguing nature, the Americanized version of the Protestant Ethic thesis, and more specifically Lenski's conclusions, have met with some criticism. At the theoretical level, questions have been raised as to whether Weber really intended to argue that the Protestant Ethic was an important cause of the rise of capitalism, and, even if so, whether he expected the Protestant-Catholic distinction to continue to lead to similar economic differences in the twentieth century.[4] More practical questions have focused on whether such gross categories as "Catholic" and "Protestant" are analytically useful in the United States, since there are important ethnic lines within American Catholicism and both ethnic and denominational differences among American Protestants.[5] Finally, at the empirical

2. For example, the article on "The Sociology of Religion" in the new and highly regarded *International Encyclopedia of the Social Sciences* (1969, Volume 13, p. 412) describes *The Religious Factor* as "perhaps the most successful attempt to apply survey research to the sociology of religion," and briefly notes the positive findings of the book.

3. Most other work on this topic investigates only the general connection between religious membership and socioeconomic variables such as income. See Glenn and Hyland (1967), which includes a fairly complete set of references to earlier studies. For more recent analyses emphasizing socioeconomic status, see Glockel (1969) and Warren (1970). Featherman (1969) provides one of the few analyses (other than Lenski's) which include intervening social psychological variables, though the intervention in this case is between different points in the achievement process for adults.

4. The wide disagreements on this point indicate that *The Protestant Ethic and the Spirit of Capitalism* (Weber, 1930) can be read in different ways. I myself see Weber's citation of religious differences in education and business (pp. 38–40) as suggesting continuation into the twentieth century of Protestant-Catholic differences in secular values. That Weber, as a careful scholar, emphasized the complexity of any causal analysis of capitalism does not mean that he lacked a bold thesis himself. In any case, the impact of Weber's writing on the Protestant Ethic has certainly been largely based on this thesis, whether or not Weber himself would today subscribe to it.

5. Glock and Stark (1965) have particularly emphasized denominational differences within Protestantism. Their dependent variables, however, are religious and moral values closely tied to the origins of American denominations, and they do not deal with values linked to the Protestant Ethic hypothesis. See Warren (1970) for a careful analysis of denominational differences in education, occupation, and income. An original review of *The Religious Factor* (Rosen, 1962) questioned the lack of attention to ethnic differences.

level enough contradictory findings have appeared to raise some doubts about the reliability of the positive findings reported in *The Religious Factor* (see especially Greely, 1964).

The present paper will not attempt to deal with the first type of question, but will assume that whatever Weber may have intended, it is not unreasonable to determine whether there are Protestant-Catholic differences in beliefs and values relevant to economic advancement. We will deal briefly at one point with the second type of question on ethnic and denominational differences within the major religions, but that is also not our primary focus. The analysis and findings described here are mainly relevant to the third question, namely, the reliability, and therefore validity, of reported Protestant-Catholic differences, using Lenski's earlier results as the focus of investigation. More simply, we shall present results from both a replication and a reanalysis of Lenski's findings, with a review along the ways of the original findings themselves.

Lenski's research was carried out in 1958 within the framework of the Detroit Area Study, a continuing survey research and training unit of the University of Michigan. It was appropriate that in 1966 the Detroit Area Study included as part of another research effort an attempt to replicate and extend certain small but important aspects of the investigation reported in *The Religious Factor*. However, the replication was by no means complete and exact, and several limitations must be stressed at the outset.

First, almost the entire focus of the 1966 replication was on the Weberian hypothesis developed and tested by Lenski in Chapter 3 ("Religion and Economics") of his book. The book deals with several other topics, such as "Religion and Politics," which are not relevant at all here, and with still other topics such as "Religion and Family Life," that are relevant but are tested only slightly, if at all, by the present data.

Second, this replication began more as an "extension" than as a simple replication. We hoped to duplicate Lenski's results and then to carry out—more carefully than his sample and techniques allowed—several further analyses, for example, on the relevance of ethnicity to religious differences. We did not, therefore, repeat quite all the questions needed for a full replication even of the economic aspect of the 1958 DAS survey, and we did not attempt seriously to follow his exact ordering of questions.

Third, replication is not a simple concept and can obviously never be carried out perfectly.[6] Apart from sampling error, which can be estimated,

---

6. The term "replication" is used here to refer to the deliberate repetition at a later point in time of part or all of a completed piece of research in order to determine whether the same results obtain. This usage is related to but not the same as that common to experimental designs (Fisher, 1951:58–60). A helpful discussion of the present usage appears in Lykken (1968). The type of replication used here would probably be termed "operational replication" by Lykken, as opposed to "constructive replication," which does not attempt to duplicate the research procedures of the original investigation but rather to operationalize the relevant constructs in other ways.

and real changes over time, which often cannot, replication turns on many subtle factors in the operational definition of the population sampled and in the actual execution of the research process. The present effort is in many ways more exact than usually possible, because essentially the same organization (although not the same people) carried out much the same type of survey within almost exactly the same geographically and socially bounded population. (Indeed, successful replication in this case would still leave open the question of whether the findings could be extended beyond the Detroit Metropolitan area. Unsuccessful replication, however, does not carry this kind of ambiguity.) Despite the similar organizational and geographic frameworks, however, there are also important differences between the 1958 and 1966 sampling designs that will be discussed below.

SAMPLE DESIGN IN 1958 AND IN 1966

Both the 1958 and 1966 data are based on samples from the metropolitan Detroit population—city and surrounding suburbs. The Detroit SMSA defined by the Bureau of the Census actually consists of three counties, but in both 1958 and 1966 thinly populated outlying parts of the counties (plus the city of Pontiac) were not included in the survey sample boundaries, primarily to reduce time and costs.[7] The sample area was defined to be somewhat larger in 1966 than in 1958 in order to accommodate expansion of actual suburban areas, but the percentage of the total SMSA population included in the total sample area was quite similar for the two years: 87% in 1958 and 85% in 1966. Suburban towns that had experienced recent growth were all included in the 1966 boundaries, and it does not appear likely that important parts of the "1958 population" had moved beyond the 1966 boundaries. Thus, we regard the total populations available for the two studies as essentially the same, except for whatever long-distance migration may have taken place between the Detroit SMSA and the rest of the United States during the intervening eight years.

Although the geographically defined populations were essentially the same for the two studies, the 1966 survey screened out parts of the general population that were included in 1958. We need to indicate the likely effect of this differential screening on comparisons between the two sets of results.

The sample used in 1958 involved essentially a cross section selection of occupied dwelling units from the geographic area described above. Within each dwelling unit, all persons age 21 and over were listed and one was selected at random for interview. No type of household appears to have been screened out. Of the 750 households selected for interview, 656 resulted in complete interviews—a response rate of 87%.

7. Information on the 1956 sampling was obtained from Lenski (1963:16–17) and from "Sampling Design for the 1957–58 Detroit Area Study" (1959). Neither of the

The sample in 1966 drew a cross section of occupied dwelling units, but considered eligible for random selection within household, only white males, ages 21 through 64, born in the United States or Canada. A total of 1,013 cases were obtained, with a response rate of 80%.[8] Each of the screening factors requires brief consideration. Included in parentheses is the number of cases that were excluded from the sample as originally drawn because of the criterion discussed.

1. *Exclusion of Negroes* (N = 332): Lenski divided the Protestant population by race in all his calculations, and his main conclusions about the effects of religion are based on differences between white Protestants and Catholics. His decision can be questioned from a theoretical standpoint, but in terms of replication it means that an all-white sample is quite adequate for re-testing his findings. One simply ignores the specific results and conclusions in *The Religious Factor* that involve the Negro subsample.
2. *Exclusion of persons born outside the United States or Canada* (N = 181): The effect of this exclusion should be to *increase* Protestant-Catholic differences, according to Lenski's 1958 results. One of his most striking conclusions is that differences between "socio-religious groups" are generally heightened when third generation Americans are studied separately.
3. *Exclusion of Women* (N = 268) *and of Native-Born Men over 65* (N = 92): In the chapter directly replicated by the 1966 study, certain of the tables are confined to men, and others include both sexes. There is no indication that results differ by sex where questions are relevant to both sexes. The same applies to age, except that the finding reported above on third generation effects suggests that Protestant-Catholic differences may well increase among younger people. Nonetheless, possible specification by age or sex must be allowed for and will be discussed below after presentation of major results.
4. *Differences in response rates:* The difference between the response rates for the two years is partly a function of the restriction of the 1966 sample to working age males—a particularly difficult category to reach. It may also reflect the general downward trend of response rates reported in most studies over the past two decades. Insofar as the latter is the case, the difference *may* reduce comparability between the obtained samples for the two years. While there is no particular reason to expect such an effect, especially given the relatively small percentage difference, the possibility cannot be ruled out. It provides a good example of the difficulty of achieving "literal replication" (Lykken, 1968).

---

above sources specified the lower age limit for the 1956 sample, referring simply to "adults." The lower cut-off of 21 mentioned below is found in the "Interviewer's Instruction Booklet" for the 1957–58 study. Information on the 1966 sampling appears in Schuman (1967).

8. The actual number of interviews obtained was 985. Twenty-eight of these interviews were weighted double for sampling reasons explained in Schuman (1967). The number involved in the weighting is assumed to be too small to require adjustments in significance tests. A design effect due to cluster sampling of about 1.1 has also been ignored here because of its trivial size.

RESULTS

Lenski's major conclusion concerning Protestant-Catholic differences in economic ethic is that "as a general rule, commitment to the spirit of capitalism . . . is especially frequent among white Protestants and Jews [and] is much less frequent among Catholics . . ." (Lenski, 1963:128). We will review the evidence he offers for this conclusion, presenting parallel results from the 1966 study where possible. Our initial focus will be on values and attitudes, rather than on indicators of occupational achievement or mobility, since as noted earlier Lenski's research remains valuable mainly because of its development of intervening social psychological variables. Our tables will include results for Jews when these were presented by Lenski, but our main focus will be on Protestant-Catholic comparisons. The Jewish subsample is quite small in both DAS surveys, and it also involves other issues not directly tied to the Weberian debate.[9]

WORK VALUES

After examining differences in upward mobility by religion, Lenski presents the first of a series of questions on work values and work-related attitudes. Each person in both the 1958 and the 1966 surveys was asked to rank the following in order of their importance when choosing a job:

1. High income
2. No danger of being fired
3. Working hours short, lots of free time
4. Chances for advancement
5. The work is important and gives a feeling of accomplishment.

The 1958 survey asked men and working women to answer for themselves, and wives to answer in terms of what they would want in their husbands' job; the 1966 survey, as mentioned earlier, did not include women.

Lenski considers the 5th alternative the one best representing the "Protestant Ethic" as conceived by Weber, the 4th also a partial indicator of the Ethic, and the 1st a popular but questionable approach to opera-

---

9. Lenski does not always present exact N's with percentage findings. It is useful to record here the total N's for the two studies, even though a few "don't know" cases are usually lost for any given question.

	Protestants	Catholics	Jews	Total*
1958 Study	267	230	27	524
1966 Study	498	433	29	960

* The 1958 sample also included 100 Negro Protestants and apparently 32 "Others" (Negro Catholics and white "other religion"), as calculated from figures in Lenski (1963:16 and 370). The 1966 sample included 53 white "other religion."

tionalizing the same construct. The 3rd alternative, and to a lesser extent the 2nd, are regarded as "completely in opposition to any conception of the Protestant Ethic" (Lenski, 1963:87).

Lenski notes "how strong a hold the Protestant Ethic, in the classical sense, has on all segments of the American population": nearly half of the 1958 sample ranked the 5th alternative highest, and two-thirds selected either the 5th or the 4th alternative. Our results in 1966 are almost identical, with 47% of the sample making the 5th alternative first choice, and another 27% selecting the 4th alternative.

Turning to differences by religion, Lenski reports that the following percentages of the three religious groups rank first the "classic Protestant Ethic" alternative ("the work is important and gives a feeling of accomplishment"):[10] Protestants, 52%; Jews, 48%; Catholics, 44%. The difference of 8 percentage points between Protestants and Catholics is not great, but it meets the .10 level of significance (one-tailed) used in *The Religious Factor*. The small Jewish subsample does not differ significantly ($p > .10$, one-tailed) from either of the other categories. Lenski also notes, without presenting data, that "application of controls for class position of respondents and of their parents, and for the education of respondents . . . revealed that the differences between white Protestants on the one hand and Jews and Catholics on the other are greater among the better educated and in the middle classes than among the less well educated and the working classes." (Lenski, 1963:91).

On the other hand, Lenski finds that Jews and Catholics are high on alternatives 1 and 4 which refer to chances for advancement and high income. He reports only the percentage for the two alternatives combined and without controls:[11] Jews, 45%; Catholics, 40%; Protestants, 31%. This difference confirms Lenski's belief that there are two somewhat separate though related systems of work values which deserve to be distinguished. Protestants tend to be higher on the "classic" Protestant Ethic, while Jews and Catholics are higher on the more contemporary version. Finally, Lenski notes that all the reported differences are small and cannot account for the major part of the relative economic success of Protestants and Jews as against Catholics. Perhaps for this reason, he does not include results for this question in his summary table comparing the size of differences by religion with the size of differences by social class (Lenski, 1963:326).

Our own findings on this question are reported in Table 1. The results

---

10. It is not completely clear that totals for religious groups were used, but absence of qualifications makes this likely. Here as elsewhere in this paper, Lenski's fourth "socio-religious" category of Negro Protestants is omitted; all respondents included in the three categories shown are white.

11. This assumes that each percentage stands for first choice of one alternative or the other—an assumption implied but not explicit (Lenski 1963:91). The percentages here, it should be noted, are largely determined by the preceding set, but the determination is not complete since there were two other possible response categories to the question.

TABLE 1. *Percent of Protestants (P), Catholics (C) and Jews (J) Giving First Rank to "Protestant Ethic Responses" (1966 Data)**

Relig. Group	1st Choice to A[a]	1st Choice to B[b] or C[c]
P	49% (498)	40% (498)
C	44 (433)	44 (433)
J	52 (29)	38 (29)

* Base N's in parentheses.
[a] "The work is important and gives a feeling of accomplishment."
[b] "Chance for advancement."
[c] "High income."

successfully replicate Lenski's work in part. A somewhat greater proportion of Protestants than Catholics give first rank to the sense of accomplishment and worth of work. The difference of 5 percentage points between the two groups would not be significant for Lenski's sample sizes, but just makes the 10% level of significance (one-tailed) for our larger subsamples. There is also a trend for Catholics to be higher (by 4 percentage points) than Protestants on first choice given to income or chances for advancement. Lenski's finding that Jews were highest on first choice of advancement or income, and Protestants lowest, does not hold up well. The differences are slight and Jews are actually lowest on these combined responses (and highest on the "classical" Protestant Ethic response).

As noted above, Lenski reports, but does not present, data showing that the religious factor operates more strongly among the middle-class and better educated. We have created social class (occupation and income) and educational controls as close as possible to those generally used by Lenski.[12]

---

12. The social class and educational criteria used in the two surveys and the resulting distributions are shown below, with cases omitted where classificatory information is lacking:

A. Percent in Each Social Class in 1958 and 1966

Social Class	Criteria	Lenski's Dist. (Whites only)	1966 Dist.
Upper-Middle Class	White collar occupation: Family head income $8,000 or more in 1958; $10,000 or more in 1966.	17%	29%
Lower-Middle Class	White collar occupation: Family head income less than $8,000 in 1958; less than $10,000 in 1966.	26	18
Upper-Working Class	Manual or service occupation; Family head income $5,000 or more in 1958; $7,000 or more in 1966.	32	39
Lower-Working Class	Manual or service occupation; Family head income less than		

Comparisons between Protestants and Catholics within class and educational categories for the work-values question are shown in Table 2. (There are too few Jews to allow for such controls.) Our results bear out the 1958 finding that differences between Protestants and Catholics are primarily located within the upper stratum. Among the upper-middle class and the college-educated, Protestant-Catholic differences increase slightly over that found for the total samples, while only small, though consistent, differences occur among the other strata. In summary, then, our results in 1966 for this question are generally in accord with those obtained by Lenski in 1958, although all associations are small.

ATTITUDES TOWARD WORK

Central to Weber's conception of the Protestant Ethic was the high valuation of work as man's vocation in this world. This contrasts with the view that work is simply a necessary evil, or indeed a consequence of Original Sin. To explore further this contrast, both the 1958 and 1966 surveys asked the following questions: "Some people tell us they couldn't really be happy unless they were working at some job. But others say that they would be a lot happier if they didn't have to work and could take life

$5,000 in 1958; less than $7,000 in 1966.	25	14
Total	100	100
N	(502)	(1004)

B. Percent in Each Category of School Years Completed in 1958 and 1966.

	Lenski's Sample	1966 Sample
13 years or more	21%	35%
12 years (high school grad.)	—⎱ 59	32⎱ 53
9 to 11 years	—⎰	21⎰
0 to 8 years	20	12
	100%	100%
N =	(524)	(1008)

The 1966 study used the same occupational groupings as Lenski, but raised the cutting point for income by $2,000 to take account of changes in income level between 1958 and 1964. Partly as a result of this change, the 1966 "social class" distribution is somewhat different from Lenski's. There is also a slight difference in occupational distributions as such, since Lenski's combined middle-class categories account for 43%, as against 47% for the 1966 sample. This may represent a change in the Detroit occupational structure, but may simply be a result of sampling error plus the 1966 exclusion of older men from the sample. The greater difference between the two distributions involves income within the two occupational categories, and since this is a relative matter it should not result in marked changes in other relationships. It is also clear that the present sample is distributed somewhat differently in education than Lenski's, no doubt in part because of the 1966 age restriction. We should also note that class differences beween Protestants and Catholics in the present sample are not great and educational differences are virtually nonexistent.

Table 2. Percent Protestants and Catholics Giving First Rank to "Work is important" by Social Class and Education (1966 Data).

Social Class	Protestants	Catholics	Education	Protestants	Catholics
Upper Middle	68% (148)	58% (94)	Some College and Above	62% (165)	50% (145)
Lower Middle	47 (86)	44 (91)	9–12 Years of School	44 (271)	42 (240)
Upper Working	40 (181)	38 (175)	0–8 Years of School	37 (62)	35 (46)
Lower Working	37 (78)	37 (68)			
	(493)	(428)		(498)	(431)

517

easy. How do you feel about this? Why is that?" Respondents were then coded into one of three general categories: 1. a completely positive attitude toward work, which emphasizes its intrinsic rewards or its moral character; 2. a neutral attitude, which involves a preference for working, but one based on extrinsic factors, such as boredom with too much leisure; 3. a negative attitude, which involves a frank assertion by the respondent that he would be happier if he did not have to work.

The 1958 survey found the following percentages of males in each religious group expressing a *positive* attitude toward work: Jews, 42%; Protestants, 30%; Catholics, 23%. The difference between Protestants and Catholics here is significant at the .10 level, according to the table Lenski provides (1963:372). He also reports that controls for generation, region of birth, and class show Protestant-Catholic differences to be on the increase rather than on the decrease. "Catholics who were northern born, third-generation Americans were much more likely to have a *negative attitude* toward work than were first- and second-generation immigrants (36% vs. 14%)" (p. 90). The *opposite* trend occurred among Protestants for *positive* attitudes toward work (30% vs. 24%). Moreover, positive attitudes toward work were directly correlated with social class for Protestants, but the correlation was inverse for Catholics (see Lenski, 1963:98, Table 10). Lenski interprets this to mean that Protestants take a more positive attitude toward more demanding and rewarding positions, while Catholics show a more positive attitude toward positions that are less demanding and hence less rewarding. None of the above controls are applied to Jews because of small sample sizes, and there is no comment on the largest percentage differences in 1958 for the question, those between Jews and *both* Protestants and Catholics.

Our own findings on this question are shown in Table 3, alongside Lenski's results where these were reported in detail. The value of placing results from both years together is to allow direct comparisons of trends in subgroup differences. Absolute percents for any given subgroup should not be compared, however, since as explained earlier the 1958 survey included parts of the population excluded in 1966. For the present question, the populations are somewhat closer than usual, since Lenski presents these data also only for males, but there are still differences by age and birth place.

Our results do not replicate those of Lenski's with regard to Protestant-Catholic differences. We find only a trivial and unreliable difference on this question for the two religious groups as a whole. When generation is introduced as a third variable, we find slight and probably unreliable effects *opposite* to those reported by Lenski. When social class is introduced as a third variable, there is little variation of any kind in *negative* attitudes toward work. There is a tendency for positive attitudes to increase with class position for *both* religious groups, rather than a reversal in direction as Lenski found. The only line of support for Lenski's original result is that there is a greater spread between the top and bottom classes for Protestants than for Catholics, but the figures are of certain reliability and meaning, and they constitute only a very partial replication of the 1958 results.

SPENDING AND SAVING

Shifting from attitudes toward work to values about consumption, Lenski "inquired into the manner in which families use their income." One question concerned installment buying: Changing the subject a bit, do you think it's a good idea or a bad idea to buy things on the installment plan? Lenski reports 46% of his total sample in favor of installment buying, 38% against, with the balance not decided. In 1966 we find 47% for, 50% against, and 3% other. The differences here are not great and could easily result from differences in sample design (e.g., Negroes included in 1958 but not in 1966), changes over time, or a combination of sampling error and format variation.[13]

Lenski reports the following percents by religious groups in terms of *dis*approval of installment buying: Jews, 56%; Protestants, 44%; Catholics, 40%. The Protestant-Catholic difference is not reliable even at the .10 level (one-tailed), but Lenski does find the same interaction with generation reported earlier: Catholics closer to immigrant status (1st and 2nd generation) are more disapproving of installment buying than are Catholics in or beyond the third generation; the opposite is true among Protestants. Table 4 presents the 1958 findings, along with comparable percentages from the present study.

Our overall findings by religion show even less of a Protestant-Catholic difference than the small one reported by Lenski. We also found a reversal for Jews, with the latter less rather than more disapproving of installment buying than the other two groups. This was such a puzzling finding that it led us to check our entire coding procedure for the question, but a count based on the original 29 raw questionnaires for the subsample of Jews confirmed the finding already reported.[14]

Simultaneous controls for generation and class produce slight trends

---

13. This question was included at the end of a five-minute attitude form which the respondent filled out himself mid-way in the hour interview. The form was completed entirely within the larger interview and does not result in loss of respondents; such a procedure was used primarily to allow observations of the house to be made by the interviewer for purposes unconnected with the present replication. The 1958 and 1966 questions were worded identically, but the 1958 version included an interview box for "unsure" if volunteered; the 1966 item did not offer such a choice explicitly. This latter minor difference in format occurs also for the "attitude toward work" question discussed earlier.

14. A control for occupation shows that this favorability toward installment buying is much stronger among Jewish businessmen (7 of 9 favoring) than among Jewish professionals (4 of 11). We suspect that this question may be ambiguous to some businessmen, and that they may interpret it as indicating favorability toward allowing installment buying by customers, rather than in terms of personal preference.

TABLE 3. Percent of White Males Expressing "Positive," "Neutral," and "Negative" Attitudes Toward Work.*

Religious Group	Lenski's Findings				1966 Findings			
	Pos.	Neut.	Neg.	N	Pos.	Neut.	Neg.	N
Protestants	30%	(not separated)		(—)	32%	58%	11%	(481)
Catholics	23	(not separated)		(—)	33	55	12	(421)
Jews	42	(not separated)		(—)	34	55	10	(29)
By Generation:								
Protestant, 3rd Gen. or More	30%	(not separated)		(40)	33%	54%	14%	(259)
Protestant, 2nd Gen. or Less	24	(not separated)		(37)	36	56	8	(125)
Catholic, 3rd Gen. or More	(not separated)	36		(22)	32	57	11	(190)
Catholic, 2nd Gen. or Less	(not separated)	14		(69)	35	52	14	(219)

* Where N's are not given for Lenski's groups, they were not presented in the book. The total N's in 1958 were no doubt the same or close to those reported in our ft. 9. Class criteria here are the same as those presented in ft. 12. With regard to generational criteria, in the 1966 study 1st-generation persons were, as mentioned earlier, excluded from the target population altogether, and only Northern-born respondents are included in the generation comparison. Lenski's survey includes 1st-generation immigrants, and his tables apparently exclude Southern-born respondents from third-generation or more categories, but not from second-generation categories.

By Class:								
Protestant:								
Upper Middle	36%	52%	12%	(25)	46%	46%	9%	(145)
Lower Middle	32	57	11	(19)	26	64	10	(84)
Upper Working	23	56	21	(39)	28	59	12	(172)
Lower Working	30	33	37	(27)	22	68	10	(78)
Catholic:								
Upper Middle	19	56	25	(16)	39	53	8	(95)
Lower Middle	18	57	25	(28)	34	57	9	(88)
Upper Working	18	64	18	(38)	30	56	15	(171)
Lower Working	33	48	19	(21)	30	55	15	(66)

TABLE 4.   *Percent Disapproving of Installment Buying.**

Religious Group	Lenski's Findings		1966 Findings	
Protestants:	44%	(—)	52%	(481)
Middle Class, 3rd Gen.	38	(60)	50	(159)
Middle Class, 1st & 2nd Gen.	34	(32)	49	(67)
Working Class, 3rd Gen.	51	(41)	54	(190)
Working Class, 1st & 2nd Gen.	42	(53)	52	(61)
Catholics:	40%	(—)	50%	(422)
Middle Class, 3rd Gen.	35	(31)	44	(94)
Middle Class, 1st & 2nd Gen.	41	(51)	49	(86)
Working Class, 3rd Gen.	35	(34)	51	(107)
Working Class, 1st & 2nd Gen.	39	(84)	53	(126)
Jews	56%	(—)	39%	(28)

* For the analysis by class, both studies exclude Southern-born respondents. Only Lenski's study includes 1st generation immigrants.

in the direction Lenski noted: third-generation Protestants are more disapproving of installment buying than second-generation Protestants, while the reverse effect is found among Catholics. However, the percentage differences are very tiny and could easily result from chance or from other differences correlated with religion, e.g., socioeconomic differences not controlled by the crude categorization into "middle-class" and "working-class." Certainly the net "interaction effect" found in the present study is much less than that reported in *The Religious Factor*.

OTHER ATTITUDES AND VALUES REGARDING WORK AND CONSUMPTION

The Religious Factor presents the results for several relevant attitude questions which we did not attempt to replicate exactly in the 1966 study. Lenski's findings on these questions will be briefly reviewed, with our reason for omitting the question or the results of modifying it also noted.

(a) *Belief in the Possibility of Success:* Lenski asked two questions designed to determine whether a respondent believed it is possible to rise from the working-class to the middle-class and whether he believed that ability rather than family connections makes for success. He reports that with class held constant (dichotomized into Middle-class vs. Working-class), over 10% more Protestants than Catholics hold such beliefs. We did not attempt to replicate these questions because we could not see a clear connection between them and Weber's central focus on the Protestant Ethic. As Lenski himself had earlier stressed, the concern with work that supposedly developed out of early Protestant views had to do not with the striving after extrinsic success, but with positive satisfaction in pursuing one's vocation in this world.

(b) *Divine Concern with Economic Striving:* A somewhat more relevant question seemed to be one that asked whether "God is more pleased when people try to get ahead, or when people are satisfied with what they have and don't try to push ahead." But Lenski found only a five percentage points difference between Protestants and Catholics on this question, though in the "right direction." He also reports that the question was difficult for respondents to answer and that many tried to avoid the forced choice. For these reasons, the question was not included in the 1966 study.

(c) *Use of Leisure Time:* In another chapter of *The Religious Factor,* Lenski reports data from an earlier (1953) Detroit Area Study, which shows a trend for Protestants to say they would use extra leisure time productively (e.g., social service work, reading, gardening) rather than indulgently (e.g., loafing, going to movies, shopping). This seems to be directly relevant to Weber's conception of a puritan work ethic, and we included the following similar (although not identical) question in our study immediately after the question on whether the respondent would be happier working or not working: "Suppose you *did* have a lot of free time. What would you most like to do with it?" Responses were coded into two basic categories of "Productive" (mainly self-improvement in content) and "Indulgent" (mainly casual social contacts, sports, and recreation). Differences by religion in 1966 are shown below:

	Productive	Indulgent	Total	N
Protestant	22	78	100%	(476)
Catholic	26	74	100%	(424)
Jewish	21	79	100%	(28)

Differences are slight, and if anything the trend is for Catholics to be less "indulgent" than Protestants.

(d) *Concern with Thrift:* Respondents in 1958 were asked how important it is to save regularly, and why? This "ant-and-grasshopper" inquiry was used to determine whether respondents emphasized ascetic self-discipline in the early Calvinist tradition or indulged themselves in more comsummatory directions. Results are not reported in detail, but apparently Protestants and Catholics did *not* differ in belief in the desirability of saving. The only difference found between the two groups was that a greater proportion of Protestants (28%) than Catholics (19%) gave more than one reason for saving. We did not find this numerical result as pertinent to the thrift argument as other questions, and therefore did not attempt to repeat the long series of inquiries used to obtain it.

(e) *Follow-up to Installment Buying*: After the question on install-ment buying reported earlier, the 1958 study asked: "Why do you feel this way?" Lenski reports that in explaining their disapproval, Protestants more often cited moral reasons than Catholics: 30% of the working-class Protes-tants, as against 18% of the working-class Catholics. Figures for middle-class respondents are not given, but by implication are less clear. Of the additional attitude questions treated in this section, this is the only one which seems both directly relevant to the main argument and somewhat promising in terms of reported results. It is unfortunate that we were not able to include it in the 1966 study.

POSITIONAL AND PERFORMANCE MEASURES

Although Lenski does not explicitly distinguish between attitudes and values on the one hand and performance indicators on the other hand, such a distinction appears essential. Weber's emphasis, although historical in its source of data, was basically social-psychological in nature. Individual Protestants were seen as developing beliefs and values which in turn led to distinctive performance in the world. Such performance finally led to changes in social position, for example, to a rise in one's occupation, income, and general status. If only one of these links can be focused upon, the psychological dimension seems most proximate for investigating the construct "Protestant Ethic." Differences in social position or even in per-formance cannot by themselves tell us very much about their origins. With this qualification in mind, we will examine the remaining evidence that Lenski offers for differences in Work Ethic between the two religious groups.

(a) *Labor Union Activity*: As suggested above, Lenski believed that "in many respects the values for which the unions stand are in opposition to the values embodied in the 'Protestant Ethic' and the 'spirit of capital-ism.' " This is because unions view work as a necessary evil and emphasize security rather than achievement. The Benjamin Franklins of today should presumably be men who wish to escape from the union rank and file, not contribute to its solidarity.

Lenski focuses on the lower middle class (clerks and salesmen) as the place in the social structure where union membership is possible but not taken for granted. He finds that 38% of the Catholics in the middle class (N=27) belong to unions, while only 15% of the middle class Protestants (N=33) have such membership. (No difference appears among working class men.) Our results do not replicate the white collar difference: among clerical and sales workers we find that 23% of the Protestants (N=66) and 23% of the Catholics (N=49) belong to unions.

The 1958 study did not include other questions on union involvement. But Lenski refers to other surveys done through the Detroit Area Study and elsewhere which show Protestant-Catholic differences. He cites the 1952 Detroit Area Study data showing that Protestant union members attend union meetings less often than Catholics and also say they are less "interested" in their union than Catholics. We did not repeat either of these questions exactly, but we did ask union members whether they felt "very involved" or "not very involved" in their union. Exactly 28% of the union members (177 Protestant union members, 166 Catholics) of each religious group claimed to be "very involved." A control for occupational level did not change this indication of no difference.

(b) *Self-Employment:* Just as unions are seen by Lenski as the locus of collectivistic and security-minded sentiments, so the self-employed are viewed as representatives of individualism. He finds little difference between Protestant and Catholic males in over-all rates of self-employment (8% and 10%, respectively). Controls for immigrant generation and region of birth alter the picture, with Protestants showing a greater representation among the self-employed. (See Table 5.) Lenski concludes from these trends (and similar trends for past self-employment) that "even in the bureaucratized modern metropolis there are real and significant differences among the major socio-religious groups in the degree to which they value occupational independence and autonomy, with Jews ranking first, white Protestants second, and Catholics third" (1963:104). The findings of the present study, however, confirm these earlier results only with regard to Jews. As Table 5 shows, we find no difference at all between Protestants and Catholics on this measure.

TABLE 5.   *Percent of Each Religious Group Self-Employed.**

Religious Group	Lenski's Findings		1966 Findings	
1st & 2nd Gen.				
Protestants	15%	(39)	11%	(266)
Catholics	8	(71)	11	(193)
3rd Gen.				
Northern Born				
Protestants	12	(42)	14	(118)
Catholics	4	(24)	13	(211)
Total				
Protestants	10	(—)	12	(384)
Catholics	8	(—)	12	(404)
Jews	">50%"	(27)	36	(25)

* 1st generation men were not included in the 1966 sample. Both samples used only males. Lenski does not report the N's for the two missing entries.

(c) *Budgeting:* Lenski was interested in discovering whether Protestants were more likely than Catholics to budget family expenditures. He found, however, no difference between the two religious groups on this question, and we therefore did not attempt to replicate the question.

(d) *Vertical Mobility:* We have saved until last the question of "vertical mobility," which Lenski treats first. Although it is obviously important to discover such differences if they exist, their origin is bound to be ambiguous. Even given the same attitudes and values, groups starting from different points will end at different points.

Lenski reports on the conflicting evidence in this area, and then presents data (p. 85) from the 1958 study showing greater Protestant than Catholic intergenerational mobility among white males. His data are not unambiguous, and this is an area where there is a fair amount of replication, often with larger national samples and using more recent analytic techniques.[15] Nevertheless, we have closely comparable data on this subject for the Detroit metropolitan area for 1966, presented in Table 6. Following the same mode of analysis that Lenski uses, we do not find much consistent support for his conclusion concerning greater Protestant mobility. Evidence in one part of the table is contradicted by evidence in another part, and the N's are too small to allow diverse conclusions based on specific pairs of cells.

TABLE 6.   *Occupational Level of White Male Respondents by Father's Occupation and Religion (1966 Data).**

Respondent's Occupational Level	Father's Occupation							
	Middle		Upper Working		Lower Working		Farmer	
	Prot.	Cath.	Prot.	Cath.	Prot.	Cath.	Prot.	Cath.
Upper Middle	54%	47%	32%	28%	22%	27%	18%	21%
Lower Middle	18	17	12	10	12	10	10	0
Upper Working	10	17	23	34	27	35	26	53
Lower Working	17	19	33	28	39	28	46	26
Total	100	100	100	100	100	100	100	100
N	153	95	112	144	147	162	77	20

* Occupational levels here and in Lenski (1963, Table 8, p. 85) are not the class levels described in ft. 12 above, but instead involve distinctions between: (1) professional and managerial, (2) clerical and sales, (3) craftsmen and foremen, and (4) operatives, service workers, and laborers. (Based on communication from Gerhard Lenski.) Note also that males over 64 and foreign-born are excluded from the 1966 sample and the above table, but not from Table 8 in *The Religious Factor.*

15. See Glockel, *op. cit.,* and Featherman, *op. cit.*

Religious Involvement and the Protestant Ethic

A problem with comparisons of "Protestants" and "Catholics" is the vague and omnibus nature of such labels. For one thing, "Protestant" covers many different denominations and sects in America, and Weber was at pains to detail differences as well as similarities among these. In addition, within religious groups, individuals differ widely in the depth of their involvement, and if indeed it is religion that is a source of attitude and values, we might expect these variations in involvement to lead to variations in adherence to the "Protestant Ethic."

Lenski handles the first problem by arguing that "denominational groupings within Detroit Protestantism no longer constitute self-contained socio-religious groups" (1963:21). He notes that his 1958 data show large "amounts" of marriage and friendship across denomination lines, and that half the Protestant respondents were in favor of denominational mergers. Most significantly, he reports that dependent variables in his data show few differences by denomination that are not simply accounted for by class position or regional background (1963:396–398).

Our own larger sample allows a somewhat more adequate analysis of denominational effects, and shows them to be about as impressive as simple Protestant-Catholic differences. Using only the four denominations on which we have at least 75 respondents, and employing the Work Values question discussed earlier, we obtain the results shown in Table 7. Even with controls for three indicators of socioeconomic status, five of the six between-denomination comparisons are as large as the original Protestant-Catholic difference we reported in Table 1, and four of the six are as large as the Protestant-Catholic difference reported for this question in *The Religious Factor*. It is not clear that the ordering of denominations is what a careful reader of Weber would anticipate, since the more "Calvinistic" Presbyterians score closest to the Catholics, while the Lutherans are unexpectedly high in giving the classic Protestant Ethic response. However, it does appear that "Protestants" constitute a rather heterogeneous category, and that at the very least we must expect responses for that category to vary depending on the varying proportions of these denominations in different parts of the United States.[16]

---

16. We also attempted to learn to what extent a control for ethnicity affected the Protestant-Catholic difference reported in Table 1. We included our three religious groups (Protestants, Catholics, Jews) and also eight nationality groupings (based on a question about "What nationality background do you think of yourself as having—that is, besides being an American?") as predictors in a single multiple classification analysis. With nationality controlled, the original five point percentage difference be-

Table 7.   *Percent Choosing "The Work is Important and Gives a Feeling of Achievement,"[a] by Denomination (1966 Data).*

Religious Group	Without Controls		Contra. for Socioecon. Status[b]	
Baptists	35%	(103)	39%	(103)
(Catholics)[c]	44	(433)	—	(433)
(All Prot.)[c]	49	(498)	—	(498)
Presbyterians	52	(75)	47	(75)
Lutherans	53	(110)	53	(110)
Methodists	59	(87)	57	(87)

[a] The "work values" question was dichotomized into the fifth alternative quoted here vs. the other four combined.

[b] The four denominations shown here were included as one set of predictors in a multiple classification analysis. The other predictors used as controls were education, occupation, and income. Results are not changed appreciably if only education is included as a control.

[c] Protestant and Catholic figures from Table 1 are also shown here for comparison purposes. Note that "all Protestants" include respondents from other denominations in addition to the four separated out here.

Let us turn now to individual differences in personal involvement in religion. Lenski deals with the important issue of depth of commitment by constructing one index of "associational involvement" in the church as a formal organization, and another index of "communal involvement" in the informal but encompassing subcommunity of co-religionists. The former is operationalized by frequency of attendance at church services, the latter by the degree to which primary relationships are limited to members of the same religion. (See Lenski, 1963:23, for details of index construction.) He shows that the two indices are only slightly related to each other, hence can usefully be treated as separate measures.

Although Lenski makes a convincing case for the general importance of "communal involvement" as a vehicle for religious influence, it turns out that the index does *not* distinguish within religious groups in terms of economic attitudes and behaviors. He concludes that "the churches, rather than the sub-communities, are the primary source of the differences in economic behavior" between Protestants and Catholics (pp. 124–125).

As the above quotations suggest, associational involvement does appear

---

tween Protestants and Catholics on the Work Values question is halved. Thus ethnicity does seem to be a relevant variable, as Rosen (1962) and others have argued. Both ethnic and denominational effects are much slighter when the dependent variable shifts to the "attitudes toward work" question. Apparently the latter variable is simply not a useful one in this study, for as we saw earlier it fails to show any significant relation to religion.

to be an important specifying variable for the 1958 data. In most of the questions where comparisons were possible, frequency of church attendance among Protestants was positively associated with the Weberian "spirit of capitalism." There was no, or even a slight, negative relationship for the same variables among Catholics. The quantitative results for each question are not presented by Lenski in tabular form, but most of the questions which are reported to show the relationship involve social positions (e.g., self-employment) rather than values or attitudes. In particular, neither the question on what is valued about work, nor positive attitudes toward work as against leisure, showed any relation in 1958 to degree of associational involvement. This lack of a relation is not treated by Lenski as a negative finding concerning the influence of the religious factor on economic behavior, but rather as a sign that "the Protestant churches have allowed the doctrine of the calling to be neglected."

Our own findings, reported in Table 8, differ considerably from Lenski's, insofar as comparisons can be made.

1. Lenski reports that the "work values" question showed little relation to associational involvement; we find a consistent trend for the more actively involved among both Protestants and Catholics to say that the significance of the work is their main concern in choosing a job. This may simply reflect uncontrolled variation within crude class categories that are related to associational involvement.

2. For attitudes toward work, we find a relation that Lenski apparently expected: positive attitudes going with frequent church attendance among Protestants but not among Catholics. However, Lenski's own *findings* appear to have been in the opposite direction.

3. Lenski finds both occupational self-employment and disapproval of installment buying greater among more actively involved Protestants. We find weak trends in the opposite direction.

3. Lenski finds both occupational self-employment and disapproval of installment buying greater among more actively involved Protestants. We find weak trends in the opposite direction for both religious groups.

4. Lenski reports that both membership and interest in unions are least among active Protestant church-goers. We find opposite trends.

More generally we find little systematic or meaningful difference in the effect of associational involvement on Protestants and Catholics. We have not been able to attempt replication of certain questions used by Lenski in this analysis because they were not included in the 1966 survey, but the results we can check are not encouraging.

Lenski reports several other ways in which some of the dependent variables under discussion seem to be influenced by type of religious commitment. For example, he finds that a "devotional" orientation, as indicated by personal prayer and concern to determine God's will when making decisions, is positively associated with a commitment to work. But

TABLE 8. *Percent of "Protestant Ethic" Responses for High and Low Associational Categories within Religious and Social Class Categories (1966 Data)**

"Protestant Ethic" Response	Protestants				Catholics			
	Middle Class		Working Class		Middle Class		Working Class	
	Active	Marg.	Active	Marg.	Active	Marg.	Active	Marg.
	(79)	(154)	(58)	(201)	(144)	(37)	(155)	(85)
Intrinsic work valuation in job choice	67%	56%	43%	38%	54%	43%	42%	29%
Positive attitude toward work	43	36	32	25	37	38	31	29
Disapproves of installment buying	43	53	47	55	46	46	48	60
Presently self-employed	16	18	2	4	22	27	4	6
Member of union**	31	21	57	64	19	36	61	67
Very involved in union**	23	4	19	16	5	9	17	20

* The measure of Associational Involvement here is slightly different from Lenski's. Lenski classifies as Active "those who attend worship services every week," plus those who attend services two or three times a month and also some church-related group at least once a month," with all others classified as Marginal. The 1966 questionnaire included only a question on frequency of attendance at religious services, and we have distinguished only between those who attend at least once a week (Active) and those who attend less often (Marginal).
** For these two questions, middle class refers only to clerical and sales workers, and the relevant N's are reduced to 13 (Protestant-Active), 53 (Protestant-Marginal), 37 (Catholic-Active), and 11 (Catholic-Marginal).

530

in this instance, as elsewhere in these supplementary findings, the relation of religious variables to other variables is not associated with Protestant-Catholic differences, but holds equally for both religious groups. Therefore, we do not attempt here to replicate such results.

Reanalysis of Lenski's 1958 Data

We have reviewed Lenski's 1958 findings bearing directly on the application of the Protestant Ethic hypothesis to Protestant-Catholic differences in the United States, and have presented evidence from a 1966 replication of most of the more promising 1958 results. The 1966 survey provides a single important confirming replication regarding work values, and we will explore it further below. Against this lone successful replication, a variety of failures to replicate have been presented.

As indicated earlier, our 1966 sample omitted women, the foreign born, and men over 65, and it also had a somewhat lower response rate than did the 1958 study. It is conceivable that these differences in target populations account for some of the differences in results. Although we have not attempted a complete reanalysis of Lenski's 1958 data, we have done so using age, sex, and nativity controls on the initial Protestant-Catholic differences for three main items: "work values," "attitudes toward work," and "installment buying." It is worth noting that the reanalysis proved a great deal more difficult than anticipated, because of the problems encountered first of all merely in reproducing the original results reported in *The Religious Factor,* before proceeding to introduce sample controls. In only one of the attitudes reviewed here were we able to obtain Lenski's published results perfectly, although in the other two cases the discrepancies were minor and very likely due to differences in placement of one or two cases. The possible explanations for such minor discrepancies are manifold: errors in our, or Lenski's use of computing equipment; errors by Lenski in preparation of tables or at later stages in writing; errors by us in interpretation of Lenski's codes and recodes; actual damage to the data over the intervening decade. The whole effort left us with a healthy respect for the variability of percentages for reasons other than either sampling or measurement error, and with a sense of how easily borderline significance levels can be altered in this size sample by minor changes in coding conventions (for example, inclusion or not of missing data when calculating percents). We suspect that these problems in reanalysis are not unique to Lenski's data, and that only with the greatest care is it possible to transmit data and codes in reliable form from one investigator to another.

When controls for age, sex, and nativity were applied to bring Lenski's sample to essentially the same composition as the 1966 replication, the results did in fact tend to converge. For the "work values" item this means that in the 1958 tables rerun using only 21- to 64-year-old, native-born males, Protestant-Catholic differences were reduced to almost the exact sizes of the 1966 results given in Table 1. For example, "the work is important . . ." shows a 6% Protestant-Catholic difference in Table 9, as

TABLE 9.   *Percent of 21–64 Year Old Native-Born Men in Each Religious Group Giving "Protestant Ethic" Responses (Reanalysis of 1958 Data)*

Religious Group	% Saying "The work is important . . ."			N
Protestants	50%			(93)
Catholics	44			(88)
	Attitude toward Work			
	Positive	Neutral	Negative	
Protestants	26%	52%	22%	(89)
Catholics	26	57	17	(86)
	Disapprove Installment Buying			
Protestants	29%			(91)
Catholics	27			(88)

compared with our 5% difference in 1966. Thus our earlier report of a successful replication for this item holds and is even improved when the 1958 and 1966 samples are brought more closely into line.

The two other items in Table 9 show a similar movement toward the 1966 results when similar age, sex, and nativity controls are applied. This means, however, that Protestant-Catholic differences for these items tend to disappear among 1958 native-born men under 65. For the "attitude toward work" item, the original difference reported by Lenski appears to come entirely from men over 64 and men born outside the United States—relegating the result either to the record of a disappearing generation or an indicator of the religious correlates of old age. Because of the difficulties noted above in this reanalysis, along with the small n's within subsample categories and the generally small percentage differences by religion found for all these items, we are reluctant to place great emphasis on such specific findings.

FURTHER PURSUIT OF OUR ONE POSITIVE FINDING

Most of our conclusions about an intrinsically religious factor must, therefore, be negative. But not quite all, for a single question on work values repeated in 1966 did, as already reported, replicate Lenski's results;

moreover, stronger findings were produced in favor of his hypothesis than were apparent in his own 1958 data. Also, the question seems theoretically closer to the conceptual meaning of the "Protestant Ethic" than most of the other variables introduced by Lenski. It is possible, of course, that the finding is due to chance, given the large number of results that have been reviewed here. But it is important to avoid Type II as well as Type I errors and for that reason the "work values" result bears closer examination.

The 1966 difference between Protestants and Catholics in their basis for evaluating jobs has proven surprisingly tenacious. In particular, under a variety of controls Protestants, significantly more often than Catholics, rank as most important their attitude that "'the work is important and gives a feeling of accomplishment." Examination of this response using combinations of socioeconomic background factors has specified the religious difference, but in the process generally sharpens rather than eliminates it. Several such controls are shown in Table 10.

The difference on this question is rather clearly located in upper middle-class and, to a lesser extent, upper blue-collar occupations. These occupational differences in turn are not much changed when either respondent's education or father's education is held constant. An interesting interpretation of the results might note that the three occupational areas in question—professional, managerial, and craftsmen—are probably the most nonroutinized parts of the occupational structure. They are types of occupations that can be entered *both* for intrinsic reasons relating to the content of the work and for extrinsic reasons having to do with advancement in income and status. Religious sources of values could thus operate to fill these positions not with differential frequency, but rather for different reasons and perhaps with different consequences in terms of actual role performance.

In the light of previous sections of this report, we will wish to regard this line of thought as merely an intriguing hypothesis for further investigation, certainly not as a conclusion based on broad empirical evidence. The findings first of all require urgent replication, since they have been selected as the only "reliable differences" from among a large number of comparisons.[17] If replicable, they then suggest the value of concentrating the search for a current equivalent of the Protestant Ethic in particular directions. This means not only locating it more specifically in the social structure, but also both clarifying and, if possible, validating the secular value dimension involved. Rather than expanding the Protestant Ethic

---

17. The application of significance tests to complex survey analysis has been attacked and defended regularly at least since Hanon Selvin's (1957) "A Critique of Tests of Significance in Survey Research." However, none of the more controversial issues are involved in the present point, which concerns only the loss of clear meaning to conventional significance levels as an analyst scans many tables and selects for interpretation the few that are "significant."

TABLE 10. *Percent Emphasizing Importance of Work (5th Alternative) in Choosing a Job, by Religion, Occupation, and Education (1966 Data)**

Respondent's Occupation

Religion	Professional	Managerial	Clerical	Sales	Craftsman	Operative & Laborer
Protestant	69 (99)	59 (68)	53 (36)	40 (30)	48 (103)	33 (157)
Catholic	58 (67)	49 (71)	52 (25)	38 (24)	41 (134)	34 (109)
Difference	+11	+10	+1	+2	+7	−1

Respondent's Occupation (Selected) and Education

Religion	Professional 0–8	9–12	13+	Managerial 0–8	9–12	13+	Craftsman 0–8	9–12	13+
Protestant	(0)	54 (22)	72 (77)	(4)	58 (31)	64 (33)	60 (20)	46 (76)	(7)
Catholic	(2)	54 (11)	57 (54)	(1)	51 (35)	46 (35)	29 (24)	37 (84)	42 (26)
Difference		0	+15		+7	+18	+31	+9	

Respondent's Occupation (Selected) and Father's Education

Religion	Professional 0–8	9–12	13+	Managerial 0–8	9–12	13+	Craftsman 0–8	9–12	13+
Protestant	68 (41)	66 (32)	80 (20)	57 (30)	79 (19)	44 (16)	44 (70)	59 (17)	(9)
Catholic	53 (17)	55 (33)	69 (16)	49 (47)	42 (19)	(5)	40 (77)	42 (36)	47 (15)
Difference	+15	+11	+11	+8	+37		+4	+17	

* Each percent is shown with its base N in parentheses. Percents are not calculated for N < 15.

534

thesis in many and diverse ways, construct specification seems very much in order.

DISCUSSION

The 1966 Detroit Area Study replication of parts of the 1958 Detroit Area Study has called into question conclusions derived from the earlier survey that bear on "religion and economics." Four explanations are available.

(1) There may have been a genuine change in Protestant or Catholic attitudes and values during the intervening eight years. This explanation seems the least plausible one to me, because the variables involved do not appear subject to rapid change on the basis of transient events. Lenski's own conclusions point toward gradual widening of Protestant-Catholic differences.

(2) Variations between the two surveys may result from the more limited population defined by the 1966 study. Women, men over 64, and the foreign-born were deliberately excluded, and the response rate was also somewhat lower in 1966. There is little in Lenski's analysis to suggest that these factors *should* affect major conclusions, but our reanalysis of Lenski's 1958 data does seem to point to such special but not especially meaningful subpopulations as the source of some of his findings.

(3) Lenski's results may point toward religious differences of a much more specific and limited character than he expected and concluded. This is the import of the one successful replication in 1966, which concerns a single but strategic question on work values and locates the religious difference mainly among men in professional and managerial occupations. Those interested in the Protestant Ethic hypothesis would seem well advised to follow up this result, staying close to whatever the item represents. It must also be kept in mind that the difference discovered here is by no means a large one.

(4) There is the real possibility that all the differences reported by Lenski, as well as the one most successfully pursued in the 1966 data, are due to "chance." The reader who has followed the detailed comparison of the 1958 and 1966 results may have noted by now that the original findings presented by Lenski were by no means uniform and large in their implications for a "religious factor" in the economic realm. For a number of variables introduced by Lenski, there were no reliable differences *even* in 1958, and in other cases the differences barely met the rather lenient demand of a one-tailed significance level of .10. In still other cases, there were no 1958 differences between Protestants and Catholics as a whole, but differences appeared in certain subgroups when controls were applied.

Such subgroups were often quite small, and selective attention to them capitalized on sampling error. A more general problem that runs through *The Religious Factor* is a tendency to assume a basic Protestant-Catholic difference as fact, and therefore to interpret negative findings as adding specific nuances in meaning to the nature of this fact, rather than as calling it into general question. For example, when "communal involvement" turns out to be unrelated to economic values, Lenski's conclusion is that "the churches, rather than the subcommunities, are the primary source of the [religious] differences in economic behavior" (1963:124–125). But another, and at least reasonable conclusion, would have been that an important linking hypothesis had been tested and disconfirmed, raising the problem of whether the earlier findings meant what they seemed to mean about religious differences.

While the specific implications of this paper have to do with the Protestant Ethic thesis as developed by Lenski, there is surely a larger implication concerning the place of replication in empirical sociology. *The Religious Factor* was an original and stimulating work, and while the analysis carried out within it seems somewhat problematic in 1969, the primary issue lies not with the book but with the need to strengthen traditions that make replication an assumed part of sociological research. This is particularly true when the original finding is a nonobvious but intuitively interesting one. As with all science, the development of sociology can be greatly stimulated by unexpected results, but the more remarkable an empirical finding, the more it requires careful scrutiny and systematic replication.

REFERENCES

Bellah, Robert N.
    1968. "The sociology of religion." In International Encyclopedia of the Social Sciences. Volume 13, pp. 406–414. New York: The Macmillan Co. and The Free Press.
Detroit Area Study
    1959. "Sampling design for the 1957–58 Detroit area study." Mimeograph, Ann Arbor: Detroit Area Study.
Featherman, David
    1969. The Socioeconomic Achievement of White Married Males in the United States: 1957–67. Ph.D. Dissertation, University of Michigan.
Fisher, Ronald A.
    1951. The Design of Experiments. New York: Hafner.
Glenn, Norval and Ruth Hyland
    1967. "Religious preference and worldly success: Some evidence from national surveys." American Sociological Review 32 (February):73–85.
Glock, Charles Y. and Rodney Stark
    1965. Religion and Society in Tension. Chicago: Rand McNally.

Glockel, Glen L.
   1969. "Income and religious affiliation." American Journal of Sociology 74 (May):632–649.
Greely, Andrew M.
   1964. "The Protestant ethic: Time for a moratorium." Sociological Analysis 24 (Spring):20–33.
Lenski, Gerhard
   1963. The Religious Factor. Garden City, N.Y.: Anchor Books.
Lykken, David T.
   1968. "Statistical significance in psychological research." Psychological Bulletin 70 (September):151–159.
Rosen, Bernard C.
   1962. "Review of The Religious Factor." American Sociological Review 27 (February):111–113.
Schuman, Howard
   1967. "Sampling memorandum on the 1965–66 Detroit area study." Multilith. Ann Arbor: Detroit Area Study.
Selvin, Hanan
   1957. "A critique of tests of significance in survey research." American Sociological Review 22 (October):1957.
Warren, Bruce
   1970. The Relationship Between Religious Preference and Socioeconomic Achievement of American Men. Ph.D. dissertation, University of Michigan.
Weber, Max
   1930. The Protestant Ethic and the Spirit of Capitalism. New York: Charles Scribner's Sons.

Chapter	Politics:
16	*Power Elite or Veto Groups?*

The protagonists in this debate are C. Wright Mills (on the left) and David Riesman (more to the right). This is one of the oldest debates included in this book, dating back to the early and middle fifties, but it continues today in essentially the same form. In Mills's view America is run by a relatively small power elite, while to Riesman America is a pluralistic society with a number of veto groups no one of which predominates for any great length of time. Mills's power elite makes all of the major decisions, while in Riesman's view the veto group which exercises power varies with the issue. There are many other points of divergence between Mills and Riesman, and these are neatly summarized by Kornhauser in the concluding selection. Mills and Riesman have presented oversimplified conceptions of the American power structure, and Kornhauser has demonstrated that the situation is far more complex than either of their positions and badly in need of solid empirical research, not polemics. Yet, Kornhauser has no more empirical support for his position than either Mills or Riesman. It may be, despite the polemical nature of their work, that either Mills or Riesman will be vindicated by future research. What do *you* think? Is America dominated by a power elite? Or, is it composed of a number of veto groups? Or, has the American power structure defied description, at least until now?

The Power Elite*

C. WRIGHT MILLS

We study history, it has been said, to rid ourselves of it, and the history of the power elite is a clear case for which this maxim is correct. Like the tempo of American life in general, the long-term trends of the power structure† have been greatly speeded up since World War II, and certain newer trends within and between the dominant institutions have also set the shape of the power elite and given historically specific meaning to its fifth epoch:

I. In so far as the structural clue to the power elite today lies in the political order, that clue is the decline of politics as genuine and public debate of alternative decisions—with nationally responsible and policy-coherent parties and with autonomous organizations connecting the lower and middle levels of power with the top levels of decision. America is now in considerable part more a formal political democracy than a democratic social structure, and even the formal political mechanics are weak.

The long-time tendency of business and government to become more intricately and deeply involved with each other has, in the fifth epoch, reached a new point of explicitness. The two cannot now be seen clearly as two distinct worlds. It is in terms of the executive agencies of the state that the rapprochement has proceeded most decisively. The growth of the executive branch of the government, with its agencies that patrol the complex economy, does not mean merely the "enlargement of government" as some sort of autonomous bureaucracy: it has meant the ascendancy of the corporation's man as a political eminence.

During the New Deal the corporate chieftains joined the political directorate; as of World War II they have come to dominate it. Long interlocked with government, now they have moved into quite full direction of the economy of the war effort and of the postwar era. This shift of the corporation executives into the political directorate has accelerated the long-term relegation of the professional politicians in the Congress to the middle levels of power.

II. In so far as the structural clue to the power elite today lies in the enlarged and military state, that clue becomes evident in the military

---

* From *The Power Elite,* by C. Wright Mills, pp. 274–283. Copyright © 1956 by Oxford University Press, Inc. Reprinted by permission.
† See above, ONE: The Higher Circles.

ascendancy. The warlords have gained decisive political relevance, and the military structure of America is now in considerable part a political structure. The seemingly permanent military threat places a premium on the military and upon their control of men, materiel, money, and power; virtually all political and economic actions are now judged in terms of military definitions of reality: the higher warlords have ascended to a firm position within the power elite of the fifth epoch.

In part at least this has resulted from one simple historical fact, pivotal for the years since 1939: the focus of elite attention has been shifted from domestic problems, centered in the 'thirties around slump, to international problems, centered in the 'forties and 'fifties around war. Since the governing apparatus of the United States has by long historic usage been adapted to and shaped by domestic clash and balance, it has not, from any angle, had suitable agencies and traditions for the handling of international problems. Such formal democratic mechanics as had arisen in the century and a half of national development prior to 1941 had not been extended to the American handling of international affairs. It is, in considerable part, in this vacuum that the power elite has grown.

III. In so far as the structural clue to the power elite today lies in the economic order, that clue is the fact that the economy is at once a permanent war economy and a private-corporation economy. American capitalism is now in considerable part a military capitalism, and the most important relation of the big corporation to the state rests on the coincidence of interests between military and corporate needs, as defined by warlords and corporate rich. Within the elite as a whole, this coincidence of interest between the high military and the corporate chieftains strengthens both of them and further subordinates the role of the merely political men. Not politicians, but corporate executives, sit with the military and plan the organization of war effort.

The shape and meaning of the power elite today can be understood only when these three sets of structural trends are seen at their point of coincidence: the military capitalism of private corporations exists in a weakened and formal democratic system containing a military order already quite political in outlook and demeanor. Accordingly, at the top of this structure, the power elite has been shaped by the coincidence of interest between those who control the major means of production and those who control the newly enlarged means of violence; from the decline of the professional politician and the rise to explicit political command of the corporate chieftains and the professional warlords; from the absence of any genuine civil service of skill and integrity, independent of vested interests.

The power elite is composed of political, economic, and military men, but this instituted elite is frequently in some tension: it comes together only on certain coinciding points and only on certain occasions of "crisis." In the long peace of the nineteenth century, the military were not in the high councils of state, not of the political directorate, and neither were the economic men—they made raids upon the state but they did not join its directorate. During the 'thirties, the political man was ascendant. Now the military and the corporate men are in top positions.

Of the three types of circle that compose the power elite today, it is the military that has benefited the most in its enhanced power, although the corporate circles have also become more explicitly intrenched in the more public decision-making circles. It is the professional politician that has lost the most, so much that in examining the events and decisions, one is tempted to speak of a political vacuum in which the corporate rich and the high warlord, in their coinciding interests, rule.

It should not be said that the three "take turns" in carrying the initiative, for the mechanics of the power elite are not often as deliberate as that would imply. At times, of course, it is—as when political men, thinking they can borrow the prestige of generals, find that they must pay for it, or, as when during big slumps, economic men feel the need of a politician at once safe and possessing vote appeal. Today all three are involved in virtually all widely ramifying decisions. Which of the three types seems to lead depends upon "the tasks of the period" as they, the elite, define them. Just now, these tasks center upon "defense" and international affairs. Accordingly, as we have seen, the military are ascendant in two senses: as personnel and as justifying ideology. That is why, just now, we can most easily specify the unity and the shape of the power elite in terms of the military ascendancy.

But we must always be historically specific and open to complexities. The simple Marxian view makes the big economic man the *real* holder of power; the simple liberal view makes the big political man the chief of the power system; and there are some who would view the warlords as virtual dictators. Each of these is an oversimplified view. It is to avoid them that we use the term "power elite" rather than, for example, "ruling class."*

In so far as the power elite has come to wide public attention, it has

---

* "Ruling class" is a badly loaded phrase. "Class" is an economic term; "rule" a political one. The phrase, "ruling class," thus contains the theory that an economic class rules politically. That short-cut theory may or may not at times be true, but we do not want to carry that one rather simple theory about in the terms that we use to define our problems; we wish to state the theories explicitly, using terms of more precise and unilateral meaning. Specifically, the phrase "ruling class," in its common political connotations, does not allow enough autonomy to the political order and its agents, and it says nothing about the military as such. It should be clear to the reader by now that we do not accept as adequate the simple view that high economic men unilaterally make all decisions of national consequence. We hold that such a simple view of "economic determinism" must be elaborated by "political determinism" and "military determinism"; that the higher agents of each of these three domains now often have a noticeable degree of autonomy; and that only in the often intricate ways of coalition do they make up and carry through the most important decisions. Those are the major reasons we prefer "power elite" to "ruling class" as a characterizing phrase for the higher circles when we consider them in terms of power.

done so in terms of the "military clique." The power elite does, in fact, take its current shape from the decisive entrance into it of the military. Their presence and their ideology are its major legitimations, whenever the power elite feels the need to provide any. But what is called the "Washington military clique" is not composed merely of military men, and it does not prevail merely in Washington. Its members exist all over the country, and it is a coalition of generals in the roles of corporation executives, of politicians masquerading as admirals, of corporation executives acting like politicians, of civil servants who become majors, of vice-admirals who are also the assistants to a cabinet officer, who is himself, by the way, really a member of the managerial elite.

Neither the idea of a "ruling class" nor of a simple monolithic rise of "bureaucratic politicians" nor of a "military clique" is adequate. The power elite today involves the often uneasy coincidence of economic, military, and political power.

3

Even if our understanding were limited to these structural trends, we should have grounds for believing the power elite a useful, indeed indispensable, concept for the interpretation of what is going on at the topside of modern American society. But we are not, of course, so limited: our conception of the power elite does not need to rest only upon the correspondence of the institutional hierarchies involved, or upon the many points at which their shifting interests coincide. The power elite, as we conceive it, also rests upon the similarity of its personnel, and their personal and official relations with one another, upon their social and psychological affinities. In order to grasp the personal and social basis of the power elite's unity, we have first to remind ourselves of the facts of origin, career, and style of life of each of the types of circle whose members compose the power elite.

The power elite is *not* an aristocracy, which is to say that it is not a political ruling group based upon a nobility of hereditary origin. It has no compact basis in a small circle of great families whose members can and do consistently occupy the top positions in the several higher circles which overlap as the power elite. But such nobility is only one possible basis of common origin. That it does not exist for the American elite does not mean that members of this elite derive socially from the full range of strata composing American society. They derive in substantial proportions from the upper classes, both new and old, of local society and the metropolitan 400. The bulk of the very rich, the corporate executives, the political outsiders, the high military, derive from, at most, the upper third of the income and occupational pyramids. Their fathers were at least of the professional and business strata, and very frequently higher than that. They are native-born Americans of native parents, primarily from urban areas, and, with the exceptions of the politicians among them, overwhelmingly from the East. They are mainly Protestants, especially Episcopalian or Presbyterian. In general, the higher the position, the greater the proportion of men within it who have derived from and who maintain connections with the upper classes. The generally similar origins of the members of the power elite are underlined and carried further by the fact of their increasingly common educational routine. Overwhelmingly college graduates, substantial proportions have attended Ivy League colleges, although the education of the higher military, of course, differs from that of other members of the power elite.

But what do these apparently simple facts about the social composition of the higher circles really mean? In particular, what do they mean for any attempt to understand the degree of unity, and the direction of policy and interest that may prevail among these several circles? Perhaps it is best to put this question in a deceptively simple way: in terms of origin and career, who or what do these men at the top represent?

Of course, if they are elected politicians, they are supposed to represent those who elected them; and, if they are appointed, they are supposed to represent, indirectly, those who elected their appointers. But this is recognized as something of an abstraction, as a rhetorical formula by which all men of power in almost all systems of government nowadays justify their power of decision. At times it may be true, both in the sense of their motives and in the sense of who benefits from their decisions. Yet it would not be wise in any power system merely to assume it.

The fact that members of the power elite come from near the top of the nation's class and status levels does not mean that they are necessarily "representative" of the top levels only. And if they were, as social types, representative of a cross-section of the population, that would not mean that a balanced democracy of interest and power would automatically be the going political fact.

We cannot infer the direction of policy merely from the social origins and careers of the policy-makers. The social and economic backgrounds of the men of power do not tell us all that we need to know in order to understand the distribution of social power. For: (1) Men from high places may be ideological representatives of the poor and humble. (2) Men of humble origin, brightly self-made, may energetically serve the most vested and inherited interests. Moreover (3), not all men who effectively represent the interests of a stratum need in any way belong to it or personally benefit by policies that further its interests. Among the politicians, in short, there are sympathetic *agents* of given groups, conscious and unconscious, paid and unpaid. Finally (4), among the top decision-makers we find men who have been chosen for their positions because of their "expert knowledge." These are some of the obvious reasons why the social origins and careers of the power elite do not enable us to infer the class interests and policy directions of a modern system of power.

Do the high social origin and careers of the top men mean nothing, then, about the distribution of power? By no means. They simply remind us that we must be careful of any simple and direct inference from origin and career to political character and policy, not that we must ignore them in our attempt at political understanding. They simply mean that we must analyze the political psychology and the actual decisions of the political directorate as well as its social composition. And they mean, above all, that we should control, as we have done here, any inference we make from the origin and careers of the political actors by close understanding of the institutional landscape in which they act out their drama. Otherwise we should be guilty of a rather simple-minded biographical theory of society and history.

Just as we cannot rest the notion of the power elite solely upon the institutional mechanics that lead to its formation, so we cannot rest the notion solely upon the facts of the origin and career of its personnel. We need both, and we have both—as well as other bases, among them that of the status intermingling.

But it is not only the similarities of social origin, religious affiliation, nativity, and education that are important to the psychological and social affinities of the members of the power elite. Even if their recruitment and formal training were more heterogeneous than they are, these men would still be of quite homogeneous social type. For the most important set of facts about a circle of men is the criteria of admission, of praise, of honor, of promotion that prevails among them; if these are similar within a circle, then they will tend as personalities to become similar. The circles that compose the power elite do tend to have such codes and criteria in common. The co-optation of the social types to which these common values lead is often more important than any statistics of common origin and career that we might have at hand.

There is a kind of reciprocal attraction among the fraternity of the successful—not between each and every member of the circles of the high and mighty, but between enough of them to insure a certain unity. On the slight side, it is a sort of tacit, mutual admiration; in the strongest tie-ins, it proceeds by intermarriage. And there are all grades and types of connection between these extremes. Some overlaps certainly occur by means of cliques and clubs, churches and schools.

If social origin and formal education in common tend to make the members of the power elite more readily understood and trusted by one another, their continued association further cements what they feel they have in common. Members of the several higher circles know one another as personal friends and even as neighbors; they mingle with one another on the golf course, in the gentleman's clubs, at resorts, on transcontinental airplanes, and on ocean liners. They meet at the estates of mutual friends, face each other in front of the TV camera, or serve on the same philanthropic committee; and many are sure to cross one another's path in the columns of newspapers, if not in the exact cafés from which many of these columns originate. As we have seen, of "The New 400" of café society, one chronicler has named forty-one members of the very rich, ninety-three political leaders, and seventy-nine chief executives of corporations.*

"I did not know, I could not have dreamed," Whittaker Chambers has written, "of the immense scope and power of Hiss' political alliances and his social connections, which cut across all party lines and ran from the Supreme Court to the Religious Society of Friends, from governors of states and instructors in college faculties to the staff members of liberal magazines. In the decade since I had last seen him, he had used his career, and, in particular, his identification with the cause of peace through his part in organizing the United Nations, to put down roots that made him one with the matted forest floor of American upper class, enlightened middle class, liberal and official life. His roots could not be disturbed without disturbing all the roots on all sides of him."

The sphere of status has reflected the epochs of the power elite. In the third epoch, for example, who could compete with big money? And in the fourth, with big politicians, or even the bright young men of the New Deal? And in the fifth, who can compete with the generals and the admirals and the corporate officials now so sympathetically portrayed on the stage, in the novel, and on the screen? Can one imagine *Executive Suite* as a successful motion picture in 1935? Or *The Caine Mutiny*?

The multiplicity of high-prestige organizations to which the elite usually belong is revealed by even casual examination of the obituaries of the big businessman, the high-prestige lawyer, the top general and admiral, the key senator: usually, high-prestige church, business associations, plus high-prestige clubs, and often plus military rank. In the course of their lifetimes, the university president, the New York Stock Exchange chairman, the head of the bank, the old West Pointer—mingle in the status sphere, within which they easily renew old friendships and draw upon them in an effort to understand through the experience of trusted others those contexts of power and decision in which they have not personally moved.

In these diverse contexts, prestige accumulates in each of the higher circles, and the members of each borrow status from one another. Their self-images are fed by these accumulations and these borrowings, and accordingly, however segmental a given man's role may seem, he comes to feel himself a "diffuse" or "generalized" man of the higher circles, a "broad-

---

* See above, FOUR: The Celebrities.

gauge" man. Perhaps such inside experience is one feature of what is meant by "judgment."

The key organizations, perhaps, are the major corporations themselves, for on the boards of directors we find a heavy overlapping among the members of these several elites. On the lighter side, again in the summer and winter resorts, we find that, in an intricate series of overlapping circles; in the course of time, each meets each or knows somebody who knows somebody who knows that one.

The higher members of the military, economic, and political orders are able readily to take over one another's point of view, always in a sympathetic way, and often in a knowledgeable way as well. They define one another as among those who count, and who, accordingly, must be taken into account. Each of them as a member of the power elite comes to incorporate into his own integrity, his own honor, his own conscience, the viewpoint, the expectations, the values of the others. If there are no common ideals and standards among them that are based upon an explicitly aristocratic culture, that does not mean that they do not feel responsibility to one another.

All the structural coincidence of their interests as well as the intricate, psychological facts of their origins and their education, their careers and their associations make possible the psychological affinities that prevail among them, affinities that make it possible for them to say of one another: He is, of course, one of us. And all this points to the basic, psychological meaning of class consciousness. Nowhere in America is there as great a "class consciousness" as among the elite; nowhere is it organized as effectively as among the power elite. For by class consciousness, as a psychological fact, one means that the individual member of a "class" accepts only those accepted by his circle as among those who are significant to his own image of self.

Within the higher circles of the power elite, factions do exist; there are conflicts of policy; individual ambitions do clash. There are still enough divisions of importance within the Republican party, and even between Republicans and Democrats, to make for different methods of operation. But more powerful than these divisions are the internal discipline and the community of interests that bind the power elite together, even across the boundaries of nations at war.

"Veto Groups"*

DAVID RIESMAN

The Veto Groups. The shifting nature of the lobby provides us with an important clue as to the difference between the present American political scene and that of the age of McKinley. The ruling class of businessmen could relatively easily (though perhaps mistakenly) decide where their interests lay and what editors, lawyers, and legislators might be paid to advance them. The lobby ministered to the clear leadership, privilege, and imperative of the business ruling class.

Today we have substituted for that leadership a series of groups, each of which has struggled for and finally attained a power to stop things conceivably inimical to its interests and, within far narrower limits, to start things. The various business groups, large and small, the movie-censoring groups, the farm groups and the labor and professional groups, the major ethnic groups and major regional groups, have in many instances succeeded in maneuvering themselves into a position in which they are able to neutralize those who might attack them. The very increase in the number of these groups, and in the kinds of interests "practical" and "fictional" they are protecting, marks, therefore, a decisive change from the lobbies of an earlier day. There is a change in method, too, in the way the groups are organized, the way they handle each other, and the way they handle the public, that is, the unorganized.

These veto groups are neither leader-groups nor led-groups. The only leaders of national scope left in the United States today are those who can placate the veto groups. The only followers left in the United States today are those unorganized and sometimes disorganized unfortunates who have not yet invented their group.

Within the veto groups, there is, of course, the same struggle for top places that goes on in other bureaucratic setups. Among the veto groups competition is monopolistic; rules of fairness and fellowship dictate how far one can go. Despite the rules there are, of course, occasional "price wars," like the jurisdictional disputes of labor unions or Jewish defense groups; these are ended by negotiation, the division of territory, and the formation of a roof organization for the previously split constituency. These big monopolies, taken as a single group, are in devastating competition with the not yet grouped, much as the fair-trade economy competes against the free-trade economy. These latter scattered followers find what protection they can in the interstices around the group-minded.[1]

Each of the veto groups in this pattern is capable of an aggressive move, but the move is sharply limited in its range by the way in which the various groups have already cut up the sphere of politics and arrayed certain massive expectations behind each cut. Both within the groups and in the situation created by their presence, the political mood tends to become one of other-directed tolerance. The vetoes so bind action that it is hard for the moralizers to conceive of a program that might in any large way alter the relations between political and personal life or between political and economic life. In the amorphous power structure created by the veto groups it is hard to distinguish rulers from the ruled, those to be aided from those to be opposed, those on your side from those on the other side. This very pattern encourages the inside-dopester who can unravel the personal linkages, and discourages the enthusiast or indignant who wants to install the good or fend off the bad. Probably, most of all it encourages the new-style indifferent who feels and is often told that his and everyone else's affairs are in the hands of the experts and that laymen, though they should "participate," should not really be too inquisitive or aroused.

By their very nature the veto groups exist as defense groups, not as leadership groups. If it is true that they do "have the power," they have it by virtue of a necessary mutual tolerance. More and more they mirror each other in their style of political action, including their interest in public relations and their emphasis on internal harmony of feelings. There is a tendency for organizations as differently oriented as, say, the Young Socialists and the 4-H Club, to adopt similar psychological methods of salesmanship to obtain and solidify their recruits.

This does not mean, however, that the veto groups are formed along the lines of character structure. As in a business corporation there is room for extreme inner-directed and other-directed types, and all mixtures between, so in a veto group there can exist complex symbiotic relationships among people of different political styles. Thus a team of lobbyists may include both moralizers and inside-dopesters, sometimes working in harness, sometimes in conflict; and the constituency of the team may be composed mainly of new-style political indifferents who have enough

---

1. It should be clear that monopolistic competition, both in business and politics, *is* competition. People are very much aware of their rivals, within and without the organization. They know who they are, but by the very nature of monopolistic competition they are seldom able to eliminate them entirely. While we have been talking of fair trade and tolerance, this should not obscure the fact that for the participants the feeling of being in a rivalrous setup is very strong. Indeed, they face the problem of so many other-directed people: how to combine the appearance of friendly, personalized, "sincere" behavior with the ruthless, sometimes almost paranoid, envies of their occupational life.

literacy and organizational experience to throw weight around when called upon. Despite these complications I think it fair to say that the veto groups, even when they are set up to protect a clear-cut moralizing interest, are generally forced to adopt the political manners of the other-directed.

In saying this I am talking about the national scene. The smaller the constituency, of course, the smaller the number of veto groups involved and the greater the chance that some one of them will be dominant. Thus, in local politics there is more indignation and less tolerance, just as even the *Chicago Tribune* is a tolerant paper in comparison with the community throwaways in many Chicago neighborhoods.

The same problem may be considered from another perspective. Various groups have discovered that they can go quite far in the amorphous power situation in America without being stopped. Our society is behaviorally open enough to permit a considerable community of gangsters a comfortable living under a variety of partisan political regimes. In their lack of concern for public relations these men are belated businessmen. So are some labor leaders who have discovered their power to hold up the economy, though in most situations what is surprising is the moderation of labor demands—a moderation based more on psychological restraints than on any power that could effectively be interposed. Likewise, it is sometimes possible for an aggresssive group, while not belonging to the entrenched veto-power teams, to push a bill through a legislature. Thus, the original Social Security Act went through Congress, so far as I can discover, because it was pushed by a devoted but tiny cohort; the large veto groups including organized labor were neither very much for it nor very much against it.

For similar reasons those veto groups are in many political situations strongest whose own memberships are composed of veto groups, especially veto groups of one. The best example of this is the individual farmer who, after one of the farm lobbies has made a deal for him, can still hold out for more. The farm lobby's concern for the reaction of other veto groups, such as labor unions, cuts little ice with the individual farmer. This fact may strengthen the lobby in a negotiation: it can use its internal public relations problems as a counter in bargaining, very much as does a diplomat who tells a foreign minister that he must consider how Senator so-and-so will react. For, no matter what the other-directedness of the lobby's leaders, they cannot bind their membership to carry out a public relations approach. Many labor unions have a similar power because they cannot control their memberships who, if not satisfied with a deal made by the union, can walk off or otherwise sabotage a job.

In contrast, those veto groups are often weaker whose other-directed orientation can dominate their memberships. Large corporations are vulnerable to a call from the White House because, save for a residual indignant like Sewell Avery, their officials are themselves other-directed and

because, once the word from the chief goes out, the factory superintendents, no matter how boiling mad, have to fall into line with the new
policy by the very nature of the centralized organization for which they
work: they can sabotage top management on minor matters but not, say, on
wage rates or tax accounting. As against this, the American Catholic
Church possesses immense veto-group power because it combines a certain
amount of centralized command—and a public picture of a still greater
amount—with a highly decentralized priesthood (each priest is in a sense
his own trade association secretary) and a membership organization of wide-
ranging ethnic, social, and political loyalties; this structure permits great
flexibility in bargaining.

These qualifications, however, do not change the fact that the veto
groups, taken together, constitute a new buffer region between the old,
altered, and thinning extremes of those who were once leaders and led. It is
both the attenuation of leaders and led, and the other-oriented doings of
these buffers, that help to give many moralizers a scene of vacuum in
American political life.

The veto groups, by the conditions their presence creates and by the
requirements they set for leadership in politics, foster the tolerant mood of
other-direction and hasten the retreat of the inner-directed indignants.

Is There a Ruling Class Left?

Nevertheless, people go on acting as if there still were a decisive
ruling class in contemporary America. In the postwar years, businessmen
thought labor leaders and politicians ran the country, while labor and the
left thought that "Wall Street" ran it, or the "sixty families." Wall Street,
confused perhaps by its dethronement as a telling barometer of capital-
formation weather, may have thought that the midwestern industrial
barons, cushioned on plant expansion money in the form of heavy depreci-
ation reserves and undivided profits, ran the country. They might have had
some evidence for this in the fact that the New Deal was much tougher
with finance capital—e.g., the SEC and the Holding Company Act—than
with industrial capital and that when, in the undistributed profits tax, it
tried to subject the latter to a stockholder and money-market control, the
tax was quickly repealed.

But these barons of Pittsburgh, Weirton, Akron, and Detroit, though
certainly a tougher crowd than the Wall Streeters, are, as we saw earlier,
coming more and more to think of themselves as trustees for their benefi-
ciaries. And whereas, from the point of view of labor and the left, these
men ran the War Production Board in the interest of their respective
companies, one could argue just as easily that the WPB experience was one
of the congeries of factors that have tamed the barons. It put them in a

situation where they had to view their company from the point of view of "the others."

Despite the absence of intensive studies of business power and of what happens in a business negotiation, one can readily get an impressionistic sense of the change in business behavior in the last generation. In the pages of *Fortune,* that excellent chronicler of business, one can see that there are few survivals of the kinds of dealings—with other businessmen, with labor, with the government—that were standard operating practice for the pre–World War I tycoons. Moreover, in its twenty-year history, *Fortune* itself has shown, and perhaps it may be considered not too unrepresentative of its audience, a steady decline of interest in business as such and a growing interest in once peripheral matters, such as international relations, social science, and other accoutrements of the modern executive.

But it is of course more difficult to know whether character has changed as well as behavior—whether, as some contend, businessmen simply rule today in a more subtle, more "managerial" way. In "Manager Meets Union" Joseph M. Goldsen and Lillian Low have depicted the psychological dependence of a contemporary sales manager on the approval of the men under him, his willingness to go to great lengths, in terms of concessions, to maintain interpersonal warmth in his relations with them, and his fierce resentment of the union as a barrier to this emotional exchange.[2] As against this, one must set the attitude of some of the auto-supply companies whose leadership still seems much more craft-oriented than people-oriented and therefore unwilling to make concessions and none too concerned with the emotional atmosphere of negotiations. Likewise, the General Motors–UAW negotiations of 1946, as reported in print, sound more like a cockfight than a Platonic symposium, although in Peter Drucker's *Concept of the Corporation,* a study of General Motors published in the same year, there is much evidence of management eagerness to build a big, happy family.

Power, indeed, is founded, in a large measure, on interpersonal expectations and attitudes. If businessmen feel weak and dependent, they do in actuality become weaker and more dependent, no matter what material resources may be ascribed to them. My impression, based mainly on experiences of my own in business and law practice, is that businessmen from large manufacturing companies, though they often talk big, are easily frightened by the threat of others' hostility; they may pound the table, but they look to others for leadership and do not care to get out of line with their peer-groupers. Possibly, attitudes toward such an irascible business-man as Sewell Avery might mark a good dividing line between the older and the newer attitudes. Those businessmen who admire Avery, though

---

2. "Manager Meets Union: a Case Study of Personal Immaturity," *Human Factors in Management,* ed. S. D. Hoslett (Parkville, Missouri, Park College Press, 1946), p. 77.

they might not dare to imitate him, are becoming increasingly an elderly minority, while the younger men generally are shocked by Avery's "high-handedness," his rebuff of the glad hand.

The desire of businessmen to be well thought of has led to the irony that each time a professor writes a book attacking business, even if almost nobody reads it, he creates jobs in industry for his students in public relations, trade association work, and market research! While the Black Horse Cavalry of an earlier era held up businessmen by threatening to let pass crippling legislation desired by anti-business moralizers, today many honest intellectuals who would not think of taking a bribe hold business or trade association jobs because their clients have been scared, perhaps by these very men, into taking cognizance of some actual or imaginary veto group. Since a large structure is built up to woo the group, no test of power is made to see whether the group has real existence or real strength. Understandably, ideologies about who has power in America are relied upon to support these amiable fictions which serve, as we shall see in Chapter XIII, to provide the modern businessman with an endless shopping list, an endless task of glad-handing. This is a far cry, I suggest, from the opportunistic glad-handing of the wealthy on which Tocqueville comments at the chapter head; very likely, what was mere practice in his day has become embedded in character in ours.

Businessmen, moreover, are not the only people who fail to exploit the power position they are supposed, in the eyes of many observers, to have. Army officers are also astonishingly timid about exercising their leadership. During the war one would have thought that the army would be relatively impervious to criticism. But frequently the generals went to great lengths to refrain from doing something about which a congressman might make an unfriendly speech. They did so even at times when they might have brushed the congressman off like an angry fly. When dealing with businessmen or labor leaders, army officers were, it seemed to me, astonishingly deferential; and this was as true of the West Pointers as of the reservists. Of course, there were exceptions, but in many of the situations where the armed services made concessions to propitiate some veto group, they rationalized the concessions in terms of morale or of postwar public relations or, frequently, simply were not aware of their power.

To be sure, some came to the same result by the route of a democratic tradition of civilian dominance. Very likely, it was a good thing for the country that the services were so self-restrained. I do not here deal with the matter on the merits but use it as an illustration of changing character and changing social structure.

All this may lead to the question: well, who really runs things? What people fail to see is that, while it may take leadership to start things running, or to stop them, very little leadership is needed once things are under way—that, indeed, things can get terribly snarled up and still go on running. If one studies a factory, an army group, or other large organization, one wonders how things get done at all, with the lack of leadership and with all the feather-bedding. Perhaps they get done because we are still trading on our reserves of inner-direction, especially in the lower ranks. At any rate, the fact they do get done is no proof that there is someone in charge.

There are, of course, still some veto groups that have more power than others and some individuals who have more power than others. But the determination of who these are has to be made all over again for our time: we cannot be satisfied with the answers given by Marx, Mosca, Michels, Pareto, Weber, Veblen, or Burnham, though we can learn from all of them.

There are also phenomena in this vast country that evade all of them (and surely, too, evade my collaborators and me). One example is the immense power, both political and economic, possessed by Artie Samish, allegedly the veto-group boss of California. Samish is a new-type lobbyist, who represents not one but scores of interests, often competing ones, from truckers to chiropractors, and who plays one veto group off against others to shake them down and strengthen his own power: he has learned how the other-orientation of the established veto groups will lead them to call still other groups into being through his auspices. Since the old-line parties have little power in California, there is no way of reaching a clear-cut decision for or against a particular veto group through the party system; instead, the state officials have become dependent on Samish for electoral support, or at least nonopposition, through his herded groups of voters and their cash contributions; moreover, he knows how to go directly to the people through the "democratic" plebiscite machinery.[3]

Carey McWilliams has observed that Samish's power rests both on the peculiar election machinery of the state and on the fact that no one industry or allied group of industries, no one union, one ethnic group or region, is dominant. The situation is very different in a state like Montana, where copper is pivotal, and one must be either for the union or for Anaconda. It is different again in Virginia where, as V. O. Key shows in *Southern Politics*, the setup of the state constitution favors control by the old courthouse crowd. In view of these divergences, rooted in local legal niceties as

---

3. Ironically enough, but typically enough, Samish craves the one power he does not have: social power in the society-page sense. A poor boy in origin, he can make or break businessmen and politicians but cannot get into the more exclusive clubs. And while consciously he is said to despise these social leaders whom he can so easily frighten and manipulate, he cannot purge himself of the childhood hurts and childhood images of power that make him vulnerable to their exclusion of him. In this, of course, he resembles other and better-known dictators.

I have drawn on Carey McWilliams, "Guy Who Gets Things Done," *Nation*, CLXIX (1949), 31–33; and Lester Velie, "Secret Boss of California," *Collier's*, CXXIV (August 13, 20, 1949), 11–13, 12–13.

well as in major social and economic factors, it is apparent that any discussion of class and power on the national scene can at best be only an approximation. Yet I would venture to say that the United States is on the whole more like California in its variety—but without its veto boss—than like Montana and Virginia in their particularity. The vaster number of veto groups, and their greater power, mean that no one man or small group of men can amass the power nationally that Artie Samish and, in earlier days, Huey Long, have held locally.

Rather, power on the national scene must be viewed in terms of issues. It is possible that, where an issue involves only two or three veto groups, themselves tiny minorities, the official or unofficial broker among the groups can be quite powerful—but only on that issue. However, where the issue involves the country as a whole, no individual or group leadership is likely to be very effective, because the entrenched veto groups cannot be budged: unlike a party that may be defeated at the polls, or a class that may be replaced by another class, the veto groups are always "in."

One might ask whether one would not find, over a long period of time, that decisions in America favored one group or class—thereby, by definition, the ruling group or class—over others. Does not wealth exert its pull in the long run? In the past this has been so; for the future I doubt it. The future seems to be in the hands of the small business and professional men who control Congress, such as realtors, lawyers, car salesmen, undertakers and so on; of the military men who control defense and, in part, foreign policy; of the big business managers and their lawyers, finance-committee men, and other counselors who decide on plant investment and influence the rate of technological change; of the labor leaders who control worker productivity and worker votes; of the black belt whites who have the greatest stake in southern politics; of the Poles, Italians, Jews, and Irishmen who have stakes in foreign policy, city jobs, and ethnic religious and cultural organizations; of the editorializers and storytellers who help socialize the young, tease and train the adult, and amuse and annoy the aged; of the farmers—themselves a warring congeries of cattlemen, corn men, dairymen, cotton men, and so on—who control key departments and committees and who, as the living representatives of our inner-directed past, control many of our memories; of the Russians and, to a lesser degree, other foreign powers who control much of our agenda of attention; and so on. The reader can complete the list. Power in America seems to me situational and mercurial; it resists attempts to locate it the way a molecule, under the Heisenberg principle, resists attempts simultaneously to locate it and time its velocity.

But people are afraid of this indeterminacy and amorphousness in the cosmology of power. Even those intellectuals, for instance, who feel themselves very much out of power and who are frightened of those who they think have the power, prefer to be scared by the power structures they conjure up than to face the possibility that the power structure they believe exists has largely evaporated. Most people prefer to suffer with interpretations that give their world meaning than to relax in the cave without an Ariadne's thread.

"Power Elite" or "Veto Groups"?*

WILLIAM KORNHAUSER

I

In the 50's two books appeared purporting to describe the structure of power in present-day America. They reached opposite conclusions: where C. Wright Mills found a "power elite," David Riesman found "veto groups." Both books have enjoyed a wide response, which has tended to divide along ideological lines. It would appear that *The Power Elite* has been most favorably received by radical intellectuals, and *The Lonely Crowd* has found its main response among liberals. Mills and Riesman have not been oblivious to their differences. Mills is quite explicit on the matter: Riesman is a "romantic pluralist" who refuses to see the forest of American power inequalities for the trees of short-run and discrete balances of power among diverse groups. [244]¹ Riesman has been less explicitly polemical, but he might have had Mills in mind when he spoke of those intellectuals "who feel themselves very much out of power and who are frightened of those who they think have the power," and who "prefer to be scared by the power structures they conjure up than to face the possibility that the power structure they believe exists has largely evaporated." [257–258)²

I wish to intervene in this controversy just long enough to do two things: (1) locate as precisely as possible the items upon which Riesman and Mills disagree; and (2) formulate certain underlying issues in the analysis of power that have to be met before such specific disagreements as those between Riesman and Mills can profitably be resolved.

We may compare Mills and Riesman on power in America along five dimensions:

---

* From *Culture and Social Character,* edited by S. M. Lipset and L. Lowenthal, pp. 252–267. Reprinted with permission of the Macmillan Company. © by The Free Press of Glencoe, Inc., 1961.
1. Page references in the text for remarks by C. Wright Mills refer to *The Power Elite* (New York: Oxford University Press, 1956).
2. Page references in the text for remarks by David Riesman refer to *The Lonely Crowd* (New York: Doubleday Anchor, 1953).

1. structure of power: how power is distributed among the major segments of present-day American society;
2. changes in the structure of power: how the distribution of power has changed the course of American history;
3. operation of the structure of power: the means whereby power is exercised in American society;
4. bases of the structure of power: how social and psychological factors shape and sustain the existing distribution of power;
5. consequences of the structure of power: how the existing distribution of power affects American society.

1. STRUCTURE OF POWER

It is symptomatic of their underlying differences that Mills entitles his major consideration of power simply "the power elite," whereas Riesman has entitled one of his discussions "who has the power?" Mills is quite certain about the location of power, and so indicates by the assertive form of his title. Riesman perceives a much more amorphous and indeterminate power situation, and conveys this view in the interrogative form of his title. These contrasting images of American power may be diagrammed as two different pyramids of power. Mills' pyramid of power contains three levels:

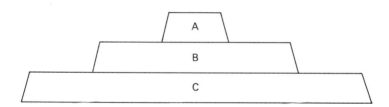

The apex of the pyramid (A) is the "power elite": a unified power group composed of the top government executives, military officials, and corporation directors. The second level (B) comprises the "middle levels of power": a diversified and balanced plurality of interest groups, perhaps most visibly at work in the halls of Congress. The third level (C) is the "mass society": the powerless mass of unorganized and atomized people who are controlled from above.

Riesman's pyramid of power contains only two major levels:

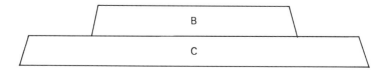

The two levels roughly correspond to Mills' second and third levels, and have been labeled accordingly. The obvious difference between the two pyramids is the presence of a peak in the one case and its absence in the other. Riesman sees no "power elite," in the sense of a single unified power group at the top of the structure, and this in the simplest terms contrasts his image of power in America with that of Mills. The upper level of Riesman's pyramid (B) consists of "veto groups": a diversified and balanced plurality of interest groups, each of which is primarily concerned with protecting its jurisdiction by blocking efforts of other groups that seem to threaten that jurisdiction. There is no decisive ruling group here, but rather an amorphous structure of power centering in the interplay among these interest groups. The lower level of the pyramid (C) comprises the more or less unorganized public, which is sought as an ally (rather than dominated) by the interest groups in their maneuvers against actual or threatened encroachments on the jurisdiction each claims for itself.

2. CHANGES IN THE STRUCTURE OF POWER

Riesman and Mills agreed that the American power structure has gone through four major epochs. They disagree on the present and prospective future in the following historical terms: Mills judges the present to represent a fifth epoch, whereas Riesman judges it to be a continuation of the fourth.

The first period, according to Mills and Riesman, extended roughly from the founding of the republic to the Jacksonian era. During this period, Riesman believes America possessed a clearly demarcated ruling group, composed of a "landed-gentry and mercantalist-money leadership." [239] According to Mills, "the important fact about these early days is that social life, economic institutions, military establishment, and political order coincided, and men who were high politicians also played key roles in the economy and, with their families, were among those of the reputable who made up local society." [270]

The second period extended roughly from the decline of Federalist leadership to the Civil War. During this period power became more widely dispersed, and it was no longer possible to identify a sharply defined ruling group. "In this society," Mills writes, "the 'elite' became a plurality of top groups, each in turn quite loosely made up." [270] Riesman notes that farmer and artisan groups became influential, and "occasionally, as with Jackson, moved into a more positive command." [240]

The third period began after the Civil War and extended through McKinley's administration in Riesman's view [240] and until the New

Deal according to Mills. [271] They agree that the era of McKinley marked the high point of the unilateral supremacy of corporate economic power. During this period, power once more became concentrated, but unlike the Federalist period and also unlike subsequent periods, the higher circles of economic institutions were dominant.

The fourth period took definite shape in the 1930's. In Riesman's view this period marked the ascendancy of the "veto groups," and rule by coalitions rather than by a unified power group. Mills judges it to have been so only in the early and middle Roosevelt administrations: "In these years, the New Deal as a system of power was essentially a balance of pressure groups and interest blocs." [273]

Up to World War II, then, Mills and Riesman view the historical development of power relations in America along strikingly similar lines. Their sharply contrasting portrayal of present-day American power relations begins with their diverging assessments of the period beginning about 1940. Mills envisions World War II and its aftermath as marking a new era in American power relations. With war as the major problem, there arises a new power group composed of corporate, governmental, and military directors.

> The formation of the power elite, as we may now know it, occurred during World War II and its aftermath. In the course of the organization of the nation for that war, and the consequent stabilization of the war-like posture, certain types of man have been selected and formed, and in the course of these institutional and psychological developments, new opportunities and intentions have arisen among them.[3]

Where Mills sees the ascendancy of a power elite, Riesman sees the opposite tendency toward the dispersal of power among a plurality of organized interests:

> There has been in the last fifty years a change in the configuration of power in America, in which a single hierarchy with a ruling class at its head has been replaced by a number of "veto groups" among which power is dispersed. [239]
>
> The shifting nature of the lobby provides us with an important clue as to the difference between the present American political scene and that of the age of McKinley. The ruling class of businessmen could relatively easily (though perhaps mistakenly) decide where their interests lay and what editors, lawyers, and legislators might be paid to advance them. The lobby ministered to the clear leadership, privilege, and imperative of the business ruling class. Today we have substituted for that leadership a

---

3. C. Wright Mills, "The Power Elite," in A. Kornhauser (ed.), *Problems of Power in American Society* (Detroit: Wayne University Press, 1957), p. 161.

series of groups, each of which has struggled for and finally attained a power to stop things conceivably inimical to its interests and, within far narrower limits, to start things. [246–247]

In short, both Mills and Riesman view the current scene from an historical perspective; but where one finds a hitherto unknown *concentration* of power, the other finds an emerging *indeterminacy* of power.

3. operation of the structure of power

Mills believes the power elite sets all important public policies, especially foreign policy. Riesman, on the other hand, does not believe that the same group or coalition of groups sets all major policies, but rather that the question of who exercises power varies with the issue at stake: most groups are inoperative on most issues, and all groups are operative primarily on those issues that vitally impinge on their central interests. This is to say that there are as many power structures as there are distinctive spheres of policy. [256]

As to the modes of operation, both Mills and Riesman point to increasing *manipulation,* rather than command or persuasion, as the favored form of power play. Mills emphasizes the secrecy behind which important policy-determination occurs. Riesman stresses not so much manipulation under the guise of secrecy as manipulation under the guise of mutual tolerance for one another's interests and beliefs. Manipulation occurs, according to Riesman, because each group is trying to hide its concern with power in order not to antagonize other groups. Power relations tend to take the form of "monopolistic competition": "rules of fairness and fellowship [rather than the impersonal forces of competition] dictate how far one can go." [247] Thus both believe the play of power takes place to a considerable extent backstage; but Mills judges this power play to be under the direction of one group, while Riesman sees it as controlled by a mood and structure of accommodation among many groups.

Mills maintains that the mass media of communication are important instruments of manipulation: the media lull people to sleep, so to speak, by suppressing political topics and by emphasizing "entertainment." Riesman alleges that the mass media give more attention to politics and problems of public policy than their audiences actually want, and thereby convey the false impression that there is more interest in public affairs than really exists in America at the present time. Where Mills judges the mass media of communication to be powerful political instruments in American society [315–316], Riesman argues that they have relatively little significance in this respect. [228–231]

4. BASES OF THE STRUCTURE OF POWER

Power tends to be patterned according to the structure of interests in a society. Power is shared among those whose interests coincide, and divides along lines where interests diverge. To Mills, the power elite is a reflection and solidification of a *coincidence of interests* among the ascendant institutional orders. The power elite rests on the "many interconnections and points of coinciding interests" of the corporations, political institutions, and military services. [19] For Riesman, on the other hand, there is an amorphous power structure, which reflects a *diversity of interests* among the major organized groups. The power structure of veto groups rests on the divergent interests of political parties, business groups, labor organizations, farm blocs, and a myriad of other organized groups. [247]

But power is not a simple reflex of interests alone. It also rests on the capabilities and opportunities for cooperation among those who have similar interests, and for confrontation among those with opposing interests. Mills argues in some detail that the power elite rests not merely on the coincidence of interests among major institutions but also on the "psychological similarity and social intermingling" of their higher circles. [19] By virtue of similar social origins (old family, upper-class background), religious affiliations (Episcopalian and Presbyterian), education (Ivy League college or military academy), and the like, those who head up the major institutions share codes and values as well as material interests. This makes for easy communication, especially when many of these people already know one another, or at least know many people in common. They share a common way of life, and therefore possess both the will and the opportunity to integrate their lines of action as representatives of key institutions. At times this integration involves "explicit co-ordination," as during war. [19–20] So much for the bases of power at the apex of the structure.

At the middle and lower levels of power, Mills emphasizes the lack of independence and concerted purpose among those who occupy similar social positions. In his book on the middle classes,[4] Mills purports to show the weakness of white-collar people that results from their lack of economic independence and political direction. The white-collar worker simply follows the more powerful group of the moment. In his book on labor leaders,[5] Mills located the alleged political impotence of organized labor in its dependence on government. Finally, the public is conceived as composed of atomized and submissive individuals who are incapable of engaging in effective communication and political action. [302 ff.]

---

4. *White Collar* (New York: Oxford University Press, 1951).
5. *The New Men of Power* (New York: Harcourt, Brace and Company, 1948).

Riesman believes that power "is founded, in large measure, on inter-personal expectations and attitudes." [253] He asserts that in addition to the diversity of interest underlying the pattern of power in America there is the psycho-cultural fact of widespread feelings of weakness and depen-dence at the top as well as at the bottom of the power structure: "If businessmen feel weak and dependent they do in actuality become weaker and more dependent, no matter what material resources may be ascribed to them." [253] In other words, the amorphousness of power in America rests in part on widespread feelings of weakness and dependence. These feelings are found among those whose position in the social structure provides resources that they could exploit, as well as among those whose position provides less access to the means of power. In fact, Riesman is concerned to show that people at all levels of the social structure tend to feel weaker than their objective position warrants.

The theory of types of conformity that provides the foundation of so much of Riesman's writings enters into his analysis of power at this point. The "other-directed" orientation in culture and character helps to sustain the amorphousness of power. The other-directed person in politics is the "inside-dopester," the person who possesses political competence but avoids political commitment. This is the dominant type in the veto groups, since other-direction is prevalent in the strata from which their leaders are drawn. "Both within the [veto] groups and in the situation created by their presence, the political mood tends to become one of other-directed tolerance." [248] However, Riesman does not make the basis of power solely psychological:

> This does not mean, however, that the veto groups are formed along the lines of character structure. As in a business corporation there is room for extreme inner-directed and other-directed types, and all mixtures between, so in a veto group there can exist complex "symbiotic" relationships among people of different political styles. . . . Despite these complications I think it fair to say that the veto groups, even when they are set up to protect a clearcut moralizing interest, are generally forced to adopt the political manners of the other-directed. [249]

Riesman and Mills agree that there is widespread apathy in American society, but they disagree on the social distribution of political apathy. Mills locates the apathetic primarily among the lower social strata, whereas Riesman finds extensive apathy in higher as well as lower strata. Part of the difference may rest on what criteria of apathy are used. Mills conceives of apathy as the lack of political meaning in one's life, the failure to think of personal interests in political terms, so that what happens in politics does not appear to be related to personal troubles.[6] Riesman extends the notion

---

6. *White Collar*, p. 327.

of apathy to include the politically uninformed as well as the politically uncommitted.[7] Thus political indignation undisciplined by political understanding is not a genuine political orientation. Riesman judges political apathy to be an important *basis* for amorphous power relations. Mills, on the other hand, treats political apathy primarily as a *result* of the concentration of power.

5. CONSEQUENCES OF THE STRUCTURE OF POWER

Four parallel sets of consequences of the structure of power for American society may be inferred from the writings of Mills and Riesman. The first concerns the impact of the power structure on the interests of certain groups or classes in American society. Mills asserts that the existing power arrangements enhance the interests of the major institutions whose directors constitute the power elite. [276 ff.] Riesman asserts the contrary: no one group or class is decisively favored over others by the culminated decisions on public issues. [257]

The second set of consequences concerns the impact of the structure of power on the quality of politics in American society. Here Mills and Riesman are in closer agreement. Mills maintains that the concentration of power in a small circle, and the use of manipulation as the favored manner of exercising power, lead to the decline of politics as public debate. People are decreasingly capable of grasping political issues, and of relating them to personal interests.[8] Riesman also believes that politics has declined in meaning for large numbers of people. This is not due simply to the ascendancy of "veto groups," although they do foster "the tolerant mood of other-direction and hasten the retreat of the inner-directed indignants." [251] More important, the increasing complexity and remoteness of politics make political self-interest obscure and aggravate feelings of impotence even when self-interest is clear.[9]

The third set of consequences of the American power structure concerns its impact on the quality of power relations themselves. Mills contends that the concentration of power has taken place without a corresponding shift in the bases of legitimacy of power: power is still supposed to reside in the public and its elected representatives, whereas in reality it resides in the hands of those who direct the key bureaucracies. As a consequence, men of power are neither responsible nor accountable for their power. [316–317] Riesman also implies that there is a growing discrepancy between the facts of power and the images of power, but for the opposite

---

7. David Riesman and Nathan Glazer, "Criteria for Political Apathy," in Alvin W. Gouldner (ed.), *Studies in Leadership* (New York: Harper & Brothers, 1950).
8. *White Collar,* pp. 342–350.
9. "Criteria for Political Apathy," p. 520.

reason from Mills: power is more widely dispersed than is generally believed. [257–258]

Finally, a fourth set of consequences concerns the impact of the power structure on democratic leadership. If power tends to be lodged in a small group that is not accountable for its power, and if politics no longer involves genuine public debate, then there will be a *severe weakening of democratic institutions,* if not of leadership (the power elite exercises leadership in one sense of the term, in that it makes decisions on basic policy for the nation). Mills claims that power in America has become so concentrated that it increasingly resembles the Soviet system of power:

> Official commentators like to contrast the ascendancy in totalitarian countries of a tightly organized clique with the American system of power. Such comments, however, are easier to sustain if one compares mid-twentieth-century Russia with mid-nineteenth-century America, which is what is often done by Tocqueville-quoting Americans making the contrast. But that was an America of a century ago, and in the century that has passed, the American elite have not remained as patrioteer essayists have described them to us. The "loose cliques" now head institutions of a scale and power not then existing and, especially since World War I, the loose cliques have tightened up. [271]

If, on the other hand, power tends to be dispersed among groups that are primarily concerned to protect and defend their interests rather than to advance general policies and their own leadership, and if at the same time politics has declined as a sphere of duty and self-interest, then there will be a *severe weakening of leadership.* Thus Riesman believes that "power in America seems to [be] situational and mercurial; it resists attempts to locate it." [257] This "indeterminacy and amorphousness" of power inhibits the development of leadership: "Where the issue involves the country as a whole, no individual or group leadership is likely to be very effective, because the entrenched veto groups cannot be budged." [257] "Veto groups exist as defense groups, not as leadership groups." [248] Yet Riesman does not claim that the decline of leadership directly threatens American democracy, at least in the short run: the dispersion of power among a diversity of balancing "veto groups" operates to support democratic institutions even as it inhibits effective leadership. The long run prospects of a leaderless democracy are of course less promising.

II

In the second part of this paper, I wish to raise certain critical questions about Riesman's and Mills' images of power. One set of questions

Two Portraits of the American Power Structure

	Mills	Riesman
Levels	a. Unified power elite b. Diversified and balanced plurality of interest groups c. Mass of unorganized people who have practically no power over elite	a. No dominant power elite b. Diversified and balanced plurality of interest groups c. Mass of unorganized people who have some power over interest groups
Changes	a. Increasing concentration of power	a. increasing dispersion of power
Operation	a. One group determines all major policies b. Manipulation of people at the bottom by group at the top	a. Who determines policy shifts with the issue b. Monopolistic competition among organized groups
Bases	a. Coincidence of interests among major institutions (economic, military, governmental)	a. Diversity of interests among major organized groups b. Sense of weakness and dependence among those in higher as well as lower status
Consequences	a. Ehancement of interests of corporations, armed forces, and executive branch of government b. Decline of politics as public debate c. Decline of responsible and accountable power—loss of democracy	a. No one group or class is favored significantly over others b. Decline of politics as duty and self-interest c. Decline of capacity for effective leadership

seeks to probe more deeply the basic area of disagreement in their views. A second set of questions concerns their major areas of agreement.

Power usually is analyzed according to its distribution among the several units of a system. Most power analysts construe the structure of power as a *hierarchy*—a rank-order of units according to their amount of power. The assumption often is made that there is only one such structure, and that all units may be ranked vis-à-vis one another. Units higher in the hierarchy have power over units lower in the structure, so there is a one-way flow of power. Mills tends to adopt this image of the structure of power.

Riesman rejects this conception of the power structure as mere hierarchy:

The determination of who [has more power] has to be made all over again for our time: we cannot be satisfied with the answers given by Marx, Mosca, Michels, Pareto, Weber, Veblen, or Burnham. [255]

The image of power in contemporary America presented [in *The Lonely Crowd*] departs from current discussions of power which are usually based on a search for a ruling class. [260]

Riesman is not just denying the existence of a power elite in contemporary American society; he is also affirming the need to consider other aspects of power than only its unequal distribution. He is especially concerned to analyze common responses to power:

If the leaders have lost the power, why have the led not gained it? What is there about the other-directed man and his life situation which prevents the transfer? In terms of situation, it seems that the pattern of monopolistic competition of the veto groups resists individual attempts at power aggrandizement. In terms of character, the other-directed man simply does not seek power; perhaps, rather, he avoids and evades it. [275]

Whereas Mills emphasizes the *differences* between units according to their power, Riesman emphasizes their *similarities* in this respect. In the first view, some units are seen as dominated by other units, while in the second view, all units are seen as subject to constraints that shape and limit their use of power *in similar directions*.

The problem of power is not simply the differential capacity to make decisions, so that those who have power bind those who do not. Constraints also operate on those who are in decision-making positions, for if these are the places where acts of great consequence occur, so are they the targets for social pressures. These pressures become translated into restriction on the alternatives among which decision-makers can choose. Power may be meaningfully measured by ascertaining the range of alternatives that decision-makers can realistically consider. To identify those who make decisions is not to say how many lines of action are open to them, or how much freedom of choice they enjoy.

A major advance in the study of power is made by going beyond a formal conception of power, in which those who have the authority to make decisions are assumed to possess the effective means of power and the will to use it. Nor can it be assumed that those not in authority lack the power to determine public policy. The identification of effective sources of power requires analysis of how *decision-makers are themselves subject to various kinds of constraint*. Major sources of constraint include (1) opposing elites and active publics; and (2) cultural values and associated psychological receptivities and resistances to power. A comparison of Mills and Riesman with respect to these categories of constraint reveals the major area of disagreement between them.

Mills implies that both sources of constraint are by and large inoperative on the highest levels of power. (1) There is little opposition among the top power-holders. Since they are not in opposition to one another, they do not constrain one another. Instead, they are unified and mutually supportive. Furthermore, there are few publics to constrain the elite. Groups capable of effective participation in broad policy determination have been replaced by atomized masses that are powerless to affect policy, since they lack the social bases for association and communication. Instead, people in large numbers are manipulated through organizations and media controlled by the elite. (2) Older values and codes no longer grip elites, nor have they been replaced by new values and codes that could regulate the exercise of power. Top men of power are not constrained either by an inner moral sense or by feelings of dependence on others. The widespread permissiveness toward the use of expedient means to achieve success produces "the higher immorality," that is to say, elites that are irresponsible in the use of power.

In sharp contrast to Mills, Riesman attaches great importance to both kinds of constraints on decision-makers. (1) There is a plethora of organized groups, "each of which has struggled for and finally attained a power to stop things conceivably inimical to its interests." [247] Furthermore, there is extensive opportunity for large numbers of people to influence decision-makers, because the latter are constrained by their competitive relations with one another to bid for support in the electoral arena and more diffusely in the realm of public relations. (2) The cultural emphasis on "mutual tolerance" and social conformity places a premium on "getting along" with others at the expense of taking strong stands. People are psychologically disposed to avoid long-term commitments as a result of their strong feelings of dependence on their immediate peers. "Other-directed" persons seek approval rather than power.

In general, the decisive consideration in respect to the restraint of power is the presence of multiple centers of power. Where there are many power groups, not only are they mutually constrained; they also are dependent on popular support, and therefore responsive to public demands. Now, there are many readily observable cases of institutionalized opposition among power groups in American society. In the economic sphere, collective bargaining between management and labor is conflict of this kind; and to the extent that "countervailing power" among a few large firms has been replacing competition among many small firms in the market place, there is a *de facto* situation of opposition among economic elites. In the political sphere, there is a strong two-party system and more or less stable factionalism within both parties, opposition among interest blocs in state and national legislatures, rivalry among executive agencies of government and the military services, and so forth.

Mills relegates these conflicting groups to the middle levels of power.

Political parties and interest groups, both inside and outside of government, are not important units in the structure of power, according to Mills. It would seem that he takes this position primarily with an eye to the sphere of foreign policy, where only a few people finally make the big decisions. But he fails to put his argument to a decisive or meaningful test: he does not examine the pattern of decisions to show that foreign policy not only is made *by* a few people (this, after all, is a constitutional fact), but that it is made *for their particular interests*. Mills' major premise seems to be that all decisions are taken by and for special interests; there is no action oriented toward the general interests of the whole community. Furthermore, Mills seems to argue that because only a very few people occupy key decision-making *positions*, they are free to decide on whatever best suits their particular interests. But the degree of *autonomy* of decision-makers cannot be inferred from the *number* of decision-makers, nor from the *scope* of their decisions. It is determined by the character of decision-making, especially the dependence of decision-makers on certain kinds of *procedure* and *support*.

Just as Mills is presenting a distorted image of power in America when he fails to consider the pressures on those in high positions, so Riesman presents a biased picture by not giving sufficient attention to *power differentials* among the various groups in society. When Riesman implies that if power is dispersed, then it must be relatively equal among groups and interests, with no points of concentration, he is making an unwarranted inference. The following statement conjures up an image of power in America that is as misleading on its side as anything Mills has written in defense of his idea of a power elite.

One might ask whether one would not find, over a long period of time, that decisions in America favored one group or class . . . over others. Does not wealth exert its pull in the long run? In the past this has been so; for the future I doubt it. The future seems to be in the hands of the small business and professional men who control Congress, such as realtors, lawyers, car salesmen, undertakers, and so on; of the military men who control defense and, in part, foreign policy; of the big business managers and their lawyers, finance-committee men, and other counselors who decide on plant investment and influence the rate of technological change; of the labor leaders who control worker productivity and worker votes; of the black belt whites who have the greatest stake in southern politics; of the Poles, Italians, Jews, and Irishmen who have stakes in foreign policy, city jobs, and ethnic, religious and cultural organizations; of the editorializers and storytellers who help socialize the young, tease and train the adult, and amuse and annoy the aged; of the farmers—themselves a warring congeries of cattlemen, corn men, dairymen, cotton men, and so on—who control key departments and committees and who, as the living representatives of our inner-directed past, control many of our memories;

of the Russians and, to a lesser degree, other foreign powers who control much of our agenda of attention; and so on. [257]

It appears that Riesman is asking us to believe that power differentials do not exist, but only differences in the spheres within which groups exercise control.

If Riesman greatly exaggerates the extent of which organized interests possess equal power, nevertheless he poses an important problem that Mills brushes aside. For Riesman goes beyond merely noting the existence of opposition among "veto groups" to suggest that they operate to smother one another's initiative and leadership. It is one thing for interest groups to constrain one another; it is something else again when they produce stalemate. Riesman has pointed to a critical problem for pluralist society: the danger that power may become fragmented among so many competing groups that effective general leadership cannot emerge.

On Mills' side, it is indisputable that American political institutions have undergone extensive centralization and bureaucratization. This is above all an *institutional* change wrought by the greatly expanded scale of events and decisions in the contemporary world. But centralization cannot be equated with a power elite. There can be highly centralized institutions and at the same time a fragmentation of power among a multiplicity of relatively independent public and private agencies. Thus Riesman would appear to be correct that the substance of power lies in the hands of many large organizations, and these organizations are not unified or coordinated in any firm fashion. If they were, surely Mills would have been able to identify the major mechanisms that could produce this result. That he has failed to do so is the most convincing evidence for their nonexistence.

To complete this analysis, we need only remind ourselves of the fundamental area of agreement between our two critics of American power relations. Both stress *the absence of effective political action* at all levels of the political order, in particular among the citizenry. For all of their differences, Mills and Riesman agree that there has been a decline in effective political participation, or at least a failure of political participation to measure up to the requirements of contemporary events and decisions. This failure has not been compensated by an increase in effective political action at the center: certainly Riesman's "veto groups" are not capable of defining and realizing the community's general aspirations; nor is Mills' "power elite" such a political agency. Both are asserting the inadequacy of political associations, including public opinion, party leadership, Congress, and the Presidency, even as they see the slippage of power in different directions. In consequence, neither is sanguine about the capacity of the American political system to provide responsible leadership, especially in international affairs.

If there is truth in this indictment, it also may have its sources in the very images of power that pervade Mills' and Riesman's thought. They are both inclined toward a negative response to power; and neither shows a willingness to confront the idea of a political system and the ends of power in it. Riesman reflects the liberal suspicion of power, as when he writes "we have come to realize that men who compete primarily for wealth are relatively harmless as compared with men who compete primarily for power." That such assertions as this may very well be true is beside the point. For certainly negative consequences of power can subsist alongside of positive ones. At times Riesman seems to recognize the need for people to seek and use power if they as individuals and the society as a whole are to develop to the fullest of their capacities. But his dominant orientation toward power remains highly individualistic and negative.

Mills is more extreme than Riesman on this matter, since he never asks what is socially required in the way of resources of power and uses of power, but instead is preoccupied with the magnitude of those resources and the (allegedly) destructive expropriation of them by and for the higher circles of major institutions. It is a very limited notion of power that construes it only in terms of coercion and conflict among particular interests. Societies require arrangements whereby resources of power can be effectively used and supplemented for public goals. This is a requirement for government, but the use of this term should not obscure that fact that government either commands power or lacks effectiveness. Mills does not concern himself with the *ends* of power, nor with the conditions for their attainment. He has no conception of the bases of political order, and no theory of the functions of government and politics. He suggests nothing that could prevent his "power elite" from developing into a full-blown totalitarianism. The logic of Mills' position finally reduces to a contest between anarchy and tyranny.

The problem of power seems to bring out the clinician in each of us. We quickly fasten on the pathology of power, whether we label the symptoms as "inside-dopesterism" (Riesman) or as "the higher immorality" (Mills). As a result, we often lose sight of the ends of power in the political system under review. It is important to understand that pivotal decisions increasingly are made at the national level, and that this poses genuine difficulties for the maintenance of democratic control. It is also important to understand that a multiplicity of public and private agencies increasingly pressure decision-makers, and that this poses genuine difficulties for the maintenance of effective political leadership. But the fact remains that there have been periods of centralized decision-making *and* democratic control, multiple constraints on power *and* effective leadership. There is no simple relationship between the extent to which power is equally distributed and the stability of democratic order. For a democratic order requires strong government as well as public consent by an informed citizenry. Unless current tendencies are measured against both sets of needs, there will be little progress in understanding how either one is frustrated or fulfilled. Finally, in the absence of more disciplined historical and comparative analysis, we shall continue to lack a firm basis for evaluating such widely divergent diagnoses of political malaise as those given us by Mills and Riesman.

Cross Reference Chart to All Basic Texts

Ritzer Chapter Headings	Toby(2)	Smelser	Green(5)	Bertrand	Lowry and Rankin	Dressler	Himes	Hodges, Jr.	McKee	Bierstedt(3)	Wilson(2)	Phillips	Broom and Selznick
1. Discipline of Sociology	1	—	1	1	1	1	1	1	1, 2	1	1, 15	1	1
2. Methods	2	—	1	3	1	2	1	2	3	1	1, 15	1	1
3. Socialization and Social Control	3, 4, 5, 13	10	7, 21	4, 5, 16	2	5, 8, 9	12, 13	4	6	7, 8, 9	4	4	4
4. Deviance	13	11	22	13–15	10	10, 18	13	—	6	—	12	—	—
5. Collective Behavior and Social Change	14	12	24, 25, 25	8	5, 11	7	15, 16	14	19, 20	20	13, 14	16, 17	8
6. Stratification	12	4	10, 11, 14	10	6	15	11	8	10	17	8	8	6
7. Minority Groups	14	—	12	—	—	20	—	15	11	18	—	9	—
8. Organizations	10	3	—	—	7	12	6	—	8	11	10	6	7
9. Urban	7	—	13	22	8	16	7	6	9	16	7	15	13
10. Community	7	2	13	22	8	16	7	6	9	16	7	15	—
11. Population	—	—	9	20, 21	—	19	10	7	21	4	2	10	9
12. Family	4	9	15, 16	17	9	24	9	9	13	15	9	5	4
13. Education	11	7	—	18	—	26	9	13	14	—	9	13	11
14. Economy	6	5	19	19	—	21, 27	8	10	15	—	10	11	14
15. Religion	8	6	17, 18	18	—	25	9	12	18	—	11	12	10
16. Politics	9	8	20	19	—	13, 27	8, 14	11	16	19	11	14	15

Anderson	J. Rose	McNall(2)	CRM	VanderZanden	Biesanz and Biesanz	Stewart and Glynn	DeFleur, D'Antonio, DeFleur	Rose and Rose(3)	Horton and Hunt	Popenoe	Worsley	Caplow	Chinoy
—	1	1, 2	36	1	1	1	Prolog Epilog	1	1	—	1	1, 4	1, 2, 5
—	2	3	—	1, 21	1	1	Epilog Prolog	1	2	—	2	2–3	
1–2	13	6	4, 23, 24, 25	3, 12	12, 13, 14	4	5	2, 3, 4, 14	5, 6, 7	3, 11	8	—	4, 18
—	14	11	24	3	15	—	12	—	7	11	—	11	19
—	16, 17	12	30–36	7	16, 17	7, 15	6, 11	—	16, 19, 20	12	—	13	20
3–6	11	10	13–16	13	8, 9	5	7	10	11–14	6	7	7	8
10, 11	12	14	17	—	10, 11	6	10	—	15	7	—	—	9
—	6	7	11	11	7	—	2	5	9	5	5	9	10
—	19	9	6, 7	20	—	9	9	13	18	13	6	6	11
—	19	9	6, 7	—	—	—	2	13	18	13	6	—	11
—	18	8	5	20	18	8	8	12	17	10	—	5	17
12	8	15	18	15	19	10	16	6	10	4	3	10	7
—	—	—	21	19	—	12	18	8	—	8	4	—	15
7, 9	—	—	12, 19	17	20	13	15	8	—	13	5	8	12
—	9	17	22	16	—	11	17	8	—	9	—	—	14
8	10	16	20	18	21	14	14	8	—	14	—	—	13